HOLLYWOOD
SCREENWRITING
DIRECTORY

SPRING/SUMMER • VOLUME 6

BURBANK, CALIFORNIA

Printed and bound in the United States of America.

Published by F+W Media, Inc.
3510 West Magnolia Boulevard
Burbank, California 91505
www.fwcommunity.com

Disclaimer

Every reasonable effort has been made to ensure the accuracy of the information contained in the *Hollywood Screenwriting Directory*. F+W Media, Inc. cannot be held responsible for any inaccuracies, or the misrepresentation of those listed in the Hollywood Screenwriting Directory.

Updates/Change Listing

Please submit corrections and updates to corrections@screenwritingdirectory.com

Print ISBN 13: 978-1-59963-973-4
Print ISBN 10: 1-59963-973-4
ePub ISBN 13: 978-1-59963-977-2
ePub ISBN 10: 1-59963-977-7
PDF ISBN 13: 978-1-59963-975-8
PDF ISBN 10: 1-59963-975-0

Contents

How to Use the *Hollywood Screenwriting Directory*

Dear Fellow Screenwriter,

Whether this is your very first copy or you update each season, this Spring/Summer Volume 6 edition of the *Hollywood Screenwriting Directory* is an essential addition to your script-selling toolkit. You'll find that much of the information—40% of it, to be exact—is still current from our previous edition. We know this because we thoroughly check each listing from season to season to ensure that it's always the most up-to-date contact information available. The updates you will find include changes to the 10% of our listings with new contact info, along with new Twitter, Facebook, and LinkedIn details, and changes to submission policies. About 10% of our listings were deleted because certain companies were no longer in business.

The *Screenwriting Directory* is also online as an active marketplace that allows you to post your project for purchase consideration in an area accessible only to verified Industry Execs looking for new writers and fresh material. Visit screenwritingdirectory.com/c/HSD15S297 now for a **free Silver subscription.** You can also use our handy one-sheet template and screenwriter experience Q&A fields to present your work and yourself as a screenwriter in a way that will catch an exec's attention. You also have the option to have your logline included in our monthly screenplay report sent out to Industry professionals.

To get your script in the very best shape it can be before you submit to these seasoned Industry Insiders, we recommend one of our top-rated ScriptXpert services. From Screenplay Coverage to Query Letter Critiques, our professional readers and coaches can quickly help you take your work to the saleable level.

The *HSD* is a very specialized directory created by The Writers Store based on our extensive experience serving the screenwriting community since 1982. It contains a range of people to contact regarding your script, from ambitious upstarts to established studio execs, along with management companies who package production deals and independent financiers/distributors with a production wing. For each listing, you'll find the kind of useable information you need: street and email addresses, whether or not they accept unsolicited material, and how they prefer to receive submissions.

While having access to this data is crucial, just as essential is an understanding of the right way to use it. These insiders are flooded with submissions daily. Any indication of incorrect format or other amateur flubs in the first few pages will quickly send your script to the trash.

Find software, books, courses and more on WritersStore.com

We can't emphasize enough how important it is that your submission is polished and professional before you send it out for consideration. Screenwriting software makes producing an Industry-standard screenplay simple and straightforward. Programs like Final Draft and Movie Magic Screenwriter put your words into proper format as you type, letting you focus on a well-told story rather than the chore of margins and spacing. In these pages, we've also included a guide to proper screenplay format, along with sample title and first pages to help you send out a professional script.

Besides a properly packaged submission, it's also wise to know your audience before you send out any materials. If your script is an action thriller with a strong female lead, don't send it to Paul Giamatti's production company. Actors establish their own companies so that they're not reliant on studios for roles. Pad an actor's vanity (and his pipeline) by submitting materials catered specifically to him.

You may find that a good number of companies do not want unsolicited submissions. It's not that they're not open to new ideas; they're not open to liability. A script is property, and with it, come ramifications if not handled properly. If you choose to disregard "no unsolicited submissions,&rdquo sending your script with a submission release form gives it a better chance of getting read. Consult with an entertainment attorney to draft an appropriate form, or consult a guide like *Clearance and Copyright* by Michael C. Donaldson, which has submission release form templates. It's also prudent to protect your work. We recommend registering your script with the WGA (Writers Guild of America, West) or the ProtectRite registration service.

A benefit of the digital age is that the same companies that are not open to receiving unsolicited submissions will gladly accept a query letter by email. Take advantage of this opportunity. Craft a well-written and dynamic query letter email that sells you and your script. We have included a sample query, and some tips and guidelines on how to write great query letters.

While Hollywood is a creative town it is, above all, professional. Do a service to yourself and the potential buyer by being courteous. If you choose to follow up by phone, don't be demanding and frustrated. These people are overworked and do not owe you anything. It's okay to follow up, but be sure to do so with respect. And if you pique a buyer's interest and she asks for a treatment, you must be ready to send off this vital selling tool at once! That's why we've also included a handy guide to writing treatments in this volume.

While it may oftentimes feel like the opposite, the Entertainment Industry *is* looking for new writers and fresh material. BUT (and this is important) they're also looking for those aspiring scribes to take the time to workshop their scripts with an experienced professional and get them to a marketable level. The Writers Store can help you get ready for the big leagues through our slate of screenwriting courses, personalized coaching and Development Notes service, which works in a format that mirrors the same process occurring in the studio ranks.

Hollywood is the pinnacle of competition and ambition. But that's not to say that dreams can't happen—they can, and they do. By keeping to these professional guidelines and working on your craft daily, you can find the kind of screenwriting success you seek.

Wishing you the best of luck,

Jesse Douma
Editor

Find software, books, courses and more on WritersStore.com

What is a Screenplay?

In the most basic terms, a screenplay is a 90-120 page document written in Courier 12pt font on 8.5" x 11" bright white three-hole punched paper. Wondering why Courier font is used? It's a timing issue. One formatted script page in Courier font equals roughly one minute of screen time. That's why the average page count of a screenplay should come in between 90 and 120 pages. Comedies tend to be on the shorter side (90 pages, or 1 ½ hours) while Dramas run longer (120 pages, or 2 hours).

A screenplay can be an original piece, or based on a true story or previously written piece, like a novel, stage play or newspaper article. At its heart, a screenplay is a blueprint for the film it will one day become. Professionals on the set including the producer, director, set designer and actors all translate the screenwriter's vision using their individual talents. Since the creation of a film is ultimately a collaborative art, the screenwriter must be aware of each person's role and as such, the script should reflect the writer's knowledge.

For example, it's crucial to remember that film is primarily a visual medium. As a screenwriter, you must show what's happening in a story, rather than tell. A 2-page inner monologue may work well for a novel, but is the kiss of death in a script. The very nature of screenwriting is based on how to show a story on a screen, and pivotal moments can be conveyed through something as simple as a look on an actor's face. Let's take a look at what a screenplay's structure looks like.

The First Page of a Screenplay

Screenwriting software makes producing an Industry-standard script simple and straightforward. While screenplay formatting software such as Final Draft, Movie Magic Screenwriter, Movie Outline, Montage and Scriptly for the iPad frees you from having to learn the nitty-gritty of margins and indents, it's good to have a grasp of the general spacing standards.

The top, bottom and right margins of a screenplay are 1". The left margin is 1.5". The extra half-inch of white space to the left of a script page allows for binding with brads, yet still imparts a feeling of vertical balance of the text on the page. The entire document should be single-spaced.

Screenplay Elements

Following is a list of items that make up the screenplay format, along with indenting information. Again, screenplay software will automatically format all these elements, but a screenwriter must have a working knowledge of the definitions to know when to use each one.

Ⓐ Fade In

The very first item on the first page should be the words FADE IN:.

Ⓑ Page Numbers

The first page is never numbered. Subsequent page numbers appear in the upper right hand corner, 0.5" from the top of the page, flush right to the margin.

Ⓒ Mores and Continueds

Use mores and continueds between pages to indicate the same character is still speaking.

Ⓓ Scene Heading

Left Indent: 0"   Right Indent: 0"   Width: 6"

A scene heading is a one-line description of the location and time of day of a scene, also known as a "slugline." It should always be in CAPS. Example: EXT. WRITERS STORE – DAY reveals that the action takes place outside The Writers Store during the daytime.

Ⓔ Subheader

Left Indent: 0"   Right Indent: 0"   Width: 6"

When a new scene heading is not necessary, but some distinction needs to be made in the action, you can use a subheader. But be sure to use these sparingly, as a script full of subheaders is generally frowned upon. A good example is when there are a series of quick cuts between two locations, you would use the term INTERCUT and the scene locations.

Ⓕ Action

Left Indent: 0"   Right Indent: 0"   Width: 6"

The narrative description of the events of a scene, written in the present tense. Also less commonly known as direction, visual exposition, blackstuff, description or scene direction. Remember—only things that can be seen and heard should be included in the action.

Sample Screenplay Page

 FADE IN:

 EXT. WRITERS STORE - DAY

In the heart of West Los Angeles, a boutique shop's large
OPEN sign glows like a beacon.

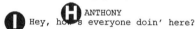 DISSOLVE TO:

INT. WRITERS STORE - SALES FLOOR - DAY

Writers browse the many scripts in the screenplay section.

ANTHONY, Canadian-Italian Story Specialist extraordinaire,
30s and not getting any younger, ambles over.

                    ANTHONY
          Hey, how's everyone doin' here?

A WRITING ENTHUSIAST, 45, reads the first page of "The
Aviator" by John Logan.

                    ENTHUSIAST
          Can John Logan write a killer first
          page or what?

                    ANTHONY
          You, sir, are a gentleman of
          refined taste. John Logan is my
          non-Canadian idol.

The phone RINGS. Anthony goes to--

THE SALES COUNTER

And answers the phone.

                    ANTHONY (CONT'D)
          Writers Store, Anthony speaking.

                    VOICE
              (over phone)
          Do you have Chinatown in stock?

I/E LUXURIOUS MALIBU MANSION - DAY

A FIGURE roams his estate, cell phone pressed to his ear.

                    ANTHONY (O.S.)
          'Course we have Chinatown!
          Robert Towne's masterpiece is
          arguably the Great American
          Screenplay...
              (MORE)

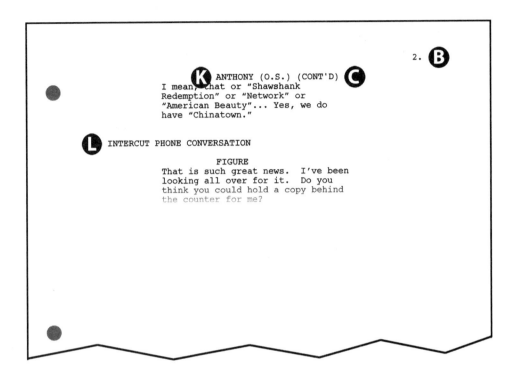

Character

Left Indent: 2" Right Indent: 0" Width: 4"

G When a character is introduced, his name should be capitalized within the action. For example: The door opens and in walks LIAM, a thirty-something hipster with attitude to spare.

H A character's name is CAPPED and always listed above his lines of dialogue. Minor characters may be listed without names, for example TAXI DRIVER or CUSTOMER.

I Dialogue

Left Indent: 1" Right Indent: 1.5" Width: 3.5"

Lines of speech for each character. Dialogue format is used anytime a character is heard speaking, even for off-screen and voice-overs.

J Parenthetical

Left Indent: 1.5" Right Indent: 2" Width: 2.5"

A parenthetical is direction for the character, that is either attitude or action-oriented. Parentheticals are used very rarely, and only if absolutely necessary. Why? First, if you need to use a parenthetical to convey what's going on with your dialogue, then it probably needs a good re-write. Second, it's the director's job to instruct an actor, and everyone knows not to encroach on the director's turf!

Ⓚ Extension

Placed after the character's name, in parentheses

An abbreviated technical note placed after the character's name to indicate how the voice will be heard onscreen, for example, if the character is speaking as a voice-over, it would appear as LIAM (V.O.).

Ⓛ Intercut

Intercuts are instructions for a series of quick cuts between two scene locations.

Ⓜ Transition

Left Indent: 4"   Right Indent: 0"   Width: 2"

Transitions are film editing instructions, and generally only appear in a shooting script. Transition verbiage includes:

```
CUT TO:
DISSOLVE TO:
SMASH CUT:
QUICK CUT:
FADE TO:
```

As a spec script writer, you should avoid using a transition unless there is no other way to indicate a story element. For example, you might need to use DISSOLVE TO: to indicate that a large amount of time has passed.

Shot

Left Indent: 0"   Right Indent: 0"   Width: 6"

A shot tells the reader the focal point within a scene has changed. Like a transition, there's rarely a time when a spec screenwriter should insert shot directions. Examples of Shots:

```
ANGLE ON --
EXTREME CLOSE UP --
LIAM'S POV --
```

Spec Script vs. Shooting Script

A "spec script" literally means that you are writing a screenplay on speculation. That is, no one is paying you to write the script. You are penning it in hopes of selling the script to a buyer. Spec scripts should stick stringently to established screenwriting rules. Once a script is purchased, it becomes a shooting script, also called a production script. This is a version of the screenplay created for film production. It will include technical instructions, like film editing notes, shots, cuts and the like. All the scenes are numbered, and revisions are marked with a color-coded system. This is done so that the production assistants and director can then arrange the order in which the scenes will be shot for the most efficient use of stage, cast, and location resources.

A spec script should never contain the elements of shooting script. The biggest mistake any new screenwriter can make is to submit a script full of production language, including camera angles and editing transitions.

It can be very difficult to resist putting this type of language in your script. After all, it's your story and you see it in a very specific way. However, facts are facts. If you want to direct your script, then try to go the independent filmmaker route. But if you want to sell your script, then stick to the accepted spec screenplay format.

Script Presentaction and Binding

Just like the format of a script, there are very specific rules for binding and presenting your script. The first page is the title page, which should also be written in Courier 12pt font. No graphics, no fancy pictures, only the title of your script, with "written by" and your name in the center of the page. In the lower left-hand or right-hand corner, enter your contact information.

In the lower left-hand or right-hand corner you can put Registered, WGA or a copyright notification, though this is generally not a requirement.

Sample Screenplay Title Page

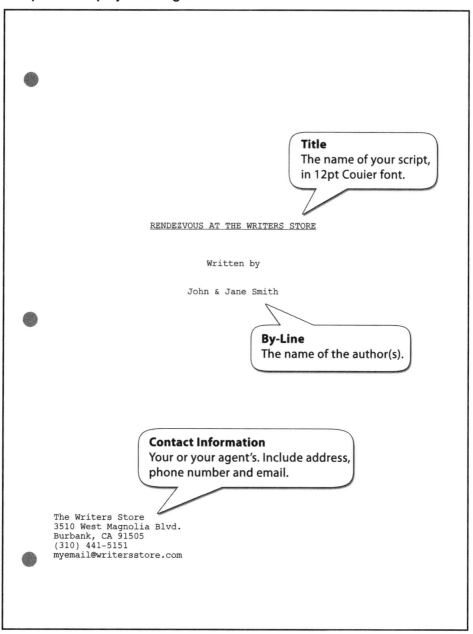

Title
The name of your script, in 12pt Couier font.

RENDEZVOUS AT THE WRITERS STORE

Written by

John & Jane Smith

By-Line
The name of the author(s).

Contact Information
Your or your agent's. Include address, phone number and email.

The Writers Store
3510 West Magnolia Blvd.
Burbank, CA 91505
(310) 441-5151
myemail@writersstore.com

Query Letters

A query is a one-page, single-spaced letter that quickly tells who you are, what the work is, and why the work is appropriate for the market in question. Just as queries are used as the first means of contact for pitching magazine articles and novels, they work just the same for scripts.

A well-written query is broken down into three parts.

Part I: Your Reason for Contacting/Script Details

Before even looking at the few sentences describing your story, a producer wants to see two other things:

1. **What is it?** State the title, genre, and whether it's a full-length script or a shorter one.
2. **Why are you contacting this market/person in particular?** There are thousands of individuals who receive scripts. Why have you chosen this person to review the material? Is it because you met them in person and they requested to see your work? Have they represented writers similar to yourself? Did you read that they were actively looking for zombie comedies? Spelling out your reason upfront shows that you've done your research, and that you're a professional.

Part II: The Elevator Pitch

If you wrote the first paragraph correctly, you've got their attention, so pitch away. Explain what your story is in about 3-6 sentences. The point here is to intrigue and pique only. Don't get into nitty-gritty details of any kind. Hesitate using a whole lot of character names or backstory. Don't say how it ends or who dies during the climax or that the hero's father betrays him in Act II. Introduce us to the main character and his situation, then get to the key part of the pitch: the conflict.

Try to include tidbits here and there that make your story unique. If it's about a cop nearing retirement, that's nothing new. But if the story is about a retiring cop considering a sex change operation in his bid to completely start over, while the police union is threatening to take away his pension should he do this, then you've got something different that readers may want to see.

Sample Query Letter

John. Q. Writer
123 Main St.
Writerville, USA
(212) 555-1234
johnqwriter@email.com

Agent
JQA & Associates
678 Hollywood St.
Hollywood, CA 90210

Dear Mr./Ms (Last Name):

My name is John Q. Writer and we crossed paths at the Screenwriters World Conference in Los Angeles in October 2012. After hearing the pitch for my feature-length thriller, October Surprise, you requested that I submit a query, synopsis and the first 10 pages of the script. All requested materials are enclosed. This is an exclusive submission, as you requested.

U.S. Senator Michael Hargrove is breaking ranks with his own political party to endorse another candidate for President of the United States. At the National Convention, he's treated like a rock star V.I.P. -- that is, until, he's abducted by a fringe political group and given a grim ultimatum: Use your speech on live TV to sabotage and derail the presidential campaign you're now supporting, or your family back home will not live though the night.

The script was co-written with my scriptwriting partner, Joe Aloysius. I am a produced playwright and award-winning journalist. Thank you for considering October Surprise. I will be happy to sign any release forms that you request. May I send the rest of the screenplay?

Best,
John Q. Writer

Part III: The Wrap Up

Your pitch is complete. The last paragraph is where you get to talk about yourself and your accomplishments. If the script has won any awards or been a finalist in a prominent competition, this is the place to say so. Mention your writing credentials and experience. Obviously, any paid screenwriting experience is most valuable, but feel free to include other tidbits such as if you're a magazine freelancer or a published novelist.

Sometimes, there won't be much to say at the end of a query letter because the writer has no credits, no contacts and nothing to brag about. As your mother would tell you: If you don't have anything nice to say, don't say anything at all. Keep the last section brief if you must, rather than going on and on about being an "active blogger" or having one poem published in your college literary magazine.

Following some information about yourself, it's time to wrap up the query and propose sending more material. A simple way to do this is by saying "The script is complete. May I send you the treatment and full screenplay?"

Here are the elements of a query letter in the example on the facing page:

A Include all of your contact information—including phone and e-mail—as centered information at the top.

B Use proper greetings and last names.

C Include a reason for contacting the reader.

D Try and keep the pitch to one paragraph.

E Regarding your credentials, be concise and honest.

Treatments and Log Lines

Introduction to the Treatment

Nobody reads a full script in Hollywood anymore. Execs don't want to put in the time to read a 90-page comedy script, much less a 180-page epic. They want to know if the goods are there before they invest their precious time, and this is where the treatment comes in. Think of it as reading the back cover of a book before you invest in buying it. You'd never just pay for a book without knowing what type of story to expect. So it is with the movie industry. The treatment is the essential selling tool that can make or break your script.

What is a Treatment

A treatment is a short document written in prose form and in the present tense that emphasizes, with vivid description, the major elements of a screenplay.

That's a very broad definition, to be sure. And while the main purpose of a treatment is as a selling tool, there are variations of the definition to consider.

1. A treatment could be your first attempt toward selling your screenplay to a producer, your first try at getting someone to pay you to write the script.
2. A treatment could be a sales tool for a script that you've already written—a shorter, prose version of the screenplay's story for producers to read, to pique their interest in your project and entice them to read your screenplay.
3. A treatment could describe how you intend to attack a rewrite, either of your own script or of another writer's script. Often when a producer hires a writer to do a rewrite, they'll ask for a treatment first.
4. A treatment could be the first step toward writing your screenplay—it could be one of the first steps toward getting your story down on paper. Maybe you don't have time to write the screenplay yet—a treatment can help cement the story in your mind (and on paper) so that you can work on it later.

Why Write a Treatment?

Ultimately, the best reason to write a treatment is that the process of writing your treatment can help you write a better script. It can be easier to find and solve structural challenges, plot incongruities, lapses in logic, etc. in the prose treatment format than it is to find and solve those challenges in the screenplay format.

Writing a screenplay is a step-by-step process, and some steps are more involved than others. Writing a treatment is a very achievable step in the screenwriting process, and taking that step from beginning to end can be a rewarding boost for your writing ego.

Writing a treatment helps give tangible shape to your story, and makes sharing your story with others simpler and more precise. If you can share your story with others, you can get feedback, which may open up more channels in your brain and help your story to grow. The treatment format is much easier to read and comprehend for people who aren't familiar with the screenplay format.

You might not be ready to write your complete screenplay yet—you might not have time, you might not be fully committed to the idea. Writing a treatment is a good stopgap measure, so that an idea doesn't just exist as an idea—it may exist as something you can sell, share with a collaborator, or simply file away for a rainy day.

When is a Treatment Used

A treatment is usually used when you begin the process of selling your script. When you pitch your script to a producer and he shows interest in your script, he will most likely ask you to send over the treatment. This way, he can review the story and see if he is interested in reading the full script.

Think of the treatment as your business card—the thing you leave behind after you've pitched your story.

You may have heard of writers who sell a script based only a treatment. Yes, this happens, but this happens only for established writers with a track record of produced scripts. They have proven to Hollywood that they can write a blockbuster script, so buyers know that if they like the treatment, they will most likely love the script.

The treatment can also be used as an outline for the writer before he begins his script. It's smart to either outline or summarize a script before you begin writing. If you can complete the story in a smaller form, you know that you'll be able to sustain it in the longer script format. Architects don't erect a building without first designing a blueprint and then creating a model of the structure. The outline is your blueprint and the treatment is your model.

Treatment vs. Synopsis, Coverage, Beat Sheet and Outline

The term treatment is thrown around loosely in Hollywood, and you can be sure that you'll hear a different definition each time you ask. Some buyers will request a treatment when they really want a synopsis, an outline or a beat sheet. So what are the definitions of the other items?

Find software, books, courses and more on WritersStore.com

Synopsis

A Synopsis is a brief description of a story's plot or a straightforward presentation of the scenes and events in a story. It is not a selling tool, but rather a summation of the story, and is typically no more than 2 pages long. It's generally used by professional script readers when writing coverage on a script.

Coverage

Coverage is the name of the document generated by the buyer's in house script readers. The main purpose of this document is to assess the commercial viability of the script. The reader supplies the buyer with the basic identifying information of the script, a synopsis, their comments on the script and a rating chart on all of the elements of the script, including characters, dialogue, action, setting, and commercial appeal. The reader then rates the script "pass" (no, thanks. Don't call us, cause we're certainly not gonna call you) "consider" (maybe someone we know can rewrite this puppy into something marketable) or "recommend" (this is the script that will move me from script reader hell to producing heaven!).

Beat Sheet

A Beat Sheet lists the sequence of major events that takes place in a script. It shows what will happen to the main character, and the order in which the events will occur. It can be anywhere from a short paragraph to three pages. Each beat is described in only 1-2 sentences.

Here is an extremely short example from "Die Hard."

1. New York Detective John McClane flies to Los Angeles to reconcile with his wife Holly at her company Christmas party.
2. When he arrives at Holly's high-rise office building, they argue and Holly leaves McClane alone in her executive bathroom.
3. From the bathroom, McClane hears terrorists, lead by Hans Gruber, break in and take over the building.
4. McClane witnesses the murder of Takagi, the CEO of the company, by Gruber and decides to take action.
5. McClane kills the brother of the lead henchman, Karl, and many other terrorists. He greatly angers Hans and Karl in the process.
6. McClane battles the terrorists with the help of a lone police officer.
7. The other police are against McClane and he feels alone in his fight. The police approach fails, so McClane is totally alone.
8. McClane fights Karl, kills him and prepares to go save Holly from Gruber.
9. Seemingly outnumbered, McClane appears to give up.
10. Using his New York wits, McClane kills Gruber and saves Holly.

Outline

An outline is a list of the scenes that make up a screenplay, from FADE IN to FADE OUT. Every writer has a different method of outlining—some are very detailed, while some list only a sentence or even just a word for each scene.

A good way to start a screenplay is to write a beat sheet, an outline and then a treatment. If you work out the story problems with these three tools, you will find that writing the actual script is a breeze.

Why Do I Need a Treatment

Besides being an important selling tool, a treatment allows you to see if your idea can sustain a feature-length film. Many writers take an idea straight to screenplay form, and then find 30 pages in that there is not enough story to continue the script. In this short summary form, you will also be able to identify any weaknesses in your plot, theme and characters.

It is much easier to find and solve these challenges in the prose treatment form than it is to locate them in the screenplay format.

How Long Should It Be?

Sadly, there is no cut and dry length for a treatment. Generally, treatments vary in length from 1-25 pages.

A general rule—the more power the executive holds, the shorter the treatment you should send them. It is recommended to have a few different versions of your treatment. Besides a lengthy summary of the story, have a quick one pager on hand.

What Is the Format?

Your treatment should be written in prose form, and in 12 point Courier font. In essence, the treatment looks like a short story. There should be one line of space between each paragraph, and no indenting.

DON'T insert dialogue, slug lines, or anything else in screenplay format.

DO use standard punctuation for dialogue.

However, be careful not to rely on much dialogue in your treatment in order to effectively tell the story in 10 pages or less. A few carefully chosen thematic lines will suffice. For instance, the treatment for "Forrest Gump" would likely use the line, "Life is like a box of chocolates. You never know what you're gonna get," because it is used throughout the script as a thematic tag line.

What Should I Aspire to Do with the Treatment?

The treatment should not look, sound or read like an outline, a beat sheet or a screenplay. The essence of the story and the characters should be evoked through exhilarating language and imagery. It should sound like an excited moviegoer recanting the details of a film he just saw that was thought provoking, exhilarating and made him feel like he just had to share all the details with his friends. The prose you use in a treatment should be different than the narrative lines of a screenplay.

The beginning of the treatment has to grab the reader and not let go until the very end. Your reader should be able to see the script play out on the silver screen in front of his or her very eyes. After reading the treatment, the reader should be on fire to get this script to her boss, pronto!

The Log Line

A Log Line is a one sentence description of your film. It's really that simple. You've seen log lines, even if you're not aware of it. In essence, TV Guide descriptions of films are log lines. A log line may describe the following elements:

- Genre—comedy, drama, thriller, love story, etc.
- Setting—time and place, locale, other pertinent information
- Plot—the main narrative thrust of the story
- Character—the lead character or group of characters
- Theme—the main subject of the movie

A log line need not contain the following elements:

- Character names (unless the characters are historical figures)
- Back story
- Qualitative judgments—"A hilarious story…" "A fascinating tale…"
- Comparisons to other films—"It's 'Jaws' meets 'Mary Poppins'…"

Here are a few examples of log lines for well-known films. See if you can guess the film being described (the answers are right below, so don't cheat!):

1. A throwback to the serial adventure films of the 1930s, this film is the story of a heroic archeologist who races against the Nazis to find a powerful artifact that can change the course of history.
2. Set at a small American college in the early 1960s, this broad comedy follows a fraternity full of misfits through a year of parties, mishaps and food fights.
3. An illiterate boy looks to become a contestant on the Hindi version of "Who Wants to be A Millionaire" in order to re-establish contact with the girl he loves, who is an ardent fan of the show.

4. A man decides to change his life by saying 'yes' to everything that comes his way. On his journey, he wins $45,000, meets a hypnotic dog, obtains a nursing degree, travels the globe, and finds romance.

5. A behind-the-scenes view of the 2000 presidential election and the scandal that ensued in the weeks following.

Get the idea? The log line is designed to describe and to tease, like a line of advertising copy for your film. It has to be accurate, it can't be misleading. It's the first sentence a producer or executive is going to read, and you've got to make sure it isn't the last. Make it count.

By the way, the log lines above are for:

1. "Raiders of the Lost Ark"
2. "Animal House"
3. "Slumdog Millionaire"
4. "Yes Man"
5. "Recount"

Why Is the Log Line Important in a Treatment?

The log line is the first sentence an executive will ever read from your hand. It's also the shorthand that executives will use to discuss your project with each other. If a junior executive reads your treatment and likes it, she'll need to tell her boss about the project in order to move it to the next step (probably a meeting between you and the boss).

The boss will ask the junior executive "What's it about?" The junior executive will respond with your log line, if you've written it well and accurately. You are helping to provide the junior executive with the tools she needs to help move your project forward. If you don't provide a log line at the beginning of your treatment, you rely on the junior executive's ability to digest your treatment and come up with a good log line of her own. Even in a collaborative art form like filmmaking, it's never a good idea to leave a job undone for someone else to do if you are more capable of doing it yourself. And who knows your story better than you do? Write a great log line for your treatment, and you'll know that your treatment is being discussed in your own words.

Who Is the Log Line For

The log line is for the buyer: the executive, the producer, the agent. By writing a log line for your treatment, you are helping them to process your material more efficiently. Getting a movie made is a sales process, a constant, revolving door sales process. You sell your work to an agent, who then sells your work to a producer, who then sells it to a director, who then sells it to actors and key crew members.

Once the movie is made, the sales process starts all over again, as the producer has to sell the movie to distributors and marketing executives, who have to sell the film to theater owners who have to sell the film to audiences. A good log line can ride the film all the way from start to finish, helping to sell it at each step.

Should the Log Line Refer to Other Movies?

No. It used to be popular to write log lines that were entirely film references. This practice became so prevalent that it became a cliché, and should be avoided if at all possible. Nothing says "schlock" as quickly as a "Die Hard" reference—the classic action movie reference that every movie strived for in the early 1990s. "Speed" was called "Die Hard" on a bus. "Passenger 57" was called "Die Hard" on a plane. Descriptive as these log lines may be, they read as lazy writing, and if your writing isn't even original in the log line, who will be interested in reading your treatment or your script? Avoid hucksterism, overselling and hype. It's a turnoff.

How Long Should the Log Line Be

Your log line should be one sentence long. Pare it down to its essence, and don't let your sentence become a run-on. Try it out loud, see if it works. You don't have to follow every twist and turn of the plot in your log line, you only have to convey the flavor of the script. One sentence will do it.

What Is the Difference Between the Log Line and the Theme?

Your log line is a sales tool that is a teaser and an invitation to read your script. The theme may be contained in the log line, but not necessarily. Theme is the real answer to "What is your script about?" and Theme need not be confined to a one sentence answer. Theme is often related to the discovery that your main character makes during the course of the film. For instance, in "Raiders of the Lost Ark," Indiana Jones discovers that people are actually more important to him than historical artifacts. In "Animal House," the Deltas discover that the camaraderie that they've discovered in their fraternity is the real lasting value of their college experience, not their class work or their social status on campus.

In Closing

You've spent months or years (or even decades) on your script, and so it may be frustrating to jump through the hoops of the submission process—but it's important. Don't give readers an excuse to ignore your work. You must craft a killer query, treatment and log line before the script gets its big shot. Compose them well, and you're on your way to selling that screenplay.

The Legal 411 for Screenwriters

By Dinah Perez

As a practicing entertainment attorney for nearly two decades, I have represented many writers. I have counseled them on the legal issues related to their writing endeavors, negotiated their agreements with agents and managers, helped them sell their screenplays, and settled their disputes with other writers and producers.

You need to be diligent when it comes to dealing with the legal issues that may arise while you are writing and selling your screenplay, including hiring an agent and manager. Otherwise, you may end up jointly owning your screenplay with another writer, though it was not your intention; may be sued for copyright infringement for incorporating copyright protected material into your screenplay that you thought was in the public domain; could waste your time writing a derivative work based on an original whose rights you cannot acquire; may not be paid compensation and rights you're entitled to when you sell your screenplay; may not be able to shop or sell your screenplay; and may find it impossible to replace your current agent or manager. Overall, consulting with an entertainment attorney up front is much more cost efficient that attempting to fix mistakes and settle disputes that could have been avoided. Whenever I say "attorney" herein, I mean "entertainment attorney."

This chapter endeavors to inform you of the legal issues that exist as you navigate through the process of writing, shopping, selling your screenplay, and hiring an agent, manager, and attorney. This is not a full exploration of the law, nor is it intended to make you an expert in the field. Rather, it is meant to help you spot the issues that may require legal counsel and the important deal terms of the agreements into which you may enter into as a screenwriter. There is a primer on the basics of copyright law up front. Thereafter, I have organized the information in a sequential manner that guides you on your journey, start to finish.

Copyright

A "copyright" is a form of protection for the authors of original content which, with few exceptions, bestows upon authors of intellectual property, such as a book, play, magazine article, news story, video game, screenplay, motion pictures, etc., the exclusive right to reproduce, distribute, perform, prepare and sell their creations.[1] Copyright protection does not extend to ideas—only to their expression. The current term of copyright is the life of the author plus 70 years.[2] Copyright is automatic the moment the work is fixed in a tangible medium, like a printed page, a hard drive, a flash drive, digital recording, film, etc.[3] Copyright law may impact your use of any of the source material you incorporate into your screenplay, and the ownership of your screenplay if you collaborate with another writer.

Copyright protection means that you own the object of your creation and that anyone who wants to use it needs to acquire the right to do so from you. In fact, absent an exception, anyone who uses your copyright protected work without your assent is infringing on your copyright. Likewise, you cannot use another's work without permission unless said work is in the public domain, or you are claiming your use is a "Fair Use." This exception to the Copyright Act allows you to utilize another's work without permission for the purpose of "criticism, comment, news reporting, teaching (including multiple copies for classroom use), scholarship, or research" without infringing copyright.[4] I advise that you proceed with caution and consult with an attorney if you are claiming a Fair Use exception to the Copyright Act, since the exception is far narrower than most people realize.

Though copyright protection is automatic, I strongly urge you to spend the $35 it costs to formally register a copyright for your treatment (if you are going to be pitching it prior to writing the screenplay) and screenplay, once you have completed them. You can register a copyright at any time, but I recommend you do so before you start shopping and submitting your treatment and/or screenplay. The benefits that you gain from the registration far outweigh the cost and time it takes to complete the registration form online. Copyright registration within five years of first publication provides proof of ownership and affords you the opportunity to litigate against infringers, since registration is a prerequisite to filing a legal claim. Registration within three month of first publication and prior to an infringement allows a court to award you statutory damages of up to $150,0000 (or actual damages and profits, if they are more than the statutory damages) as well as attorneys' fees. You may only be awarded actual damages and profits if you do not register within the first three months of publication or prior to an infringement.[5]

Registration of your copyright with the U.S. Copyright Office is the only registration that affords the benefits in the preceding paragraph. The "poor man's copyright," which entails you mailing your screenplay (or other creation) to yourself and you saving the unopened package, provides no more protection than the unregistered copyright. The Writers Guild of America ("WGA") script registration service, which allows you to register ideas, treatments, screenplays, and teleplays, may serve to potentially provide proof as to the day of existence of your registered material. I recommend registering with WGA when a production company requests it, or when what you have created is not entitled to copyright protection, e.g., an idea. WGA registration costs $20 for non-members and $10 for members. Note that WGA script registration does not trump the Copyright Act.

Note that in order for anyone to infringe on your screenplay's copyright they actually have to copy it. There is no infringement unless the party you are accusing had access to your screenplay and there is substantial similarity of the copyright protected elements in your screenplay and the screenplay or picture you are claiming is infringing on yours. You have no copyright infringement claim if someone independently creates a screenplay that is similar to yours.

Ready, Set ... Pause

You have come up with an idea for a screenplay which you want to begin writing. I suggest that you stop and ponder what you intend to write and the potential legal issues that may exist at this juncture. Pausing long enough to consider what may be required legally of you at the start of every writing endeavor will help you avoid legal errors and costly mistakes that may undermine your goals.

Ask yourself the questions that follow in order to determine if you need to consult with and/or hire an attorney. Are you writing by yourself or with a writing partner? Is the story you want to tell completely fictional and original to you? Is your screenplay based on, or inspired by, outside source material, like a book, play, news article, magazine article, or trial transcript? Are you writing about a living person? It is important that you ask yourself these questions at the outset so that you do not waste time writing something you cannot sell.

Resist the temptation to use a boilerplate agreement not specifically drafted for you by an attorney. Chances are you do not know enough about the law, or crafting an agreement, to revise the agreement without creating a litigation worthy mistake, or one that forces you to shelve your screenplay. The time that you are investing writing warrants the cost of hiring an attorney to do things right.

Writing the Screenplay

Collaborations

A "collaboration" occurs when you write with another writer. You have to consider the long-term implications of any writing partnership because the term of copyright, in the proceeds of your collaboration, is your life plus 70 years. As such, it is important that your writing partner and you share a similar vision for the screenplay you intend to write, that you agree on the deal terms of your partnership, and that you assess the relationship and its long term viability. Note that your writing partner and you will equally co-own the screenplay you write together the moment you fix it in a tangible medium, since copyright automatically attaches regardless of oral agreements or intention to the contrary.

I strongly urge that you retain an attorney, if you do not already have one, and that you enter into a "Collaboration Agreement," a three to four page agreement that addresses all of the pertinent terms of your writing partnership, e.g., split of copyright and revenues, who gets the first position credit, who gets to make the final decision if you disagree on a creative or business issue, who will be responsible for shopping the screenplay, who approves the sale, etc.

Your attorney will help you compromise when your writing partner and you cannot seem to agree on a deal term so that you both feel fairly treated. When a client and collaborator cannot agree on the credit, I suggest that one take the first position credit on screen and the other in ads. When both want final approval, I suggest that one have it on business decisions and the other on creative ones. You can start writing once you have executed the Collaboration Agreement. If you cannot agree, despite the attorney's efforts, then you both just walk away, only having expended the legal fees. This is a small price to pay to avoid a time-intensive and potentially costly dispute down the line.

What happens if you started writing without a Collaboration Agreement and now realize that you do not want to complete the screenplay with your writing partner? You may not have to shelve what you have written thus far if your writing partner is willing to assign it to you. To "assign" means to transfer an asset. You want the other writer to transfer his/her interest in the screenplay to you. This is done via an "Assignment," since copyright law requires that a transfer of a copyright interest be affected by a written document signed by the party assigning rights.[6] I suggest that you execute an Assignment, even if what you have written does not qualify for copyright protection. In addition to drafting the Assignment, an attorney can motivate a recalcitrant collaborator by negotiating terms whereby he/she is paid a portion of the screenplay's sale price. Unfortunately, you may have to chalk this experience up to a lesson learned if your collaborator and you are at an impasse. The alternative, in such a circumstance, is that you assign the results and proceeds of your collaboration to the other writer.

Original Fictional Screenplays

You can proceed to write without regard to any legal issues if you are writing a completely original screenplay either on your own or with a writing partner, as long as you have entered into a Collaboration Agreement. For the purposes of this chapter, "completely original to you" means that you are writing a work of fiction that is not based on outside material, be it a book, play, magazine article, life story, video game, etc. If you are doing research, then it is best that you determine if any of the other sections of this chapter apply to your use of the source materials you may be incorporating into your screenplay.

Screenplays Based on Public Domain Material

You may write a screenplay that is an adaptation of, or based upon, a work that is in the public domain without infringing its copyright. A work is in "Public Domain" when no one owns that work's copyright or if the work never qualified for copyright protection. A work is in the public domain because it was not registered for copyright at a time when an actual registration was mandatory, did not comply with the formalities of the Copyright Act, or the copyright term has expired. You can use a work that is in public domain without securing permission to do so from the author. Works in the public domain include the following: Works published between 1923 and 1977 that were never registered for copyright; works published prior to 1923; works published between 1923 and 1963 that were registered for copyright but published without a copyright notice; works published between 1978 and March 1, 1989 without a copyright notice and without a subsequent registration (within 5 years); unpublished works from authors who died prior to 1944; unpublished anonymous or pseudonymous works created prior to 1894; unpublished works created prior to 1894 when the author's date of death is unknown; and, foreign works that are in the public domain in their country of origin.[7]

Facts, numbers, events, government works (written by government employees), and ideas do not qualify for copyright protection and are, therefore, also in the public domain. Keep in mind that though the aforementioned are in the public domain, their expression and any theories that are original to the author may be protected by copyright. Be extremely careful when using material in historical biographies. Do extensive research in order to separate the historical facts from the author's theories and expression thereof.

Keep your notes and research and annotate your screenplay if you are including any public domain works or information in your screenplay; this may seem burdensome, but you will be grateful you did it if you are ever accused of copyright infringement, since you may have to provide it to prove your innocence. Furthermore, whoever produces your screenplay is going to purchase Errors and Omissions Insurance which, among other things, insures producers against copyright infringement law suits. The insurance carrier may require an opinion letter from an attorney, who may request the annotated script from you. It is far easier to annotate a script as you write than to try to piece it together after the fact.

You are not required to credit the source of your public domain materials. Notwithstanding, I recommend that you credit the author and work if your screenplay is an adaptation of it, or if your screenplay is based upon the work. You do not need to credit your research sources for facts, numbers and such.

Derivative Works

You need to secure the author's or publisher's ("author/publisher") permission if you want to adapt or write a screenplay based upon or inspired by another literary work, such as a book, play, magazine article, essay, etc. Do not take the risk of writing first and attempting to acquire rights afterwards. You are not only infringing copyright when you do this—you are also potentially wasting your time because the author/publisher of the literary work may refuse to let you acquire the rights you need to proceed. They do not always want to have their literary works adapted to the big screen and, even if they do, may prefer to do business with a studio, which is more likely to pay them hefty option fees and purchase prices. If that is the case, it is best that you discover it up front before you invest your time.

Copyright protection applies to that portion of a derivative work created by you, but not to the original work itself. If you adapt a book, your adaptation is protected by copyright, but you acquire no rights in the original materials from the underlying book. In other words, the characters, locations, dialogue, storyline and other elements from the book belong to its author/publisher. The same goes any for public domain facts you incorporate into your screenplay; they remain in the public domain while your expression of those facts is subject to copyright protection.

You acquire the rights to a literary work by entering into an "Option/Purchase Agreement" whereby you have the exclusive option to buy said literary work for a determined period of time. The Option/Purchase Agreement has two components: the Option Agreement ("Option") itself states how much time you have to buy the literary work, and the purchase agreement includes the sale price and rights to be granted. You purchase the literary work by exercising the Option and paying the purchase price prior to the Option's expiration date. You do not actually purchase the literary work until the commencement of principal photography—when you know that the picture is being produced.

Options usually run in one year increments ("option period(s)") and can have one or more extensions. I recommend a one year initial option period with a minimum of two one year extension periods. You pay an "option fee" at the commencement of each option period. Option fees are considered advances and, therefore, may be applicable against the purchase price. If you have paid $20,000 in applicable option fees, when you exercise the Option, you pay $80,000 of the total $100,000 purchase price. If you do not make the option fees applicable, then you would pay the full purchase price irrespective of the option fees paid. The Option expires if you let it lapse due to non-payment of the applicable option fee, so be sure to extend the Option one week prior to its expiration; to avoid any mishaps mail the option fee and notice of extension via registered mail return receipt requested.

My clients have paid option fees as low as $1 and as high as $25,000 per option period. Expect to deplete your bank account if you are entering into an Option/Purchase Agreement on behalf of a best-selling book or play, or a magazine article or news story from a well known publication. Authors/publishers in the know expect an option fee equal to 10% of the purchase price. Some may consider this an industry standard—I do not because this is a point of negotiation versus a hard and fast rule. If you cannot afford to pay an option fee equal to 10% of the purchase price, then offer what you can pay, keeping in mind that you do not want to insult the author/publisher. Among other things, I may offer to make one or more of the option fees non-applicable if they are on the low end and it seems like they may be keeping the author/publisher from agreeing to the Option/Purchase Agreement. A "free" Option may be possible if you are acquiring a self-published or obscure book or play, or an article published in a relatively unknown publication. Notwithstanding that the Option is free, you should pay at least one dollar per option period so that the Option/Purchase Agreement does not fail for lack of consideration of some kind. "Consideration" is necessary for the formation of a binding contract—each party to the transaction needs to get a benefit.

The Option/Purchase Agreement for the literary work upon which you are basing your screenplay will determine whether you can sell your creation upon its completion. You will not be able to sell your screenplay if you go about it incorrectly or offer too high a purchase price. I advise that you hire an attorney to help you negotiate and draft an Option/Purchase Agreement that provides you with all the rights you need to deliver to your screenplay's buyer.

Remakes and Sequels Based on Pre-Existing Pictures

Do not write a screenplay based on a previously released motion picture or television show. This is not only copyright infringement—it is a monumental waste of your time! Under no uncertain terms will the motion picture studio or television network ("studio/network") which produced the original ever give you permission to write a sequel or remake based on their original motion picture or television show; they do not let third parties acquire an interest in their library. When the studio/network is ready, it will develop the remake or sequel in-house, with writers of their own choosing. Delete the screenplay if you have already written it, since you cannot use it as a writing sample or share it with anyone due to copyright infringement. Do not waste your money hiring an attorney to attempt to make a submission for you since the studio/network always responds with a resounding, "no." They do not want to read your screenplay because they do not want to risk you filing a copyright infringement, unjust enrichment, and/or breach of implied contract law suit against them, when they produce a remake or sequel that contains elements that were in your submitted screenplay. This happened to MGM and Sylvester Stallone when a writer submitted his version of "Rocky IV" to them. MGM and Sylvester Stallone prevailed over the writer because the "Rocky" characters were entitled to copyright protection.

Life Stories

"Private Persons"

Every living person has the "right of privacy"—the right to be left alone and the right to keep private facts from the public. As a consequence thereof, you need to enter into a Life Story Agreement if the subject of your screenplay is a "private person" whose story has not been in the national news and, hence, is not known by the general public. Do not commence writing until you have entered into a Life Story Agreement. The only exception here is if you are writing about a deceased person, since the right of privacy terminates upon death.

A Life Story Agreement is an agreement whereby the person whose life story you are writing (the "subject" of your screenplay) gives you permission to base your screenplay on his/her life story. It also allows your screenplay's buyer to produce and distribute the picture based on your screenplay. The Life Story Agreement is an Option/Purchase Agreement which takes into account the personal nature of the rights being acquired. The option fee and purchase price for a private person's Life Story Agreement are generally on the low end, because the life story is arguably not in big demand. Both tend to be far lower than the subject usually expects. It is more likely that the purchase price will be in the $80,000 range than the $1 million—the sum a subject asked of a client of mine a couple of years ago. You will not be able to find a buyer for your screenplay if you overpay for the rights, so that is something to always keep in mind.

The Life Story Agreement will give you access to the subject's life story via any news clippings, journals, and interviews. Do not be surprised if the subject wants "final approval" of the screenplay. You can grant the subject the right to comment on a draft of your screenplay, but never final approval. The former is just feedback, the latter means that the subject can stop you from producing any version of the screenplay he/she does not like. Needless-to-say, you never give a subject final approval of the screenplay.

The Life Story Agreement conveys upon you the right to write the screenplay, but it does not give you permission to defame or portray the subject of your screenplay in a false light without legal repercussions. You can take certain dramatic license with the story, but cannot depict the subject in an untrue and in an inaccurate manner—especially one that would be offensive or damaging to him/her. Let the subject comment on the screenplay so that you know where you have potential issues. It is much easier and cost efficient to fix the issues during the writing process than to address them in a court of law. Note that defamation and false light are not the same thing: the former is making false statements that harm a person's reputation and the latter is making untrue statements that depict a person in a false light and are offensive or cause the person embarrassment.

"Public Persons"

Celebrities, politicians, and other persons in whom the general public has great interest are all considered "public persons" because they have disclosed their private facts and live so much of their lives out in the public. As a consequence, public persons have a more limited right of privacy than the private person, and have a lesser expectation of it.

You have a lot of leeway to write about a politician because of the First Amendment and the public's right and need to know about any individual running for, or in, political office.[8] You may disclose truthful facts about politicians, e.g., that a politician is taking bribes, is an alcoholic or drug addict, has cancer, etc. Limit disclosure to facts that impact the politician's ability to do his/her job or how he/she carries out the responsibilities of office. You do not have the same berth where a living celebrity is concerned. If you want to avoid a costly judgment in favor of a celebrity, use facts that are already in the public consciousness, garnered from the likes of a trial transcript, news story, magazine article, biography, autobiography, television interviews, etc.

In the category of public persons are criminals whose crimes have catapulted them to celebrity status. Casey Anthony, Amy Fisher, Ted Bundy, and David Berkowitz aka the Son of Sam are what I call "celebrity criminals." The aforementioned have all had pictures produced about them, but not all entered into Life Story Agreements with the television networks that produced movies about them. In fact, two of the three networks that produced pictures about

Amy Fisher, the "Long Island Lolita," did so without a Life Story Agreement. You can write about a celebrity criminal as long as you stick to the facts disclosed in court during a trial and/or are in the public domain.

Notwithstanding, since the public person has a right to privacy, limited though it may be, I always recommend that you consult with an attorney and that you enter into a Life Story Agreement rather than proceed without one. In order to sell your screenplay, you are going to have to warrant and represent that you have not invaded anyone's right of privacy, and will be required to agree to indemnify and hold harmless the producer if you breach that warranty and representation. This means that you have to reimburse the producer for any damages the producer suffers due to your breach of the right of privacy via your screenplay. The Life Story Agreement greatly eliminates the risk of litigation and a costly judgment, as long as you do not defame or portray your subject in a false light (there has to be an element of maliciousness where celebrities are concerned). The producer and distributor may want the assurances and rights granted via the Life Story Agreement and may make it a condition of financing and distribution. Also, you may want the public person's cooperation either because you may want to interview him/her to gain access to information that was not previously disclosed and/or need his/her help in securing any releases from other individuals integral to the life story.

The Right of Publicity

Every person, be they private or public, also has the "right of publicity," which gives everyone the right to control the commercial exploitation of their name, likeness, voice, and any other identifying aspect of their persona. In other words, your screenplay's producer cannot advertise and distribute a picture based on your screenplay unless you acquired the subject's right of publicity. This is best done via a Life Story Agreement, which grants the buyer the right to use the subject's, name, voice and likeness to produce, advertise, and distribute the picture.

Also, though the right of privacy terminates at death, the right of publicity does not always because state law determines whether the right dies or survives. For example, in New York, the right of publicity is extinguished at death for persons domiciled there[9] and, as per California statute, the right of publicity is a descendible property right that currently survives death by 70 years (for persons who died there prior to 1985).[10] You need to know where the subject of your screenplay died in order to ascertain whether the right of publicity ended with, or outlived, your subject's life.

Representation: Signing with an Agent or Manager

You are going to need representation via an agent or manager once you are done writing your screenplay. The California Talent Agency Act ("TAA") says that only licensed "agents" may procure, offer, promise, or attempt to procure employment or engagements for you. Agents must limit their commissions to 10% of what you earn, post a $50,000 surety bond with the Labor Commissioner, submit their artist agreement for approval by the Labor Commissioner, and segregate client monies from agency monies in a client trust fund.[11] In addition, agents are not supposed to have a conflict of interest with their clients, which means that they do not attach themselves to produce their clients' screenplays.

Managers are not licensed agents and, therefore, are not supposed to engage in agent type activities, such as pitching, shopping screenplays, and attempting to secure writing assignments. Because of the TAA, managers are limited to advising their clients on matters related to their careers, helping their clients secure agency representation, and assisting in the development of their clients' screenplays. They cannot procure, promise to procure or attempt to procure work. Since managers are not agents, they are not required to post a surety bond or maintain a client trust account, and have no limit on their commissions—though the industry standard is 10%. Notwithstanding the TAA, most literary managers do engage in agent type activities on behalf of their clients when their clients lack agency representation. Managers risk rescission of the management agreement with you, and forfeiture of past and future commissions from you, if you file a complaint against them with the California Labor Commissioner alleging that the manager engaged in activities in violation of the TAA, and the California Labor Commissioner determines your allegations to be true.

I am grateful for every reputable manager who works to create and improve the career of any writer—more so when the writer is not represented by an agent. I believe managers should be paid for the value of services they render regardless of the TAA. They should get to collect commissions if their services contributed to your success and earnings. The only problem I have with managers is that their interests are very often in conflict with those of their clients. This occurs when managers attempt to attach themselves to produce their clients' screenplays. A manager friend tells me that she should be credited and paid as a producer because the development work that she does with her clients is actually a producer's job. I disagree.

My biggest concern with managers attaching themselves to produce is that it might deter a producer from going forward—especially if the manager has not produced before. It's best to have an agreement with the manager whereby the manager does not insist on being attached, or will step aside if his/her attachment negatively impacts the negotiation. If necessary, I would offer the manager a higher commission (up to 20% total) to compensate him/her for development services.

Notwithstanding the possible drawbacks, there are a couple of advantages when a manager produces: you have someone advocating on your behalf and you pay a lower commission because the manager's producing fee is credited against the commission you owe. (A commission of $100,000 gets reduced to $20,000 if the manager's producing fee is $80,000.) Whether you want a manager/producer representing you is something that you need to consider prior to entering into the management agreement. Very often, managers will decline representation if they cannot produce the material they develop.

Standard agency and management agreements include a variety of clauses related to your relationship with the agent and/or manager, their duties, compensation, the term of the agreement, how you may be able to terminate the agreement do to non-performance, etc. The agreement you sign most likely will not contain a "sunset clause" unless your attorney makes it a requirement.

A "sunset clause" reduces and eventually terminates continuing commissions owed to the agent and/or manager once the agreement terminates. The need for a sunset clause most often arises when your agent and/or manager secures you a position as a staff writer on a television series, sells your screenplay and it spins off into a series, or your screenplay becomes a studio franchise. The agent or manager wants to receive his/her commission on any monies earned by you, in perpetuity, from agreements you entered into during the term of their representation—even after their agreement with you terminates. The problem with this is that whoever represents you next is going to want to commission *all* your earnings as payment for the services they are rendering in the present. Since agents individually or jointly cannot charge you in excess of 10%, you are in the position of not being able to hire any agent that wants to commission the pre-existing deal, which is likely most of them. You could end up paying a double commission to your managers, since there is no restriction as to how much they can charge.

The alternative is the sunset clause whereby the commission to the previous agent and/or manager is reduced by 33 ⅓% per year until it zeroes out—you pay the new agent or manager that commission on an escalating basis until he/she is receiving 100% of the commission on those earnings. You will only reap the benefit of the sunset clause if it is negotiated into your agreement up front, since the agent will not incorporate it after the fact; it impacts them negatively.

Whether you need both an agent and manager depends on where you are in your career. As I said above, the agent's job is to sell you while the manager's job is to develop you. You are more likely to need a manager earlier in your career, when you do not have an agent, need help getting your career off the ground, and need help developing your talent. You always need an agent. It is highly unlikely that you are going to be able to secure an agent or manager with the top five companies early in your career—unless you are introduced by someone whose opinion they value or you have been extremely successful in another medium, e.g., you have a best-selling novel, graphic novel or video game. Sign with the agent and/or manager you can at this time. You can upgrade later if the opportunity presents itself.

Your relationship with your agent or manager, how much money you get to keep, what expenses you are reimbursing the manager for, how much help you get from both, and how long you are tied to them is going to be dictated by the agreement you sign. You will regret not having hired an attorney to advise you where this agreement is concerned when you realize that you could have made a better deal and/or that the deal you made has drawbacks.

As far as your attorney goes, be sure to keep him/her in the loop at all times. My clients always end up with a better deal when their representatives and I work together. I always improve the financial terms, credit, make sure that my client reaps the benefits of a box office success, and/ or include clauses that protect my client and maintain my client's involvement if the picture or series has a life beyond the original production.

Shopping and Submissions

Shopping

Your agent (or manager if you do not have an agent) will shop and submit your screenplay once you have completed it. "Shopping" is defined in the industry to mean marketing your screenplay in an effort to entering into an Option/Purchase Agreement. A "pitch" is a three to four minute oral summary of your screenplay. The producer and your agent will negotiate the terms of the Option/Purchase Agreement if the producer wants to develop and potentially produce a picture based on your screenplay. Again, I strongly recommend that you insist that your agent work jointly with your attorney to get you the best option fee, purchase price, and overall terms. Whatever additional monies you have to pay your attorney will be justified by the end result.

You can shop your screenplay directly to producers if you do not have an agent or manager. This directory includes within it the information you need to contact producers. When dealing with a producer that has a development department, contact a development executive, unless you have a pre-existing relationship with the producer. You will pitch your screenplay on that first call if you make contact, so be sure to have a prepared pitch and logline. A "logline" is a sentence summary of your script.

Protecting Your Ideas

You have to be careful not to "blurt out" the idea for your screenplay, since ideas are not protected by copyright law. A "blurt out" most often occurs when a writer meets a producer by chance, like at a party, restaurant, or in an elevator, and takes advantage of the moment by sharing the idea without asking for permission to do so. Producers do not want to be liable for hearing an unsolicited idea, nor should they be. Since it is not entitled to copyright protection, your idea is in the public domain and is up for grabs once you blurt it out. For the reasons stated below, I prefer that you pitch in a formal setting even if the producer grants you permission to pitch during the chance encounter.

Pitching your idea and/or screenplay in a business meeting goes a long way in protecting it because contract law fills the void that exists in copyright law. You can protect your idea by setting up an oral agreement or an implied-in-fact contract. Both require that you work smart and be patient enough to pitch in formal settings only.

An oral agreement is a spoken versus written contract. You protect your idea by creating an oral agreement with the producer for that purpose. You create the oral agreement during your pitch meeting by making disclosure of the idea contingent on the producer's agreement to your terms. Prior to pitching say, "As you know, I'm here to pitch my screenplay (or the idea for a screenplay), but before I do, I just want to make sure you are willing to credit me and purchase my screenplay for no less than WGA minimum if you use it. Can we agree to that?" Oral agreements are difficult to prove so be sure to create a paper trail to substantiate its existence. You do this by sending an email to confirm the scheduled meeting and its purpose beforehand. Afterwards, send the producer an email thanking him/her for the meeting, the purpose of the meeting, and reiterate the agreed upon oral agreement.

You can also protect an idea via an implied-in-fact contract, which is formed when you pitch in a formal setting and it is clear from the conduct that you met with the producer for the purpose of selling your idea and, hence expect payment for its use. The idea can even be based on material that is in the public domain, like a Shakespearean play, as was the case with *Blaustein v. Burton*.

Julian Blaustein, came up with the idea to produce "The Taming of the Shrew", starring Elizabeth Taylor and Richard Burton. He pitched the idea to Richard Burton's agent. Blaustein conditioned the disclosure on the agent being interested in his idea and Burton and Taylor being available to star in it. The agent confirmed both. Blaustein went ahead with the pitch. The agent responded positively and confirmed that it was something Burton and Taylor had not previously considered. Burton and Taylor went ahead and produced the picture without Blaustein's involvement. Blaustein sued for breach of an implied-in-fact contract and prevailed even though the idea was for material in the public domain.[12]

You see here why the conduct and circumstances under which the idea is pitched are so important. Blaustein would not have prevailed if the agent had informed him that Burton and Taylor were already developing the idea, had previously considered it, if they had produced the picture based on a screenplay they had received from an independent source, or if Blaustein had blurted out the idea in an informal setting. As with the oral agreement, I recommend that you create a paper trail as evidence of your meeting and your intentions. Send an email confirming the meeting and its purpose. Send another afterward to evidence the fact that the meeting took place, what you pitched, and why.

Notwithstanding, the above, be aware that idea theft is rather rampant and difficult to prove. The trend is for courts tend to side with the studios/networks and producers versus the writers. The conundrum is that you risk theft when you pitch, but that you can never sell anything unless you do. In light of that, do everything you can to protect your idea. Never pitch without permission to do so, only do so in a formal setting, and create a paper trail. Do not pitch the idea for your completed screenplay until you have registered it with the U.S. Copyright Office since, among other things, it is prima facie evidence as to the date of your screenplay's existence. If you are pitching an idea for a screenplay that you have yet to write, at least write up a summary and register it with the WGA; this does not provide copyright protection, but you at least have proof as to the date of your idea's existence.

Submission Releases

If you are not represented by an agent or manager, it is likely that you will be required to sign a "Submission Release" when you ask to submit your screenplay to a producer or studio/network. A "Submission Release" is a written agreement whereby you relieve the recipient of your screenplay from liability should he/she use any of the content in your screenplay that is not protected by copyright, such as your idea or the public domain material incorporated therein. It also relieves the producer and studio/network of the obligation to pay you if it independently creates material similar to yours, or comes by it from an independent source. Furthermore, the Submission Release also states that the recipient will pay you fair market value if they use of your screenplay, or any portion thereof that is protected by copyright. The Submission Release is going to override any oral agreement you have made to the contrary with the producer once you sign it.

As onerous as Submission Releases are, I understand that producers and studios/networks require them as a form of protection against lawsuits that may or may not be warranted. You can pay an attorney to explain the Submission Release to you, but it is unlikely that the attorney will be able to convince the producer to revise it. You might be tempted to throw caution to the wind and sign the Submission Release if you are unrepresented by an agent or manager. I recommend that you ask the producer if he/she will accept an attorney submission instead. Your lawyer can make the submission for you if the producer agrees to accept it. If not, then I suggest that you continue pounding doors until you do find an agent or manager willing to represent you. I know that it is difficult to walk away from what you may think is your only opportunity, but you have to be patient unless you are willing to risk your screenplay.

Note that agents will also require that you sign a Submission Release as a condition to reading your screenplay. You cannot submit otherwise. Be aware that agents can share your screenplay with other agents and the agency's clients with impunity once you sign the Submission Release. You might try having your manager make the submission, or asking if the agent will accept an attorney submission. Otherwise, you will have to take the risk if you want to the agent to consider representing you.

Sample Submission Release

_____ (Name of Production Company)

_____ (Title of Screenplay)

Dear _____:

I am submitting to you herewith the above referenced screenplay (hereinafter referred to as the "material") pursuant to the following terms and conditions.

1. I am interested in having you evaluate my material. I know that because of your stature in the industry that you receive many screenplays, treatments, ideas, stories, formats, and suggestions for screenplays. As a consequence thereof, I understand that you cannot read, accept, and evaluate the material unless I sign and return this Submission Release.

[The production company wants to protect itself from copyright infringement and breach of implied or oral contract claims on behalf of your submitted screenplay. This Submission Release, which is a binding agreement, will release the production company from liability for the aforementioned types of legal claims initiated by the person submitting the material.]

2. I represent and warrant that I am the material's author; that I am sole owner of the right, title and interest in and to the material; that I have the authority to make this submission and to grant the rights being conveyed to you hereunder; that the material does not infringe upon a third party's copyright; that the material does not violate anyone's right of privacy nor is it defamatory. I agree to indemnify you and hold you harmless from any claims, losses, judgments, and expenses (including reasonable legal fees and costs) that are incurred by you due to my breach of the aforementioned warranties and this Submission Release.

[You own the screenplay because you either wrote it or commissioned it as a work-for-hire. The production company wants you to warrant that you have the legal right and authority to submit the screenplay and to contract on its behalf. The production company wants an assurance that the screenplay is not going to result in a third party copyright infringement, right of privacy, or defamation claim against it should they to produce your screenplay. Via this clause, you agree to pay all of the losses and costs incurred by the production company if a legal claim is brought against the production company due to you breach of the warranties in this clause and the overall Submission Release.]

3. I understand that you create screenplays in-house and, as such, that you may be developing a screenplay that is similar to the material that I am submitting to you. Furthermore, I am also aware that a third party may submit a screenplay to you that is comparable to mine, which you may decide to acquire and produce. You may produce said screenplay, without any obligation

to me of any kind, a screenplay that though similar to the material was independently created by a third party or you.

[The production company is disclosing the scenarios under which it may produce a screenplay that may resemble yours but which it asserts is independently created by the production company or a third party. You are agreeing that the production company does not have to pay or credit you under these circumstances.]

4. I agree that any portion of the material that may be freely used by the public, because it is not protected under copyright law or is in the public domain, may be utilized by you. The material which you are free to use without any obligation to me shall be referred to as "unprotected material" henceforth. If all or any part of said material is not unprotected material because it is protected under copyright law, then it shall be referred to herein as "protected material."

[Ideas, theories, names, titles, formats, and content in the public domain are not protected by copyright law. The production company wants the right to use this unprotected material without having to credit or pay you. For example, if you adapt, update and give an urban spin to a Jane Austen book, the production company can do the same without paying you because Austen's works are in the public domain. The production company cannot use your exact word for word adaptation, but it take utilize your idea without payment to you if you sign this Submission Release.]

5. If you use or cause to be used any of the protected material, you will pay me industry standard compensation or the fair market value of said material, whichever is greater.

[I have seen many different clauses regarding use of protected material and compensation therefor. Some companies will wait to reach an agreement with you prior to using the protected material—others want free reign to use it at will. Some will agree to pay you fair market value while others agree to industry standards, or what they say they typically pay for similar material. Regardless of the formula, you usually give up your ability to negotiate the purchase price of your protected material via the agreement.]

6. I acknowledge that no fiduciary or confidential relationship now exists or will ever exist between us by reason of this agreement or submission of the material to you. No express or implied agreements will be exist between us as a consequence of this unsolicited submission or conversations in reference thereto.

[This eliminates the possibility that you may be paid for use of the unprotected material in your screenplay. If you will remember, I discuss in the chapter how contract law protects elements of your screenplay that are not protected by copyright law—this clause eliminates that possibility.]

7. This agreement shall be governed by the laws of the state of California applicable to agreements executed and to be fully performed therein.

[This means that California state law will apply to this agreement regardless of where you reside.]

8. In the event of any dispute concerning the material or concerning any claim of any kind or nature whatsoever, arising in connection with the material or arising in connection with this agreement, such dispute will be submitted to arbitration. We hereby waive any and all rights and benefits, which we may otherwise have or be entitled to under the laws of California to litigate any such dispute in court, it being the intention of the parties to arbitrate, according to the provisions hereof, all such disputes. Either party may commence arbitration proceedings by giving the other party written notice thereof by registered mail and proceeding thereafter in accordance with the rules and procedures of the American Arbitration Association. The arbitration shall be conducted in the County of Los Angeles, State of California and shall be governed by and subject to the laws of the State of California and the then prevailing rules of the American Arbitration Association. The arbitrators' award shall be final and binding and a judgment upon the award may be enforced by any court of competent jurisdiction.

[An arbitration is a proceeding that takes place outside of a court room. There is no judge or jury—just an arbitrator. Furthermore, the prevailing party usually recuperates reasonable legal fees and expenses associated with the arbitration proceeding. Arbitration clauses are touted by the production entities as more financially efficient and less time consuming than litigation. After discussing the issue of arbitration clauses with various transactional and litigation attorneys and witnessing my own clients' arbitrations, I have come to the conclusion that I prefer for my clients to litigate than arbitrate: arbitration is not necessarily less costly than litigation, it is most definitely not less time consuming, can result in an unprecedented decisions, and may result in an outcome that is biased in favor of a motion picture studio or television network. I make an effort to negotiate out of the arbitration clause whenever possible.]

9. I hereby state that I have read and understand this agreement and that no oral representations of any kind have been made to me and that this agreement states our entire understanding with reference to the subject matter hereof. Any modification or waiver of any of the provisions of this agreement must be in writing and signed by both of us.

[This clause eliminates the possibility of an oral agreement that contradicts the terms of the Submission Release. Modifications after-the-fact need to be agreed to in writing by the production company and you.]

Sincerely,

_____   Date: _____
(Writer's Signature)

[The Submission Release is a contract of adhesion, which means that the agreement is presented to you on a take or leave it basis. They will not modify the Submission Release if you object to any of

its content, and they will not accept your material without it if you lack an agent or manager and the production company does not accept attorney submissions.

I have presented the most basic of Submission Releases. Every company has their own basic form. It is a good idea to have an attorney explain a Submission Release to you at least once, so that you may know up front how signing it may negatively impact you.

You may download a PDF edition of this Sample Submission Release form here: http://www.scriptmag.com/features/submission-releases]

Selling Your Screenplay: The Option/Purchase Agreement

The Option

Any producer who is serious about producing a picture based on your screenplay will offer to Option it. The "Option/Purchase Agreement," in this instance, is a written agreement whereby a producer acquires the exclusive right to develop, produce and distribute a picture based on your screenplay. The Option automatically expires at the end of each option term unless the producer renews it (if it has any remaining terms), or the producer exercises it and purchases the screenplay. The producer will not buy your screenplay until the commencement of principal photography.

Typically, producers want a minimum one year option term with a one year extension. This is not excessive considering that it takes an average of seven years to get a picture produced. You need to give the producer a realistic amount of time to develop the screenplay with you, to attach talent and a director, and to shop it for financing. In fact, do not be surprised if the producer wants an extension at the end of the second option term. I advise my clients to extend if the producer is paying a decent option fee, or has made good use of the time, e.g., talent or a director capable of attracting funding are attached.

The option fee that the producer offers to pay you is influenced by a number of factors: your track record, the producer's track record, the heat generated by your screenplay (if any), the subject's notoriety if the screenplay is based on a true life story, whether you are a WGA member, the screenplay's purchase price, the option term, and whether the producer is a studio or independent producer. Due to the foregoing, I disagree with the notion that the industry standard option fee is 10% of the purchase price. I always try to negotiate the highest option fee possible; in my experience, they generally tend to be under 10% for unproduced writers unless the purchase price is less than WGA low budget minimum. They are in the 10% range for writers with a successful track record.

Whether a writer is a WGA member will influence the option fee because the WGA requires that its members be paid an option fee equal to no less than 10% of the applicable WGA minimum purchase price (for a term not to exceed 18 months). As of May 2014, the WGA minimums for a low budget and high budget completed screenplay are $44,445 and $90,982 respectively. The option fee required for a purchase price of $250,000 is only $9,098. The producer can offer a higher option fee, but he/she is not required to do so by the WGA. If the producer does so, it will depend on the above factors.

When considering option fees, you have to take into account the fact that most independent producers lack development funds. As such, be flexible and consider the entirety of the circumstances, e.g., the producer's track record, connections, and ability to raise financing. I do recommend that you consider an earnest and reasonable offer. I consider a reasonable offer to be one that takes into consideration the benefit the producer gets by having your screenplay available to develop and produce and the legal fees you will incur to enter into the Option/Purchase Agreement. I appreciate the time, effort and money that the producer is going to invest in getting your screenplay made; I also believe you should not be out-of-pocket on the legal fees.

Options fees are technically advances against the purchase price, but whether they are applied against the purchase price is up to negotiation. Most often, the end result is that the first option fee is applicable against the purchase price and the subsequent ones are not.

I advise you against entering into "free" Options. Free Options usually result in a waste of time, money and opportunity, since you are out-of-pocket on legal fees, cannot shop the screenplay while it is under Option, and producers tend to be less productive when they have no money at stake. An alternative to the free Option is a "Shopping Agreement" wherein you allow the producer to shop the screenplay without acquiring the right to purchase it from you. This arrangement usually works well when you are dealing with a proven producer, who has studio or production company connections, and who could potentially enter into an Option/Purchase Agreement directly with you and pay you an option fee. Shopping Agreements are usually in the 60-90 day range and get extended if you are in the midst of negotiations with a studio/network or production company interested in entering into an Option/Purchase Agreement with you. The producer does not negotiate the terms of the Option/Purchase Agreement on your behalf. He/she only gets the ball rolling so that your agent and attorney can step in and negotiate for you. Keep in mind that if the producer is not successful, that you will not be able to shop your screenplay where he/she shopped it for at least a year—or until there are new executives working there. Other producers may not be interested in paying you for an Option if the previous producer has limited his/her opportunities for success, so this is something to keep in mind.

Purchase Price

There is no such thing as a "standard" purchase price for a screenplay. WGA members cannot accept less than the sum prescribed in the WGA Schedule of Minimums, but can exceed the minimum, and non-WGA members can sell their screenplays for any price they are able to negotiate. Sale prices typically range between 1% and 3% of the cash production budget of the picture. How much you are offered for your screenplay depends on who you are and what you bring to the table. Producers consider your track record; whether there is a bidding war for your screenplay; whether the screenplay is based on a best-selling novel; whether it is about a salacious, interesting or well publicized person or event; the screenplay's genre; and, if known ahead of time, the picture's potential production budget. If the production budget is not known going into the negotiations, I suggest a purchase price based on a sliding scale, e.g., "for a picture not to exceed $15,000,000 dollars, the purchase price shall be 2 ½% of the cash budget of the picture, but in no event less than WGA low budget minimum and no more than $250,000. The purchase price will be increased by $10,000 for every $1 million increase in the picture's production above $15,000,000 not to exceed a total purchase price equal to $500,000." The attorney attempts to secure the highest ceiling possible while the producer tries to limit it.

Additional Compensation

If the purchase price is on the lower end due to limited financing, I ask for additional compensation in the form of a deferment. "Deferred compensation" is a sum of money that is paid at a future date, from first revenues on a pari passu basis with the other parties being paid on a deferred basis. "Pari passu" means dollar for dollar. For example, if you and four cast members are entitled to deferred monies, where you are due $100,000 and each cast member $25,000, and the production company receives $100,000 in revenues, then you each receive $20,000 from the $100,000. Monies received by the production company will be distributed this way until each deferral is satisfied. Deferred compensation is usually paid prior to investor recoupment, since it is considered part of the screenplay's purchase price and is a production cost.

Whenever possible, I negotiate for my clients to receive a "Box Office Bonus," which is not guaranteed and only gets paid when, and if, the picture reaches a specific and pre-determined sales goal. Box Office Bonus compensation may be expressed as follows: "Writer shall be entitled to a Box Office Bonus of $50,000 when, and if, the picture's domestic and international gross box office, as reported in Variety, exceeds three times the picture's production budget." The bonus is only paid if you are a credited writer. I also negotiate for Nomination/Award Bonus that is paid for award nominations and wins, e.g., Golden Globes and Academy Awards.

Sequels, Remakes...

It is standard for a producer to pay the writer of an original screenplay additional monies if he/she produces a sequel, remake, or television series based on the writer's original screenplay. These additional monies are passive payments, which means that the writer does not have to render additional writing services in order receive them. As per industry standard, if a sequel based on your original screenplay is produced, you are paid 50% of the original screenplay's purchase price and 50% of the profit participation allocated to you for the original screenplay. The passive payment drops from 50% to 33 ⅓% on behalf of remakes based on your original screenplay. As such, if you were paid a $100,000 purchase price and 5% of picture's net profits for your original screenplay, you will be paid $50,000 plus 2 ½% of picture's net profits for any sequels and $33,333 plus 1 ⅔% of picture's net profits for any remakes produced. For any television series based on your screenplay, you will receive passive payments based on the running time of each episode, on its first airing and a portion thereof up to the sixth rerun. I usually refer to the WGA schedule of minimums to calculate the television payments even if my client is not a WGA member.

I always negotiate for my clients to have the Right of First Refusal to write any subsequent versions of their original screenplay, be it a sequel, remake, prequel, television series, or television motion picture. How much you are paid to write any of the aforementioned may depend on whether you are a WGA member, the success of your original screenplay, whether you were credited on your original screenplay (sometimes requires sole credit), and whether you are a working writer at the time of the subsequent version's negotiation. The terms for these writing services will not be negotiated until your services are required, and whether you are engaged to write is contingent upon the producer and you coming to an agreement for your services, since this is just a "Right of First Refusal." Passive payments are generally offered in lieu of writing fees.

Separated Rights

The WGA may determine that you are entitled to "Separated Rights" if you are a WGA member: these are a bundle of rights that the WGA has determined belong to writers of original screenplays. Dramatic stage and publication rights are both included in Separated Rights, as is the mandatory first rewrite of your original screenplay for WGA minimum; the right to meet with a senior production executive if the producer wants to replace you with another writer; the right to reacquire the screenplay if it has not been produced within five years; and, WGA minimum payment for sequel theatrical motion pictures, television movies, and television series.

As far as the dramatic stage rights are concerned, you will be entitled to a royalty free license to produce the screenplay as a dramatic stage play after the producer's holdback period of two years from the picture's general release or five years from the purchase agreement. A "holdback period" is a period of time during which the producer has exclusivity to exploit the right. If the producer exploits the dramatic stage rights prior to expiration of the holdback period, then you shall be paid 50% of the minimum sum paid to authors under the Minimum Basic Contract of the Dramatist Guild of the Author's League of America, Inc. Regarding publishing, you will be able to publish the script or novelization of the script subject to a holdback period equal to six months from the picture's general release or three years from date of the purchase agreement. The producer has to give you the opportunity to negotiate directly with the publisher to write a novel based on your screenplay, if the producer publishes it during the holdback period. The producer has to pay you WGA minimum if you do not write the novel and it is published.

Remember, the compensation and the rights guaranteed via the WGA Basic Agreement are the bare minimum to which you are entitled as a WGA member. Sometimes industry standards are higher, as is the case for passive payments for sequels and remakes. Your attorney can always negotiate for more rights and compensation than that required by the WGA.

Profit Participation

"Net Profits," an additional form of remuneration, are paid when, and if, the Picture based on your screenplay reaches a profit position. Net profits are usually calculated by subtracting all of the costs incurred in the making, marketing and distributing the Picture; this calculation includes the production budget, all financing costs, legal fees, bank interest, production company overhead, collection costs, prints, ads, distribution fees, residuals paid to any union, etc. I negotiate for my clients to have net profits allocated, knowing that it is unlikely that they will ever receive them due to the industry's accounting practices and distribution expenses. In other words, it would be nice if you received net profits—just do not count on it.

It is standard to allocate writers 5% of the picture's net profits, though independent producers tend to offer 5% of producer's net profits instead. It is important for you to understand the difference between the two calculations: "Picture's net profits" refers to 100% of the net profits of the picture whereas "producer's net profits" accounts for only 50% of the net profits. Independent producers prefer the latter formula because they generally only retain 50% of the picture's net profits themselves. Rather than push for 5% of Picture's Net Profits, my clients prefer for me to negotiate a Box Office Bonus instead.

Credit

You are entitled to a "Written by" credit if the screenplay was completely original to you, or "Screenplay by" credit if the screenplay is derived from another work, e.g., a book or play. Your credit should appear in the main credits of the picture, on a single card, in a size and type equal to the size and type of the director's credit. The credit should also appear on screen, in the position prior to the director's credit, and in paid ads whenever the director or producers are credited (excepting paid ads which are award/congratulatory type ads). If you are not the only credited writer, as happens so often, then you will have to share the writing credit on the same card with the other credited writer(s).

The WGA has a credit determination process[13] whereby it decides who gets credited (and how) when there are multiple writers on any one screenplay. The WGA compares the written drafts against the produced draft and then determines who gets the credit and in what order, and who does not. The basic credit determination rule is this: Any writer whose work equals 33% of a non-original screenplay, e.g., an adaptation, or 50% an original screenplay will be credited. Credits are limited to two writers unless the credit determination rules otherwise.

Non-members of the WGA do not get the benefit of the WGA's credit determination process. Notwithstanding, I always negotiate into my client's agreements that the producer will apply the WGA rules to determine my client's credit if he/she is not the only writer who worked on the screenplay. This way the subsequent writer only receives a credit if his/her contribution to the screenplay is substantial. I avoid credit provisions whereby the producer is given sole discretion over all aspects of your credit.

If the writer is not a member of the WGA and is entering into an Option/Purchase Agreement with a producer, who is not a WGA signatory, it is a good idea to include language in the credits clause that states that the writer will be "upgraded" (and become a WGA member) if the production company becomes a WGA signatory, or finances the Picture through a WGA signatory company, such as a studio/network. I suggest this additional terminology because a writer, who is not WGA member, will not get the benefit of a WGA credit determination or the credit he/she agreed to in the Option/Purchase Agreement, if the screenplay is rewritten by a WGA member.

Rewrites

You always want the opportunity to do the first paid rewrite of your screenplays, since whether you are credited or share credit hinges on how much of your writing ends up in the final screenplay. I attempt to secure this right for my client regardless of their WGA membership status. I always ask for the rewrite fee to be no less than WGA minimum—more if the writer has a track record. Sometimes producers attempt to credit the rewrite fee against the purchase price—whether it is will depend on your bargaining power. Either way, the goal is to not only do the first rewrite but all of them. The better you rewrite and collaborate with the producer, the more likely it is that you will be the only credited writer. I had a client who Optioned her screenplay to a major studio, refused to do the rewrite that the development executive wanted, breached her contract with the studio, and gave up the career she could have had. You may not believe in the rewrite the producer wants of you, but you have to do it if you want to stay on board and get that credit.

Occasionally, an independent producer without development funding may ask you to do a free rewrite if you are not a WGA member. Whether or not you should do it is contingent on the circumstances. I would not advise you to undertake writing for free for a producer without a good track record, since you will likely be wasting your time. If you are unproduced or need to get a screenplay produced, and a producer asks you to rewrite for free, then I might advise you to do it if the producer lacks development funding, has a very good track record, has the ability to help you develop a production worthy screenplay, and has the connections and capacity to get your screenplay produced. The caveat here is that you have to own the rewrite.

Warranties & Representations

The Option/Purchase Agreement will include a paragraph whereby you will have to make certain representations and warranties in order to sell the screenplay. You will have to warrant and represent the following: that your screenplay is original; that if any material in the screenplay is not original, that said material came from the public domain; that if any material in the screenplay is not original or in the public domain, that it is included with the permission of the original material's author; that your screenplay does not defame anyone; that it does not infringe on another person's right to privacy, and that you are the screenplay's sole and exclusive proprietor and, hence, have the authority to enter into the Option/Purchase Agreement. You cannot enter into the Option/Purchase Agreement knowing that you will be in breach of this clause the moment you sign it because the repercussions are great: you are going to be liable for whatever damages are caused to the producer via an indemnification and hold harmless clause whereby you have to reimburse the producer for any and all damages and legal fees. You need for there to be a reciprocal indemnity and hold harmless clause from the producer to you for damages incurred by you as a consequence of the production and distribution of the picture.

Rights Sold

The Option/Purchase Agreement will, at the very least, require that you sell exclusively and forever all motion picture rights, all television motion picture, all television series and all television spin-off rights and all allied and ancillary rights for the term of the copyright and all renewals and extensions thereof. The allied and ancillary rights include the right to create and sell the picture's soundtrack, merchandise, video games, etc.

In the end, what rights you get to reserve for yourself will depends on your bargaining position and the buyer. For example, studios/networks want to acquire any and all rights in and to your screenplay, whether now in existence or yet to be invented, because in addition to creating filmed entertainment, they may want the right to sell books, create theme parks or theme park rides, stage plays, etc. I try to reserve dramatic, publishing and radio rights. It is next to impossible to reserve them if you are an unproduced writer entering into an Option/Purchase Agreement with a studio/network and more likely with an independent producer. Notwithstanding, you may be entitled to Separated Rights as a WGA member.

Option Reversion

The Option on your screenplay expires if the producer does not renew or exercise the Option prior to its termination date. All rights in and to the screenplay automatically revert to you when the Option expires. You retain any and all option and writing fees paid to you by the producer without the obligation of repayment.

Turnaround Right

You will have a "turnaround right" that provides you with the opportunity to buy back your screenplay if the producer purchased the screenplay, but did not produce it within the time specified in the Option/Purchase Agreement—usually five years. You will have an 18 to 24 month window to reacquire the screenplay. You, or whoever is buying your screenplay, will have to reimburse the producer's direct out-of-pocket cost to purchase and develop the screenplay.

Works-For-Hire: Getting Paid to Write

Most working writers in the film industry work on a for hire basis. A "work-for-hire", as it is known, means that the writer is specifically hired and paid to write on behalf of someone who employs his/her services. In the film industry, this usually occurs when a producer hires you to write a treatment, outline, or screenplay either based on the producer's idea or assigned material, such as a book, news story, or life story. I strongly recommend that you engage an attorney to negotiate and review the producer's draft of the Work-for-Hire Agreement.

Copyright in the Work-For-Hire

Although copyright normally vests in the author of an original work, copyright to your work vests in the producer if the producer and you entered into a written Work-for-Hire Agreement prior to the commencement of services. The Work-for-Hire Agreement will, among other things, clearly state that you are working on a for-hire basis and, therefore, that all results and proceeds of your labor and the copyright to your work are the property of the producer. It is imperative that the producer and you enter into the Work-for-Hire Agreement beforehand so that the copyright vests in the producer versus you. Otherwise, you will have to assign the results and proceeds of your labor and the copyright to the producer.

Compensation

Any producer who asks you to write for "free" is not treating you with respect and, is likely, a producer without the power and ability to get the screenplay he/she expects you to write produced. You have to value yourself and your talent if you expect anyone else to do the same. Whether I advise my client to write depends on the reasonableness of the compensation and terms offered by the producer.

Work-for-Hire Agreements are done on a "flat deal" or "step deal" basis. "Flat deal" means that the producer is going to pay you a lump sum to write the treatment, outline, first draft, second draft, final draft, polish, etc. It is important that the flat deal be well defined in the agreement, so that you know exactly how many steps you need to write for that flat deal payment. Otherwise, you could end up writing an infinite number of steps until the producer is satisfied, if ever. Payments pursuant to the Work-for-Hire Agreement occur at commencement and delivery of each step, e.g., treatment/outline, first draft, second draft, and final draft. A "step deal" means that the producer is hiring you on a step-by-step basis, so that he/she has the discretion to order the next step in the writing process, or not, and only paying for the steps ordered.

The compensation the producer offers you will take into account your track record, whether you are a member of the WGA, and whether the producer has a development deal or financing. "Development deal" refers to an arrangement between a studio/network and producer whereby the studio/network funds the producer's overhead and development expenses. It is unlikely that the producer will offer you WGA minimum compensation if you are not a WGA member, and not much beyond it if you are, but do not have track record that warrants more.

Additional Compensation

I ask the producer for deferred compensation if you are being offered a less than competitive flat deal or step deal. In addition, I negotiate for a Set Up Bonus, Box Office Bonus and a Nomination/Award Bonus. A "Set Up Bonus" gets paid when, and if, the producer sets up the screenplay at a studio/network.

Profit Participation

The producer should agree to allocate you a portion of net profits as part of your overall compensation, which as per industry standard is five percent (5%) of the net profits of the picture or producer's net profits. If I have to choose between net profits and actual money, I always chose the latter. Whether you are paid net profits, even assuming the picture is profitable, is going to depend on whether you are a credited writer (more on credits below). Your five percent (5%) will get cut in half if you share the credit. Uncredited writers get zero net profits unless the Work-for-Hire Agreement specifically states otherwise.

Credit

Your credit is not eliminated because the copyright is vesting in the producer. You are the screenplay's writer irrespective of copyright law because you wrote it. How, when, and if you are credited is more a function of the WGA or the Work-for-Hire Agreement. There is nothing you can do about your credit if the producer is a WGA signatory, you are WGA member, and you are not the screenplay's only writer due to the WGA's credit determination process. Your credit is completely up to the terms of the Work-For-Hire Agreement if you are not a WGA writer and the producer is not a WGA signatory. Notwithstanding, I try to make the producer follow the WGA's rules for credit determination, so that you are treated fairly should another writer be engaged after you.

Sequels, Remakes...

You may be entitled to passive payments if you are not a WGA member and your attorney was successful in negotiating for them. Whether you need to be the sole writer in order to get paid passive payments will be a function of the Work-for-Hire Agreement. The WGA will determine whether you are entitled to Separated Rights if you are WGA member; this is possible even though you worked on assigned material if your screenplay is substantially different from what was assigned to you, or the assigned material was not available to you, i.e., you adapt a book without referring to it.

Right of First Refusal

You may have the ability to write subsequent versions of your original screenplay, e.g., sequel, remakes, television series, if you are granted the Right of First Refusal in your Work-for-Hire Agreement and are a credited writer. I find that it is always worth asking for this right, since you should benefit if your work resulted in a screenplay with a life beyond the original. As I previously mentioned, how much you are paid to write any of the aforementioned will depend on whether you are a WGA member, the success of your original screenplay, and whether you are a working writer. Whether you get to write the subsequent version will depend on whether the producer and you are able to reach an agreement for your engagement to do so.

Warranties and Representations

As with the Option/Purchase Agreement, you will have to warrant and represent that whatever you write is original to you with the exception of any material assigned to you. You will have to indemnify and hold harmless the producer should you breach this warranty and representation. You need for there to be a reciprocal indemnity and hold harmless clause for any of the assigned materials provided by the producer and producer's production and distribution of the picture, since you do not want to be legally and financially liable for the producer's actions.

Becoming a WGA Member

Joining the WGA requires that you earn 24 units in the three years preceding the application and payment of a $2,500 initiation fee. You accumulate units by writing for, selling, or by entering into an Option/Purchase Agreement on behalf your screenplay with a WGA signatory producer. Below is the WGA Schedule of Units that applies to screenplays:

- 8 units for a short subject theatrical screenplay.
- 12 units for story for a feature-length theatrical screenplay.
- 24 units for a feature-length theatrical screenplay.

A rewrite will earn you half of the units applicable to the category, e.g., you get four units for rewriting a short subject theatrical screenplay.

A polish will earn you one-quarter of the units applicable to the category, e.g., you get two units for polishing a short subject theatrical screenplay.

An Option will earn one-half of the units you would be entitled to on the purchase up to a maximum of eight units per year, e.g., you are allocated four units if you Option a short subject theatrical screenplay. You are only entitled to units for the initial option period. You receive no units for extensions and renewals.

You can refer to WGA's website for the Schedule of Units available for television, radio, and New Media.[14]

Hiring an Attorney

I have discussed above the reasons why and when you may need to retain an attorney. Now the issue is, how do you find the attorney that is right for you? I suggest you do a little research: ask friends and colleagues for referrals, read legal articles and books written by attorneys, and refer to the posts by attorneys you have read and liked on Linkedin.com or another social forum. Narrow your list down to five attorneys and then interview them. Most attorneys offer a free half hour initial consultation, which is for both your benefit and the attorney's. Take advantage of it. I use the consultation to get to know the potential client, his/her needs and expectations, the likelihood that I can be of service, and to determine if our personalities are compatible. My advice to you is that you retain an attorney that you feel comfortable asking questions, who respects you, who tells you the truth—even if you do not want to hear it—and who you feel is going to be a good advocate for you. If you want an attorney for the long term, which I recommend, steer clear of attorneys that intimidate you or are arrogant. Use the free consultation to shop for an attorney—not for the purpose of picking the attorney's brain when you have no intention of retaining legal counsel.

Attorneys most often get paid an hourly fee, a flat fee, or a percent of the gross monies earned by you. Hourly rates run the gamut. How much you pay by the hour is going to depend on the attorney's experience and whether the attorney is with a large law firm. The average hourly rate is in the $300-$500 range. When billing on an hourly basis, the attorney charges for all the time spent on your behalf: negotiating, drafting, redlining (revising agreements presented to you), phone calls on your behalf or with you, copies, messenger, etc. You might be able to convince an attorney to represent you on a flat fee basis if your financial resources are limited. A flat fee entails the attorney quoting you a price that is inclusive of all the phone calls and work to be done by the attorney on your behalf. The attorney gets no more than the flat fee quoted regardless of how long it takes to conclude the task. Flat fees are on a task by task basis. Either way, you are going to have to provide an up-front deposit based on the attorney's guesstimate or flat fee quote. Whether an attorney will represent you on a percentage basis will depend on whether you are currently making money writing, are represented by a reputable agency or manager, have a track record, or have an offer on the table that will result in a payment to you large enough to compensate the attorney. It is unlikely that an attorney will represent you on a percentage basis otherwise. The average percent is 5%, but it can be as high as 10% if the attorney is representing you on a very low paying matter. Sometimes an attorney will structure a hybrid billing arrangement so that you are paying a portion of your fee up front and the other portion as a percent of the monies earned by you. Attorneys do this sometimes to accommodate a client's limited financial resources.

You will have to sign an engagement agreement with the attorney, which explains the basis of the representation, the fees, deposits (if any), and contains any necessary disclosures. The California State Bar requires one whenever the matter is going to result in payment to the attorney exceeding $1,000 and in contingent fee arrangements. The deposit that you give the attorney will go into an Attorney/Client Trust Account until it is earned by the attorney. Any monies remaining at the end of representation, if any, are returned to you. If you do not understand the engagement agreement have the attorney explain it to you, or consult with another attorney about it.

Is the cost of hiring an attorney worth it if you have an agent or manager? Absolutely, yes! The attorney is an important part of your team who is responsible for not only improving the deal terms but, also, making sure you are protected. I have yet to work on a negotiation with an agent or manager where I did not substantially improve the overall deal. Among other things, I have secured deferrals and bonuses for my clients that were not offered up front and improved my client's credit and the likelihood that he/she would retain it. I always say, "When you think you cannot afford attorney is exactly when you cannot afford to go without one."

Conclusion

As I hope you have realized by reading this chapter, writing is not just about sitting down and creating, it is also about working smart to avoid the types of situations that might detour your writing career. When in doubt, consult with an attorney. Do not rely on advice from "friends," or attorneys who are not familiar with entertainment and intellectual property law. Do not use boilerplates or attempt to draft your own agreements. It is better that you consult and determine that you are in the clear, than discover that you have made a very costly mistake.

This chapter is not a complete review of the subject matter. You should consult with an attorney if you have questions, need additional information, or require legal representation.

About the Author

Dinah Perez graduated from Loyola Law School and has been in the practice of entertainment law since 1996. She practices film, television, theater, music, new media, publishing, copyright, and trademark law. She enjoys her practice because she has great respect for the arts and those who create, and relishes helping her clients attain their professional goals.

Ms. Perez has been published in *Story Board Magazine*, *Release Print*, and *Script Magazine*, *The Screenwriter's Guide to Agents and Managers*, and the *Hollywood Screenwriting Directory*. She has been quoted in *Entertainment Weekly*, *Wired Magazine*, *Wired.Com*, and *Alone in a Room*.

Ms. Perez has participated in panels and/or spoken at the Black Hollywood Film Festival, the Latin Heat Film Festival, Women in Film, Cinewomen, Independent Feature Project West,

American Film Market, the Inktip Pitch Summit, The Writers Store, the Showbiz Store and Cafe, and the Screenwriters World Conference.

She is a member of the Beverly Hills Bar Association (Entertainment Law Section, Executive Committee) and the California State Bar. She was a founding board member of Cinewomen in Los Angeles, CA.

Ms. Perez is available for consultation. She may be reached by phone at (323) 935-7955, via her website at www.dinahperezlaw.com, or email at dinahperezlaw@gmail.com.

[1] 17 U.S.C. §302.

[2] 17 U.S.C. §102

[3] 17 U.S.C. §102.

[4] 17 U.S.C. §107.

[5] U.S. Copyright Office, *Copyright Basics Circular 1*, Library of Congress, May 2012.

[6] 17 U.S.C. §107.

[7] http://www.unc.edu/~unclng/public-d.htm

[8] Michael C. Donaldson, *Clearance & Copyright* (Silman James Press 2008), 332-335.

[9] N.Y. CVR. LAW § 50 and 51.

[10] CAL. CIV. CODE §3344.1

[11] Cal. Labor Code §1700.4.

[12] *Blaustein v. Burton* (1970) 9 Cal.App.3d 161, 88 Cal.Rptr. 319.

[13] http://www.wga.org/subpage_Writersresources.aspx?id=170

[14] http://www.wga.org/

The Directory

100% ENTERTAINMENT

200 N. Larchmont Blvd.
Los Angeles, CA 90004
323-461-6360 (phone)
323-871-8203 (fax)

100percent@iname.com
100percentent.com
imdb.com/company/co0077804

Accepts query letter from unproduced, unrepresented writers via email. Project types include TV. Preferred genres include Drama, Non-Fiction, and Science Fiction. Established in 1998.

Stanley Isaacs

President
323-461-6360
sisaacs100@mac.com
imdb.com/name/nm0410570
linkedin.com/pub/stanley-isaacs/4/50b/5bb
twitter.com/Stanley100

100% TERRYCLOTH

1334 3rd St. Promenade, Ste. 201
Santa Monica, CA 90401
310-393-8585

1801 Ave of the Stars, Ste.1150
Century City, CA 90067
310-785-0300

2000 Ave of the Stars
Los Angeles, CA 90067
424-288-8000

contact@terencemichael.com
imdb.com/company/co0194989
facebook.com/pages/100-Percent-Terry-Cloth-Inc/
    147268518656038
terencemichael.com

Accepts query letter from unproduced, unrepresented writers via email. Project types include TV. Preferred genres include Comedy and Reality.

Terence Michael

Producer
310-823-3432
tm@terencemichael.com
imdb.com/name/nm0006709

Erik Adams

Development
linkedin.com/in/erikmichaeladams
twitter.com/ErikMAdams

1019 ENTERTAINMENT

1680 N Vine St, Suite 600
Hollywood, CA 90028
323-645-6840 (phone)
323-645-6841 (fax)

info@1019ent.com
twitter.com/1019Ent
1019ent.com
imdb.com/company/co0263748

Does not accept any unsolicited material. Project types include TV. Preferred genres include Comedy, Drama, and Non-Fiction.

Terry Botwick

Partner
imdb.com/company/co0263748

Ralph Winter

Partner
imdb.com/name/nm0003515
linkedin.com/pub/ralph-winter/7/1a8/8a9

10 BY 10 ENTERTAINMENT

1950 Sawtelle Blvd.
Suite 200
Los Angeles, CA 90025
310-575-1235 (phone)
310-575-1237 (fax)

imdb.com/company/co0112253
facebook.com/pages/10x10-Entertainment/
    114948301852714

Accepts query letter from unproduced, unrepresented writers. Project types include TV. Preferred genres include Comedy, Drama, and Non-Fiction.

Brad Austin

Director of Development
310-575-1235
imdb.com/name/nm4114614

Ken Mok
Principle
310-575-1235
imdb.com/name/nm0596298

1821 PICTURES

205 S. Beverly Dr.
Suite 206
Beverly Hills, CA 90212
310-860-1121 (phone)
310-860-1123 (fax)

asst@1821pictures.com
1821pictures.com
imdb.com/company/co0237259
facebook.com/1821Pictures

Accepts query letter from unproduced, unrepresented writers via email. Project types include TV. Preferred genres include Animation, Comedy, Drama, and Non-Fiction. Established in 2005.

Billy Piché
Director of Development
310-860-1121
imdb.com/name/nm5046038
linkedin.com/pub/billy-pich%C3%A9/16/7b9/9b4

Paris Latsis
310-860-1121
imdb.com/company/co0237259

Terry Douglas
Principle
310-860-1121
imdb.com/name/nm0234806
facebook.com/td007

19 ENTERTAINMENT

8560 W Sunset Blvd, 9th Floor
West Hollywood, CA 90069
310-777-1940 (phone)
310-777-1949 (fax)

1071 Ave of the Americas,
New York, NY 10018
212-784-7770

inquiries@19entertainment.com
coremediagroup.com/19.html

linkedin.com/company/19-entertainment
imdb.com/company/co0085773
facebook.com/19EntertainmentLtd
twitter.com/COREMediaGrp

Does not accept any unsolicited material. Project types include TV. Preferred genres include Animation, Comedy, and Drama.

Peter Hurwitz
President
310-777-1940
linkedin.com/pub/peter-hurwitz/b/a6b/7b7

21 LAPS/ADELSTEIN

10201 W. Pico Blvd.
Building 41, Suite 500B
Los Angeles, CA 90064
310-369-7402

imdb.com/company/co0372539

Does not accept any unsolicited material.

Marty Adelstein
Producer
310-270-4570
imdb.com/name/nm1374351

21 LAPS ENTERTAINMENT

c/o Twentieth Century Fox
10201 W Pico Blvd
Building 41, Suite 400
Los Angeles, CA 90064
310-369-7170 (phone)
310-969-0443 (fax)

imdb.com/company/co0158853
facebook.com/pages/21-Laps-Entertainment/
    185829081580687

Does not accept any unsolicited material. Project types include Feature Films and TV. Preferred genres include Action, Comedy, and Drama.

Dan Levine
President of Production
imdb.com/name/nm0505782

Shawn Levy
Principal
310-369-4466
imdb.com/name/nm0506613

Billy Rosenberg
Senior Vice President Development
310-369-7170
imdb.com/name/nm1192785

Will Rack
Director of Development
310-369-7170
imdb.com/name/nm5211280

25/7 PRODUCTIONS

4119 Burbank Blvd.
Burbank, CA 91505
818-432-2800 (phone)
818-432-2810 (fax)

info@257productions.com
257productions.com
imdb.com/company/co0200336

Accepts query letter from unproduced, unrepresented writers. Project types include TV. Preferred genres include Animation, Comedy, Drama, and Non-Fiction. Established in 2003.

David Broome
President
818-432-2800
imdb.com/company/co0200336

26 FILMS

8748 Holloway Dr
Los Angeles, CA, 90069
310-205-9922 (phone)
310-206-9926 (fax)

asst@26films.com

Accepts query letter from unproduced, unrepresented writers via email.

Nathalie Marciano
Principal
310-205-9922
asst@26films.com
imdb.com/name/nm0545695

Elena Brooks
Director of Development
310-205-9922
asst@26films.com
imdb.com/name/nm4542983
linkedin.com/pub/elena-brooks/7/229/4b5

2929 PRODUCTIONS

1437 Seventh St, Suite 250
Santa Monica, CA 90401
310-309-5200 (phone)
310-309-5716 (fax)

2929entertainment.com

Accepts query letter from unproduced, unrepresented writers. Preferred genres include Action, Drama, and Non-Fiction.

Todd Wagner
Principal
310-309-5200
todd@2929entertainment.com
imdb.com/company/co0005596
linkedin.com/pub/todd-wagner/52/977/ba4

Shay Weiner
Director of Development
310-309-5200
sweiner@2929ent.com
imdb.com/name/nm1674317

Michael Merlob
Creative Executive

2S FILMS

10390 Santa Monica Blvd
Suite 210
Los Angeles, CA 90025
310-789-5450 (phone)
310-789-3060 (fax)

info@2sfilms.com
imdb.com/company/co0238996
2sfilms.whoiskenjackson.com

Does not accept any unsolicited material. Project types include Feature Films. Preferred genres include Comedy and Romance. Established in 2007.

Molly Smith
Principle
310-789-5450
info@2sfilms.com
imdb.com/company/co0238996

Allison Rayne
Vice President of Development
310-789-5450
info@2sfilms.com
imdb.com/name/nm2588349
linkedin.com/pub/allison-rayne/5/56/9a8

Jon Schumacher
Development Executive
imdb.com/name/nm2749499

2WAYTRAFFIC - A SONY PICTURES ENTERTAINMENT COMPANY

Middenweg 1
PO Box 297
Hilversum 1217 HS
The Netherlands
+31(0)357508000 (phone)
+31(0)357508020 (fax)

info@2waytraffic.com
2waytraffic.com
imdb.com/company/co0211160
linkedin.com/company/2waytraffic

Does not accept any unsolicited material. Project types include Feature Films and TV. Established in 2004.

3311 PRODUCTIONS

3522 Hayden Ave
Culver City, CA 90232
323-319-5060 (phone)
323-306-5534 (fax)

info@3311productions.com
3311productions.com
imdb.com/company/co0312478
linkedin.com/company/3311-productions-inc

Accepts query letter from produced or represented writers. Project types include Feature Films. Preferred genres include Comedy and Drama.

Mark Roberts
Executive
imdb.com/name/nm4224736

Eddie Vaisman
imdb.com/name/nm4224744

Ross Jacobson
CEO
imdb.com/name/nm2278951
linkedin.com/pub/ross-jacobson/6/6bb/60a

34TH STREET FILMS

8200 Wilshire Blvd, Suite 300
Beverly Hills, CA 90211
323-315-7963 (phone)
323-315-7117 (fax)

facebook.com/34thstreetfilms
imdb.com/company/co0248547

Does not accept any unsolicited material. Project types include Feature Films. Preferred genres include Action, Comedy, Family, and Romance.

Matt Moore
Executive Vice President
323-315-7963
imdb.com/name/nm0601597

Amber Rasberry
Director of Development
323-315-7963
imdb.com/name/nm2248393
linkedin.com/in/amberrasberry
twitter.com/arazz

Poppy Hanks
Senior Vice President (Production & Development)
323-315-7963
imdb.com/name/nm1585325
linkedin.com/pub/poppy-hanks/6/9b8/4a0

3 ARTS ENTERTAINMENT

9460 Wilshire Blvd 7th Floor
Beverly Hills, CA 90212
310-888-3200 (phone)
310-888-3210 (fax)

16 W 22nd St
Suite 201
New York, NY 10010

3arts.com
imdb.com/company/co0070636
linkedin.com/company/3-arts-entertainment

Accepts query letter from unproduced, unrepresented writers. Project types include Feature Films and TV. Preferred genres include Comedy and Drama. Established in 1992.

Howard Klein
Partner
310-888-3200
hklein@3arts.com
imdb.com/name/nm2232433

Erwin Stoff
Partner (Chairman)
310-888-3200
estoff@3arts.com
imdb.com/name/nm0831098
linkedin.com/pub/erwin-stoff/41/70a/a1b

3 BALL PRODUCTIONS

3650 Redondo Beach Ave
Redondo Beach, CA 90278
424-236-7500 (phone)
424-236-7501 (fax)

3ball.reception@eyeworks.tv
3ballproductions.com
imdb.com/company/co0100000
linkedin.com/company/3-ball-productions

Accepts query letter from unproduced, unrepresented writers via email. Project types include TV. Preferred genres include Drama.

J.D. Roth
CEO
424-236-7500
imdb.com/name/nm0744870

Brandt Pinvidic
President
424-236-7500
imdb.com/name/nm1803480

40 ACRES & A MULE FILMWORKS, INC.

75 S Elliot Place
Brooklyn, NY 11217
718-624-3703 (phone)
718-624-2008 (fax)

40acres.com
imdb.com/company/co0029134
facebook.com/40AcresAndAMuleFilmworks

Does not accept any unsolicited material. Project types include TV. Preferred genres include Action, Comedy, Drama, and Non-Fiction.

Spike Lee
Chairman
718-624-3703
imdb.com/name/nm0000490
facebook.com/SpikeLee
twitter.com/SpikeLee

44 BLUE PRODUCTIONS, INC.

4040 Vineland Ave, Suite 105
Studio City, CA 11217
818-760-4442 (phone)
818-760-1509 (fax)

reception@44blue.com
44blue.com
imdb.com/company/co0012712
twitter.com/44blue
linkedin.com/company/44-blue-productions
facebook.com/44blueproductions

Does not accept any unsolicited material. Project types include TV. Preferred genres include Comedy, Drama, and Non-Fiction.

Rasha Drachkovitch
President
818-760-4442
reception@44blue.com
imdb.com/name/nm0236624
linkedin.com/pub/rasha-drachkovitch/8/735/598
facebook.com/rasha.drachkovitch

Stephanie Drachkovitch
Executive Vice-President
818-760-4442
reception@44blue.com
imdb.com/name/nm1729517
linkedin.com/pub/stephanie-drachkovitch/47/218/113

495 PRODUCTIONS

4222 Burbank Blvd, 2nd Floor
Burbank, CA 91505
818-840-2750 (phone)
818-840-7083 (fax)

info@495productions.com
495productions.com
imdb.com/company/co0192481
facebook.com/495Productions
twitter.com/495Prods

Does not accept any unsolicited material. Project types include TV. Preferred genres include Comedy, Drama, Non-Fiction, and Reality.

SallyAnn Salsano
President
818-840-2750
info@495productions.com
imdb.com/name/nm1133163
linkedin.com/pub/sallyann-salsano/38/2a2/3b5
twitter.com/sallyannsalsano

James Bianco
Head (Production)
imdb.com/name/nm1291179

4TH ROW FILMS

27 W 20th St, Suite 1006
New York, NY 10011
212-974-0082 (phone)
212-627-3090 (fax)

info@4throwfilms.com
4throwfilms.com
linkedin.com/company/4th-row-films
facebook.com/4thRowFilmsNYC
twitter.com/4thRowFilms
imdb.com/company/co0117932

Does not accept any unsolicited material. Project types include TV. Preferred genres include Comedy, Drama, and Non-Fiction.

Susan Bedusa
Senior Vice President, Production & Development
imdb.com/name/nm1513256
linkedin.com/pub/susan-bedusa/5/578/aa0

Douglas Tirola
President
imdb.com/name/nm0864263
linkedin.com/pub/douglas-tirola/4/427/856
facebook.com/douglas.tirola

51 MINDS ENTERTAINMENT

5200 Lankershim Blvd. Ste. 200
North Hollywood CA 91601
818-643-8200 (phone)
323-466-9202 (fax)

info@51minds.com
51minds.com
imdb.com/company/co0166565
facebook.com/pages/51-Minds-Entertainment/
   162815400414419
linkedin.com/company/51-minds-entertainment

Accepts query letter from unproduced, unrepresented writers via email. Project types include TV. Preferred genres include Comedy, Drama, and Reality.

Mark Cronin
Co-President
323-466-9200
info@51minds.com
imdb.com/name/nm0188782

David Caplan
Vice President (Development)
323-466-9200
info@51minds.com
imdb.com/name/nm4933376

Cris Abrego
Co-President
323-466-9200
info@51minds.com
imdb.com/name/nm0009312

59TH STREET FILMS

101 Destiny Dr
Lafayette, LA 70506
337-280-9370

59thstreetfilms@gmail.com
59thstreetfilms.com
imdb.com/company/co0285087
facebook.com/59thStreetFilms
twitter.com/59thstreetfilms
linkedin.com/company/59th-street-films

Accepts scripts from unproduced, unrepresented writers. Project types include TV. Preferred genres include Comedy and Drama.

Sarah Agor
Producer
imdb.com/name/nm2706070
linkedin.com/pub/sarah-agor/7/36/216

Jennifer Jarrett
Producer
imdb.com/name/nm1838264

Alfred Rubin Thompson
Producer
imdb.com/name/nm0867022

Nicholas Scott
imdb.com/name/nm4641966

Steve Sirkis
imdb.com/name/nm2401659
linkedin.com/pub/dir/nicholas/scott

5IVE SMOOTH STONES PRODUCTIONS

8500 Wilshire Blvd, Suite #527
Beverly Hills, CA 90211

5ivesmoothstones.com
imdb.com/company/co0332052

Accepts query letter from unproduced, unrepresented writers via email. Project types include Feature Films. Preferred genres include Comedy and Family.

Robert Wise
President Scripted Development

Terry Crews
Actor/CEO
imdb.com/name/nm0187719
facebook.com/realterrycrews
twitter.com/terrycrews

72ND STREET PRODUCTIONS

1041 N Formosa Ave
Formosa Building, Suite 3
West Hollywood, CA 90046
323-850-3139 (phone)
323-850-3179 (fax)

contact@72ndstreetproductions.com
imdb.com/company/co0180596
72ndstreetproductions.com

Accepts query letter from unproduced, unrepresented writers via email. Project types include Feature Films, TV, and Commercials. Preferred genres include Drama.

Tim Harms
Principle
323-850-3139
tharms@72ndstreetproductions.com
imdb.com/name/nm0363608

Lee Toland Krieger
Principle
323-850-3139
lkrieger@72ndstreetproductions.com
imdb.com/name/nm1767218

Steven Krieger
Principle
323-850-3139
skrieger@72ndstreetproductions.com
imdb.com/name/nm2544844

72 PRODUCTIONS

39 mesa streets, no 207, san francisco, CA 94129
415-292-7100 (phone)
310-278-1224 (fax)

72productions.com
imdb.com/company/co0196483

Accepts query letter from unproduced, unrepresented writers. Project types include Feature Films. Preferred genres include Science Fiction and Thriller.

Jennifer Chaiken
Principle
310-278-1221
imdb.com/name/nm0149671
linkedin.com/pub/jen-chaiken/37/779/945

Sebastian Dungan
Principle
310-278-1221
imdb.com/name/nm0242253
facebook.com/sebastian.dungan

777 GROUP

158 Beddington Ln
Croydon, Surrey CR0 4TE
020 8689 6861 (phone)
020 8689 7176 (fax)

777group@gmail.com
the777group.com
imdb.com/company/co0133127
twitter.com/777group

Accepts query letter from unproduced, unrepresented writers via email. Project types include TV. Preferred genres include Animation, Comedy, Drama, and Non-Fiction.

Marcello Robinson
CEO
312-834-7770
info@the777group.com
imdb.com/name/nm0732883
linkedin.com/pub/marcello-robinson/6/56/912

7ATE9 ENTERTAINMENT

740 N. La Brea Ave
Los Angeles, CA 90038
323-936-6789 (phone)
323-937-6713 (fax)

info@7ate9.com
andrea@7ate9.com
7ate9.com
imdb.com/company/co0171281

Does not accept any unsolicited material. Project types include TV.

Artur Spigel
Creative Director
imdb.com/name/nm1742493
linkedin.com/pub/artur-spigel/25/982/926
facebook.com/art.spigel

8:38 PRODUCTIONS

10390 Santa Monica Blvd.
Suite 200
Los Angeles, CA 90064
310-789-3056 (phone)
310-789-3077 (fax)

imdb.com/company/co0252672

Does not accept any unsolicited material. Preferred genres include Family and Romance.

Kira Davis
Principle
310-789-3056
imdb.com/name/nm0204987

8790 PICTURES, INC.

11400 W Olympic Blvd, Suite 590
Los Angeles, CA 90064
310-471-9983 (phone)
310-471-6366 (fax)

8790pictures@gmail.com
imdb.com/company/co0159892

Accepts query letter from unproduced, unrepresented writers via email. Project types include Feature Films and TV. Preferred genres include Action, Animation, Comedy, Drama, and Romance.

Joan Singleton
310-471-9983
8790pictures@gmail.com
imdb.com/name/nm0802306
linkedin.com/pub/joan-singleton/4/336/62b

Ralph Singleton
310-471-9983
8790pictures@gmail.com
imdb.com/name/nm0802326

8TH WONDER ENTERTAINMENT

7961 W 3rd St
Los Angeles, CA 90048

info@8thwonderent.com
imdb.com/company/co0226729
facebook.com/pages/8th-wonder-entertainment

Accepts query letter from unproduced, unrepresented writers via email.

David Luong
Director of Development
info@8thwonderent.com

Michael McQuarn
mcq@8thwonderent.com
linkedin.com/pub/michael-mcquarn/33/953/793
facebook.com/Iammcq
twitter.com/IamMcQ

900 FILMS

1611A South Melrose Dr
Vista, CA 92081
760-477-2470 (phone)
760-477-2478 (fax)

asst@900films.com
900films.com
imdb.com/company/co0086829
facebook.com/900films

Accepts query letter from unproduced, unrepresented writers via email. Project types include Feature Films, TV, and Commercials. Preferred genres include Non-Fiction and Reality.

Tony Hawk
Skateboarder/Principle
imdb.com/name/nm0005000

Angela Rhodehamel
Production Manager/ Producer
linkedin.com/pub/angela-rhodehamel/86/520/979

9.14 PICTURES

1804 Chestnut St, Suite 2
Philadelphia, PA 19103
215-238-0707 (phone)
215-238-0663 (fax)

info@914pictures.com
914pictures.com
imdb.com/company/co0145535
facebook.com/pages/914-Pictures/117299371642553

Accepts query letter from unproduced, unrepresented writers via email. Established in 2002.

Sheena Joyce
Owner
215-238-0707 ext. 11#
info@914pictures.com
imdb.com/name/nm1852224
linkedin.com/pub/sheena-joyce/6/230/852
twitter.com/sheenamjoyce

Don Argott
Owner
215-238-0707 ext. 12#
info@914pictures.com
imdb.com/name/nm0034531
linkedin.com/pub/don-argott/6/7a5/634
twitter.com/dargott

AARDMAN ANIMATIONS

Gas Ferry Rd
Bristol BS1 6UN
United Kingdom
+44117-984-8485 (phone)
+44117-984-8486 (fax)

1410 Aztec West
Bristol
BS32 4RT
014-548-59000

mail@aardman.com
aardman.com
imdb.com/company/co0103531
twitter.com/aardman

Does not accept any unsolicited material. Preferred genres include Animation.

Alicia Gold
Head (Feature Development)
+44117-984-8485
mail@aardman.com
imdb.com/name/nm1664759imdb.com/name/nm4211100
linkedin.com/pub/alicia-gold/50/1a6/575

AARON KOGAN PRODUCTIONS

10474 S. Santa Monica Blvd., Ste. 301
Los Angeles, CA 90025
310-474-4000 (phone)
310-474-4431 (fax)

Does not accept any unsolicited material. Project types include Feature Films. Preferred genres include Crime and Drama.

Aaron Kogan
Producer/Manager
imdb.com/name/nm1179939

ABANDON INTERACTIVE ENTERTAINMENT

711 Route 302
Pine Bush, NY 12566
845-361-9317 (phone)
845-361-9150 (fax)

info@abandoninteractive.com
imdb.com/company/co0025591
linkedin.com/company/abandon-interactive-
    entertainment

Does not accept any unsolicited material.

Karen Lauder
COO
845-361-9317
info@abandoninteractive.com
imdb.com/name/nm0490746

ABANDON PICTURES

711 Route 302
Pine Bush, NJ 12566
845-361-9317 (phone)
212-397-8361 (fax)

imdb.com/company/co0025591

Does not accept any unsolicited material. Project types include Feature Films. Preferred genres include Thriller.

Karen Lauder
Producer
imdb.com/name/nm0490746

Deborah Marcus
imdb.com/name/nm3359316

Lizzie Friedman
Producer
imdb.com/name/nm0295288

ABBOLITA PRODUCTIONS

New York, NY

abbolita.com
imdb.com/company/co0419092
twitter.com/abbolita13

Accepts scripts from unproduced, unrepresented writers via email. Project types include Feature Films. Established in 2014.

Tim Nye
Principle
imdb.com/name/nm5470167

ABC SIGNATURE

500 S Buena Vista St
Burbank, CA 91521

imdb.com/company/co0492993

Does not accept any unsolicited material. Project types include TV. Preferred genres include Comedy and Drama.

Wei Chen
Manager

Tracy Underwood
Head
imdb.com/name/nm0881046

ABC STUDIOS

500 S Buena Vista St
Burbank, CA 91505
818-460-7777

twitter.com/ABCNetwork
facebook.com/ABCNetwork
imdb.com/company/co0209226

Does not accept any unsolicited material. Project types include TV and Commercials. Preferred genres include Comedy and Drama.

Patrick Moran
Executive Vice President (Creative & Production)
imdb.com/name/nm3988896
facebook.com/patrick.moran.18400

Gary French
Senior Vice President (Production)
imdb.com/name/nm2380686

Brenda Kyle
Vice President (Television Production)
imdb.com/name/nm0477368
linkedin.com/pub/brenda-kyle/1/a09/9b1

ABERRATION FILMS

1425 N Crescent Heights Blvd, #203
West Hollywood, CA 90046
323-656-1830

aberrationfilms@yahoo.com
info@aberrationfilms.com
aberrationfilms.com
imdb.com/company/co0164476

Accepts query letter from unproduced, unrepresented
writers. Project types include Feature Films. Preferred
genres include Drama.

Susan Dynner
323-656-1830
aberrationfilms@yahoo.com
imdb.com/name/nm1309839
linkedin.com/pub/susan-dynner/8/739/83

A BIGGER BOAT

275 S. Beverly Dr, Suite 210
Beverly Hills, CA 90212
310-860-1113

Does not accept any unsolicited material. Project types
include Feature Films.

Beth Essick
Development

Peter Block
Producer
imdb.com/name/nm0088756

Amanda Essick
imdb.com/name/nm2302699

ABOMINABLE PICTURES

3400 Cahuenga Blvd. West Building, 2nd Floor
Los Angeles, CA 90068

info@abominablepictures.com
abominablepictures.com
twitter.com/AbominablePix
facebook.com/pages/Abominable-Pictures/
    337127229732998
imdb.com/company/co0295946

Does not accept any unsolicited material. Project types
include TV. Preferred genres include Comedy.

Jonathan Stern
Producer
imdb.com/name/nm0827746

ABSURDA FILMS

16782 Redhill Ave., Suite B
Irvine, CA 92606
949-250-8090

Does not accept any unsolicited material. Project types
include Feature Films. Preferred genres include Drama
and Horror.

Eric Bassett
Producer

David Lynch
Producer/Director/Writer
imdb.com/name/nm0000186

Norm Hill
Producer
imdb.com/name/nm2147362

ACAPPELLA PICTURES

8271 Melrose Ave, Suite 101
Los Angeles, CA 90046
323-782-8200 (phone)
323-782-8210 (fax)

charmaine@acappellapictures.com
acappellapictures.com
imdb.com/company/co0055414

Accepts query letter from unproduced, unrepresented
writers via email.

Charles Evans
President
323-782-8200
charmaine@acappellapictures.com
imdb.com/name/nm0262509
linkedin.com/pub/dir/Charlie/Evans

Charmaine Parcero
Development Executive
323-782-8200
charmaine@acappellapictures.com
imdb.com/name/nm0661019
linkedin.com/pub/charmaine-parcero/7/200/520

ACCELERATED ENTERTAINMENT LLC

10201 W Pico Blvd, Building 6
Los Angeles, CA 90064

cleestorm@acceleratedent.com
acceleratedent.com
imdb.com/company/co0208920

Does not accept any unsolicited material. Project types include Feature Films. Preferred genres include Drama and Non-Fiction.

Christina Lee Storm
cleestorm@acceleratedent.com
imdb.com/name/nm0497028
linkedin.com/pub/dir/christina/storm

Jason Perr
jperr@acceleratedent.com
imdb.com/name/nm1280790
linkedin.com/pub/dir/%20/Perr

A.C. LYLES PRODUCTIONS, INC.

5555 Melrose Ave, Hart Building 409
Hollywood, CA 90038-3197
323-956-5819

imdb.com/company/co0074718

Accepts query letter from unproduced, unrepresented writers via email.

ACME PRODUCTIONS

4000 Warner Blvd, Building 19, Room 221-B
Burbank, CA 91522
818-954-7779

imdb.com/company/co0066048

Does not accept any unsolicited material. Project types include TV. Preferred genres include Comedy and Family.

Mindy Schultheis
Partner/Producer
imdb.com/name/nm0995547
linkedin.com/pub/mindy-mindy-schultheis/43/967/507

Michael Hanel
Partner/Producer
imdb.com/name/nm0995625

ACT III PRODUCTIONS

100 N Crescent Dr, Suite 250
Beverly Hills, CA 90210
310-385-4111 (phone)
310-385-4148 (fax)

normanlear.com/act_iii.html
imdb.com/company/co0030401

Accepts query letter from unproduced, unrepresented writers.

Norman Lear
310-385-4111
normanl@actiii.com
normanlear.com
imdb.com/name/nm0005131

Lara Bergthold
Director of Development
310-385-4111
imdb.com/name/nm2401887

ACTION!!! ENTERTAINMENT

12165 Viewcrest Rd
Studio City, CA 91604
818-980-0889

aaandaction.com
facebook.com/pages/ActionVisuals/142054852531756

twitter.com/actionvisuals

Does not accept any unsolicited material. Project types include Feature Films. Preferred genres include Drama.

Susan Feiles
Producer
imdb.com/name/nm4716424
facebook.com/fourthrt

Chris Darling
Producer
imdb.com/name/nm3827939

ACTIVE ENTERTAINMENT

1000 Celtic Dr
Baton Rouge, LA 70809
225-906-5440 (phone)
225-906-5445 (fax)

170 Camino Viejo
Santa Barbara, CA 93108
805-969-2151 (phone)
310-388-0496 (fax)

activeentertainment.com
facebook.com/activentertainment
twitter.com/ActiveEntertain
imdb.com/company/co0098277

Does not accept any unsolicited material. Project types include TV. Preferred genres include Fantasy and Horror.

Daniel Lewis
COO
imdb.com/name/nm2786983
linkedin.com/pub/daniel-lewis/22/bbb/846

Kenneth M. Badish
President/Producer
imdb.com/name/nm0046168
linkedin.com/pub/ken-badish/a/126/9a1
facebook.com/kenneth.badish
twitter.com/kbadish

Griff Furst
Creative Director/Producer
imdb.com/name/nm0975225
linkedin.com/pub/griff-furst/47/246/b49
facebook.com/griff.furst
twitter.com/GEFURST

ACTUAL REALITY PICTURES

310-202-1272 (phone)
310-202-1502 (fax)

questions@arp.tv
actualreality.tv
imdb.com/company/co0004087

Does not accept any unsolicited material.

R.J. Cutler
President
310-202-1272
imdb.com/name/nm0191712

ADAM FIELDS PRODUCTIONS

1601 Cloverfield Suite 2000 North
Santa Monica, CA 90404
310-745-5454 (phone)
310-859-4795 (fax)

imdb.com/company/co0064962

Accepts query letter from unproduced, unrepresented writers.

Adam Fields
President
310-859-9300
imdb.com/name/nm0276178
linkedin.com/pub/adam-fields/3/685/907

ADAPTIVE STUDIOS

3623 Hayden Ave
Culver City, CA 90232

info@adaptivestudios.com
adaptivestudios.com
facebook.com/adaptivestudios
linkedin.com/company/adaptive-studios
twitter.com/adaptivestudios
imdb.com/company/co0394662

Does not accept any unsolicited material. Project types include TV.

TJ Barrack
Founder/President/COO

Perrin Chiles
Founder/CEO
imdb.com/name/nm1406232
linkedin.com/pub/perrin-chiles/2/b18/351
facebook.com/perrin.chiles
twitter.com/perrinchiles

Marc Joubert
Founder/Head of Business Development
linkedin.com/pub/marc-joubert/2b/82a/571

ADDICTIVE PICTURES

Los Angeles, CA

Does not accept any unsolicited material. Project types include Feature Films. Established in 2014.

John Schoenfelder
imdb.com/name/nm4964008

Russell Ackerman
imdb.com/name/nm1652438

ADES FILMS, MIKE

1028 12th St, Suite 8
Santa Monica, CA 90403
310-699-0242

Does not accept any unsolicited material. Project types include Feature Films.

Mike Ades
Producer
imdb.com/name/nm1400460

AD HOMINEM ENTERPRISES

506 Santa Monica Blvd
Suite 400
Santa Monica, CA 90401
310-394-1444 (phone)
310-394-5401 (fax)

imdb.com/company/co0171502

Does not accept any unsolicited material. Project types include Feature Films.

Jim Burke
Partner
310-394-1444
jwb@adhominem.us
imdb.com/name/nm0121724
Assistant: Adam Wagner

Alexander Payne
Partner
310-394-1444
imdb.com/name/nm0668247

Adam Wagner
Director of Development
310-394-1444
twitter.com/linkedin.compubadam-wagner15326b07

ADITI PICTURES

244 5th Ave, Suite 2658
New York, NY 10001
646-861-8777

borozco@aditipictures.com
aditipictures.com
imdb.com/company/co0416283
facebook.com/pages/Aditi-Pictures-Incorporated/
167187393297937

Accepts query letter from unproduced, unrepresented writers via email. Project types include Feature Films and TV. Preferred genres include Comedy and Family.

Janeth Herrera
Vice President

Shante Evans
Executive Assistant

Beverly Orozco
President/CEO
imdb.com/name/nm3869619
linkedin.com/pub/beverly-orozco/4/7a/750
twitter.com/beverlyorozco

ADJACENT PRODUCTIONS

10351 Santa Monica Blvd., Suite 250
Los Angeles, CA 90025
310-228-1001

imdb.com/company/co0490085

Does not accept any unsolicited material. Project types include TV. Preferred genres include Drama.

Michael Brooks
SVP of Entertainment Programming

ADVENTURES IN FILM

Burbank, CA 91505
310-880-0222 (phone)
310-867-2004 (fax)

ira@adventuresinfilm.com
jeff@adventuresinfilm.com
adventuresinfilm.com
imdb.com/company/co0348285
facebook.com/AdventuresInFilm

Does not accept any unsolicited material. Project types include Feature Films. Preferred genres include Drama.

Ira Besserman
Producer
imdb.com/name/nm0078810
linkedin.com/pub/ira-besserman/12/1a9/b55
facebook.com/ira.besserman

AEGIS FILM GROUP

7510 Sunset Blvd
Ste 275
Los Angeles, CA 90046
818-588-3545 (phone)
323-650-9954 (fax)

aegisfilmgroup@ca.rr.com
aegisfilmgroup.com
imdb.com/name/nm1985255
facebook.com/pages/Aegis-Film-Group

Does not accept any unsolicited material. Project types include Feature Films. Preferred genres include Documentary. Established in 2003.

Arianna Eisenberg
CEO
323-848-7977
imdb.com/name/nm1985255
linkedin.com/pub/arianna-eisenberg/22/818/b21

Steven Shultz
President (Production)
323-848-7977
imdb.com/name/nm0795789

AEI - ATCHITY ENTERTAINMENT INTERNATIONAL, INC.

9601 Wilshire Blvd, #1202
Beverly Hills, CA 90210
323-932-0407 (phone)
323-932-0321 (fax)

kja@aeionline.com
aeionline.com
imdb.com/company/co0010944
twitter.com/kennja

Does not accept any unsolicited material.

David Angsten
Development Executive

Ken Atchity
Writer
kja@aeionline.com
imdb.com/name/nm0040338

A&E NETWORK

235 E 45th St
New York, NY 10017
212-210-1400 (phone)
212-210-9755 (fax)

2049 Century Park East Tenth Floor
Los Angeles, CA 90067
310-556-7500

feedback@aetv.com
aetv.com
imdb.com/company/co0056790
facebook.com/AETV
twitter.com/intentuser

Does not accept any unsolicited material.

Thomas Moody
Senior Vice President
212-210-1400
feedback@aetv.com
imdb.com/name/nm1664759

AESOP ENTERTAINMENT

269 S Beverly Dr, Suite 950
Beverly Hills, CA 90212

12-13 Greek St
Soho W1D 4DL London

la@aesopentertainment.com
uk@aesopentertainment.com
aesopentertainment.com
imdb.com/name/nm5764189
linkedin.com/company/aesop-entertainment-limited

Does not accept any unsolicited material. Project types include Feature Films. Preferred genres include Comedy.

Lizzie Tayloer
Producer

Michael Kasher
Head
imdb.com/name/nm1183606

A&E STUDIOS

2049 Century Park East Tenth Floor
Los Angeles, CA 90067
310-556-7500

aetv.com
facebook.com/AETV

Does not accept any unsolicited material. Project types include Feature Films. Established in 2014.

Barry Jossen
Vice President
imdb.com/name/nm0430904

Robert DeBitetto
President
imdb.com/name/nm2248039

AFFIRMATIVE ENTERTAINMENT

425 N Robertson Blvd.
West Hollywood, CA 90048
310-858-3200

imdb.com/company/co0244988

Does not accept any unsolicited material. Project types include Feature Films and TV. Preferred genres include Comedy, Drama, and Thriller.

Melanie Greene
Producer/Manager
linkedin.com/pub/melanie-greene/3a/782/912

Nicholas Bogner
Producer/Manager
imdb.com/name/nm0091851
linkedin.com/pub/nicholas-bogner/2b/312/912
facebook.com/nicholas.bogner.75

AFFIRM FILMS

10202 W. Washington Blvd., Stage 6/513
Culver City, CA 90232
310-244-4000

af-acquisitions@spe.sony.com
sonypictures.com/homevideo/affirmfilms
facebook.com/sonyaffirm
imdb.com/company/co0248867
twitter.com/AFFIRMFilms

Does not accept any unsolicited material. Project types include Feature Films. Preferred genres include Drama and Family.

Rich Peluso
VP
imdb.com/name/nm3553062
linkedin.com/in/richpeluso

AFTER DARK FILMS

844 Seward St
Los Angeles, CA 90038
310-270-4260 (phone)
310-270-4262 (fax)

info@afterdarkfilms.com
afterdarkfilms.com
imdb.com/company/co0166161
twitter.com/afterdarkfilms
facebook.com/afterdarkfilms
linkedin.com/company/after-dark-films

Does not accept any unsolicited material. Preferred genres include Horror. Established in 2006.

Richard Cardona
Creative Executive
linkedin.com/pub/richard-cardona/3/b63/591

Courtney Solomon
CEO

AGAMEMNON FILMS

650 N Bronson Ave, Suite B225
Los Angeles, CA 90004
323-960-4066

agamemnon.com
imdb.com/company/co0004137

Accepts query letter from unproduced, unrepresented
writers via email. Project types include TV. Preferred
genres include Action, Drama, Family, Non-Fiction,
Reality, and Thriller. Established in 1981.

Fraser Heston
President
imdb.com/name/nm0381699
linkedin.com/pub/fraser-heston/34/419/936
Assistant: Heather Thomas

Alex Butler
Senior Partner
imdb.com/name/nm0124808

AGGREGATE FILMS

100 Universal City Plaza
Bungalow 4144
Universal City, CA 91608
818-777-8180

imdb.com/company/co0369082

Does not accept any unsolicited material. Project types
include Feature Films. Preferred genres include
Comedy and Family.

Jim Garavente
President
imdb.com/name/nm4814574

Jason Bateman
Founder
imdb.com/name/nm0000867

AGILITY STUDIOS

11928 Ventura Blvd
Studio City, CA 91604
310-314-1440 (phone)
310-496-3292 (fax)

info@agilitystudios.com
agilitystudios.com
imdb.com/company/co0293230
linkedin.com/company/agility-studios-llc

Accepts query letter from unproduced, unrepresented
writers via email. Established in 2008.

Scott Ehrlich
Principle
310-314-1440
info@agilitystudios.com
imdb.com/name/nm3796990
linkedin.com/in/scottehrlich

AGRON PRODUCTIONS, CHARLES

PO Box 7302
Beverly Hills, CA
310-203-1450

info@charlesagronproductions.com
charlesagronproductions.com
imdb.com/company/co0361904
facebook.com/pages/Charles-Agron-Productions/
    284039284962368

Does not accept any unsolicited material. Project types
include Feature Films. Preferred genres include
Horror.

Charles Agron
Producer
imdb.com/name/nm4469602
facebook.com/charles.agron.7
twitter.com/CAgronProducer

AGUA FILMS

5482 Wilshire Blvd., Suite 193
Los Angeles, CA 90036
323-571-2723 (phone)
323-571-0210 (fax)

information@aguafilms.com
aguafilms.com

imdb.com/company/co0175993

Does not accept any unsolicited material. Project types include Feature Films and TV. Preferred genres include Drama.

Lourdes Diaz
Producer
imdb.com/name/nm0969006
linkedin.com/in/lourdesdiaz

Leyani Diaz
Creative Executive
imdb.com/name/nm2250587
facebook.com/leyanid
twitter.com/LEYANIWRITER

AHIMSA FILMS

6671 Sunset Blvd, Suite 1593
Los Angeles, CA 90028
323-464-8500 (phone)
323-464-8535 (fax)

imdb.com/company/co0202538

Accepts query letter from unproduced, unrepresented writers.

Rebecca Yeldham
President
imdb.com/name/nm0947344
Assistant: Alex Killian

AHIMSA MEDIA

8060 Colonial Dr, Suite 204
Richmond, BC V7C 4V1
Canada
604-785-3602

info@ahimsamedia.com
ahimsamedia.com
imdb.com/company/co0222513
facebook.com/ahimsamedia
twitter.com/ahimsamedia
linkedin.com/company/ahimsa-media

Accepts query letter from unproduced, unrepresented writers via email. Project types include Commercials.

Erica Hargreave
President/Head of Creative and Interactive
604-785-3602
info@ahimsamedia.com
imdb.com/name/nm2988128
twitter.com/EricaHargreave

AIRMONT PICTURES

1115 Berkeley St
Santa Monica, CA 90403

imdb.com/company/co0176167

Accepts query letter from unproduced, unrepresented writers.

Matthew Gannon
Producer
imdb.com/name/nm0304478
linkedin.com/pub/matt-gannon/5/b28/385

AKIL PRODUCTIONS

Los Angeles, CA
212-608-2000

info@akilproductions.com
akilproductions.com
twitter.com/AKILPRODUCTIONS
imdb.com/company/co0372929
facebook.com/akilproductionstv

Project types include TV. Preferred genres include Drama. Established in 2000.

Mara Brock Akil
Founder
imdb.com/name/nm0015327
linkedin.com/pub/mara-akil/74/50/3b7

Salim Akil
Founder
imdb.com/name/nm0015328

ALAMO DRAFTHOUSE FILMS

Austin, TX

info@drafthousefilms.com
drafthousefilms.com
imdb.com/company/co0313579
facebook.com/drafthousefilms

twitter.com/DrafthouseFilms

Does not accept any unsolicited material. Project types include Feature Films. Preferred genres include Action, Comedy, Documentary, Drama, and Thriller. Established in 1997.

James Emanuel Shapiro
COO
imdb.com/name/nm4874938

Tim League
CEO
imdb.com/name/nm1382506
linkedin.com/in/timleague
facebook.com/timleague
twitter.com/timalamo

Evan Husney
Creative Director
imdb.com/name/nm3432889
linkedin.com/pub/evan-husney/9/3b0/5aa
facebook.com/evanhusney
twitter.com/evanhusney

ALAN BARNETTE PRODUCTIONS

8899 Beverly Blvd # 800
Los Angeles, CA 90048
310-922-2688

dabarnette@aol.com
imdb.com/company/co0056462

Does not accept any unsolicited material.

Alan Barnette
Executive Producer
imdb.com/name/nm0056002
linkedin.com/pub/alan-barnette/6/122/752

Nancy Mosher Hall
Development Executive
imdb.com/name/nm0355945

ALAN DAVID MANAGEMENT

8840 Wilshire Blvd,
Suite 200
Beverly Hills, CA 90211
310-358-3155 (phone)
310-358-3256 (fax)

ad@adgmp.com
imdb.com/company/co0097077

Does not accept any unsolicited material.

Alan David
President
310-358-3155
ad@adgmp.com
imdb.com/name/nm2220960

ALAN GASMER & FRIENDS

10877 Wilshire Blvd., Suite 1404
Los Angeles, CA 90024
310-208-7338

imdb.com/company/co0283191

Does not accept any unsolicited material. Project types include Feature Films. Preferred genres include Comedy.

Alan Gasmer
Producer/Manager
imdb.com/name/nm2231517

ALAN SACKS PRODUCTIONS

11684 Ventura Blvd, Suite 809
Studio City, CA 91604
323-957-1952

asacks@pacbell.net
imdb.com/company/co0013945

Does not accept any unsolicited material.

Alan Sacks
Executive Producer
imdb.com/name/nm0755286

ALCHEMY ENTERTAINMENT

7024 Melrose Ave, Suite 420
Los Angeles, CA 90038
323-937-6100 (phone)
323-937-6102 (fax)

imdb.com/company/co0094892

Does not accept any unsolicited material.

Jason Barrett
Principle (Manager)
323-937-6100
imdb.com/name/nm2249074

ALCIDE BAVA PICTURES

Los Angeles, CA

imdb.com/company/co0482803

Does not accept any unsolicited material. Project types include Feature Films. Preferred genres include Comedy and Horror. Established in 2014.

Johnny Galecki
Principle

ALCON ENTERTAINMENT, LLC

10390 Santa Monica Blvd, Suite 250
Los Angeles, CA 90025
310-789-3040 (phone)
310-789-3060 (fax)

info@alconent.com
alconent.com
imdb.com/company/co0054452
facebook.com/AlconEntertainment

Does not accept any unsolicited material. Project types include Feature Films.

Broderick Johnson
Co-CEO/Co-Founder
310-789-3040
info@alconent.com
imdb.com/name/nm0424663

Steven Wegner
Executive Vice President of Production
310-789-3040
info@alconent.com
imdb.com/name/nm1176853

ALEXANDER CONTENT

8033 Sunset Blvd. Suite 507
Los Angeles, CA 90046

alexandercontent.com
twitter.com/Alexanderrcc

Does not accept any unsolicited material. Project types include Feature Films. Preferred genres include Action, Science Fiction, and Thriller.

Rick Alexander
President/Producer
imdb.com/name/nm1006153

ALEXANDER/MITCHELL PRODUCTIONS

201 Wilshire Blvd Third Floor
Santa Monica, CA 90401
310-458-3003 (phone)
310-393-7238 (fax)

imdb.com/company/co0241249

Accepts query letter from unproduced, unrepresented writers via email. Project types include Feature Films and TV. Preferred genres include Drama.

Les Alexander
imdb.com/name/nm0018573

Jonathan Mitchell
imdb.com/name/nm2927057

ALEX ROSE PRODUCTIONS

8291 Presson Place
Los Angeles, CA 90069
323-654-8662 (phone)
323-654-0196 (fax)

imdb.com/company/co0177705

Accepts query letter from unproduced, unrepresented writers.

Alexandra Rose
President
imdb.com/name/nm0741228

ALIANZA FILMS INTERNATIONAL

11941 Weddington St, Suite #106
Studio City, CA 91607
310-933-6250 (phone)
310-388-0874 (fax)

shari@alianzafilms.com
alianzafilms.com

imdb.com/company/co0022267

Accepts query letter from unproduced, unrepresented writers. Established in 1984.

Shari Hamrick
Executive
shari@alianzafilms.com
imdb.com/name/nm0359089

ALIGNED ENTERTAINMENT

1093 Broxton Ave., Suite 240
Los Angeles, CA 90024

aligned-ent.com

Does not accept any unsolicited material. Project types include Feature Films. Preferred genres include Comedy.

Frank Gonzales
VP of Talent

Mohammed Ali
Manager

Brett Carducci
Producer/Manager
imdb.com/name/nm2248023
linkedin.com/pub/brett-carducci/1a/4b8/71a
facebook.com/brett.carducci.7
twitter.com/BrettCarducci

A-LINE PICTURES

info@a-linepictures.com
a-linepictures.com
imdb.com/company/co0156447

Does not accept any unsolicited material. Established in 2005.

Caroline Baron
Producer
212-496-9496
info@a-linepictures.com
imdb.com/name/nm0056205

ALIVE ENTERTAINMENT

7955 W. 3rd St, Unit C
Los Angeles, CA 90048

323-939-3130 (phone)
323-939-3132 (fax)

84 Franklin St.
New York, NY 10013
646-797-2794

info@aliveentertainment.com
aliveentertainment.com
linkedin.com/company/alive-entertainment
imdb.com/company/co0008174

Does not accept any unsolicited material.

Philip von Alvensleben
Partner/Producer
imdb.com/name/nm0901880

Isabell von Alvensleben
Partner/Producer
imdb.com/name/nm0901879
facebook.com/isabell.vonalvensleben

ALLEGIANCE THEATER, THE

269 S Beverly Dr, Suite 822
Beverly Hills, CA 90212
424-260-3340

theallegiancetheater.com
facebook.com/TheAllegianceTheater/timeline
imdb.com/company/co0370262

Does not accept any unsolicited material. Project types include Feature Films. Preferred genres include Comedy, Drama, and Thriller.

Lara Alameddine
Partner/Producer
imdb.com/name/nm1240783
facebook.com/lara.alameddine

Timothy Crane
Partner/Producer
linkedin.com/pub/tim-crane/a/605/29b

Daniel Dubiecki
Partner/Producer
imdb.com/name/nm0239277
linkedin.com/pub/daniel-dubiecki/a/256/10a
facebook.com/daniel.dubiecki
twitter.com/danieldubiecki

Torus Tammer
Partner (Australia)
imdb.com/name/nm0848709
linkedin.com/pub/torus-tammer/7/208/b27
facebook.com/pages/Torus-Tammer/
139179796109857

Carly Norris
Head of Development
imdb.com/name/nm1771200

ALLENTOWN PRODUCTIONS

100 Universal City Plaza
Building 2372B, Suite 114
Universal City, CA 91608
818-733-1002 (phone)
818-866-4181 (fax)

writetous@allentownproductions.com
allentownproductions.com
imdb.com/company/co0122945
facebook.com/AllentownProductions
twitter.com/JamesMoll

Does not accept any unsolicited material. Preferred genres include Non-Fiction. Established in 1994.

James Moll
Principle
imdb.com/name/nm0002224

Chris W. King
Director of Development
imdb.com/name/nm1648242

ALLIANCE FILMS

9465 Wilshire Blvd.
Suite 500
Beverly Hills, CA 90212

22 Harbor Park Dr
Port Washington, NY 11050

145 Kings St East
Suite 300
Toronto, ON, Canada, M5C2Y7
416-309-4200 (phone)
416-309-4290 (fax)

info@alliancefilms.com
imdb.com/company/co0224509

alliancefilms.com

Does not accept any unsolicited material. Project types include Feature Films. Preferred genres include Action, Comedy, Crime, Drama, Fantasy, Horror, Romance, Science Fiction, and Thriller.

Xavier Marchand
President
imdb.com/name/nm0545421

ALL NIPPON ENTERTAINMENT WORKS

5225 Wilshire Blvd., Suite 700
Los Angeles, CA 90036
323-904-3787 (phone)
323-904-3788 (fax)

an-ew.com
imdb.com/company/co0349144
facebook.com/pages/All-Nippon-Entertainment-
Works/137524653039188

Does not accept any unsolicited material. Project types include Feature Films and TV. Preferred genres include Action and Science Fiction.

Hiro H. Shimizu
COO

Sandy Climan
CEO
imdb.com/name/nm0166787

Annmarie Sairrino Bailey
VP of Creative Affairs
imdb.com/name/nm2913118

ALLOY ENTERTAINMENT

4000 Warner Blvd.
Building 146, Room 203
Burbank, CA 91522
818-954-3074 (phone)
818-954-3508 (fax)

151 W. 26th St
11th Floor
New York, NY 10001
212-329-8448

laassistant@alloyentertainment.com
alloyentertainment.com

imdb.com/company/co0142434
facebook.com/alloyent
twitter.com/alloyent

Accepts query letter from unproduced, unrepresented writers via email.

Josh Bank
Executive Vice President
212-329-8448
imdb.com/name/nm2987370

ALOE ENTERTAINMENT

433 N Camden Dr.
Suite 600
Beverly Hills, CA 90210
310-288-1886 (phone)
310-288-1801 (fax)

info@aloeentertainment.com
aloeentertainment.com
facebook.com/theofficialaloeentertainment
imdb.com/company/co0261920

Does not accept any unsolicited material. Established in 1999.

Mary Aloe
imdb.com/name/nm0022053

ALORIS ENTERTAINMENT

275 W Natick Rd
Warwick, RI 02886
401-374-0249

alorisentertainment.com
facebook.com/Alorisentertainment
imdb.com/company/co0301850
twitter.com/AlorisEnt

Does not accept any unsolicited material. Project types include Feature Films. Preferred genres include Crime, Horror, and Thriller.

John Santilli
Producer
imdb.com/name/nm2530923
linkedin.com/pub/john-santilli/6/480/82b

AL ROKER PRODUCTIONS

250 W 57th St
Suite 1525
New York, NY 10019
212-757-8500 (phone)
212-757-8513 (fax)

info@alroker.com
alrokerproductions.com
facebook.com/AlRokerEntertainment
twitter.com/AlRoker_Entmnt
imdb.com/company/co0095131

Does not accept any unsolicited material. Project types include Feature Films. Established in 1994.

Al Roker
CEO
imdb.com/name/nm0737963
twitter.com/alroker

Tracie Brennan
imdb.com/name/nm2200420
linkedin.com/in/traciebrennan

ALTA LOMA ENTERTAINMENT

9346 Civic Center Dr.
Beverly Hills, CA 90210
310-424-1800

alta-loma.com
imdb.com/company/co0008514

Does not accept any unsolicited material.

J.W. Starrett
Director of Development
323-276-4211
imdb.com/name/nm2852786

ALTERNATIVE STUDIO

100 Universal City Plaza
Universal City, CA 91608
818-777-1000

nbcuni.com
linkedin.com/company/universal-pictures
twitter.com/UniversalTV
facebook.com/UniversalTV
imdb.com/company/co0096447

Does not accept any unsolicited material. Project types include TV. Preferred genres include Comedy.

Paul Telegdy
President, Alter.Prgrmming/Late Night
imdb.com/name/nm2350150

ALTURAS FILMS

2403 Main St Santa Monica, CA 90405
310-230-6100 (phone)
310-314-2135 (fax)

info@alturasfilms.com
reception@alturasfilms.com
alturasfilms.com
imdb.com/company/co0169508

Does not accept any unsolicited material. Established in 2004.

Marshall Rawlings
CEO (Producer)
310-401-6200
reception@alturasfilms.com
imdb.com/name/nm1987844
linkedin.com/pub/marshall-rawlings/0/a63/489

AMADEUS PICTURES

578 Washington Blvd., Suite 578
Marina Del Rey, CA 90292
310-923-4356

info@amadeuspictures.com
amadeuspictures.com
facebook.com/amadeuspictures
imdb.com/company/co0224596

Does not accept any unsolicited material. Preferred genres include Drama.

Damian Chapa
Writer/Producer/Director/Actor
imdb.com/name/nm0152082
facebook.com/pages/Damian-Chapa/
    108140612539942

A-MARK ENTERTAINMENT

233 Wilshire Blvd, Suite 200
Santa Monica, CA 90401
310-255-0900

info@amarkentertainment.com
amarkentertainment.com
imdb.com/company/co0135086
linkedin.com/company/a-mark-entertainment

Does not accept any unsolicited material. Established in 2004.

Bruce McNall
Co-Chairman
310-255-0900
info@amarkentertainment.com
imdb.com/name/nm1557652

AMBASSADOR ENTERTAINMENT, INC.

310-862-5200 (phone)
310-496-3140 (fax)

aspeval@ambassadortv.com
ambassadortv.com
imdb.com/company/co0175998

Does not accept any unsolicited material. Established in 1999.

Albert Spevak
President
aspeval@ambassadortv.com
imdb.com/name/nm0818411
linkedin.com/in/albertspevak

AMBER ENTERTAINMENT

21 Ganton St, 4th Floor
London
United Kingdom
W1F 98N
+44207-292-7170

info@amberentertainment.com
amberentertainment.com
imdb.com/company/co0266476
linkedin.com/company/amber-entertainment
twitter.com/amber_ent

Does not accept any unsolicited material. Project types include Feature Films. Preferred genres include Crime,

Drama, Fantasy, Horror, and Thriller. Established in 2010.

Lawrence Elman
Executive Producer
imdb.com/name/nm3793846

Ileen Maisel
Executive
+44207-292-7170
info@amberentertainment.com
imdb.com/name/nm0537884

AMBLIN ENTERTAINMENT

100 Universal Plaza
Bldg 5121
Universal City, CA 91608
818-733-7000

imdb.com/company/co0009119
facebook.com/pages/Amblin-Entertainment

Does not accept any unsolicited material. Project types include Feature Films. Preferred genres include Action, Comedy, Drama, Fantasy, and Science Fiction.

Steven Spielberg
Chairman
imdb.com/name/nm0000229
facebook.com/pages/Steven-spielberg

AMBUSH ENTERTAINMENT

360 N. La Cienega Blvd. Third Floor
Los Angeles, CA 90048
323-951-9197 (phone)
323-951-9998 (fax)

info@ambushentertainment.com
ambushentertainment.com
imdb.com/company/co0091524
linkedin.com/company/ambush-entertainment

Accepts scripts from produced or represented writers. Established in 2000.

Miranda Bailey
Partner (CEO)
323-951-9197
323-951-9998
imdb.com/name/nm0047419

Amanda Marshall
Head (Production)
imdb.com/name/nm1622973

AMERICAN CHAINSAWS

10950 Washington Blvd., Suite 300
Culver City, CA 90232
213-241-9500

americanchainsaws.com
imdb.com/company/co0361572

Project types include TV.

Royal Malloy
Producer
imdb.com/name/nm3735876
linkedin.com/pub/royal-malloy/31/950/749
facebook.com/royal.malloy
twitter.com/royalmalloy

Duke Straub
Producer
imdb.com/name/nm0833702
linkedin.com/pub/duke-straub/12/b63/437

Colt Straub
Producer
imdb.com/name/nm2324836
linkedin.com/pub/colt-straub/48/a74/886
facebook.com/colt.straub.92
twitter.com/cougarcolt

AMERICAN CINEMA INTERNATIONAL

15363 Ventura Blvd.
Sherman Oaks, CA 91406
818-907-8700

aci-americancinema.com
facebook.com/pages/American-Cinema-International/
166267290065693
imdb.com/company/co0004425

Does not accept any unsolicited material. Project types include Feature Films. Preferred genres include Action, Drama, and Romance.

George Shamieh
CEO
imdb.com/name/nm0787864

Chevonne O'Shaughnessy
President
imdb.com/name/nm1367679
linkedin.com/pub/chevonne-o-shaughnessy/11/8a2/
    5b8
facebook.com/chevonne.oshaughnessy.5

AMERICAN UNITED ENTERTAINMENT

7119 W. Sunset Blvd., Suite 403
Hollywood, CA 90046
424-235-0030

info@americanunitedent.com
americanunitedent.com
facebook.com/pages/Beverly-Hills-CA/American-
    United-Entertainment/210968482563
imdb.com/company/co0223507

Does not accept any unsolicited material. Project types
include Feature Films and TV. Preferred genres
include Action, Comedy, Drama, and Family.

Wallace Pidgeon
Director of Entertainment

Art Camacho
VP of Entertainment
imdb.com/name/nm0131064

Kevin Hicks
President
imdb.com/name/nm1649077

Todd Chamberlain
President of Production
imdb.com/name/nm1956927

Robert Rodriguez
CEO/Producer
imdb.com/name/nm0001675

AMERICAN WORK INC.

7030 Delongpre
Los Angeles, CA 90028
323-668-1100 (phone)
323-668-1133 (fax)

imdb.com/company/co0167015

Accepts query letter from unproduced, unrepresented
writers. Preferred genres include Comedy.

Ravi Nandan
imdb.com/name/nm2249298

Scot Armstrong
Partner
imdb.com/name/nm0035905

AMERICAN WORLD PICTURES

8255 Sunset Blvd.
West Hollywood, CA 90046
323-848-7700 (phone)
323-848-7744 (fax)

info@americanworldpictures.com
americanworldpictures.com
imdb.com/company/co0054536

Accepts scripts from unproduced, unrepresented
writers. Project types include Feature Films. Preferred
genres include Action, Comedy, Drama, Family,
Horror, Romance, and Thriller.

Mark Lester
818-340-9004
mark@americanworldpictures.com
imdb.com/name/nm0504495
linkedin.com/pub/mark-l-lester/44/503/a57

Dana Dubovsky
818-340-9004
dana@americanworldpictures.com
imdb.com/name/nm0239541
linkedin.com/pub/dana-dubovsky/40/868/268

AMERICAN ZOETROPE

916 Kearny St Sentinel Building
San Francisco, CA 94133
415-788-7500 (phone)
415-989-7910 (fax)

1641 N Ivar Ave
Los Angeles, CA 90028

contests@zoetrope.com
zoetrope.com
imdb.com/company/co0020958

Accepts scripts from unproduced, unrepresented
writers. Preferred genres include Action, Crime, Non-
Fiction, and Thriller. Established in 1972.

Francis Coppola
Emeritus
415-788-7500
imdb.com/name/nm0000338

Michael Zakin
Vice President (Production & Acquisitions)
323-460-4420
imdb.com/name/nm2943902

AM PRODUCTIONS & MANAGEMENT

8899 Beverly Blvd. Suite 713
Los Angeles , CA 90048
310-275-9081 (phone)
310-275-9082 (fax)

imdb.com/company/co0094894

Does not accept any unsolicited material.

Roger Smith
Producer/Manager

Alan Marguilies
Producer/Manager
imdb.com/name/nm0546865

ANCHOR BAY FILMS

9242 Beverly Blvd Suite 201
Beverly Hills, CA 90210
424-204-4166

1699 Stutz Dr.
Troy, MI 48084
248-816-0909 (phone)
248-816-3335 (fax)

questions@anchorbayent.com
anchorbayent.com
imdb.com/company/co0249289

Preferred genres include Crime, Horror, and Thriller.
Established in 1997.

Bill Clark
President
424-204-4166
imdb.com/name/nm0163694

ANDELL ENTERTAINMENT

10877 Wilshire Blvd. Suite 2200
Los Angeles , CA 90024
310-954-4890 (phone)
310-954-4881 (fax)

imdb.com/company/co0064187

Does not accept any unsolicited material. Project types include Feature Films. Preferred genres include Drama.

Andrew Hauptman
Producer

Eric Hayes
President

Lisbeth Vitallo-Hook
Development

ANDELL ENTERTAINMENT

10877 Wilshire Blvd. Suite 2200
Los Angeles , CA 90024
310-954-4890 (phone)
310-954-4881 (fax)

imdb.com/company/co0064187

Does not accept any unsolicited material. Project types include Feature Films. Preferred genres include Drama.

Eric Hayes
President
imdb.com/name/nm2498510
linkedin.com/pub/eric-hayes/5/b77/540

Andrew Hauptman
Producer
imdb.com/name/nm0369448
facebook.com/pages/Andrew-Hauptman/
143071572375642
twitter.com/andrew_hauptman

Lisbeth Vitallo-Hook
Development
imdb.com/name/nm1025460

ANDERSON PRODUCTIONS, CRAIG

444 N. Larchmont Blvd., Suite 109
Los Angeles, CA 90004
323-463-2000 (phone)
323-463-2022 (fax)

info@cappix.com
cappix.com
imdb.com/company/co0062854
linkedin.com/company/craig-anderson-productions

Accepts query letter from produced or represented writers. Project types include TV. Preferred genres include Drama.

Peter Karabots
Executive Producer

Craig Anderson
Producer
imdb.com/name/nm0026544
linkedin.com/pub/craig-anderson/5/839/14

David Markus
VP of Development
imdb.com/name/nm0549007

Nathan Santell
Development
imdb.com/name/nm2731214

ANDREA SIMON ENTERTAINMENT

4230 Woodman Ave.
Sherman Oaks, CA 91423
818-380-1901 (phone)
818-380-1932 (fax)

asimon@andreasimonent.com
imdb.com/company/co0102747
linkedin.com/company/andrea-simon-entertainment

Accepts query letter from unproduced, unrepresented writers. Project types include Feature Films and TV. Preferred genres include Comedy and Drama.

Andrea Simon
Principle
asimon@andreasimonent.com
imdb.com/name/nm2231084
linkedin.com/pub/andrea-simon/18/AB/885

ANDREW LAUREN PRODUCTIONS

36 E 23rd St, Suite 6F
New York, NY 10010
212-475-1600 (phone)
212-529-1095 (fax)

asst@andrewlaurenproductions.com
andrewlaurenproductions.com
imdb.com/company/co0032488
linkedin.com/company/andrew-lauren-productions

Accepts scripts from unproduced, unrepresented writers. Project types include Feature Films and TV. Preferred genres include Drama.

Andrew Lauren
Principle
212-475-1600
asst@andrewlaurenproductions.com
imdb.com/name/nm0491054

Dave Platt
Creative Executive
212-475-1600
asst@andrewlaurenproductions.com
imdb.com/name/nm5255879

AND THEN PRODUCTIONS

1023 1/2 Abbot Kinney Blvd.
Venice, CA 90291
310-260-7073 (phone)
310-260-7060 (fax)

imdb.com/company/co0202735

Does not accept any unsolicited material. Project types include Feature Films. Preferred genres include Drama.

David Duchovny
Principal, Producer, Actor
imdb.com/name/nm0000141
facebook.com/DavidDuchovnyOfficial
twitter.com/davidduchovny

Tea Leoni
Principal, Producer, Actor
imdb.com/name/nm0000495
facebook.com/TeaLeoni
twitter.com/TheTeaLeoni

Susanna Jolly
Executive Vice President
imdb.com/name/nm3104740

Eric Knight
Development
imdb.com/name/nm0460896
linkedin.com/in/theericknight

ANGEL ARK PRODUCTIONS

5042 Wilshire Blvd,. Suite 592
Los Angeles, CA 90036
818-981-8833

imdb.com/company/co0030722

Does not accept any unsolicited material. Project types include TV. Preferred genres include Comedy and Crime.

Jason Alexander
Partner
imdb.com/name/nm0004517
facebook.com/pages/Jason-Alexander/
    108011235885841
twitter.com/IJasonAlexander

Jenny Birchfield-Eick
Partner
imdb.com/name/nm0083316
linkedin.com/pub/jenny-birchfield-eick/27/b7/50b
facebook.com/jenny.birchfieldeick

Michael A. Jackman
Partner
imdb.com/name/nm0413182
linkedin.com/pub/michael-a-jackman/1/74/a63
twitter.com/jackmantwo

ANGELWORLD ENTERTAINMENT LTD.

New Bridge House
30-34 New Bridge St
London
EC4 V6BJ

6 Triq Ta Fuq Il Widien
Mellieha
Malta

asst@angelworldentertainment.com
angelworldentertainment.com

Accepts query letter from unproduced, unrepresented writers via email. Project types include Feature Films. Established in 2007.

Darby Angel
CEO/Producer
chris@angelworldentertainment.com
imdb.com/name/nm3786007
linkedin.com/pub/darby-angel/0/963/b50
Assistant: Christopher Tisa

John Michaels
Head of Production

ANGRY FILMS

1416 N. La Brea Ave
Los Angeles, CA
323-802-1715 (phone)
323-802-1720 (fax)

donmurphy.net
imdb.com/company/co0000612

Does not accept any unsolicited material. Project types include Feature Films. Preferred genres include Action, Drama, and Thriller.

Don Murphy
Producer
donmurphy.net
imdb.com/name/nm0006613
facebook.com/pages/Don-Murphy/100330733356089

Susan Montford
Producer
imdb.com/name/nm1848205
facebook.com/pages/Susan-Montford/
    141299689229919

ANIMAL KINGDOM

242 W 30th St Suite 602
New York, NY 10001
212-206-1801

info@animalkingdomfilms.com
animalkingdomfilms.com
twitter.com/AnimalFilms
facebook.com/pages/Animal-Kingdom-Films/
    472303949497226

Does not accept any unsolicited material. Project types include Feature Films. Preferred genres include Drama. Established in 2014.

Frederick Green
Principle
imdb.com/name/nm2677259

Joshua Astrachan
Principle
imdb.com/name/nm0040120
linkedin.com/pub/joshua-astrachan/16/602/2a5
facebook.com/joshua.astrachan

ANIMA SOLA PRODUCTIONS

1041 N. Formosa Ave Writers Building, Suite 6
West Hollywood, CA 90046
323-850-3530

info@animasolaproductions.com
animasolaproductions.com
facebook.com/animasolaproductions
twitter.com/animasolaprods
linkedin.com/company/anima-sola-productions
imdb.com/company/co0050662

Does not accept any unsolicited material. Project types include TV. Preferred genres include Comedy and Drama.

Will Scheffer
Writer/Producer
imdb.com/name/nm0770504
linkedin.com/in/willscheffer
facebook.com/pages/Will-Scheffer/110837282298444

Mark V. Olsen
Writer/Producer
imdb.com/name/nm0647739

Lisa Bellomo
SVP of Production & Development
imdb.com/name/nm0069185
linkedin.com/pub/lisa-bellomo/6/403/98b
facebook.com/lisa.bellomo.71
twitter.com/lisagbellomo

ANIMUS FILMS

914 Hauser Blvd
Los Angeles, CA 90036

323-988-5557 (phone)
323-571-3361 (fax)

info@animusfilms.com
imdb.com/company/co0092860
animusfilms.com
facebook.com/AnimusFIlms

Accepts query letter from unproduced, unrepresented writers. Preferred genres include Non-Fiction and Thriller. Established in 2003.

Jim Young
Principle
323-988-5557
info@animusfilms.com
imdb.com/name/nm1209063
linkedin.com/pub/jim-young/8/176/28

ANNAPURNA PICTURES

310-724-5678

annapurnapics.com
imdb.com/company/co0323215
twitter.com/annapurnapics
facebook.com/annapurnapics

Does not accept any unsolicited material. Project types include Feature Films and TV. Preferred genres include Action, Comedy, Crime, Drama, Non-Fiction, and Thriller.

David Distenfeld
Development Executive
imdb.com/name/nm3367048

Megan Ellison
Principle
imdb.com/name/nm2691892

AN OLIVE BRANCH PRODUCTIONS, INC.

9100 Wilshire Blvd, Suite 616
East Tower
Beverly Hills, CA 90212
310-860-6088 (phone)
310-362-8922 (fax)

38 Highbridge Place
Toronto, ON M1V4R9

info@anolivebranchmedia.com
anolivebranchmedia.com
imdb.com/company/co0055694imdb.com/company/
co0308344
facebook.com/AnOliveBranchMedia
linkedin.com/company/an-olive-branch-productions-
inc-

Accepts scripts from produced or represented writers.
Project types include Feature Films. Preferred genres
include Drama.

Cybill Lui
310-860-6088
info@anolivbranchmedia.com
imdb.com/name/nm3359236

George Zakk
310-860-6088
info@anolivbranchmedia.com
imdb.com/name/nm0952327
linkedin.com/pub/george-zakk/b/863/2a6

ANONYMOUS CONTENT

3532 Hayden Ave
Culver City, CA 90232
310-558-3667 (phone)
310-558-2724 (fax)

588 Broadway Suite 308
New York, NY 10012
212-925-0055 (phone)
212-925-5030 (fax)

filmtv@anonymouscontent.com
litmanagement@anonymouscontent.com
anonymouscontent.com
imdb.com/company/co0017525
linkedin.com/company/23201

Accepts query letter from unproduced, unrepresented
writers via email. Project types include Feature Films,
TV, and Commercials. Preferred genres include
Action, Comedy, Crime, Drama, Family, Non-
Fiction, and Thriller. Established in 1999.

Steve Golin
CEO
imdb.com/name/nm0326512

Emmeline Yang
Executive (Features)
310-558-3667
imdb.com/name/nm2534779
linkedin.com/pub/emmeline-yang/5/b2a/65a

Matt DeRoss
Vice President (Features)
310-558-3667
mattd@anonymouscontent.com
imdb.com/name/nm2249185
linkedin.com/pub/matt-derossi/18/582/229

ANOVA PICTURES

12400 Wilshire Blvd., Suite 1275
Los Angeles, CA 90025
310-985-7335 (phone)
310-362-8922 (fax)

info@anovapictures.com
anovapictures.com
imdb.com/company/co0442499

Accepts query letter from produced or represented
writers. Project types include Feature Films.

Cybill Lui
Producer
imdb.com/name/nm3359236
linkedin.com/profile/view
facebook.com/cyb.lui
twitter.com/TheCybills

ANTHEM PICTURES

5137 Clareton Dr, Suite 120
Agoura Hills, CA 91301
818-597-2344 (phone)
818-706-8553 (fax)

info@anthemdvd.com
anthemdvd.com
imdb.com/company/co0106574

Does not accept any unsolicited material. Project types
include Feature Films and TV.

Keith Walley
Vice President
imdb.com/name/nm0909120
linkedin.com/pub/keith-walley/37/185/96b

Charles Adelman
President
imdb.com/name/nm0011828
linkedin.com/in/charlesadelman
facebook.com/chuck.adelman
twitter.com/charles_adelman

ANTIDOTE FILMS

PO Box 150566
Brooklyn, NY 11215-0566
646-486-4344

info@antidotefilms.com
antidotefilms.com

Does not accept any unsolicited material. Project types include Feature Films. Preferred genres include Documentary. Established in 2000.

Jeffrey Kusama-Hinte
President
646-486-4344 x301
jeff@antidotefilms.com
imdb.com/name/nm0506664

Takeo Hori
646-486-4344 x300
imdb.com/name/nm0394659
linkedin.com/in/takeohori

Gerry Kim
imdb.com/name/nm2332388
linkedin.com/pub/dir/gerald/kim

James Debbs
646-486-4344 x305
imdb.com/name/nm0999455
linkedin.com/pub/james-debbs/9/9b/1a5

APARTMENT 3B

3000 W Olympic Blvd., Suite 2363
Santa Monica, CA 90404
310-264-4264

imdb.com/company/co0117528

Does not accept any unsolicited material. Project types include Feature Films and TV. Preferred genres include Comedy, Drama, Horror, and Thriller.

Jennifer Klein
Producer/President
imdb.com/name/nm0458813

APATOW PRODUCTIONS

11788 W Pico Blvd
Suite 141
Los Angeles, CA 90064
310-943-4400 (phone)
310-479-0750 (fax)

imdb.com/company/co0073081

Does not accept any unsolicited material. Project types include Feature Films and TV. Preferred genres include Action, Comedy, Documentary, Drama, and Romance. Established in 2000.

Judd Apatow
imdb.com/name/nm0031976
twitter.com/JuddApatow
Assistant: Amanda Glaze, Rob Turbovsky, Michael Lewen

APERTURE ENTERTAINMENT

7620 Lexington Ave
West Hollywood, CA 90046
323-848-4069

agasst@aperture-ent.com
imdb.com/company/co0265611
facebook.com/pages/Aperture-Entertainment
twitter.com/aperturee
aperture-ent.com

Accepts scripts from unproduced, unrepresented writers. Project types include Feature Films and TV. Preferred genres include Action, Fantasy, Horror, Science Fiction, and Thriller. Established in 2009.

Adam Goldworm
Principle
323-848-4069
adam@aperture-ent.com
imdb.com/name/nm0326411
linkedin.com/in/adamgoldworm
twitter.com/goldworm

APOSTLE

568 Broadway, Suite 301
New York, NY 10012
212-541-4323 (phone)
212-541-4330 (fax)

9696 Culver Blvd Suite 108
Culver City, CA 90232
310-945-2991

apostlenyc.com
facebook.com/pages/Apostle/123688471019932
twitter.com/ApostleTvFilm
imdb.com/company/co0072799

Does not accept any unsolicited material. Project types
include Feature Films and TV.

Jim Serpico
President/Producer
jimserpico.com
imdb.com/name/nm0785351
linkedin.com/pub/jim-serpico/10/b67/2a8
facebook.com/pages/Jim-Serpico/140494332642978
twitter.com/jimserpico

Denis Leary
Producer/Director/Actor
denisleary.com
imdb.com/name/nm0001459
facebook.com/denisleary
twitter.com/denisleary

Tom Sellitti
SVP of Production/Producer
imdb.com/name/nm0783418
linkedin.com/pub/tom-sellitti/25/9b7/195
facebook.com/tom.sellitti.3

Molly Irwin
Assistant
imdb.com/name/nm2630329
linkedin.com/pub/molly-irwin/6/664/9bb

APPARATUS PRODUCTIONS

8633 Washington Blvd.
Culver City, CA 90232
310-424-1300

imdb.com/company/co0073189

Does not accept any unsolicited material. Project types
include Feature Films. Preferred genres include
Drama.

Matt Livadory
Story Editor

Marc Forster
Director, Producer
imdb.com/name/nm0286975
facebook.com/pages/Marc-Forster/112920088719735
twitter.com/MarcForster

Brad Simpson
Producer
imdb.com/name/nm0800922
linkedin.com/pub/brad-simpson/99/987/459

Jessica Kumai Scott
Creative Executive
imdb.com/name/nm1869626
linkedin.com/pub/jessica-kumai-scott/a/64/a96
facebook.com/jkumai
twitter.com/jkumai

APPIAN WAY

9255 Sunset Blvd., Suite 615
West Hollywood, CA 90069
310-300-1390 (phone)
310-300-1388 (fax)

imdb.com/company/co0088354
facebook.com/LeonardoDiCaprio
twitter.com/LeoDiCaprio

Does not accept any unsolicited material. Project types
include Feature Films and TV. Preferred genres
include Crime, Drama, Horror, Science Fiction, and
Thriller.

James Ward
Creative Executive

Michael Hampton
Co-VP
imdb.com/name/nm6280536

Leonardo DiCaprio

CEO, Actor, Producer
leonardodicaprio.com
imdb.com/name/nm0000138
facebook.com/LeonardoDiCaprio
twitter.com/LeoDiCaprio

Jennifer Davisson Killoran

President/Producer
imdb.com/name/nm2248832

Nathaniel Posey

Co-VP
imdb.com/name/nm2929952

Aaron Criswell

Creative Executive
imdb.com/name/nm2082839
linkedin.com/pub/aaron-criswell/52/b89/a58

APPLE CART PRODUCTIONS

11684 Ventura Blvd. #544
Studio City, CA 91604
818-274-9609 (phone)
818-763-5319 (fax)

info@applecartproductions.com
applecartproductions.com
imdb.com/company/co0221107

Does not accept any unsolicited material. Project types include Feature Films. Preferred genres include Drama and Romance.

Benjamin Oberman

President / Producer
boberman@applecartproductions.com
imdb.com/name/nm2589353
linkedin.com/pub/benjamin-oberman/0/649/b1
facebook.com/BenjaminOberman
twitter.com/TheFilmChampion

Jordana Oberman

VP of Development/Producer
joberman@applecartproductions.com
resumes.actorsaccess.com/JordanaOberman
imdb.com/name/nm3037696
linkedin.com/pub/jordana-oberman/8/330/831
facebook.com/jordana.oberman
twitter.com/jordanaoberman

APPLESEED ENTERTAINMENT

7715 W Sunset Blvd
Hollywood, CA 90046
818-718-6000 (phone)
818-556-5610 (fax)

films@appleseedent.com
appleseedent.com
imdb.com/company/co0176039

Does not accept any unsolicited material. Project types include Feature Films. Preferred genres include Comedy, Drama, and Family.

Ben Moses

Founder
ben@appleseedent.com
imdb.com/name/nm0608558

Lynne Moses

Founder
lynne@appleseedent.com
imdb.com/name/nm1030988
facebook.com/lynne.moses
twitter.com/lynne_moses

APPLOFF ENTERTAINMENT

5900 Wilshire Blvd, Suite 2250
Los Angeles, CA 90036
310-975-9707

imdb.com/company/co0213781
facebook.com/pages/Apploff-Entertainment/
    137269886288644

Does not accept any unsolicited material. Project types include TV.

Jeff Apploff

Executive Producer
imdb.com/name/nm2201741
linkedin.com/pub/jeff-apploff/0/439/b55
facebook.com/japploff
twitter.com/japploff

APRIL FILMS

17644 Rancho St
Encino, CA 91316
818-757-7680 (phone)
818-757-7437 (fax)

info@aprilfilms.com
aprilfilms.com
imdb.com/company/co0089035

Does not accept any unsolicited material. Project types include Feature Films.

Rudy Cohen
Producer
imdb.com/company/co0080027
linkedin.com/pub/rudy-cohen/7/764/450

Adam Dunlap
Producer
imdb.com/name/nm318441

ARAD PRODUCTIONS, AVI

10203 Santa Monica Blvd., Suite 301
Los Angeles, CA 90067
310-772-2723

imdb.com/company/co0180492

Does not accept any unsolicited material. Project types include Feature Films. Preferred genres include Action.

Avi Arad
Producer
imdb.com/name/nm0032696
facebook.com/pages/Avi-Arad/110917875627509
twitter.com/AviArad

Alexandra Bland
Executive
imdb.com/name/nm6348549

Emmy Yu
Development
linkedin.com/pub/emmy-yu/35/226/454

ARCHER GRAY PRODUCTIONS

142 Greene St, 4th Floor
New York, NY 10012

info@archergray.com
archergrayproductions.com
facebook.com/ArcherGrayProductions
imdb.com/company/co0423953
linkedin.com/company/archer-gray-productions
twitter.com/Archer_Gray

Does not accept any unsolicited material. Project types include Feature Films and TV. Preferred genres include Drama.

Amy Nauiokas
Founder/CEO
amynauiokas.com
imdb.com/name/nm2602846
linkedin.com/in/amynauiokas
facebook.com/amy.nauiokas
twitter.com/AmyNauiokas

Anne Carey
President of Production
imdb.com/name/nm0136904
linkedin.com/pub/anne-carey/28/237/661
facebook.com/pages/Anne-Carey/112360425443946

Shani Geva
Creative Executive
imdb.com/name/nm2802616
linkedin.com/pub/shani-geva/54/165/752
facebook.com/shani.geva.7
twitter.com/shanigeva

ARCHETYPE PRODUCTIONS

1608 Argyle Ave
Los Angeles, CA 90028
323-468-3600 (phone)
323-784-7842 (fax)

info@archetypela.com
archetypela.com
facebook.com/ArchetypeLA
twitter.com/ArchetypeLA
imdb.com/company/co0156755
linkedin.com/company/archetype

Does not accept any unsolicited material. Project types include Feature Films. Preferred genres include Action.

David Server
Producer
imdb.com/name/nm2159992
facebook.com/david.server.3

Ray Miller
Producer/Manager
ray.miller@archetypela.com
linkedin.com/pub/ray-miller/1/b31/63b
facebook.com/raymillerla
twitter.com/LARayRay

ARCLIGHT FILMS

9107 Wilshire Blvd, Suite 600
Beverly Hills, CA 90210
310-777-8855 (phone)
310-777-8882 (fax)

90/330 Wattle St
Ultimo NSW 2007, Australia
06028-353-2440

info@arclightfilms.com
arclightfilms.com
facebook.com/ArclightFilms

Accepts query letter from unproduced, unrepresented writers via email. Project types include Feature Films.

Gary Hamilton
Co-Chairman
310-528-5888
gary@arclightfilms.com
imdb.com/name/nm0357861
linkedin.com/pub/hamilton-gary/32/ba/a12

Mike Gabrawy
CCO
310-475-2330
info@arclightfilms.com
imdb.com/name/nm0300166
linkedin.com/pub/mike-gabrawy/1/667/729

ARDABAN

1741 Ivar Ave
Los Angeles, CA 90028
323-790-8000

chachi@ardaban.com
ardaban.com
imdb.com/company/co0396320
linkedin.com/company/shine-group
facebook.com/ShineGroup.tv
twitter.com/ShineGroupTV

Does not accept any unsolicited material. Project types include TV.

Chachi Senior
CEO
imdb.com/name/nm1551847
linkedin.com/pub/chachi-senior/5/544/a5
facebook.com/chachi.senior
twitter.com/ChachiSenior

ARENAS ENTERTAINMENT

3375 Barham Blvd
Los Angeles, CA 90068
323-785-5555 (phone)
323-785-5560 (fax)

2121 N. Bayshore Dr.
Miami, FL 33137

general@arenasgroup.com
arenasgroup.com
imdb.com/company/co0051527
twitter.com/ArenasEnt
facebook.com/ArenasEntertainment

Does not accept any unsolicited material. Project types include Feature Films. Established in 1988.

Santiago Pozo
CEO
imdb.com/name/nm0694815

ARGONAUT PICTURES

310-359-8481

info@argonaughtpictures.co.uk
argonautpictures.co.uk
imdb.com/company/co0015041
twitter.com/ArgonautPicture

Does not accept any unsolicited material. Project types include Feature Films. Preferred genres include Drama.

Scott Bloom
Owner
imdb.com/name/nm0089231
linkedin.com/in/scottbloomedit1

Karim Mashouf
Owner
imdb.com/name/nm3196690

Manny Mashouf
Owner
imdb.com/name/nm3196705

Giovanni Agnelli
Owner
imdb.com/name/nm1278301
facebook.com/public/Giovanni-Agnelli

Paul Marashlian
paul@argonautpictures.com
imdb.com/name/nm2281671

Carter Hall
carter@argonautpictures.com
imdb.com/name/nm3050292

ARIESCOPE PICTURES

10750 Cumpston St
North Hollywood, CA 91601

info@ariescope.com
ariescope.com

Does not accept any unsolicited material. Project types include Feature Films and TV. Preferred genres include Comedy, Crime, Drama, Fantasy, Horror, Romance, and Thriller. Established in 1998.

Will Barratt
Principle
imdb.com/name/nm1701139
facebook.com/pages/Will-Barratt-Productions

Cory Neal
Principle
imdb.com/name/nm1425628

Adam Green
Principle
imdb.com/name/nm1697112
facebook.com/AdamFnGreen

ARLOOK GROUP

205 S Beverly Dr, Suite 209
Beverly Hills, CA 90212

310-550-5714 (phone)
310-550-8714 (fax)

arlookgroup.com
facebook.com/pages/The-Arlook-Group/
    366944246680789
imdb.com/company/co0242042

Does not accept any unsolicited material. Project types include Feature Films. Preferred genres include Drama.

Richard Arlook
Producer/Manager
imdb.com/name/nm0035207
facebook.com/pages/Richard-Arlook/
    143404012338857
twitter.com/richardarlook

ARMORY FILMS

6671 W. Sunset Blvd., Suite 1585
Los Angeles, CA 90028
323-461-1613

armoryfilms.com
facebook.com/pages/Armory-Films/
    221193544620551
imdb.com/company/co0368217

Does not accept any unsolicited material. Project types include Feature Films. Preferred genres include Action, Comedy, Horror, and Thriller.

Christopher Lemole
CCO
imdb.com/name/nm4043287
linkedin.com/pub/chris-lemole/76/805/927
twitter.com/clemole

Tim Zajaros
Partner/Producer
imdb.com/name/nm2591283
linkedin.com/pub/tim-zajaros/4/9a6/434
facebook.com/TimZajaros
twitter.com/TimZajaros

ARROYO PICTURES

3000 Olympic Blvd., Suite 1100
Santa Monica, CA 90404

imdb.com/company/co0067151

Does not accept any unsolicited material. Project types include Feature Films and TV. Preferred genres include Crime, Drama, and Thriller.

Scott Frank
President/Writer/Producer
imdb.com/name/nm0291082

ARSENAL PICTURES

6363 Wilshire Blvd., Suite 550
Los Angeles, CA 90048
323-852-0011 (phone)
323-852-0013 (fax)

info@arsenal-pictures.com
facebook.com/ArsenalPictures
twitter.com/ArsenalPictures
imdb.com/company/co0176772
arsenal-pictures.com

Does not accept any unsolicited material. Project types include Feature Films. Preferred genres include Action, Comedy, Drama, and Thriller.

Yarek Danielak
Founder/Producer
imdb.com/name/nm1345948
linkedin.com/pub/yarek-danielak/1/4ba/560
facebook.com/yarek.danielak

ARS NOVA

511 W 54th St
New York, NY 10019
212-586-4200 (phone)
212-489-1908 (fax)

info@arsnovaent.com
arsnovaent.com
imdb.com/company/co0176042
twitter.com/arsnova

Accepts scripts from unproduced, unrepresented writers. Preferred genres include Action, Comedy, Fantasy, Myth, and Science Fiction.

Jon Steingart
Producer
212-586-4200
japfelbaum@arsnovaent.com
imdb.com/name/nm0826050

Jillian Apfelbaum
Producer
212-586-4200
japfelbaum@arsnovaent.com
imdb.com/name/nm2249752
linkedin.com/pub/jillian-apfelbaum/5/294/51b

ARTHAUS PICTURES

Granville Towers, 1424 N. Crescent Heights, Suite 57
West Hollywood, CA 90046
323-848-8257 (phone)
323-848-8267 (fax)

imdb.com/company/co0211409

Does not accept any unsolicited material. Preferred genres include Drama.

Chuck Rock
Producer
imdb.com/name/nm3066606

ARTICLE19 FILMS

247 Centre St, Suite 7W
New York, NY 10013
212-777-1987

info@article19films.com
facebook.com/pages/Article-19-Films/
    410967495625491
imdb.com/company/co0164965

Accepts query letter from unproduced, unrepresented writers. Preferred genres include Non-Fiction. Established in 2006.

Filippo Bozotti
Executive
imdb.com/name/nm1828075

ARTICULUS ENTERTAINMENT

9440 Santa Monica Blvd., Suite 708
Beverly Hills, CA 90210
310-691-1401 (phone)
877-724-8651 (fax)

articulusentertainment.com
imdb.com/company/co0097887

Does not accept any unsolicited material. Project types include Feature Films. Preferred genres include Action and Drama.

Steven Sawalich
Founder, Producer
imdb.com/name/nm1367960
linkedin.com/in/stevesawalich
facebook.com/steven.sawalich
twitter.com/stevensawalich

Jennifer Perchalla
Director of Development
imdb.com/name/nm1339702
linkedin.com/pub/jen-perchalla/23/54a/1b

ARTINA FILMS

1416 N La Brea Ave
Los Angeles, CA 90028
323-802-1500

info@artinafilms.com
artinafilms.com
imdb.com/company/co0193161

Does not accept any unsolicited material. Project types include Feature Films. Preferred genres include Comedy, Drama, and Thriller.

Robert Salerno
Producer/Director
imdb.com/name/nm0007011
facebook.com/pages/Robert-Salerno/
    133011346736225

Naomi Despres
Producer
imdb.com/name/nm0221638
linkedin.com/pub/naomi-despres/16/baa/117

ARTISTS PRODUCTION GROUP

2601 Colorado Ave
Santa Monica, CA 90404
310-300-2400

imdb.com/company/co0024601

Does not accept any unsolicited material.

Chris George
Development
imdb.com/name/nm0313383

ARTISTS PUBLIC DOMAIN

225 W 13th St
New York, NY 10011

info@artistspublicdomain.com
artistspublicdomain.com
twitter.com/apdfilms
facebook.com/artistspublicdomain

Accepts query letter from unproduced, unrepresented writers. Project types include Feature Films. Preferred genres include Comedy, Drama, Family, Non-Fiction, Romance, Sociocultural, and Thriller.

Hunter Gray
Producer
imdb.com/name/nm0336683

Alex Orlovsky
Producer
imdb.com/name/nm0650164

Andrew Adair
imdb.com/name/nm4253715

ARTIST VIEW ENTERTAINMENT

4425 Irvine Ave
Studio City, CA 91602
818-752-2480 (phone)
818-752-9339 (fax)

info@artistviewent.com
imdb.com/company/co0054865
linkedin.com/company/artist-view-entertainment
facebook.com/artistviewent
artistviewent.com

Does not accept any unsolicited material. Project types include Feature Films. Preferred genres include Action, Comedy, Drama, and Romance.

Jay E. Joyce
Vice President
imdb.com/name/nm0431543
linkedin.com/in/jayjoyce1

Scott J. Jones
President
imdb.com/name/nm0429222
linkedin.com/pub/scott-j-jones/89/508/272
facebook.com/profile.php

ASCENDANT PICTURES

406 Wilshire Blvd.
Santa Monica CA 90401
310-288-4600 (phone)
310-288-4601 (fax)

info@ascendantpictures.com
ascendantpictures.com
facebook.com/pages/Ascendant-Pictures/
   154899421215569
imdb.com/company/co0094902

Does not accept any unsolicited material. Project types
include Feature Films. Preferred genres include
Comedy.

Christopher Roberts
CEO/Founder
imdb.com/name/nm0730932
linkedin.com/pub/chris-roberts/39/132/351
facebook.com/pages/Chris-Roberts-game-developer/
   427661267297625
twitter.com/croberts68

ASIS PRODUCTIONS

316 N Rossmore Ave, Suite 400
Los Angeles, CA 90004

imdb.com/company/co0420272

Does not accept any unsolicited material. Project types
include Feature Films and TV. Preferred genres
include Drama.

Jeff Bridges
President/Actor
jeffbridges.com
imdb.com/name/nm0000313
facebook.com/JeffBridgesOfficial
twitter.com/TheJeffBridges

A. SMITH & COMPANY PRODUCTIONS

9911 W Pico Blvd
Suite 250
Los Angeles, CA 90035
310-432-4800 (phone)
310-551-3085 (fax)

4130 Cahuenga Blvd. Suite 108
Toluca Lake, CA 91602
818-432-2900 (phone)
818-432-2940 (fax)

info@asmithco.com
asmithco.com
imdb.com/company/co0095150
facebook.com/ASmithCoProductions
linkedin.com/company/a.-smith-&-compan

Accepts query letter from unproduced, unrepresented
writers via email.

Arthur Smith
CEO
imdb.com/name/nm0807368
linkedin.com/pub/arthur-smith/B/A76/91B

Christmas Rini
Senior Vice President (Development)
imdb.com/name/nm2859471

A SQUARED ENTERTAINMENT (A2)

9401 Wilshire Blvd. #608
Beverly Hills, CA 90212
310-273-4442 (phone)
310-273-4202 (fax)

info@a2entertain.com

Does not accept any unsolicited material. Preferred
genres include Animation and Family.

Andy Heyward
Partner/Co--President/Producer

Amy Moynihan Heyward
Partner/Co--President/Producer

Gregory Payne
COO

Darren Romanelli
Creative Director

Sidney Iwanter
Story Editor

ASYLUM ENTERTAINMENT

15503 Ventura Blvd.
Suite 240
Encino, CA 91436
310-696-4600

info@asylument.com
asylument.com
facebook.com/AsylumEnt
twitter.com/AsylumEnt
imdb.com/company/co0017595

Accepts scripts from unproduced, unrepresented writers. Project types include TV. Preferred genres include Action, Crime, Drama, Fantasy, Horror, Non-Fiction, Science Fiction, and Thriller.

Steve Michaels
CEO

Jonathan Koch
CCO

A THING OR TWO PRODUCTIONS

Los Angeles, CA

imdb.com/company/co0476877
facebook.com/pages/A-Thing-or-Two-Productions/
    563880260365062

Does not accept any unsolicited material. Project types include Feature Films. Preferred genres include Drama. Established in 2014.

Logan Marshall-Green
imdb.com/name/nm1334869

Benjamin McKenzie
imdb.com/name/nm1360270

ATLAS ENTERTAINMENT (PRODUCTION BRANCH OF MOSAIC)

9200 W Sunset Blvd, 10th Floor
Los Angeles, CA 90069
310-786-4900

imdb.com/company/co0028338

Does not accept any unsolicited material. Project types include Feature Films and TV.

Andy Horwitz
Producer
imdb.com/name/nm2191045

Alex Gartner
Producer
imdb.com/name/nm0308672
linkedin.com/pub/alex-gartner/1a/695/69a

Jake Kurily
Vice-President
imdb.com/name/nm2464228
linkedin.com/pub/jake-kurily/1/785/26b

ATLAS MEDIA CORPORATION

242 W 36th St
New York, NY, 10018
212-714-0222 (phone)
212-714-0240 (fax)

info@atlasmediacorp.com
atlasmedia.tv
facebook.com/atlasinteractiveagency
twitter.com/atlasinteract
imdb.com/company/co0280783

Does not accept any unsolicited material. Preferred genres include Non-Fiction.

Glen Freyer
Senior Vice President (Development)
imdb.com/name/nm0294662
linkedin.com/pub/glen-freyer/4/18b/62b

Andrew Jacobs
Director of Development
linkedin.com/in/andrewejacobs
facebook.com/manofstats

ATMOSPHERE ENTERTAINMENT MM, LLC

5970 Wilshire Blvd Ste 450
Los Angeles, CA 90036
323-556-0056

imdb.com/company/co0014103

Accepts scripts from produced or represented writers. Preferred genres include Fantasy, Horror, and Thriller. Established in 2003.

David Hopwood
Senior Vice President (Production & Development)
imdb.com/name/nm2055027

Mark Canton
Principal

ATOMIC ENTERTAINMENT

Los Angeles, CA
323-739-3999

Mississippi
800-859-0450

info@atomicent.com
atomicent.com

Does not accept any unsolicited material. Project types include Feature Films. Preferred genres include Drama. Established in 2014.

Adam Rosenfelt
Principle
imdb.com/name/nm0742580

Maureen Meulen
Principle
imdb.com/name/nm1371473

ATO PICTURES

44 Wall St, 23rd Floor
New York, NY 10005
646-292-7500 (phone)
646-292-7550 (fax)

info@atopictures.com
atopictures.com

Does not accept any unsolicited material. Project types include Feature Films. Preferred genres include Comedy.

Jonathan Dorfman
Partner, Producer

Temple Fennell
Partner, Producer

Dave Matthews
Partner, Producer

ATTABOY FILMS

8335 Sunset Blvd., Suite 102
Los Angeles, CA 90069
323-337-9037

info@attaboyfilms.com
attaboyfilms.com

Does not accept any unsolicited material. Project types include Feature Films and TV. Preferred genres include Comedy and Drama.

Alexandra Ryan
Principal/Producer

Leigh Ann Maynard
Development

ATTICUS ENTERTAINMENT

7025 Santa Monica Blvd.
Hollywood, CA 90038
310-550-2720

Does not accept any unsolicited material. Project types include Feature Films and TV.

Jim Lampley
Producer

Adam Fratto
President

AUDAX FILMS

100 Wilshire Blvd, Suite 650
Santa Monica, CA 90401
310-870-3771

info@audaxfilms.com
audaxfilms.com
facebook.com/AudaxFilms
twitter.com/audaxfilms

Does not accept any unsolicited material. Project types include Feature Films. Preferred genres include Drama.

AU FILMS

2319 Fargo St, Los Angeles, CA 90039
213-926-9098

david@aufilms.com
aufilms.com

Does not accept any unsolicited material. Project types include Feature Films. Preferred genres include Drama. Established in 2014.

David Au
Producer
david@aufilms.com
imdb.com/name/nm1614404

AUTOMATIC PICTURES

5225 Wilshire Blvd
Suite 525
Los Angeles, CA 90036
323-935-1800 (phone)
323-935-8040 (fax)

automaticstudio@mail.com
automaticpictures.net

Accepts query letter from unproduced, unrepresented writers via email. Project types include Video Games. Preferred genres include Fantasy.

Frank Beddor
imdb.com/name/nm0065980
linkedin.com/pub/frank-beddor/6/191/4ba
facebook.com/goaskalyss
Assistant: Bo Liebman

Liz Cavalier
Creative Executive
imdb.com/name/nm2248983
linkedin.com/pub/liz-cavalier/59/b66/b27

Nate Barlow
nate@automaticpictures.net
imdb.com/name/nm0055269
linkedin.com/in/natebarlow
facebook.com/natebarlowfans

AUTONOMOUS FILMS

10203 Santa Monica Blvd. Suite 300A
Los Angeles, CA 90067
310-270-4260

Does not accept any unsolicited material. Project types include Feature Films. Preferred genres include Action and Comedy.

Courtney Solomon
Producer

Allan Zeman
Producer

AVALON PICTURES

435 W. 19th St., 4th Floor
New York, NY 10011
212-691-2211 (phone)
212-691-2212 (fax)

Avalon Pictures
P.O. Box 2409
La Jolla, CA 92038
858-551-6865 (phone)
858-551-6871 (fax)

avalon.com/avalon_pictures.htm

Does not accept any unsolicited material. Project types include Feature Films. Preferred genres include Drama.

Ted Waitt
Principal/Producer

Kevin Hyman
President/Producer

AVALON TELEVISION

9171 Wilshire Blvd, Suite 320
Beverly Hills, CA 90210
310-887-5030

4a Exmoor St
London W10 6BD
United Kindom
44 0 20 7598 8000 (phone)
44 0 20 7598 7300 (fax)

Avalon New York
666 Broadway, Suite 800
New York, NY 10012
212-400-4822

television@avalonuk.com
avalon-usa.com
avalonuk.com

Does not accept any unsolicited material. Project types
include TV. Preferred genres include Comedy.

Richard Allen-Turner
Joint Managing Director (UK)

Jon Thoday
Joint Managing Director (UK)

David Martin
President of Avalon USA

Dan Lubetkin
SVP of Production & Development

Kara Baker
Producer/Manager

AVENUE PICTURES

1105 Glendon Ave
Beverly Hills, CA 90024
310-209-0600 (phone)
310-744-0002 (fax)

avenuepictures.com

Does not accept any unsolicited material. Project types
include Feature Films. Preferred genres include
Drama.

Cary Brokaw
CEO/Producer

AVERSANO FILMS

2011 Benedict Canyon
Beverly Hills , CA 90210
310-246-2392

Does not accept any unsolicited material. Project types
include Feature Films and TV. Preferred genres
include Action, Comedy, Drama, and Science Fiction.

Scott Aversano
Producer

AVIATION CINEMAS PRODUCTIONS

231 W Jefferson Blvd.
Oak Cliff, TX 75208

info@aviationcinemas.com
aviationcinemas.com

Does not accept any unsolicited material. Project types
include Feature Films. Preferred genres include
Drama.

Eric Steele
Partner/Director

Adam Donaghey
Partner/Producer

Barak Epstein
Partner

Jason Reimer
Partner

AWAAZ PRODUCTIONS

1850 Houret Court
Mipitas, CA 95035
408-823-4811

awaazproduction.com

Does not accept any unsolicited material. Project types
include Feature Films. Preferred genres include
Horror.

Fasi Khurram
CEO

Sami Akram
President

Si Lai
CFO

AWOUNDEDKNEE

48 W 25th St, 9th Floor
New York, NY 10010
212-255-4440 (phone)
212-255-4494 (fax)

info@awkfilms.com
awkfilms.com

Does not accept any unsolicited material. Preferred genres include Crime.

Lance Doty
Producer, Writer, Director

Sam Welch
Producer

BACK LOT PICTURES

1351 N. Genesee Ave.
Los Angeles, CA 90046
323-876-1057

imdb.com/company/co0143583

Does not accept any unsolicited material. Project types include Feature Films. Preferred genres include Comedy, Drama, and Horror.

Glenn Williamson
Owner/Producer
imdb.com/name/nm0932037

Brian Schornak
VP of Production
imdb.com/name/nm1935985

BACK ROADS ENTERTAINMENT

7 Penn Plaza, Suite 1105
New York, NY 10001

contact@backroadsentertainment.com
facebook.com/BackRoadsEntertainment
twitter.com/backroadsent
backroadsentertainment.com
imdb.com/company/co0464900
linkedin.com/company/back-roads-entertainment

Does not accept any unsolicited material. Project types include TV. Preferred genres include Comedy.

Juliet Barrack
Manager of Development

Colby Gaines
Founder
imdb.com/name/nm1454469

Charles Taylor Goubeaud
Producer
imdb.com/name/nm3982977

Zach Messner
Development Associate
imdb.com/name/nm4130410

BAD BOY WORLDWIDE ENTERTAINMENT

1440 Broadway, 30th Floor
New York, NY 10036
212-381-1540 (phone)
212-381-1599 (fax)

badboyonline.com
facebook.com/bbweg
imdb.com/company/co0125541

Does not accept any unsolicited material. Project types include Feature Films. Preferred genres include Action, Comedy, Crime, and Thriller.

Sean Combs
Chairman/Producer/Actor
imdb.com/name/nm0004835

Anthony Maddox
VP
imdb.com/name/nm1474016

BAD HAT HARRY PRODUCTIONS

10201 W Pico Blvd
Building 50
Los Angeles, CA 90064
310-369-2260

imdb.com/company/co0057712

Accepts scripts from produced or represented writers. Project types include TV. Preferred genres include Action, Drama, Fantasy, Myth, Science Fiction, and Thriller.

Bryan Singer
CEO
imdb.com/name/nm0001741
twitter.com/BryanSinger

Mark Berliner
Vice President (Development)
imdb.com/name/nm2249392

BAD ROBOT

1221 Olympic Blvd
Santa Monica, CA 90404
310-664-3456 (phone)
310-664-3457 (fax)

badrobot.com
twitter.com/bad_robot
imdb.com/company/co0021593

Does not accept any unsolicited material. Project types
include Feature Films and TV. Preferred genres
include Action, Drama, Fantasy, and Science Fiction.
Established in 2001.

J.J. Abrams
CEO
imdb.com/name/nm0009190

Jonathan Cohen
Executive (Film)
Assistant: Veronica Baker

Kevin Jarzynski
Executive (Film)
imdb.com/name/nm1704653
Assistant: Veronica Baker

Bryan Burk
Partner (Vice President)
imdb.com/name/nm1333357
Assistant: Max Taylor

David Baronoff
Executive (New Media, Film, & Television)
imdb.com/name/nm2343623

Kathy Lingg
Head (Television)
imdb.com/name/nm2489727
Assistant: Matthew Owens

Lindsey Paulson Weber
Head (Film)
imdb.com/name/nm1439829
Assistant: Corrine Aquino

Athena Wickham
Executive (Television)
imdb.com/name/nm2204043
Assistant: Casey Haver

BAGDASARIAN PRODUCTIONS

1192 C. Mountain Dr
Montecito, CA 93108
805-969-3349 (phone)
805-969-7466 (fax)

chipmunks.com
facebook.com/AlvinAndTheChipmunks
twitter.com/officialalvinnn
imdb.com/company/co0026227

Does not accept any unsolicited material. Project types
include Feature Films. Preferred genres include
Comedy and Family.

Janice Karman
Producer
imdb.com/name/nm0439739

Ross Bagdasarian Jr.
Producer
imdb.com/name/nm0046559

BAIN FILMS, BARNET

4250 Wilshire Blvd.
Los Angeles, CA 90010
323-656-8829

imdb.com/company/co0123754
facebook.com/pages/Barnet-Bain-Films/
   548666401854501

Does not accept any unsolicited material. Project types
include Feature Films. Preferred genres include Drama
and Fantasy.

Barnet Bain
Producer
barnetbain.com
imdb.com/name/nm0047685
linkedin.com/pub/barnet-bain/1/112/441
facebook.com/barnet.bain
twitter.com/BarnetBain

BAKER ENTERTAINMENT INC, DAVID E.

146 N San Fernando Blvd. Suite 206
Burbank, CA 91502
818-843-8700

info@davidebaker.com
davidebaker.com
imdb.com/company/co0129945
linkedin.com/company/david-e-baker-entertainment-
     inc-

Accepts query letter from unproduced, unrepresented writers via email. Project types include Feature Films and TV. Preferred genres include Action, Animation, Comedy, Crime, Detective, Documentary, Drama, Family, Fantasy, Horror, Myth, Non-Fiction, Period, Reality, Romance, Science Fiction, Sociocultural, and Thriller.

Will Sweet
Executive Producer

Matt Alarcon
Associate Producer

John Scoville
Associate Producer

David E. Baker
Executive Producer
imdb.com/name/nm0048380

BALDWIN ENTERTAINMENT GROUP, LTD.

3000 W Olympic Blvd
Suite 2510
Santa Monica, CA
310-243-6634

225 Parkway North
Waterford, CT 06385
806-326-2870

info@baldwinent.com
imdb.com/company/co0057712mdb.com/company/
     co0145519

Does not accept any unsolicited material. Project types include Feature Films. Preferred genres include Action, Comedy, Drama, Non-Fiction, and Romance. Established in 2009.

Howard Baldwin
President
310-243-6634
imdb.com/name/nm0049920

Karen Baldwin
Executive Vice President
310-243-6634
imdb.com/name/nm0049945

BALLYHOO, INC.

6738 Wedgewood Place
Los Angeles, CA 90068
323-874-3396

imdb.com/company/co0094858

Accepts scripts from unproduced, unrepresented writers. Project types include Feature Films. Preferred genres include Action and Comedy.

Michael Besman
Producer
323-874-3396
imdb.com/name/nm0078698
linkedin.com/pub/michael-besman/4/b9/455

BALTIMORE PICTURES

8306 Wilshire Blvd
PMB 1012
Beverly Hills, CA 90211
310-234-8988

levinson.com/index_bsc.htm
imdb.com/company/co0038108

Does not accept any unsolicited material. Project types include Feature Films. Preferred genres include Comedy, Crime, Drama, Romance, Science Fiction, and Thriller.

Jason Sosnoff
Director of Development
imdb.com/name/nm0815369

Barry Levinson
Principle
imdb.com/name/nm0001469
facebook.com/pages/Barry-Levinson/50880796633

BANDAI ENTERTAINMENT

5551 Katella Ave
Cypress , CA 90630
1-877-77-ANIME

bandai-ent.com
imdb.com/company/co0040281

Does not accept any unsolicited material.

BANDITO BROTHERS

Hangar 102
14850 NW 44th Court
Miami, FL 33054

3249 S. La Cienega Blvd,
Los Angeles, CA 90016
310-559-5404 (phone)
310-559-5230 (fax)

info@banditobrothers.com
jay@banditobrothers.com
banditiobrothers.com
imdb.com/company/co0195602
facebook.com/BanditoBrothers
twitter.com/BanditoBrothers

Does not accept any unsolicited material. Project types include Feature Films. Preferred genres include Action, Comedy, Drama, Fantasy, Science Fiction, and Thriller.

Max Leitman
COO
imdb.com/name/nm2649648

Mike McCoy
CEO
imdb.com/name/nm0566788

Scott Waugh
Founder
imdb.com/name/nm0915304

Suzanne Hargrove
Managing Director
imdb.com/name/nm2597628

Jacob Rosenberg
CTO
imdb.com/name/nm0742230

BARBARA LIEBERMAN PRODUCTIONS

10510 Culver Blvd.
Culver City, CA 90232
310-204-0404

imdb.com/company/co0021842

Does not accept any unsolicited material. Project types include TV. Preferred genres include Comedy and Drama.

Barbara Lieberman
Executive Producer
imdb.com/name/nm0509365

Devlin McCluskey
Development
imdb.com/name/nm3052185

BARBARIAN FILM FUND

1801 Century Park East, 25th Floor
Los Angeles, CA 90067
310-553-2300 (phone)
310-553-2345 (fax)

imdb.com/company/co0228488

Does not accept any unsolicited material. Project types include Feature Films. Preferred genres include Comedy and Thriller.

Aaron Kaufman
Principal, Producer
imdb.com/name/nm2721926

Doug Kuber
Principal, Producer
imdb.com/name/nm2739787

Ron Hartenbaum
Producer
imdb.com/name/nm2735439

BARNSTORM FILMS

73 Market St
Venice, CA 90291
310-396-5937 (phone)
310-450-4988 (fax)

tbtb@comcast.net
imdb.com/company/co0044065
barnstormfilms.com

Accepts query letter from unproduced, unrepresented writers.

Tony Bill
Producer
tbtb@comcast.net
imdb.com/name/nm0082300

BARNYARDGROUP ENTERTAINMENT

175 Atlantic St - 3rd Floor
Stamford, CT 06901
646-532-1512

15 Central Park West, Suite G104
New York, NY 10023

thebarnyardgroup.com
facebook.com/TheBarnYardGroup
linkedin.com/company/thebarnyardgroup
twitter.com/BarnyardGroup

Elaine Rogers
Co-Founder/Co-CEO/Producer
imdb.com/name/nm1199976

BARRY FILMS

4081 Redwood Ave
Los Angeles, CA 90066
310-871-3392

mail@barryfilms.com
barryfilms.com
imdb.com/company/co0075789

Does not accept any unsolicited material. Project types
include Feature Films. Preferred genres include Action,
Animation, Detective, Fantasy, and Romance.

Benito Mueller
Principle
benito@barryfilms.com
imdb.com/name/nm1762339

BARRY MENDEL PRODUCTIONS

11788 W. Pico Blvd. 3rd Floor
Los Angeles, CA 90064
310-943-4473

Does not accept any unsolicited material. Project types
include Feature Films. Preferred genres include
Comedy, Drama, and Horror.

Barry Mendel
Producer
imdb.com/name/nm0578814

BARWOOD FILMS

5670 Wilshire Blvd., Suite 2400
Los Angeles, CA 90036
323-653-1555 (phone)
323-653-1593 (fax)

imdb.com/company/co0073376
facebook.com/barbrastreisand
linkedin.com/company/barwood-films

Does not accept any unsolicited material. Project types
include Feature Films. Preferred genres include
Drama.

Barbra Streisand
Actor/Director/Producer
imdb.com/name/nm0000659
facebook.com/barbrastreisand
twitter.com/BarbraStreisand

Cis Corman
Chairman/Producer
imdb.com/name/nm0180015

Jason Gould
President
imdb.com/name/nm0332410

BASE PRODUCTIONS

4540 W Valerio St
Burbank, CA 91505
818-333-5700

info@baseproductions.com
baseproductions.com
imdb.com/company/co0010298
facebook.com/pages/BASE-Productions/
   109436385749283
linkedin.com/company/base-productions

Does not accept any unsolicited material. Project types
include TV.

Sara Hansemann
VP of Development

John Brenkus
Co-CEO
imdb.com/name/nm0107228

Mickey Stern
Co-CEO (Washington, DC)
imdb.com/name/nm0827790

BASRA ENTERTAINMENT

68-444 Perez Rd, Suite O
Cathedral City, CA 92234
760-324-9855 (phone)
760-324-9035 (fax)

daniela@basraentertainment.com
info@basraentertainment.com
basraentertainment.com
imdb.com/company/co0092056

Accepts query letter from unproduced, unrepresented writers via email. Established in 2002.

Daniela Ryan
Producer
daniela@basraentertainment.com
imdb.com/name/nm0752491
linkedin.com/pub/daniela-ryan/10/7b9/815

Tony Shawkat
President
tony@basraentertainment.com
imdb.com/name/nm0790059
linkedin.com/pub/abdul-tony-shawkat/27/7a/a2b

Dina Burke
Producer
dina@basraentertainment.com
imdb.com/name/nm1318482

BASS FILMS, EDWARD

358 Broadway, 3A
New York, NY 10013
212-937-5999 (phone)
310-601-7628 (fax)

511 Stonewood Dr
Beverly Hills, CA 90210

info@edwardbassfilms.com
edwardbassfilms.com
twitter.com/EdwardBassFilm

facebook.com/pages/Edward-Bass-Films/
   163000960933

Does not accept any unsolicited material. Project types include Feature Films. Preferred genres include Comedy and Romance.

Edward Bass
Producer/Writer/Financier
linkedin.com/in/edwardbass1

BATTAGLIA PRODUCTIONS, MATT

8033 Sunset Blvd. #902
Los Angeles, CA 90046
323-851-2868

info@mattbattagliaproductions.com
http/www.mattbattagliaproductions.com
imdb.com/company/co0286886

Does not accept any unsolicited material. Project types include Feature Films. Preferred genres include Drama.

Matt Battaglia
Producer
mattbattaglia.com
imdb.com/name/nm0061307
linkedin.com/pub/matt-battaglia/23/5a8/56b
facebook.com/matt.battaglialouisville
twitter.com/mattbattaglia

BATTLE GROUND

1948 N Van Ness Ave
Los Angeles, CA 90068
323-962-9913

imdb.com/company/co0295113

Does not accept any unsolicited material. Project types include Feature Films. Preferred genres include Action and Drama.

David Mackay
Producer/Director
imdb.com/name/nm0533145

Mark Witsken
Producer
imdb.com/name/nm0936837

BATTLEPLAN PRODUCTIONS

1041 N. Formosa Ave.
West Hollywood, CA 90046
323-850-2940

imdb.com/company/co0089304

Does not accept any unsolicited material. Project types include Feature Films and TV. Preferred genres include Action and Drama.

Marc Frydman
Partner/Producer
imdb.com/name/nm0296827

Rod Lurie
Partner/Writer/Director
imdb.com/name/nm0527109

BAUER MARTINEZ STUDIOS

601 Cleveland St, Suite 501
Clearwater, FL 33755
727-210-1408 (phone)
727-210-1470 (fax)

cindy@bauermartinez.com
sales@bauermartinez.com
bauermartinez.com
imdb.com/company/co0025891

Accepts query letter from unproduced, unrepresented writers.

Philippe Martinez
CEO
imdb.com/name/nm0553662
linkedin.com/pub/philippe-martinez/2b/71a/b11

BAUMGARTEN MANAGEMENT AND PRODUCTION

9595 Wilshire Blvd., Suite 1000
Beverly Hills, CA 90212
310-445-1601 (phone)
310-996-1892 (fax)

imdb.com/company/co0191075

Does not accept any unsolicited material. Project types include Feature Films. Preferred genres include Thriller.

Craig Baumgarten
Producer/Manager
imdb.com/name/nm0062332

BAUM PRODUCTIONS, CAROL

8899 Beverly Blvd., Suite 721
Los Angeles , CA 90048
310-550-4575 (phone)
310-550-2088 (fax)

imdb.com/company/co0058685

Does not accept any unsolicited material. Project types include Feature Films and TV. Preferred genres include Comedy and Drama.

Carol Baum
Producer
imdb.com/name/nm0062071

BAY FILMS

631 Colorado Ave
Santa Monica, CA 90401
310-319-6565 (phone)
310-319-6570 (fax)

imdb.com/company/co0049752

Does not accept any unsolicited material. Project types include Feature Films. Preferred genres include Action, Comedy, Drama, Fantasy, Science Fiction, and Thriller.

Michael Bay
CEO
michaelbay.com
imdb.com/name/nm0000881
linkedin.com/company/bay-films
facebook.com/MichaelBayMovies
Assistant: Talley Singer

Matthew Cohan
Vice President
imdb.com/name/nm0169134
linkedin.com/in/matthewcohan

BAYONNE ENTERTAINMENT

8560 W Sunset Blvd
9th Floor

West Hollywood, CA 90069
310-777-1940

assistant@bayonne-ent.com
imdb.com/company/co0070871

Accepts query letter from produced or represented writers. Project types include TV. Preferred genres include Comedy, Drama, Fantasy, and Science Fiction.

Rob Lee
President
imdb.com/name/nm0498098
linkedin.com/pub/rob-lee/14/46B/295

BAZELEVS PRODUCTIONS

9229 Sunset Bvld.
Suite 820
West Hollywood, CA 90069
424-288-4822

Pudovkina St
6/1
Moscow, Russia, 119285
Moscow 119285
Russia
+7 495-223-04-00

film@bazelevs.ru
bazelevs.ru
imdb.com/company/co0042742

Does not accept any unsolicited material. Project types include Feature Films.

Alan Khamoui
Development Executive
imdb.com/name/nm3081242
linkedin.com/pub/alan-khamoui/44/12/641

Timur Bekmambetov
Founder
+7 495-223-04-00
film@bazelevs.ru
imdb.com/name/nm0067457
linkedin.com/pub/timur-bekmambetov/4/9b1/863

BBC FILMS

Zone A, 7th Floor BBC Broadcasting House Portland Place

London, United Kingdom, W1A 1AA
011-440-2036144445

bbc.co.uk/bbcfilms
imdb.com/company/co0103694
twitter.com/BBCFilms

Accepts scripts from unproduced, unrepresented writers. Project types include Feature Films and TV. Preferred genres include Action, Comedy, Crime, Detective, Drama, Fantasy, Horror, Myth, Non-Fiction, Romance, Science Fiction, and Thriller.

Nichola Martin
Development Executive
imdb.com/name/nm1660581

Beth Pattinson
Development Executive
imdb.com/name/nm3179273

BBCG FILMS

466 W. Montgomery Ave
Haverford, PA 19041

imdb.com/company/co0396231

Does not accept any unsolicited material. Project types include Feature Films. Preferred genres include Comedy.

Tommy Joyner
Producer

Tammy Tiehel-Stedman
Producer
imdb.com/name/nm0862843

BCDF PICTURES

7 Old Pilgrims Way
Kerhonkson, NY 12446
845-834-4300 (phone)
917-591-7589 (fax)

submissions@bcdfpictures.com
info@bcdfpictures.com
bcdfpictures.com
linkedin.com/company/bcdf-pictures

Accepts query letter from unproduced, unrepresented writers via email. Project types include Feature Films.

Preferred genres include Comedy, Crime, Drama, Family, Romance, and Thriller.

Claude Dal Farra
Principal
imdb.com/name/nm3894387

Lauren Munsch
Producer
imdb.com/name/nm3907323

Paul Prokop
COO (Executive Producer)
imdb.com/name/nm2373782

Brice Dal Farra
Principal
imdb.com/name/nm3894454
facebook.com/brice.dalfarra

BCII PRODUCTIONS

16135 Roscoe Blvd.
North Hills, CA 91343
818-333-3680 (phone)
818-487-2713 (fax)

bciitv.com
imdb.com/company/co0398777

Does not accept any unsolicited material. Project types include TV.

Bud Brutsman
CEO/Producer
imdb.com/name/nm0116782

Ashley Yoder
Producer
imdb.com/name/nm1825095

Greg Glass
President
greg@bciitv.com
imdb.com/name/nm2374944

Cynthia Whorton
Director of Operations
cynthia@bciitv.com
imdb.com/name/nm1469778

BDE ENTERTAINMENT

9903 Santa Monica Blvd., Suite 230
Beverly Hills, CA 90212
310-497-9190

imdb.com/company/co0186277
facebook.com/pages/BDE-Entertainment/
170850746292249

Does not accept any unsolicited material. Project types include Feature Films and TV. Preferred genres include Comedy and Drama.

Marc Jeffries
Development

Bob Debrino
Producer
imdb.com/name/nm1754593

BEACHSIDE

625 Mildred Ave.
Venice, CA 90291
310-230-3999

info@beachsidefilms.com
beachsidefilms.com
facebook.com/beachsidefilms
twitter.com/Beachsidefilms
imdb.com/company/co0421107

Does not accept any unsolicited material. Project types include Feature Films. Preferred genres include Comedy, Drama, and Romance.

Alex Turtletaub
Partner/Producer
imdb.com/name/nm2801211

Michael B. Clark
Partner/Producer
imdb.com/name/nm0164290

BEACON PICTURES

2900 Olympic Blvd
2nd Floor
Santa Monica, CA 90404
Santa Monica, CA 90404
310-260-7000 (phone)
310-260-7096 (fax)

contactus@beaconpictures.com
info@beaconpictures.com
beaconpictures.com

Does not accept any unsolicited material. Project types include Feature Films and TV. Preferred genres include Action, Comedy, Crime, Detective, Drama, Family, Fantasy, Romance, Science Fiction, and Thriller. Established in 1990.

Armyan Berstein
Chairman
imdb.com/name/nm0077000

Suzann Ellis
President
sellis@beaconpictures.com
imdb.com/name/nm0255104

Glenn Klekowski
Vice President (Internet Content)
imdb.com/name/nm0459192
linkedin.com/pub/glenn-klekowski/17/3b3/8b3

Joeanna Sayler
Executive (Television)
imdb.com/media/rm2798096896/nm1376366

Jeffrey Crooks
Director (Special Projects)
imdb.com/name/nm3715349
linkedin.com/pub/dir/jeff/crooks

BEALLOR PRODUCTIONS, JUNE

100 Universal City Plaza, Bldg. 6147
Universal City, CA 91608
818-777-9000

info@junebeallorproductions.com
junebeallorproductions.com
imdb.com/company/co0044270

Does not accept any unsolicited material. Project types include Feature Films and TV.

Susan Baker
VP

June Beallor
Producer
imdb.com/name/nm0063706

BECKER COMPANY, THE WALT

8530 Wilshire Blvd., Suite 550
Beverly Hills, CA 90212
310-855-2212

imdb.com/company/co0405377

Does not accept any unsolicited material. Project types include TV. Preferred genres include Comedy.

Walt Becker
Writer/Producer
imdb.com/name/nm0065608

Ross Putman
Development
imdb.com/name/nm3819444

Kelly Hayes
Director of Development & Production
imdb.com/name/nm0971886
linkedin.com/pub/kelly-hayes/2a/845/717

BEDFORD FALLS COMPANY

409 Santa Monica Blvd
Penthouse Suite
Santa Monica, CA 90401
310-394-5022 (phone)
310-394-5825 (fax)

imdb.com/company/co0110946
linkedin.com/company/bedford-falls-productions
facebook.com/pages/Bedford-Falls-Productions/
    143292225689760

Does not accept any unsolicited material. Project types include Feature Films. Preferred genres include Action and Drama. Established in 1985.

Troy Putney
Creative Executive
imdb.com/name/nm1586726

Marshall Herskovitz
Executive Producer

Edward Zwick
Executive Producer

Joshua Gummersall
Producer

Scott Saccoccio
Creative Executive

BEDROCK STUDIOS

2115 Colorado Ave
Santa Monica, CA 90404
310-264-6480

imdb.com/company/co0299258

Accepts query letter from produced or represented writers. Project types include Feature Films and TV. Preferred genres include Family.

Ed Jones
Co-Founder/Producer

Spike Seldin
Head of Television
imdb.com/name/nm1749292

Cary Granat
Co-Founder/Producer
imdb.com/name/nm0334665

BEECH HILL FILMS

330 W 38th St, Suite 1405
New York, NY 10018
212-594-8095

imdb.com/company/co0064667
facebook.com/pages/Beech-Hill-Film-Inc/
    120092768006274

Does not accept any unsolicited material. Project types include Feature Films and TV. Preferred genres include Comedy and Drama.

Alexa Fogel
Producer
imdb.com/name/nm0283881

Joseph Infantolino
Producer
imdb.com/name/nm0408642

BEE HOLDER PRODUCTIONS

310-860-1005 (phone)
310-860-1007 (fax)

asst@beeholder.com

imdb.com/company/co0136434

Accepts query letter from unproduced, unrepresented writers. Project types include Feature Films. Preferred genres include Comedy, Crime, Detective, Documentary, Drama, and Thriller.

Michelle Jones
Executive
imdb.com/name/nm4786947

John Hill
imdb.com/name/nm4787026

Dan Fugardi
Vice President (New Media)
dan@beeholder.com
imdb.com/name/nm2809882
linkedin.com/in/danfugardi

Steven L. Jones
Principle
imdb.com/name/nm2831867
linkedin.com/pub/steve-jones/9/1A4/ABB

BEFORE THE DOOR PICTURES

323-644-5525

staff@beforethedoor.com
beforethedoor.com
imdb.com/company/co0271126
facebook.com/beforethedoor

Does not accept any unsolicited material. Project types include Feature Films, TV, and Commercials. Preferred genres include Action, Comedy, Crime, Drama, Science Fiction, and Thriller.

Zachary Quinto
Partner
zacharyquinto.com/before-the-door.html
imdb.com/name/nm0704270
facebook.com/zacharyquintoofficial

Corey Moosa
Partner
imdb.com/name/nm0602161
facebook.com/corey.moosa

Neal Dodson
Partner
imdb.com/name/nm0230306

Sean Akers
Development Executive
imdb.com/name/nm3577109

BE GOOD PRODUCTIONS

1327 Ocean Ave., Suite L
Santa Monica, CA 90491
310-458-1600 (phone)
310-458-1665 (fax)

info@begoodinc.com
begoodinc.com
imdb.com/company/co0202350

Does not accept any unsolicited material. Project types
include Feature Films.

BEHOLD MOTION PICTURES

Oklahoma City, OK
213-260-1670

info@beholdmotionpictures.com
beholdmotionpictures.com

Does not accept any unsolicited material. Project types
include Feature Films. Preferred genres include
Documentary. Established in 2014.

BELIEVE ENTERTAINMENT

13032 Aztec St
Sylmar, CA 91342
818-336-6775

info@believe-entertainment.com
believe-entertainment.com
facebook.com/pages/Believe-Entertainment/
    149232458511959
imdb.com/company/co0158325
linkedin.com/company/believe-entertainment

Does not accept any unsolicited material. Project types
include Feature Films and TV. Preferred genres
include Drama and Family.

Cary Solomon
Producer
imdb.com/name/nm0813301

Chuck Konzelman
Producer
imdb.com/name/nm0465484

BELISARIUS PRODUCTIONS

1901 Ave of the Stars
Second Floor
Los Angeles, CA 90067
310-461-1361 (phone)
310-461-1362 (fax)

imdb.com/company/co0114905

Does not accept any unsolicited material. Project types
include TV. Preferred genres include Crime, Detective,
Drama, and Thriller.

David Bellisario
Producer
imdb.com/name/nm0069072

John C. Kelley
imdb.com/name/nm0445931

Chas Floyd Johnson
imdb.com/name/nm0424759

Shane Brennan
Producer
imdb.com/name/nm0107402

Mark Horowitz
imdb.com/name/nm0395317

Donald Bellisario
Executive Producer
imdb.com/name/nm0069074
linkedin.com/pub/donald-bellisario/15/99/355

BELLADONNA PRODUCTIONS

164 W 25th St 9th Floor
New York, NY 10001
212-807-0108 (phone)
212-807-6263 (fax)

mail@belladonna.bz
belladonna.bz
twitter.com/belladonnaprods
imdb.com/company/co0003224
facebook.com/belladonnaproductions

Accepts scripts from unproduced, unrepresented writers via email. Project types include Feature Films and Commercials. Preferred genres include Comedy, Non-Fiction, and Thriller. Established in 1994.

René Bastian
Owner/Producer
212-807-0108
mail@belladonna.bz
imdb.com/name/nm0060459
linkedin.com/company/belladonna-productions
facebook.com/rene.bastian.167
twitter.com/renebastian

BELLTOWER FILMS

11684 Ventura Blvd., Suite 685
Studio City, CA 91604
877-355-1388 (phone)
310-598-222 (fax)

belltowerfilms.com

Does not accept any unsolicited material. Project types include Feature Films. Preferred genres include Drama.

BELLUM ENTERTAINMENT

2901 W. Alameda Ave Suite 500
Burbank, CA 91505

bellument.com
facebook.com/BellumEntertainment
twitter.com/BellumEnt
linkedin.com/company/bellum-entertainment
imdb.com/company/co0361925

Does not accept any unsolicited material. Project types include TV.

BELLWETHER PICTURES

73 Moody Rd
Tunbridge, VT 05077
802-889-3474 (phone)
802-889-3412 (fax)

john@bellwetherfilms.com
imdb.com/company/co0359041
twitter.com/BellwetherPics
bellwetherfilms.com

Accepts query letter from unproduced, unrepresented writers via email. Project types include Feature Films and Commercials. Preferred genres include Action, Comedy, Drama, and Science Fiction. Established in 2011.

Joss Whedon
Principle
imdb.com/name/nm0923736

Kai Cole
Principle
imdb.com/name/nm4740874

BENAROYA PICTURES

8383 Wilshire Blvd
Suite 310
Beverly Hills, CA 90212
USA
323-883-0056 (phone)
866-220-5520 (fax)

general@benaroyapics.com
benaroyapics.com
facebook.com/pages/Benaroya-Pictures
imdb.com/company/co0232586

Accepts query letter from unproduced, unrepresented writers via email. Project types include Feature Films. Preferred genres include Drama. Established in 2006.

Michael Benaroya
CEO
323-883-0056
imdb.com/name/nm2918260

Joe Jenckes
Head (Production)
323-883-0056
joel@benaroyapics.com
imdb.com/name/nm3765270
linkedin.com/pub/joe-jenckes/7/bb7/5a8

Clayton Young
323-883-0056
clay@benaroyapics.com
imdb.com/name/nm4464240
facebook.com/clayton.young.5851

BENDERSPINK

8447 Wilshire Blvd.
Suite 250
Los Angeles, CA 90211
323-904-1800 (phone)
323-297-2442 (fax)

info@benderspink.com
benderspink.com
imdb.com/company/co0044439
facebook.com/pages/Benderspink/177855663106

Does not accept any unsolicited material. Project types include TV. Preferred genres include Action, Comedy, Crime, Detective, Drama, Fantasy, Horror, Myth, Non-Fiction, Romance, Science Fiction, and Thriller.

J.C. Spink
Founder
imdb.com/name/nm0818940

Chris Bender
Founder
imdb.com/name/nm0818940
linkedin.com/pub/chris-bender/10/B22/569

BENGE, WENDY

15 Brooks Ave
Venice, CA 90291

wb@wbesquire.com
wbesquire.com
imdb.com/name/nm3076187

Does not accept any unsolicited material. Project types include Feature Films. Preferred genres include Comedy, Crime, Drama, and Thriller.

Wendy Benge
Producer/Attorney
imdb.com/name/nm3076187
linkedin.com/in/wendybenge
facebook.com/wendy.benge.9

BENNETT ROBBINS PRODUCTIONS

116 Thompson St. – 2A
New York, NY 10012
212-586-0500 (phone)
212-918-9138 (fax)

info@bennettrobbins.com
bennettrobbins.com
imdb.com/company/co0233377

Does not accept any unsolicited material. Project types include Feature Films. Preferred genres include Crime and Thriller.

John M. Bennett
Producer

Lawrence Robbins
imdb.com/name/nm2797178

BENTO BOX ENTERTAINMENT

2600 W Magnolia Blvd.
Burbank, CA 91505
818-333-7700

info@bentoboxent.com
bentoboxent.com
facebook.com/bentoboxent
twitter.com/BentoBoxEnt
imdb.com/company/co0239674
linkedin.com/company/bento-box-entertainment-llc

Does not accept any unsolicited material. Project types include Short Films. Preferred genres include Comedy and Family.

Mike Clements
Head of Creative Development

Scott Greenberg
Principal/Producer
imdb.com/name/nm2092115

Joel Kuwahara
Principal/Producer
imdb.com/name/nm0476669

Mark McJimsey
Principal/Producer
imdb.com/name/nm0570877

BERK/LANE ENTERTAINMENT

9595 Wilshire Blvd, Suitee 900
Beverly Hills, CA 90212
310-300-8410

info@berklane.com
berklane.com

imdb.com/company/co0183891

Does not accept any unsolicited material. Preferred genres include Action, Comedy, and Crime.

Jason Berk
imdb.com/name/nm1357809

Matt Lane
imdb.com/name/nm2325262

BERLANTI TELEVISION

4000 Warner Blvd.
Burbank, CA 91522
818-954-4319 (phone)
818-977-9728 (fax)

imdb.com/company/co0192672

Accepts query letter from unproduced, unrepresented writers. Project types include TV. Preferred genres include Drama.

Ryan Lindenberg
Director of Development
imdb.com/name/nm1742204

Greg Berlanti
Principle
imdb.com/name/nm0075528

BERNERO PRODUCTIONS

500 S. Buena Vista St, Suite 2D-4
Burbank, CA 91521
818-560-1442

info@berneroproductions.com
berneroproductions.com
imdb.com/company/co0281008

Accepts query letter from unproduced, unrepresented writers via email.

Bob Kim
Producer
imdb.com/name/nm2344755

BETH GROSSBARD PRODUCTIONS

5168 Otis Ave
Tarzana, CA 91356

818-758-2500 (phone)
818-705-7366 (fax)

bgpix@sbcglobal.net
imdb.com/company/co0037144

Accepts query letter from produced or represented writers. Project types include TV. Preferred genres include Comedy and Drama.

Beth Grossbard
Executive Producer
bgpix@sbcglobal.net
imdb.com/name/nm0343526
linkedin.com/pub/beth-grossbard/12/989/996

BET NETWORKS

1443 Park Ave.
New York, NY 10029
212-975-4048

BET Atria West
10635 Santa Monica Blvd.
Second Floor
Los Angeles, CA 90025
310-481-3700

One BET Plaza
1235 W St NE
Washington, DC 20018-1211
202-608-2000 (phone)
206-608-2631 (fax)

bet.com
imdb.com/company/co0176390
facebook.com/BET
twitter.com/BET

Does not accept any unsolicited material. Project types include Feature Films and TV. Preferred genres include Comedy, Documentary, and Drama.

Austyn Biggers
Director of Development
310-481-3741
austyn.biggers@bet.net
imdb.com/name/nm2056137
linkedin.com/in/austynb

BICKFORD PRODUCTIONS, LAURA

10153 1/2 Riverside Dr, Suite 683
Toluca Lake, CA 91602
323-850-8191

lbprods.com
imdb.com/company/co0214437
facebook.com/pages/Laura-Bickford-Productions/
    507372106020086

Does not accept any unsolicited material. Project types include Feature Films. Preferred genres include Comedy, Drama, and Romance.

Laura Bickford
Producer
imdb.com/name/nm0081046
facebook.com/laura.bickford.526

Patrick Reese
Assistant
imdb.com/name/nm3101321

BIGEL ENTERTAINMENT, LLC

1450 Broadway, 41st Floor
New York, NY 10018
212-475-4333

info@bigelentertainment.com
bigelentertainment.com
linkedin.com/company/bigel-entertainment
imdb.com/company/co0163248

Accepts query letter from produced or represented writers. Project types include Feature Films and TV. Preferred genres include Comedy and Drama.

Daniel Bigel
Producer
imdb.com/name/nm0081730

BIG FISH ENTERTAINMENT

609 Greenwich St, 7th Floor
New York, NY 10014
646-797-4102

info@bigfishusa.com
bigfishusa.com
imdb.com/company/co0203789

facebook.com/pages/Big-Fish-Entertainment/
    199241686772035
twitter.com/BigFishUSA

Does not accept any unsolicited material. Project types include TV.

Doug DePriest
Co-Owner/Producer
imdb.com/name/nm2685128

Dan Cesareo
Co-Owner/Producer
imdb.com/name/nm2389863

BIG FOOT ENTERTAINMENT, LTD.

Bigfoot Entertainment Inc.
246 W Broadway
New York NY 10013
212-666-9000

info@bigfoot.com
help@bigfoot.com
bigfoot.com
imdb.com/company/co0261687

Accepts query letter from unproduced, unrepresented writers via email. Project types include Feature Films and TV. Preferred genres include Action, Animation, Drama, Fantasy, Myth, Science Fiction, and Thriller. Established in 2004.

Ashley Jordan
CEO
ashley@bigfootcorp.com
imdb.com/name/nm1248442
linkedin.com/pub/dir/ashley/jordan

BIG INDIE PICTURES

55 Main St, 2nd Floor
Yonkers, NY 10701
914-420-1447

declanbaldwin@gmail.com
corey@bigindiepictures.com
bigindiepictures.com
imdb.com/company/co0203259

Does not accept any unsolicited material. Project types include Feature Films. Preferred genres include Drama.

Declan Baldwin
Producer
declanbaldwin@gmail.com
imdb.com/name/nm0049888

Corey Deckler
Producer
corey@bigindiepictures.com
imdb.com/name/nm4224057

BIG JOURNEY PRODUCTIONS

9100 Wilshire Blvd., Suite 400W
Beverly Hills, CA 90212
310-595-0100

Project types include TV. Preferred genres include Drama.

Steve Shill
Writer/Producer/Director
imdb.com/name/nm0793455

BIG KID PICTURES

9000 Sunset Blvd., Suite 1010
West Hollywood, CA 90069

bigkidpictures.com
imdb.com/company/co0246151
facebook.com/pages/David-Dobkin/
    107565629266878

Does not accept any unsolicited material. Project types include Feature Films. Preferred genres include Action and Comedy.

David Dobkin
Writer/Producer
imdb.com/name/nm0229694

BIG LIGHT PRODUCTIONS

500 S. Buena Vista St, Animation Bldg.
Burbank, CA 91521
818-560-4782

biglightquestions@gmail.com
biglight.com
facebook.com/biglightprod
twitter.com/FrankSpotnitz
imdb.com/company/co0172688

Does not accept any unsolicited material. Project types include Feature Films and TV. Preferred genres include Crime, Drama, Science Fiction, and Thriller.

BIG PITA, LIL' PITA

231 Park Place, Suite 31
Brooklyn, NY 11238
646-395-3371

imdb.com/company/co0184052

Does not accept any unsolicited material. Project types include Feature Films and TV. Preferred genres include Family and Fantasy.

Jeff Robinson
Partner

Susan Lewis
Executive

Alicia Keys
Partner/Producer
imdb.com/name/nm1006024

BIG SCREEN ENTERTAINMENT GROUP

5555 Melrose Ave, Wallis Bldg. Suite 221
Hollywood, CA 90038
323-956-4321 (phone)
323-862-1172 (fax)

5440 W. Sahara Ave, Suite 202
Las Vegas, Nevada 89146

info@bigscreenent.com
bigscreenentertainmentgroup.com
facebook.com/BigScreenEntertainmentGroup
twitter.com/bigscreenbuzz
linkedin.com/company/big-screen-entertainment-
    group
imdb.com/company/co0145769

Does not accept any unsolicited material. Project types include Feature Films. Preferred genres include Drama, Romance, and Thriller.

BIG STAR PICTURES

1041 Formosa Ave, Writer's Building, Suite 317
West Hollywood, CA 90046
424-245-0015

info@bigstarpictures.com
bigstarpictures.com
facebook.com/bigstarpix
twitter.com/BigStarPictures

Does not accept any unsolicited material. Project types include Feature Films. Preferred genres include Drama. Established in 2013.

Christopher Quinn
Principle
imdb.com/name/nm1077724
linkedin.com/pub/christopher-quinn/b/2b2/855
facebook.com/christopher.quinn.940
twitter.com/BigStarPictures

BIG TALK PRODUCTIONS

26 Nassau St
London
W1W 7AQ
+44 (0) 20-7255-1131 (phone)
+44 (0) 20-7255-1132 (fax)

info@bigtalkproductions.com
bigtalkproductions.com
twitter.com/bigtalk
facebook.com/bigtalk

Does not accept any unsolicited material. Project types include TV. Preferred genres include Action, Comedy, Crime, Drama, and Science Fiction.

Rachael Prior
Head (Development/Film)
imdb.com/name/nm0975099

BILL'S MARKET & TELEVISION PRODUCTIONS

17328 Ventura Blvd., Suite 191
Encino, CA 91316

imdb.com/company/co0410317

Does not accept any unsolicited material. Project types include TV.

Gelila Asres-Hurwitz
Co-Founder/Partner

David Hurwitz
Co-Founder/Partner
imdb.com/name/nm0975188

BILL THOMPSON PRODUCTIONS

149 N Cambridge St
Orange, CA 92866
714-450-9000

Does not accept any unsolicited material. Project types include TV. Preferred genres include Drama. Established in 2014.

Bill Thompson
Principle
imdb.com/name/nm0859892
linkedin.com/pub/bill-thompson/8/A54/8B8

BIRCH TREE ENTERTAINMENT

10620 Southern Highlands Parkway
Suite 103
Las Vegas, NV 89141
Las Vegas, NV 89141
702-858-2782 (phone)
702-583-7928 (fax)

sales@birchtreefilms.com
birchtreeentertainment.com
imdb.com/company/co0114722
facebook.com/pages/Las-Vegas-NV/Birch-Tree-
    Entertainment/178085089631
twitter.com/BIRCHTREEFILMS

Accepts scripts from produced or represented writers. Project types include Feature Films. Preferred genres include Action.

Art Birzneck
CEO
sales@birchtreefilms.com
imdb.com/name/nm1010723
linkedin.com/pub/art-birzneck/36/ab8/5a7
linkedin.com/pub/art-birzneck/36/ab8/5a7

BISCAYNE PICTURES

Los Angeles, CA
310-777-2007

info@biscaynepictures.com
imdb.com/company/co0152645
biscaynepictures.com

Does not accept any unsolicited material. Project types include Feature Films and TV. Preferred genres include Action, Animation, Crime, Detective, Drama, Fantasy, Myth, Science Fiction, and Thriller.

Jeffrey Silver
Principle
310-777-2007
info@biscaynepictures.com
imdb.com/name/nm0798711
linkedin.com/pub/jeffrey-silver/16/833/503

BISCHOFF-HERVEY ENTERTAINMENT

1033 N Hollywood Way, Suite F
Burbank, CA 91505

bhe.tv
facebook.com/bischoffhervey
twitter.com/bhetv
imdb.com/company/co0165662
linkedin.com/company/bischoff-hervey-entertainment-television-llc

Does not accept any unsolicited material. Project types include TV.

Eric Bischoff
Partner/Producer
imdb.com/name/nm0083888

Jason Hervey
Partner/Producer
imdb.com/name/nm0381155

BIX PIX ENTERTAINMENT

11630 Tuxford St.
Sun Valley, CA 91352
818-252-7474 (phone)
818-252-7410 (fax)

info@bixpix.com
jodidowns@bixpix.com

bixpix.com
imdb.com/company/co0187260

Accepts query letter from unproduced, unrepresented writers. Preferred genres include Fantasy. Established in 1998.

Kelli Bixler
Founder
imdb.com/name/nm1064778
linkedin.com/pub/kelli-bixler/4/577/426

BLACK BEAR PICTURES

185 Franklin St
4th Floor
New York, NY 10013
New York, NY 10013
212-931-5714 (phone)
212-966-3311 (fax)

info@blackbearpictures.com
blackbearpictures.com
facebook.com/pages/Black-Bear-Pictures/
    166891590022937
twitter.com/blackbearpics

Accepts query letter from produced or represented writers. Project types include Feature Films. Preferred genres include Comedy, Drama, and Romance. Established in 2011.

Ben Stillman
Creative Executive
imdb.com/name/nm4212466
linkedin.com/pub/ben-stillman/2b/11b/433

Teddy Schwarzman
imdb.com/name/nm3267061
linkedin.com/pub/teddy-schwarzman/11/50a/27a

Amanda Greenblatt
imdb.com/name/nm1716375
linkedin.com/pub/amanda-greenblatt/0/8b/829

BLACK BULL MEDIA

1101 The Plaza
Tenafly, NJ 07670

blackbull.com
twitter.com/blackbullnews

facebook.com/pages/Black-Bull-Media/
178772705557048

Does not accept any unsolicited material. Preferred genres include Action and Drama.

Gareb Shamus
Principle/Producer
imdb.com/name/nm1347437
linkedin.com/in/garebshamus

BLACK CASTLE PRODUCTIONS

1041 N Formosa Ave., Formosa Bldg. Suite 195
West Hollywod, CA 90046
323-426-9208

blackcastleproductions@ymail.com
blackcastleprod.com
facebook.com/BlackCastleProductions
twitter.com/BlackCastleProd
imdb.com/company/co0311113
linkedin.com/company/black-castle-productions

Does not accept any unsolicited material. Project types include Feature Films. Preferred genres include Drama, Horror, and Thriller.

Sabrina Cooper
Producer
imdb.com/name/nm3735458

BLACKFIN

25 Broadway, 9th Floor
New York, NY 10004

info@blackfin.tv
facebook.com/pages/Blackfin/589135057798131
twitter.com/GENO_TV
imdb.com/company/co0466165
blackfin.tv

Does not accept any unsolicited material. Project types include TV. Preferred genres include Reality.

Alexa Conway
Partner/Exec. in Charge of Production

Geno McDermott
Partner/CEO/Producer
imdb.com/name/nm6183414

Joanne Inglott
Partner/Producer
imdb.com/name/nm1531940

BLACK FOREST FILM GROUP

8383 Wilshire Blvd. Suite 355
Beverly Hills, CA 90210
310-990-8680

info@blackforestfg.com
blackforestfilmgroup.com
twitter.com/BlackForestFG
imdb.com/company/co0369400

Does not accept any unsolicited material. Project types include Feature Films. Preferred genres include Thriller.

Brett Hudson
Partner
imdb.com/name/nm0399791

Mark Morgan
Partner
imdb.com/name/nm0604878

Kami Garcia
Partner
imdb.com/name/nm3721581

Eric Thompson
Partner
imdb.com/name/nm0860095

BLACKLIGHT

9560 Wilshire Blvd
4th Floor
Beverly Hills, CA 90212
310-285-9000

contact@blacklighttransmedia.com
pr@blacklighttransmedia.com
blacklighttransmedia.com
imdb.com/company/co0333337
facebook.com/BlacklightTransmedia
twitter.com/BlacklightMedia

Accepts scripts from produced or represented writers. Project types include Feature Films.

Zak Kadison
CEO
imdb.com/name/nm1780162
linkedin.com/in/zakkadison

Justin Catron
Director of Development
imdb.com/name/nm2031037

BLACKMALED PRODUCTIONS

5700 Arlington Ave
Bronx, NY 10471
718-601-5353

malcolmdlee.com
imdb.com/company/co0425503
facebook.com/pages/Malcolm-D-Lee-Blackmaled-
    Productions/408778477872
linkedin.com/company/blackmaled-productions

Does not accept any unsolicited material. Project types
include Feature Films. Preferred genres include
Comedy and Drama.

Malcolm D. Lee
Writer/Director/Producer
imdb.com/name/nm0002700
twitter.com/malcolmdlee

BLANK PAIGE PRODUCTIONS

611 N. Bronson Ave, Suite 2
Los Angeles, CA 90004
323-461-2300 (phone)
323-461-1320 (fax)

info@blankpaige.com
blankpaige.com
imdb.com/company/co0324748
twitter.com/blankpaigetv
facebook.com/BlankPaigeProductions

Does not accept any unsolicited material. Project types
include TV.

Edward Paige
Executive Producer
imdb.com/name/nm2302761
linkedin.com/pub/edward-paige/1b/ba9/4a8

Liane Su
Executive Producer
imdb.com/name/nm1015692

BLEIBERG ENTERTAINMENT

225 S Clark Dr
Beverly Hills, CA 90211
310-273-1034 (phone)
310-273-0007 (fax)

info@bleibergent.com
sales@bleibergent.com
bleibergent.com
facebook.com/ehud.bleiberg.9
imdb.com/company/co0165151

Accepts query letter from unproduced, unrepresented
writers via email. Project types include Feature Films
and TV.

Melanie Kollar
Vice President of Operations

Ehud Bleiberg
Chairman
ehud@bleibergent.com
imdb.com/name/nm0088173
linkedin.com/pub/ehud-bleiberg/11/679/595

Nicholas Donnermeyer
Vice President of Acquisitions & Development
nick@bleibergent.com
imdb.com/name/nm2223730

BLINDING EDGE PICTURES

1055 Westlakes Dr
Berwyn, PA 19312
610-251-9200 (phone)
610-260-9879 (fax)

imdb.com/company/co0054054

Does not accept any unsolicited material. Project types
include Feature Films. Preferred genres include
Drama, Horror, and Thriller.

Ashwin Rajan
Head of Production/Producer
imdb.com/name/nm2248864

M. Night Shyamalan

Writer/Director/Producer
mnightshyamalan.com
imdb.com/name/nm0796117
facebook.com/pages/M-Night-Shyamalan/
116097218498409
twitter.com/MNightShyamalan

BLINDWINK PRODUCTIONS

8 Mills Place 2nd Floor
Pasadena, CA 91105
626-600-4100

info@blindwink.com
blindwink.com
imdb.com/company/co0230970
facebook.com/pages/Blind-Wink-Productions

Does not accept any unsolicited material. Project types include Feature Films. Preferred genres include Action, Comedy, Crime, Drama, Family, Fantasy, Science Fiction, and Thriller.

Josh Pincus
Director of Development

Gore Verbinski
Principal
imdb.com/name/nm0893659

Nils Peyron
Executive Vice President
imdb.com/name/nm3741163

Jonathan Krauss
Head of Film Production & Development
imdb.com/name/nm0470310

BLONDIE GIRL PRODUCTIONS

Relativity Television
1040 N. Las Palmas Ave.
Building 40
Hollywood, CA 90038
323-860-8610 (phone)
323-860-8601 (fax)

jessica@blondiegirlprod.com
blondiegirlproductions.com
facebook.com/BlondieGirlProductions
twitter.com/blondiegirlprod

imdb.com/company/co0261290

Does not accept any unsolicited material. Project types include TV.

Jennifer Rhoades
VP Development and Production
imdb.com/name/nm1056279

Ashley Tisdale
Owner
misstisdale.net/jessica-rhoades-of-blondie-girl-prod-
interview
imdb.com/name/nm0864308

BLOOD MOON PRODUCTIONS

75 Saint Marks Place
Staten Island, NY 10301
718-556-9410 (phone)
718-816-4092 (fax)

bloodmoonproductions.com
facebook.com/pages/Blood-Moon-Productions-Ltd/
258733018503
twitter.com/BloodyandLunar
imdb.com/company/co0511521

Does not accept any unsolicited material. Project types include Feature Films. Preferred genres include Drama.

Danforth Prince
Publisher/Executive Producer
imdb.com/name/nm3362710

BLUE BAY PRODUCTIONS

1119 Colorado Ave., Ste. 100
Santa Monica, CA 90401
310-440-9904

imdb.com/company/co0176188
facebook.com/bluebayprod/timeline

Does not accept any unsolicited material. Project types include Feature Films. Preferred genres include Comedy, Drama, and Romance.

Rodney Liber
Producer
imdb.com/name/nm0508764

BLUE COLLAR PRODUCTIONS

1041 N. Formosa Ave., S. M. East Bldg. Suite 210
West Hollywood, CA 90046
323-850-2530 (phone)
323-850-2531 (fax)

bluecollarproductions.com
twitter.com/BlueCollarLA
facebook.com/pages/Blue-Collar-Productions-Inc/
    152776894868030
imdb.com/company/co0121663
linkedin.com/company/blue-collar-productions-inc.

Does not accept any unsolicited material. Project types include Feature Films.

Mark Rowen
Producer
imdb.com/name/nm0746651

Jeffrey Lerner
Partner
imdb.com/company/co0121663

BLUEGRASS FILMS

100 Universal City Plaza
Bungalow 4171
Universal City, CA 91608
818-777-3200 (phone)
818-777-0020 (fax)

imdb.com/company/co0376117

Does not accept any unsolicited material. Project types include Feature Films and TV. Preferred genres include Action, Crime, Drama, Fantasy, Romance, Science Fiction, and Thriller.

Scott Stuber
Principle
imdb.com/name/nm0835959

Nicholas David Nesbitt
Vice President
imdb.com/name/nm1704779

Michael Clear
Vice President
imdb.com/name/nm2752795
linkedin.com/pub/mike-clear/4/90/42b

BLUE PRINT PICTURES

43-45 Charlotte St
London W1T 1RS
United Kingdom
+44 0207-580-6915

enquiries@blueprintpictures.com
asst@blueprintpictures.com
blueprintpictures.com

Does not accept any unsolicited material. Established in 2004.

Graham Broadbent
Principle
asst@blueprintpictures.com
imdb.com/name/nm0110357

BLUE RIDER PICTURES

2801 Ocean Park Blvd., Suite 193
Santa Monica, CA 90405
310-314-8405 (phone)
310-314-8402 (fax)

info@blueriderpictures.com
blueriderpictures.com
imdb.com/company/co0042650
linkedin.com/company/blue-rider-pictures

Does not accept any unsolicited material. Project types include Feature Films and TV. Preferred genres include Comedy.

Walter Josten
CEO/Executive Producer
imdb.com/name/nm0430943

Jeff Geoffray
CFO/Executive Producer
imdb.com/name/nm0313258

BLUE SHIRT PRODUCTIONS

506 Santa Monica Blvd., Suite. 200
Santa Monica, CA 90401
310-917-5000

blueshirtmusic@gmail.com
facebook.com/BluShirtProductions/timeline
imdb.com/company/co0255230

Does not accept any unsolicited material. Project types include Feature Films. Preferred genres include Family.

Jennifer Moyer
Senior Executive

Karey Kirkpatrick
Writer/Director
imdb.com/name/nm0456732

BLUE SKY STUDIOS

One American Ln
Greenwich, CT 06831
203-992-6000 (phone)
203-992-6001 (fax)

info@blueskystudios.com
blueskystudios.com
facebook.com/BlueSkyStudios
imdb.com/company/co0047265

Does not accept any unsolicited material. Project types include Feature Films. Established in 1997.

Chris Wedge
Vice-President (Creative Director)
imdb.com/name/nm0917188
linkedin.com/in/chrispinkuswesselman

Lisa Fragner
Head (Feature Development)
imdb.com/name/nm0289591
linkedin.com/in/lisafragner

BLUE TULIP PRODUCTIONS

2128 Narcissus Court
Venice, CA 90291
310-458-2166

imdb.com/company/co0007610

Does not accept any unsolicited material. Project types include Feature Films and TV. Preferred genres include Action, Science Fiction, and Thriller.

Jan De Bont
Director/Producer
imdb.com/name/nm0000957
linkedin.com/pub/jan-de-bont/36/b24/25a

Chris Stanley
Vice President
imdb.com/name/nm0000957

BLUEWATER RANCH ENTERTAINMENT

1433 Sixth St
Santa Monica, CA 90401
310-395-1882

rancher@bluewaterranch.com
bluewaterranch.com
twitter.com/BluewaterRanch
facebook.com/profile.php
linkedin.com/company/bluewater-ranch-entertainment
imdb.com/company/co0201577

Does not accept any unsolicited material. Project types include Feature Films. Preferred genres include Comedy, Drama, and Thriller.

Mindy Marin
Producer
imdb.com/name/nm0547484

BLUMHOUSE PRODUCTIONS

2401 Beverly Blvd.
Los Angeles, CA 90057
213-835-1000

blumhouseproductionsinfo@gmail.com
imdb.com/company/co0098315
blumhouse.com/index.php
twitter.com/blumhouse
facebook.com/Blumhouse

Accepts query letter from unproduced, unrepresented writers. Preferred genres include Action, Horror, and Thriller. Established in 2000.

Jason Blum
President
imdb.com/name/nm0089658

Jessica Hall
Director of Development
imdb.com/name/nm4148859
linkedin.com/pub/jessica-hall/1/703/a07

BLUR STUDIO INC.

589 Venice Blvd.
Venice, CA 90291
310-581-8848 (phone)
310-851-8850 (fax)

blur.com

Does not accept any unsolicited material. Project types include Feature Films. Preferred genres include Action, Animation, and Science Fiction.

Tim Miller
Writer, Director

Chris Kubsch
Executive Producer

BLUR STUDIO INC.

589 Venice Blvd.
Venice, CA 90291
310-581-8848 (phone)
310-851-8850 (fax)

blur.com
twitter.com/TheBlurStudio
facebook.com/therealblurstudio
imdb.com/company/co0064973
linkedin.com/company/blur-studio

Project types include Feature Films. Preferred genres include Action and Science Fiction.

Tim Miller
Writer, Director
imdb.com/name/nm1783265

Chris Kubsch
Executive Producer
imdb.com/name/nm5477852

BMP LATIN

6007 Sepulveda Blvd.
Van Nuys, CA 91411
818-756-5100

bunim-murray.com/bmp-latin
twitter.com/bunimmurray
facebook.com/BunimMurrayProductions
imdb.com/company/co0031439
linkedin.com/company/bunim-murray-productions

Does not accept any unsolicited material. Project types include TV.

Julio Caro
Co-Head

Gabriela Cocco-Sanchez
Co-Head
imdb.com/name/nm6419869

BN FILMS

1531 14th St
Santa Monica, CA 90404
310-881-6334

info@bnfilms.tv
bnfilms.tv
facebook.com/bnfilmsLA
twitter.com/BNFilmsLA
imdb.com/company/co0403621

Does not accept any unsolicited material. Project types include Feature Films. Preferred genres include Drama and Thriller.

Lucas Akoskin
Producer
imdb.com/name/nm1993666

Alex Garcia
Producer
imdb.com/name/nm4111213

Katrina Wolfe
President of Production/Producer
imdb.com/name/nm2302501

Jonathan Gray
Executive (NY)
imdb.com/name/nm1807745

BOBBCAT FILMS

1320 Ellsworth Industrial Blvd. Bldg. A – 900
Atlanta, GA
404-351-5353 (phone)
404-351-5327 (fax)

bobbcatfilms.com
facebook.com/pages/bobbcatfilms/224619900913110
twitter.com/bobbcatfilms
linkedin.com/company/bobbcat-films

imdb.com/company/co0351552

Does not accept any unsolicited material. Project types include TV. Preferred genres include Drama.

Roger Bobb
CEO/Producer/Director
imdb.com/name/nm0090292

BOBKER/KRUGAR FILMS

1416 N La Brea Ave
Hollywood, CA 90028
323-469-1440 (phone)
323-802-1597 (fax)

imdb.com/company/co0163148

Accepts query letter from unproduced, unrepresented writers.

Daniel Bobker
Producer
imdb.com/name/nm0090394
linkedin.com/pub/daniel-bobker/62/1b9/59b

Ehren Kruger
imdb.com/name/nm0472567

BOB STICKS WORLDWIDE

nikki@bobsticks.com
bobsticks.com

Does not accept any unsolicited material. Project types include Feature Films and TV. Preferred genres include Action, Comedy, and Thriller. Established in 2014.

Nikki Stanghetti
Producer
nikki@bobsticks.com
imdb.com/name/nm2325595

BOGNER ENTERTAINMENT INC.

269 S Beverly Dr, Suite 8
Beverly Hills, CA 90212
310-569-7525

Relativity / Bogner Entertainment
1040 N. Las Palmas Ave., Bldg 40

Hollywood, CA 90028
323-860-8670

info.beitv@gmail.com
bognerentertainment.com
twitter.com/share
facebook.com/beitv
imdb.com/company/co0068550

Accepts scripts from unproduced, unrepresented writers. Preferred genres include Action, Comedy, Family, Horror, and Thriller. Established in 2000.

Oliver Bogner
oliverbogner@gmail.com
imdb.com/name/nm3331124
linkedin.com/in/oliverbogner
facebook.com/oliverbogner
twitter.com/oliver_bogner

Jonathan Bogner
President
jsbogner@aol.com
imdb.com/name/nm0091845
linkedin.com/pub/jonathan-bogner/1/37b/91a

BOKU FILMS

1438 N Gower St
Box 87
Hollywood, CA 90028
323-860-7710 (phone)
323-860-7706 (fax)

leon@bokufilms.com
katgoh@bokufilms.com
imdb.com/company/co0047458
bokufilms.com

Does not accept any unsolicited material. Project types include TV. Preferred genres include Drama and Thriller.

Alan Poul
Principle
imdb.com/name/nm0693561

BOLD FILMS

6464 Sunset Blvd,
Suite 800
Los Angeles, CA 90028

323-769-8900 (phone)
323-769-8954 (fax)

info@boldfilms.com
boldfilms.com
imdb.com/company/co0135575

Does not accept any unsolicited material. Project types include Feature Films and TV. Preferred genres include Action, Fantasy, Horror, and Thriller.

Stephanie Wilcox
Director of Development
imdb.com/name/nm3432545

Garrick Dion
Senior Vice President (Development)
imdb.com/name/nm1887182

BONA FIDE PRODUCTIONS

8899 Beverly Blvd
Suite 804
Los Angeles, CA 90048
310-273-6782 (phone)
310-273-7821 (fax)

imdb.com/company/co0063938

Accepts query letter from unproduced, unrepresented writers. Project types include Feature Films. Established in 1993.

Albert Berger
Partner
imdb.com/name/nm0074100
linkedin.com/pub/albert-berger/6/b49/493

BORDERLINE FILMS

545 8th Ave
11th Floor
New York, NY 10018

contact@blfilm.com
blfilm.com
imdb.com/company/co0155943

Does not accept any unsolicited material. Project types include Feature Films. Preferred genres include Crime, Detective, Drama, and Thriller. Established in 2003.

Sean Durkin
Principle
imdb.com/name/nm1699934

Antonio Campos
Principle
imdb.com/name/nm1290515

Josh Mond
Principle
imdb.com/name/nm1317614
linkedin.com/pub/dir/Josh/Mond/us-70-Greater-New-York-City-Area

BOSS MEDIA

9440 Santa Monica Blvd.
Suite 200
Beverly Hills, CA 90210
310-205-9900 (phone)
310-205-9909 (fax)

imdb.com/company/co0341936
boss-media.com
linkedin.com/company/boss-media-ab
twitter.com/bossmediacomm

Does not accept any unsolicited material. Preferred genres include Comedy, Science Fiction, and Thriller.

Frank Mancuso
President
310-205-9900
imdb.com/name/nm0541548

Jennifer Nieves Gordon
Vice President (Development)
310-205-9900
imdb.com/name/nm2707034

BOW & ARROW ENTERTAINMENT

Los Angeles, CA

imdb.com/company/co0488623
facebook.com/pages/Bow-and-Arrow-Entertainment/
1468827943363517
linkedin.com/company/bow-and-arrow-entertainment

Does not accept any unsolicited material. Project types include Feature Films. Preferred genres include Documentary and Drama. Established in 2014.

Michael Sherman
Principle
imdb.com/name/nm5554634

Matthew Perniciaro
Principle
imdb.com/name/nm0674362
linkedin.com/pub/matthew-perniciaro/47/976/73b

BOX INC.

4440 El Camino Real
Los Altos, CA 94022
877-729-4269

box.com
twitter.com/boxHQ

Does not accept any unsolicited material. Project types include TV. Preferred genres include Drama.

Josh C. Kline
Head of Media & Entertainment/Producer

Aaron Levie
CEO
imdb.com/name/nm3085736

BOXING CAT PRODUCTIONS

11500 Hart St
North Hollywood, CA 91605
818-765-4870 (phone)
818-765-4975 (fax)

bradb@boxingcats.ca
imdb.com/company/co0080834
boxingcats.ca

Does not accept any unsolicited material. Project types include Feature Films and TV. Preferred genres include Comedy and Family.

Tim Allen
timallen.com/misc/bcf.php?xpt=1
imdb.com/name/nm0000741

BOY WONDER PRODUCTIONS

347-632-2961 (phone)
347-332-6953 (fax)

info@boywonderproductions.net
boywonderproductions.net
facebook.com/pages/Boy-Wonder-Productions/
 239113204508
imdb.com/company/co0255525

Accepts query letter from unproduced, unrepresented writers via email. Project types include TV. Preferred genres include Comedy, Drama, and Non-Fiction. Established in 2006.

BOZ PRODUCTIONS

323-697-5340

bozenga@sbcglobal.net
bozproductions.com
imdb.com/company/co0068487

Accepts query letter from unproduced, unrepresented writers.

Bo Zenga
bozenga@sbcglobal.net
imdb.com/name/nm0954848

BRAD LACHMAN PRODUCTIONS

4450 Lakeside Dr, Suite 280
Burbank, CA 91505
818-954-0473

reception@bradlachmanprods.com
bradlachmanprods.com
imdb.com/company/co0091962

Does not accept any unsolicited material. Project types include TV.

Brad Lachman
Producer
imdb.com/name/nm0480044

BRAINWAVE FILM GROUP

827 Hollywood Way, Suite 539
Burbank, CA 91505
818-429-4238

info@brainwavefilms.net
brainwavefilms.net
facebook.com/brainwavefilms01
twitter.com/BrainwaveFilms

Does not accept any unsolicited material. Project types include Feature Films. Preferred genres include Drama.

Duane Andersen
Producer
imdb.com/name/nm1104565

Emily Pearson
Producer
imdb.com/name/nm0962588

BRANDED FILMS

4000 Warner Blvd
Building 139, Suite 107
Burbank, CA 91522
818-954-7969

info@branded-films.com
branded-films.com
imdb.com/company/co0347637

Does not accept any unsolicited material. Project types include Feature Films and TV. Preferred genres include Comedy. Established in 2011.

Russell Brand
Principle
imdb.com/name/nm1258970
Assistant: Lee Sacks

Nik Linnen
Producer
imdb.com/name/nm3800556

BRAUN ENTERTAINMENT GROUP

3685 Motor Ave, Suite 150
Los Angeles, CA 90034
310-204-6000 (phone)
310-204-6005 (fax)

braunent@aol.com
braunentertainmentgroup.com
imdb.com/company/co0150508
linkedin.com/company/braun-entertainment-group

Accepts query letter from unproduced, unrepresented writers via email. Project types include Feature Films and TV. Preferred genres include Drama.

Zev Braun
CEO/President
imdb.com/name/nm0105881

Philip M. Krupp
EVP
imdb.com/name/nm0472803

Michael Swidler
Development
imdb.com/name/nm4522103

BRAUNSTEIN FILMS, HOWARD

12301 Wilshire Blvd., Suite 110
Los Angeles, CA 90025
310-207-6600

imdb.com/company/co0462935

Does not accept any unsolicited material. Preferred genres include Drama.

Howard Braunstein
Producer
imdb.com/name/nm0105946

BRAVERMAN PRODUCTIONS

3000 Olympic Blvd.
Santa Monica, CA 90404
310-264-4184 (phone)
310-388-5885 (fax)

chuck@bravermanproductions.com
bravermanproductions.com
imdb.com/company/co0093100
facebook.com/pages/Braverman-Productions-Inc/
    411951145571125

Does not accept any unsolicited material. Project types include Feature Films.

Chuck Braverman
Producer/Director
imdb.com/name/nm0106015
facebook.com/chuck.braverman

BREAKFAST ANYTIME PRODUCTIONS

13701 Riverside Dr, Suite 400
Sherman Oaks, CA 91423

breakfastanytime.tv
imdb.com/company/co0333901

Does not accept any unsolicited material. Project types include TV.

Ari Shofet
Producer
imdb.com/name/nm1597896

Rick Hurvitz
President/Producer
imdb.com/name/nm1539523

BREAKOUT WORLDWIDE ENTERTAINMENT

1438 N. Gower St, Bldg. 70, Suite 226 Box 70
Hollywood, CA 90028
323-860-7100 (phone)
323-468-4665 (fax)

breakoutent.com

Does not accept any unsolicited material. Project types include Feature Films. Preferred genres include Horror.

Sherri Strain
President
imdb.com/name/nm0833173

Christina Rosenberg
VP of Development
imdb.com/name/nm0479447

BREGMAN PRODUCTIONS, MARTIN

34-12 36th St, Suite 2/201
Astotia, NY 11106
718-706-4700

Does not accept any unsolicited material. Project types include Feature Films. Preferred genres include Thriller.

Martin Bregman
Producer
imdb.com/name/nm0106840

Michael Bregman
Director/Writer
imdb.com/name/nm0106841

BRIDGE FILMS

149 S Barrington Ave #762
Los Angeles, CA 90049
310-472-0780 (phone)
310-472-4781 (fax)

mriklin@bridgefilms.com
bridgefilms.com
imdb.com/company/co0013928

Does not accept any unsolicited material. Project types include Feature Films. Preferred genres include Thriller.

Matthew Riklin
President/Producer
imdb.com/name/nm1930450

BRIDGET JOHNSON FILMS

1416 N. La Brea Ave
Los Angeles, CA 90028
323-802-1749

imdb.com/company/co0095018

Does not accept any unsolicited material. Project types include Feature Films and TV. Preferred genres include Comedy, Drama, and Thriller.

Bridget Johnson
Producer
imdb.com/name/nm0424660

BRIGHTLIGHT PICTURES

The Bridge Studios
2400 Boundary Rd
Burnaby, BC V5M 3Z3
Canada
604-628-3000 (phone)
604-628-3001 (fax)

info@brightlightpictures.com
brightlightpictures.com
imdb.com/company/co0065717

Does not accept any unsolicited material. Project types include Feature Films and TV. Preferred genres include Comedy and Drama. Established in 2001.

Shawn Williamson
Chairman
imdb.com/name/nm0932144
linkedin.com/pub/shawn-williamson/13/442/124

BRILLIANT DIGITAL ENTERTAINMENT

14011 Ventura Blvd, Suite 501
Sherman Oaks, CA 91423
818-386-2179

brilliantdigital.com
imdb.com/company/co0004768
linkedin.com/company/brilliant-digital-entertainment

Does not accept any unsolicited material. Project types include TV.

BROKEN CAMERA PRODUCTIONS

San Antonio, TX
210-446-8103

info@brokencameraproductions.com
brokencameraproductions.com

Accepts query letter from unproduced, unrepresented writers via email. Project types include Feature Films. Preferred genres include Comedy, Drama, and Thriller.

Sommer Bostick
Editor
830-998-5017
sommer@brokencameraproductions.com
imdb.com/name/nm5223266

Matthew Garth
Producer
210-454-8103
matthew@brokencameraproductions.com
imdb.com/name/nm2123288

David Y. Duncan
Producer
210-884-5234
dave@brokencameraproductions.com
imdb.com/name/nm2839229

Lynette C. Aleman
Producer
210-317-4647
lynette@brokencameraproductions.com
imdb.com/name/nm4074593

BROOKLYN FILMS

3815 Hughes Ave.
Culver City, CA 90232
310-838-2500 (phone)
310-204-3464 (fax)

inquiries@brooklynfilms.com
brooklynfilms.com
facebook.com/pages/New-York-NY/Brooklyn-Films/
    12482289393
imdb.com/company/co0088618

Accepts query letter from unproduced, unrepresented writers. Project types include Feature Films and TV. Preferred genres include Crime and Drama.

Michael Helman
michael.helman@brooklynfilms.com

Robin Adams
Co-Founder
robin.adams@brooklynfilms.com
linkedin.com/in/robincadams

Jon Avnet
Principle
imdb.com/name/nm0000816

Marsha Oglesby
Executive Producer
imdb.com/name/nm0644749

BROOKSFILMS

9336 W. Washington Blvd.
Culver City , CA 90232
310-202-3292 (phone)
310-202-3225 (fax)

imdb.com/company/co0000858
facebook.com/pages/Mel-Brooks/109496505734925

Does not accept any unsolicited material. Project types include Feature Films. Preferred genres include Comedy and Drama.

Mel Brooks
President/Director/Writer
imdb.com/name/nm0000316

BROOKSIDE ARTIST MANAGEMENT

250 W. 57th St
New York, NY 10019
212-489-4929 (phone)
212-489-9056 (fax)

facebook.com/pages/Brookside-Artist-Management/
170654672948747
imdb.com/company/co0084962
linkedin.com/company/brookside-artist-management

Does not accept any unsolicited material. Project types include Feature Films. Preferred genres include Comedy.

Emily Gerson Saines
President/Producer/Manager
imdb.com/name/nm0756593

BROTHERS DOWDLE PRODUCTIONS

13323 W Washington Blvd.
Los Angeles, CA 90066

imdb.com/company/co0114058

Project types include Feature Films. Preferred genres include Drama and Thriller.

Drew Dowdle
Producer/Writer
imdb.com/name/nm1803105

John Dowdle
Director/Writer
imdb.com/name/nm0235719

BROWNSTONE PRODUCTIONS

100 Universal Plaza
Universal City, CA 91608

imdb.com/company/co0019749

Does not accept any unsolicited material. Project types include Feature Films and TV. Preferred genres include Comedy, Drama, and Fantasy.

Elizabeth Banks
Actor/Producer
imdb.com/name/nm0006969

Max Handelman
Producer
imdb.com/name/nm2583641

BRUCE COHEN PRODUCTIONS

8292 Hollywood Blvd
Los Angeles, CA 90069
323-650-4567 (phone)
323-843-9534 (fax)

Does not accept any unsolicited material. Project types include TV. Preferred genres include Drama.

Jessica Leventhal
Director of Development
imdb.com/name/nm4202199
linkedin.com/pub/jessica-leventhal/25/453/196

Bruce Cohen
Principle
imdb.com/name/nm0169260
facebook.com/bruce.cohen.908

BRUCKS ENTERTAINMENT

6363 Wilshire Blvd., Suite 416
Los Angeles, CA 90046
323-556-6419

imdb.com/company/co0284585

Does not accept any unsolicited material. Project types include Feature Films. Preferred genres include Action.

Bryan Brucks
Producer/Manager
imdb.com/name/nm1834398

BS PRODUCTIONS

9229 Sunset Blvd., Suite 608
Los Angeles, CA 90069
310-717-5187

barrett_stuart@bsproductions.org
bsproductions.org
imdb.com/company/co0191476

Preferred genres include Drama.

Barrett Stuart
Producer
imdb.com/name/nm2302967

BUFFALO JUMP PRODUCTIONS

6100 Primrose St, Suite 12
Los Angeles, CA 90068
323-461-3422

info@buffalojumpproductions.com
buffalojumpproductions.com
imdb.com/company/co0061609

Bill Kalmenson
Actor/Writer/Director
imdb.com/name/nm0436105

BUNGALOW MEDIA + ENTERTAINMENT

7 Penn Plaza, Suite 1105
New York, NY 10001
646-753-5037

1888 Century Park East, 7th Floor
Los Angeles, CA 90067
310-734-0451

info@bungalowentertainment.com
ahoffman@bungalowentertainment.com
bungalowentertainment.com
linkedin.com/company/bungalow-media-
    entertainment

Does not accept any unsolicited material. Project types include Feature Films and TV. Preferred genres include Comedy and Drama.

Todd Hoffman
Partner/Producer

Robert Friedman
CEO/Producer
imdb.com/name/nm2473259

BUNIM-MURRAY PRODUCTIONS

6007 Sepulveda Blvd
Van Nuys, CA 91411

818-756-5100 (phone)
818-756-5140 (fax)

contactus@bunim-murray.com
bmp@bunim-murray.com
bunim-murray.com
linkedin.com/company/bunim-murray-productions

Does not accept any unsolicited material. Project types include TV. Preferred genres include Documentary and Reality.

Jeff Jenkins
Executive Vice President
imdb.com/name/nm0420870
linkedin.com/pub/jeff-jenkins/9/B09/79B

Cara Goldberg
Production Executive
linkedin.com/in/caraleigh

Erin Cristall
Vice President (Development)
imdb.com/name/nm0188058
linkedin.com/pub/dir/erin/cristall

Jonathan Murray
Chairman
imdb.com/name/nm0615086

Gil Goldschein
President
imdb.com/name/nm2251455
linkedin.com/pub/gil-goldschein/0/a33/17

Scott Freeman
Executive Vice President (Current Programming and Development)
imdb.com/name/nm1321720
linkedin.com/pub/dir/Scott/Freeman

John Greco
Vice President (Production)
linkedin.com/pub/erin-cristall/9/545/549

BUREAU OF MOVING PICTURES

1548 Hedgepath Ave
Hacienda Heights, CA 91745
626-961-3465

imdb.com/company/co0211360

Does not accept any unsolicited material. Project types include Feature Films. Preferred genres include Drama.

Andrew Meieran
Producer/Financier
imdb.com/name/nm2677942

Matthew Tabak
Producer
imdb.com/name/nm0845860

BURLEIGH FILMWORKS

22287 Mulholland Highway, Suite 129
Calabasas, CA 91302
818-224-4686 (phone)
818-223-9089 (fax)

imdb.com/company/co0176271

Accepts query letter from unproduced, unrepresented writers.

Steve Burleigh
Principle
steve.burleigh@burleighfilmworks.com
imdb.com/name/nm0122114
linkedin.com/pub/steve-burleigh/8/a35/813
facebook.com/steve.burleigh

BURNSIDE ENTERTAINMENT, INC.

265 W 19th St
New York, NY 10011
323-902-7384

mail@burnsideentertainment.com
imdb.com/company/co0180518

Accepts query letter from unproduced, unrepresented writers.

Seth William Meier
Partner
323-902-7384
sethwilliammeier@burnsideentertainment.com
imdb.com/name/nm0576720

Glen Trotiner
Owner
212-727-7665
gtrotiner@burnsideentertainment.com
imdb.com/name/nm0873641

BUSBOY PRODUCTIONS

375 Greenwich St, Fifth Floor
New York, NY 10013
212-965-4700

imdb.com/company/co0176273
facebook.com/pages/Busboy-Productions/
112760302071089

Does not accept any unsolicited material. Project types include Feature Films and TV. Preferred genres include Comedy.

Jon Stewart
Principal
imdb.com/name/nm0829537

Chris McShane
Co-Head of Production and Development
imdb.com/name/nm1457370

C2 ENTERTAINMENT

2917 W Olive Ave
Burbank, CA 91505
818-450-3425

info@c2creates.com
c2creates.com
facebook.com/pages/C2-Entertainment/
106245599449496
twitter.com/c2creates

Project types include Feature Films. Preferred genres include Action.

CABIN CREEK FILMS

270 Lafayette St, Suite 710
New York, NY 10012
212-343-2545 (phone)
212-343-2585 (fax)

info@cabincreekfilms.com
cabincreekfilms.com

twitter.com/cabincreekfilms
facebook.com/pages/Cabin-Creek-Films/
    196118677070312
imdb.com/company/co0050052
linkedin.com/company/cabin-creek-films

Does not accept any unsolicited material. Project types
include Feature Films and TV. Preferred genres
include Drama.

Barbara Kopple
Producer/Director
imdb.com/name/nm0465932

CAIRO/SIMPSON ENTERTAINMENT

10764 Rochester Ave.
Los Angeles, CA 90024
310-470-9309

imdb.com/company/co0039501

Does not accept any unsolicited material. Project types
include Feature Films. Preferred genres include Horror
and Romance.

Michael A. Simpson
Producer/Director/Writer
imdb.com/name/nm0801121

Judy Cairo
Producer
imdb.com/name/nm0003437

CALIBER MEDIA COMPANY

5670 Wilshire Blvd.
Ste 1600
Los Angeles, CA 90036
310-786-9210

calibermediaco.com
imdb.com/company/co0228420
twitter.com/calibermediaco
facebook.com/CALIBERMEDIACO

Accepts query letter from unproduced, unrepresented
writers. Project types include Feature Films. Preferred
genres include Action, Crime, Drama, Family, Horror,
Sociocultural, and Thriller. Established in 2008.

Jack Heller
Partner
imdb.com/name/nm2597331
linkedin.com/pub/jack-heller/12/60/967

Dallas Sonnier
Partner
imdb.com/name/nm2447772

CALLAHAN FILMWORKS

4000 Warner Blvd.
Building 138, Room 209
Burbank, CA 91522
323-878-0645 (phone)
323-878-0649 (fax)

imdb.com/company/co0113274

Does not accept any unsolicited material. Project types
include Feature Films and TV. Preferred genres
include Action, Comedy, Crime, Drama, Family,
Fantasy, and Romance.

Peter Segal
Partner
imdb.com/name/nm0781842
linkedin.com/pub/pete-segal/11/996/a90

Michael Ewing
Partner
imdb.com/name/nm0263989
linkedin.com/pub/michael-ewing/56/545/728

Chris Osbrink
Creative Executive
imdb.com/name/nm1644713
linkedin.com/pub/chris-osbrink/6/b33/a1a

CALLA PRODUCTIONS

3019 Effie St
Los Angeles, CA 90026
310-392-3775 (phone)
310-399-5594 (fax)

debcalla@callaproductions.com
callaproductions.com
imdb.com/company/co0131004
facebook.com/pages/Calla-Productions/
    166894293323398
linkedin.com/company/calla-productions

Does not accept any unsolicited material. Project types include Feature Films and TV. Preferred genres include Drama.

Deborah Calla
Producer
imdb.com/name/nm0130111

CAMELOT ENTERTAINMENT GROUP

8001 Irvine Center Dr
Suite 400
Irvine, CA 92618
949-754-3030

submissions@camelotfilms.com
info@camelotfilms.com
imdb.com/company/co0006731
camelotent.com

Accepts scripts from unproduced, unrepresented writers. Project types include Feature Films and TV. Preferred genres include Action, Animation, Comedy, Drama, Family, Horror, Non-Fiction, Romance, Science Fiction, and Thriller.

Robert Atwell
Chairman
imdb.com/name/nm0041164

Steven Istock
Partner
imdb.com/name/nm1916408

CAMPBELL GROBMAN FILMS

9461 Charleville Blvd, Suite 301
Beverly Hills, CA 90212
310-422-8444

facebook.com/pages/Campbell-Grobman-Films/
336999609674457
imdb.com/company/co0360646

Does not accept any unsolicited material. Project types include Feature Films. Preferred genres include Comedy, Drama, and Horror.

Lati Grobman
Partner/Producer
imdb.com/name/nm0342788

Christa Campbell
Partner/Actor/Producer
imdb.com/name/nm0132300

CAMP GREY PRODUCTIONS

9229 W Sunset Blvd.
West Hollywood, CA 90069
424-283-3900

Does not accept any unsolicited material. Project types include Feature Films. Preferred genres include Drama and Thriller.

Colleen Camp
Producer

CANADIAN BROADCASTING COMPANY (CBC)

181 Queen St
Ottawa, ON, Canada, K1P 1K9
613-288-6000

liaison@cbc.ca
cbc.ca
imdb.com/company/co0045850
linkedin.com/company/cbc

Does not accept any unsolicited material. Project types include Feature Films and TV. Preferred genres include Action, Animation, Comedy, Crime, Documentary, Drama, Family, Non-Fiction, and Period. Established in 2007.

Suzanne Colvin-Goulding
imdb.com/name/nm0003681
linkedin.com/pub/suzanne-colvin-goulding/17/704/
10B

Hubert Lacroix
President
imdb.com/name/nm4522750

Trevor Walton
imdb.com/name/nm4280633

Kim Wilson
linkedin.com/pub/dir/Kimberly/Wilson

CANNELL STUDIOS

7083 Hollywood Blvd., Ste. 600
Hollywood , CA 90028
323-465-5800 (phone)
323-856-7390 (fax)

questions@cannell.com
cannell.com
facebook.com/StephenCannell
imdb.com/company/co0369010
linkedin.com/company/cannell-studios

Does not accept any unsolicited material. Preferred genres include Action, Drama, and Horror.

Theresa Peoples
Development
imdb.com/name/nm1323919

CANNY LADS PRODUCTIONS

500 S. Buena Vista St, Animation 3B-10
Burbank, CA 91521
818-560-1314

cannyladsproductions.com

Does not accept any unsolicited material. Project types include TV. Preferred genres include Comedy and Drama.

Julie Anne Robinson
Director/Producer
imdb.com/name/nm1455688

CAPACITY PICTURES

310-247-8534

capacitypictures@gmail.com
imdb.com/company/co0192878

Does not accept any unsolicited material. Project types include Feature Films. Preferred genres include Comedy, Crime, Drama, Horror, and Thriller. Established in 2008.

Wayne Rice
Principle
imdb.com/name/nm0723573

Richard Heller
Principle
imdb.com/name/nm0375378
linkedin.com/pub/richard-heller/10/8B5/95A
twitter.com/richardheller

CAPITAL ARTS ENTERTAINMENT

23315 Clift on Plaza
Valencia, CA 91354
818-343-8950 (phone)
818-343-8962 (fax)

info@capitalarts.com
imdb.com/company/co0009722
facebook.com/CapitalLArtsandEntertainment
sandmancommunications.com

Accepts query letter from unproduced, unrepresented writers via email. Preferred genres include Action, Comedy, Horror, and Thriller. Established in 1995.

Mike Elliot
imdb.com/name/nm0254291
linkedin.com/pub/mike-elliott/8/443/509

Joe Genier
Partner
imdb.com/name/nm0312856
linkedin.com/pub/joe-genier/11/a67/851

Rob Kerchner
Partner
imdb.com/name/nm0449246

CAPTIVATE ENTERTAINMENT

3111 Camino Del Rio North, Suite 400
San Diego, CA 92108
323-658-7760 (phone)
818-733-4303 (fax)

imdb.com/company/co0263292
captive-entertainment.com

Does not accept any unsolicited material. Project types include Feature Films and TV. Preferred genres include Action, Comedy, Drama, Fantasy, Myth, Romance, Science Fiction, and Thriller.

Tony Shaw
Creative Executive
tony.shaw@univfilms.com
imdb.com/name/nm4130192
linkedin.com/pub/tony-shaw/9/958/86a
facebook.com/public/Tony-Shaw

Jeffrey Weiner
Chairman (CEO)
imdb.com/name/nm1788648

Ben Smith
President
imdb.com/name/nm3328356
linkedin.com/in/bensmithonline

CAREER ARTIST MANAGEMENT

1100 Glendon Ave, Suite 1100
Los Angeles, CA 90024
310-776-7640 (phone)
310-776-7659 (fax)

camanagement.com
linkedin.com/company/career-artist-management
facebook.com/pages/Career-Artist-Management-
    CAM/1571532839756068
imdb.com/company/co0175522

Project types include TV. Preferred genres include
Comedy and Drama.

Jordan Feldstein
Producer
imdb.com/name/nm3206443

CARNIVAL FILMS

1 Central St. Giles, St. Giles High St, London WC2H
8NU, United Kingdom
440203-618-6600 (phone)
440206-618-8900 (fax)

55 New Oxford St.
London, England, WC1A 1BS
United Kingdom
0203-618-6600 (phone)
0203-618-8900 (fax)

info@carnivalfilms.co.uk
carnivalfilms.co.uk
twitter.com/Carnival_Films

imdb.com/company/co0106806
facebook.com/carnivalfilm

Does not accept any unsolicited material. Project types
include TV. Preferred genres include Documentary,
Drama, and Thriller.

Sam Symons
Development Executive
imdb.com/name/nm1599585
linkedin.com/pub/symons-sam/23/647/2

Kimberly Hikaka
Production Executive
imdb.com/name/nm2529465
linkedin.com/pub/kimberley-hikaka/5/10/aa4

CAROUSEL TELEVISION

12925 Riverside Dr, 4th Floor
Sherman Oaks, CA 90068
818-849-3900

imdb.com/company/co0303652

Does not accept any unsolicited material. Project types
include TV. Preferred genres include Comedy.

Steve Carell
Actor/Owner/President
imdb.com/name/nm0136797

Campbell Smith
Co-Head of TV
imdb.com/name/nm0962607

CARRIE PRODUCTIONS

2625 Alcatraz Ave, Suite 243
Berkeley, CA 94705
510-450-2500

imdb.com/company/co0059331
facebook.com/pages/Carrie-Productions-Inc/
    113680898643029

Does not accept any unsolicited material. Project types
include Feature Films and TV. Preferred genres
include Drama.

Danny Glover
Producer/Actor
imdb.com/name/nm0000418

Karen Bolt
Development Executive
imdb.com/name/nm1163463

CARSON SIGNATURE FILMS

10 Universal City Plaza, 20th Floor
Universal City, CA 91608
818-753-2333 (phone)
818-753-2310 (fax)

imdb.com/company/co0176330

Does not accept any unsolicited material. Project types
include Feature Films. Preferred genres include
Thriller.

Beaux Carson
President/Producer
imdb.com/name/nm0141185

Darby Connor
Sr. Vice President/ Writer
imdb.com/name/nm1915279

CARTOON NETWORK

300 N 3rd St.
6th Floor
Burbank, CA 91502
818-729-4000 (phone)
818-729-4220 (fax)

10 Columbus Circle
New York, NY 10019
212-275-7800

1065 Techwood Dr. NW
Atlanta, GA 30318
404-885-2263 (phone)
404-885-4312 (fax)

adultswim.com
imdb.com/company/co0153115

Accepts query letter from unproduced, unrepresented
writers. Project types include Video Games.

Mike Lazzo
Executive Vice President (Creative Director, Adult
Swim)
imdb.com/name/nm0494020

Katie Krentz
Development Executive (Comedy Animation)
imdb.com/name/nm1872617
twitter.com/katiekrentz

CARYN MANDABACH PRODUCTIONS

135 Bay St, Unit 7
Santa Monica, CA 90405
310-399-6700

info@mandabachtv.com
imdb.com/company/co0275656
mandabachtv.com

Does not accept any unsolicited material. Project types
include TV. Preferred genres include Comedy, Crime,
and Drama.

Michael Besman
Executive
imdb.com/name/nm0078698

Caryn Mandabach
Producer
imdb.com/name/nm0541591

CASEY SILVER PRODUCTIONS

1411 5th St
Santa Monica, CA 90401
310-566-3750 (phone)
310-566-3751 (fax)

imdb.com/company/co0058884

Does not accept any unsolicited material. Project types
include Feature Films. Preferred genres include Action,
Comedy, Drama, Family, and Thriller.

Casey Silver
Owner
casey@caseysilver.com
imdb.com/name/nm0798661
facebook.com/pages/Casey-Silver-Productions

Matthew Reynolds
Creative Executive
matthew@caseysilver.com
imdb.com/name/nm2303863
linkedin.com/pub/matthew-reynolds/66/345/258

CASPIAN PICTURES

839 E. Orange Grove Ave
Burbank, CA 91501
818-567-1565 (phone)
818-567-1560 (fax)

info@caspianpictures.net
caspianpictures.net
imdb.com/company/co0246517
facebook.com/pages/Caspian-Pictures/
   221682464537498

Does not accept any unsolicited material. Project types
include Feature Films. Preferred genres include
Drama.

Will Raee
Producer, Director
imdb.com/name/nm0706091

Brian Bullock
Producer
imdb.com/name/nm3068149

CASTLE ROCK ENTERTAINMENT

9169 W. Sunset Blvd.
Los Angeles, CA 90069
310-285-2300 (phone)
310-285-2345 (fax)

imdb.com/company/co0040620

Accepts scripts from produced or represented writers.

Andrew Scheinman
andres.scheinman@castle-rock.com
imdb.com/name/nm0770650

Rob Reiner
rob.reiner@castle-rock.com
imdb.com/name/nm0001661

CATAPULT FILM FUND

39 Mesa St, Suite 209
San Francisco, CA 94129
415-738-8337

info@catapultfilmfund.org
catapultfilmfund.org
facebook.com/pages/Catapult-Film-Fund/
   199055386793333

twitter.com/CatapultFilmFnd

Accepts scripts from unproduced, unrepresented
writers. Preferred genres include Documentary.
Established in 2014.

Lisa Kleiner Chanoff
Founder
imdb.com/name/nm5137916

Bonni Cohen
Founder
imdb.com/name/nm1010896

CATAPULT FILMS INC.

832 Third St, Suite 303
Santa Monica, CA 90403-1155
310-395-1470 (phone)
310-401-0122 (fax)

info@catapult.ee
imdb.com/company/co0100754
catapult.ee

Accepts scripts from produced or represented writers.

Lisa Josefsberg
Producer
imdb.com/name/nm2248853

Lawrence Levy
Executive
imdb.com/name/nm0506504

CATCHPHRASE ENTERTAINMENT

3575 Cahuenga Blvd West, Suite 360
Los Angeles, CA 90068
310-622-4273 (phone)
310-826-6886 (fax)

info@catchphraseentertainment.com
catchphraseentertainment.com
imdb.com/company/co0205963
facebook.com/pages/Catchphrase-Entertainment/
   159079530776013
linkedin.com/company/catchphrase-entertainment

Does not accept any unsolicited material. Project types
include Feature Films and TV.

Shahrook Oomer
Producer
imdb.com/name/nm1551082

Dean Shull
CEO
imdb.com/name/nm1306561

CATEGORY 5 ENTERTAINMENT

9229 Sunset Blvd., Suite 601
Los Angeles, CA 90069
310-273-9400 (phone)
310-273-9494 (fax)

imdb.com/company/co0231993
linkedin.com/company/category-5-entertainment

Brian Sher
Producer/Manager
imdb.com/name/nm0792033

CBS FILMS

11800 Wilshire Blvd
Los Angeles, CA 90025
310-575-7700

cbsfilms.com
imdb.com/company/co0047306
twitter.com/CBSFilms
facebook.com/pages/CBS-Films/86622447300

Does not accept any unsolicited material. Project types include Feature Films. Preferred genres include Action, Drama, Fantasy, Romance, and Science Fiction.

Terry Press
imdb.com/name/nm1437110

Maria Faillace
imdb.com/name/nm1299267

Mark Ross
imdb.com/name/nm0743653

Wolfgang Hammer
imdb.com/name/nm1424985

CECCHI GORI PRODUCTIONS

5555 Melrose Ave
Bob Hope 203

Los Angeles, CA 90038
323-956-5954 (phone)
323-862-2254 (fax)

info@cgglobalmedia.com
cecchigoripictures.com
imdb.com/company/co0078943

Project types include Feature Films. Preferred genres include Drama, Family, Horror, Romance, and Thriller.

Niels Juul
CEO
imdb.com/name/nm3887220

Jennifer Parker
Development Executive
imdb.com/name/nm4487725

Andy Scott
Art Director
imdb.com/name/nm4866101

Dana Galinsky
imdb.com/name/nm1919300

Alex Shub
VP of Business and Legal Affairs
linkedin.com/pub/alex-shub/24/467/971
facebook.com/alex.shub.1

CELADOR ENTERTAINMENT

39 Long Acre
London, WC2E 9LG
United Kingdom
+44 20-7845-6800 (phone)
+44 20-7845-6801 (fax)

imdb.com/company/co0152921
celador.co.uk

Accepts scripts from produced or represented writers. Established in 1989.

Paul Smith
psmith@celador.co.uk
imdb.com/name/nm0809531

Michelle Davies
44 020 7845 6800
mdavies@celador.co.uk

CENTROPOLIS ENTERTAINMENT

1445 N Stanley
3rd Floor
Los Angeles, CA 90046
Los Angeles, CA 90046
323-850-1212 (phone)
323-850-1201 (fax)

info@centropolis.com
imdb.com/company/co0050111
centropolis.com
twitter.com/rolandemmerich

Accepts scripts from produced or represented writers. Preferred genres include Action, Fantasy, Myth, Non-Fiction, and Romance. Established in 1985.

Roland Emmerich
imdb.com/name/nm0000386

Ute Emmerich
imdb.com/name/nm0256498

CENTSLESS PICTURES

580 8th Ave 4th Floor
New York, NY 10018
917-688-1561

info@centslesspictures.com
facebook.com/CentslessPictures
imdb.com/company/co0326610
twitter.com/centslesspix

Does not accept any unsolicited material. Project types include Feature Films. Preferred genres include Crime, Drama, and Thriller. Established in 2014.

Stephen Cavaliero
Principle
imdb.com/name/nm3308912
facebook.com/stephen.cavaliero
twitter.com/centslesspix

CHAIKEN FILMS

802 Potrero Ave
San Francisco, CA 94110
415-826-7880 (phone)
415-826-7882 (fax)

info@chaikenfilms.com

imdb.com/company/co0064208
chaikenfilms.com

Accepts query letter from unproduced, unrepresented writers. Preferred genres include Non-Fiction. Established in 1998.

Jennifer Chaiken
Producer
jen@chaikenfilms.com
imdb.com/name/nm0149671

CHAMPION ENTERTAINMENT

2620 Fountain View, Suite 220
Houston, TX 77057
713-522-4701 (phone)
713-522-0426 (fax)

info@championentertainment.com
championentertainment.com
facebook.com/CEI-Information
twitter.com/filmsbychampion
imdb.com/company/co0036127

Does not accept any unsolicited material. Project types include Feature Films and TV. Preferred genres include Drama, Family, and Horror.

Bob Willems
Owner/Producer
imdb.com/name/nm0929721

CHARLOTTE STREET FILMS

1901 Ave of the Stars, Suite 200
Los Angeles, CA 90067
310-499-4949

imdb.com/company/co0157676

Does not accept any unsolicited material. Project types include Feature Films and TV.

Jeffrey Auerbach
Producer

CHARTOFF PRODUCTIONS

1250 Sixth St, Suite 101
Santa Monica, CA 90401
310-319-1960 (phone)
310-319-3469 (fax)

hendeechartoff@cs.com
imdb.com/company/co0094865

Accepts scripts from produced or represented writers. Established in 1986.

Robert Chartoff
imdb.com/name/nm0153590

CHERNIN ENTERTAINMENT

1733 Ocean Ave, Suite 300
Santa Monica, CA 90401
310-899-1205

imdb.com/company/co0286257

Accepts scripts from produced or represented writers. Project types include Feature Films and TV. Preferred genres include Action, Comedy, and Drama. Established in 2009.

Peter Chernin
Principle
imdb.com/name/nm1858656

Dylan Dark
dc@cherninent.com
imdb.com/name/nm1249995

Jenno Topping
jt@cherninent.com
imdb.com/name/nm0867768

Ivana Schechter-Garcia
Creative Executive
imdb.com/name/nm1190974

Pavun Shetty
ps@cherninent.com
imdb.com/name/nm0792904

Katherine Pope
kp@cherninent.com
imdb.com/name/nm0691142

CHERRY SKY FILMS

2100 Sawtelle Blvd.,
Suite 101
Los Angeles, CA 90025
310-479-8001 (phone)
310-479-8815 (fax)

contact@cherryskyfilms.com
cherryskyfilms.com
imdb.com/company/co0032062
twitter.com/cherryskyfilms
facebook.com/pages/Cherry-Sky-Films/
    172702119443857

Does not accept any unsolicited material. Project types include Feature Films. Preferred genres include Comedy, Drama, Family, and Romance. Established in 2001.

Joan Huang
Producer
imdb.com/name/nm0399009

Jeffrey Gou
Producer
imdb.com/name/nm2370188

CHESTNUT RIDGE PRODUCTIONS

8899 Beverly Blvd, Suite 800
Los Angeles, CA
310-285-7011

imdb.com/company/co0273538

Does not accept any unsolicited material. Established in 2009.

Paula Wagner
imdb.com/name/nm0906048

CHEYENNE ENTERPRISES LLC

406 Wilshire Blvd
Santa Monica, CA 90401
310-455-5000 (phone)
310-688-8000 (fax)

imdb.com/company/co0041195

Accepts scripts from produced or represented writers. Established in 2000.

Arnold Rifkin
imdb.com/name/nm0726476

Joshua Rowley
Director of Development
imdb.com/name/nm2282373

CHICAGOFILMS

253 W 72nd St
Suite 1108
New York, NY 10023
USA
212-721-7700 (phone)
212-721-7701 (fax)

imdb.com/company/co0012485

Accepts scripts from produced or represented writers.

Bob Balaban
imdb.com/name/nm0000837

CHICKFLICKS

8861 St Ives Dr
Los Angeles, CA 90069
310-854-7210

info@chickflicksinc.com
imdb.com/company/co0156986
chickflicksinc.com

Accepts scripts from produced or represented writers. Preferred genres include Comedy, Fantasy, Myth, Non-Fiction, and Romance.

Stephanie Austin
310-854-7210
stephanie@chickflicksinc.com
imdb.com/name/nm0042520

Sara Risher
310-854-7210
sara@chickflicksinc.com
imdb.com/name/nm0728260

CHIPSHOT FILMS

1140 Highland Ave. #123
Manhattan Beach, CA 90266
310-772-8126

tbennett@chipshotfilms.com
chipshotfilms.com

Does not accept any unsolicited material. Project types include Feature Films. Preferred genres include Thriller.

Tracy Bennett
Producer
imdb.com/name/nm0072100

Lee Ross
Producer
imdb.com/name/nm0743605

CHOCKSTONE PICTURES

22355 Carbon Mesa Rd
Malibu, CA 90265
310-456-2945

steves@chockstonepictures.com
chockstonepictures.com
imdb.com/company/co0192912
facebook.com/chockstonepictures

Accepts query letter from unproduced, unrepresented writers via email. Project types include Feature Films. Established in 2004.

Roger Schwartz
Development Executive
310-600-6840
rogers@chockstonepictures.com
imdb.com/name/nm0970118
linkedin.com/pub/roger-schwartz/1a/2a5/2b6

Paula Mae Schwartz
CEO
paulamae@chockstonepictures.com
imdb.com/name/nm2445382

Steve Schwartz
President
steves@chockstonepictures.com
imdb.com/name/nm0777455
linkedin.com/pub/steve-schwartz/1b/8/329

CHOTZEN/JENNER PRODUCTIONS

4178 Dixie Canyon Ave.
Sherman Oaks, CA 91423
323-465-9877 (phone)
323-460-6451 (fax)

imdb.com/company/co0176334

Accepts scripts from produced or represented writers. Project types include TV. Preferred genres include Comedy and Drama. Established in 1990.

William Jenner
imdb.com/name/nm0421076

Yvonne Chotzen
Movie Producer
imdb.com/name/nm0159278

CHRIS/ROSE PRODUCTIONS

3131 Torreyson Place
Los Angeles, CA 90046
323-851-8772 (phone)
323-851-0662 (fax)

imdb.com/company/co0040069

Accepts scripts from produced or represented writers.
Project types include TV. Preferred genres include
Comedy, Drama, and Non-Fiction.

Robert Christiansen
Executive Producer
310-781-0833
imdb.com/name/nm0160222

CHUBBCO FILM CO.

751 N. Fairfax Ave.
#10
Los Angeles, CA 90046
310-729-5858 (phone)
310-933-1704 (fax)

1550 E. Valley Rd.
Santa Barbara, CA 93108

chubbco@gmail.com
imdb.com/company/co0026094

Does not accept any unsolicited material. Preferred
genres include Action, Crime, and Non-Fiction.

Caldecot Chubb
Producer
chubbco@gmail.com
imdb.com/name/nm0160941

CHUCK FRIES PRODUCTIONS, INC.

1880 Century Park East
Suite 213
Los Angeles, CA 90067

310-203-9520 (phone)
310-203-9519 (fax)

imdb.com/company/co0040068

Accepts scripts from produced or represented writers.
Preferred genres include Crime and Detective.

Charles Fries
imdb.com/name/nm0295594

CHUCK LORRE PRODUCTIONS

4000 Warner Blvd, Bldg. 160
Burbank, CA 91522

imdb.com/company/co0004981

Does not accept any unsolicited material. Project types
include Feature Films and TV. Preferred genres
include Comedy and Drama.

Chuck Lorre
Producer/Writer
imdb.com/name/nm0521143

Robert Broder
Executive
imdb.com/name/nm2516638

CINDY COWAN ENTERTAINMENT

8265 W Sunset Blvd
Suite 205
Los Angeles, CA 90046
323-822-1082 (phone)
323-822-1086 (fax)

info@cowanent.com
cowanent.com
imdb.com/company/co0094925

Does not accept any unsolicited material. Established
in 1999.

Cindy Cowan
President
imdb.com/name/nm0184546

CINEMA EPHOCH

2600 W. Olive Ave.
5th Floor

Burbank, CA 91505
818-753-2345

acquisitions@cinemaepoch.com
info@cinemaepoch.com
imdb.com/company/co0028810
cinemaepoch.com

Does not accept any unsolicited material. Preferred genres include Action, Comedy, Crime, Detective, Horror, Myth, Non-Fiction, and Thriller. Established in 2001.

Gregory Hatanaka
imdb.com/name/nm0368693

CINEMAGIC ENTERTAINMENT

9229 Sunset Blvd, Suite 610
West Hollywood, CA 90069
310-385-9322 (phone)
310-385-9347 (fax)

imdb.com/company/co0183883
cinemagicent.com

Accepts query letter from unproduced, unrepresented writers. Preferred genres include Action, Crime, Detective, Fantasy, Horror, Myth, Science Fiction, and Thriller.

Lee Cohn
imdb.com/name/nm2325144

CINEMA LIBRE STUDIO

120 S. Victory Blvd, First Floor
Burbank, CA 91502
818-588-3033 (phone)
818-349-9922 (fax)

project@cinemalibrestudio.com
imdb.com/company/co0132224
cinemalibrestudio.com
facebook.com/cinemalibrestudio
twitter.com/cinemalibre

Accepts query letter from unproduced, unrepresented writers. Established in 2003.

Philippe Diaz
imdb.com/name/nm0225034

CINE MOSAIC

130 W 25th St, 12th Floor
New York, NY 10001
212-625-3797 (phone)
212-625-3571 (fax)

info@cinemosaic.net
imdb.com/company/co0124029
cinemosaic.net
facebook.com/cinemosaic
twitter.com/queendean

Accepts scripts from produced or represented writers. Project types include TV. Preferred genres include Action, Drama, and Non-Fiction. Established in 2002.

Lydia Pilcher
imdb.com/name/nm0212990

CINERGI

406 Wilshire Blvd.
Santa Monica, CA 90401
310-315-6000 (phone)
310-315-6015 (fax)

imdb.com/company/co0009350

Does not accept any unsolicited material. Project types include Feature Films. Preferred genres include Action and Drama.

Andrew Vajna
CEO
imdb.com/name/nm0883351

CINESON ENTERTAINMENT

4519 Varna Ave.
Sherman Oaks, CA 91423
818-501-8246 (phone)
818-501-3647 (fax)

cineson@cineson.com
imdb.com/company/co0127539

Does not accept any unsolicited material. Project types include Feature Films and TV. Preferred genres include Comedy, Crime, Drama, Non-Fiction, Period, Romance, and Thriller. Established in 1999.

Andy Garcia
imdb.com/name/nm0000412

CINETELFILMS

8255 Sunset Blvd
Los Angeles, CA 90046
323-654-4000 (phone)
323-650-6400 (fax)

info@cinetelfilms.com
imdb.com/company/co0017447
cinetelfilms.com

Does not accept any unsolicited material. Project types include TV. Preferred genres include Crime, Drama, Horror, and Thriller. Established in 1985.

Paul Hertzberg
imdb.com/name/nm0078473

CINEVILLE

3400 Airport Ave
Santa Monica, CA 90405
310-397-7150 (phone)
310-397-7155 (fax)

info@cineville.com
imdb.com/company/co0063993
cineville.com
facebook.com/cinevilleUSA

Accepts query letter from unproduced, unrepresented writers. Preferred genres include Comedy, Non-Fiction, and Romance. Established in 1990.

Carl Colpaert
President
imdb.com/name/nm0173207

CIRCLE OF CONFUSION

8931 Ellis Ave
Los Angeles, CA 90034
310-691-7000 (phone)
310-691-7099 (fax)

queries@circleofconfusion.com
imdb.com/company/co0090153
facebook.com/pages/Circle-of-Confusion/
    258459361785
twitter.com/ofconfusion
circleofconfusion.com

Accepts query letter from unproduced, unrepresented writers. Project types include TV. Preferred genres

include Action, Comedy, Crime, Detective, Drama, Fantasy, Horror, Myth, Non-Fiction, Romance, Science Fiction, and Thriller.

Stephen Emery
Executive Vice-President Production and Development
stephen@circleofconfusion.com
imdb.com/name/nm1765323

CITY ENTERTAINMENT

266 1/2 S Rexford Dr
Beverly Hills, CA 90212
310-273-3101 (phone)
310-273-3676 (fax)

imdb.com/company/co0093881

Does not accept any unsolicited material.

Joshua Maurer
imdb.com/name/nm0561027

CLARITY PICTURES, LLC

1107 Fair Oaks Ave
Ste 155
South Pasadena, CA 91030
USA
310-226-7046 (phone)
310-388-5846 (fax)

info@claritypictures.net
imdb.com/company/co0151012

Does not accept any unsolicited material. Project types include Feature Films and TV. Preferred genres include Comedy, Documentary, and Horror. Established in 2004.

David Basulto
imdb.com/name/nm0060617

Loren Basulto
imdb.com/name/nm1457923

CLASS 5 FILMS

200 Park Ave South, 8th Floor
New York, NY 10003
917-414-9404

imdb.com/company/co0113781

Accepts query letter from unproduced, unrepresented writers.

Edward Norton
imdb.com/name/nm0001570

CLEAR PICTURES ENTERTAINMENT

12400 Ventura Blvd, Suite 306
Studio City, CA 91604
818-980-5460 (phone)
818-980-4716 (fax)

clearpicturesinc@aol.com
imdb.com/company/co0171732
linkedin.com/.../clear-pictures-entertainment

Accepts query letter from unproduced, unrepresented writers via email. Project types include Feature Films and TV. Preferred genres include Drama and Non-Fiction. Established in 2009.

Elizabeth Fowler
Principle
imdb.com/name/nm2085583

CLEARVIEW PRODUCTIONS

1180 S Beverly Dr, Suite 700
Los Angeles, CA 90035
310-271-7698 (phone)
310-278-9978 (fax)

imdb.com/company/co0464904

Does not accept any unsolicited material.

Albert Ruddy
Producer
imdb.com/name/nm0748665

CLICK PRODUCTIONS

6399 Wilshire Blvd, Suite 1007
Los Angeles, CA 90048
323-655-6845

Alain Sirtzky Productions
23 Rue Raynouard
Paris 75016, France

asproductions@usa.net

asproductions.net
imdb.com/company/co0011751

Does not accept any unsolicited material. Project types include Feature Films and TV. Preferred genres include Comedy and Drama.

Alain Sirtzky
President
imdb.com/name/nm0802852

CLIFFORD WERBER PRODUCTIONS INC.

232 S Beverly Dr, Suite 224
Beverly Hills, CA 90212
310-288-0900 (phone)
310-288-0600 (fax)

imdb.com/company/co0097249

Accepts query letter from produced or represented writers.

Clifford Werber
Producer
imdb.com/name/nm0921222

CLINICA ESTETICO

308 Mott St
New York, NY 10012
212-219-2800

imdb.com/company/co0093046
facebook.com/pages/Clinica-Estetico/
     137878189593335

Does not accept any unsolicited material. Project types include Feature Films. Preferred genres include Drama and Science Fiction.

Jonathan Demme
Producer/Director/Writer
imdb.com/name/nm0001129

CLOSED ON MONDAYS ENTERTAINMENT

3800 Barham Blvd Suite 100
Los Angeles, CA 90068
818-526-6707

imdb.com/company/co0186526

Does not accept any unsolicited material. Established in 2003.

Joe Nozemack
imdb.com/name/nm1060496

CLOUD EIGHT FILMS

39 Long Acre
London WC2E 9LG
United Kingdom
+44 20-7845-6877

imdb.com/company/co0265704

Accepts scripts from produced or represented writers. Established in 2009.

Christian Colson
+44 20 7845 6988
imdb.com/name/nm1384503

CMT FILMS

2600 Colorado Blvd.
Santa Monica, CA 90404
310-752-8000

cmt.com
imdb.com/company/co0155665
facebook.com/cmt

Does not accept any unsolicited material. Project types include Feature Films. Preferred genres include Drama.

COALITION GROUP

11222 Weddington St
North Hollywood, CA 91601
818-755-7941

contact@thecoalition-group.com
thecoalition-group.com
facebook.com/coalitiongroup
twitter.com/coalitiongroup
imdb.com/company/co0425053

Does not accept any unsolicited material. Project types include Feature Films. Preferred genres include Action and Fantasy.

CODEBLACK ENTERTAINMENT

111 Universal Hollywood Dr, Suite 2260
Universal City, CA 91608
818-286-8600 (phone)
818-286-8649 (fax)

info@codeblackentertainment.com
imdb.com/company/co0172361
codeblack.com
codeblack.com
twitter.com/codeblack.comfilter

Does not accept any unsolicited material. Established in 2005.

Jeff Clanagan
CEO
imdb.com/name/nm0163335

CODE ENTERTAINMENT

9229 Sunset Blvd, Suite 615
Los Angeles, CA 90069
310-772-0008 (phone)
310-772-0006 (fax)

contact@codeentertainment.com
imdb.com/company/co0143069
codeentertainment.com

Accepts scripts from produced or represented writers. Established in 2005.

Bart Rosenblatt
Producer
310-772-0008 ext. 3
imdb.com/name/nm0742386

COHEN PICTURES

15332 Antioch St, Suite 215
Pacific Palisades, CA 90272
310-462-2040

imdb.com/company/co0206264

Does not accept any unsolicited material. Project types include Feature Films. Preferred genres include Comedy and Drama.

Bobby Cohen
Producer

COLLEEN CAMP PRODUCTIONS

6464 Sunset Blvd, Suite 800
Los Angeles, CA 90028
323-463-1434 (phone)
323-463-4379 (fax)

asst@ccprods.com
imdb.com/company/co0092983

Accepts query letter from unproduced, unrepresented writers.

Colleen Camp
Producer
imdb.com/name/nm0131974

COLLETON COMPANY

20 Fifth Ave, Suite 13F
New York, NY 10011
212-673-0916 (phone)
212-673-1172 (fax)

imdb.com/company/co0176685

Accepts scripts from produced or represented writers. Project types include Feature Films and TV. Preferred genres include Crime, Detective, Drama, Non-Fiction, and Thriller.

Sara Colleton
imdb.com/name/nm0171780

COLOR FORCE

1524 Cloverfield Blvd, Suite C
Santa Monica, CA 90404
310-828-0641 (phone)
310-828-0672 (fax)

imdb.com/company/co0212151

Accepts query letter from unproduced, unrepresented writers. Preferred genres include Action and Comedy. Established in 2007.

Nina Jacobson
Producer
nina.jacobson@colorforce.com
imdb.com/name/nm1749221

COLOSSAL ENTERTAINMENT

PO Box 461010
Los Angeles, CA 90046
323-656-6647

clsslent@aol.com
imdb.com/company/co0176684

Accepts query letter from unproduced, unrepresented writers.

Kelly Rowan
Producer
imdb.com/name/nm0746414

Graham Ludlow
imdb.com/name/nm0524905

COLUMBIA PICTURES

10202 W Washington Blvd Thalberg Building
Culver City, CA 90232
310-244-4000 (phone)
310-244-2626 (fax)

imdb.com/company/co0071509
sonypictures.com
facebook.com/SonyPictures
twitter.com/sonypictures

Does not accept any unsolicited material. Project types include Feature Films. Preferred genres include Action, Animation, Comedy, Crime, Drama, Family, Fantasy, Horror, Non-Fiction, Period, Romance, Science Fiction, and Thriller. Established in 1939.

Amy Pascal
Chairman
imdb.com/name/nm1166871

Doug Belgrad
President
imdb.com/name/nm1000411

Elizabeth Cantillon
Executive Vice President of Production
imdb.com/name/nm0134578
Assistant: Katherine Spada
katherine_spada@spe.sony.com

Samuel C. Dickerman
Executive Vice President of Production
imdb.com/name/nm0225385

Andrea Giannetti
Executive Vice President of Production
imdb.com/name/nm1602150

Foster Driver
Creative Executive
imdb.com/name/nm5372839

Eric Fineman
Creative Executive
imdb.com/name/nm2349857

Hannah Minghella
imdb.com/name/nm1098742
Assistant: Mahsa Moayeri
mahsa_moayeri@spe.sony.com

Pete Corral
imdb.com/name/nm0180707

DeVon Franklin
imdb.com/name/nm2035952

Andy Given
imdb.com/name/nm0321429

Jonathan Kadin
imdb.com/name/nm2142367
Assistant: Ashley Johnson
ashley_johnson@spe.sony.com

Rachel O'Connor
imdb.com/name/nm1471418

Lauren Abrahams
imdb.com/name/nm1036268

Debra Bergman
imdb.com/name/nm2984630

Adam Moos
imdb.com/name/nm0602149

COMEDY ARTS STUDIOS

2500 Broadway
Santa Monica, CA 90404
310-382-3677 (phone)
310-382-3170 (fax)

imdb.com/company/co0220109

Accepts query letter from unproduced, unrepresented writers. Project types include TV. Preferred genres include Comedy and Drama.

Stu Smiley
imdb.com/name/nm0806979

COMPANY 3

1661 Lincoln Blvd., Suite 400
Santa Monica, CA 90404
310-255-6600

company3.com
facebook.com/Company3
twitter.com/Company3
imdb.com/company/co0028470
linkedin.com/company/company-3

Does not accept any unsolicited material. Project types include Feature Films. Preferred genres include Horror.

COMPLETION FILMS

60 E 42nd St, Suite 4600
New York, NY 10165
718-693-2057 (phone)
888-693-4133 (fax)

info@completionfilms.com
completionfilms.com
imdb.com/company/co0175660

Accepts query letter from unproduced, unrepresented writers. Preferred genres include Non-Fiction.

Kisha Imani Cameron
President
imdb.com/name/nm0131650

CONCEPT ENTERTAINMENT

334 1/2 N Sierra Bonita Ave
Los Angeles, CA 90036
323-937-5700 (phone)
323-937-5720 (fax)

enquiries@conceptentertainment.biz
imdb.com/company/co0096670
conceptentertainment.biz

Accepts query letter from unproduced, unrepresented writers. Project types include TV. Preferred genres include Action, Comedy, Crime, Detective, Drama, Fantasy, Horror, Myth, Non-Fiction, Romance, Science Fiction, and Thriller.

David Faigenblum
imdb.com/name/nm1584960

CONCRETE ENTERTAINMENT

468 N Camden Dr, Suite 200
Beverly Hills, CA 90210
310-860-5611

imdb.com/company/co0182126

Does not accept any unsolicited material. Project types
include Feature Films and TV. Preferred genres
include Comedy.

Alicia Silverstone
Producer/Actress
imdb.com/name/nm0000224

Carolyn Kessler
Manager/Producer
imdb.com/name/nm0450315

CONSTANTIN FILM

9200 W Sunset Blvd, Suite 800
West Hollywood, CA 90069
310-247-0300 (phone)
310-247-0305 (fax)

Feilitzschstr. 6
Munich, Bavaria D-80802
Germany
+49-89-44-44-60-0 (phone)
+49-89-44-44-60-666 (fax)

zentrale@constantin-film.de
imdb.com/company/co0002257
constantin-film.de
facebook.com/constantinfilm

Accepts query letter from produced or represented
writers. Project types include Feature Films and TV.
Preferred genres include Action, Crime, and Thriller.
Established in 1950.

Robert Kultzer
Executive
310-247-0300 ext. 3
robert.kultzer@constantin-film.de
imdb.com/name/nm0474709

CONTENT HOUSE

3500 Overland Ave. Suite 110-16
Los Angeles, CA 90034
310-277-7701 (phone)
310-277-7708 (fax)

info@contenthousela.com
contenthousela.com
imdb.com/company/co0119743
facebook.com/contenthousela/timeline

Does not accept any unsolicited material. Project types
include Feature Films. Preferred genres include Action,
Drama, Horror, and Science Fiction.

Josh Morris
Partner/Producer/Manager

Mark Saffian
Partner/Producer/Manager
imdb.com/name/nm2948427

CONTENT MEDIA CORPORATION PLC

225 Arizona Ave, Suite #250
Santa Monica, CA 90401
310-576-1059 (phone)
310-576-1859 (fax)

19 Heddon St
London,
W1B 4BG
UK
+44 20 7851 6500 (phone)
+44 20 7851 6506 (fax)

80 Richmond St West
Toronto
Ontario M5H 2A4 CANADA
+416-360-6103 (phone)
416-360-6065 (fax)

jcassistant@contentmediacorp.com
la@contentmediacorp.com
imdb.com/company/co0366223
contentmediacorp.com

Accepts query letter from unproduced, unrepresented
writers.

Jamie Carmichael
jamie.carmichael@contentmediacorp.com
imdb.com/name/nm0138430

CONTRADICTION FILMS

3103 Neilson Way
Santa Monica, CA 90405
310-396-8558

contradictionfilms.com
imdb.com/company/co0306436

Does not accept any unsolicited material. Project types include Feature Films. Preferred genres include Horror and Thriller.

Tim Carter
Writer/Producer
imdb.com/name/nm3939975

Tomas Harlan
Producer
imdb.com/name/nm3938576

CONTRAFILM

1531 N Cahuenga Blvd
Los Angeles, CA 90028
323-467-8787 (phone)
323-467-7730 (fax)

imdb.com/company/co0128546

Accepts query letter from unproduced, unrepresented writers. Project types include Feature Films. Preferred genres include Drama, Horror, and Thriller.

Tripp Vinson
Producer
imdb.com/name/nm1246087
Assistant: Tara Farney

Alexandra Church
Creative Executive
imdb.com/name/nm0161344

Tucker Williams
Creative Executive
imdb.com/name/nm2606099

CONUNDRUM ENTERTAINMENT

325 Wilshire Blvd, Suite 201
Santa Monica, CA 90401
310-319-2800 (phone)
310-319-2808 (fax)

imdb.com/company/co0030016

Accepts scripts from produced or represented writers. Preferred genres include Comedy.

Peter Farrelly
Executive
imdb.com/name/nm0268380

Bobby Farrelly
Executive
imdb.com/name/nm0268370

COOPER'S TOWN PRODUCTIONS

302A West 12th St, Suite 214
New York, NY 10014
212-255-7566 (phone)
212-255-0211 (fax)

info@copperstownproductions.com
imdb.com/company/co0132168
copperstownproductions.com

Accepts query letter from unproduced, unrepresented writers. Project types include Feature Films. Preferred genres include Non-Fiction.

Phillip Hoffman
Partner
imdb.com/name/nm0000450

Sara Murphy
imdb.com/name/nm2072976

COQUETTE PRODUCTIONS

8105 W Third St
Los Angeles, CA 90048
323-801-1000 (phone)
323-801-1001 (fax)

imdb.com/company/co0142408

Does not accept any unsolicited material. Project types include TV. Preferred genres include Comedy, Crime, Drama, and Romance.

Thea Mann
Head of Development
imdb.com/name/nm0542996

Jeff Bowland
Executive
imdb.com/name/nm0101188

David Arquette
imdb.com/name/nm0000274

Courtney Cox
imdb.com/name/nm0001073

CORNER STORE ENTERTAINMENT

9615 Brighton Way
Ste 201
Beverly Hills, CA 90210
310-276-6400 (phone)
310-276-6410 (fax)

cornerstore-ent.com
imdb.com/company/co0223726

Does not accept any unsolicited material. Project types
include Feature Films. Preferred genres include
Comedy, Drama, and Romance.

Matthew Weaver
imdb.com/name/nm2822461

Scott Prisand
imdb.com/name/nm1964055

CORNICE ENTERTAINMENT

421 S Beverly Dr, 8th Floor
Beverly Hills, CA 90212
310-279-4080

imdb.com/company/co0094922

Does not accept any unsolicited material. Project types
include Feature Films and TV.

Michael Marcus
Producer

CORONET FILMS

736 Seward St
Los Angeles, CA 90038
323-957-3213 (phone)
323-957-5405 (fax)

coronetentertainment@gmail.com
coronetfilms.net

imdb.com/company/co0273550

Does not accept any unsolicited material. Project types
include Feature Films. Preferred genres include
Drama.

Deborah Del Prete
Producer
imdb.com/name/nm0215769

COURT FIVE

6030 Wilshire Blvd., Suite 300
Los Angeles, CA 90036
310-242-6445

information@courtfive.com
courtfive.com
facebook.com/courtfive
twitter.com/court_five
linkedin.com/company/court-five
imdb.com/company/co0242577

Does not accept any unsolicited material. Project types
include Feature Films. Preferred genres include Family
and Fantasy.

Mark Ordesky
Producer
imdb.com/name/nm0649507

Jane Fleming
Producer
imdb.com/name/nm3794057

COVENANT ROAD ENTERTAINMENT

334 4th Ave
Venice, CA 90291
310-598-3317

imdb.com/company/co0355555

Does not accept any unsolicited material. Project types
include TV.

CRAFTSMAN FILMS

4108 Riverside Dr, Suite 2
Burbank, CA 91505
818-567-0700

craftsmanfilms.com/main.html?src=%2F

imdb.com/company/co0176721
linkedin.com/company/craftsman-films

Does not accept any unsolicited material. Project types
include TV.

Kerry McCluggage
Producer
imdb.com/name/nm1394315

CRAVE FILMS

3312 Sunset Blvd
Los Angeles, CA 90026
323-669-9000 (phone)
323-669-9002 (fax)

imdb.com/company/co0146364
cravefilms.com

Does not accept any unsolicited material. Project types
include Feature Films. Preferred genres include
Drama.

David Ayer
david@cravefilms.com
imdb.com/name/nm0043742

Alex Ott
alex@cravefilms.com
imdb.com/name/nm1944773

CREANSPEAK PRODUCTIONS, LLC

120 S El Camino Dr
Beverly Hills, CA 90212
310-273-8217

info@creanspeak.com
imdb.com/company/co0097231
linkedin.com/pub/creanspeak-productions/3/a16/8ab

Accepts query letter from unproduced, unrepresented
writers via email. Project types include Feature Films,
TV, and Commercials. Preferred genres include
Action, Comedy, Drama, Family, Non-Fiction, and
Reality.

Kelly Crean
310-273-8217
info@creanspeak.com
imdb.com/name/nm1047631

Jon Freis
310-273-8217
info@creanspeak.com
imdb.com/name/nm2045371

CREATED BY

9415 Culver Blvd.
Culver City, CA 90232
424-298-2500

imdb.com/company/co0471110

Does not accept any unsolicited material. Preferred
genres include Drama, Science Fiction, and Thriller.

Ralph M. Vicinanza
President
imdb.com/name/nm2088223

Vincent Gerardis
Manager
imdb.com/name/nm1136210

CREATIVE CONTROL ENTERTAINMENT

3427 Overland Ave
Los Angeles, CA 90034
310-273-5311 (fax)

info@creativecontrolent.com
creativecontrolent.com
twitter.com/cre8ve_ctrl
imdb.com/company/co0372971
facebook.com/pages/Creative-Control/
173142216084589

Does not accept any unsolicited material. Project types
include TV. Preferred genres include Drama.

Joel C. High
President/Producer
imdb.com/name/nm0383573

CREATIVE PROJECTS GROUP

14011 Ventura Blvd. Suite 206 East
Sherman Oaks, CA 91423
818-763-0374

900 Third Ave, 20th Floor
New York, NY 10022

212-751-3001 (phone)
212-751-3113 (fax)

wnix@creativeprojectsgroup.com
creativeprojectsgroup.com
imdb.com/name/nm2773807
linkedin.com/profile/view
facebook.com/pages/Creative-Projects-Group/
139727129373379

Does not accept any unsolicited material. Project types include Feature Films. Preferred genres include Drama.

CRESCENDO PRODUCTIONS

252 N Larchmont Blvd, Suite 200
Los Angeles, CA 90004
323-465-2222 (phone)
323-464-3750 (fax)

imdb.com/company/co0025116

Accepts query letter from unproduced, unrepresented writers. Project types include Feature Films and TV. Preferred genres include Non-Fiction and Reality.

Don Cheadle
323-465-2222
imdb.com/name/nm0000332

CREST ANIMATION PRODUCTIONS, INC.

333 N Glenoaks Blvd, Suite 300
Burbank, CA 91502
818-846-0166 (phone)
818-846-6074 (fax)

info@crestcgi.com
imdb.com/company/co0218880

Accepts query letter from unproduced, unrepresented writers via email. Project types include Feature Films. Preferred genres include Animation.

Richard Rich
818-846-0166
info@crestcgi.com
imdb.com/name/nm0723704

Gregory Kasunich
818-846-0166
gkasunich@crestcgi.com
imdb.com/name/nm3215310

CRIME SCENE PICTURES

3450 Cahuenga Blvd W, Suite 701
Los Angeles, CA 90068
323-963-5136 (phone)
323-963-5137 (fax)

info@crimescenepictures.net
imdb.com/company/co0326645

Does not accept any unsolicited material. Project types include Feature Films. Established in 2010.

Brett Hedblom
Director of Development
imdb.com/name/nm3916261

Jennifer Marmor
Creative Executive
imdb.com/name/nm4420063

Adam Ripp
imdb.com/name/nm0728063

CROSS CREEK PICTURES

9220 W Sunset Blvd, Suite 100
West Hollywood, CA 90069
310-248-4061 (phone)
310-248-4068 (fax)

info@crosscreekpictures.com
crosscreekpictures.com
imdb.com/company/co0285648
facebook.com/crosscreekpictures

Does not accept any unsolicited material. Project types include Feature Films and TV. Preferred genres include Drama.

Brian Oliver
President
brian@crosscreekpicture.com
imdb.com/name/nm1003922
linkedin.com/pub/brian-oliver/3a/806/3a8

John Shepherd
Creative Executive
310-248-4061
info@crosscreekpicture.com
imdb.com/name/nm3005173
linkedin.com/pub/john-hilary-shepherd/5a/560/456

Stephanie Hall
stephanie@crosscreekpicture.com
imdb.com/name/nm24206

CROSSROADS FILMS

1722 Whitley Ave
Los Angeles, CA 90028
310-659-6220 (phone)
310-659-3105 (fax)

imdb.com/company/co0061179
crossroadsfilms.com

Accepts query letter from unproduced, unrepresented writers. Project types include Feature Films, TV, and Commercials. Preferred genres include Comedy, Crime, Drama, Romance, and Thriller.

Camille Taylor
310-659-6220
imdb.com/name/nm0852088

CRUCIAL FILMS

2220 Colorado Ave, 5th Floor
Santa Monica, CA 90404
310-865-8249 (phone)
310-865-7068 (fax)

crucialfilms.asst@gmail.com
imdb.com/company/co0049027

Does not accept any unsolicited material. Project types include Feature Films and TV. Preferred genres include Action, Comedy, Crime, Drama, Fantasy, Horror, Romance, and Thriller.

Daniel Schnider
310-865-8249
crucialfilms.asst@gmail.com
imdb.com/name/nm3045845

CRYBABY MEDIA

130 W 25th St, Suite 5C
New York, NY 10001

info@crybaby-media.com
crybaby-media.squarespace.com
twitter.com/crybabymedia
linkedin.com/company/936927
facebook.com/pages/Crybaby-Media/
    142392552443351
twitter.com/crybabymedia
linkedin.com/company/936927

Does not accept any unsolicited material. Project types include TV. Preferred genres include Drama and Reality. Established in 2014.

Alyssa Lomuscio
Editor
imdb.com/name/nm5143588
linkedin.com/pub/alyssa-lomuscio/56/589/17
facebook.com/alyssa.lomuscio

Dan Passman
Founder
imdb.com/name/nm0664908
linkedin.com/pub/danny-passman/3/779/708
facebook.com/passmand

Salil Gandhi
Legal Counsel
linkedin.com/pub/salil-gandhi/3/937/7b0

CRYSTAL LAKE ENTERTAINMENT, INC.

4420 Hayvenhurst Ave
Encino, CA 91436
818-995-1585 (phone)
818-995-1677 (fax)

sscfilms@earthlink.net
contact@crystallakeentertainment.com
imdb.com/company/co0067362
facebook.com/crystallakeent
twitter.com/clecampdirector

Accepts query letter from unproduced, unrepresented writers via email. Project types include Feature Films and TV. Preferred genres include Horror, Science Fiction, and Thriller.

Sean Cunningham
818-995-1585
sscfilms@earthlink.net
imdb.com/name/nm0192446

Geoff Garrett
818-995-1585
sscfilms@earthlink.net
imdb.com/name/nm0308117

CRYSTAL SKY PICTURES, LLC

10203 Santa Monica Blvd, 5th Floor
Los Angeles, CA 90067
310-843-0223 (phone)
310-553-9895 (fax)

info@crystalsky.com
imdb.com/company/co0004724
crystalsky.com

Accepts query letter from unproduced, unrepresented writers via email. Project types include Feature Films. Preferred genres include Action, Comedy, Crime, Drama, Family, Fantasy, Horror, Science Fiction, and Thriller.

Florent Gaglio
Executive
310-843-0223
info@crystalsky.com
imdb.com/name/nm2904382

Eric Breiman
310-843-0223
info@crystalsky.com

Steven Paul
310-843-0223
info@crystalsky.com
imdb.com/name/nm0666999

CUBEVISION

9000 W Sunset Blvd
West Hollywood, CA 90069
310-461-3490 (phone)
310-461-3491 (fax)

icecube.com
imdb.com/company/co0044714
facebook.com/IceCube

twitter.com/icecube

Accepts query letter from unproduced, unrepresented writers. Project types include Feature Films and TV. Preferred genres include Action, Animation, Comedy, Crime, Drama, Family, Non-Fiction, Reality, Romance, and Thriller.

Matt Alvarez
Partner
310-461-3490
imdb.com/name/nm0023297
Assistant: Lawtisha Fletcher

Ice Cube
310-461-3495
imdb.com/name/nm0001084
Assistant: Nancy Leiviska

CURB ENTERTAINMENT

3907 W Alameda Ave
Burbank, CA 91505
818-843-8580 (phone)
818-566-1719 (fax)

info@curbentertainment.com
curbentertainment.com
imdb.com/company/co0089886

Accepts query letter from unproduced, unrepresented writers via email. Project types include Feature Films and TV. Preferred genres include Animation, Comedy, Crime, Drama, Family, Horror, Romance, Science Fiction, and Thriller. Established in 1984.

Carole Nemoy
818-843-8580
ccurb@curb.com
imdb.com/name/nm0626002

Mona Kirton
818-843-8580
mkirton@curb.com
imdb.com/name/nm1310398

Christy Peterson
818-843-8580
cpeterson@curb.com

CYAN PICTURES

410 Park Ave, 15th Floor
New York, NY 10022
212-274-1085

info@cyanpictures.com
imdb.com/company/co0080910
linkedin.com/company/cyan-pictures

Accepts query letter from unproduced, unrepresented writers via email. Project types include Feature Films and TV. Preferred genres include Comedy, Crime, Drama, Horror, Non-Fiction, Reality, Romance, Science Fiction, and Thriller.

Alexander Burns
CFO
212-274-1085
info@cyanpictures.com

Joshua Newman
CEO
212-274-1085
newman@cyanpictures.com
imdb.com/name/nm1243333

Wes Schrader
212-274-1085
schrader@cyanpictures.com

CYPRESS FILMS, INC.

630 Ninth Ave, Suite 415
New York, NY 10036

kmoarefi@cypressfilms.com
cypressfilms.com
imdb.com/company/co0044830

Accepts query letter from unproduced, unrepresented writers via email. Project types include Feature Films. Preferred genres include Comedy, Drama, Family, Romance, and Science Fiction.

Jessica Forsythe

Jon Glascoe
212-262-3900
imdb.com/name/nm0321797

Joseph Pierson
212-262-3900
imdb.com/name/nm0682777

CYPRESS POINT PRODUCTIONS

3000 Olympic Blvd
Santa Monica, CA 90404
310-315-4787 (phone)
310-315-4785 (fax)

cppfilms@earthlink.net
imdb.com/company/co0038030

Accepts query letter from unproduced, unrepresented writers via email. Project types include TV. Preferred genres include Action, Comedy, Crime, Drama, Family, Non-Fiction, Romance, Science Fiction, and Thriller.

Gerald Abrams
Chairman
310-315-4787
cppfilms@earthlink.net
imdb.com/name/nm0009181

Michael Waldron
310-315-4787
cppfilms@earthlink.net
imdb.com/name/nm1707236

DAHLIA STREET FILMS

199 Monitor St
Brookyln, NY 11222
347-535-4746

info@dahliastreetfilms.com
dahliastreetfilms.com
imdb.com/company/co0022350

Does not accept any unsolicited material. Project types include Feature Films. Preferred genres include Comedy and Science Fiction.

Molly Mayeux
Owner/Producer
imdb.com/name/nm0562617

DAKOTA PICTURES

4633 Lankershim Blvd
North Hollywood, CA 91602
818-760-0099 (phone)
818-760-1070 (fax)

info@dakotafilms.com

dakotafilms.com
imdb.com/company/co0009221
twitter.com/dakotafilms
facebook.com/pages/Dakota-Pictures/
    154008627979358

Does not accept any unsolicited material. Project types
include Feature Films and TV. Preferred genres
include Action, Animation, Comedy, Crime, Drama,
Family, Fantasy, Non-Fiction, Reality, and Thriller.

Troy Miller
818-760-0099
info@dakotafilms.com
imdb.com/name/nm0003474

A.J. DiAntonio
818-760-0099
info@dakotafilms.com
imdb.com/name/nm1472504

Matt Magielnicki
818-760-0099
info@dakotafilms.com
imdb.com/name/nm2616148

DANCING ORANGE PRODUCTIONS

708 17th St
Santa Monica, CA 90402

Does not accept any unsolicited material. Project types
include Feature Films. Preferred genres include
Drama.

Lisa Todd
Producer
imdb.com/name/nm0865217

Jason Benesh
Producer
imdb.com/name/nm1200394

DAN GORDON PRODUCTIONS

2060-D Ave. Suite #250
Thousand Oaks , CA 91362
805-496-2566

zaki.yc.edu
imdb.com/company/co0094966

Does not accept any unsolicited material. Project types
include Feature Films and TV.

Dan Gordon
Writer/Producer
imdb.com/name/nm0330108

DANIEL L. PAULSON PRODUCTIONS

9056 Santa Monica Blvd, Suite 203A
West Hollywood, CA 90069
310-278-9747 (phone)
310-278-3751 (fax)

dlpprods@sbcglobal.net
imdb.com/company/co0034720

Does not accept any unsolicited material. Project types
include Feature Films and TV. Preferred genres
include Action, Comedy, Crime, Detective, Drama,
Family, Non-Fiction, Reality, Romance, and Thriller.

Daniel Paulson
310-278-9747
dlpprods@sbcglobal.net
imdb.com/name/nm0667340

Steve Kennedy
310-278-9747
dlpprods@sbcglobal.net
imdb.com/name/nm0448346

DANIEL OSTROFF PRODUCTIONS

2046 N Hillhurst Ave. #120
Los Angeles, CA 90027
323-284-8824

oteamthe@gmail.com
imdb.com/company/co0138101

Accepts query letter from unproduced, unrepresented
writers. Project types include Feature Films and TV.
Preferred genres include Comedy, Detective, Non-
Fiction, and Reality.

Daniel Ostroff
Producer
323-284-8824
oteamthe@gmail.com
imdb.com/name/nm0652491
linkedin.com/pub/daniel-ostroff/6/856/28a

DANIEL PETRIE JR. & COMPANY

18034 Ventura Blvd, Suite 445
Encino, CA 91316
818-708-1602 (phone)
818-774-0345 (fax)

imdb.com/company/co0120842

Accepts query letter from unproduced, unrepresented writers. Project types include Feature Films and TV. Preferred genres include Action, Comedy, Crime, Detective, Drama, Horror, Romance, Science Fiction, and Thriller.

Daniel Petrie,
818-708-1602
imdb.com/name/nm0677943

Rick Dugdale
818-708-1602
imdb.com/name/nm1067987

DANIEL SLADEK ENTERTAINMENT CORPORATION

8306 Wilshire Blvd, Suite 510
Beverly Hills, CA 90211
323-934-9268 (phone)
323-934-7362 (fax)

danielsladek@mac.com
danielsladek.com

Does not accept any unsolicited material. Project types include Feature Films and TV. Preferred genres include Action, Comedy, Crime, Drama, Fantasy, Horror, Non-Fiction, Reality, Romance, Science Fiction, and Thriller. Established in 1998.

Daniel Sladek
Talent Manager
323-934-9268
danielsladek@mac.com
imdb.com/name/nm0805202

DANJAQ PRODUCTIONS

2400 Broadway
Ste 310
Santa Monica, CA 90404
310-449-3185

imdb.com/company/co0024134

Does not accept any unsolicited material. Project types include Feature Films. Preferred genres include Action.

David Pope
CEO
310-449-3185
imdb.com/name/nm0691102

Michael Wilson
President
310-449-3185
imdb.com/name/nm0933865

Barbara Broccoli
imdb.com/name/nm0110483

DAN LUPOVITZ PRODUCTIONS

936 Alandele Ave
Los Angeles, CA 90036
323-930-0769 (phone)
310-385-0196 (fax)

dlupovitz@aol.com
imdb.com/company/co0027986

Accepts query letter from unproduced, unrepresented writers via email. Project types include Feature Films and TV. Preferred genres include Comedy, Drama, and Romance.

Randy Albelda
323-930-0769

Dan Lupovitz
323-930-0769
dlupovitz@aol.com
imdb.com/name/nm0526991

DAN WINGUTOW PRODUCTIONS

534 Laguardia Pl., Suite 3
New York, NY 10012
212-477-1328 (phone)
212-254-6902 (fax)

imdb.com/company/co0018565

Accepts query letter from unproduced, unrepresented writers. Project types include Feature Films and TV. Preferred genres include Comedy, Crime, Drama,

Fantasy, Horror, Romance, Science Fiction, and Thriller.

Dan Wigutow
Executive Producer
212-477-1328
imdb.com/name/nm0927887

Caroline Moore
212-477-1328
imdb.com/name/nm0601006

DARIUS FILMS INCORPORATED

9255 Sunset Blvd
Suite 1100
Los Angeles, CA 90069
310-728-1342 (phone)
310-494-0575 (fax)

349 Carlaw Ave
Suite 204
Toronto, ON M4M 2T1
416-922-0007 (phone)
416-406-0034 (fax)

info@dariusfilms.com
imdb.com/company/co0133523
dariusfilms.com

Accepts query letter from produced or represented writers. Project types include Feature Films and TV. Preferred genres include Comedy, Crime, Detective, Drama, Fantasy, Non-Fiction, Romance, Science Fiction, and Thriller.

Nicholas Tabarrok
310-728-1342
info@dariusfilms.com
imdb.com/name/nm0002431

Daniel Baruela
310-728-1342
info@dariusfilms.com
imdb.com/name/nm3758990

DARK ARTS

65 Eckford St, Suite 4
Brooklyn, NY 11222

info@darkartsfilm.com
darkartsfilm.com

imdb.com/company/co0422626

Does not accept any unsolicited material. Project types include Feature Films. Preferred genres include Comedy.

Alicia Van Couvering
Producer
imdb.com/name/nm0885900

Andrea Roa
Producer
imdb.com/name/nm1978398

DARK CASTLE ENTERTAINMENT

1601 Main St
Venice, CA 90291
310-566-6100 (phone)
310-566-6188 (fax)

imdb.com/company/co0050870

Accepts query letter from produced or represented writers. Project types include Feature Films. Preferred genres include Action, Crime, Drama, Horror, and Thriller. Established in 1999.

Joel Silver
Partner
imdb.com/name/nm0005428

Steve Richards
imdb.com/name/nm0724345

Andrew Rona
imdb.com/name/nm0739868
Assistant: Dash Boam

DARK HORSE ENTERTAINMENT

12711 Ventura Blvd.
Suite 270
Studio City, CA 91604
323-655-3600 (phone)
323-655-2430 (fax)

dhentertainment.com
imdb.com/company/co0020061
facebook.com/darkhorsecomics
twitter.com/darkhorsecomics

Does not accept any unsolicited material. Project types include Feature Films. Preferred genres include Action,

Animation, Comedy, Crime, Drama, Family, Fantasy, Horror, Non-Fiction, Romance, Science Fiction, and Thriller.

Mike Richardson
323-655-3600
miker@darkhorse.com
imdb.com/name/nm0724700
Assistant: Pete Cacioppo

Keith Goldberg
323-655-3600
keithg@darkhorse.com
imdb.com/name/nm1378991

DARKO ENTERTAINMENT

7164 Melrose Ave.
2nd Floor
Los Angeles, CA 90046
323-592-3460 (phone)
323-850-2481 (fax)

info@darko.com
darko.com
imdb.com/company/co0118694
facebook.com/pages/Darko-Entertainment/
    184834071562799
twitter.com/darko_ent

Does not accept any unsolicited material. Project types include Feature Films and TV. Preferred genres include Fantasy, Horror, and Thriller.

Jeff Cullota
imdb.com/name/nm2261214

DARK SKY FILMS

16101 S 108th Ave
Orland Park, IL 60467
800-323-0442

info@darkskyfilms.com
darkskyfilms.com
twitter.com/darkskyfilms
facebook.com/DarkSkyFilms

Does not accept any unsolicited material. Project types include Feature Films. Preferred genres include Horror and Thriller.

Malik Ali
Executive
imdb.com/name/nm0019446

Greg Newman
Executive
imdb.com/name/nm0628103

Todd Wieneke
Producer
imdb.com/name/nm2663562

DARK TOY ENTERTAINMENT

3800 Barham Blvd. Suite 207
Los Angeles, CA 90068

imdb.com/company/co0317488

Does not accept any unsolicited material. Project types include TV. Preferred genres include Comedy and Drama.

Todd Holland
Producer
imdb.com/name/nm0390844

DARKWOODS PRODUCTIONS

301 E Colorado Blvd, Suite 705
Pasadena, CA 91101
323-454-4580 (phone)
323-454-4581 (fax)

imdb.com/company/co0029398
twitter.com/AMC_TV
facebook.com/amc
http//www.darkwoodsproductions.com

Does not accept any unsolicited material. Project types include Feature Films. Preferred genres include Comedy, Crime, Drama, Fantasy, Horror, Non-Fiction, Romance, Science Fiction, and Thriller.

Frank Darobont
323-454-4582
imdb.com/name/nm0001104
Assistant: Alex Whit

DARREN STAR PRODUCTIONS

9200 Sunset Blvd, Suite 430
Los Angeles, CA 90069

310-274-2145 (phone)
310-274-1455 (fax)

d.star.prodco@gmail.com
imdb.com/company/co0020963

Accepts query letter from unproduced, unrepresented writers. Project types include Feature Films and TV. Preferred genres include Comedy, Crime, Drama, Non-Fiction, and Romance.

Darren Star
310-274-2145
imdb.com/name/nm0823015

Charles Pugliese
310-274-2145
imdb.com/name/nm1551399

DAVE BELL ASSOCIATES

3211 Cahuenga Blvd West
Los Angeles, CA 90068
323-851-7801 (phone)
323-851-9349 (fax)

dbamovies@aol.com
imdb.com/company/co0033679

Accepts query letter from unproduced, unrepresented writers via email. Project types include Feature Films and TV. Preferred genres include Drama, Family, Horror, Non-Fiction, Reality, Romance, and Science Fiction.

Ted Weiant
323-851-7801
dbamovies@aol.com
imdb.com/name/nm1059707

Dave Bell
President
323-851-7801
dbamovies@aol.com
imdb.com/name/nm1037012

Fred Putman
323-851-7801
imdb.com/name/nm1729656

DAVID EICK PRODUCTIONS

100 Universal City Plaza
Universal City, CA 91608
818-501-0146 (phone)
818-733-2522 (fax)

imdb.com/company/co0176813

Accepts query letter from unproduced, unrepresented writers. Project types include TV. Preferred genres include Action, Drama, Science Fiction, and Thriller.

David Eick
President
818-501-0146
imdb.com/name/nm0251594

Stephanie Stanley
Writer's Assistant
linkedin.com/pub/stephanie-stanley/40/491/b01

DAVID E. KELLEY PRODUCTIONS

1600 Rosecrans Ave., Bldg. 4B
Manhattan Beach , CA 90266
310-727-2200

imdb.com/company/co0050201

Does not accept any unsolicited material. Project types include Feature Films and TV. Preferred genres include Drama.

Robert Breeech
President of Development
imdb.com/name/nm010666

David E. Kelley
CEO/Writer/Producer
imdb.com/name/nm0005082

DAVIS ENTERTAINMENT

10201 W Pico Blvd
31-301
Los Angeles, CA 90064
310-556-3550 (phone)
310-556-3688 (fax)

150 S. Barrington Place
Los Angeles, CA 90049

imdb.com/company/co0022730

Accepts scripts from produced or represented writers.

John Davis
imdb.com/name/nm0204862

John Fox
imdb.com/name/nm2470810

DAYBREAK PRODUCTIONS

3000 W. Olympic Blvd. Bldge 5
Santa Monica, CA 90404
310-264-4202 (phone)
310-264-4222 (fax)

imdb.com/company/co0030602

Does not accept any unsolicited material. Project types include Feature Films and TV.

Charles Gordon
Producer
imdb.com/name/nm0330077

James Abraham
Development
imdb.com/name/nm1673506

DCI-LOS ANGELES

2001 Wilshire Blvd., Suite 600
Santa Monica, CA 90403
310-586-5600 (phone)
310-586-5898 (fax)

dentsuentertainment.com
imdb.com/company/co0293867

Does not accept any unsolicited material. Project types include TV. Preferred genres include Science Fiction.

DEED FILMS

419-685-4842

sdonely@deedfilms.com
imdb.com/company/co0323092
deedfilms.com

Accepts query letter from unproduced, unrepresented writers via email. Project types include Feature Films. Preferred genres include Comedy and Crime. Established in 2008.

Scott Donley
President
imdb.com/name/nm4238094

DEEDLE-DEE PRODUCTIONS

1875 Century Park East
Los Angeles, CA 90025

imdb.com/company/co0093771

Does not accept any unsolicited material. Project types include TV. Preferred genres include Comedy.

Greg Daniels
Writer/Producer
imdb.com/name/nm0199939

DEERJEN FILMS

222 W 23rd St
New York, NY 10011

deerjen.com
imdb.com/company/co0190929
imdb.com/company/co0190929

Accepts query letter from produced or represented writers. Project types include Feature Films. Preferred genres include Comedy, Drama, Period, Romance, and Thriller.

Jen Gatien
Producer
jen@deerjen.com
imdb.com/name/nm0309684

DEFIANCE ENTERTAINMENT

6605 Hollywood Blvd, Suite 100
Los Angeles, CA 91401
323-393-0132

info@defiance-ent.com
imdb.com/company/co0236811

Accepts query letter from unproduced, unrepresented writers via email. Project types include Feature Films, TV, and Commercials. Preferred genres include Action, Comedy, Crime, Drama, Fantasy, Horror, Myth, Science Fiction, and Thriller. Established in 2006.

Clare Kramer
COO
clare@defiance-ent.com
imdb.com/name/nm0004456

Brian Keathley
brian@defiance-ent.com
imdb.com/name/nm0444080

DEFIANT PICTUREHOUSE

Los Angeles, CA

defiant@defiantfilmhaus.com
twitter.com/titanpicturesme
defiantfilmhaus.com

Does not accept any unsolicited material. Project types include Feature Films and Short Films. Preferred genres include Drama. Established in 2013.

Aaron Jackson
Producer
imdb.com/name/nm2980930
linkedin.com/pub/aaron-jackson/13/99b/611
facebook.com/aaronthejack

DE FINA PRODUCTIONS

443 Greenwich St, 5th Floor
New York, NY 10013
212-219-1525 (phone)
212-219-1859 (fax)

imdb.com/company/co0276457

Does not accept any unsolicited material. Project types include Feature Films. Preferred genres include Thriller.

Barbara De Fina
Principal, Producer
imdb.com/name/nm0208381

Sarah Feinberg
Head
imdb.com/name/nm5963270

DE LINE PICTURES

4000 Warner Blvd Building 66, Room 147
Burbank, CA 91522

818-954-5200 (phone)
818-954-5430 (fax)

imdb.com/company/co0033149

Does not accept any unsolicited material. Project types include Feature Films. Preferred genres include Action, Animation, Comedy, Crime, Drama, Family, Fantasy, Period, Romance, Science Fiction, and Thriller. Established in 2001.

Donald De Line
President
imdb.com/name/nm0209773
Assistant: Matt Gamboa matt@delinepictures.com

Jacob Robinson
imdb.com/name/nm1563784

DEL TORO PRODUCTIONS

1000 Flower St
Glendale, CA 91201
818-695-6363

imdb.com/company/co0247699

Does not accept any unsolicited material. Project types include Feature Films and TV. Preferred genres include Crime, Drama, Horror, and Thriller.

Guillermo del Toro
Producer/Director
imdb.com/name/nm0868219

DELVE FILMS

20727 High Desert Ct
Suite 4+5
Bend, OR 97701
424-703-3583

info@delvefilms.com
delvefilms.com
imdb.com/company/co0315636

Accepts query letter from produced or represented writers. Project types include Feature Films. Preferred genres include Comedy, Documentary, Drama, Fantasy, Romance, and Thriller.

Isaac Testerman
President
isaac@delvefilms.com
imdb.com/name/nm4107099

Nate Salciccioli
541-788-6139
nate@delvefilms.com
imdb.com/name/nm4244606

DEMAREST FILMS

100 N Crescent Dr
Suite 350
Beverly Hills, CA 90210
310-385-4310

imdb.com/company/co0317576

Does not accept any unsolicited material. Project types include Feature Films and TV. Preferred genres include Comedy, Crime, Drama, Fantasy, and Thriller.

Sam Englebardt
imdb.com/name/nm1583132
Assistant: Linda Goetz

Brian Flanagan

William D. Johnso
imdb.com/name/nm4207924

Michael Lambert
imdb.com/name/nm2236003

DEON TAYLOR ENTERPRISES

320 N 10th St, Suite E
Sacramento, CA 95811
United States
916-448-2388

info@deontaylorenterprises.com
deontaylorenterprises.com

Does not accept any unsolicited material. Project types include Feature Films. Preferred genres include Horror.

Deon Taylor
Producer/Writer/Director

DE PASSE ENTERTAINMENT

9200 Sunset Blvd., Suite 510
West Hollywood, CA 90069
310-858-3734

imdb.com/company/co0063390

Does not accept any unsolicited material. Project types include Feature Films and TV. Preferred genres include Drama.

Rose Caraet
Creative Affairs
imdb.com/name/nm1122044

Suzanne de Passe
Producer
imdb.com/name/nm0210867

DEPTH OF FIELD

1724 Whitley Ave
Los Angeles, CA 90028
323-466-6500 (phone)
323-466-6501 (fax)

imdb.com/company/co0113177

Accepts scripts from produced or represented writers. Project types include Feature Films.

Andrew Miano
Executive Producer
imdb.com/name/nm0583948

Chris Weitz
imdb.com/name/nm0919363

DESERT WIND FILMS

13603 Marina Pointe Dr
Ste D529
Marina Del Rey, CA 90292
310-437-0740 (phone)
310-499-5254 (fax)

media@desertwindfilms.com
info@desertwindstudios.com
desertwindfilms.com
facebook.com/pages/Desert-Wind-Films/
489420855503
imdb.com/company/co0298614

Accepts query letter from unproduced, unrepresented writers. Project types include Feature Films.

T.J. Amato
President
imdb.com/name/nm2125600

Steven Camp
CFO
imdb.com/name/nm3823972

Danny Amato
imdb.com/name/nm3824734

Jeffrey James Ward
imdb.com/name/nm3823932

Josh Mills
imdb.com/name/nm1836231

DESTINY PICTURES

destiny@destinypictures.biz
destinypictures.biz
imdb.com/company/co0176808
facebook.com/pages/Destiny-Pictures/
    185479521464859

Accepts query letter from unproduced, unrepresented writers via email. Preferred genres include Drama, Non-Fiction, and Thriller.

Christine Redlin
Executive Producer
linkedin.com/pub/christine-redlin/1/24b/502
twitter.com/ChristineRedlin

Mark Castaldo
Founder
imdb.com/name/nm0144431
linkedin.com/pub/mark-castaldo/6/966/90b
facebook.com/markcastaldoproducer

DEUCE THREE PRODUCTIONS

1041 N Formosa Ave., Santa Monica Building
Los Angeles, CA 90046

imdb.com/company/co0086846

Does not accept any unsolicited material. Project types include Feature Films. Preferred genres include Drama.

Carol Fenelon
Partner/Producer
imdb.com/name/nm0271770

Curtis Hanson
Partner/Producer/Director
imdb.com/name/nm0000436

DEVAN CLAN PRODUCTIONS

Los Angeles, CA
818-732-9902

devanclan5@gmail.com
imdb.com/company/co0475409
facebook.com/devanclanproductions
devanclan.com
twitter.com/devanclan

Does not accept any unsolicited material. Project types include Feature Films. Preferred genres include Drama and Thriller. Established in 2014.

Kim Williams
Producer

Dylan Matlock
Producer

George Troester

Jason DeVan
CEO
imdb.com/name/nm1755962

Heather DeVan
CEO
imdb.com/name/nm2860951

DEVIANT FILM

6715 Hollywood Blvd., Suite 103
Hollywood, CA 90028
323-839-1345

info@deviantfilm.com

Does not accept any unsolicited material. Project types include Feature Films. Preferred genres include Comedy and Drama.

Tim Peternel
Producer

David Hillary
Producer
imdb.com/name/nm0975187

DFZ PRODUCTIONS

9465 Wilshire Blvd., Suite 920
Beverly Hills, CA 90212
310-274-5735

imdb.com/company/co0013073

Does not accept any unsolicited material. Project types
include Feature Films.

Dean Zanuck
Producer
imdb.com/name/nm0953124

DI BONAVENTURA PICTURES

5555 Melrose Ave
DeMille Building, 2nd Floor
Los Angeles, CA 90038
323-956-5454 (phone)
323-862-2288 (fax)

imdb.com/company/co0117723

Does not accept any unsolicited material. Project types
include Feature Films. Preferred genres include Action,
Fantasy, Science Fiction, and Thriller.

Lorenzo di Bonaventura
President
imdb.com/name/nm0225146

David Ready
VP (Executive)
imdb.com/name/nm2819401

Mark Vahradian
President of Production
(Executive)http://www.imdb.com/name/nm1680607/
imdb.com/name/nm1680607

Edward Fee
Director of Development
imdb.com/name/nm1825537

Erik Howsam
Senior Vice-President Production
imdb.com/name/nm1857184

DI BONAVENTURA PICTURES TELEVISION

500 S Buena Vista St Animation Building, Suite 3F-3
Burbank, CA 91521

imdb.com/company/co0341152

Does not accept any unsolicited material. Project types
include TV. Preferred genres include Drama, Science
Fiction, and Thriller. Established in 2011.

Lorenzo di Bonaventura
Partner
imdb.com/name/nm0225146
Assistant: Elizabeth Kiernan

Dan McDermott
Partner
imdb.com/name/nm1908145

DIC ENTERTAINMENT

4100 W. Alamdea Ave, 4th Floor
Burbank, CA 91502
818-955-5400 (phone)
818-955-5696 (fax)

info@dicentertainment.com
dicentertainment.com
imdb.com/company/co0112669

Does not accept any unsolicited material.

DIFFERENT DUCK FILMS

18 Wardell Ave.,
Rumson, NJ 07760

differentduckfilms@hotmail.com
imdb.com/company/co0215662

Does not accept any unsolicited material. Project types
include Feature Films. Preferred genres include
Comedy, Drama, Family, Fantasy, and Thriller.

Rob Margolies
imdb.com/name/nm1827689

DIGITAL DOMAIN FILMS

300 Rose Ave
Venica, CA 90291

310-314-2800 (phone)
310-664-2701 (fax)

digitaldomain.com

Does not accept any unsolicited material. Project types include Feature Films.

Mark Miller
President & CEO
imdb.com/name/nm0588903

DIGNITY FILM FINANCE

22647 Ventura Blvd, Suite 1004
Woodland Hills, CA 91364
818-436-2410

info@dignity-distribution.com
dignity-distribution.com
imdb.com/company/co0381376

Does not accept any unsolicited material. Project types include Feature Films.

Chris Heltzel
Creative Executive
imdb.com/name/nm3810728

Maggie Monteith
President/CEO
imdb.com/name/nm1803406

DIMENSION FILMS

99 Hudson St
4th Floor
New York, NY 10013
212-845-8600

9100 Wilshire Blvd.
Suite 700W
Beverly Hills, CA 90212
424-204-4800

weinsteinco.com
imdb.com/company/co0019626
twitter.com/WeinsteinFilms
facebook.com/weinsteinco

Does not accept any unsolicited material. Project types include Feature Films. Preferred genres include Action, Comedy, Horror, Science Fiction, and Thriller.

Bob Weinstein
imdb.com/name/nm0918424

Jeff Maynard
imdb.com/name/nm0963230

Matthew Signer
imdb.com/name/nm1529449

DINO DE LAURENTIIS COMPANY

100 Universal City Plaza Bungalow 5195
Universal City, CA 91608
818-777-2111 (phone)
818-886-5566 (fax)

ddlcoffice@ddlc.net
ddlc.net
imdb.com/company/co0014380
twitter.com/DeLaurentiisCo
facebook.com/DeLaurentiisCo

Does not accept any unsolicited material. Project types include Feature Films and TV. Preferred genres include Action, Crime, Detective, Drama, Horror, Romance, Science Fiction, and Thriller.

Martha De Laurentiis
President
imdb.com/name/nm0776646

Lorenzo De Maio
imdb.com/name/nm1298951

Stuart Boros
imdb.com/name/nm0097214

Bobby Gonzales
imdb.com/name/nm5260285

Meryl Pestano
imdb.com/name/nm2535378

DINOVI PICTURES

720 Wilshire Blvd, Suite 300
Santa Monica, CA 90401
310-458-7200 (phone)
310-458-7211 (fax)

imdb.com/company/co0062957

Accepts scripts from produced or represented writers. Project types include Feature Films. Preferred genres include Drama and Romance. Established in 1993.

Alison Greenspan
President
imdb.com/name/nm1327019
Assistant: Rebecca Rajkowski

Denise Di Novi
Producer
imdb.com/name/nm0224145
Assistant: Maureen Poon Fear

DI NOVI PICTURES

720 Wilshire Blvd., Suite 300
Santa Monica , CA 90401
310-458-7200 (phone)
310-458-7211 (fax)

imdb.com/company/co0062957

Does not accept any unsolicited material. Project types include Feature Films and TV. Preferred genres include Action, Drama, Fantasy, Romance, and Sociocultural.

Denise Di Novi
Producer
imdb.com/name/nm0224145

Alison Greenspan
President/Producer
imdb.com/name/nm1327019

DISCOVERY STUDIOS

962 N. La Cienega Blvd.
Los Angeles, CA 90069
310-734-3400

1 Discovery Place
Silver Spring, MD 20910
240-662-2000 (phone)
301-272-1529 (fax)

discoverystudios.com
imdb.com/company/co0225759

Does not accept any unsolicited material. Project types include TV.

DISTANT HORIZON

519 Bainum Dr
Los Angeles, CA 90290
310-455-0759 (phone)
323-848-4144 (fax)

28 Vernon Dr
Stanmore
Middlesex
Hat 7 2bt
United Kingdom
44 0 20 8861 5500 (phone)
44208-861-4411 (fax)

la@distant-horizon.com
distant-horizon.com
imdb.com/company/co0037852

Does not accept any unsolicited material. Project types include Feature Films and TV. Preferred genres include Action, Drama, and Thriller.

Brian Cox
Producer
imdb.com/name/nm0004051

Anant Singh
Producer
imdb.com/name/nm0802081

DIVIDE PICTURES

11601 W Pico Blvd
Los Angeles, CA 90064
310-473-1213

info@dividepictures.com
dividepictures.com
imdb.com/company/co0178545

Does not accept any unsolicited material. Project types include Feature Films and TV. Preferred genres include Comedy and Drama.

Russ Cundiff
Executive Producer
imdb.com/name/nm0192096

Milo Ventimiglia
Actor/Executive Producer
imdb.com/name/nm0893257

DJ2 ENTERTAINMENT

612 Santa Monica Blvd.
Santa Monica, CA 90401
424-777-6603

contact@dj2.co
dj2.co
imdb.com/company/co0339509

Does not accept any unsolicited material. Project types include Feature Films. Preferred genres include Action and Science Fiction.

Dmitri Johnson
Producer

Dan Jevons
Producer

DLT ENTERTAINMENT

124 E 55th St
New York, NY 10022
212-245-4680 (phone)
212-315-1132 (fax)

UK Headquarters
10 Bedford Square
London England WC1B 3RA
44 020 7631-1184 (phone)
44 020 7636-4571 (fax)

dltentertainment.com
imdb.com/company/co0111885

Does not accept any unsolicited material. Project types include TV. Preferred genres include Comedy and Drama.

Don Taffner Jr.
Head
imdb.com/name/nm0846397

D-MENTED ENTERTAINMENT

1635 N Cahuenga Blvd.
Los Angeles, CA 90028
323-860-1572 (phone)
323-860-1574 (fax)

d-mented3d.com

Does not accept any unsolicited material. Project types include Feature Films. Preferred genres include Horror.

Carter Reese
Partner
imdb.com/name/nm4490803

Dave Phillips
Partner
imdb.com/name/nm1707109

DMG ENTERTAINMENT

No.466 Xietu Rd,
Luwan District,
Shanghai, China
0086-010-53027711 (phone)
0086-010-53012820 (fax)

Level 25, Tower A
26 Chaoyangmenwai St,
Beijing, China
0086-010-85653333 (phone)
0086-010-85653555 (fax)

info@dmg-entertainment.com
imdb.com/company/co0338904
linkedin.com/pub/dmg-dmg/12/11b/2b9
dmg-entertainment.com

Accepts query letter from unproduced, unrepresented writers. Project types include Feature Films and TV. Preferred genres include Action, Comedy, Drama, Horror, Romance, Science Fiction, and Thriller.

Chris Cowles
Producer
imdb.com/name/nm1038319
facebook.com/chris.cowles.397

DM PRODUCTIONS

10201 W. Pico Blvd., Bldg. 12
Los Angeles, CA 90035
310-455-5526

imdb.com/company/co0325060

Does not accept any unsolicited material. Project types include Feature Films. Preferred genres include Drama, Romance, and Thriller.

David Matalon
Producer
imdb.com/name/nm0558061

DNA FILMS

10 Amwell St
London EC1R 1UQ
+44 020-7843-4410 (phone)
+44 020-7843-4411 (fax)

info@dnafilms.com
dnafilms.com
imdb.com/company/co0103974

Does not accept any unsolicited material. Project types include Feature Films. Preferred genres include Comedy, Crime, Drama, Horror, Romance, and Thriller. Established in 1999.

Andrew Macdonald
Partner
+44 020 7843 4410
imdb.com/name/nm0531602

Allon Reich
Partner
+44 020 7843 4410
imdb.com/name/nm0716924

DOBRE FILMS

310-926-6439

dobrefilms@dobrefilms.com
dobrefilms.com
imdb.com/company/co0251623
twitter.com/DobreFilms

Accepts scripts from unproduced, unrepresented writers. Project types include Feature Films and TV. Preferred genres include Action, Comedy, Crime, Detective, Drama, Fantasy, Horror, Myth, Romance, and Science Fiction.

Christopher D'Elia
Producer
310-926-6439
cdelia@dobrefilms.com
imdb.com/name/nm3179988

Michael Klein
Producer
323-510-0818
mklein@dobrefilms.com
imdb.com/name/nm3180840

DOLPHIN ENTERTAINMENT

804 S Douglas Rd, Suite 365
Miami, FL 33134
305-774-0407

dolphinentertainment.com
imdb.com/company/co0061061

Does not accept any unsolicited material. Project types include Feature Films and TV. Preferred genres include Action and Science Fiction.

Sarah Soboleski
SVP
imdb.com/name/nm1274279

Bill O'Dowd
President/Producer
imdb.com/name/nm1199803

DOMINANT PICTURES

5750 Wilshire Blvd., 5th Floor
Los Angeles, CA 90036
323-850-1340

Does not accept any unsolicited material. Project types include Feature Films and TV. Preferred genres include Comedy.

Betty Thomas
Director/Producer
imdb.com/name/nm0858525

DONNERS' COMPANY

9465 Wilshire Blvd
Ste 430
Beverly Hills, CA 90212
310-777-4600 (phone)
310-777-4610 (fax)

imdb.com/company/co0001946

Does not accept any unsolicited material. Project types include Feature Films. Preferred genres include Action, Fantasy, and Science Fiction.

Richard Donner
Principle
imdb.com/name/nm0001149

Drew Cooke
Director of Development

DOODLE FILMS

9255 Sunset Blvd., Suite 600
West Hollywood, CA 90069

doodlefilms.net
imdb.com/title/tt0225544

Does not accept any unsolicited material. Project types include Feature Films. Preferred genres include Drama.

DOOR 24 ENTERTAINMENT

115 W 29th St, Suite 1102
New York, NY 10001

Does not accept any unsolicited material. Project types include Feature Films.

Jill McGrath
Producer/Manager
imdb.com/name/nm0569814

Rebecca Atwood
Producer/Manager
imdb.com/name/nm2344105

DOOZER PRODUCTIONS

9336 W Washington Blvd., Bldg. K
Culver City, CA 90232
310-202-3566

Does not accept any unsolicited material. Project types include TV. Preferred genres include Comedy.

Bill Lawrence
Producer
imdb.com/name/nm0492639

Jeff Ingold
President/Executive Producer
imdb.com/name/nm1264835

DOS TONTOS

10201 W. Pico Blvd.
Los Angeles, CA 90035
310-369-8701

imdb.com/company/co0265100

Does not accept any unsolicited material. Project types include Feature Films. Preferred genres include Comedy.

Michael Aguila
Partner/Producer

DOUBLE DUTCH PRODUCTIONS

8033 W. Sunset Blvd., Suite 852
Los Angeles, CA 90046
310-858-5581

doubledutchproductions.biz
imdb.com/company/co0147245

Does not accept any unsolicited material. Project types include Feature Films. Preferred genres include Drama.

Jim Evering
Writer/Producer
imdb.com/name/nm026342

David LaCour Simien
Development/Producer
imdb.com/name/nm1427504

DOUBLE EDGE ENTERTAINMENT

12228 Venice Blvd, Suite 499
Los Angeles, CA 90066
310-882-5502 (phone)
310-606-2088 (fax)

inquiry@deegroup.com
doubleedgeentertainment.com

Does not accept any unsolicited material. Project types include Feature Films. Preferred genres include Horror.

DOUBLE ENTENTE FILMS

1041 N Formosa Ave, Pickford Bldg. #204
Los Angeles, CA 90046
323-782-1363

3, Rue Alfred Dehodencq
75116 Paris France
336-09-94-06-59

info@doubleententefilms.com
doubleententefilms.com
imdb.com/company/co0200552

Does not accept any unsolicited material. Project types include Feature Films.

Bailey Kobe
Writer/Director
imdb.com/name/nm1054636

Frederic Imbert
Producer
imdb.com/name/nm0408124

DOUBLE FEATURE FILMS

8425 W 3rd St.
Suite 201
Los Angeles, CA 90048
310-887-1100

dffproducerdesk@gmail.com
imdb.com/company/co0118437
twitter.com/_ericx13
facebook.com/pages/Double-Feature/18081094353

Does not accept any unsolicited material. Project types include Feature Films. Preferred genres include Action, Comedy, Drama, Fantasy, Myth, and Thriller. Established in 2005.

Ameet Shukla
Creative Executive
imdb.com/name/nm2627415

Michael Shamberg
imdb.com/name/nm0787834

Stacey Sher
imdb.com/name/nm0792049

Taylor Latham
imdb.com/name/nm2281897

DOUBLE NICKEL ENTERTAINMENT

234 W 138th St
New York, NY 10030
646-435-4390 (phone)
212-694-6205 (fax)

311 N. Robertson Blvd.
Suite 385
Beverly Hills, CA 90211

admin@doublenickelentertainment.com
doublenickelentertainment.com
imdb.com/company/co0112616

Accepts query letter from unproduced, unrepresented writers via email. Project types include Feature Films. Preferred genres include Drama.

Jenette Kahn
imdb.com/name/nm1986495

Adam Richman
imdb.com/name/nm0725013

Adam Callan
Creative Executive
imdb.com/name/nm2565555

DREAM BALLOON PRODUCTIONS

1000 Universal Studios Plaza Backlot Building # 22A
Orlando, FL 32819
407-224-6809 (phone)
407-224-5171 (fax)

Dream Balloon Animation Studio
5750 Major Blvd.; Ste. 510
Orlando, FL 32819
407-704-7914 (phone)
407-704-7916 (fax)

mattardi@dbastudios.com
dbestudios.com
dreamballoon.wordpress.com

Does not accept any unsolicited material. Project types include Feature Films. Preferred genres include Comedy and Family.

Michael Attardi
Director/Producer
imdb.com/name/nm2558815

DREAMBRIDGE FILMS

207 W 25th St
6th Floor
New York, NY 10001
323-927-1907 (phone)
323-927-1907 (fax)

dreambridgefilms.com
imdb.com/company/co0248660

Accepts query letter from unproduced, unrepresented writers. Project types include Feature Films. Preferred genres include Comedy, Drama, and Family.

Todd J. Labarowski
CEO/Founder
todd27@mac.com
imdb.com/name/nm1132640

DREAM MERCHANT 21 ENTERTAINMENT

1416 N. La Brea Ave.
Hollywood, CA 90028
323-802-1874

imdb.com/company/co0203107

Does not accept any unsolicited material. Project types include TV.

Randy Jackson
Producer
imdb.com/name/nm1193098

DREAMWORKS ANIMATION

1000 Flower St
Glendale, CA 91201
818-695-5000 (phone)
818-695-3510 (fax)

dreamworksanimation.com
imdb.com/company/co0129164

Does not accept any unsolicited material. Project types include Feature Films, Short Films, TV, and Video Games. Preferred genres include Action, Animation, Comedy, Documentary, Family, Fantasy, Horror, and Science Fiction. Established in 2004.

Suzanne Buirgy
Production Executive
imdb.com/name/nm1330174

Gregg Taylor
Head of Development
Assistant: Diana Theobald
Diana.Theobald@dreamworks.com

Kyle Arthur Jefferson
Director
imdb.com/name/nm2200868

Ben Cawood
Creative Executive
imdb.com/name/nm1374730

Bill Damaschke
Chief Creative Officer
imdb.com/name/nm0198632

Karen Foster
Development Executive
imdb.com/name/nm2259946

Jeffrey Katzenberg
imdb.com/name/nm0005076

Chris Kuser
Senior Executive (Development)
imdb.com/name/nm1936914
Assistant: Beth Cannon

Damon Ross
Senior Executive (Development)
imdb.com/name/nm1842613

Nancy Bernsein
imdb.com/name/nm0077110

Tom McGrath
imdb.com/name/nm0569891

Jeffrey Wike
imdb.com/name/nm5204969

Amie Karp
Creative Executive (Development)
imdb.com/name/nm2047897

DREAMWORKS STUDIOS

100 Universal City Plaza
Building 5121

Universal City, CA 91608
818-733-7000

info@dreamworksstudios.com
dreamworksstudios.com
imdb.com/company/co0252576
facebook.com/DreamWorksStudios

Does not accept any unsolicited material. Project types include Feature Films and TV. Preferred genres include Action, Comedy, Crime, Drama, Fantasy, Period, Romance, Science Fiction, and Thriller.

Mia Maniscalco
Creative Executive
mia_maniscalco@dreamworksstudios.com
imdb.com/name/nm4103271
linkedin.com/pub/mia-maniscalco/6/28a/652

Holly Bario
President
info@wif.org
imdb.com/name/nm2302370

Steven Spielberg
Chairman
imdb.com/name/nm0000229

DREYFUSS/JAMES PRODUCTIONS

2420 Laurel Pass
Los Angeles, CA 90046
323-822-0140 (phone)
323-822-0440 (fax)

djprods.com
imdb.com/company/co0021491

Does not accept any unsolicited material. Project types include Feature Films. Preferred genres include Action, Animation, Comedy, Crime, Detective, Documentary, Drama, Family, Fantasy, Horror, Myth, Non-Fiction, Period, Reality, Romance, Science Fiction, Sociocultural, and Thriller.

Richard Dreyfuss
Principal
imdb.com/name/nm0000377

Judith James
Principal
imdb.com/name/nm0416648

D STREET PICTURES

Oranienburger Strasse 27
Berlin, 10117 Germany

1133 Broadway, Suite 708
New York, NY 10010

info@www.dstreetmediagroup.com
dstreetmediagroup.com

Does not accept any unsolicited material. Project types include Feature Films. Preferred genres include Drama.

Dexter Davis
CEO
imdb.com/name/nm2089464

Javier Krause
VP
imdb.com/name/nm4040018

DSW ENTERTAINMENT

116 E 16th St, 9th Floor
New York, NY 10003
212-974-5322

dsimone@dswent.com
primarywavemusic.com
imdb.com/company/co0352823

Does not accept any unsolicited material. Project types include TV.

Winston Simone
Producer
imdb.com/name/nm4483051

David Simone
Producer
imdb.com/name/nm0800108

DUALSTAR ENTERTAINMENT

1801 Century Park East, 12th Floor
Los Angeles, CA 90067
310-553-9000 (phone)
310-945-3750 (fax)

dualstarentertainmentgroup.com

Does not accept any unsolicited material. Project types include TV. Preferred genres include Comedy and Family.

Ashley Olsen
Actor/Producer
imdb.com/name/nm0001580

Mary Kate Olsen
Actor/Producer
imdb.com/name/nm0001581

DUCK SOUP STUDIOS

2205 Stoner Ave.
Los Angeles , CA 90064
310-478-0771 (phone)
310-478-0773 (fax)

info@duckstudios.com
duckstudios.com
imdb.com/company/co0172556

Does not accept any unsolicited material.

DULY NOTED

5225 Wilshire Blvd., Suite 418
Los Angeles, CA 90036
323-525-1855

info@dulynotedinc.com
dulynotedinc.com
imdb.com/company/co0142547

Does not accept any unsolicited material. Project types include Feature Films. Preferred genres include Drama, Horror, and Thriller.

DUNE ENTERTAINMENT

2121 Ave of the Stars
Suite 2570
Los Angeles, CA 90067
310-432-2288

623 Fifth Ave.
New York, NY 10022
212-301-8400

imdb.com/company/co0174373

Does not accept any unsolicited material. Project types include Feature Films. Preferred genres include Action,

Comedy, Drama, Fantasy, Horror, Romance, Science Fiction, and Thriller.

Wendy Weller
imdb.com/name/nm2956152

Larry Bernstein
imdb.com/name/nm2955628

Greg Coote
imdb.com/name/nm0178505

DUNLOP ENTERTAINMENT

30346 Esperanza, Suite B
Rancho Santa Margarita, CA 92688
949-709-7727 (phone)
949-709-7737 (fax)

sdunlop@dunlop-group.com
dunlopgrp.com
imdb.com/company/co0171053

Does not accept any unsolicited material. Project types include TV.

Scott Dunlop
Producer
imdb.com/name/nm0242472

DUPLASS BROTHERS PRODUCTIONS

902 E Fifth St
Austin, TX 78702

info@duplassbrothers.com
duplassbrothers.com
imdb.com/company/co0117723

Accepts query letter from unproduced, unrepresented writers via email. Project types include Feature Films. Preferred genres include Comedy, Drama, Horror, and Thriller.

Jay Duplass
Producer
imdb.com/name/nm0243231
twitter.com/jayduplass

Stephanie Langhoff
Producer
imdb.com/name/nm1293297

Mark Duplass
Producer
imdb.com/name/nm0243233
twitter.com/markduplass

DUTCHMEN FILMS

500 N Rossmore Ave Suite 201
Los Angeles, CA 90004
310-772-8210

franklin@dutchmenfilms.com
dutchmenfilms.com
imdb.com/company/co0246561

Does not accept any unsolicited material. Project types include Feature Films. Preferred genres include Drama.

Franklin Martin
Director/Writer/Producer/Actor
imdb.com/name/nm0552294

DYNAMIC TELEVISION

8530 Wilshire Blvd, 5th Floor
Beverly Hills, CA 90211

dmarch@dynamictelevision.com
dynamictelevision.com
imdb.com/company/co0466320

Does not accept any unsolicited material. Project types include TV. Preferred genres include Action, Drama, and Fantasy.

Daniel March
Founder
imdb.com/name/nm4883495

Klaus Zimmermann
Managing Partner
imdb.com/name/nm0956842

DYNAMITE ENTERTAINMENT

155 E. 9th Ave., Ste. B
Runnemede, NJ 08078
856-312-1040 (phone)
856-312-1050 (fax)

dynamiteentertainment.com
imdb.com/company/co0010018

Project types include Feature Films. Preferred genres include Action.

Nick Barrucci
President, Producer
imdb.com/name/nm2262057

EALING STUDIOS

Ealing Green
W5 5EP
United Kingdom
+44-0-20-8567-6655 (phone)
+44-0-20-8758-8658 (fax)

info@ealingstudios.com
ealingstudios.co.uk
imdb.com/company/co0040024
facebook.com/ealingstudios
twitter.com/ealingstudios

Does not accept any unsolicited material. Project types include Feature Films and TV. Preferred genres include Comedy, Documentary, Drama, Family, Romance, and Thriller.

Sophie Meyer
Head of Development
imdb.com/name/nm1623306

Barnaby Thompson
Producer
imdb.com/name/nm0859877

James Spring
Producer
imdb.com/name/nm2020191

Gary Stone
Manager
gary.stone@ealingstudios.com

EBS WORLD ENTERTAINMENT

3000 W. Olympic Blvd
Santa Monica, CA 90404
310-449-4065 (phone)
310-449-4061 (fax)

ebsla.com
imdb.com/company/co0158692

Does not accept any unsolicited material. Project types include Feature Films. Preferred genres include Action, Comedy, Drama, and Horror.

Richard Cooper
Co-Chairman/CEO

Wayne Wong
Co-Chairman/President
imdb.com/name/nm1373710

ECHELON STUDIOS

1440 Flower St
Glendale, CA 91201
818-500-1640

corporate@echelonstudios.us
echelonstudios.us
imdb.com/company/co0192323

Does not accept any unsolicited material. Project types include Feature Films. Preferred genres include Comedy, Drama, Horror, and Thriller.

Eric Louzil
President/CEO
imdb.com/name/nm0522218

ECHO BRIDGE ENTERTAINMENT

75 Second Ave
Suite 500
Needham, MA 02494
781-444-6767 (phone)
781-444-6472 (fax)

3089 Airport Rd
La Crosse, WI 54603
608-784-6620 (phone)
608-784-6635 (fax)

info@ebellc.com
info@echobridgehe.com
echobridgeentertainment.com
imdb.com/company/co0127873
facebook.com/echobridgehe
twitter.com/ebhomeent
linkedin.com/company/echo-bridge-home-
    entertainment

Does not accept any unsolicited material. Project types include Feature Films. Preferred genres include Action, Detective, Drama, Fantasy, Horror, Romance, Science Fiction, and Thriller.

CJ Laychak
SVP, Legal and Operations

Michael Rosenblatt
CEO
mrosenblatt@ebellc.com

Tom Hammond
CFO
thammond@ebellc.com

Nathan Hart
President, Home Entertainment
nhart@echobridgehe.com

ECHO FILMS

c/o Allen Keshishian/Brillstein Entertainment
Partners
9150 Wilshire Blvd, Suite 350
Beverly Hills, CA 90212
323-935-2909

imdb.com/company/co0234791

Does not accept any unsolicited material. Project types include Feature Films. Preferred genres include Comedy, Drama, and Romance. Established in 2008.

Jennifer Aniston
Producer

Kristin Hahn
Producer

ECHO LAKE ENTERTAINMENT

421 S Beverly Dr,
6th Floor
Beverly Hills, CA 90212
310-789-4790 (phone)
310-789-4791 (fax)

contact@echolakeproductions.com
imdb.com/company/co0076285
facebook.com/pages/Echo-Lake-Productions/
    160303590658581
linkedin.com/company/echo-lake-productions

Does not accept any unsolicited material. Project types include Feature Films and TV. Preferred genres include Drama, Non-Fiction, Reality, and Thriller.

Douglas Mankoff
Producer
imdb.com/name/nm0542551

Jessica Staman
Producer
imdb.com/name/nm1698445

Ida Diffley
Director of Development
imdb.com/name/nm3000066

Andrew Spaulding
Producer
imdb.com/name/nm1051748

ECHOLIGHT STUDIOS

1200 Lakeside Parkway. Bldg. 1
Flower Mound, TX 75028

echolight.com
facebook.com/echolightstudios
twitter.com/echolightstudio
imdb.com/company/co0391226

Does not accept any unsolicited material. Project types include Feature Films. Preferred genres include Drama and Family.

ECLECTIC PICTURES

7510 W Sunset Blvd Ste. 517
Hollywood, CA 90046
323-656-7555 (phone)
323-848-7761 (fax)

info@eclecticpictures.com
eclecticpictures.com
imdb.com/company/co0147213
facebook.com/eclecticpictures
twitter.com/eclecticpics
linkedin.com/company/2949479

Accepts query letter from unproduced, unrepresented writers via email. Project types include Feature Films. Established in 2004.

John Yarincik
Development Executive
john@eclecticpictures.com
imdb.com/name/nm2432490

Heidi Jo Markel
CEO
Assistant: Jessica Yang

Conor Charles
Senior Vice President, Production & Operations

Cem Gursel
Creative Executive

Natalie Wadlert
Executive

Kyle Cooper
Development Executive

Meric Aydin
Jr. Development Executive

ECLECTIK VISION

Building 19 Fox Studios,
Moore Park Sydney, NSW 2021
02-9383-4590 (phone)
02-9383-4581 (fax)

9461 Charleville Blvd # 431
Beverly Hills, CA 90212
310-382-7730

imdb.com/company/co0479919
eclectikvision.com.au

Does not accept any unsolicited material. Project types include Feature Films. Established in 2007.

Brett Thornquest
Founder
brett@eclectikvision.com

Steven Matusko
steven@eclectikvision.com

Emma Dewhurst
Executive Assistant
evasst@eclectikvision.com

EDEN ROCK MEDIA, INC.

1416 N LaBrea Ave
Hollywood, CA 90028
323-802-1718 (phone)
323-802-1832 (fax)

taugsberger@edenrockmedia.com
edenrockmedia.com
imdb.com/company/co0156805

Does not accept any unsolicited material. Project types include Feature Films, TV, and Commercials. Preferred genres include Crime, Drama, Family, Non-Fiction, Science Fiction, and Thriller.

Thomas Ausberger
Producer
imdb.com/name/nm0041835

EDGEN FILMS

Austin, TX
512-522-8410

contact@edgenfilms.com
info@edgenfilms.com
edgenfilms.com
imdb.com/company/co0191909
twitter.com/edgenfilms
facebook.com/pages/Edgen-Films/136229063085550
linkedin.com/company/edgen-films

Does not accept any unsolicited material. Project types include Feature Films. Preferred genres include Drama, Horror, and Thriller. Established in 2014.

Justin Durban
CCO
justin@edgenfilms.com
justindurban.com
imdb.com/name/nm0243943

Nicholle Walton-Durban
CEO
nicholle@edgenfilms.com
imdb.com/name/nm3546871

Leah Weinberger
Director of Development
leah@edgenfilms.com
imdb.com/name/nm3733040

EDMONDS ENTERTAINMENT

1635 N Cahuenga Blvd, 6th Floor
Los Angeles, CA 90028
323-860-1550 (phone)
323-860-1537 (fax)

edmondsent.com/site/main.html
imdb.com/company/co0034440

Accepts scripts from produced or represented writers. Project types include Feature Films and TV. Preferred genres include Drama, Family, Non-Fiction, Reality, and Romance.

Sheila Ducksworth
Sr. Vice-President
imdb.com/name/nm0239923

Kenneth Edmonds
Executive Producer
imdb.com/name/nm0004892

Tracey Edmonds
CEO
imdb.com/name/nm0249525
Assistant: Amy Ficken

EDWARD R. PRESSMAN FILM CORPORATION

9469 Jefferson Blvd, Suite 119
Los Angeles, CA 90232
310-450-9692 (phone)
310-450-9705 (fax)

47 Murray St
New York, NY 10007
212-489-3333 (phone)
212-489-2103 (fax)

pressman.com
imdb.com/company/co0006728
twitter.com/pressmanfilm
facebook.com/PressmanFilm
linkedin.com/company/edward-r-pressman-film-corp

Does not accept any unsolicited material. Project types include Feature Films. Preferred genres include Action, Comedy, Drama, Fantasy, Myth, and Thriller. Established in 1969.

Jonathan Katz
COO

Edward Pressman
CEO
imdb.com/name/nm0696299
Assistant: Kelly McKee

Melissa Robyn Glassman
Director of Development

Sam Pressman
Creative Consultant

EDWARD SAXON PRODUCTIONS

1526 14th St #105
Santa Monica, CA 90404
310-246-7700

esaxon@saxonproductions.net
imdb.com/company/co0182559
linkedin.com/company/edward-saxon-productions
facebook.com/pages/Edward-Saxon-Production/
   109832089080967

Accepts query letter from unproduced, unrepresented writers via email. Project types include Feature Films and TV. Preferred genres include Action, Drama, Family, Non-Fiction, and Romance. Established in 1988.

Edward Saxon
Producer
imdb.com/name/nm0768324

EFISH ENTERTAINMENT, INC.

4236 Arch St, Suite 407
Studio City, CA 91604
818-509-9377

info@efishentertainment.com
efishentertainment.com
imdb.com/company/co0272699
facebook.com/pages/eFish-Entertainment/
   105303619508702

Accepts query letter from unproduced, unrepresented writers via email. Project types include Feature Films. Preferred genres include Action, Crime, Horror, and Science Fiction. Established in 2009.

Brianna Johnson
Producer
briannaasst@efishentertainment.com
imdb.com/name/nm3776636

Eric Fischer
Producer
ericasst@efishentertainment.com
imdb.com/name/nm2737789
Assistant: Tatjana Bluchel

EFO FILMS

8200 Wilshire Blvd, Suite 300
Beverly Hills, CA 90211
323-213-4650

efofilms.com

Does not accept any unsolicited material. Project types include Feature Films and TV. Preferred genres include Action, Drama, and Horror.

George Furla
Partner/Producer
imdb.com/name/nm0298915

Randall Emmett
Partner/Producer
imdb.com/name/nm0256542

EGO FILM ARTS

80 Niagara St
Toronto, ON M5V 1C5
Canada
310-859-4000 (phone)
310-859-4440 (fax)

questions@egofilmarts.com
egofilmarts.com
imdb.com/company/co0093742

Does not accept any unsolicited material. Project types include Feature Films and TV. Preferred genres include Action, Comedy, Crime, Documentary, Drama, Horror, Romance, and Thriller.

Atom Egoyan
Founder
imdb.com/name/nm0000382

EIGHTH SQUARE ENTERTAINMENT

606 N Larchmont Blvd, Suite 307
Los Angeles, CA 90004
323-469-1003 (phone)
323-469-1516 (fax)

imdb.com/company/co0100233
facebook.com/pages/Eighth-Square-Entertainment/
167378796607994

Does not accept any unsolicited material. Project types include Feature Films, TV, and Theater. Preferred genres include Comedy, Crime, Drama, and Thriller. Established in 1998.

Jeff Melnick
Producer
imdb.com/name/nm0578179

EISENBERG-FISHER PRODUCTIONS

5555 Melrose Ave.
Los Angeles, CA 90038

Does not accept any unsolicited material. Project types include Feature Films. Preferred genres include Action.

ELECTRIC CITY ENTERTAINMENT

8409 Santa Monica Blvd
West Hollywood, CA 90069
323-654-7800 (phone)
323-654-7808 (fax)

electriccityent.com
imdb.com/company/co0366362

Accepts query letter from unproduced, unrepresented writers via email. Project types include Feature Films. Preferred genres include Comedy, Drama, and Romance. Established in 2012.

Lynette Howell
imdb.com/name/nm1987578
Assistant: Jess Engel

Jamie Patricof
imdb.com/name/nm1364232
Assistant: Jack Hart

Crystal Powell
imdb.com/name/nm2476235

Katie McNeill
imdb.com/name/nm3336352
linkedin.com/pub/katie-mcneill/a/758/581

ELECTRIC DYNAMITE

1741 Ivar Ave
Los Angeles, CA 90028
323-790-8040 (phone)
818-733-2651 (fax)

electricdynamite.com
imdb.com/company/co0190357
twitter.com/el_dynamite

Accepts query letter from unproduced, unrepresented writers. Project types include Feature Films, TV, and Commercials. Preferred genres include Comedy, Fantasy, and Science Fiction.

Jack Black
323-790-8000
imdb.com/name/nm0085312

Priyanka Mattoo
imdb.com/name/nm3339192

ELECTRIC ENTERTAINMENT

940 N Highland Ave, Suite A
Los Angeles, CA 90038
323-817-1300 (phone)
323-467-7155 (fax)

electric-entertainment.com
imdb.com/company/co0003899

Does not accept any unsolicited material. Project types include Feature Films, TV, and Commercials. Preferred genres include Action, Animation, Comedy, Drama, Non-Fiction, Reality, Science Fiction, and Thriller.

Dean Devlin
President
imdb.com/name/nm0002041
Assistant: Chase Friedman

Rachel Olschan
imdb.com/name/nm1272673

Marc Roskin
imdb.com/name/nm0743059

ELECTRIC FARM ENTERTAINMENT

3000 Olympic Blvd
Building 3, Suite 1366
Santa Monica, CA 90404
310-264-4199 (phone)
310-264-4196 (fax)

contact@electricfarment.com
imdb.com/company/co0217444
linkedin.com/pub/brent-friedman/4/342/72

Accepts query letter from unproduced, unrepresented writers via email. Project types include Feature Films, TV, and Commercials. Preferred genres include Action, Drama, Fantasy, and Science Fiction.

Stan Rogow
CEO
linkedin.com/pub/stan-rogow/11/903/335
Assistant: Allison Lurie

Brent Friedman
linkedin.com/pub/brent-friedman/4/342/72

ELECTRIC SHEPHERD PRODUCTIONS, LLC

c/o Anonymous Content
3532 Hayden Ave
Culver City, CA 90232
310-558-6538

admin@electricshepherdproductions.com

Accepts query letter from unproduced, unrepresented writers via email. Project types include Feature Films, TV, and Commercials. Preferred genres include Action, Drama, Fantasy, Myth, Science Fiction, and Thriller.

Kalen Egan
imdb.com/name/nm2290810

Isa Dick Hackett
imdb.com/name/nm2357313

Laura Leslie

ELEMENT PICTURES

14 Newburgh St
London, W1F7RT

44207-287-5420 (phone)
44207-434-0146 (fax)

21 Mespil Rd
Dublin 4
Ireland
353-1-618-5032 (phone)
353-1-664-3737 (fax)

info@elementpictures.ie
elementpictures.ie

Does not accept any unsolicited material. Project types include Feature Films and TV. Preferred genres include Action, Comedy, Documentary, Drama, Horror, and Science Fiction.

Lee Magiday
Producer
imdb.com/name/nm3717662
linkedin.com/pub/lee-magiday/3/6a8/863

Emma Norton
Head of Development
imdb.com/name/nm4499999
linkedin.com/pub/dir/Emma/Norton

Ed Guiney
Company Director
imdb.com/name/nm0347384
linkedin.com/pub/dir/Ed/Guiney

Andrew Lowe
imdb.com/name/nm1103466
linkedin.com/pub/andrew-lowe/20/1a/66

ELEPHANT EYE FILMS

89 Fifth Ave
Ste 306
New York, NY 10003
212-488-8877 (phone)
212-488-8878 (fax)

info@elephanteyefilms.com
elephanteyefilms.com
imdb.com/company/co0223262
facebook.com/pages/Elephant-Eye-Films/110546058997554
twitter.com/eeffilms

Does not accept any unsolicited material. Project types include Feature Films. Preferred genres include Action, Comedy, Drama, Fantasy, and Non-Fiction.

Kim Jose
kim@elephanteyefilms.com

Dave Robinson
dave@elephanteyefilms.com

Toni Branson
toni@elephanteyefilms.com

ELEVATE ENTERTAINMENT

6255 W Sunset Blvd Suite 800
Los Angeles, CA 90028
310-494-0101 (phone)
323-848-9867 (fax)

info@elevate-ent.com

Accepts query letter from unproduced, unrepresented writers via email. Project types include Feature Films and TV. Preferred genres include Action, Animation, Comedy, Crime, Drama, Family, Fantasy, Non-Fiction, Romance, and Science Fiction.

Dave Moody
CEO
davemoody.com/about
imdb.com/name/nm2628340
linkedin.com/in/davemoody

Josh Moody
CCO
linkedin.com/pub/josh-moody/25/47/569
facebook.com/josh.moody.319

ELIXIR FILMS

8033 W Sunset Blvd, Suite 867
West Hollywood, CA 90046
323-848-9867 (phone)
323-848-5945 (fax)

info@elixirfilms.com
elixirfilms.com
imdb.com/company/co0082095
facebook.com/ELIXIRFILMSelixirfilms

Does not accept any unsolicited material. Project types include Feature Films. Preferred genres include Drama and Family.

David Alexanian
Producer
imdb.com/name/nm1256362

Alexis Alexanian
Producer
imdb.com/name/nm0018936
Assistant: Joe Brinkman

ELKINS ENTERTAINMENT

8306 Wilshire Blvd
PMB 3643
Beverly Hills, CA 90211
323-932-0400 (phone)
323-932-6400 (fax)

info@elkinsent.com
elkinsent.com
imdb.com/company/co0041590

Accepts query letter from unproduced, unrepresented writers via email. Project types include Feature Films and TV. Preferred genres include Comedy, Drama, Non-Fiction, Reality, and Romance.

Sandi Love
imdb.com/name/nm0522418

ELLEN RAKIETEN ENTERTAINMENT

1040 N Las Palmas
Los Angeles, CA 90038
United States
323-860-8900

Does not accept any unsolicited material. Project types include TV. Preferred genres include Reality.

Ellen Rakieten
President/Producer

Jennifer Danska
SVP of Development

Matthew Vafiadis
SVP of Development

ELYSIAN ENTERTAINMENT

6735 Yucca St. #207
Hollywood, CA 90028
323-230-8224

info@elysian-entertainment.com
submissions@elysian-entertainment.com
elysian-entertainment.com

Accepts query letter from unproduced, unrepresented writers via email. Project types include Feature Films and TV.

Sheri Fults
Producer/Manager
imdb.com/name/nm2433977

EMBASSY ROW, LLC

325 Hudson St
Ste 601
New York, NY 10013
212-507-9700 (phone)
212-507-9701 (fax)

6565 Sunset Blvd Suite 200
Los Angeles, CA 90028
323-417-6560 (phone)
323-469-0015 (fax)

info@embassyrow.com
embassyrow.com

Does not accept any unsolicited material. Project types include Feature Films, TV, and Commercials. Preferred genres include Action, Comedy, Drama, Fantasy, Non-Fiction, Reality, and Science Fiction.

Michael Davies
imdb.com/name/nm0203863

Tammy Johnston
imdb.com/name/nm1183748

EMBER ENTERTAINMENT GROUP

11718 Barrington Court, Suite 116
Los Angeles, CA 90049
310-230-9759 (phone)
310-589-4850 (fax)

eeg.bronson@verizon.net
contact@ember-entertainment.com

ember-entertainment.com
imdb.com/company/co0176815
facebook.com/EmberEntertainment

Accepts query letter from unproduced, unrepresented writers via email. Project types include Feature Films and TV. Preferred genres include Action, Comedy, Drama, Fantasy, and Science Fiction.

Ryan Geithman
President
linkedin.com/pub/ryan-geithman/57/242/446

Lindsay Dunlap
Producer
imdb.com/name/nm0242397

Randall Frakes
President
imdb.com/name/nm0289696

Max Wagner
linkedin.com/pub/max-wagner/2/599/bba
linkedin.com/pub/max-wagner/2/599/bba
twitter.com/emeyex

EMERALD CITY PRODUCTIONS, INC.

c/o Stankevich-Gochman
9777 Wilshire Blvd, Suite 550
Beverly Hills, CA 90212
321-253-4335

ingrid@emeraldcityprod.com
facebook.com/emeraldcityrecords
emeraldcityprod.com

Does not accept any unsolicited material. Project types include Feature Films. Preferred genres include Drama, Fantasy, and Science Fiction.

Barrie M. Osborne
Producer
imdb.com/name/nm0651614

Stephen Walen
imdb.com/company/co0284758

EMERGENCE ENTERTAINMENT

1508 E Wildflower Ln
Spokane, WA 99224
509-939-7206

mark.kratter@alumni.stanford.org
emergenceentertainment.com

Accepts query letter from unproduced, unrepresented writers via email. Project types include Feature Films and TV. Preferred genres include Action, Animation, Comedy, Crime, Detective, Documentary, Drama, Family, Fantasy, Horror, Myth, Non-Fiction, Period, Reality, Romance, Science Fiction, Sociocultural, and Thriller.

EMJAG PRODUCTIONS

9200 W Sunset Blvd., Suite 550
West Hollywood, CA 90069
310-786-7875

imdb.com/company/co0223721

Does not accept any unsolicited material. Project types include Feature Films and TV. Preferred genres include Crime, Drama, and Thriller.

Stephanie Dziczek
Story Editor
imdb.com/name/nm2933823

Alexandra Milchan
Producer
imdb.com/name/nm0586968

EM MEDIA

Em-Media, Inc. 2728 Sunset Blvd. Steubenville, OH 43952
740-264-2186

info@em-media.com
em-media.com
imdb.com/company/co0091923

Accepts query letter from unproduced, unrepresented writers. Project types include Feature Films. Preferred genres include Comedy, Drama, and Romance. Established in 2002.

Anna Seifert-Speck
Development Executive
imdb.com/name/nm3527106

Debbie Williams
CEO
0115-993-2333
debbie.williams@em-media.org.uk
imdb.com/name/nm3527737

John Tobin
imdb.com/name/nm3527690

Suzanne Alizart
suzanne.alizart@em-media.org
imdb.com/name/nm2355251

EMMETT/FURLA FILMS

8200 Wilshire Blvd, Suite 300
Beverly Hills, CA 90211
323-213-4650

imdb.com/company/co0017712

Does not accept any unsolicited material. Project types include Feature Films and TV. Preferred genres include Comedy and Drama.

George Furla
Producer
imdb.com/name/nm0298915

Randall Emmett
Producer
imdb.com/name/nm0256542

EMPIRE PICTURES, INC.

360 E First St, Suite 774
Tustin, CA 92780
323-939-2100

imdb.com/company/co0090070

Does not accept any unsolicited material. Project types include Feature Films and TV. Preferred genres include Comedy and Drama.

Michael Birnbaum
Producer
imdb.com/name/nm0083688

ENDEMOL ENTERTAINMENT

9255 W Sunset Blvd
Suite 1100

Los Angeles, CA 90069
310-860-9914 (phone)
310-860-0073 (fax)

1000 Brickell Ave.
Suite 1015
Miami, Florida 33131
305-576-4949 (phone)
305-576-4980 (fax)

endemolusa.tv
imdb.com/company/co0011366
twitter.com/endemolUS
facebook.com/EndemolUS

Accepts query letter from produced or represented writers. Project types include TV. Preferred genres include Comedy, Drama, and Reality.

Cris Abrego
Co-Chairman and Co-CEO
imdb.com/name/nm0918141

ENDGAME ENTERTAINMENT

9100 Wilshire Blvd, Suite 100W
Beverly Hills, CA 90212
310-432-7300 (phone)
310-432-7301 (fax)

reception@endgameent.com
imdb.com/company/co0112971

Does not accept any unsolicited material. Project types include Feature Films, TV, and Theater. Preferred genres include Action, Animation, Comedy, Crime, Detective, Drama, Non-Fiction, Reality, Romance, Science Fiction, and Thriller.

Adam Del Deo
imdb.com/name/nm0215534

Lucas Smith
imdb.com/name/nm0809156

James Stern
imdb.com/name/nm0827726

Julie Goldstein
imdb.com/name/nm0326252

ENERGY ENTERTAINMENT

9107 Wilshire Blvd Suite #600
Beverly Hills, CA 90212
310-746-4872

info@energyentertainment.net
energyentertainment.net
imdb.com/company/co0120782

Does not accept any unsolicited material. Project types include Feature Films. Preferred genres include Comedy, Drama, Fantasy, Horror, Non-Fiction, Science Fiction, and Thriller. Established in 2001.

Angelina Chen
Manager
imdb.com/name/nm3255914

Brooklyn Weaver
imdb.com/name/nm0915819
Assistant: David Binns

Michelle Arenal
imdb.com/name/nm2797145

ENSEMBLE PRODUCTIONS

3000 W Olympic Blvd., Suite 2405
Santa Monica, CA 90404
310-264-3930

Does not accept any unsolicited material. Project types include TV. Preferred genres include Drama.

ENTERTAINMENT BY BONNIE AND CLYDE

1440 Colt Circle
Castle Rock, CO 80109
303-681-2955

Does not accept any unsolicited material. Project types include TV.

Beth Chapman
Producer
imdb.com/name/nm1726593

Duane Chapman
Producer
imdb.com/name/nm2406592

ENTERTAINMENT ONE GROUP

9465 Wilshire Blvd, Suite 500
Los Angeles, CA 90212
310-407-0960

22 Harbor Park Dr
Port Washington
New York
United States of America
11050

eonetv@entonegroup.com
entonegroup.com

Does not accept any unsolicited material. Project types
include Feature Films, TV, and Commercials.
Preferred genres include Animation, Comedy, Drama,
Family, Horror, Non-Fiction, Reality, Romance, and
Thriller.

Michael Rosenberg
imdb.com/name/nm0742283

Jeff Hevert
imdb.com/name/nm2062114

ENTERTAINMENT STUDIOS

9903 Santa Monica Blvd., Suite 418
Beverly Hills, CA 90212
310-277-3500

es.tv
imdb.com/company/co0127629

Does not accept any unsolicited material. Project types
include TV.

Caroylyn Folks
Executive Producer

Byron Allen
CEO/Executive Producer
imdb.com/name/nm2902750

ENTICING ENTERTAINMENT

701 Brazos St, Suite 1050
Austin, TX 78701

imdb.com/company/co0296449

Does not accept any unsolicited material. Project types
include Feature Films. Preferred genres include Drama
and Thriller.

David Tice
Producer
imdb.com/name/nm3790215

ENTITLED ENTERTAINMENT

2038 Redcliff St
Los Angeles, CA 90039
323-469-9000 (phone)
323-660-5292 (fax)

entitledentertainment.com/index.html
imdb.com/company/co0076662

Does not accept any unsolicited material. Project types
include Feature Films, TV, and Theater. Preferred
genres include Comedy, Crime, Drama, Family, and
Non-Fiction.

James Burke
Partner
imdb.com/name/nm0121711

Scott Disharoon
Partner
imdb.com/name/nm0228318

ENVISION MEDIA ARTS

EMA, LLC
c/o Raleigh Studios
5300 Melrose Ave
Suite 419 East
Los Angeles, CA 90038
310-459-8080 (phone)
310-459-8080 (fax)

EMA, LLC
c/o R2
16 W 46th St.
12th floor
NY, NY 10036
212-647-8464

info@envisionma.com
envisionma.com
imdb.com/company/co0340433
facebook.com/EnvisionMediaArts

Accepts query letter from unproduced, unrepresented writers via email. Project types include Feature Films and TV. Preferred genres include Action, Comedy, Drama, Family, Fantasy, Myth, and Romance. Established in 2002.

Lee Nelson
CEO
310-459-8080
ln@ema.la
imdb.com/name/nm0625540

David Buelow
310-459-8080
db@ema.la
imdb.com/name/nm2149164

David Tish
Director of Development
dtish@envisionma.com
imdb.com/name/nm2953843

EPIC LEVEL ENTERTAINMENT, LTD.

7095 Hollywood Blvd #688
Hollywood, CA 91604
818-752-6800 (phone)
818-752-6814 (fax)

info@epiclevel.com
epiclevel.com
imdb.com/company/co0183217

Accepts query letter from unproduced, unrepresented writers via email. Project types include Feature Films, TV, and Commercials. Preferred genres include Action, Animation, Fantasy, Horror, Myth, Non-Fiction, Reality, Science Fiction, and Thriller.

Paige Barnett
imdb.com/name/nm1831309

Cindi Rice
Producer
imdb.com/name/nm1394761
linkedin.com/in/cindirice
twitter.com/cindirice

John Rosenblum
Producer
jfr@jfr.com
jfr.com

EPIGRAM ENTERTAINMENT

3745 Longview Valley Rd
Sherman Oaks, CA 91423
818-461-8937 (phone)
818-461-8919 (fax)

epigrament@sbcglobal.net
imdb.com/company/co0176819

Accepts query letter from unproduced, unrepresented writers via email. Project types include Feature Films, TV, and Commercials. Preferred genres include Comedy, Drama, and Romance.

Ellen Baskin
imdb.com/name/nm2302395

Val McLeroy
Partner
imdb.com/name/nm0572890

EPIPHANY PICTURES, INC.

10625 Esther Ave
Los Angeles, CA 90064
310-815-1266 (phone)
310-815-1269 (fax)

epiphanysubmissions@gmail.com.com
epiphanysubmissions@gmail.com.com
epiphanypictures.com
imdb.com/company/co0023944

Accepts query letter from unproduced, unrepresented writers via email. Project types include Feature Films, TV, and Commercials. Preferred genres include Action, Animation, Comedy, Drama, Family, Fantasy, Myth, Non-Fiction, Reality, Romance, Science Fiction, Sociocultural, and Thriller.

Scott Frank
scott@epiphanypictures.com
imdb.com/name/nm0291082

Dan Halperin
310-452-0242
dan@epiphanypictures.com
imdb.com/name/nm0356917

Dave Schilling
Story Editor
dwsreader@gmail.com

EPOCH FILMS

435 Hudson St, 3rd Floor
New York, NY 10014
212-226-0661 (phone)
212-226-4893 (fax)

112-114 Great Portland St., 1st Floor
London, England W1W6PA
44207-908-6060 (phone)
44207-908-6061 (fax)

9290 Civic Center
Drive Beverly Hills, CA 90210
310-275-9333

ny@epochfilms.com
lon@epochfilms.com
epochfilms.com
imdb.com/company/co0130058

Does not accept any unsolicited material. Project types include Feature Films. Preferred genres include Comedy and Drama.

Jerry Solomon
Managing Partner/Executive Producer (LA)
imdb.com/name/nm0813355

Mindy Goldberg
Founder/Producer (NY)
imdb.com/name/nm1666061

EQUILIBRIUM MEDIA COMPANY

1259 S. Orange Grove Ave.
Los Angeles, CA 90019
323-939-3555 (phone)
323-939-7523 (fax)

info@eq-ent.com
eq-ent.com
imdb.com/company/co0232623
facebook.com/EquilibriumEnt
twitter.com/EquilibriumEnt

Accepts query letter from unproduced, unrepresented writers. Project types include Feature Films. Preferred genres include Action and Comedy.

Peter Ferentinos
Executive Producer

Demian Lichtenstein
CEO
demian@eq-ent.com

Cherif Aziz
Senior Vice President Sales & Marketing
cherif@eq-ent.com

Yoram Barzilai
Head of Production
yoram@eq-ent.com

Susan Newell
Vice-President
susan@eq-ent.com

Shajen Lichtenstein
Director of Operations
shajen@eq-ent.com

Miklos Wright
Head of Post Production & Senior Editor
miklos@eq-ent.com

Dave Hagen
Editor
dave@eq-ent.com

Alex Wood
Creative Executive
alex@eq-ent.com

ESCAPE ARTISTS

10202 W Washington Blvd
Astaire Building, 3rd Floor
Culver City, CA 90232
310-244-8833 (phone)
310-204-2151 (fax)

info@escapeartistsent.com
escapeartistsent.com
facebook.com/EscapeArtistsEnt
twitter.com/EAfilms
imdb.com/company/co0035535

Does not accept any unsolicited material. Project types include Feature Films and TV. Preferred genres include Action, Comedy, Drama, Fantasy, Myth, Reality, Romance, and Science Fiction.

Todd Black
Founder
todd_black@spe.sony.com
imdb.com/name/nm0085542

Steve Tisch
Partner
steve_tisch@spe.sony.com

Jason Blumenthal
Producer
jason_blumenthal@spe.sony.com
imdb.com/name/nm0089820

David Bloomfield
Executive Producer

ESCAPE REALITY

3815 Hughes Ave
Culver City, CA 90232
310-841-4369

escapereality.tv

Accepts query letter from produced or represented writers. Project types include Feature Films and TV. Preferred genres include Drama, Period, and Thriller. Established in 2001.

Frank Sutera
Executive Producer
imdb.com/name/nm1281372

Laura Fuest Silva
Producer
imdb.com/name/nm1557596

Steve Tisch
Producer
imdb.com/name/nm0005494

Lacy Boughn
Development Executive
imdb.com/name/nm2064419

Jason Blumenthal
Producer
imdb.com/name/nm0089820

Todd Black
Partner
imdb.com/name/nm0085542

David Bloomfield
Executive Producer
imdb.com/name/nm1837022

ESPARAZA-KATZ PRODUCTIONS

1201 W 5th St, Suite T210
Los Angeles , CA 90017
213-542-4420

imdb.com/company/co0061612

Does not accept any unsolicited material. Project types include Feature Films and TV. Preferred genres include Drama.

Robert Katz
Executive Producer
imdb.com/name/nm0441831

ESPERANZA FILMS

1014 Cedar St
Santa Monica, CA 90405
310-314-1164 (phone)
310-581-9967 (fax)

info@esperanza.com
esperanza.com

Does not accept any unsolicited material. Project types include Feature Films and TV. Preferred genres include Drama and Thriller.

Rene Simon Cruz, Jr.
Producer/Director
imdb.com/name/nm0989083

E-SQUARED

531A North Hollywood Way
Suite 237
Burbank, CA 91505
818-760-1901

info@e2-esquared.com
e2-esquared.com
imdb.com/company/co0109424

Accepts query letter from unproduced, unrepresented writers.

Chris Emerson
esquaredasst@sbcglobal.net
imdb.com/name/nm0256193

Matt Cavanaugh
Post Production Sound Assistant
linkedin.com/pub/matt-cavanaugh/19/283/511

ESSENTIAL ENTERTAINMENT

9000 Sunset Blvd. Suite 600
Los Angeles, CA 90069
310-550-9100

info@essential-ent.com
essential-ent.com
imdb.com/company/co0048134

Project types include Feature Films. Preferred genres include Comedy and Drama.

James Kohlberg
Chairman/Producer

ETERNE FILMS

99 Main St, Suite 100
Colleyville, TX 76034
817-337-4900

info@eternefilms.com
eterne.org
imdb.com/company/co0292041

Does not accept any unsolicited material. Project types include Feature Films. Preferred genres include Drama.

Steve Riach
CEO
imdb.com/name/nm3727746

EVAMERE

38 W 21st St. 12th Floor
New York, NY 10010
212-337-3327

contact@evamere.com
evamere.com

Does not accept any unsolicited material. Project types include Feature Films.

John Hart
Producer
imdb.com/name/nm0366359

EVENSTART FILMS

212-219-2020 (phone)
212-219-2323 (fax)

info@evenstarfilms.com
evenstarfilms.com
twitter.com/evenstarfilms
facebook.com/evenstarfilms

Does not accept any unsolicited material. Project types include Feature Films. Preferred genres include Drama.

Elizabeth Cuthrell
Producer
imdb.com/name/nm0193876

David Urrutia
Producer
imdb.com/name/nm0882102

Jeremy Bloom

Steven Rinehart

EVERYMAN PICTURES

Santa Monica
1512 16th St Suite 3
Santa Monica, CA 90404
310-460-7080 (phone)
310-460-7081 (fax)

imdb.com/company/co0136709

Does not accept any unsolicited material. Project types include Feature Films and TV. Preferred genres include Comedy and Drama.

Jay Roach
jay.roach@fox.com
imdb.com/name/nm0005366

Jennifer Perini
imdb.com/name/nm0673805
Assistant: Kristopher Fogel and Lauren Downey

EVERYWHERE STUDIOS

14724 Ventura Blvd., Suite 400
Sherman Oaks, CA 91403
310-461-3060

mrengrudkij@everywhere-studios.com
everywhere-studios.com
linkedin.com/company/everywhere-studios
twitter.com/EW_Studios

Does not accept any unsolicited material. Project types
include Feature Films. Preferred genres include
Drama, Family, and Fantasy. Established in 2014.

DAN ANGEL
CCO
imdb.com/name/nm0029445

DAVID CALVERT-JONES
Chairman
imdb.com/name/nm1965869

Tom Mazza
CEO

David Putt
Executive

Lori Nelson
Vice President Development

EVOLVING PICTURES ENTERTAINMENT

15303 Ventura Blvd., 9th Floor
Sherman Oaks, CA 91403
877-215-3646

info@evolvingpicturesentertainment.com
evolvingpicturesentertainment.com
imdb.com/company/co0047632

Does not accept any unsolicited material. Project types
include Feature Films and TV. Preferred genres
include Comedy, Drama, and Horror.

Jeff Beltzner
President

Jean-Pierre Pereat
VP
imdb.com/name/nm0673004

EXCLUSIVE MEDIA

9100 Wilshire Blvd,
Suite 401 East,
Beverly Hills,
310-300-9000 (phone)
310-300-9001 (fax)

33 St James's St,
London,
SW1A 1HD, United Kingdom
44-0203-002-9510

info@exclusivemedia.com
exclusivemedia.com
facebook.com/ExclusiveMedia
twitter.com/ExclusiveEMG

Does not accept any unsolicited material. Project types
include Feature Films. Preferred genres include Action,
Comedy, Crime, Documentary, Drama, Fantasy,
Horror, Romance, and Thriller.

Nigel Sinclair
nigelsinclair@spitfirepix.com
imdb.com/name/nm0801691
Assistant: Patricia Scott

Guy East
geast@exclusivemedia.com
imdb.com/name/nm0247524

Marc Schipper
CEO
imdb.com/name/nm2649227

Simon Oakes
Vice President, CEO & President of Hammer
imdb.com/name/nm0642975

EXILE ENTERTAINMENT

732 El Medio Ave.
Pacific Palisades, CA 90272
310-573-1523 (phone)
310-573-0109 (fax)

exile_ent@yahoo.com
imdb.com/company/co0063047

Accepts query letter from unproduced, unrepresented
writers. Project types include Feature Films. Preferred
genres include Comedy, Drama, and Horror.

Gary Ungar
imdb.com/name/nm1316083

EXODUS FILM GROUP

1211 Electric Ave
Venice, CA 90291
310-684-3155

info@exodusfilmgroup.com
imdb.com/company/co0080906
exodusfilmgroup.com

Does not accept any unsolicited material. Project types
include Feature Films. Preferred genres include
Animation, Comedy, and Family.

Max Howard
Producer
max@exodusfilmgroup.com
imdb.com/name/nm0397492

EYEBOOGIE

6425 Hollywood Blvd., 3rd Floor
Los Angeles, CA 90028
323-315-5750

info@eyeboogie.com
eyeboogie.com
twitter.com/eyeboogie
imdb.com/company/co0146935

Does not accept any unsolicited material. Project types
include TV.

Tom Herschko
Head of TV
imdb.com/name/nm1929330

Woody Thompson
Producer
imdb.com/name/nm0860853

EYE ON THE BALL

PO Box 46877
Los Angeles, CA 90046
323-935-0634 (phone)
323-935-4188 (fax)

imdb.com/company/co0102936

Accepts query letter from unproduced, unrepresented
writers. Project types include Feature Films. Preferred
genres include Comedy.

Yareli Arizmendi
Producer
arauarizmendi@aol.com
imdb.com/name/nm0034976

Sergio Arau
Producer
keepyoureye@aol.com
imdb.com/name/nm0033190

FABRICATION FILMS

8701 W. Olympic Blvd.
Los Angeles, CA 90035
310-289-1232 (phone)
310-289-1292 (fax)

fabricationfilms.com
imdb.com/company/co0136539

Does not accept any unsolicited material. Project types
include Feature Films. Preferred genres include Action,
Drama, and Thriller.

Jodie Skalla
Vice President of Acquisitions
imdb.com/name/nm2431792

Kjehl Rasmussen
CEO
imdb.com/name/nm0711365

FACE PRODUCTIONS

335 N Maple Dr, Suite 135
Beverly Hills, CA 90210
310-205-2746 (phone)
310-285-2386 (fax)

facebook.com/faceproductions
faceproductions.com.hk
twitter.com/faceprodlv

Does not accept any unsolicited material. Project types
include Feature Films. Preferred genres include Action,
Comedy, and Drama.

Billy Crystal
imdb.com/name/nm0000345
Assistant: Kia Hellman

Samantha Sprecher
imdb.com/name/nm0819616
Assistant: Kia Hellman

FADE TO BLACK PRODUCTIONS

9120 Sunset Blvd. Suite 100
Los Angeles, CA 90069
310-278-9440 (phone)
310-278-9443 (fax)

imdb.com/company/co0251339

Does not accept any unsolicited material. Project types include Feature Films. Preferred genres include Drama.

Tom Ford
Principal, Producer, Writer
imdb.com/name/nm1053530

FAKE EMPIRE FEATURES

5555 Melrose Ave
Marx Brothers Building #207
Hollywood, CA 90038
323-956-8766

imdb.com/company/co0299663
fakeempire.com

Accepts scripts from produced or represented writers. Project types include Feature Films. Preferred genres include Comedy, Drama, and Family.

Jay Marcus
Creative Executive
imdb.com/name/nm1682408

Lisbeth Rowinski
President
imdb.com/name/nm2925164
Assistant: Ritu Moondra

FAKE EMPIRE TELEVISION

400 Warner Blvd
Building 138, Room 1101

Burbank, CA 91522
818-954-2420

fakeempire.com/about
facebook.com/FakeEmpire6
twitter.com/fakeempireteam

Accepts scripts from produced or represented writers. Project types include TV. Preferred genres include Comedy, Drama, and Family.

Josh Schwatz
imdb.com/name/nm0777300

Leonard Goldstein
imdb.com/name/nm2325264
Assistant: Brittany Sever

Stephanie Savage
imdb.com/name/nm1335634

Stephanie Savage
imdb.com/name/nm1335634
Assistant: Kendall Sand

FALCONER PICTURES

100 Wilshire Blvd. Suite 400
Santa Monica, CA 90401
310-452-3350 (phone)
310-388-5910 (fax)

imdb.com/company/co0395531
falconerpictures.com

Does not accept any unsolicited material. Project types include Feature Films. Preferred genres include Action, Comedy, Crime, Drama, and Thriller.

Douglas Falconer
CEO
doug@falconerpictures.com
imdb.com/name/nm0266000

Sam Saab
Partner
imdb.com/name/nm5668114
twitter.com/samfalc

FAMILY CHRISTIAN ENTERTAINMENT

5300 Patterson Ave SE
Grand Rapids, MI 49530

familychristian.com
imdb.com/company/co0516222

Does not accept any unsolicited material. Project types include Feature Films. Preferred genres include Drama.

Rick Jackson
Owner
imdb.com/name/nm7040528

FARAH FILMS & MANAGEMENT

11640 Mayfield, Suite 208
Los Angeles, CA 90049
310-979-4533

info@farahfilms.com
submissions@farahfilms.com
farahfilms.com
imdb.com/company/co0194807

Accepts query letter from unproduced, unrepresented writers via email. Project types include Feature Films. Preferred genres include Action, Drama, and Science Fiction.

FARRELL/MINOFF PRODUCTIONS

14011 Ventura Blvd., Suite 401
Sherman Oaks , CA 91423
818-789-5766 (phone)
818-789-7459 (fax)

Does not accept any unsolicited material. Project types include TV. Preferred genres include Drama.

Mike Farrell
Producer/Director/Actor
imdb.com/name/nm0268286

Marvin Minoff
Producer
imdb.com/name/nm0591545

FARRELL PAURA PRODUCTIONS

11150 Santa Monica Blvd., Suite 450
Los Angeles, CA 90025
310-477-7776

imdb.com/company/co0134381

Does not accept any unsolicited material. Project types include Feature Films and TV. Preferred genres include Comedy.

Joseph Farrell
Principal
imdb.com/name/nm1289705

Catherine Paura
Principal
imdb.com/name/nm0667474

FASTBACK PICTURES

323-469-5719

info@fastbackpictures.com
imdb.com/company/co0151624
fastbackpictures.com

Accepts query letter from unproduced, unrepresented writers. Project types include Feature Films. Preferred genres include Drama and Thriller.

Pascal Franchot
Producer
323-717-5569
pascal@fastbackpictures.com
imdb.com/name/nm0289994

FASTLANE ENTERTAINMENT

1316 Third St Promenade, Suite 109
Santa Monica, CA 90401
310-857-6868 (phone)
310-388-5830 (fax)

nfo@fastlaneent.com
fastlaneent.com
imdb.com/company/co0173838

Does not accept any unsolicited material. Project types include Feature Films.

Frank Miniaci
Founder/CEO
imdb.com/name/nm2131455

FASTNET FILMS

20 Herbert Place
Dublin 2, Ireland

+353 1 639 4000 (phone)
+353 1 657 6678 (fax)

enquiries@fastnetfilms.com
fastnetfilms.com
imdb.com/company/co0010293
twitter.com/FastnetFilms

Does not accept any unsolicited material. Project types include Feature Films. Preferred genres include Documentary, Drama, and Reality.

Aoife McGonigal
imdb.com/name/nm3502464

Megan Everett
Head of Development
imdb.com/name/nm3210746

Ian Jackson
Head of Development
imdb.com/name/nm4127212

FEDORA ENTERTAINMENT

11846 Ventura Blvd
Suite 140
Studio City, CA 91604
818-508-5310

imdb.com/company/co0287780
linkedin.com/company/fedora-entertainment

Does not accept any unsolicited material. Project types include TV. Preferred genres include Comedy and Drama.

Peter Tolan
Producer
imdb.com/name/nm0865847

Michael Wimer
Producer
imdb.com/name/nm1057590

Marla A. White
imdb.com/name/nm0925187
linkedin.com/in/marlawhite

FEVERPITCH PICTURES

1810 Markley St
Norristown, PA 19401

928-563-1915 (phone)
928-484-9028 (fax)

info@feverpitchpictures.com
feverpitchpictures.com
imdb.com/company/co0206272

Does not accept any unsolicited material. Project types include Feature Films. Preferred genres include Action, Comedy, Drama, and Horror.

Jeffrey D. Erb
Partner
imdb.com/name/nm2075994

FIERCE ENTERTAINMENT

7656 Sunset Blvd.
Los Angeles, CA 90046
310-860-1174 (phone)
310-860-9446 (fax)

fierceentertainment.com
imdb.com/company/co0095383

Does not accept any unsolicited material. Project types include Feature Films and TV.

Christopher Petzel
Founder/CEO
imdb.com/name/nm0678850

FILAMENT PRODUCTIONS

1000 Dean St, Suite 303
Brooklyn, NY 11238

office@filamentprods.com
filamentprods.com
facebook.com/profile.php
twitter.com/FilamentProds
imdb.com/company/co0363211

Does not accept any unsolicited material. Project types include Feature Films. Preferred genres include Drama.

Adam Spielberg
Producer
imdb.com/name/nm1437616

FILM 360

9111 Wilshire Blvd
Beverly Hills, CA 90210
310-272-7000

imdb.com/company/co0192833

Does not accept any unsolicited material. Project types include Feature Films. Preferred genres include Action, Comedy, Crime, Drama, Family, Fantasy, Period, Science Fiction, and Thriller. Established in 2009.

Eric Kranzler
Producer
imdb.com/name/nm1023394

Daniel Rappaport
Producer
imdb.com/name/nm0710883

Scott Lambert
Producer
imdb.com/name/nm0483300

FILM 44

1526 Cloverfield Blvd
Santa Monica, CA 90404
310-586-4940

info@film44.com
imdb.com/company/co0152188

Does not accept any unsolicited material. Project types include Feature Films and TV. Preferred genres include Action, Drama, Fantasy, Myth, Science Fiction, and Thriller.

Peter Berg
Partner
imdb.com/name/nm0000916

Rebecca Hobbs
imdb.com/name/nm1778008

Braden Aftergood
imdb.com/name/nm2302240

FILMCOLONY

4751 Wilshire Blvd Third Floor
Los Angeles, CA 90010

323-549-4343 (phone)
323-549-9824 (fax)

info@filmcolony.com
filmcolony.com
imdb.com/company/co0159642
linkedin.com/company/filmcolony
twitter.com/filmcolony

Does not accept any unsolicited material. Project types include Feature Films and TV. Preferred genres include Comedy, Crime, Drama, Family, Fantasy, Romance, and Thriller. Established in 1995.

Melanie Donkers
Director of Development
imdb.com/name/nm1410650

Anand Shah
imdb.com/name/nm4337795

Richard Gladstein
President
imdb.com/name/nm0321621
twitter.com/filmcolony

FILMDISTRICT

1540 2nd St
Suite 200
Santa Monica, CA 90401
310-315-1722 (phone)
310-315-1723 (fax)

contact@filmdistrict.com
filmdistrict.com
imdb.com/company/co0314851
facebook.com/FDFilms
twitter.com/FilmDistrict

Does not accept any unsolicited material. Project types include Feature Films. Preferred genres include Action, Crime, Drama, Fantasy, Horror, Romance, and Thriller. Established in 2010.

Tim Headington
Partner
imdb.com/name/nm2593874

Graham King
Partner
imdb.com/name/nm0454752

Josie Liang
imdb.com/name/nm4169347

Josh Peters
imdb.com/name/nm5444016

Lia Buman
imdb.com/name/nm2513975
Assistant: Patrick Reese

Peter Schlessel
Founder
imdb.com/name/nm0772283
Assistant: Jessica Freenborn

FILMED IMAGINATION

8017 Hemet Place
Los Angeles, CA 90046
323-963-4880

info@filmedimagination.com
filmedimagination.com
imdb.com/company/co0229508

Does not accept any unsolicited material. Project types include Feature Films. Preferred genres include Fantasy.

Daniel Dreifuss
Producer
imdb.com/name/nm1897448

Marius Haugan
Producer
imdb.com/name/nm2235104

FILM GARDEN ENTERTAINMENT

22287 Mulholland Hwy. #206
Calabasas, CA 91302
818-783-3456 (phone)
818-752-8186 (fax)

filmgarden.tv
imdb.com/company/co0011492
facebook.com/pages/Film-Garden-Entertainment/
    202254163142169
linkedin.com/company/film-garden-entertainment

Project types include TV. Preferred genres include Non-Fiction, Period, and Reality. Established in 1994.

Nancy Jacobs Miller
President

Toni Gray
Director of Production

Michelle Van Kempen
Executive Vice-President

FILM HARVEST

750 Lillian Way, Suite 6
LA, CA 90038
310-926-4131 (phone)
323-481-8499 (fax)

info@filmharvest.com
filmharvest.com
imdb.com/company/co0251161

Does not accept any unsolicited material. Project types include Feature Films. Preferred genres include Action, Documentary, Drama, Horror, Non-Fiction, Science Fiction, and Thriller. Established in 2009.

Joseph McKelheer
Executive Producer
joe@filmharvest.com
imdb.com/name/nm1559624

Eben Kostbar
Producer
eben@filmharvest.com
imdb.com/name/nm1670295

Elana Kostbar
info@filmharvest.com
imdb.com/name/nm3657939

FILMNATION ENTERTAINMENT

345 N Maple Dr, Suite 202
Beverly Hills, CA 90210
310-859-0088 (phone)
310-859-0089 (fax)

150 W 22nd St.
9th Floor
New York, NY 10011
917-484-8900 (phone)
917-484-8901 (fax)

wearefilmnation.com

imdb.com/company/co0251858
facebook.com/filmnation

Accepts query letter from unproduced, unrepresented writers. Project types include Feature Films. Preferred genres include Action, Crime, Drama, Fantasy, Horror, and Thriller. Established in 2008.

Patrick Chu
Director of Development
pchu@wearefilmnation.com
imdb.com/name/nm1776958

Glen Basner
gbasner@wearefilmnation.com
imdb.com/name/nm0059984

FILM SCIENCE

201 Lavaca St Suite 502
Austin, TX 78701
917-501-5197

info@filmscience.com
filmscience.com

Accepts query letter from unproduced, unrepresented writers. Project types include Feature Films. Preferred genres include Comedy, Drama, and Family.

Anish Savjani
Executive
anish@filmscience.com
imdb.com/name/nm1507013

FILMSMITH PRODUCTIONS

3400 Airport Dr
Bldg D
Santa Monica, CA 90405
310-260-8866 (phone)
310-397-7155 (fax)

filmsmith@mac.com
imdb.com/company/co0017423
filmsmithproductions.net

Accepts query letter from unproduced, unrepresented writers. Project types include Feature Films and TV. Preferred genres include Comedy, Crime, Drama, and Thriller.

Ian Smith
CEO
317-345-2959

FIPPY & THUMP INTERNATIONAL PRODUCTIONS

215 W. 88th St, Suite 3C
New York, NY 10024
212-873-9841 (phone)
212-787-6875 (fax)

curkau@msn.com
geocities.ws/gitawei

Does not accept any unsolicited material. Project types include Feature Films. Preferred genres include Drama. Established in 2014.

Curt Kaufman
Producer

Gita Kaufman
Producer

FIRST RUN FEATURES

The Film Center Building, 630 Ninth Ave, Suite 1213
New York City, NY 10036
212-243-0600 (phone)
212-989-7649 (fax)

info@firstrunfeatures.com
firstrunfeatures.com
imdb.com/company/co0002318
facebook.com/firstrunfeatures

Does not accept any unsolicited material. Project types include Feature Films and Short Films. Preferred genres include Comedy, Drama, Fantasy, Romance, and Thriller. Established in 1979.

Seymour Wishman
President
imdb.com/name/nm0936544

Marc Mauceri
imdb.com/name/nm1439609

FIVE BY EIGHT PRODUCTIONS

4312 Clarissa Ave
Los Angeles, CA 90027
917-658-7545

sean@fivebyeight.com
fivebyeight.com
imdb.com/company/co0173956

Accepts query letter from unproduced, unrepresented writers via email. Project types include Feature Films and TV. Preferred genres include Drama. Established in 2006.

Michael Connors
mike@fivebyeight.com
imdb.com/name/nm2155421

Sean Mullen
sean@fivebyeight.com
imdb.com/name/nm2013693

FIVE SMOOTH STONE PRODUCTIONS

106 Oakland Hills Court
Duluth, GA 30097
770-476-7171

imdb.com/company/co0332052

Does not accept any unsolicited material. Project types include Feature Films. Preferred genres include Action, Drama, and Non-Fiction.

Morgan Middlemas
Partner

Rick Middlemas
Partner
linkedin.com/in/rickmiddlemass

FLASHPOINT ENTERTAINMENT

1318 San Ysidro Dr
Beverly Hills, CA 90210
310-205-6300

info@flashpointentertainment.com
imdb.com/company/co0177280

Does not accept any unsolicited material. Project types include Feature Films. Preferred genres include Drama and Romance.

Andrew Tennenbaum
imdb.com/name/nm0990025

Tom Johnson
310-205-6300
imdb.com/name/nm1927361

Laura Roman-Rockhold
310-205-6300
info@flashpointent.com
imdb.com/name/nm4099178

FLAVOR UNIT ENTERTAINMENT

119 Washington Ave, Suite 400
Miami Beach, FL 33139
201-333-4883 (phone)
973-556-1770 (fax)

155 Morgan St.
Jersey City, NJ 07302

info@flavorunitentertainment.com
flavorentertainment.com
imdb.com/company/co0050873

Accepts query letter from unproduced, unrepresented writers via email. Project types include Feature Films and TV. Preferred genres include Comedy, Drama, Family, and Romance.

Queen Latifah
CEO
201-333-4883
imdb.com/name/nm0001451

Otis Best
201-333-4883
imdb.com/name/nm1454006

Shakim Compere
CEO
201-333-4883
imdb.com/name/nm1406277
Assistant: Mark Jean

FLOREN SHIEH PRODUCTIONS

20 W 22nd St
Ste 415
New York, NY 10010
212-898-0890

katherine@florenshieh.com
imdb.com/company/co0287709

Accepts query letter from unproduced, unrepresented writers. Project types include Feature Films. Preferred genres include Drama.

Clay Floren
Producer
imdb.com/name/nm2850202

Aimee Shieh
Producer
imdb.com/name/nm1848263

Sean Woodruff
Story Editor
linkedin.com/in/seanswoodruff

FLOWER FILMS INC.

7360 Santa Monica Blvd
West Hollywood, CA 90046
323-876-7400 (phone)
323-876-7401 (fax)

imdb.com/company/co0148520

Accepts scripts from produced or represented writers. Project types include Feature Films and TV. Preferred genres include Comedy, Drama, Family, Fantasy, Romance, and Thriller. Established in 1995.

Drew Barrymore
Partner
imdb.com/name/nm0000106

Chris Miller
imdb.com/name/nm0588091
Assistant: Steven Acosta

Ember Truesdell
ember@flowerfilms.com
imdb.com/name/nm1456092

FOCUS FEATURES

100 Universal City Plaza Building 9128
Universal City, CA 91608
818-777-7373

press@filminfocus.com
focusfeatures.com
imdb.com/company/co0042399

twitter.com/focusfeatures
facebook.com/FocusFeatures

Does not accept any unsolicited material. Project types include Feature Films and TV. Preferred genres include Action, Animation, Comedy, Crime, Documentary, Drama, Fantasy, Horror, Non-Fiction, Romance, and Thriller. Established in 1975.

James Schamus
imdb.com/name/nm0770005

Jeb Brody
imdb.com/name/nm1330162
Assistant: Rebecca Arzoian

Andrew Karpen
imdb.com/name/nm2537917

Peter Kujawski
imdb.com/name/nm1081654

Josh McLaughlin
imdb.com/name/nm2249958

Christopher Koop
imdb.com/name/nm3096137

FORENSIC FILMS

1 Worth St, 2nd Floor
New York, NY 10013
212-966-1110 (phone)
212-966-1125 (fax)

forensicfilms@gmail.com
imdb.com/company/co0024292
twitter.com/forensicfilms

Accepts query letter from unproduced, unrepresented writers via email. Project types include Feature Films. Preferred genres include Comedy, Crime, Drama, Romance, and Thriller.

Robin O'Hara
Producer
imdb.com/name/nm0641327

Scott Macauley
Producer
imdb.com/name/nm0531337
linkedin.com/in/scottmacaulay

FORESIGHT UNLIMITED

2934 1/2 Beverly Glen Circle
Suite 900
Bel Air, CA 90077
310-275-5222 (phone)
310-275-5202 (fax)

info@foresight-unltd.com
foresight-unltd.com
imdb.com/company/co0139768
facebook.com/foresightunlimited

Accepts query letter from unproduced, unrepresented
writers via email. Project types include Feature Films.
Preferred genres include Action, Comedy, Crime,
Drama, Romance, Science Fiction, and Thriller.

Mark Damon
CEO
imdb.com/name/nm0198941

Tamara Birkemoe
imdb.com/name/nm1736077

Scott Collette

FOREST PARK PICTURES

11210 Briarcliff Ln
Studio City, CA 91604-4277
323-654-2735 (phone)
323-654-2735 (fax)

imdb.com/company/co0042178

Accepts query letter from unproduced, unrepresented
writers. Project types include Feature Films. Preferred
genres include Drama, Horror, and Thriller.
Established in 2002.

Hayden Christensen
Partner
323-848-2942 ext. 265
imdb.com/name/nm0159789

Tove Christensen
Partner
323-848-2942 ext. 265
imdb.com/name/nm0159922

FORGET ME NOT PRODUCTIONS

New York

info@4getmenotproductions.com
4getmenotproductions.com
linkedin.com/company/forget-me-not-productions
facebook.com/ForgetMeNotProductions

Accepts query letter from unproduced, unrepresented
writers via email. Project types include Feature Films.
Preferred genres include Drama.

Jennifer Gargano
jennifergargano@4getmenotproductions.com
imdb.com/name/nm2470854

Harry Azano
Producer
harryazano@gmail.com

FORTIS FILMS

8581 Santa Monica Blvd, Suite 1
West Hollywood, CA 90069
310-659-4533 (phone)
310-659-4373 (fax)

imdb.com/company/co0015475
linkedin.com/company/fortis-films

Accepts query letter from unproduced, unrepresented
writers. Project types include Feature Films and TV.
Preferred genres include Comedy, Drama, and
Romance.

Sandra Bullock
Partner
310-659-4533
imdb.com/name/nm0000113

Bryan Moore

Maggie Biggar
Partner
310-659-4533
imdb.com/name/nm0081772

FORTRESS FEATURES

2727 Main St
Santa Monica, CA 90405
323-467-4700

fortressfeatures.com
twitter.com/fortressmovies
imdb.com/company/co0194394

facebook.com/FortressMovies

Does not accept any unsolicited material. Project types include Feature Films. Preferred genres include Action, Comedy, Crime, Drama, Horror, and Thriller. Established in 2004.

Brett Forbes
Partner
imdb.com/name/nm1771405

Patrick Rizzotti
Partner
imdb.com/name/nm0729948

Bonnie Forbes
imdb.com/name/nm1424832

FORWARD ENTERTAINMENT

9255 Sunset Blvd, Suite 805
West Hollywood, CA 90069
310-278-6700 (phone)
310-278-6770 (fax)

Accepts query letter from unproduced, unrepresented writers via email. Project types include Feature Films and TV. Preferred genres include Non-Fiction.

Connie Tavel
Partner
ctavel@forward-ent.com
imdb.com/name/nm0851679

Vera Mihailovich
Partner
vmihailovich@forward-ent.com
imdb.com/name/nm2250568

FORWARD PASS

12233 W Olympic Blvd
Ste 340
Los Angeles, CA 90064
310-207-7378 (phone)
310-207-3426 (fax)

imdb.com/company/co0035930
linkedin.com/company/forward-pass-inc

Does not accept any unsolicited material. Project types include Feature Films. Preferred genres include Crime,

Detective, Drama, Non-Fiction, Period, Sociocultural, and Thriller.

Michael Mann
imdb.com/name/nm0000520

FOURBOYS FILMS

4000 Warner Blvd
Burbank, CA 91522
818-954-4378 (phone)
818-954-5359 (fax)

info@fourboysfilms.com
fourboysfilms.com
imdb.com/company/co0106524
twitter.com/FourBoysEnt

Does not accept any unsolicited material. Project types include Feature Films and TV. Preferred genres include Animation, Comedy, and Drama. Established in 2001.

David Hunt
Partner
imdb.com/name/nm0402408
linkedin.com/pub/david-hunt/24/888/742

A.J. Morewitz
President
818-954-4378
imdb.com/name/nm1031450

Patricia Heaton
Partner
imdb.com/name/nm0005004

FOX 2000 PICTURES

10201 W Pico Blvd
Los Angeles, CA 90035
310-369-1000 (phone)
310-369-4258 (fax)

foxmovies.com
imdb.com/company/co0017497
facebook.com/pages/Fox-2000-Pictures/
    106316459407327
twitter.com/20thcenturyfox
linkedin.com/groups/20th-Century-Fox-3745273

Does not accept any unsolicited material. Preferred genres include Action, Animation, Comedy, Crime,

Drama, Family, Fantasy, Horror, Myth, Romance, Science Fiction, and Thriller. Established in 1996.

Elizabeth Gabler
elizabeth.gabler@fox.com
imdb.com/name/nm1992894

Riley Kathryn Ellis
Executive
riley.ellis@fox.com

FOX DIGITAL STUDIOS

10201 W Pico Blvd
Los Angeles, CA 90035
310-369-1000

david.brooks@fox.com
foxdigitalstudios.com
facebook.com/FoxDigitalStudio
imdb.com/company/co0365818

Accepts query letter from produced or represented writers. Project types include Feature Films and TV. Preferred genres include Comedy, Crime, Drama, Horror, and Thriller.

David Worthen Brooks
Creative Director
imdb.com/name/nm3652161

FOX INTERNATIONAL PRODUCTIONS (FIP)

10201 W Pico Blvd
Los Angeles, CA 90035
310-369-1000

foxinternational.com
imdb.com/company/co0237611

Does not accept any unsolicited material. Preferred genres include Action, Crime, Drama, Family, Romance, and Thriller. Established in 2008.

Sanford Panitch
President
310-369-1000
sanford.panitch@fox.com
imdb.com/name/nm0659529

Anna Kokourina
imdb.com/name/nm3916463

Marco Mehlitz
imdb.com/name/nm0576438

FOX SEARCHLIGHT PICTURES

10201 W Pico Blvd
Building 38
Los Angeles, CA 90035
310-369-1000 (phone)
310-369-2359 (fax)

foxsearchlight.com
facebook.com/foxsearchlight
twitter.com/foxsearchlight
linkedin.com/company/fox-searchlight-pictures
imdb.com/company/co0028932

Does not accept any unsolicited material. Preferred genres include Action, Comedy, Crime, Drama, Family, Fantasy, Horror, Romance, and Thriller. Established in 1994.

Stephen Gilula
310-369-1000
stephen.gilula@fox.com
imdb.com/name/nm2322989

FRAME 29 FILMS

7070 Bruns Dr
Mobile, AL 36695

drew@frame29films.com
horst@frame29films.com
frame29films.com
facebook.com/frame29films
imdb.com/company/co0413096

Does not accept any unsolicited material. Project types include Feature Films. Preferred genres include Action, Drama, and Thriller. Established in 2012.

Drew Hall
Creative Executive
drew@frame29films.com
imdb.com/name/nm0355527

Horst Sarubin
Creative Executive
horst@frame29films.com
imdb.com/name/nm0765689

FRANCISCO PRODUCTIONS

franciscoproductions.net
facebook.com/pages/Francisco-Productions-LLC/
    231000013617995
imdb.com/company/co0306508

Accepts query letter from unproduced, unrepresented
writers via email. Project types include Feature Films.
Preferred genres include Drama and Period.
Established in 2012.

Gabriel Francisco
Producer
imdb.com/name/nm3943533
twitter.com/therealgabef

Rafael Francisco
Producer
imdb.com/name/nm3315277
twitter.com/therealrafe

Jeremy Profe
Director
imdb.com/name/nm3942977
twitter.com/mrprofe

FREDERATOR STUDIOS

2829 N. Glenoaks Blvd., Ste. 203
Burbank CA 91504
818-848-8348

22 W 21st St, 7th Floor
New York City, NY 10010
212-779-4133 (phone)
917-591-7577 (fax)

hey@frederator.com
frederator.com
imdb.com/company/co0070267
facebook.com/frederatorstudios
linkedin.com/company/frederator-networks-inc-
twitter.com/channelfred

Accepts query letter from unproduced, unrepresented
writers via email. Project types include Short Films and
TV. Preferred genres include Animation, Comedy, and
Family. Established in 1998.

Fred Selbert
646-274-4601
fred@frederator.com
imdb.com/name/nm0782288
twitter.com/fredseibert
Assistant: Zoe Barton - zoe@frederator.com

Eric Homan
eric@frederator.com
imdb.com/name/nm2302704

Kevin Kolde
kevin@frederator.com

Carrie Miller
carrie@frederator.com

FREDERIC GOLCHAN PRODUCTIONS

c/o Radar Pictures
10900 Wilshire Blvd, 14th Floor
Los Angeles, CA 90024
310-208-8525 (phone)
310-208-1764 (fax)

fgfilm@aol.com
imdb.com/company/co0093754

Does not accept any unsolicited material. Preferred
genres include Action, Comedy, Crime, Drama, and
Thriller.

Frederic Golchan
asstgolchan@gmail.com
imdb.com/name/nm0324907
linkedin.com/pub/frederic-golchan/0/625/b16
Assistant: Gaillaume Chiasoda

FRED KUENERT PRODUCTIONS

1601 Hilts Ave. #2
Los Angeles, CA 90024
310-470-3363 (phone)
310-470-0060 (fax)

Accepts query letter from unproduced, unrepresented
writers via email. Project types include Feature Films.
Preferred genres include Action, Fantasy, Horror,
Science Fiction, and Thriller.

Sandra Chouinard
Partner

Fred Kuenert
fkuehnert@earthlink.net
imdb.com/name/nm0473896
linkedin.com/pub/fred-kuehnert/4/352/848

FREEDOM FILMS

15300 Ventura Blvd. #508
Sherman Oaks, CA 91403
818-906-2339 (phone)
818-906-2342 (fax)

info@freedomfilmsllc.com
freedomfilms.com

Does not accept any unsolicited material. Project types include Feature Films. Preferred genres include Action, Crime, Drama, Family, Horror, and Thriller.

Warren Davis
Head of Development

Carissa Buffel-Matusow

Kevin J Matusow

Brain Presley
CEO
imdb.com/name/nm0696169

Alexandria Klipstein
Creative Executive
imdb.com/name/nm2317077

Scott Robinson
imdb.com/name/nm1558904

FRELAINE

8383 Wilshire Blvd
5th Fl
Beverly Hills, CA 90211
323-848-9729 (phone)
323-848-7219 (fax)

imdb.com/company/co0176000

Accepts query letter from unproduced, unrepresented writers. Project types include Feature Films. Preferred genres include Action, Fantasy, Period, and Thriller.

James Jacks
Executive
imdb.com/name/nm0413208

FRESH & SMOKED

Studio City
10700 Ventura Blvd. Ste. 2D
Studio City, CA 91604
818-505-1311 (phone)
818-301-2135 (fax)

bdtd@freshandsmoked.com
freshandsmoked.com
imdb.com/company/co0223352
twitter.com/freshandsmoked
facebook.com/pages/Fresh-Smoked/
    116615628395984

Accepts scripts from unproduced, unrepresented writers. Project types include Feature Films, TV, and Commercials. Preferred genres include Action, Animation, Comedy, Crime, Detective, Drama, Family, Fantasy, Horror, Myth, Non-Fiction, Reality, Romance, Science Fiction, and Thriller.

Monika Gosch
Producer
monika@freshandsmoked.com
imdb.com/name/nm2815838

Jeremy Gosch
Director
jeremy@freshandsmoked.com
imdb.com/name/nm0331443

Angela McIntyre
angela@freshandsmoked.com

FRIED FILMS

100 N Crescent Dr, Suite 350
Beverly Hills, CA 90210
310-694-8150 (phone)
310-861-5454 (fax)

imdb.com/company/co0053780

Accepts query letter from unproduced, unrepresented writers. Project types include Feature Films and TV. Preferred genres include Action, Comedy, Crime, Detective, Drama, Family, Romance, and Thriller. Established in 1990.

Robert Fried
Producer
imdb.com/name/nm0294975

Tyrrell Shaffner
Development Executive
424-210-3607
imdb.com/name/nm1656222

FRIENDLY FILMS

100 N Crescent Dr, Suite 350
Beverly Hills, CA 90210
310-432-1818 (phone)
310-432-1801 (fax)

info@friendly-films.com
friendly-films.com
imdb.com/company/co0186321

Accepts query letter from unproduced, unrepresented writers. Project types include Feature Films. Preferred genres include Comedy, Crime, Drama, Family, and Science Fiction. Established in 2006.

David Friendly
310-432-1800
imdb.com/name/nm0295560

FRONT STREET PICTURES

1950 Franklin St
Vancouver, BC V5L 1R2
Canada
604-257-4720 (phone)
604-257-4739 (fax)

info@frontstreetpictures.com
frontstreetpictures.com
imdb.com/company/co0149567

Accepts query letter from unproduced, unrepresented writers. Project types include Feature Films and TV. Preferred genres include Action, Comedy, Crime, Drama, Fantasy, and Thriller.

Harvey Kahn
Producer
harvey@frontstreetpictures.com
imdb.com/name/nm0434838

FR PRODUCTIONS

1531 Colorado Ave.
Santa Monica, CA 90404

310-470-9212 (phone)
310-470-4905 (fax)

imdb.com/company/co0168898

Accepts query letter from unproduced, unrepresented writers via email. Project types include Feature Films. Preferred genres include Comedy, Crime, Drama, Family, Romance, and Thriller.

Fred Roos
frprod@earthlink.net
imdb.com/name/nm0740407

FULLER FILMS

P.O. BOX 976
Venice, CA 90294
310-717-8842

imdb.com/company/co0066675

Does not accept any unsolicited material. Project types include Feature Films. Preferred genres include Comedy, Crime, and Drama.

Paul De Souza
Producer
gopics@verizon.net
imdb.com/name/nm0996278

Henry Bean
imdb.com/name/nm0063785

FUN LITTLE FILMS

2227 W Olive Ave
Burbank, CA 91506
323-467-6868

contact@funlittlemovies.com
funlittlemovies.com
imdb.com/company/co0161105

Accepts query letter from unproduced, unrepresented writers. Project types include TV. Preferred genres include Animation and Comedy.

Frank Chindamo
President
frank@funlittlemovies.com
imdb.com/name/nm0157828

FURLINED

2803 Colorado Ave
Santa Monica, CA 90404
310-496-5060

info@furlined.com
facebook.com/furlinedproductions
furlined.com
twitter.com/furlined_

Does not accept any unsolicited material. Project types include Commercials. Established in 2005.

Diane Mcarter
President
diane@furlined.com

David Thorne
Executive Producer
david@furlined.com

Meghan Lang
Executive Producer
meghan@furlined.com

FURST FILMS

8954 W Pico Blvd
2nd Floor
Los Angeles, CA 90035
310-278-6468 (phone)
310-278-7401 (fax)

info@furstfilms.com
furstfilms.com
imdb.com/company/co0022433

Accepts query letter from unproduced, unrepresented writers via email. Project types include Feature Films and TV. Preferred genres include Action, Crime, Detective, Drama, Horror, Non-Fiction, Reality, and Thriller.

Bryan Furst
Principal/Producer
imdb.com/name/nm1227576

Sean Furst
Partner
imdb.com/name/nm0299120

FURTHUR FILMS

100 Universal City Plaza
Building 5174
Universal City, CA 91608
818-777-6700 (phone)
818-866-1278 (fax)

imdb.com/company/co0002647
twitter.com/furtherfilms

Accepts query letter from unproduced, unrepresented writers. Project types include Feature Films. Preferred genres include Comedy, Crime, Drama, Romance, and Thriller.

Michael Douglas
Producer
imdb.com/name/nm0000140

Andy Ziskin

FUSEFRAME

2332 Cotner Ave, Suite 200
Los Angeles, CA 90064
424-208-1765

imdb.com/company/co0353810

Does not accept any unsolicited material. Project types include Feature Films. Preferred genres include Horror and Thriller. Established in 2011.

Marcus Chait
Director of Film and New Media
imdb.com/name/nm1483939

Eva Konstantopoulos
imdb.com/name/nm2192285

FUSION FILMS

2355 Westwood Blvd, Suite 117
Los Angeles, CA 90064
310-441-1496

info@fusionfilms.net
imdb.com/company/co0337140

Accepts query letter from unproduced, unrepresented writers. Project types include Feature Films and TV. Preferred genres include Action, Animation, Comedy, Crime, Drama, Fantasy, Horror, and Thriller.

Jay Judah
Creative Executive

John Baldecchi
imdb.com/name/nm0049689

FUZZY DOOR PRODUCTIONS

1925 Century Park E
Los Angeles, CA 90067
323-857-8826 (phone)
323-857-8945 (fax)

imdb.com/company/co0065872
facebook.com/FuzzyDoorProductions

Does not accept any unsolicited material. Project types include Feature Films and TV. Preferred genres include Animation, Comedy, and Family. Established in 1998.

Seth MacFarlane
Founder
sethmacfarlane.org
imdb.com/name/nm0532235

GAETA/ROSENZWEIG FILMS

6399 Wilshire Blvd, Ste 510
Santa Monica, CA 90048
310-399-7101

imdb.com/company/co0248894

Accepts query letter from unproduced, unrepresented writers. Project types include Feature Films and TV. Preferred genres include Comedy, Crime, Drama, Horror, and Thriller.

Alison Rosenzweig
Producer
imdb.com/name/nm0742851
linkedin.com/pub/alison-rosenzweig/64/519/b03

Michael J. Gaeta
Partner
imdb.com/name/nm1357812

GALATEE FILMS

19 Ave de Messine
Paris, France 75008

+33 1 44 29 21 40 (phone)
+33 1 44 29 25 90 (fax)

mail@galateefilms.com
imdb.com/company/co0058643
facebook.com/pages/Galat%C3%A9e-Films/
   434039390064500
linkedin.com/company/galatee-films-sas

Accepts query letter from unproduced, unrepresented writers via email. Project types include Feature Films. Preferred genres include Drama, Non-Fiction, and Romance.

Nicolas Mauvernay
Producer
imdb.com/name/nm1241814

Nicolas Elghozi
Producer

Jacques Perrin
President
imdb.com/name/nm0674742

Christophe Barratier
Producer
imdb.com/name/nm0056725

GALLANT ENTERTAINMENT

16161 Ventura Blvd, Suite 664
Encino, CA 91436
818-905-9848

mog@gallantentertainment.com
gallantentertainment.com
twitter.com/GallantEntGroup
linkedin.com/company/the-gallant-entertainment-
   group
imdb.com/company/co0018692

Accepts query letter from unproduced, unrepresented writers via email. Project types include Feature Films, TV, and Commercials. Preferred genres include Drama, Family, Non-Fiction, Reality, Romance, and Thriller. Established in 1992.

K.R. Gallant
Operations
krg@gallantentertainment.com

Michael Gallant
Producer
imdb.com/name/nm0302572
linkedin.com/pub/michael-o-gallant/45/733/506

GAMBIT PICTURES

10100 Santa Monica Blvd., Suite 1300
Los Angeles, CA 90067

Does not accept any unsolicited material. Project types include Feature Films and TV. Preferred genres include Drama, Science Fiction, and Thriller.

George Nolfi
Partner/Producer/Writer/Director
imdb.com/name/nm1079776

Michael Hackett
Partner/Producer
imdb.com/name/nm0352489

GARLIN PICTURES

11640 Woodbridge St, Suite #106
Studio City, CA 91604
310-991-7754 (phone)
818-506-7122 (fax)

info@garlinpictures.com
garlinpictures.com
imdb.com/company/co0136730

Does not accept any unsolicited material. Project types include Feature Films.

Josh Etting
CEO/Producer
imdb.com/name/nm0262186

Brian R. Etting
CEO/Producer
imdb.com/name/nm0262188

GARY HOFFMAN PRODUCTIONS

3931 Puerco Canyon Rd
Malibu, CA 90265
310-456-1830 (phone)
310-456-8866 (fax)

garyhofprods@charter.net
imdb.com/company/co0014302

Accepts query letter from unproduced, unrepresented writers via email. Project types include Feature Films and TV. Preferred genres include Action, Comedy, Crime, Drama, Romance, and Thriller. Established in 1988.

Ann Ryan

Gary Hoffman
President
imdb.com/name/nm0388888

GARY SANCHEZ PRODUCTIONS

729 Seward St
2nd Fl
Los Angeles, CA 90038
USA
323-465-4600 (phone)
323-465-0782 (fax)

gary@garysanchezprods.com
garysanchezprods.com
imdb.com/company/co0186190
facebook.com/pages/Gary-Sanchez-Productions/
    553932381341300
linkedin.com/company/gary-sanchez-productions

Does not accept any unsolicited material. Project types include Feature Films and TV. Preferred genres include Comedy.

Will Ferrell
imdb.com/name/nm0002071

Gary Sanchez
gary@garysanchezprods.com
facebook.com/garysanchezprods

GAUCHO PRODUCTIONS

12810 Westella Dr
Houston, TX 77077
713-397-7135 (phone)
713-937-9309 (fax)

martin@gauchop.com
gauchop.com
imdb.com/company/co0091826

Does not accept any unsolicited material. Project types include Feature Films. Preferred genres include Drama.

Andrea Elustondo-Sanchez
Executive Producer
imdb.com/name/nm1326834

Martin Delon
Producer/Director
imdb.com/name/nm1312872

GENEXT FILMS

1650 E 4th St, Ste 101
Santa Ana, CA 92701
714-552-2731

contact@genextfilms.com
genextfilms.com
imdb.com/company/co0234963
facebook.com/pages/GenextT-FILMS-Productions/
    686554521437240

Accepts query letter from unproduced, unrepresented
writers via email. Project types include Feature Films
and TV. Preferred genres include Comedy.

Carlos Salas
imdb.com/name/nm2972624
Assistant: Kathy Snyder

Rossana Salas
imdb.com/name/nm2970664

GENREBEND PRODUCTIONS

233 Wilshire Blvd, Suite 400
Santa Monica, CA 90401
310-860-0878

genrebend@elvis.com
imdb.com/company/co0094959
twitter.com/genrebend

Accepts query letter from unproduced, unrepresented
writers via email. Project types include Feature Films
and TV. Preferred genres include Comedy and Drama.

Tom Lavagnino
imdb.com/name/nm0491706

David Nutter
imdb.com/name/nm0638354
twitter.com/genrebend

GENRE FILMS

10201 W. Pico Blvd.
Los Angeles, CA 90035

Does not accept any unsolicited material. Project types
include Feature Films. Preferred genres include Action,
Family, and Fantasy.

Simon Kinberg
Writer/Producer
imdb.com/name/nm1334526

Aditya Sood
President of Production
imdb.com/name/nm1533078

GEORGE LITTO PRODUCTIONS

339 N Orange Dr
Los Angeles, CA 90401
323-936-6350

imdb.com/company/co0050602

Does not accept any unsolicited material. Project types
include Feature Films. Preferred genres include Action,
Drama, and Thriller.

George Litto
CEO/Producer
imdb.com/name/nm0514788

Andria Litto
President
imdb.com/name/nm0514787

GERARD BUTLER ALAN SIEGEL ENTERTAINMENT

11755 Wilshire Blvd
9th Fl
Los Angeles, CA 90025
310-278-8400

imdb.com/company/co0332840

Does not accept any unsolicited material. Project types
include Feature Films. Preferred genres include
Comedy, Drama, and Thriller.

Danielle Robinson
Director of Development

Gerard Butler
imdb.com/name/nm0124930

Alan Siegel
Executive

GERBER PICTURES

4000 Warner Blvd
Building 138, Suite 1205
Burbank, CA 91522
818-954-3046 (phone)
818-954-3706 (fax)

imdb.com/company/co0062831
linkedin.com/company/gerber-pictures
gerberpics.com
facebook.com/pages/Gerber-Pictures/
    100942556613624

Does not accept any unsolicited material. Project types
include Feature Films and TV. Preferred genres
include Action, Animation, Comedy, Drama, Family,
and Romance.

Bill Gerber
President
imdb.com/name/nm0314088
Assistant: James Leffler

GG FILMZ

5028 Vanalden Ave
Tarzana, CA 91356

ggfilmz.com
facebook.com/pizzafilms
twitter.com/DeborahGGFilmz
imdb.com/company/co0195008

Does not accept any unsolicited material. Project types
include Feature Films. Preferred genres include Action,
Crime, and Drama.

Deborah Giarratana
Producer
imdb.com/name/nm1072937

Ray Giarratana
Producer/Director/Writer
imdb.com/name/nm1568265

GHOST HOUSE PICTURES

315 S Beverly Dr, Suite 216
Beverly Hills, CA 90212
310-785-3900 (phone)
310-785-9176 (fax)

info@ghosthousepictures.com
ghosthousepictures.com
imdb.com/company/co0116611

Does not accept any unsolicited material. Project types
include Feature Films and TV. Preferred genres
include Comedy, Drama, Horror, and Thriller.

Sam Raimi
imdb.com/name/nm0000600

GHOULARDI FILM COMPANY

2301 Nottingham Ave
Los Angeles, CA 90027
818-487-7444

imdb.com/company/co0027686

Does not accept any unsolicited material. Project types
include Feature Films. Preferred genres include
Drama.

Paul Thomas Anderson
Writer/Director/Producer
imdb.com/name/nm0000759

JoAnne Sellar
Producer
imdb.com/name/nm0783280

GIANT SCREEN FILMS

990 Grove St, Suite 200
Evanston, IL 60201
847-475-9140

info@gsfilms.com
gsfilms.com
imdb.com/company/co0082191

Does not accept any unsolicited material. Project types
include Feature Films. Preferred genres include Non-
Fiction.

Don Kempf
Founder/Producer
imdb.com/name/nm0447437

Andy Wood
SVP of Development and Operations
imdb.com/name/nm2012559

GIDDEN MEDIA

10202 W. Washington Blvd. David Lean Bldg. Ste
230
Culver City, CA 90232
310-244-2988

info@giddenmedia.com
giddenmedia.com
imdb.com/company/co0386252

Does not accept any unsolicited material. Project types
include Feature Films and TV. Preferred genres
include Drama and Non-Fiction.

Amy Baer
Producer
imdb.com/name/nm1616124

Christopher Ceccotti
Head of Development
imdb.com/name/nm5153580

GIGANTIC PICTURES

164 W 25th St
Suite 4M
New York, NY 10001
212-925-5075 (phone)
212-925-5061 (fax)

info@giganticpictures.com
giganticpictures.com
facebook.com/pages/Gigantic-Pictures/
    223176104540602

Accepts query letter from produced or represented
writers. Project types include Feature Films and TV.
Preferred genres include Comedy, Drama, Non-
Fiction, and Romance.

Brian Devine
Founder
imdb.com/name/nm0222601

Jason Orans
Producer
jason@giganticpictures.com
imdb.com/name/nm0649346

Pamela Ryan
Producer
pamela@giganticpictures.com
imdb.com/name/nm2135347

GIGAPIX STUDIOS

9333 Oso Ave
Chatsworth, CA 91311
818-592-0755 (phone)
800-862-7656 (fax)

info@gigapixstudios.com
gigapixstudios.com
imdb.com/company/co0190777

Does not accept any unsolicited material. Project types
include Feature Films. Preferred genres include Action
and Comedy.

Chris Blauvelt
Chairman

David Pritchard
President
imdb.com/name/nm0698021

GIL ADLER PRODUCTIONS

9000 W Sunset Blvd, Ste 504
West Hollywood, CA 90069
310-550-6265

Does not accept any unsolicited material. Project types
include Feature Films, TV, and Commercials.
Preferred genres include Action, Horror, Non-Fiction,
Reality, and Thriller. Established in 2001.

Gil Adler
Producer
imdb.com/name/nm0012155
linkedin.com/pub/gil-adler/6/a66/63b
Assistant: Ryan Lough

GILBERT FILMS

8409 Santa Monica Blvd.
West Hollywood, CA 90069
323-650-6800 (phone)
323-650-6810 (fax)

info@gilbertfilms.com
imdb.com/company/co0084122
gilbertfilms.com

Accepts query letter from unproduced, unrepresented writers via email. Project types include Feature Films. Preferred genres include Comedy, Drama, and Family.

Gary Gilbert
President
imdb.com/name/nm1344784

Jordan Horowitz
Vice-President, Production and Development
imdb.com/name/nm0395302

GIL NETTER PRODUCTIONS

1645 Abbot Kinney Blvd, Suite 320
Venice, CA 90291
310-566-5477 (phone)
310-899-6722 (fax)

facebook.com/pages/Gil-Netter-Productions/
   110136129048415
linkedin.com/company/gil-netter-production

Does not accept any unsolicited material. Project types include Feature Films. Preferred genres include Action, Comedy, Drama, Family, and Romance.

Gil Netter
Producer
imdb.com/name/nm0626696

Jennifer Ho
Executive

GI PICTURES

545 8th Ave Suite 401
New York, NY 10018

info@nehst.com
gipictures.com

Accepts query letter from unproduced, unrepresented writers via email. Project types include Feature Films. Preferred genres include Action and Drama.

Dana Offenbach
President of Nehst Studios
imdb.com/name/nm0644382

Larry Meistrich
Producer
imdb.com/name/nm0577134

GIRLS CLUB ENTERTAINMENT

30 Sir Francis Drake Blvd
PO Box 437
Ross, CA 94957
415-233-4060 (phone)
415-233-4082 (fax)

info@girlsclubentertainment.com
girlsclubentertainment.com
imdb.com/company/co0119654

Does not accept any unsolicited material. Project types include Feature Films and TV. Preferred genres include Comedy, Crime, Drama, Non-Fiction, Reality, and Romance.

Jennifer Siebel Newsom
Founder
jennifersiebelnewsom.com
imdb.com/name/nm1308076

Regina Kulik Scully
Founder

Wendi Gilbert
Producer

Jessica Congdon
Writer

GITLIN PRODUCTIONS

1310 Montana Ave Second Floor
Santa Monica, CA 90403
310-209-8443 (phone)
310-728-1749 (fax)

gitlinproduction@aol.com

Accepts query letter from unproduced, unrepresented writers via email. Project types include Feature Films and TV. Preferred genres include Action, Comedy, Drama, Non-Fiction, and Reality.

Mimi Polk Gitlin
Producer
imdb.com/name/nm0689316

Richard Gitlin

GITTES, INC.

16615 Park Ln Place
Los Angeles, CA 90049
310-472-2689

Accepts query letter from unproduced, unrepresented writers. Project types include Feature Films. Preferred genres include Comedy and Drama.

Harry Gittes
Producer
harry_gittes@spe.sony.com
imdb.com/name/nm0321228

Edward Wang
Director of Development
310-244-4334
edward_wang@spe.sony.com
imdb.com/name/nm0910882

GK FILMS

1540 2nd St, Suite 200
Santa Monica, CA 90401
310-315-1722 (phone)
310-315-1723 (fax)

contact@gk-films.com
gk-films.com
facebook.com/GKFilms
twitter.com/gkfilms
imdb.com/company/co0209646

Does not accept any unsolicited material. Project types include Feature Films and TV. Preferred genres include Action, Animation, Comedy, Crime, Drama, Family, Fantasy, Non-Fiction, Romance, Science Fiction, and Thriller. Established in 2007.

David Crocket
Creative Executive

Graham King
CEO
imdb.com/name/nm0454752
Assistant: Leah Williams, Michelle Reed

GLORY ROAD PRODUCTIONS

23638 Lyons Ave.
Newhall, CA 91321
424-202-2510

info@gloryroadproductions.com
facebook.com/pages/Glory-Road-Productions/
    152847784771624

Does not accept any unsolicited material. Project types include Feature Films. Preferred genres include Action, Comedy, Drama, Family, Fantasy, and Horror.

Michael Reymann
President
imdb.com/name/nm1478831

Erik Elseman
Executive Vice President
imdb.com/name/nm4831920

Tara Bonacci
Producer
imdb.com/name/nm1742721

Val Mancini
Director of Development
imdb.com/name/nm4441689

GOFF-KELLAM PRODUCTIONS

8491 Sunset Blvd. Suite 1000
West Hollywood, CA 90069
323-656-2001 (phone)
323-656-1002 (fax)

goffkellam.com
imdb.com/company/co0043362

Does not accept any unsolicited material. Project types include Feature Films.

Gina G. Goff
Partner/Producer
imdb.com/name/nm0324574

Laura A. Kellam
Partner/Producer
imdb.com/name/nm044549

GO FISH PICTURES

1000 Flower St
Glendale, CA 91201
818-695-7742

gofishpictures.com
imdb.com/company/co0108632

Does not accept any unsolicited material. Project types
include Feature Films.

GO GIRL MEDIA

3450 Cahuenga Blvd West #802
Los Angeles, CA 90068
310-472-8910

info@gogirlmedia.com
gogirlmedia.com
imdb.com/company/co0177675
facebook.com/pages/Go-Girl-Media/
185402498145525

Accepts query letter from unproduced, unrepresented
writers via email. Project types include Feature Films
and TV. Preferred genres include Animation, Comedy,
Drama, Family, Non-Fiction, and Reality. Established
in 2004.

Don Priess
Head of Production
don@gogirlmedia.com
imdb.com/name/nm1043744

Susie Singer Carter
CEO
susie@gogirlmedia.com
imdb.com/name/nm0802053

GOLD CIRCLE FILMS

233 Wilshire Blvd, Suite 650
Santa Monica, CA 90401
310-278-4800 (phone)
310-278-0885 (fax)

info@goldcirclefilms.com

goldcirclefilms.com
imdb.com/company/co0076476
facebook.com/pages/Gold-Circle-Films/
109649739054057
linkedin.com/company/gold-circle-films

Does not accept any unsolicited material. Project types
include Feature Films. Preferred genres include Action,
Comedy, Drama, Family, Horror, Romance, Science
Fiction, and Thriller. Established in 2000.

Paul Brooks
President
imdb.com/name/nm0112189

Brad Kessell
imdb.com/name/nm1733186

Guy Danella
Producer
twitter.com/GADanella

GOLDCREST FILMS

1 Lexington St
London W1F 9AF
United Kingdom
+44207-437-8696 (phone)
+44207-437-4448 (fax)

799 Washington St.
New York City, NY 10014
212-243-4700 (phone)
212-624-1701 (fax)

info@goldcrestfilms.com
goldcrestfilms.com
facebook.com/GoldcrestPost
twitter.com/Goldcrest_Films
imdb.com/company/co0045569
linkedin.com/company/goldcrest-films
imdb.com/company/co0045569
twitter.com/goldcrest_films

Does not accept any unsolicited material. Project types
include Feature Films and TV. Preferred genres
include Animation, Comedy, Drama, Non-Fiction,
Reality, and Romance. Established in 1977.

Stephen Johnston
President
imdb.com/name/nm1158125

Rob Farris
Head of Production
+44 (0)20 7437 7972
rfarris@goldcrestfilms.com

Patrick Malone
Managing Director
+44 (0)20 7437 7972
pmalone@goldcrestfilms.com

Martin Poultney
Director
+44 (0)20 7437 7972
mpoultney@goldcrestfilms.com

Laurent Treherne
Chief Technology Officer
+44 (0)20 7437 7972
ltreherne@goldcrestfilms.com

Tim Spitzer
Managing Director
212-897-3882
tspitzer@goldcrestfilms.com

Jim Gardner
Director of Operations
212-897-3890
jgardner@goldcrestfilms.com

Margaret Lewis
Producer
212-897-3966
mlewis@goldcrestfilms.com

GOLDENLIGHT FILMS

818-904-2667 (phone)
818-994-9124 (fax)

info@goldenlightfilms.com
goldenlightfilms.com
imdb.com/company/co0072737

Does not accept any unsolicited material. Project types include Feature Films, Short Films, and Commercials. Preferred genres include Drama and Thriller. Established in 1998.

Theodore Melfi
Founder
imdb.com/name/nm0577647
twitter.com/theodoremelfi

Jason Gibb
Development Executive

Kimberly Quinn
Founder
imdb.com/name/nm0703910

Shawn Askinosie
CCO
imdb.com/name/nm2999202

GOLDENRING PRODUCTIONS

4804 Laurel Canyon Blvd
Room 570
Valley Village, CA 91607
818-508-7425

info@goldenringproductions.net
goldenringproductions.net
imdb.com/company/co0047633

Accepts query letter from unproduced, unrepresented writers via email. Project types include Feature Films and TV. Preferred genres include Animation, Comedy, Drama, Family, and Non-Fiction.

Jane Goldenring
imdb.com/name/nm0325553
linkedin.com/pub/jane-goldenring/6/480/71

Jon King
jonnyfking@gmail.com

GOLDOVE ENTERTAINMENT

Los Angeles, CA
818-355-7670

info@goldove.com
twitter.com/GoldoveEnt
goldove.com
facebook.com/GoldoveEntertainment

Accepts query letter from unproduced, unrepresented writers via email. Project types include Feature Films and Short Films. Preferred genres include Action, Drama, and Thriller. Established in 2012.

Lynda McKoy
CEO

Gino McKoy
Director

Hudson McKoy
Vice-President

GOLDSMITH-THOMAS PRODUCTIONS

239 Central Park West, Suite 6A
New York, NY 10024
212-243-4147 (phone)
212-799-2545 (fax)

imdb.com/company/co0186672

Accepts query letter from unproduced, unrepresented writers. Project types include Feature Films and TV. Preferred genres include Comedy, Drama, Family, Non-Fiction, and Romance.

Elaine Goldsmith-Thomas
imdb.com/name/nm0326063
linkedin.com/pub/elaine-goldsmith-thomas/20/a85/498
Assistant: Anabel Graff

GOOD CLEAN FUN

3733 Motor Ave
Los Angeles, CA 90034
310-842-9300

goodcleanfunllc.com
imdb.com/name/nm2275176

Does not accept any unsolicited material. Project types include TV.

Jason Carbone
Producer

Matthew Wrablik
VP of Development
imdb.com/name/nm0136160

GOOD GAME ENTERTAINMENT

4000 Warner Blvd., Building 34
Burbank, CA 91522
818-954-3414

Does not accept any unsolicited material. Project types include TV. Preferred genres include Comedy and Drama.

Lauren Graham
Actor/Producer/Writer
imdb.com/name/nm0334179

Kathy Ebel
VP
imdb.com/name/nm1889799

GOOD HUMOR TELEVISION

9255 W Sunset Blvd #1040
West Hollywood, CA 90069
310-205-7361 (phone)
310-550-7962 (fax)

imdb.com/company/co0227256

Accepts query letter from unproduced, unrepresented writers. Project types include TV. Preferred genres include Animation and Comedy.

Tom Werner
imdb.com/name/nm0921492

GORDONSTREET PICTURES

2241 N.Cahuenga Blvd.
Los Angeles, CA
323-467-6267

imdb.com/company/co0137407

Does not accept any unsolicited material. Project types include Feature Films. Preferred genres include Drama and Thriller.

Ram Bergman
Producer
imdb.com/name/nm0074851

Raymond Izaac
Development
imdb.com/name/nm0412691

GORILLA PICTURES

2000 W Olive Ave
Burbank, CA 91506
818-848-2198 (phone)
818-848-2232 (fax)

info@gorillapictures.net
gorillapictures.net

Does not accept any unsolicited material. Project types include Feature Films. Preferred genres include Action, Animation, Crime, Drama, Family, Fantasy, Science Fiction, and Thriller. Established in 1999.

Bill Gottlieb
CEO
bill.gottlieb@gorillapictures.net
imdb.com/name/nm1539281

Don Wilson
don.wilson@gorillapictures.net
imdb.com/name/nm0933310

GOTHAM ENTERTAINMENT GROUP

Los Angeles, CA

85 John St Penthouse 1
New York City, NY 10038
814-253-5151 (phone)
801-439-6998 (fax)

newyork@gothamcity.com
losangeles@gothamcity.com
gothamentertainmentgroup.com
linkedin.com/company/gotham-entertainment-group

Accepts query letter from unproduced, unrepresented writers via email. Project types include Feature Films and TV. Preferred genres include Action, Comedy, Crime, Drama, Non-Fiction, Reality, Romance, Science Fiction, and Thriller.

Joel Roodman
Partner
joel@gothamentertainmentgroup.com
imdb.com/name/nm0740211

Eric Kopeloff
Partner
imdb.com/name/nm0465740

GRACE HILL MEDIA

12211 Huston St
Valley Village, CA 91607
818-762-0000

rsvp@gracehillmedia.com
gracehillmedia.com
facebook.com/GraceHillMedia
twitter.com/GraceHillTweets

linkedin.com/company/grace-hill-media

Does not accept any unsolicited material. Project types include Feature Films. Preferred genres include Documentary and Family. Established in 2000.

Jonathon Bock
Founder

GRACIE FILMS

10201 W. Pico Blvd., Bldg. 41/42 Los Angeles, CA 90064
310-369-7222

graciefilms@aol.com
graciefilms.com
imdb.com/company/co0035761

Does not accept any unsolicited material. Project types include Feature Films and TV. Preferred genres include Animation, Comedy, Drama, Family, Non-Fiction, and Romance.

James Brooks
imdb.com/name/nm0000985

Richard Sakai
President
imdb.com/name/nm0757017

Julie Ansell
imdb.com/name/nm0030572

GRADE A ENTERTAINMENT

149 S Barrington Ave, Suite 719
Los Angeles, CA 90049
310-358-8600 (phone)
310-919-2998 (fax)

development@gradeaent.com
gradeaent.com
imdb.com/company/co0092463

Accepts query letter from unproduced, unrepresented writers via email. Project types include Feature Films and TV. Preferred genres include Fantasy.

Andy Cohen
andy@gradeaent.com
imdb.com/name/nm2221597

GRAMMNET PRODUCTIONS

2461 Santa Monica Blvd #521
Santa Monica, CA 90404
310-317-4231 (phone)
310-317-4260 (fax)

imdb.com/company/co0067942

Does not accept any unsolicited material. Project types include Feature Films, TV, and Theater. Preferred genres include Comedy, Drama, Family, Non-Fiction, and Reality.

Stella Bulochnikov
Executive
310-255-5089
Assistant: Melissa Panzer, mpanzer@lionsgate.com

Kelsey Grammar
imdb.com/name/nm0001288
Assistant: Xochitl L. Olivas

GRANAT ENTERTAINMENT

2115 Colorado Ave
Santa Monica, CA 90404

imdb.com/company/co0282230

Does not accept any unsolicited material. Project types include Feature Films.

Cary Granat
President
imdb.com/name/nm0000026

GRAND CANAL FILM WORKS

1187 Coast Village Rd
Montecito, CA 93108
818-259-8237

11135 Magnolia, SU 160
North Hollywood, CA 91601

Does not accept any unsolicited material. Project types include Feature Films, TV, and Theater. Preferred genres include Non-Fiction and Reality.

Rick Brookwell
Partner
rbrookwell@grandcanalfw.com
imdb.com/name/nm2162558
linkedin.com/pub/rick-brookwell/9/906/407

Craig Haffner
Partner
chaffner@grandcanalfw.com
imdb.com/name/nm0353121
linkedin.com/pub/craig-haffner/9/1a6/193

GRAND HUSTLE ENTERTAINMENT

PMB 161 541 10th St
Atlanta, GA 30318

grandhustle.com
imdb.com/company/co0184618

Does not accept any unsolicited material. Preferred genres include Comedy.

T. I.
Producer, Actor
imdb.com/name/nm1939267

Jason Geter
Producer
imdb.com/name/nm2327951

GRAND PRODUCTIONS

16255 Venture Blvd, Suite 400
Encino, CA 91436
818-981-1497 (phone)
818-380-3006 (fax)

grandproductions@mac.com
twitter.com/grndproductions
imdb.com/company/co0000803

Does not accept any unsolicited material. Project types include Feature Films and TV. Preferred genres include Comedy and Drama.

Gary Randall
imdb.com/name/nm0709592

GRANDVIEW PICTURES

230 Central Park West
New York, NY 10024
212-595-2206

imdb.com/company/co0076728

Does not accept any unsolicited material. Project types include Feature Films. Preferred genres include Drama.

Jon Kilik
Producer
imdb.com/name/nm0453091

GRANITE ENTERTAINMENT

8539 Sunset Blvd Ste. 4-136
Los Angeles, CA 90069
310-854-6220

imdb.com/company/co0272032

Does not accept any unsolicited material. Project types include Feature Films and TV.

Robert Knotek
Partner/Producer

Hank McCann
Partner/Producer/Casting
imdb.com/name/nm0564869

GRAN VIA PRODUCTIONS

1888 Century Park East
14th Floor
Los Angeles, CA 90067
310-859-3060 (phone)
310-859-3066 (fax)

imdb.com/company/co0071947

Does not accept any unsolicited material. Project types include Feature Films and TV. Preferred genres include Comedy, Drama, Fantasy, and Science Fiction.

Mark Ceryak
Creative Executive
imdb.com/name/nm1641437

Mark Johnson
imdb.com/name/nm0425741
Assistant: Emily Eckert (Story Editor)

GRAPHIC FILM COMPANY

3450 Cahuenga Blvd. W, Bldg. 609
Los Angeles, CA 90068
323-845-0821

imdb.com/company/co0074086
thegraphicfilmcompany.com

Does not accept any unsolicited material. Project types include Feature Films. Preferred genres include Drama.

GRAY ANGEL PRODUCTIONS

69 Windward Ave
Venice, CA 90291
310-581-0010 (phone)
310-396-0551 (fax)

facebook.com/grayangelproductions
imdb.com/company/co0177683

Accepts query letter from unproduced, unrepresented writers. Project types include Feature Films.

Anjelica Huston
imdb.com/name/nm0001378

Jaclyn Bashoff
imdb.com/name/nm1902472

GRAZKA TAYLOR PRODUCTIONS

409 N Camden Dr, Suite 202
Beverly Hills, CA 90210
310-246-1107

grazkat.com
imdb.com/company/co0115289

Does not accept any unsolicited material. Project types include Feature Films and TV. Preferred genres include Drama, Non-Fiction, Reality, and Romance.

Grazka Taylor
Producer
grazka@grazkat.com
imdb.com/name/nm0852429

GREASY ENTERTAINMENT

6345 Balboa Blvd
Building 4, Suite 375

Encino, CA 91316
310-586-2300

info@greasy.biz
greasy.biz
imdb.com/company/co0176928

Accepts query letter from unproduced, unrepresented writers via email. Project types include Feature Films and TV. Preferred genres include Action and Comedy.

Dan Heder
Executive

Doug Heder

Jon Heder
imdb.com/name/nm1417647

GREEN COMMUNICATIONS

255 Parkside Dr
San Fernando, CA 91340
818-557-0050

info@greenfilms.com
greenfilms.com
imdb.com/company/co0049963

Does not accept any unsolicited material. Project types include Feature Films and TV.

Talaat Captan
President
imdb.com/name/nm0135708

D'Arcy Conrique
CEO
imdb.com/name/nm1330256

GREEN HAT FILMS

4000 Warner Blvd
Building 66
Burbank, CA 91522
818-954-3210 (phone)
818-954-3214 (fax)

imdb.com/company/co0221959

Does not accept any unsolicited material. Project types include Feature Films. Preferred genres include Comedy, Drama, Non-Fiction, and Thriller.

Mark O'Connor
Director of Development

Todd Phillips
imdb.com/name/nm0680846
Assistant: Joseph Garner

Diana Davis-Dyer

GREENSTREET FILMS

430 W Broadway 2nd Floor
New York City, NY 10012
212-609-9000 (phone)
212-609-9099 (fax)

general@gstreet.com
greenestreetfilms.com

Accepts query letter from unproduced, unrepresented writers via email. Project types include Feature Films. Preferred genres include Comedy, Drama, Horror, Romance, and Thriller.

John M Penotti
President
imdb.com/name/nm0006597

Matthew Honovic
Creative Executive
http://www.imdb.com/name/
nm2416270/?ref_=fn_al_nm_1

GREENTREES FILMS

854-A 5th St
Santa Monica, CA 90403
310-899-1522 (phone)
310-496-2082 (fax)

info@greentreesfilms.com
greentreesfilms.com
twitter.com/greentreesfilms
imdb.com/company/co0184723
facebook.com/greentreesfilms

Accepts query letter from unproduced, unrepresented writers via email. Project types include Feature Films, TV, and Commercials. Preferred genres include Comedy, Drama, Non-Fiction, and Reality.

Jack Binder
imdb.com/name/nm0082784

GRINDSTONE ENTERTAINMENT GROUP

2700 Colorado Ave
Suite 200
Santa Monica, CA 90404
310-255-5761 (phone)
310-255-3766 (fax)

thegrindstone.net
imdb.com/company/co0209560

Accepts query letter from produced or represented writers. Project types include Feature Films. Preferred genres include Action, Drama, Period, and Thriller.

Barry Brooker
President
barry@thegrindstone.net
imdb.com/name/nm1633269

Ryan Black
Director of Development
ryan@thegrindstone.net
imdb.com/name/nm3337383

Stan Wertlieb
stanwertlieb@gmail.com
imdb.com/name/nm0921627

Teresa Sabatine
teresa@thegrindstone.net
imdb.com/name/nm3466608

GRIZZLY ADAMS PRODUCTIONS

201 Five Cities Dr SPC 172, Pismo Beach
CA 93449
877-556-8536 (phone)
805-556-0393 (fax)

imdb.com/company/co0076591
twitter.com/_grizzlyadams_
grizzlyadams.com

Does not accept any unsolicited material. Project types include Feature Films and TV. Preferred genres include Documentary, Drama, Family, Non-Fiction, and Reality.

David W. Balsiger
imdb.com/name/nm1901322

GROSSO JACOBSON COMMUNICATIONS CORP.

767 Third Ave
New York, NY 10017

373 Front St East
Toronto, Ontario MSA 1G4
Canada

1801 Ave of the Stars, Suite 911
Los Angeles, CA 90067
310-788-8900

grossojacobson@grossojacobson.com

Accepts query letter from unproduced, unrepresented writers via email. Project types include Feature Films, TV, and Theater. Preferred genres include Comedy, Crime, Drama, Horror, Non-Fiction, Reality, and Thriller. Established in 1999.

Sonny Grosso
Executive Producer
212-644-6909
imdb.com/name/nm0343780

Keith Johnson
Sr. VP Development
310-788-8900
imdb.com/name/nm1702242
linkedin.com/pub/keith-johnson/6/A09/A74

GROSS-WESTON PRODUCTIONS

10560 Wilshire Blvd, Suite 801
Los Angeles, CA 90024
310-777-0010 (phone)
310-777-0016 (fax)

gross-weston@sbcglobal.net
imdb.com/company/co0032431
linkedin.com/company/gross-weston-productions

Accepts scripts from produced or represented writers. Project types include Feature Films, TV, and Theater. Preferred genres include Action, Comedy, Drama, Family, Non-Fiction, Reality, Romance, Science Fiction, and Thriller.

Mary Gross
Executive Producer
imdb.com/name/nm0343437

Ann Weston
Executive Producer
imdb.com/name/nm0922912

GROUNDSWELL PRODUCTIONS

12424 Wilshire Blvd.
Suite 1120
Los Angeles, CA 90025
310-385-7540 (phone)
310-385-7541 (fax)

info@groundswellfilms.com
groundswellfilms.com
imdb.com/company/co0173527
linkedin.com/company/groundswell-productions

Does not accept any unsolicited material. Project types include Feature Films, TV, and Theater. Preferred genres include Action, Comedy, Crime, Drama, Horror, Non-Fiction, Romance, and Thriller. Established in 2006.

Kelly Mullen
Vice-President
imdb.com/name/nm4133402

Janice Williams
imdb.com/name/nm1003921

GUARDIAN ENTERTAINMENT, LTD

71 5th Ave
New York, NY 10003
212-727-4729 (phone)
212-727-4713 (fax)

guardian@guardianltd.com
guardianltd.com

Accepts query letter from unproduced, unrepresented writers via email. Project types include Feature Films, TV, and Commercials. Preferred genres include Drama, Horror, Non-Fiction, Reality, Science Fiction, and Thriller.

Richard Miller
rmiller@guardianltd.com

Anita Agair
agair@guardianltd.com

GUNN FILMS

500 S Buena Vista St
Old Animation Building, Suite 3-A7
Burbank, CA 91521
818-560-6156 (phone)
818-842-8394 (fax)

imdb.com/company/co0007784

Does not accept any unsolicited material. Project types include Feature Films and TV. Preferred genres include Action, Comedy, Drama, Family, Fantasy, Romance, Science Fiction, and Thriller. Established in 2001.

Andrew Gunn
Producer
andrew.gunn@disney.com
imdb.com/name/nm0348151

GUSH PRODUCTIONS

San Francisco, CA
415-644-8741

info@gushproductions.com
gushproductions.com/index.php
facebook.com/pages/GUSH-productions/
    183116245059192
imdb.com/company/co0475971

Preferred genres include Documentary. Established in 2009.

Samantha Grant
Founder
linkedin.com/in/gushproductions

GUY WALKS INTO A BAR

236 W 27th St #1000
New York, NY 10001
212-941-1509

info@guywalks.com
guywalks.com

Does not accept any unsolicited material. Project types include Feature Films, TV, and Commercials. Preferred genres include Animation, Comedy, Family, Fantasy, Romance, and Science Fiction.

Jonathan Coleman
Director of Development

Todd Komarnicki
imdb.com/name/nm0464548

H2O MOTION PICTURES

8549 Hedges Place
Los Angeles, CA 90069
323-654-5920 (phone)
323-654-5923 (fax)

23 Denmark St., 3rd Floor
London, WC2H 8NH, U.K
44207-240-5656

h2o@h2omotionpictures.com
h2omotionpictures.com
imdb.com/company/co0333174

Does not accept any unsolicited material. Project types include Feature Films.

Andras Hamori
President
imdb.com/name/nm0358877

HAFT ENTERTAINMENT

38 Gramercy Park North, #2C
New York, NY 10010
212-586-3881 (phone)
212-459-9798 (fax)

imdb.com/company/co0045494

Accepts query letter from produced or represented writers. Project types include Feature Films and Short Films.

Steven Haft
President/Producer
imdb.com/name/nm0353187

HALESTORM ENTERTAINMENT

5132 N 300 West
Provo, UT
801-655-5180 (phone)
801-655-5181 (fax)

contact@hstorm.com

imdb.com/company/co0000345
halestormentertainment.com

Does not accept any unsolicited material. Project types include Feature Films. Preferred genres include Comedy.

Kurt Hale
Partner/COO/Producer
imdb.com/name/nm1109378

Dave Hunter
Partner/Writer/Director
imdb.com/name/nm111268

HALF FULL ENTERTAINMENT

500 S. Buena Vista St. Old Animation Bldg., Ste. 2F3
Burbank, CA 91521
818-560-6868

imdb.com/company/co0308384

Does not accept any unsolicited material. Project types include TV. Preferred genres include Comedy.

HALFIRE ENTERTAINMENT

8730 W Sunset Blvd., Penthouse West
Los Angeles, CA 90069

HALFIRE ENTERTAINMENT
2021 Killarney Dr
Ottawa Ontario K2A 1P9
Canada

halfireentertainment.com
imdb.com/company/co0432767

Does not accept any unsolicited material.

Noreen Halpern
President/Producer
imdb.com/name/nm0356957

Stephanie Fontana
Director of Development
imdb.com/name/nm0284952

HAMMER FILMS

52 Haymarket
London, United Kingdom,

SW1Y 4RP
+44 20 3002 9510

info@hammerfilms.com
hammerfilms.com
imdb.com/company/co0103101

Does not accept any unsolicited material. Project types include Feature Films and TV. Preferred genres include Action, Comedy, Documentary, Drama, Horror, and Thriller. Established in 1934.

Simon Oakes
imdb.com/name/nm2649227

HAMZEH MYSTIQUE FILMS

61 Blaney St
Swampscott , MA 01907-2546
781-596-1281 (phone)
781-599-2424 (fax)

info@hamzehmystiquefilms.com
hamzehmystiquefilms.com
imdb.com/company/co0057291

Does not accept any unsolicited material.

Ziad H. Hamzeh
President
imdb.com/name/nm0359144

Marc Sandler
VP of Development/Creative Affairs
imdb.com/name/nm0761983

HANDPICKED FILMS

2893 Sea Ridge Dr
Malibu, CA 90265
310-361-6832 (phone)
310-456-1166 (fax)

info@handpickedfilms.net
handpickedfilms.net

Does not accept any unsolicited material. Project types include Feature Films, TV, and Commercials. Preferred genres include Animation, Comedy, Detective, Drama, Horror, Non-Fiction, and Reality. Established in 2005.

Anthony Romano
Producer
imdb.com/name/nm0738853

Michel Shane
imdb.com/name/nm0788062

Darren VanCleave
Executive
imdb.com/name/nm2168166

HANDSOMECHARLIE FILMS

1720-1/2 Whitley Ave
Los Angeles, CA 90028
323-462-6013

Does not accept any unsolicited material. Project types include Feature Films. Preferred genres include Action, Comedy, Drama, Non-Fiction, and Romance.

Kimberly Barton
Creative Executive

Natalie Portman
President
imdb.com/name/nm0000204

Annette Savitch

HANNIBAL PICTURES

8265 Sunset Blvd, Suite 107
West Hollywood, CA 90046
323-848-2945 (phone)
323-848-2946 (fax)

contactus@hannibalpictures.com
hannibalpictures.com
facebook.com/pages/Hannibal-Pictures/
    158994507487285

Accepts query letter from unproduced, unrepresented writers via email. Project types include Feature Films. Preferred genres include Action, Comedy, Crime, Drama, Non-Fiction, Romance, Science Fiction, and Thriller. Established in 1999.

Cam Cannon
Director of Development
imdb.com/name/nm1359191

Patricia Rionda Del Castro
President

Kristy Eberle-Adams
imdb.com/name/nm5554723

Richard Rionda Del Castro
imdb.com/name/nm0215502

HANNOVER HOUSE

1428 Chester St
Springdale, AR 72764
479-751-4500 (phone)
479-751-4999 (fax)

hannoverhouse.com
imdb.com/company/co0098047

Does not accept any unsolicited material. Project types include Feature Films. Preferred genres include Drama, Family, and Science Fiction.

Eric Parkinson
President / CEO
imdb.com/name/nm0003826

HAPPY MADISON PRODUCTIONS

10202 W Washington Blvd Judy Garland Building
Culver City, CA 90232
310-244-3100 (phone)
310-244-3353 (fax)

imdb.com/company/co0059609
twitter.com/happymadison

Does not accept any unsolicited material. Project types include Feature Films, Short Films, and TV. Preferred genres include Action, Animation, Comedy, Drama, Fantasy, Romance, and Thriller. Established in 1999.

Jack Giarraputo
Partner
imdb.com/name/nm0316406
Assistant: Rachel Simmer

Judit Maull
Executive
imdb.com/name/nm1263796

Billy Wee

Doug Robinson
imdb.com/name/nm2120562
Assistant: Brianna Riofrio

Adam Sandler
Partner
imdb.com/name/nm0001191
twitter.com/AdamSandler

Heather Parry
imdb.com/name/nm1009782
twitter.com/heatherparry

HARBOR LIGHT ENTERTAINMENT

1438 N Gower St
Los Angeles, CA 90028
323-397-4928

imdb.com/company/co0213272

Does not accept any unsolicited material. Project types include Feature Films.

Edwin Marshall
Producer
imdb.com/name/nm0550862

Stuart Calcote
Producer
imdb.com/name/nm3129931

HARMS WAY PRODUCTIONS

4158 Camellia Ave
Studio City, CA 91604
818-486-0946

Does not accept any unsolicited material. Project types include Feature Films and TV.

Kristin Harms
Producer
imdb.com/name/nm0363599

HARPO FILMS, INC.

345 N Maple Dr, Suite 315
Beverly Hills, CA 90210
310-278-5559

sylvia@myagsc.com

facebook.com/pages/Harpo-Productions/
108466999178602

Does not accept any unsolicited material. Project types
include Feature Films and TV. Preferred genres
include Comedy, Drama, Fantasy, Horror, Non-
Fiction, and Romance.

Oprah Winfrey
imdb.com/name/nm0001856
facebook.com/oprahwinfrey
twitter.com/Oprah

HARTBREAK FILMS

14622 Ventura Blvd. Suite 102
Sherman Oaks, CA 91403

info@hartbreak.com
hartbreak.com
imdb.com/company/co0035722

Does not accept any unsolicited material. Project types
include TV. Preferred genres include Family.

Paula Hart
Producer
imdb.com/name/nm0366472

HARTSWOOD FILMS

3A Paradise Rd
Richmond
Surrey
TW9 1RX
+44 (0) 20-3668-3060 (phone)
+44 (0) 20-3668-3050 (fax)

Nations and Regions Office
17 Cathedral Rd
Cardiff
CF11 9HA
+44 (0)29-2023-3333 (phone)
+44 (0)29-2022-5878 (fax)

films.tv@hartswoodfilms.co.uk
hartswoodfilms.co.uk
imdb.com/company/co0023675
facebook.com/pages/Hartswood-Films/
132967313406613
twitter.com/hartswoodfilms

Does not accept any unsolicited material. Project types
include TV. Preferred genres include Comedy, Crime,
Detective, Drama, Horror, and Thriller. Established in
1980.

Elaine Cameron
Head of Development
imdb.com/name/nm0131569

Beryl Vertue
Chairman
imdb.com/name/nm0895054

Debbie Vertue
Director of Operations
imdb.com/name/nm0895055

Sue Vertue
Producer
imdb.com/name/nm0895056
twitter.com/suevertue

HASBRO, INC./HASBRO FILMS

Burbank
2950 N Hollywood Way Suite 100
Burbank, CA 91504
818-478-4320

hasbro.com/?US

Accepts query letter from unproduced, unrepresented
writers. Project types include Feature Films. Preferred
genres include Action, Animation, Comedy, Family,
Fantasy, Non-Fiction, and Science Fiction.

Daniel Persitz
Creative Executive
imdb.com/name/nm1974626
linkedin.com/pub/daniel-persitz/35/224/36a

HAYMAKER

4146 Lankershim Blvd. Suite 401
North Hollywood, CA 91602

150 W 22nd St., 3rd Fl.
New York, NY 10011

contact@haymakertv.com
haymakertv.com
imdb.com/title/tt162099

Aaron Rothman
Producer
imdb.com/name/nm4169818

Irad Eyal
Producer
imdb.com/name/nm1164455

HAZY MILLS PRODUCTIONS

4024 Radford Ave
Building 7 - 2nd Floor
Studio City, CA 91604
818-840-7568

hazymills.com
imdb.com/company/co0147414

Does not accept any unsolicited material. Project types include Feature Films and TV. Preferred genres include Comedy, Drama, Family, Horror, Non-Fiction, and Reality. Established in 2004.

Sean Hayes
imdb.com/name/nm0005003
facebook.com/seanhayesmusic
twitter.com/theseanhayes
Assistant: Jessie Kalick

Kiel Elliott
Development Executive
linkedin.com/pub/kiel-elliott/28/644/b3b
twitter.com/KielElliott

HBO FILMS

1100 Ave of the Americas
New York, NY 10036
212-512-1208

contacthbo@hbo.com
facebook.com/pages/HBO-Films/104072436296883
imdb.com/company/co0005861
hbo.com/movies
twitter.com/HBO
linkedin.com/company/hbo

Does not accept any unsolicited material. Project types include TV. Preferred genres include Comedy, Drama, Family, Non-Fiction, Romance, and Thriller. Established in 1983.

Len Amato
President, Films
imdb.com/name/nm0024163
facebook.com/len.amato1

Glenn Whitehead
Executive Vice President, Business Affairs & Production

Jeffrey Guthrie
Senior VP/Chief Counsel

Janet Graham Borba
Senior VP, Production

Jenni Sherwood
Senior VP, Development & Production, Films

Carrie Frazier
Senior VP, Casting

Suzanne Young
Vice President, Business Affairs

Amy Berman
Vice President, Casting

Cynthia Davis Kanner
VP, Post Production

Molly Wilson
VP/Chief Labor Counsel

Ginny Nugent
VP, Production

John Murchison
VP, Development & Production, Miniseries

Maria Zuckerman
VP, Development & Production, Films (NY)

Mark Hoerr
VP, Post Production

Holly Schiffer Zucker
VP, Post Production

Susanna Felleman
VP, Business Affairs

Tara Grace
VP, Development & Production, Films

Kary Antholis
President, Miniseries
imdb.com/name/nm0030794

HD FILMS, INC

4000 Warner Blvd., Bldg. 34 Suite 316
Burbank, CA 91522
818-954-4990 (phone)
818-954-4440 (fax)

hdfilms.com

Does not accept any unsolicited material. Project types include TV. Preferred genres include Science Fiction.

Jace Hall
Principal/Producer
imdb.com/name/nm0995727

HDNET FILMS

8269 E. 23rd Ave
Denver, CO 80238
303-542-5600

viewer@axs.tv
imdb.com/company/co0094788
hdnetmovies.com
twitter.com/HDNetMovies
facebook.com/hdnetmovies
linkedin.com/company/hdnet

Accepts query letter from unproduced, unrepresented writers. Project types include Feature Films and TV. Preferred genres include Comedy, Crime, Documentary, Drama, Reality, Romance, Science Fiction, and Thriller. Established in 2001.

Mark Cuban
CEO
mcuban@axs.tv

HEAVY DUTY ENTERTAINMENT

6121 Sunset Blvd, Ste 103
Los Angeles, CA 90028
323-209-3545 (phone)
323-653-1720 (fax)

info@heavydutyentertainment.com
heavydutyentertainment.com

imdb.com/company/co0205983

Does not accept any unsolicited material. Project types include Feature Films and TV. Preferred genres include Action, Comedy, Drama, Horror, and Science Fiction.

Rhoades Rader
Producer
imdb.com/name/nm0705476

Jeff Balis
Producer
imdb.com/name/nm0050276
linkedin.com/pub/jeff-balis/3/a45/659

HEEL & TOE PRODUCTIONS

2058 Broadway
Santa Monica, CA 90404
310-288-6289

imdb.com/company/co0022072
facebook.com/pages/Heel-and-Toe-Films/
129670757225127

Does not accept any unsolicited material. Project types include Feature Films and TV. Preferred genres include Action, Drama, and Romance. Established in 2001.

Paul Attanasio
Executive Producer
paul.attanasio@fox.com
imdb.com/name/nm0001921

Katie Jacobs
Executive Producer
katie.jacobs@fox.com
imdb.com/name/nm0414498

John Krauss
Director of Development

HEMISPHERE ENTERTAINMENT

20058 Ventura Blvd
#316
Woodland Hills, CA 91364
818-888-2263 (phone)
818-888-3651 (fax)

hemisphereentertainment.com

imdb.com/company/co0184074

Accepts query letter from unproduced, unrepresented writers. Project types include Feature Films. Preferred genres include Action, Crime, Drama, Family, Horror, Romance, and Thriller.

Ralph E. Portillo
CEO
imdb.com/name/nm1589685

Jamie Elliot
COO
imdb.com/name/nm0254242

Brad Wilson
Vice President of Development & Production
imdb.com/name/nm0933085

HENCEFORTH PICTURES

15260 Ventura Blvd Ste 1040
Sherman Oaks, CA 91403
424-832-5517 (phone)
424-832-5564 (fax)

inquiries@henceforthpictures.com
imdb.com/company/co0375280
henceforthpictures.com

Does not accept any unsolicited material. Project types include Feature Films and TV. Preferred genres include Action, Crime, Drama, and Thriller. Established in 2009.

William Monahan
Principal
imdb.com/name/nm1184258

Justine Jones
VP, Development
imdb.com/name/nm3540960

HENDERSON PRODUCTIONS

4252 W Riverside Dr
Burbank, CA 91505
805-966-5832 (phone)
805-701-0918 (fax)

info@henderson-productions.com
henderson-productions.com
imdb.com/company/co0050874

twitter.com/HendersonProd

Does not accept any unsolicited material. Project types include Feature Films and Theater. Preferred genres include Comedy, Drama, Family, and Romance.

Garry Marshall
Producer
imdb.com/name/nm0005190

Bill Henderson
Founder
bill@henderson-productions.com

HENRY ISLAND PRODUCTIONS

610 Venice Blvd.
Venice, CA 90291
310-577-5200

info@henryislandproductions.com
henryislandproductions.com
imdb.com/company/co0242278

Does not accept any unsolicited material. Project types include Feature Films and TV.

Debbie Shepard
Producer

Brian Neal
Producer
imdb.com/name/nm5563983

HENSON ALTERNATIVE

1416 N LaBrea Ave
Hollywood, CA 90028
323-802-1500 (phone)
323-802-1825 (fax)

henson.com/alternative.php
imdb.com/company/co0250340

Does not accept any unsolicited material. Project types include TV. Preferred genres include Comedy.

Lisa Henson
CEO of The Jim Henson Co.
imdb.com/name/nm0378229

HERE NOW PRODUCTIONS

9107 Wilshire Blvd.
Beverly Hills, CA 90210
310-461-3530

imdb.com/company/co0220218

Does not accept any unsolicited material. Project types
include Feature Films. Preferred genres include
Comedy and Drama.

Mark Webber
Actor/Producer/Director/Writer
imdb.com/name/nm0916406

HERO PICTURES INTERNATIONAL

12016 Wilshire Blvd., Suite 1
Los Angeles, CA 90025
310-207-4280 (phone)
310-207-4515 (fax)

info@heropictures.net
heropicturesinternational.com

Accepts query letter from unproduced, unrepresented
writers via email. Project types include Feature Films.

Luis Prats
CEO

Koldo Eguren
President
imdb.com/name/nm3222573

HEYDAY FILMS

4000 Warner Blvd
Building 81, Room 207
Burbank, CA 91522
818-954-3004 (phone)
818-954-3017 (fax)

office@heydayfilms.com

Does not accept any unsolicited material. Project types
include Feature Films and TV. Preferred genres
include Action, Comedy, Crime, Drama, and Fantasy.

David Heyman
Partner
imdb.com/name/nm0382268
Assistant: Ollie Wiseman (011) 442078366333

Jeffrey Clifford
President
imdb.com/name/nm0166641
Assistant: Kate Phillips

HGTV

9721 Sherrill Blvd
Knoxville, TN 37932
865-694-2700 (phone)
865-690-6595 (fax)

hgtv.com
imdb.com/company/co0004908

Does not accept any unsolicited material. Project types
include Feature Films and TV. Preferred genres
include Documentary and Reality.

Burton Jablin

Freddy James

Chris Moore

Steven Lerner

Courtney White

HIGH HORSE FILMS

100 Universal City Plaza
Building 2128, Suite E
Universal City, CA 91608
323-939-8802 (phone)
323-939-8832 (fax)

Accepts query letter from unproduced, unrepresented
writers. Project types include Feature Films and TV.
Preferred genres include Comedy, Drama, and
Romance. Established in 1990.

Cynthia Chvatal
Producer
imdb.com/name/nm0161558

William Petersen
imdb.com/name/nm0676973

HIGH INTEGRITY PRODUCTIONS

11054 Ventura Blvd
Suite 324

Studio City, CA 91604 USA
714-313-9606

highintegrityproductions.com
facebook.com/pages/High-Integrity-Productions/
    166109760098778
imdb.com/company/co0188415

Accepts query letter from unproduced, unrepresented writers. Project types include Feature Films. Preferred genres include Animation, Horror, Romance, and Thriller.

Dale Noble
909-883-0417
dale@highintegrityproductions.com
imdb.com/name/nm2303672
linkedin.com/pub/dale-noble/11/414/a0a

HIGHLAND FILM GROUP

9200 Sunset Blvd. Suite 600
West Hollywood, CA 90069
310-271-8400 (phone)
310-278-7500 (fax)

sales@highlandfilmgroup.com
highlandfilmgroup.com
facebook.com/pages/Highland-Film-Group/
    437170369637020
twitter.com/thehighlandfilm
imdb.com/company/co0303030

Does not accept any unsolicited material. Project types include Feature Films. Preferred genres include Crime, Drama, and Thriller.

HIGH TREASON PRODUCTIONS

8200 Wilshire Blvd, Suite 200
Beverly Hills, CA 90211
323-556-0727 (phone)
323-556-0827 (fax)

info@hightreasonproductions.com
hightreasonproductions.com
imdb.com/company/co0192071

Does not accept any unsolicited material. Project types include Feature Films. Preferred genres include Comedy, Horror, and Thriller.

Eduardo Levy
Producer
imdb.com/name/nm2037687

James Martin
Producer
imdb.com/name/nm1006311

HIT ENTERTAINMENT

230 Park Ave, 12th Fl
New York City, NY 10003
212-463-9623

hitentertainment.biz
imdb.com/company/co0029268

Does not accept any unsolicited material. Project types include TV. Preferred genres include Comedy and Family.

Sangeeta Desai
CEO

HIT & RUN PRODUCTIONS

222 Riverside Dr. Suite 8B
New York, NY 10025
212-864-0800

imdb.com/company/co0011026

Does not accept any unsolicited material. Project types include Feature Films.

Hilary Shor
President/Producer
imdb.com/name/nm0794892

HOLDING PICTURES

120 Broadway, Suite 200
Santa Monica, CA 90401
310-260-7070 (phone)
310-260-7050 (fax)

holdingpictures.com

Does not accept any unsolicited material. Project types include Feature Films. Preferred genres include Comedy, Drama, and Horror.

Charlie Lyons
CEO/Producer
imdb.com/name/nm1854001

Jamie Gregor
Story Editor
imdb.com/name/nm1439017

HOLLYWOOD GANG PRODUCTIONS

4000 Warner Blvd
Building 139, Room 201
Burbank, CA 91522
818-954-4999 (phone)
818-954-4448 (fax)

imdb.com/company/co0129244

Does not accept any unsolicited material. Project types include Feature Films. Preferred genres include Action, Drama, Fantasy, Science Fiction, and Thriller.

Gianni Nunnari
imdb.com/name/nm0638089

HOME BOX OFFICE (HBO)

2500 Broadway Suite 400
Santa Monica, CA 90404
310-382-3000 (phone)
310-201-9293 (fax)

1100 Ave of the Americas
Room H13-16
New York City, New York 10036
212-512-1000 (phone)
212-512-5698 (fax)

homeboxoffice.com
imdb.com/company/co0008693

Does not accept any unsolicited material. Project types include Feature Films and TV. Preferred genres include Action, Comedy, Crime, Documentary, Drama, Family, Fantasy, Non-Fiction, Period, Romance, Science Fiction, and Sociocultural. Established in 1972.

HOMEGROWN PICTURES

1684 Ventura Blvd, Suite 800
Studio City, CA 91604

http://omegrownfilms@mac.com
imdb.com/company/co0069694

Does not accept any unsolicited material. Project types include Feature Films and TV. Preferred genres include Drama and Romance.

Stephanie Allain
Producer
imdb.com/name/nm0019858

HONEST ENGINE TV

432 W 45th St, 7th Floor
New York, NY 10036
212-947-2341 (phone)
646-867-2782 (fax)

feedback@honestenginetv.com
honestenginetv.com
imdb.com/company/co0252513

Does not accept any unsolicited material. Project types include TV. Preferred genres include Comedy.

Nick McKinney
Founder/Producer
imdb.com/name/nm0571903

Meghan O'Hara
Founder/Producer
imdb.com/name/nm0641306

HOOSICK FALLS PRODUCTIONS

1633 Stanford St
Santa Monica, CA 90404
310-453-2700 (phone)
310-453-2701 (fax)

hoosickfallsla.com
imdb.com/company/co0097609

Does not accept any unsolicited material. Project types include TV. Preferred genres include Comedy.

George Verschoor
Executive Producer
imdb.com/name/nm0004461

HOPSCOTCH PICTURES

616 N Robertson Blvd., Suite B
Beverly Hills, CA 90211
310-358-0630 (phone)
310-358-0631 (fax)

imdb.com/company/co0177700

Does not accept any unsolicited material. Project types include Feature Films.

Sukee Chew
Manager/Producer
imdb.com/name/nm0156819

HORIZON ALTERNATIVE TELEVISION

4000 Warner Blvd.
Burbank, CA 91522

Does not accept any unsolicited material. Project types include TV.

HORIZON ENTERTAINMENT

1025 S Jefferson Parkway
New Orleans, LA 70125
504-483-1177 (phone)
504-483-1173 (fax)

jsasst@horizonent.tv
horizonent.tv
imdb.com/company/co0225725

Accepts query letter from unproduced, unrepresented writers. Project types include Feature Films and TV. Preferred genres include Action, Comedy, Crime, Drama, Family, Reality, Romance, and Thriller. Established in 2000.

Jason Sciavicco
Executive Producer
imdb.com/name/nm2217296

Melissa Dembrun Sciavicco
imdb.com/name/nm2847926

HORROR, INC.

54 Jaconnet St
Newton, MA 02461

Does not accept any unsolicited material. Project types include Feature Films and TV. Preferred genres include Horror.

Robert Barsamian
President/Producer
imdb.com/name/nm6452819

HOTPLATE PRODUCTIONS

16000 Ventura Blvd, Suite 600
Encino, CA 91436
818-385-1934

Does not accept any unsolicited material. Project types include TV. Preferred genres include Crime and Drama.

Kathryn Morris
Actor/Producer
imdb.com/name/nm0606700

Josh Gold
VP of Production & Development
imdb.com/name/nm2236268

HUGHES CAPITAL ENTERTAINMENT

22817 Ventura Blvd, Suite 471
Woodland Hills, CA 91364
818-484-3205

info@trihughes.com
trihughes.com

Accepts scripts from produced or represented writers. Project types include Feature Films. Preferred genres include Action, Comedy, Drama, Family, and Romance.

Jacob Clymore
jc@trihughes.com

Patrick Hughes
imdb.com/name/nm1449018
linkedin.com/pub/patrick-hughes/19/911/141

HUMANOIDS

8033 Sunset Blvd. # 628
Hollywood, CA 90046

77 Beak St, Suite 149
Soho, London W1F 9DB
United Kingdom

contact@humanoids.com
humanoids.com
facebook.com/humanoidsinc
twitter.com/humanoidsinc

Does not accept any unsolicited material. Project types include Feature Films. Preferred genres include Action, Drama, Fantasy, Horror, and Science Fiction.

HUNTER FILMS

500 23rd St South
Birmingham, AL 35233
205-870-4996

Does not accept any unsolicited material. Project types include Feature Films. Preferred genres include Drama.

Alan Hunter
Partner/Producer
imdb.com/name/nm0402694

Hugh Hunter
Partner/Producer
imdb.com/name/nm1227818

HUTCH PARKER ENTERTAINMENT

204 Santa Monica Blvd Suite A
Santa Monica, CA 90401

hutchparkerentertainment@gmail.com

Accepts scripts from produced or represented writers. Project types include Feature Films. Preferred genres include Romance and Thriller. Established in 2012.

Aaron Ensweiler
Vice-President
imdb.com/name/nm3943221

Hutch Parker
Founder
imdb.com/name/nm0404446

HYDE PARK ENTERTAINMENT

14958 Ventura Blvd Suite 100
Sherman Oaks, CA 91423
818-783-6060 (phone)
818-783-6319 (fax)

hydeparkentertainment.com

Does not accept any unsolicited material. Project types include Feature Films and Commercials. Preferred genres include Action, Comedy, Crime, Drama, Fantasy, Romance, Science Fiction, and Thriller. Established in 1999.

Marc Fiorentino

Ashtok Amritraj
imdb.com/name/nm0002170

HYPNOTIC

12233 W Olympic Blvd, Suite 255
Los Angeles, CA 90064
310-806-6930 (phone)
310-806-6931 (fax)

Does not accept any unsolicited material. Project types include Feature Films and TV. Preferred genres include Action, Comedy, Crime, Drama, Horror, and Thriller.

Lindsay Sloane
Development Executive

Doug Liman
imdb.com/name/nm0510731

IAC GROUP

555 W 18th St
New York, NY 10011
212-314-7300

iac.com

Does not accept any unsolicited material. Project types include Feature Films. Preferred genres include Documentary.

Barry Diller
Chairman & Senior Executive
imdb.com/name/nm1660377

Victor Kaufman
Victor Kaufman
imdb.com/name/nm3215413

IBID FILMWORKS

515 Fifth Ave, Suite 3A
Brooklyn, NY 11215

info@ibidfilmworks.com
ibidfilmworks.com
imdb.com/company/co0182518

Does not accept any unsolicited material. Project types include Feature Films. Preferred genres include Comedy, Crime, and Drama.

Marc Meyers
Partner/Producer
imdb.com/name/nm1836315

Jody Girgenti
Partner/Producer
imdb.com/name/nm1761255

ICARUS PRODUCTIONS

1100 Madison Ave, Suite 6A
New York, NY 10028
212-581-3020

imdb.com/company/co0125551

Does not accept any unsolicited material. Project types include Feature Films. Preferred genres include Comedy and Drama.

Mike Nichols
Director/Producer/Writer
imdb.com/name/nm0001566

ICON ENTERTAINMENT INTERNATIONAL

Charlotte Building
17 Gresse St
London W1T 1QL
United Kingdom
+44 (0)20 7927 6900 (phone)
+44 (0)20 7927 6901 (fax)

imdb.com/company/co0000700
iconmovies.net

linkedin.com/company/icon-entertainment-
    international

Does not accept any unsolicited material. Project types include Feature Films and TV. Preferred genres include Action, Comedy, Crime, Drama, Horror, Non-Fiction, Science Fiction, and Thriller. Established in 1989.

Mel Gibson
Founder
imdb.com/name/nm0000154

ICONIC MEDIA PRODUCTIONS

5670 Wilshire Blvd. #19264
Los Angeles, CA 90036

judibell@iconicmediaprod.com
iconicmediaprod.com
facebook.com/IconicMediaProductions
imdb.com/company/co0382482

Does not accept any unsolicited material. Project types include Feature Films. Preferred genres include Drama.

Judi Bell
CEO/Producer
imdb.com/name/nm2230559

Matt Nicholas
Writer/Producer
imdb.com/name/nm3818521

IDEAL PARTNERS

630 Fifth Ave, Suite 1465
New York, NY 10111
212-396-9209

imdb.com/company/co0195669

Does not accept any unsolicited material. Project types include Feature Films. Preferred genres include Drama and Thriller.

Rachel Cohen
Partner/Producer
imdb.com/name/nm1707602

Jana Edelbaum
Partner/Producer
imdb.com/name/nm0248944

IDENTITY FILMS

8520 Mulholland Dr
Los Angeles, CA 90046
323-654-3000 (phone)
323-654-3010 (fax)

info@identityfilm.com
identityfilm.com

Does not accept any unsolicited material. Project types include Feature Films and TV. Preferred genres include Drama.

Tara Ahamed
Director of Development
imdb.com/name/nm3925704

Anthony Mastromauro
Co-Founder/CEO/Producer
imdb.com/name/nm0557829

IDG FILMS

One Exeter Plaza, 15th Floor
Boston, MA 02116
617-534-1200

idg.com

Does not accept any unsolicited material. Project types include Feature Films.

Steven Squillante
Producer
imdb.com/name/nm1115325

David Lee
Producer
imdb.com/name/nm0497115

IDW PUBLISHING

5080 Santa Fe
San Diego, CA 92109

idwpublishing.com
imdb.com/company/co0188055

Does not accept any unsolicited material. Project types include Feature Films. Preferred genres include Horror.

Robbie Robbins
Founder/Executive
imdb.com/name/nm4730671

Ted Adams
Founder/CEO/Executive Producer
imdb.com/name/nm0011389

IKM PRODUCTIONS

601 W 26th St, Suite 1255
New York, NY 10001
212-533-1951 (phone)
212-255-3382 (fax)

imdb.com/company/co0205492

Does not accept any unsolicited material. Project types include Feature Films and TV. Preferred genres include Comedy and Thriller.

James K. Jones
Producer
imdb.com/name/nm1300158

Patrick Moses
Producer
imdb.com/name/nm2095313

ILLUMINATION ENTERTAINMENT

info@illuminationent.com
imdb.com/company/co0221986
behindthegoggles.net
facebook.com/pages/Illumination-Entertainment/
    173587985995833

Does not accept any unsolicited material. Project types include Feature Films and Short Films. Preferred genres include Animation, Comedy, Drama, and Family. Established in 2007.

Christopher Meledandri
Founder
imdb.com/name/nm0577560
Assistant: Rachel Feinberg and Katie Kirnan

ILLUSION INDUSTRIES

2424 N Ontario St
Burbank, CA 91504
818-565-5986

10000 Celtic Dr, O'Connor Building
Baton Rouge, LA 70809

admin@illusionindustries.com
illusionindustries.com
imdb.com/company/co0304148

Does not accept any unsolicited material. Project types include Feature Films. Preferred genres include Horror.

Todd Tucker
President
imdb.com/name/nm2586719

Ronald Halvas
CEO
imdb.com/name/nm359772

IMAGEMOVERS

100 Universal City
Bungalow 5170
Los Angeles, CA 91608
818-733-4000

imdb.com/company/co0038131
facebook.com/pages/ImageMovers/114718638545017

Does not accept any unsolicited material. Project types include Feature Films and TV. Preferred genres include Action, Animation, Comedy, Drama, Family, Fantasy, Period, Romance, and Thriller. Established in 1997.

Jimmy Skodras
Development Executive

Steve Starkey
Partner
imdb.com/name/nm0823330

Robert Zemeckis
Partner
imdb.com/name/nm0000709

Jack Rapke
Partner
imdb.com/name/nm0710759

Jackie Levine

IMAGINE ENTERTAINMENT

9465 Wilshire Blvd
7th Floor
Beverly Hills, CA 90212
310-858-2000

imagine-entertainment.com
imdb.com/company/co0003687
facebook.com/pages/Imagine-Entertainment/
    103825922989076
twitter.com/ImaginEntertain

Does not accept any unsolicited material. Project types include Feature Films and TV. Preferred genres include Action, Animation, Comedy, Crime, Drama, Family, Fantasy, Horror, Non-Fiction, Romance, Science Fiction, and Thriller. Established in 1986.

Ron Howard
Founder
r.howard@imagine-entertainment.com
imdb.com/name/nm0000165

Brian Grazer
Founder

IM GLOBAL

8201 Beverly Blvd.
5th Floor
Los Angeles, CA 90048
310-777-3590 (phone)
323-657-5354 (fax)

info@imglobalfilm.com
imglobalfilm.com
imdb.com/company/co0323227
facebook.com/imglobalfilm
twitter.com/imglobalfilm

Does not accept any unsolicited material. Project types include Feature Films and TV. Preferred genres include Action, Comedy, Fantasy, and Thriller.

Brian Kavanaugh-Jones
Head (Automatik Film Division)
office@automatikent.com
imdb.com/name/nm2271939
Assistant: Alex Saks

IMPACT PICTURES

9200 W Sunset Blvd, Suite 800
West Hollywood, CA 90069
310-247-1803

Accepts query letter from unproduced, unrepresented writers via email. Project types include Feature Films. Preferred genres include Action, Comedy, Crime, Drama, Fantasy, Horror, Romance, Science Fiction, and Thriller.

Jeremy Bolt
Producer
imdb.com/name/nm0093337

Paul Anderson
imdb.com/name/nm0027271
Assistant: Sarah Crompton

IMPACT PRODUCTIONS

3939 S. Harvard Ave
Tulsa, OK 74135
918-87-2000

info@impactprod.org
impactproductions.com
facebook.com/impactproductions01
twitter.com/tcnewman
imdb.com/company/co0089412

Does not accept any unsolicited material. Project types include Feature Films. Preferred genres include Drama and Family.

IMPRINT ENTERTAINMENT

100 Universal City Plaza
Bungalow 7125
Universal City, CA 91608
818-733-5410 (phone)
818-733-4307 (fax)

info@imprint-ent.com
imprint-ent.com
facebook.com/pages/IMPRINT-
    ENTERTAINMENT/120818451267628
twitter.com/ImprintEnt
imdb.com/company/co0247764

Does not accept any unsolicited material. Project types include Feature Films, TV, and Commercials.

Preferred genres include Action, Comedy, Crime, Drama, Fantasy, Horror, Non-Fiction, Reality, Romance, and Thriller. Established in 2008.

Michael Becker
CEO

IN CAHOOTS

4024 Radford Ave
Editorial Building 2, Suite 7
Studio City, CA 91604
818-655-6482 (phone)
818-655-8472 (fax)

Does not accept any unsolicited material. Project types include Feature Films and TV. Preferred genres include Comedy, Drama, and Thriller.

Ken Kwapis
imdb.com/name/nm0477129

Reynolds Anderson
Creative Executive
imdb.com/name/nm1568030

INCOGNITO PICTURES

16027 Ventura Blvd
Suite 650
Encino, CA 91436
818-724-4727

info@incognitopictures.com
incognitopictures.com
facebook.com/pages/Incognito-Pictures/
    167198753371256
imdb.com/company/co0295349

Does not accept any unsolicited material. Project types include Feature Films. Preferred genres include Crime, Drama, and Thriller.

Scott G. Stone
CEO
imdb.com/name/nm1680597
linkedin.com/pub/scott-stone/53/162/214

Jack Selby
Chairman
imdb.com/name/nm3095212

INDEPENDENT TELEVISION GROUP

8306 Wilshire Blvd., Suite 995
Beverly Hills, CA 90211
310-854-2300

indytvgroup.com
imdb.com/company/co0286591

Does not accept any unsolicited material. Project types include TV. Preferred genres include Drama.

Steven Jensen
Producer
imdb.com/name/nm0421688

INDIAN PAINTBRUSH

1660 Euclid St
Santa Monica, CA 90404
310-566-0160

imdb.com/company/co0215519

Does not accept any unsolicited material. Project types include Feature Films. Preferred genres include Action, Animation, Comedy, Drama, Family, Horror, Romance, Science Fiction, and Thriller.

Steven Rales
Owner

INDIA TAKE ONE PRODUCTIONS

7955 W 3rd St
Los Angeles, CA 90048
323-634-1566 (phone)
323-634-1566 (fax)

M-165, Greater Kailash, Part 2
New Delhi - 110048, India
91 11 4163 8648 (fax)

info@indiatakeone.com
indiatakeone.com
imdb.com/company/co0210547

Does not accept any unsolicited material. Project types include Feature Films. Preferred genres include Drama and Non-Fiction.

Tabrez Noorani
Producer
imdb.com/name/nm0634782

INDICAN PRODUCTIONS

New York, NY

Does not accept any unsolicited material. Project types include Feature Films. Preferred genres include Crime, Drama, and Non-Fiction.

Julia Ormond
Founder
julia.ormond@fox.com
imdb.com/name/nm0000566

INDIE GENIUS PRODUCTIONS

361 Stryker Ave
St. Paul, MN 55107
646-596-0937

imdb.com/company/co0097647

Accepts query letter from unproduced, unrepresented writers. Project types include Feature Films. Preferred genres include Documentary. Established in 2007.

Curt Johnson
curt_johnson@indiegeniusprod.com

INDIEVEST PICTURES

1416 N La Brea Ave
Los Angeles, CA 90028
888-299-9961

info@indievest.com
indievest.com
imdb.com/company/co0198316

Does not accept any unsolicited material. Project types include Feature Films.

Mark Burton
President
imdb.com/name/nm0123666

Matt Wall
Vice President of Development
imdb.com/name/nm0908457

INDIGO FILMS

155 N Redwood Dr. Suite 250
San Rafael, CA 94903

415-444-1700 (phone)
415-444-1720 (fax)

info@indigofilms.com
indigofilms.com
imdb.com/company/co0033065

Does not accept any unsolicited material. Project types include TV. Preferred genres include Drama and Horror.

David Frank
President

James Cox
VP of Development
imdb.com/name/nm0185063

INDOMITABLE ENTERTAINMENT

225 Varick St
Ste 304
New York, NY 10014
212-352-1071 (phone)
212-727-3860 (fax)

1920 Main St, Suite A
Santa Monica, CA 90405
310-664-8700 (phone)
310-664-8711 (fax)

info@indomitable.com
indomitableentertainment.com
facebook.com/pages/Indomitable-Entertainment/
    20750471594844
imdb.com/company/co0274022
twitter.com/IndomitableEnt

Accepts query letter from unproduced, unrepresented writers via email. Project types include Feature Films and TV. Preferred genres include Action, Comedy, Drama, and Thriller.

Dominic Ianno
Founder, CEO
imdb.com/name/nm1746156

Chris Mirosevic
Director of Film Services
imdb.com/name/nm1746156

Stuart Pollok
Executive Producer
imdb.com/name/nm0689415

Robert Deege
Vice President of Business & Creative Affairs
imdb.com/name/nm1830098
linkedin.com/in/rdproducerdirector
twitter.com/rdeege

INDUSTRY ENTERTAINMENT

955 S Carrillo Dr, Suite 300
Los Angeles, CA 90048
323-954-9000

imdb.com/company/co0024345

Accepts scripts from produced or represented writers. Project types include Feature Films and TV. Preferred genres include Comedy, Drama, Family, Fantasy, Horror, Romance, and Thriller. Established in 1982.

Keith Addis
Partner
imdb.com/name/nm0011688

INEFFABLE PICTURES

9247 Alden Dr
Beverly Hills, CA 90210
424-653-1122

info@ineffablepictures.com
ineffablepictures.com
imdb.com/company/co0343339
facebook.com/pages/Ineffable-Pictures
twitter.com/IneffablePics

Does not accept any unsolicited material. Project types include Feature Films. Preferred genres include Action, Comedy, Drama, Fantasy, and Science Fiction. Established in 2010.

Raphael Kryszek
President
imdb.com/name/nm1398360
linkedin.com/pub/raphael-kryszek/0/a6/a75

Jesse Israel
Executive
imdb.com/name/nm2368220
linkedin.com/pub/dir/jesse/israel

Ross Putman
Creative Executive
imdb.com/name/nm3819444
linkedin.com/pub/ross-putman/29/78b/68

INEVITABLE FILM GROUP

8484 Wilshire Blvd, Suite 465
Beverly Hills, CA 90211
310-220-4360

inevitablefilmgroup.com
imdb.com/company/co0206616

Does not accept any unsolicited material. Project types
include Feature Films and TV. Preferred genres
include Drama and Horror.

Stephen Wozniak
Principal/Producer
imdb.com/name/nm0941966

Ron Farber
Principal/Producer
imdb.com/name/nm2618786

INFERNO ENTERTAINMENT

Does not accept any unsolicited material. Project types
include Feature Films. Preferred genres include Action,
Comedy, Crime, Drama, Family, Fantasy, Horror,
Romance, Science Fiction, and Thriller.

INFINITUM NIHIL

infinitumnihil.com
imdb.com/company/co0135149
facebook.com/pages/Infinitum-Nihil/
    108165115878775
twitter.com/infinitumnihil

Does not accept any unsolicited material. Project types
include Feature Films. Preferred genres include Action,
Comedy, Family, Fantasy, Myth, and Romance.

Christi Dembrowski
President
imdb.com/name/nm0218259
Assistant: Dawn Sierra & Erik Schmudde

Norman Todd
Director of Development
imdb.com/name/nm0865249

Margaret French Isaac
imdb.com/name/nm0410504
Assistant: Brandon Zamel

Sam Sarkar
imdb.com/name/nm0765274

Bobby DeLeon
imdb.com/name/nm3765677

Johnny Depp
Founder
imdb.com/name/nm0000136

INFORMANT MEDIA

Los Angeles, CA

informantmedia.com
imdb.com/company/co0242459
facebook.com/InformantMedia
twitter.com/InformantMedia

Accepts query letter from unproduced, unrepresented
writers via email. Project types include Feature Films
and TV. Preferred genres include Action, Comedy,
Drama, Fantasy, Romance, and Thriller. Established in
2008.

Rick Bitzelberger
development@informantmedia.com

Elsa Ramo
Legal Counsel
imdb.com/name/nm1721649

Michael Simpson
CEO
michaelasimpson@informantmedia.com
imdb.com/name/nm0801121

Judy Cairo
Partner
judycairo@informantmedia.com
imdb.com/name/nm0003437

Eric Brenner
Partner
ericbrenner@informantmedia.com
imdb.com/name/nm3665102

Tracey Becker
Producer
tracey@informantmedia.com
imdb.com/name/nm1240204

Howard Meltzer
howardmeltzer@informantmedia.com

Jeremy Po
jeremypo@informantmedia.com

Melina Lizette
melina@informantmedia.com

IN FRONT PRODUCTIONS

imdb.com/company/co0077065

Project types include TV. Established in 1992.

Danny Jacobson
Manager
imdb.com/name/nm0414816

INK FACTORY

73 Wells St
London W1T 3QG
UK
+44-20-7096-1698

2105 Colorado Ave
suite 101
Santa Monica, CA 90404
310-721-5409

info@inkfactoryfilms.com
inkfactoryfilms.com
twitter.com/the_ink_factory

Does not accept any unsolicited material. Project types include Feature Films. Preferred genres include Action, Drama, and Thriller. Established in 2010.

Stephen Cornwell
Principle
310-721-5409
steven@inkonscreen.co.uk
imdb.com/name/nm4051169
linkedin.com/pub/stephen-cornwell/18/b5b/788

Rhodri Thomas
Executive
rhodri@inkonscreen.co.uk
imdb.com/name/nm2905579
facebook.com/rhodri.thomas.908
twitter.com/rodwan1

INPHENATE

9701 Wilshire Blvd
10th Floor
Beverly Hills, CA 90212
310-601-7117 (phone)
310-601-7110 (fax)

imdb.com/company/co0145670
inphenate.com
twitter.com/Inphenate

Does not accept any unsolicited material. Project types include Feature Films and TV. Preferred genres include Comedy, Drama, Non-Fiction, and Reality.

Glenn Rigberg
Owner
imdb.com/name/nm0726572
linkedin.com/in/phenate

INTEGRATED FILMS & MANAGEMENT

2912 Colorado Ave. Ste. 100
Santa Monica, CA 90404
310-998-8648 (phone)
310-998-8680 (fax)

integratedfilms.net
imdb.com/company/co0085255

Does not accept any unsolicited material. Project types include Feature Films. Preferred genres include Horror.

Andy Trapani
Producer

Chris Winvick
Development
imdb.com/name/nm0936111

INTERLOPER FILMS

1622 Pepper Dr
Los Angeles, CA 90068
626-296-0068

coordinator@interloperfilms.com
interloperfilms.com
imdb.com/company/co0101529

Does not accept any unsolicited material. Project types include Feature Films. Preferred genres include Non-Fiction.

David Timoner
Principal
imdb.com/name/nm0863755

Ondi Timoner
Principal
imdb.com/name/nm0863756

INTERMEDIA FILMS

9242 Beverly Blvd., Suite 201
Beverly Hills, CA 90210
310-777-0007 (phone)
310-777-0008 (fax)

info@intermediafilm.com
imdb.com/company/co0010183
intermediafilm.com

Does not accept any unsolicited material. Project types include Feature Films. Preferred genres include Action, Comedy, and Drama.

Konstantin Thoeren
Chairman
imdb.com/name/nm0858328

Linda Benjamin
President
imdb.com/name/nm0071326

INTERNATIONAL ARTS ENTERTAINMENT

8899 Beverly Blvd., Ste 800
Los Angeles, CA 90048
310-550-6760 (phone)
310-550-8839 (fax)

internationalartsentertainment.com

imdb.com/company/co0062824

Does not accept any unsolicited material.

Alan Greenspan
Producer
imdb.com/name/nm2325162

Robyn Morrison
Development
imdb.com/name/nm1308467

INTERVISION PARTNERS

122 E 42nd St., Suite 2900
New York, NY 10168
212-949-3400 (phone)
212-949-7534 (fax)

usa@intervisionsitv.com
intervisionsitv.com
imdb.com/company/co0209777

Does not accept any unsolicited material. Project types include Feature Films and TV. Preferred genres include Drama.

Jerry Wolff
Partner/Producer
imdb.com/name/nm2872765

INTREPID PICTURES

10323 SANTA MONICA BLVD., SUITE 111 LOS ANGELES, CA 90025
310-566-5000

info@intrepidpictures.com
intrepidpictures.com

Does not accept any unsolicited material. Project types include Feature Films. Preferred genres include Action, Comedy, Horror, and Thriller. Established in 2004.

Marc D. Evans
Founder
imdb.com/name/nm2162955

Trevor Macy
Founder
imdb.com/name/nm1006167

Melinda Nishioka
Director of Development
melinda@intrepidpictures.com
imdb.com/name/nm2325559

INTRINSIC VALUE FILMS

1 State St Plaza, 24th Floor
New York, NY 10004
212-989-7200 (phone)
212-202-7808 (fax)

406 Grand Blvd
Venice, CA 90291
310-857-6733

info@intrinsicvaluefilms.com
intrinsicvaluefilms.com
imdb.com/company/co0072994

Accepts query letter from unproduced, unrepresented writers via email. Project types include Feature Films. Preferred genres include Comedy, Drama, Horror, and Thriller.

Aimee Schoof
Producer
imdb.com/name/nm0774779

Isen Robbins
Producer
imdb.com/name/nm0730358

INTUITION PRODUCTIONS

1635 N Cahuenga Blvd
Los Angeles, CA 90028
323-464-1682

imdb.com/company/co0119811

Does not accept any unsolicited material. Project types include TV. Preferred genres include Drama.

Keri Selig
Producer
imdb.com/name/nm0783146

INVENTURE ENTERTAINMENT

44 E 32nd St, 9th Floor
New York, NY 10016
212-863-9656

info@inventureentertainment.com
inventureentertainment.com
imdb.com/company/co0180061

Does not accept any unsolicited material. Project types include Feature Films.

Daniel Rosenberg
Producer
imdb.com/name/nm1360674

IRISH DREAMTIME

imdb.com/company/co0088199

Does not accept any unsolicited material. Project types include Feature Films and TV. Preferred genres include Action, Comedy, Crime, Drama, Non-Fiction, Romance, and Thriller. Established in 1996.

Pierce Brosnan
Founder
imdb.com/name/nm0000112

Keith Arnold
Head of Development
imdb.com/name/nm2993265

Beau St. Clair
imdb.com/name/nm0820429

IRONCLAD PICTURES

25 Broadway, 12th Floor
New York, NY 10004
646-370-5793 (phone)
646-390-6576 (fax)

assistant@ironcladpictures.com
ironcladpictures.com

Does not accept any unsolicited material. Project types include Feature Films. Preferred genres include Crime and Drama.

Jordan Yale Levine
Founder/Producer
imdb.com/name/nm2775149

Ash Christian
Founder/Producer
imdb.com/name/nm1101381

IRON OCEAN FILMS

1317 Luanne Ave
Fullerton, CA 92831
323-957-9706

Does not accept any unsolicited material. Project types include Feature Films. Preferred genres include Crime, Drama, and Thriller.

Jessica Biel
imdb.com/name/nm0004754

Michelle Purple
imdb.com/name/nm0321977

IRONWORKS PRODUCTIONS

517 W 35th St 2nd Floor
New York City, NY 10001
212-216-9780 (phone)
212-239-9180 (fax)

IRONWORKS PRODUCTIONS INC.
131 GORE DRIVE, BARRIE, ONTARIO CANADA
L4N 0A8
705-333-1679

ironworksproductions@pobox.com
imdb.com/company/co0159206
ironworksproductions.ca

Accepts query letter from unproduced, unrepresented writers via email. Project types include Feature Films and TV. Preferred genres include Comedy, Drama, Non-Fiction, Reality, Romance, and Thriller.

Bruce Weiss
imdb.com/name/nm0918933

Isa Freeling
imdb.com/name/nm2303742

IRWIN ENTERTAINMENT

710 Seward St
Los Angeles, CA 90038
323-468-0700 (phone)
323-464-1001 (fax)

Collin Reno
William Morris Endeavor
9601 Wilshire Blvd,

Beverly Hills, CA 90210
310-859-4526

imdb.com/company/co0193199
twitter.com/irwinent
irwinentertainment.com
linkedin.com/company/irwin-entertainment

Does not accept any unsolicited material. Project types include Feature Films and TV. Preferred genres include Comedy and Reality.

John Irwin
President
john@irwinentertainment.com
imdb.com/name/nm1685815

ISH ENTERTAINMENT

104 W 27th St Second Floor
New York, NY 10001
212-654-6445

info@ish.tv
ish.tv
imdb.com/name/nm4851905
twitter.com/ishteevee

Does not accept any unsolicited material. Project types include Feature Films, Short Films, and TV. Preferred genres include Documentary and Reality. Established in 2008.

Wendy Roth
Executive Vice President of Production
imdb.com/name/nm0745046

Melissa Cooper
Director of Development
imdb.com/name/nm2435108

Larissa Neal

Michael Saffran
Executive
imdb.com/name/nm5249575

Madison Merritt
imdb.com/name/nm3117402

Chris Choun
imdb.com/name/nm1780111

Michael Hirschorn
President
imdb.com/name/nm1337695
linkedin.com/pub/michael-hirschorn/41/451/483

IS OR ISN'T ENTERTAINMENT

8391 Beverly Blvd., Suite 125
Los Angeles, CA 90048
310-854-0972

info@isorisnt.com
isorisnt.com
imdb.com/company/co0116545

Does not accept any unsolicited material. Project types include TV. Preferred genres include Drama.

Lisa Kudrow
Actor/Partner
imdb.com/name/nm0001435

Dan Bucatinsky
Partner/Producer/Writer
imdb.com/name/nm0117857

ITHACA PICTURES

8711 Bonner Dr
West Hollywood, CA 90048
310-967-0112 (phone)
310-967-3053 (fax)

Does not accept any unsolicited material. Project types include Feature Films. Preferred genres include Drama and Non-Fiction.

Michael Fitzgerald
Executive
imdb.com/name/nm028033

Richard Romero
Producer
imdb.com/name/nm2484143

JACKHOLE PRODUCTIONS

6834 Hollywood Blvd
Los Angeles, CA 90028
323-860-5900

imdb.com/company/co0071163

facebook.com/pages/Jackhole-Productions/
112075485472368

Accepts query letter from produced or represented writers. Project types include TV. Preferred genres include Comedy and Reality.

Jimmy Kimmel
Partner
imdb.com/name/nm0453994

Adam Carolla
Partner
imdb.com/name/nm0004805

Daniel Kellison
Partner
imdb.com/name/nm0446058

Doug DeLuca
Producer
imdb.com/name/nm0217891

JAFFE/BRAUNSTEIN FILMS

12301 Wilshire Blvd Suite 110 Los Angeles, CA
90025
310-207-6600 (phone)
310-207-6069 (fax)

imdb.com/company/co0012412

Accepts scripts from produced or represented writers. Project types include Feature Films and TV. Preferred genres include Comedy, Drama, Horror, Romance, Science Fiction, and Thriller.

Howard Braunstein
imdb.com/name/nm0105946
linkedin.com/pub/howard-braunstein/0/a6/3a6

Michael Jaffe
Partner
imdb.com/name/nm0415468
Assistant: Lynn Delaney

JAKKS PACIFIC

21749 Baker Parkway
Walnut, CA 91789
877-875-2557

jakkspacific.com
imdb.com/company/co0072553

Does not accept any unsolicited material. Project types include TV. Preferred genres include Science Fiction.

Stephen G. Berman
President/CEO

Joel Bennett
CFO/EVP
imdb.com/name/nm0071547

JANE STARTZ PRODUCTIONS

244 Fift h Ave, 11th Floor
New York, NY 10001
212-545-8910 (phone)
212-545-8909 (fax)

imdb.com/company/co0048322

Accepts query letter from unproduced, unrepresented writers. Project types include Feature Films and TV. Preferred genres include Animation, Comedy, Drama, Family, Fantasy, Romance, and Thriller.

Jane Startz
President
imdb.com/name/nm0823661

Kane Lee
Vice-President
imdb.com/name/nm1634508

JANE STREET ENTERTAINMENT

100 Ave Of The Americas, 11th Floor
New York, NY 10013

janestreetentertainment.com
imdb.com/company/co0363484

Does not accept any unsolicited material. Project types include TV.

Linda Lea
Producer
imdb.com/name/nm1103775

Donna Macletchie
Producer
imdb.com/name/nm2338190

JARET ENTERTAINMENT

6973 Birdview Ave
Malibu, CA 90265
310-589-9600

info@jaretentertainment.com
jaretentertainment.com
imdb.com/company/co000426

Does not accept any unsolicited material. Project types include Feature Films and TV.

Seth Jaret
Producer/Manager
imdb.com/name/nm0418684

JEAN DOUMANIAN PRODUCTIONS

595 Madison Ave Suite 2200
New York City, NY 10022
212-486-2626 (phone)
212-688-6236 (fax)

jdpnyc.com
imdb.com/company/co0028809
facebook.com/jeandoumanianproductions
twitter.com/jdp_theater

Accepts query letter from unproduced, unrepresented writers. Project types include Feature Films and TV. Preferred genres include Comedy, Drama, Horror, Non-Fiction, Period, Romance, and Thriller.

Jean Doumanian
Founder
imdb.com/name/nm0235389

Kathryn Willingham
Development Associate
imdb.com/name/nm5187379
linkedin.com/pub/kathryn-willingham/a/a85/1a5

Patrick Daly
Vice-President
imdb.com/name/nm4794210
linkedin.com/pub/patrick-daly/20/449/aa

Saul Nathan-Kazis
Associate Director of Theatrical Development
imdb.com/name/nm2651163
linkedin.com/pub/saul-nathan-kazis/23/3/910

Preston Copley
Director of Theatrical Development

JEFF MORTON PRODUCTIONS

10201 W Pico Blvd Building 226
Los Angeles, CA 90035
310-467-1123 (phone)
818-981-4152 (fax)

Does not accept any unsolicited material. Project types include Feature Films and TV.

Jeff Morton
Producer
scoutspence@mindspring.com
imdb.com/name/nm0608005

JERRY BRUCKHEIMER FILMS

1631 10th St
Santa Monica, CA 90404
310-664-6260 (phone)
310-664-6261 (fax)

imdb.com/company/co0217391
facebook.com/JBFilms
jbfilms.com

Does not accept any unsolicited material. Project types include Feature Films and TV. Preferred genres include Action, Comedy, Crime, Detective, Drama, Family, Fantasy, Horror, Myth, Non-Fiction, Reality, Science Fiction, and Thriller.

Jerry Bruckheimer
imdb.com/name/nm0000988
linkedin.com/in/jerrybruckheimer
twitter.com/BRUCKHEIMERJB

Charlie Vignola
Director of Development
linkedin.com/pub/charlie-vogel/38/213/398

Mike Stenson
President
imdb.com/name/nm0826679

JERRY WEINTRAUB PRODUCTIONS

190 N Canon Dr, Suite 204
Beverly Hills, CA 90210

310-273-8800 (phone)
310-273-8502 (fax)

imdb.com/company/co0024560

Does not accept any unsolicited material. Project types include Feature Films. Preferred genres include Action, Comedy, Crime, Drama, Family, Non-Fiction, Science Fiction, and Thriller.

Jerry Weintraub
Producer
Assistant: Kimberly Pinkstaff

Susan Ekins
Vice-President
Assistant: Betsy Dennis

JERSEY FILMS

PO Box 491246
Los Angeles, CA 90049
310-550-3200 (phone)
310-550-3210 (fax)

imdb.com/company/co0010434

Accepts query letter from unproduced, unrepresented writers. Project types include Feature Films. Preferred genres include Action, Comedy, Drama, Non-Fiction, Romance, and Thriller.

Danny DeVito
Executive
imdb.com/name/nm0000362

Nikki Grosso
310-477-7704
imdb.com/name/nm0343777

JET TONE PRODUCTIONS

21/F Park Commercial Centre
No. 180 Tung Lo Wan Rd
Hong Kong
China
852-2336-1102 (phone)
852-2337-9849 (fax)

jettone@netvigator.com
jettone.net
imdb.com/company/co0074316

Accepts query letter from unproduced, unrepresented writers via email. Project types include Feature Films. Preferred genres include Action, Animation, Comedy, Crime, Drama, Romance, Science Fiction, and Thriller.

Wong Kar-wai
imdb.com/name/nm0939182

J.K. LIVIN' PRODUCTIONS

64 Market St
Venice, CA 90291
310-857-1555

imdb.com/company/co0097218

Does not accept any unsolicited material. Project types include Feature Films. Preferred genres include Action.

Matthew McConaughey
Partner/Producer/Actor
imdb.com/name/nm0000190

Mark Gustawes
President of Production
imdb.com/name/nm0349126

JOEL SCHUMACHER PRODUCTIONS

10960 Wilshire Bvld. Suite 1900
Los Angeles, CA 90024
310-472-7602 (phone)
310-270-4618 (fax)

imdb.com/company/co0094915

Does not accept any unsolicited material. Project types include Feature Films, TV, and Commercials. Preferred genres include Action, Comedy, Crime, Drama, Fantasy, Romance, Science Fiction, and Thriller.

Joel Schumacher
310-472-7602
imdb.com/name/nm0001708
Assistant: Jeff Feuerstein

Aaron Cooley
Producer
818-260-6065
imdb.com/name/nm0177583
linkedin.com/pub/aaron-cooley/39/2b7/432

JOHN CALLEY PRODUCTIONS

10202 W Washington Blvd
Crawford Building
Culver City, CA 90232
310-244-7777 (phone)
310-244-4070 (fax)

imdb.com/company/co0125552

Does not accept any unsolicited material. Project types include Feature Films and TV. Preferred genres include Action, Comedy, Detective, Drama, Romance, and Thriller.

John Calley
Producer
310-244-7777
imdb.com/name/nm1886942
linkedin.com/pub/john-calley/8/252/4a0

Lisa Medwid
310-244-7777
imdb.com/name/nm1886942

JOHN CARRABINO MANAGEMENT

5900 Wilshire Blvd., Suite 406
Los Angeles, CA 90036
323-857-4650

facebook.com/pages/John-Carrabino-Management/
161867210499754
imdb.com/name/nm4222011

Does not accept any unsolicited material. Project types include TV.

Gladys Gonzalez
Producer/Manager

John Carrabino
Owner/Manager
imdb.com/name/nm0139920

JOHN DOE MEDIA

8265 Sunset Blvd., Suite 105
West Hollywood, CA 90046
424-235-3688

info@johndoemedia.com
johndoemedia.com
imdb.com/company/co0268174

Does not accept any unsolicited material. Project types include TV.

D. Renard Young
Producer
imdb.com/name/nm1511022

JOHN GOLDWYN PRODUCTIONS

5555 Melrose Ave, Dressing Room. 112
Los Angeles, CA 90038
323-956-5054 (phone)
323-862-0055 (fax)

imdb.com/company/co0177677

Does not accept any unsolicited material. Project types include Feature Films and TV. Preferred genres include Action, Comedy, Crime, Detective, Drama, Non-Fiction, and Thriller. Established in 1991.

John Goldwyn
President
imdb.com/name/nm0326415
Assistant: Jasen Laks

Hilary Marx
Creative Executive
imdb.com/name/nm1020576
Assistant: Rebecca Crow

Erin David
Creative Executive
imdb.com/name/nm1716252
Assistant: Rebecca Crow

JOHN WELLS PRODUCTIONS

4000 Warner Blvd
Building 1
Burbank, CA 91522-0001
818-954-1687 (phone)
818-954-3657 (fax)

jwppa@warnerbros.com
imdb.com/company/co0037310

Accepts query letter from unproduced, unrepresented writers. Project types include Feature Films and TV. Preferred genres include Action, Comedy, Drama, Family, Horror, Romance, Science Fiction, and Thriller.

Claire Polstein
President
imdb.com/name/nm0689856
Assistant: Tessie Groff

Jinny Joung
Vice-President
Assistant: Irene Lee irene.lee@jwprods.com

Andrew Stearn
President
imdb.com/name/nm1048942
Assistant: Quinn Tivey quinn.tivey@jwprods.com

John Wells
Principle
imdb.com/name/nm2187561
Assistant: Kristin Martini

JON SHESTACK PRODUCTIONS

409 N Larchmont Blvd
Los Angeles, CA 90004
323-468-1113

imdb.com/company/co0168855

Does not accept any unsolicited material. Project types include Feature Films. Preferred genres include Animation, Comedy, Crime, Drama, Family, Fantasy, Romance, Science Fiction, and Thriller. Established in 2006.

Jonathan Shestack
imdb.com/name/nm0792871

Ginny Brewer Pennekamp
imdb.com/name/nm2555285

JOSEPHSON ENTERTAINMENT

1201 W 5th St Suite M-170 Los Angeles, CA 90017
213-534-3995

imdb.com/company/co0046572

Does not accept any unsolicited material. Project types include Feature Films and TV. Preferred genres include Action, Animation, Comedy, Crime, Drama, Family, Fantasy, Horror, Romance, Science Fiction, Sociocultural, and Thriller.

Tia Maggini
Assistant: Mekita Faiye
mekita.faiye@josephsonent.com

Barry Josephson
Principle
imdb.com/name/nm0430742
Assistant: Sean Bennett

JOURNEYMAN PICTURES

225 W 13th St
New York, NY 10011
212-989-1038 (phone)
212-989-3907 (fax)

info@journeyman-pictures.com
journeyman-pictures.com
imdb.com/company/co0065292

Does not accept any unsolicited material. Project types include Feature Films. Preferred genres include Drama.

Paul Mezey
Producer
imdb.com/name/nm0583796

Becky Glupczynski
Producer
imdb.com/name/nm1014894

JUNCTION FILMS

9615 Brighton Way, Suite M110
Beverly Hills, CA 90210
310-246-9799 (phone)
310-246-3824 (fax)

info@junctionfilms.com
imdb.com/company/co0099841
junctionfilms.com

Accepts query letter from unproduced, unrepresented writers. Preferred genres include Action, Comedy, Crime, Drama, Horror, Reality, Science Fiction, and Thriller. Established in 2001.

Brad Wyman
Producer
310-246-9799
imdb.com/name/nm0943829

Donald Kushner
Producer
imdb.com/name/nm0476291

Alwyn Kushner
Producer
imdb.com/name/nm1672379

JUNIPER PLACE PRODUCTIONS

4024 Radford Ave, Bungalow 1
Studio City, CA 91604
818-655-5043 (phone)
818 655-8402 (fax)

Accepts query letter from unproduced, unrepresented writers. Project types include TV. Preferred genres include Drama.

Jeffrey Kramer
Principle
imdb.com/name/nm0469552
linkedin.com/pub/jeffrey-kramer/6/89/850

Jennifer Stempel
Director of Development
imdb.com/name/nm4009105

KAMALA FILMS

375 Greenwich St, 5th Floor
New York, NY 10013
212-219-4161

info@kamalafilms.com
kamalafilms.com
imdb.com/company/co0172185

Does not accept any unsolicited material. Project types include Feature Films. Preferred genres include Drama.

Marissa McMahon
Producer
imdb.com/name/nm0997470

KAPITAL ENTERTAINMENT

8687 Melrose Ave
9th Floor
West Hollywood, CA 90069
310-854-3221

imdb.com/company/co0275279

Does not accept any unsolicited material. Project types include TV. Preferred genres include Comedy and Drama.

Aaron Kaplan
akaplan@kapital-ent.com
imdb.com/name/nm3483168

Cailey Buck
Director of Development
linkedin.com/pub/cailey-buck/19/120/980

KAPLAN/PERRONE ENTERTAINMENT

280 S Beverly Dr, #513
Beverly Hills, CA 90212
310-285-0116

imdb.com/company/co0094257

Accepts scripts from produced or represented writers. Project types include Feature Films and TV. Preferred genres include Action, Comedy, Drama, Romance, and Thriller.

Josh Goldenberg
Manager

Sean Perrone
Partner

Tobin Babst

Alex Lerner
Manager
linkedin.com/pub/alex-lerner/1a/64b/845

Aaron Kaplan
Partner
linkedin.com/pub/aaron-kaplan/3/74b/507

KARTEMQUIN FILMS

1901 W. Wellington
Chicago, IL 60657
773-472-3348

info@kartemquin.com
kartemquin.com
imdb.com/company/co0076348

Does not accept any unsolicited material. Project types include Feature Films. Preferred genres include Drama and Non-Fiction.

Ed Bachrach
Board Member/Producer

KARZ ENTERTAINMENT

4000 Warner Blvd Building 138, Suite 1205
Burbank, CA 91522
818-954-1698 (phone)
818-954-1700 (fax)

karzent@aol.com
imdb.com/company/co0033868

Does not accept any unsolicited material. Project types include Feature Films and TV. Preferred genres include Action, Comedy, Crime, Documentary, Drama, Family, Fantasy, Horror, Romance, and Thriller. Established in 1998.

Mike Karz
President
imdb.com/name/nm0440344

KASDAN PICTURES

9220 W Sunset Blvd, Suite 108
West Hollywood, CA 90069
310-281-2340

Does not accept any unsolicited material. Project types include Feature Films. Preferred genres include Comedy, Drama, and Thriller.

Lawrence Kasdan
Writer/Producer/Director
imdb.com/name/nm0001410

KASSEN BROTHERS PRODUCTIONS

141 W 28th St, Suite 301
New York, NY 10001
212-244-2865 (phone)
212-244-2874 (fax)

imdb.com/company/co0183529

Accepts query letter from unproduced, unrepresented writers. Project types include TV. Preferred genres include Action, Comedy, Drama, and Non-Fiction.

Mark Kassen
President
imdb.com/name/nm0440860

Patrick Petrocelli
imdb.com/name/nm2332569

Mark Olsen
Director of Development
imdb.com/name/nm1565746

Adam Kassen
212-244-2865
imdb.com/name/nm0440859

KATALYST FILMS

6806 Lexington Ave
Los Angeles, CA 90038
323-785-2700 (phone)
323-785-2715 (fax)

info@katalystfilms.com
imdb.com/company/co0102320
katalystfilms.com
facebook.com/katalyst

Accepts scripts from unproduced, unrepresented writers. Project types include Feature Films and TV. Preferred genres include Action, Animation, Comedy, Crime, Drama, Reality, Romance, Science Fiction, and Thriller.

Ashton Kutcher
Partner
imdb.com/name/nm0005110
facebook.com/Ashton

Jason Goldberg
Partner
imdb.com/name/nm0325229
linkedin.com/pub/jason-goldberg/22/120/131

KATCO

8687 Melrose Ave
West Hollywood, CA 90069
310-854-3223

Does not accept any unsolicited material. Project types include Feature Films and TV. Established in 2014.

Tracy Katsky
Executive
818-789-1182
tracykb@gmail.com
Assistant: Danyelle Foord

KAUFMAN COMPANY

15030 Ventura Blvd, Suite 510
Sherman Oaks, CA 91403
818-223-9840

info@thekaufmancompany.com
thekaufmancompany.com
imdb.com/company/co0043378

Paul Kaufman
Producer
imdb.com/name/nm2092500

KELLER ENTERTAINMENT GROUP

1093 Broxton Ave, Suite #246
Los Angeles, CA 90024
310-443-2226 (phone)
310-443-2194 (fax)

kellerentertainment.com
imdb.com/company/co0007667

Does not accept any unsolicited material. Project types include Feature Films and TV. Preferred genres include Action, Drama, and Family.

Max Keller
Chairman/CEO
imdb.com/name/nm0445720

Micheline Keller
President
imdb.com/name/nm0445732

KENNEDY/MARSHALL COMPANY

619 Arizona Ave
Santa Monica, CA 90401
310-656-8400 (phone)
310-656-8430 (fax)

kennedymarshall.com
twitter.com/KenedyMarshall

facebook.com/pages/The-KennedyMarshall-Company/
274557862638636
imdb.com/company/co0013175

Does not accept any unsolicited material. Project types
include Feature Films and TV. Preferred genres
include Action, Comedy, Detective, Drama, Family,
Non-Fiction, Romance, Science Fiction, and Thriller.

Robert D. Zotnowski

Frank Marshall
imdb.com/name/nm0550881

Grey Rembert
imdb.com/name/nm0718880

KERNER ENTERTAINMENT COMPANY

1888 Century Park East
Suite 1005
Los Angeles, CA 90067
310-815-5100 (phone)
310-815-5110 (fax)

imdb.com/company/co0127668

Does not accept any unsolicited material. Project types
include Feature Films. Preferred genres include Action,
Animation, Comedy, Drama, Family, and Fantasy.

Jordan Kerner
President
imdb.com/name/nm0449549
linkedin.com/pub/jordan-kerner/29/48/a96

Ben Haber
imdb.com/name/nm1852209

KESTREL COMMUNICATIONS

1100 Spring St, Suite 770
Atlanta, GA 30309
404-888-0336

contact@kestrelcom.com
kestrelcom.com
imdb.com/company/co0197764

Does not accept any unsolicited material. Project types
include Feature Films and TV. Preferred genres
include Comedy and Drama.

Robert L. Rearden Jr.
Producer
imdb.com/name/nm4299673

KEY CREATIVES

1800 N. Highland Ave., Suite 500
Los Angeles, CA 90028
323-785-7950

imdb.com/company/co0124523

Does not accept any unsolicited material. Project types
include Feature Films and TV. Preferred genres
include Science Fiction.

Ken Kamins
CEO, Producer
imdb.com/name/nm1353341

KEY FILMS

5613 Versailles Ct.
Colleyville, TX 76034

imdb.com/company/co0136532

Does not accept any unsolicited material. Project types
include Feature Films. Preferred genres include Crime
and Drama.

Charles Key
Producer
imdb.com/name/nm2105495

KGB FILMS

5555 Melrose Ave, Lucy Bungalow 101
Los Angeles, CA 90038
323-956-5000 (phone)
323-224-1876 (fax)

turbo@kgbfilms.com
kgbfilms.com
facebook.com/kgbfilms
linkedin.com/company/kgb-films

Accepts query letter from unproduced, unrepresented
writers via email. Project types include Feature Films,
Short Films, and TV. Preferred genres include
Comedy, Crime, Drama, Non-Fiction, and Romance.
Established in 1994.

Justin Hogan
Producer
imdb.com/name/nm0389556
linkedin.com/pub/frank-scherma/0/332/440

Rosser Goodman
President
rossergoodman.com
imdb.com/name/nm0329223

KICKSTART PRODUCTIONS

343 Railway St suite 101
Vancouver,
British Columbia
V6A 1A4
604-684-3465

594 Broadway,
Ninth Floor
New York, New York
10012

3212 Nebraska Ave
Santa Monica, CA 90404
310-264-1757

1066 Tung Chau West St,
Alexandria Industrial Bldg,
Suite 306, 3/F, Block A
Lai Chi Kok, Kowloon
852-9528-0442

hila@kickstartent.com
hiny@kickstartent.com
kickstartent.com
twitter.com/kickstartpro
facebook.com/pages/Kick-Start-Productuons-Inc/
    170721556324763
imdb.com/company/co0163548

Does not accept any unsolicited material. Project types include Feature Films. Preferred genres include Action, Animation, Comedy, Family, and Science Fiction. Established in 1999.

Jason Netter
President
imdb.com/name/nm0626697

Susan Norkin
imdb.com/name/nm0635379

Loris Kramer Lunsford
Executive Producer
imdb.com/name/nm0469603
linkedin.com/in/loriskl

Samantha Olsson Shear
imdb.com/name/nm2427387
linkedin.com/pub/samantha-shear/6/a67/a18

KILLER FILMS

18th East 16th St, 4th Floor
New York, NY 10003
212-473-3950 (phone)
212-807-1456 (fax)

killerfilms.com
imdb.com/company/co0030755
facebook.com/killerfilms

Accepts query letter from unproduced, unrepresented writers. Project types include Feature Films, Short Films, and TV. Preferred genres include Comedy, Crime, Drama, Family, Horror, Romance, and Thriller. Established in 1995.

Christine Vachon
Partner
imdb.com/name/nm0882927
Assistant: Gabrielle Nadig

Pamela Koffler
Partner
imdb.com/name/nm0463025
Assistant: Gabrielle Nadig

David Hinojosa
Director of Development
imdb.com/name/nm3065267
Assistant: Gabrielle Nadig

KIM AND JIM PRODUCTIONS

787 N. Palm Canyon Dr
Palm Springs, CA 92262
760-574-1858

info@kimandjimproductions.com
kimandjimproductions.com
facebook.com/kimandjimproductions
twitter.com/kimwaltrip
imdb.com/company/co0338692

Accepts query letter from unproduced, unrepresented writers. Project types include Feature Films. Preferred genres include Action, Comedy, Drama, Fantasy, Horror, Romance, and Thriller.

Jim Casey
Vice Chairman
jim@kimandjimproductions
imdb.com/name/nm2816633

Kim Waltrip
Vice Chairman
assist@kimandjimproductions.com
imdb.com/name/nm0910601
linkedin.com/in/kimwaltrip

KINETIC FILMWORKS

6660 Suset Blvd #1193
Hollywood, CA 90028
818-505-3347

kineticfilmworks@aol.com
imdb.com/company/co0224342
kineticfilmworks.com

Accepts query letter from unproduced, unrepresented writers via email. Project types include Feature Films. Preferred genres include Horror. Established in 2013.

Jeffrey Miller
Partner
imdb.com/name/nm0588577

Gary Jones
Partner
imdb.com/name/nm0428109
linkedin.com/in/garybjones

KINGDOM COUNTY PRODUCTIONS

106 Main St, Suite 2
Burlington, VT 05401
802-357-4616

info@kingdomcounty.com
kingdomcounty.com
imdb.com/company/co0154942

Does not accept any unsolicited material. Project types include Feature Films. Preferred genres include Drama.

KING MIDAS WORLD ENTERTAINMENT

3960 Howard Hughes Parkway, Suite 500
Las Vegas, NV 89169
702-990-3979 (phone)
702-562-1541 (fax)

imdb.com/company/co0242105
kingmidasworldentertainment.com

Does not accept any unsolicited material. Project types include Feature Films. Preferred genres include Action and Drama.

Fabrizio Boccardi
Founder/Chairman of the Board

KINGSBOROUGH PICTURES

361 Beloit Ave
Los Angeles, CA 90049
310-476-1613

446, Boul Saint-Laurent, Bureau 805
Montreal, Quebec
Canada H2W1Z5
514-985-2272

info@kingsboroughpictures.com
kingsboroughpictures.com
imdb.com/company/co0025097

Does not accept any unsolicited material. Project types include Feature Films. Preferred genres include Drama.

KINGSGATE FILMS, INC.

7024 Melrose Ave, Suite 420
Los Angeles, CA 90038
323-937-6110 (phone)
323-937-6102 (fax)

kingsgatefilms.com
imdb.com/company/co0013909

Does not accept any unsolicited material. Project types include Feature Films. Preferred genres include Comedy and Drama.

Greg Shapiro
Producer
imdb.com/name/nm0788513

KING'S INDIAN PRODUCTIONS

335 E 5 St, Suite 2F
New York, NY 10003

info@kingsindian.com
kingsindian.com

Does not accept any unsolicited material. Project types include Feature Films. Preferred genres include Drama and Thriller.

John Hume
President
imdb.com/name/nm1124685

KING SIZE FILM PRODUCTIONS

32302 Camino Capistrano #203
San Juan Capistrano, CA 92675
714-928-7600

imdb.com/company/co0286028

Does not accept any unsolicited material. Project types include Feature Films. Preferred genres include Drama.

Michael Zanetis
President/Producer/Writer
imdb.com/name/nm4509769

KINTOP PICTURES

7955 W 3rd St
Los Angeles, CA 90048
323-634-1570 (phone)
323-634-1575 (fax)

kintopfilm@aol.com
info@indiatakeone.com
imdb.com/company/co0004925
linkedin.com/company/kintop-pictures
indiatakeone.com
facebook.com/pages/Kintop-Pictures/
162544103769669

Accepts query letter from unproduced, unrepresented writers. Project types include Feature Films and TV. Preferred genres include Comedy, Documentary, Drama, Family, Horror, Romance, and Thriller.

Deepak Nayar
Founder
imdb.com/name/nm0623235

KIPPSTER ENTERTAINMENT

420 W End Ave, Suite 1G
New York, NY 10024
212-496-1200

imdb.com/company/co0310346

Does not accept any unsolicited material. Project types include Feature Films and TV. Preferred genres include Drama and Non-Fiction.

Perri Kipperman
Founder
imdb.com/name/nm1069530

David Sterns
Founder
imdb.com/name/nm3992907
linkedin.com/pub/david-stern/46/85/711

KIRMSER PONTURO GROUP

10 Rockefeller Plaza, Suite 910
New York, NY 10020
212-554-3430

info@kirmserponturo.com
kirmserponturo.com

Does not accept any unsolicited material. Project types include Feature Films. Preferred genres include Drama and Non-Fiction.

Fran Kirmser
Producer
imdb.com/name/nm6134040

Tony Ponturo
Producer
imdb.com/name/nm5501182

KISMET ENTERTAINMENT GROUP

8350 Wilshire Blvd., Suite 200
Beverly Hills, CA 90211
323-556-0748 (phone)
323-556-0601 (fax)

info@kismetent.com
kismetent.com
imdb.com/company/co0076370

Accepts query letter from unproduced, unrepresented writers. Project types include Feature Films. Preferred genres include Action and Horror.

Todd Knowlton
Vice President
imdb.com/name/nm1539856

David E. Allen
Chairman/CEO/Producer
imdb.com/name/nm0020431

KLASKY-CSUPO

1238 N. Higland Blvd.
Hollywood , CA 90038
323-468-2600

mail@klaskycsupo.com
klaskycsupo.com

Does not accept any unsolicited material. Project types include Feature Films and TV.

Gabor Csupo
Chairman
imdb.com/name/nm0190780

Arlene Klasky
Chairman
imdb.com/name/nm0458312

KNIGHTSBRIDGE THEATRE FILMS

1944 Riverside Dr
Los Angeles, CA 90039
323-667-0955

knightsbridgetheatre.com
facebook.com/pages/Knightsbridge-Theatre/
    119758671421319
imdb.com/company/co0351642

Does not accept any unsolicited material. Project types include Feature Films. Preferred genres include Thriller.

Joseph P. Stachura
Founder/Producer/Director/Writer
imdb.com/name/nm0821018

KOMIXX ENTERTAINMENT

Amadeus House
27b Floral St
Covent Garden
London
WC2E 9DP
+44203-428-5396

9155 W Sunset Blvd
Los Angeles, CA 90069
310-385-7140

info@komixx.com
komixx.com
twitter.com/komixx
linkedin.com/company/komixx-entertainment-
    komixx-films
imdb.com/company/co0296470

Does not accept any unsolicited material. Project types include Feature Films, Short Films, and TV. Preferred genres include Action, Comedy, and Romance.

Edward Glauser
CEO

Andrew Cole-Bulgin
CEO

Melanie Halsall
Head of Development

Maddie Stewart
Creative Assistant

Michael Ashton
Chairman

Dave Wilson
Director

Richard Randolph
Creative Director
+44207-861-3869
info@komixx.com
Assistant: Maddie Stewart

KOMUT ENTERTAINMENT

imdb.com/company/co0028360

Does not accept any unsolicited material. Project types include TV. Preferred genres include Comedy, Drama, and Thriller.

David Kohan

Partner

imdb.com/name/nm0463172

Assistant: Melissa Strauss

Melissa.Strauss@wbconsultant.com

Max Mutchnick

Partner

imdb.com/name/nm0616083

twitter.com/MaxMutchnick

K/O PAPER PRODUCTS

100 Universal City Plaza

Building 5125

Universal City, CA 91608

818-733-9645 (phone)

818-733-6988 (fax)

imdb.com/company/co0315120

Does not accept any unsolicited material. Project types include Feature Films and TV. Preferred genres include Action, Animation, Drama, Fantasy, and Science Fiction. Established in 1997.

Alex Kurtzman

Principle

imdb.com/name/nm0476064

Roberto Orci

Principle

imdb.com/name/nm0649460

KRAININ PRODUCTIONS, INC.

25211 Summerhill Ln

Stevenson Ranch, CA 91381

661-259-9700

imdb.com/company/co0016568

Does not accept any unsolicited material. Project types include Feature Films and TV.

Julian Krainin

Producer/Director

imdb.com/name/nm0469313

Joel Adams

Development

imdb.com/name/nm0011073

KRANE MEDIA, LLC.

7932 Woodrow Wilson Dr

Los Angeles, CA 90046

323-650-0942 (phone)

323-650-9132 (fax)

info@thekranecompany.com

imdb.com/company/co0323526

Does not accept any unsolicited material. Project types include Feature Films and TV. Preferred genres include Action, Comedy, Crime, Drama, Romance, Science Fiction, and Thriller. Established in 1993.

Konni Corriere

konni@thekranecompany.com

imdb.com/name/nm0180955

Jonathan Krane

imdb.com/name/nm0006790

KRASNOFF FOSTER ENTERTAINMENT

5555 Melrose Ave Marx Brothers Building, Suite 110

Los Angeles, CA 90038

323-956-4668

imdb.com/company/co0174525

Accepts query letter from unproduced, unrepresented writers. Project types include Feature Films and TV. Preferred genres include Action, Comedy, Drama, Non-Fiction, and Romance.

Russ Krasnoff

Partner

310-244-3282

imdb.com/name/nm0469929

Assistant: Beth Maurer

Gary Foster

Partner

imdb.com/name/nm0287811

Assistant: Haley Totten

KRASNOW PRODUCTIONS

3450 Cahuenga Blvd. West #202

Los Angeles, CA 90068

323-798-5560

imdb.com/company/co0112977

Does not accept any unsolicited material. Project types include TV.

Stuart Krasnow
Founder/President
imdb.com/name/nm0469950

KROFFT PICTURES

4024 Radford Ave
Building 5, Suite 102
Studio City, CA 91604
818-655-5314 (phone)
818-655-8235 (fax)

smkroft@aol.com
imdb.com/company/co0068404

Accepts query letter from unproduced, unrepresented writers via email. Project types include Feature Films and TV. Preferred genres include Animation, Comedy, and Family.

Marty Krofft
President
marty@krofft pictures.com
imdb.com/name/nm0471897

Sid Krofft
imdb.com/name/nm0471898

LACANADA DISTRIBUTION

9056 Santa Monica Blvd. Suite 203A
West Hollywood, CA 90069
310-278-9747

Does not accept any unsolicited material. Project types include TV. Preferred genres include Crime, Drama, and Thriller.

Dan Paulson
Producer
imdb.com/name/nm0667340

LADY IN THE TREE PRODUCTIONS

21700 Oxnard St, Suite 2030
Woodland Hills, CA 91367

imdb.com/company/co0338875

Does not accept any unsolicited material. Project types include Feature Films.

Jessalyn Gilsig
Actor/Producer
imdb.com/name/nm0319698

LAGO FILM GMBH

6399 Wilshire Blvd, Suite 1002
Los Angeles, CA 90048
310-653-7826

lago@lagofilm.com
lagofilm.com

Does not accept any unsolicited material. Project types include Feature Films. Preferred genres include Comedy, Drama, and Horror.

Marco Mehlitz
Producer
imdb.com/name/nm0576438

Luane Gauer
imdb.com/name/nm4293864
linkedin.com/pub/luane-gauer/30/775/950

LAGUNA RIDGE PICTURES

3452 E. Foothill Blvd., Suite 125
Pasadena, CA 91107

imdb.com/company/co0371912

Does not accept any unsolicited material. Project types include Feature Films. Preferred genres include Action and Drama.

Brandon Birtell
Producer
imdb.com/name/nm1771385

Matt Luber
Producer
imdb.com/name/nm1825319

LAHA FILMS

137 W 57th St, 7th Floor
New York, NY 10019
914-834-3311 (phone)
914-833-2717 (fax)

imdb.com/company/co0117940

Does not accept any unsolicited material. Project types include Feature Films. Preferred genres include Drama.

Leslie Holleran
Producer
imdb.com/name/nm039097

LAINIE PRODUCTIONS

18389 E Main St
Galliano, LA 70354

imdb.com/company/co0391080

Does not accept any unsolicited material. Project types include Feature Films. Preferred genres include Comedy.

Lainie Guidry
Producer
imdb.com/name/nm461371

Cynthia Guidry
Producer
imdb.com/name/nm4789595

LAKE PARADISE ENTERTAINMENT

13547 Ventura Blvd. Ste 186
Sherman Oaks, CA 91423

imdb.com/company/co0251365

Does not accept any unsolicited material. Project types include TV.

Viki Cacciatore
Principal
imdb.com/name/nm0127972

Holly M Wofford
Principal
imdb.com/name/nm1033680

LAKESHORE ENTERTAINMENT

9268 W Third St
Beverly Hills, CA 90210
310-867-8000 (phone)
310-300-3015 (fax)

info@lakeshoreentertainment.com
lakeshoreentertainment.com
imdb.com/company/co0005323
linkedin.com/company/lakeshore-entertainment

Accepts query letter from produced or represented writers. Project types include Feature Films. Preferred genres include Action, Comedy, Crime, Drama, Fantasy, Horror, Romance, Science Fiction, and Thriller. Established in 1994.

Tom Rosenberg
CEO
310-867-8000
imdb.com/name/nm0742347
Assistant: Tiffany Shinn

Robert McMinn
Sr. Vice-President
310-867-8000
imdb.com/name/nm0573372

Richard Wright
Executive Vice President of Production
imdb.com/name/nm0002999

LANDING PATCH PRODUCTIONS

8491 Sunset Blvd., Suite 700
West Hollywood, CA 90069
323-650-0150

landingpatchprods.com
facebook.com/OfficialPaulyShore
twitter.com/PaulyShore
imdb.com/company/co0178803

Does not accept any unsolicited material. Project types include Feature Films. Preferred genres include Comedy.

LANDSCAPE ENTERTAINMENT

9465 Wilshire Blvd Suite 500, Beverly Hills, CA 90212
310-248-6200 (phone)
310-248-6300 (fax)

imdb.com/company/co0070807
facebook.com/pages/Landscape-Entertainment/
    103457323053017

Accepts query letter from unproduced, unrepresented writers. Project types include Feature Films and TV. Preferred genres include Action, Animation, Comedy, Crime, Drama, Family, Non-Fiction, Science Fiction, and Thriller. Established in 2007.

Bob Cooper
Chairman
imdb.com/name/nm0178341
Assistant: Sandy Shenkman

Tyler Mitchell
Head of Development
imdb.com/name/nm1624685

LANGLEY PARK PRODUCTIONS

4000 Warner Blvd
Building 144
Burbank, CA 91522
818-954-2930

langleyparkpix.com
imdb.com/company/co0297907

Does not accept any unsolicited material. Project types include Feature Films. Preferred genres include Action, Comedy, Crime, Drama, Romance, and Thriller.

Kevin McCormick
Producer
818-954-2930
imdb.com/name/nm0566557
Assistant: Shamika Pryce

Aaron Schmidt
Creative Executive
818-954-2930
aaron.schmidt@langleyparkpix.com
imdb.com/name/nm2087164

Rory Koslow
818-954-2930
imdb.com/name/nm1739372
Assistant: Kari Cooper

LARCO PRODUCTIONS

2111 Coldwater Canyon Dr
Beverly Hills, CA 90210
323-350-5455

imdb.com/company/co0077868

Does not accept any unsolicited material. Project types include Feature Films. Preferred genres include Drama and Thriller.

Larry Cohen
Producer/Director/Writer

LARRIKIN ENTERTAINMENT

1801 Ave Of The Stars, Suite 921
Los Angeles, CA 90067
310-461-3030

imdb.com/company/co0369620

Accepts scripts from produced or represented writers. Project types include Feature Films.

Greg Coote
imdb.com/name/nm0178505
Assistant: Wayne Lin

David Jones
Producer
imdb.com/name/nm1965869

Robert Lundberg
Producer
imdb.com/name/nm2302909

LARRY LEVINSON PRODUCTIONS

500 S. Sepulveda Blvd., Suite 610
Los Angeles, CA 90049
310-440-7834

imdb.com/company/co0045255

Does not accept any unsolicited material. Project types include Feature Films and TV. Preferred genres include Drama.

Larry Levinson
President/Producer
imdb.com/name/nm0506062

LARRY THOMPSON ORGANIZATION

9663 Santa Monica Blvd, Suite 801
Beverly Hills, CA 90210
United States
310-288-0700 (phone)
310-288-0711 (fax)

ltbeverlyhills@aol.com
larrythompsonorg.com

Does not accept any unsolicited material. Project types include Feature Films. Preferred genres include Drama and Thriller.

Kelly Thompson
Development

Robert Endara
Development

Larry Thompson
CEO/Chairman/Producer

LAST STRAW PRODUCTIONS

4000 Warner Blvd., Bldg. 133, Suite 209
Burbank, CA 91522
818-954-1064

imdb.com/company/co0055726

Does not accept any unsolicited material. Project types include Feature Films and TV. Preferred genres include Drama.

Anthony LaPaglia
President/Actor/Producer
imdb.com/name/nm0001439

LATHAM ENTERTAINMENT

3200 Northline Ave
Greensboro, NC
United States
336-315-1440

lathamentertainment.com
imdb.com/title/tt0368833

Does not accept any unsolicited material. Project types include Feature Films and TV.

Walter Latham
Producer/President
imdb.com/name/nm0490124

LATIN WORLD ENTERTAINMENT

9777 Wilshire Blvd. Suite 811
Beverly Hills, CA 90210

310-275-5757 (phone)
310-275-5759 (fax)

3470 NW 82nd Ave, Suite 670
Doral, FL 33122
305-572-1515 (phone)
305-572-1510 (fax)

latinwe.com
imdb.com/company/co0106344

Does not accept any unsolicited material. Project types include TV. Preferred genres include Drama.

Sofia Vergara
Partner/Actor/Producer
imdb.com/name/nm0005527

Luis Balaguer
Partner/Producer/Manager
imdb.com/name/nm2230500

LATITUDE PRODUCTIONS

833 20th St, Suite 201
Santa Monica, CA 90403
310-488-8448

curtis.burch@latitudeproductions.com
latitudeproductions.com
imdb.com/company/co0191689

Does not accept any unsolicited material. Project types include Feature Films. Preferred genres include Comedy.

LATIUM ENTERTAINMENT

1616 Vista Del Mar
Hollywood, CA 90028
323-836-7330

latiument.com
facebook.com/LatiumEntertainment
twitter.com/latiumartists

Does not accept any unsolicited material. Project types include TV.

Charles Chavez
Producer/Manager
imdb.com/name/nm7042525

LAUNCHPAD PRODUCTIONS

4335 Van Nuys Blvd Suite 339
Sherman Oaks, CA 91403
818-788-4896

imdb.com/company/co0164701

Accepts query letter from unproduced, unrepresented writers via email. Project types include Feature Films. Preferred genres include Comedy, Crime, Drama, Horror, Period, Science Fiction, and Thriller. Established in 2005.

David Higgins
Partner
imdb.com/name/nm0383370

Angelique Higgins
President
ahiggins@launchpadprods.com
imdb.com/name/nm1583157

LAURA ZISKIN PRODUCTIONS

10202 W Washington Blvd
Astaire Building, Suite 1310
Culver City, CA 90232
310-244-7373 (phone)
310-244-0073 (fax)

imdb.com/company/co0095403

Accepts query letter from unproduced, unrepresented writers. Project types include Feature Films and TV. Preferred genres include Action, Drama, Fantasy, Romance, Science Fiction, and Thriller. Established in 1995.

Pamela Williams
President
imdb.com/name/nm0931423
linkedin.com/pub/pam-williams/39/650/246

David Jacobson
Director of Development
imdb.com/name/nm5138376

LAURENCE MARK PRODUCTIONS

10202 W Washington Blvd
Poitier Building
Culver City, CA 90232

310-244-5239 (phone)
310-244-0055 (fax)

imdb.com/company/co0027956

Accepts query letter from unproduced, unrepresented writers. Project types include Feature Films and TV. Preferred genres include Action, Comedy, Drama, Family, Fantasy, Horror, Romance, Science Fiction, and Thriller.

Tamara Chestna
Director of Development
310-244-5239
imdb.com/name/nm2309894

Laurence Mark
Principle
310-244-5239
imdb.com/name/nm0548257

David Blackman
310-244-5239
imdb.com/name/nm1844320
linkedin.com/pub/david-blackman/64/92a/b50
Assistant: Peter Richman

LAVA BEAR FILMS

3201-B South La Cienega Blvd
Los Angeles, CA 90016
310-815-9600

imdb.com/company/co0296971
lavabear.com
twitter.com/lavabearfilms
facebook.com/pages/Lava-Bear-Films/
    186604781434034

Does not accept any unsolicited material. Project types include Feature Films. Preferred genres include Action, Comedy, Crime, Drama, Family, Fantasy, Romance, Science Fiction, and Thriller. Established in 2011.

Tory Metzger
President
tmetzger@lavabear.com
imdb.com/name/nm0582762
Assistant: Jon Frye

David Linde
Principle
310-815-9603
dlinde@lavabear.com
imdb.com/name/nm0511482
Assistant: Allison Warren

LAWLESS ENTERTAINMENT

11279 Dona Lisa Dr
Studio City, CA 91604
323-201-2678 (phone)
323-654-2516 (fax)

info@lawlessent.com
lawlessent.com

Does not accept any unsolicited material. Project types include Feature Films. Preferred genres include Family and Fantasy.

Bryan Taw
VP

Catherine Malatesta
President/Producer
imdb.com/name/nm5116055

LAWRENCE BENDER PRODUCTIONS

8530 Wilshire Blvd Ste 520
Beverly Hills, CA 90211
323-951-1180

imdb.com/company/co0093776
facebook.com/pages/Lawrence-Bender-Productions/
    154135381289513

Accepts query letter from unproduced, unrepresented writers. Project types include Feature Films. Preferred genres include Action, Comedy, Crime, Drama, and Thriller.

Lawrence Bender
Partner
imdb.com/name/nm0004744
Assistant: Vincent Gatewood

Janet Jeffries
imdb.com/name/nm0420377
linkedin.com/pub/janet-jeffries/6/b02/760

Kevin Brown
imdb.com/name/nm0114019

LAWRENCE GORDON PRODUCTIONS

12011 San Vicente Blvd., Suite 350
Los Angeles, CA 90049
310-472-4786

imdb.com/company/co0041635

Does not accept any unsolicited material. Preferred genres include Action, Comedy, Drama, and Horror.

Lawrence Gordon
Producer
imdb.com/name/nm0330383

Phillip Westgren
Director of Development
imdb.com/name/nm4043152

LD ENTERTAINMENT

9000 Sunset Blvd
Suite 600
West Hollywood, CA 90069
310-275-9600

14301 Caliber Dr, Suite 300
Oklahoma City, OK 73134
405-463-7100

info@ldentertainment.com
linkedin.com/company/ld-entertainment
imdb.com/company/co0192696
ldentertainment.com
facebook.com/pages/LD-Entertainment/
    268087043237145
twitter.com/tweetLD

Does not accept any unsolicited material. Project types include Feature Films. Preferred genres include Action, Comedy, Crime, Drama, Horror, and Thriller. Established in 2007.

Mickey Liddell
CEO
imdb.com/name/nm0509176

LEE DANIELS ENTERTAINMENT

315 W 36th St
New York City, NY 10018
212-334-8110 (phone)
212-334-8290 (fax)

info@leedanielsentertainment.com
leedanielsentertainment.com
facebook.com/lee.daniels.71868
twitter.com/leedanielsent
imdb.com/company/co0048235

Accepts query letter from unproduced, unrepresented writers via email. Project types include Feature Films and TV. Preferred genres include Comedy, Crime, Drama, Period, Romance, and Thriller. Established in 2001.

Lee Daniels
imdb.com/name/nm0200005
Assistant: Tito Crafts

Lisa Cortes
imdb.com/name/nm0181263

LEFT HOOK ENTERTAINMENT

2008 S Bentley Ave. #202
Los Angeles, CA 90025

imdb.com/company/co0227075

Does not accept any unsolicited material. Project types include Feature Films. Preferred genres include Horror and Thriller.

Justin Hogan
Producer
imdb.com/name/nm0389556

LEGACY ENTERTAINMENT PARTNERS

8424 Santa Monica Blvd., A140
West Hollywood, CA 90069
310-903-0356

gena@2elevenfilms.com
legacyentp.com
imdb.com/company/co0355526

Accepts query letter from unproduced, unrepresented writers via email. Project types include Feature Films

and TV. Preferred genres include Action, Crime, and Horror.

Gena Vazquez
Executive
imdb.com/name/nm3220594

Lonnie Ramati
Executive of Business Affairs
imdb.com/name/nm1252942

LEGENDARY PICTURES

The Pointe 2900 W. Alameda Ave
Burbank, CA 91505
818-954-3888 (phone)
818-954-3884 (fax)

imdb.com/company/co0159111
facebook.com/legendary
twitter.com/Legendary
legendary.com/home
linkedin.com/company/legendary-entertainment

Does not accept any unsolicited material. Project types include Feature Films and TV. Preferred genres include Action, Comedy, Crime, Drama, Family, Fantasy, Non-Fiction, Romance, Science Fiction, and Thriller. Established in 2004.

Alex Hedlund
Creative Executive
818-954-3888
imdb.com/name/nm2906163

Thomas Tull
818-954-3888
imdb.com/name/nm2100078

Jennifer Preston Bosari
Creative Executive
jpreston@legendary.com

Alex Garcia
Senior Vice President
imdb.com/name/nm1247503
linkedin.com/pub/alex-garcia/40/166/19a

Jillan Share
Vice President, Creative Affairs
jillian.zaks@legendarypictures.com
imdb.com/name/nm2949271
linkedin.com/pub/jillian-share/a/69/624

LE GRISBI PRODUCTIONS

8733 W Sunset Blvd., Suite 101
West Hollywood, CA 90069
310-652-6120

Does not accept any unsolicited material. Project types include Feature Films and TV. Preferred genres include Comedy and Drama.

John Lesher
Producer
imdb.com/name/nm0971956

Sean Murphy
Director of Development
imdb.com/name/nm0614699

LEOMAX ENTERTAINMENT

8439 Sunset Blvd., Suite 300
Los Angeles, CA 90069
323-785-3000 (phone)
323-785-3010 (fax)

info@leomaxe.com
imdb.com/company/co0200371
leomaxentertainment.com

Does not accept any unsolicited material. Project types include Feature Films. Preferred genres include Horror.

Ingo Vollkammer
Producer
imdb.com/name/nm1703840

LESLIE IWERKS PRODUCTIONS

1322 2nd St Suite 35
Santa Monica, 90401 CA
310-458-0490 (phone)
310-458-7212 (fax)

info@leslieiwerks.com
leslieiwerks.com/new
imdb.com/company/co0188417
twitter.com/leslieiwerks
facebook.com/pages/Leslie-Iwerks-Productions/
    121694324555254
linkedin.com/company/leslie-iwerks-productions-inc-

Does not accept any unsolicited material. Project types include Feature Films, Short Films, and TV. Preferred genres include Documentary. Established in 2006.

Jane Kelly Kosek
Producer
imdb.com/name/nm1165704

Michael Tang
imdb.com/name/nm4046664
linkedin.com/pub/michael-e-tang/21/140/11a

Leslie Iwerks
President
leslie@leslieiwerks.com
imdb.com/name/nm0412649
linkedin.com/pub/leslie-iwerks/9/94b/882
facebook.com/leslie.iwerks
twitter.com/leslieiwerk

LEVEL 10 FILMS

6399 Wilshire Blvd. Suite 1018
Los Angeles, CA 90048
310-424-5063

level10films.com
imdb.com/company/co0278157

Does not accept any unsolicited material. Project types include Feature Films and TV. Preferred genres include Comedy, Horror, and Thriller.

Michael Wormser
Producer
imdb.com/name/nm2347031

Micah Goldman
Producer
imdb.com/name/nm2542772

LIAISON FILMS

44 Rue Des Acacias
Paris 75017
France
+33-1-55-37-28-28 (phone)
+33-1-55-37-98-44 (fax)

contact@liasonfilms.com
imdb.com/company/co0120310

Does not accept any unsolicited material. Project types include Feature Films. Preferred genres include Action, Crime, Drama, and Thriller.

Stephane Sperry
President
stephane.sperry@liasonfilms.com
imdb.com/name/nm0818373

LIBERTY STUDIOS INC.

9948 Hibert St, Suite 200
San Diego, CA 92131
858-271-0695 (phone)
858-271-0330 (fax)

info@libertystudiosinc.com
libertystudiosinc.com
imdb.com/company/co0043672
facebook.com/pages/Liberty-Studios/
    394349677244686
twitter.com/LibertyStudios_

Does not accept any unsolicited material. Project types include Feature Films. Preferred genres include Drama and Period. Established in 2014.

Mark Schmidt
Founder
imdb.com/name/nm2005149

Randy Williams
Founder
imdb.com/name/nm3623229

LICHT ENTERTAINMENT

132 S Lasky Dr, Suite 200
Beverly Hills, CA 90212
310-205-5500

imdb.com/company/co0183802

Does not accept any unsolicited material. Project types include Feature Films and TV.

Andy Licht
Producer
imdb.com/name/nm0508988

Aaron Wilder
Producer
imdb.com/name/nm1198288

LIGHTHOUSE ENTERTAINMENT

409 N Camden Dr, Suite 202
Beverly Hills, CA 90210
310-246-0499 (phone)
310-246-0899 (fax)

imdb.com/company/co0018183

Does not accept any unsolicited material. Project types include Feature Films and TV. Preferred genres include Drama and Thriller.

Steven Siebert
Manager, Producer
imdb.com/name/nm0796796

LIGHTNING ENTERTAINMENT

301 Arizona Ave, 4th Floor
Santa Monica, CA 90401
310-255-7999 (phone)
310-255-7998 (fax)

lightning-ent.com
imdb.com/company/co0003258

Does not accept any unsolicited material. Project types include Feature Films. Preferred genres include Drama.

Richard Guardian
Co-President
imdb.com/name/nm1862651

Joseph Dickstein
SVP of Acquisitions
imdb.com/name/nm0225737

LIGHTSTORM ENTERTAINMENT

919 Santa Monica Blvd
Santa Monica, CA 90401
310-656-6100 (phone)
310-656-6102 (fax)

imdb.com/company/co0038663
linkedin.com/company/lightstorm-entertainment

Does not accept any unsolicited material. Project types include Feature Films. Preferred genres include Action, Crime, Drama, Family, Fantasy, Horror, Romance, Science Fiction, and Thriller.

Jon Landau
COO
imdb.com/name/nm0484457
linkedin.com/pub/jon-landau/8/35b/509

Geoff Burdick
imdb.com/name/nm0120971
linkedin.com/pub/geoff-burdick/8/592/a2a

Rae Sanchini
Partner
imdb.com/name/nm0761093

James Cameron
CEO
imdb.com/name/nm0000116

LIKELY STORY

150 W 22nd St, 9th Floor
New York, NY 10011
917-484-8931

345 N. Maple Dr.
Suite 202
Beverly Hills, CA 90210

info@likely-story.com
imdb.com/company/co0190175

Does not accept any unsolicited material. Project types include Feature Films.

Anthony Bregman
917-484-8931
info@likely-story.com
imdb.com/name/nm0106835

Stefanie Azpiazu
Vice President (Development & Production)
917-484-8931
info@likely-story.com
imdb.com/name/nm1282412

LINCOLN SQUARE PRODUCTIONS

77 W 66th St
New York, NY 10023
212-456-2020

imdb.com/company/co0253555

Does not accept any unsolicited material. Project types include TV. Preferred genres include Drama.

Phyllis McGrady
SVP, Creative Development
imdb.com/name/nm0569735

Ben Sherwood
President, ABC News
imdb.com/name/nm1639636

LIN OLIVER PRODUCTIONS

8271 Beverly Blvd.
Los Angeles , CA 90068
323-782-1495

info@linoliverproductions.com
linoliverproductions.com

Does not accept any unsolicited material. Project types include TV. Preferred genres include Animation.

Lin Oliver
Producer

Kim Turrsi
Development

LIN PICTURES

4000 Warner Blvd. Bldg 143
Burbank, CA 91522
818-954-6759 (phone)
818-954-2329 (fax)

linpictures.com
imdb.com/company/co0226345
facebook.com/LinPictures

Does not accept any unsolicited material. Project types include Feature Films and TV. Preferred genres include Action, Comedy, Crime, Drama, Family, Fantasy, Romance, Science Fiction, and Thriller.

Mark Bauch
Creative Executive
imdb.com/name/nm3113076

Dan Lin
CEO
imdb.com/name/nm1469853
linkedin.com/pub/dan-lin/11/338/893
Assistant: Ryan Halprin

Jennifer Gwartz
imdb.com/name/nm0350311
Assistant: Jeremy Katz

Seanne Winslow Wehrenfennig
Head of Development
imdb.com/name/nm2253990
linkedin.com/pub/seanne-winslow-wehrenfennig/11/
    aba/4a2

LIONSGATE

2700 Colorado Ave
Santa Monica, CA 90404
310-449-9200 (phone)
310-255-3870 (fax)

general-inquiries@lgf.com
lionsgate.com
imdb.com/company/co0173285
linkedin.com/company/lionsgate
twitter.com/Lionsgate
facebook.com/lionsgate

Does not accept any unsolicited material. Project types
include Feature Films and TV. Preferred genres
include Action, Comedy, Crime, Drama, Family,
Fantasy, Horror, Non-Fiction, Romance, Science
Fiction, and Thriller. Established in 1997.

Jon Feltheimer
CEO
jfeltheimer@lionsgate.com
imdb.com/name/nm1410838

Matthew Janzen
Vice President of Production & Development
imdb.com/name/nm0418432
linkedin.com/pub/matthew-janzen/49/950/b0a

Michael Burns
Vice Chairman

Steve Beeks
COO

Brian Goldsmith
COO

Wayne Levin
Legal Counsel

James Barge
CFO

Jina Jones
Creative Executive
imdb.com/name/nm1061205
linkedin.com/pub/jina-jones/7/311/97b

LIONS GATE FAMILY ENTERTAINMENT

2700 Colorado Blvd.
Santa Monica, CA 90404
310-449-9200

general-inquiries@lgf.com
lionsgatefilms.com
imdb.com/company/co0150906

Does not accept any unsolicited material. Project types
include Feature Films. Preferred genres include Family.

Ken Katsumoto
Executive VP
imdb.com/name/nm0441546

LIQUID THEORY

4425 W. Riverside Dr
Burbank, CA 91505
818-859-7903

liquid-theory.com
imdb.com/company/co0113186
facebook.com/pages/Liquid-Theory-Inc/
    173907856002737
twitter.com/TheLiquidTheory
linkedin.com/company/liquid-theory

Accepts query letter from produced or represented
writers. Project types include Feature Films and TV.
Preferred genres include Animation, Comedy,
Documentary, Drama, Horror, Reality, Romance,
Science Fiction, and Thriller. Established in 2001.

Austin Reading
President
imdb.com/name/nm1474879
linkedin.com/pub/austin-reading/4/328/782
twitter.com/TheLiquidTheory

Matt Lambert
matt@liquid-theory.com
imdb.com/name/nm1479457

Julie Reading
President
imdb.com/name/nm1474880
linkedin.com/pub/julie-reading/4/329/3b

Mike Goldberg
mgoldberg@apa-agency.com

Marc Kamler
mkamler@apa-agency.com

Julius Saito
jsaito@liquid-theory.com

LITTLE AIRPLANE PRODUCTIONS

207 Front St
New York, NY 10038
212-965-8999 (phone)
212-965-0834 (fax)

hello@littleairplane.com
littleairplane.com
imdb.com/company/co0174821

Does not accept any unsolicited material. Project types include Feature Films. Preferred genres include Family.

Josh Selig
Founder
imdb.com/name/nm1012154

Tom Brown
Head of Production
imdb.com/name/nm0114805

LITTLE ENGINE PRODUCTIONS

500 S Buena Vista St
Animation Building 3F-6
Burbank, CA 91521
323-459-6199 (phone)
818-560-4014 (fax)

stacy@littleenginefilms.com
littleenginefilms.com
imdb.com/company/co0014340

Accepts query letter from unproduced, unrepresented writers. Project types include Feature Films and TV. Preferred genres include Comedy, Crime, Drama, Non-Fiction, Reality, and Romance.

Gina Matthews
Partner
imdb.com/name/nm0560033

Grant Scharbo
Partner
imdb.com/name/nm0770090
linkedin.com/pub/grant-scharbo/12/734/43b

Stacy Jorgensen
stacy@littleenginefilms.com

LITTLE MAGIC FILMS

130 N Sycamore Ave
Los Angeles, CA 90036
323-424-4822

kiki@littlemagicfilms.com
littlemagicfilms.com
imdb.com/company/co0042025

Does not accept any unsolicited material. Project types include Feature Films and TV. Preferred genres include Drama, Horror, Romance, and Thriller.

Kiki Miyake
Founder/President/Producer
imdb.com/name/nm0594380

LIVING DEAD GUY PRODUCTIONS

100 Universal City Plaza, Hitchcock Bungalow 5195
Universal City, CA 91608
818-777-1000

hello@livingdeadguy.com
livingdeadguy.com
imdb.com/company/co0138108

Does not accept any unsolicited material. Project types include TV. Preferred genres include Drama, Fantasy, Science Fiction, and Thriller.

Bryan Fuller
Writer/Producer
imdb.com/name/nm0298188

LIZARD TRADING COMPANY

9696 Culver Blvd. West, Suite 203
Culver City, CA 90232
310-558-8110

lizardtradingcompany.com
imdb.com/company/co0313428

Does not accept any unsolicited material. Project types include TV.

Matt Cabral
SVP of Production
imdb.com/name/nm0127746

Elyse Seder
VP of Development
imdb.com/name/nm2100138

LJS COMMUNICATIONS

1841 Broadway, Suite 812
New York, NY 10023
646-374-3940

lschiller@ljscommunications.com
lawrenceschiller.com

Does not accept any unsolicited material. Project types include Feature Films. Preferred genres include Drama.

LLEJU PRODUCTIONS

3050 Post Oak Blvd.,
Suite 460
Houston, Texas 77056
866-579-6444 (phone)
713-583-2214 (fax)

info@lleju.com
lleju.com/index.html
facebook.com/pages/Houston-TX/Lleju-Productions-
   and-Films/111483634134
twitter.com/LLeju
imdb.com/company/co0250136

Accepts query letter from unproduced, unrepresented writers. Project types include Feature Films. Preferred genres include Action, Comedy, Crime, Drama, Horror, and Thriller. Established in 2008.

Bill Perkins
Executive
imdb.com/name/nm2645116

Keith Perkins
imdb.com/name/nm1344801

Cooper Richey
imdb.com/name/nm3295785

LLOYD ENTERTAINMENT

610 S Main St, #513
Los Angeles, CA 90014
213-489-1485

Does not accept any unsolicited material. Project types include Feature Films and TV. Preferred genres include Drama.

Lauren Lloyd
Producer/Manager
imdb.com/name/nm0516056

LOGO

1540 Broadway, 31st Floor
New York, NY 10036
212-654-3005

logoonline.com

Does not accept any unsolicited material. Project types include Feature Films and TV. Preferred genres include Drama.

Brian Graden
President
imdb.com/name/nm0333536

Dave Mace
VP of Original Programming
imdb.com/name/nm0532069

LONDINE PRODUCTIONS

1626 N. Wilcox Ave.
Ste. 480
Hollywood, CA 90028
310-822-9025 (fax)

imdb.com/company/co0183894

Accepts query letter from unproduced, unrepresented writers via email. Project types include Feature Films and TV. Preferred genres include Comedy, Drama, and Thriller. Established in 1983.

Cassius Weathersby
President
cassiusii@aol.com
imdb.com/name/nm0915780

Joshua Weathersby
imdb.com/name/nm1500833

Nadine Weathersby
imdb.com/name/nm2325321

LONDINIUM FILMS

9025 Wilshire Blvd, Suite 400
Beverly Hills, CA 90211
310-883-5101

Ealing Studios
Ealing Green
London W5 5EP UK
44 (0) 20 8584 5282

thelondinium.com
imdb.com/company/co0398495

Does not accept any unsolicited material. Project types include Feature Films. Preferred genres include Comedy.

Ben Latham-Jones
Producer
imdb.com/name/nm4695347

LONE STAR FILM GROUP

335 N. Maple Dr, Suite 127
Beverly Hills, CA 90210
310-285-0700

imdb.com/company/co0041075

Does not accept any unsolicited material. Project types include Feature Films. Preferred genres include Comedy.

Fred Westheimer
CEO
imdb.com/name/nm2120938

Erica Westheimer
Production Executive
imdb.com/name/nm0922757

LONE WOLF MEDIA

10 Cottage Rd
South Portland, ME 04106
207-799-9500

info@lonewolfdg.com
lonewolfmedia.com
facebook.com/lonewolfdg
twitter.com/LoneWolf_Media

Does not accept any unsolicited material. Project types include TV. Preferred genres include Non-Fiction.

Kirk Wolfinger
President
imdb.com/name/nm0938367

Lisa Quijano Wolfinger
Producer/Director/Writer
imdb.com/name/nm0938368

LOOK AT THE MOON PRODUCTIONS

12917 Stallion Court
Potomac, MD 0854
240-672-1414

lookatthemoonproductions.com
imdb.com/company/co0243594

Does not accept any unsolicited material. Project types include Feature Films. Preferred genres include Comedy and Romance.

Sig Libowitz
Producer
imdb.com/name/nm0508904

LOOKOUT ENTERTAINMENT

54 Hermosa Ave
Hermosa Beach, CA 90254
310-798-3000

yvonne@lookoutentertainment.com
lookoutentertainment.com
imdb.com/company/co0045796

Does not accept any unsolicited material. Project types include Feature Films. Preferred genres include Crime and Drama.

Yvonne Bernard
Producer
imdb.com/name/nm1017627

LOST MARBLES PRODUCTIONS

10866 Wilshire Blvd., Floor 10
Los Angeles, CA 90024

imdb.com/company/co0278999

Does not accept any unsolicited material. Project types
include TV. Preferred genres include Comedy.

Marty Adelstein
Producer
imdb.com/name/nm137435

LOTUS PICTURES

10760 Missouri Ave. #304
Los Angeles, CA 90025
310-435-5770

lotuspics@aol.com
imdb.com/company/co0351849

Does not accept any unsolicited material. Project types
include Feature Films and TV.

Michele Berk
Producer
imdb.com/name/nm0075277

Joseph Salemi
VP
imdb.com/name/nm3687589

LOUVERTURE FILMS

101 W. 23rd St, #283
New York, NY 10011

info@louverturefilms.com
louverturefilms.com
imdb.com/company/co0176028

Does not accept any unsolicited material. Project types
include Feature Films. Preferred genres include
Drama.

Danny Glover
Partner/Actor/Producer
imdb.com/name/nm0000418

Joslyn Barnes
Partner/Writer/Producer
imdb.com/name/nm0055656

LUCASFILM LTD.

PO Box 29919
San Francisco, CA 94129
415-662-1800

facebook.com/lucasfilm
lucasfilm.com
imdb.com/company/co0071326
linkedin.com/company/lucasfilm

Does not accept any unsolicited material. Project types
include Feature Films. Preferred genres include Action,
Fantasy, and Science Fiction. Established in 1971.

George Lucas
imdb.com/name/nm0000184

Kathleen Kennedy
President
imdb.com/name/nm0005086

Howard Roffman
Executive Vice-President

Kiri Hart
Vice President, Development

Jason McGatlin
Executive Vice-President

LUCKY 50 PRODUCTIONS

801 W Bay Dr Ste 800
Largo, FL 33770

imdb.com/company/co0191774

Does not accept any unsolicited material. Project types
include Feature Films.

Philippe Martinez
Chairman/CEO
imdb.com/name/nm0553662

Martin Barab
President
imdb.com/name/nm0052774

LUCKY CROW FILMS

4335 Van Nuys Blvd.
Suite 355
Sherman Oaks, CA 91403
818-783-7529 (phone)
818-783-7594 (fax)

info@indieproducer.net
imdb.com/company/co0102838

Accepts query letter from unproduced, unrepresented writers via email. Project types include Feature Films and TV. Preferred genres include Documentary and Drama. Established in 2004.

Jon Gunn
President
imdb.com/name/nm0348197

Kerry David
President
kerrydavid.com
imdb.com/name/nm0202968
linkedin.com/in/kerrydavid

LUCKY DAY STUDIOS

129 Hawthorne Dr
Nicholasville, KY 40356
310-737-8576

info@luckydaystudios.com
luckydaystudios.com
imdb.com/company/co0273765

Does not accept any unsolicited material. Project types include Feature Films. Preferred genres include Horror and Thriller.

Tom Lockridge
Co-Founder/President
imdb.com/name/nm3330959

Jeff Day
Co-Founder/CEO
imdb.com/name/nm3026263

LUCKY HAT ENTERTAINMENT

1438 N. Gower St.
Hollywood, CA 90028

323-993-7001 (phone)
323-993-7002 (fax)

info@lucky-hat.com
lucky-hat.com
imdb.com/company/co0238733

Does not accept any unsolicited material. Project types include Feature Films.

LUCKY MONKEY PICTURES

125 E. 95th St
New York, NY 10128
212-860-1642 (phone)
212-860-1152 (fax)

lmpassist@luckymonkeypictures.com
luckymonkeypictures.com
twitter.com/luckymonkeypics
imdb.com/company/co0101005
facebook.com/pages/Lucky-Monkey-Pictures/
    136269279775936

Does not accept any unsolicited material. Project types include Feature Films. Preferred genres include Thriller.

LUMANITY PRODUCTIONS

8391 Beverly Blvd. Suite 461
Los Angeles, CA 90048
323-448-6949 (phone)
416-823-6650 (fax)

info@lumanity.com
lumanity.com
imdb.com/company/co0117925

Does not accept any unsolicited material. Project types include Feature Films. Preferred genres include Comedy, Drama, and Thriller.

Robert Budreau
President/Producer/Director/Writer
imdb.com/name/nm1519253

Charles Roberts
Development
imdb.com/name/nm0730905

LUMEN ACTUS

4119 Burbank Blvd.
Burbank, CA 91505

lumenactus.com
imdb.com/name/nm4300383

Does not accept any unsolicited material. Project types include Feature Films. Preferred genres include Horror, Science Fiction, and Thriller.

Thomas Konkle
Partner/Writer/Director
imdb.com/name/nm1015100

David Beeler
Partner/Writer/Producer
imdb.com/name/nm0066417

LUMENAS STUDIOS

625 S. 600 West
Salt Lake City, UT 84101
801-355-1510 (phone)
801-665-1240 (fax)

info@lumenas.com
lumenas.com
imdb.com/company/co0241441

Does not accept any unsolicited material. Preferred genres include Family.

Darin McDaniel
Producer/Director/Writer
imdb.com/name/nm0567388

LYNDA OBST PRODUCTIONS

10202 W Washington Blvd
Astaire Building, Suite 1000
Culver City, CA 90232
310-244-6122 (phone)
310-244-0092 (fax)

imdb.com/company/co0071668
lyndaobstproductions.com
facebook.com/pages/Lynda-Obst-Productions/
770496236344357

Does not accept any unsolicited material. Project types include Feature Films and TV. Preferred genres include Action, Comedy, Crime, Drama, Family, Fantasy, Romance, and Thriller.

Lynda Obst
Producer
lyndaobst.com
imdb.com/name/nm0643553
twitter.com/LyndaObst

Rachel Abarbanell
President
imdb.com/name/nm1561964

M8 ENTERTAINMENT, INC.

15260 Ventura Blvd, Suite 710
Sherman Oaks, CA 91403
818-325-8000 (phone)
818-325-8020 (fax)

info@media8ent.com

Does not accept any unsolicited material. Project types include Feature Films and TV. Preferred genres include Action, Comedy, Drama, and Romance. Established in 1993.

Stewart Hall
President
818-826-8000
info@media8ent.com
imdb.com/name/nm1279593

MACARI/EDELSTEIN

439 N Canon, Suite 220
Los Angeles, CA 90036
310-550-9909

imdb.com/company/co0094798

Does not accept any unsolicited material. Project types include Feature Films.

Mike Macari
Producer/Partner
imdb.com/name/nm1079551

Neal Edelstein
Producer/Partner
imdb.com/name/nm0249050

MACMILLAN ENTERTAINMENT

175 Fifth Ave
New York, NY 10010
646-307-5151

us.macmillan.com

Does not accept any unsolicited material. Project types include Feature Films and TV. Preferred genres include Action, Crime, Drama, Science Fiction, and Thriller.

John Sargent
CEO of Macmillan Publishers
imdb.com/name/nm0765120

Brendan Deneen
Producer
imdb.com/name/nm1559263

MADBROOK FILMS

15 E 62nd St
New York, NY 10065
212-981-2626

info@madbrookfilms.com
madbrookfilms.com
facebook.com/madbrookfilms
twitter.com/MadbrookFilms

Does not accept any unsolicited material. Project types include Feature Films. Preferred genres include Drama, Science Fiction, and Thriller.

Madeleine Sackler
Producer/Director
imdb.com/name/nm2153450

Boyd Holbrook
Actor/Director
imdb.com/name/nm2933542

MAD CHANCE PRODUCTIONS

4000 Warner Blvd
Building 81, Room 208
Burbank, CA 91522
818-954-3500 (phone)
818-954-3586 (fax)

imdb.com/company/co0034487
facebook.com/pages/Mad-Chance-Productions

Does not accept any unsolicited material. Project types include Feature Films. Preferred genres include Action, Comedy, Drama, Family, Fantasy, Romance, Science Fiction, and Thriller.

Andrew Lazar
Producer
imdb.com/name/nm0493662
Assistant: Wynn Wygal

MAD COW PRODUCTIONS

17530 Ventura Blvd, Suite 201
Encino, CA 91316

imdb.com/company/co0093766

Does not accept any unsolicited material. Project types include TV. Preferred genres include Comedy.

Madeleine Smithberg
President/Producer
imdb.com/name/nm0810431

MAD HATTER ENTERTAINMENT

9229 Sunset Blvd, Suite 225
West Hollywood, CA 90069
310-860-0441

imdb.com/company/co0266260
facebook.com/pages/Mad-Hatter-Entertainment/
　223926789347

Accepts scripts from unproduced, unrepresented writers. Project types include Feature Films and TV. Preferred genres include Action, Animation, Comedy, Crime, Drama, Family, Fantasy, Horror, Myth, Science Fiction, and Thriller.

Michael Connolly
mike@madhatterentertainment.com
imdb.com/name/nm0175326
Assistant: Kyle Smeehuyzen (Development Assistant)

MAD HORSE FILMS

16000 Ventura Blvd, Suite 900
Encino, CA 91436
310-571-8048

queries@madhorsefilms.com
madhorsefilms.com

facebook.com/mad.horse.films
imdb.com/company/co0382776

Accepts query letter from unproduced, unrepresented writers via email. Project types include Feature Films. Preferred genres include Action, Horror, Science Fiction, and Thriller.

Alexandru Celea
Vice President of Production
imdb.com/name/nm5088556
linkedin.com/pub/dir/%20/Celea

John Swetnam
Principal
imdb.com/name/nm4291727

MADHOUSE ENTERTAINMENT

10390 Santa Monica Blvd
Suite 110
Los Angeles, CA 90025
310-587-2200 (phone)
323-782-0491 (fax)

query@madhouseent.net
madhouseent.net
imdb.com/company/co0202761
twitter.com/madhouse_ent

Does not accept any unsolicited material. Project types include Feature Films and TV. Preferred genres include Action, Comedy, Crime, Drama, Romance, Science Fiction, and Thriller. Established in 2010.

Robyn Meisinger
President
imdb.com/name/nm1159733
linkedin.com/pub/robyn-meisinger/13/523/403

Adam Kolbrenner
imdb.com/name/nm2221807

Ryan Cunningham
Manager
imdb.com/name/nm1400515
linkedin.com/pub/ryan-cunningham/23/459/649

Chris Cook
Manager
imdb.com/name/nm2303601
linkedin.com/pub/chris-cook/10/82A/7B7

MADJACK ENTERTAINMENT

13400 Riverside Dr, Suite 108
Sherman Oaks, CA 91423
818-728-7660 (phone)
818-461-8818 (fax)

madjackentertainment.com

Does not accept any unsolicited material. Project types include TV.

Sam Mettler
Executive Producer
imdb.com/name/nm1457529

MADRIK MULTIMEDIA

4439 Sunnycrest Dr
Los Angeles, CA 90065
323-255-0216

info@madrik.com
madrik.com
imdb.com/company/co0150567

Accepts query letter from unproduced, unrepresented writers. Project types include Feature Films, TV, and Commercials. Preferred genres include Comedy and Romance. Established in 2003.

Chris Adams
Partner
chris@madrik.com
imdb.com/name/nm1886228
linkedin.com/in/madrikadams

Erik Adams
Founder

Steve Mellon
Founder

MAGIC ELEVATOR

13636 Ventura Blvd, Suite 370
Sherman Oaks, CA 91423

contact@magicelevator.com
magicelevator.com
imdb.com/company/co0339493

Does not accept any unsolicited material. Preferred genres include Drama, Family, Horror, and Science Fiction.

Berenika Maciejewicz
Producer
imdb.com/name/nm3559189

Jeff Solema
VP/Producer
imdb.com/name/nm4221414

MAGIC LANTERN ENTERTAINMENT

2304 Dunlavy St
Houston, TX 77006
713-626-0644

info@magiclanternent.com
magiclanternent.com

Does not accept any unsolicited material. Project types include Feature Films and TV. Preferred genres include Family.

Jack Crosby
Chairman
imdb.com/name/nm0188997

Jeff Segal
President/Founder
imdb.com/name/nm0781796

MAGIC STONE PRODUCTIONS

7319 Beverly Blvd.
Los Angele, CA 90036
323-549-9020

imdb.com/company/co0219979

Does not accept any unsolicited material. Project types include Feature Films. Preferred genres include Comedy.

Lindsay Stephenson
Producer

Michael Stephenson
Producer/Director
imdb.com/name/nm0827294

MAGNET RELEASING

49 W 27th St
7th Floor
New York, NY 10001
212-924-6701 (phone)
212-924-6742 (fax)

1614 W. 5th St
Austin, Texas 78703
512-474-0303 (phone)
512-474-0305 (fax)

booking@magpictures.com
magnetreleasing.com
imdb.com/company/co0219575
facebook.com/magnetreleasing

Does not accept any unsolicited material. Project types include Feature Films. Preferred genres include Action, Comedy, Crime, Family, Fantasy, Horror, Myth, Romance, Science Fiction, and Thriller.

Peter Van Steemberg
Director (Acquisitions)

Eamonn Bowles
President
imdb.com/name/nm2113054
linkedin.com/pub/eamonn-bowles/9/363/42

MAGNOLIA ENTERTAINMENT

9595 Wilshire Blvd., Suite 601
Beverly Hills, CA 90212
310-247-0450 (phone)
310-247-0451 (fax)

imdb.com/company/co0096710

Does not accept any unsolicited material. Project types include Feature Films. Preferred genres include Drama and Thriller.

Shelley Browning
CEO/Producer/Manager
imdb.com/name/nm0115212

MAGNOLIA MAE FILMS

285 W Broadway, Suite 300
New York, NY 10013
212-366-5044

info@magnoliamaefilms.com
magnoliamaefilms.com
imdb.com/company/co0002648

Does not accept any unsolicited material. Project types include Feature Films. Preferred genres include Drama.

Gabrielle Tana
Producer
imdb.com/name/nm0848932

MAINLINE RELEASING

301 Arizona Ave, 4th Floor Penthouse
Santa Monica, CA 90401
310-255-7999 (phone)
310-255-7998 (fax)

info@mainlinereleasing.com
mainlinereleasing.com
imdb.com/company/co0036169

Does not accept any unsolicited material. Project types include Feature Films and TV. Preferred genres include Drama, Family, Horror, and Thriller.

Rich Goldberg
Founder
imdb.com/name/nm5304088

Marc Greenberg
Founder
imdb.com/name/nm0338554

MAIN STREET FILMS

1176 Main St, Suite C
Irvine, CA 92614
949-660-9000 (phone)
949-468-2854 (fax)

825 Little Farms Ave, Suite B
Metaire, LA 70003
504-636-6555

mainstreetfilms.net
facebook.com/MSFilms
twitter.com/MainStreet_Film
imdb.com/company/co0423950

Does not accept any unsolicited material. Project types include Feature Films and TV. Preferred genres include Comedy and Drama.

Craig Chang
Chairman/Producer
imdb.com/name/nm4978624

Harrison Kordestani
President/Producer
imdb.com/name/nm1626595

MAJESTIC ENTERTAINMENT

2747 Paradise Rd, Suite 501
Las Vegas, NV 89109
702-369-6978 (phone)
310-470-0932 (fax)

lorenzo@majesticfilmworks.com
majesticfilmworks.com
imdb.com/company/co0305423

Lorenzo Doumani
CEO
imdb.com/name/nm0235387

MALPASO PRODUCTIONS

4000 Warner Blvd
Building 81
Suite 101
Burbank, CA 91522-0811
818-954-3367 (phone)
818-954-4803 (fax)

imdb.com/company/co0010258

Does not accept any unsolicited material. Project types include Feature Films. Preferred genres include Crime, Drama, Fantasy, Non-Fiction, Romance, and Thriller. Established in 1967.

Clint Eastwood
imdb.com/name/nm0000142

Robert Lorenz
imdb.com/name/nm0520749

MALTMAN ENTERTAINMENT

29219 Canwood St, Suite 100
Agoura Hills, CA 91301
818-707-7786

info@maltmanentertainment.com
maltmanentertainment.com

Does not accept any unsolicited material. Project types include Feature Films and TV. Preferred genres include Comedy and Horror.

Mark A. Altman
Producer
imdb.com/name/nm0022913

MANAGE-MENT

1103 1/2 Glendon Ave
Los Angeles, CA 90024
310-208-4411 (phone)
310-208-6736 (fax)

info@manage-ment.com
imdb.com/company/co0223070
manage-ment.com

Does not accept any unsolicited material. Project types include TV. Preferred genres include Comedy and Drama.

MANDALAY PICTURES

4751 Wilshire Blvd, 3rd Floor
Los Angeles, CA 90010
323-549-4300

380 Lafayette St Suite 202
New York City, NY 10003
212-725-3550

info@mandalay.com
mandalay.com
imdb.com/company/co0013922
facebook.com/pages/Mandalay-Pictures/
    109759129042274
linkedin.com/company/mandalay-pictures

Accepts query letter from produced or represented writers. Project types include Feature Films. Preferred genres include Action, Comedy, Drama, Family, Horror, Romance, and Thriller. Established in 1995.

Peter Guber
imdb.com/name/nm0345542

MANDALAY TELEVISION

4751 Wilshire Blvd, 3rd Floor
Los Angeles, CA 90010

323-549-4300 (phone)
323-549-9832 (fax)

info@mandalay.com
mandalay.com
imdb.com/company/co0018094
facebook.com/pages/Mandalay-Entertainment/
    112716635409080

Does not accept any unsolicited material. Project types include TV. Preferred genres include Action, Comedy, Drama, Period, Romance, and Thriller.

MANDATE PICTURES

2700 Colorado Ave, Suite 501
Santa Monica, CA 90404
310-360-1441 (phone)
310-360-1447 (fax)

info@mandatepictures.com
imdb.com/company/co0142446
facebook.com/MandatePictures/timeline
twitter.com/MandatePictures

Accepts query letter from unproduced, unrepresented writers via email. Project types include Feature Films. Preferred genres include Comedy, Crime, Drama, Fantasy, Horror, Romance, Science Fiction, and Thriller. Established in 2003.

Nathan Kahane
President
310-255-5700
imdb.com/name/nm1144042

Aaron Ensweiler
Creative Executive
310-255-5721
aensweiler@mandatepictures.com
imdb.com/name/nm3943221

Nicole Brown
310-255-5710
nbrown@mandatepictures.com
imdb.com/name/nm0114352

MANDEVILLE FILMS

500 S Buena Vista St
Animation Building, 2G
Burbank, CA 91521-1783

818-560-1000 (phone)
818-842-2937 (fax)

mandfilms.com
imdb.com/company/co0064942

Does not accept any unsolicited material. Project types include Feature Films and TV. Preferred genres include Action, Drama, Family, and Romance. Established in 1994.

David Hoberman
Partner
imdb.com/name/nm0387674
Assistant: Derek Steiner

Todd Lieberman
Partner
imdb.com/name/nm0509414
Assistant: Jacqueline Lesko

Laura Cray
Creative Executive
imdb.com/name/nm1733050
twitter.com/lauracray
Assistant: Liz Bassin

MANDY FILMS

9201 Wilshire Blvd, Suite 206
Beverly Hills, CA 90210
310-246-0500 (phone)
310-246-0350 (fax)

imdb.com/company/co0032786

Accepts query letter from unproduced, unrepresented writers. Project types include Feature Films and TV. Preferred genres include Action, Comedy, Drama, Fantasy, Science Fiction, and Thriller.

Leonard Goldberg
President
imdb.com/name/nm0325252

Amanda Goldberg
imdb.com/name/nm0325144

MANGUSTA PRODUCTIONS

145 6th Ave
Suite #6E

New York, NY 10013
212-463-9503

Ojai, CA
805-646-8800

info@mangustaproductions.com
mangustaproductions.com
facebook.com/MangustaProductions
imdb.com/company/co0203045
twitter.com/Mangu_tv

Project types include Feature Films. Preferred genres include Comedy, Documentary, Drama, and Romance.

Giancarlo Canavesio
Owner
imdb.com/name/nm2184875
linkedin.com/pub/giancarlo-canavesio/11/6a2/938

Shannon McCoy Cohn
Producer
imdb.com/name/nm3101571

Sol Tryon
Producer
imdb.com/name/nm0874501
linkedin.com/pub/sol-tryon/4/611/746

Blake Ashman
imdb.com/name/nm0039137

MANIFEST FILM COMPANY

5709 Franklin Ave.
Los Angeles, CA 90028
412-996-8410

info@manifestfilms.com
imdb.com/company/co0005048
manifestfilm.com
facebook.com/ManifestFilm
twitter.com/ManifestFilm

Accepts query letter from unproduced, unrepresented writers. Project types include Feature Films. Preferred genres include Comedy, Crime, Drama, Period, and Thriller. Established in 1998.

Janet Yang
President
janetyang2013@gmail.com
janetyang.com
imdb.com/name/nm0946003

MAN IN HAT

175 Varick St
New York, NY 10013
646-494-3837

info@maninhat.com
maninhat.com
twitter.com/ManInHatNY
facebook.com/pages/ManInHat/195266753840189
imdb.com/company/co0351336
linkedin.com/company/man-in-hat

Does not accept any unsolicited material. Project types include Feature Films, Short Films, and Commercials. Preferred genres include Drama. Established in 2011.

Bruno Mourral
Director
imdb.com/name/nm3681751

Alessandro Penazzi
Producer
imdb.com/name/nm3958443

D. H. Bhatt
Producer

Jonathan Whittaker
Director

Duccio Fabbri
Producer

Franck Allera
Director

Shelly Carmel
Director

Thinesh Kumar Lachumanan
Producer

Paul Weekes
Producer

Greg Montano
Legal Counsel

Matthew Blute
Cinematographer

Chris Whittaker
Producer

MANKIND ENTERTAINMENT

1717 W 6th St, Suite #445
Austin, TX 78703

john@mankind-ent.com
mankind-ent.com
imdb.com/company/co0297190

Does not accept any unsolicited material. Project types include Feature Films. Preferred genres include Drama.

Joey Lamy
Producer

John Torres Martinez
Producer
imdb.com/name/nm2336847

MAPLE SHADE FILMS

4000 Warner Blvd
Building 138, Room 1103
Burbank, CA 91522
818-954-3137

imdb.com/company/co0100155

Accepts query letter from unproduced, unrepresented writers. Project types include Feature Films. Preferred genres include Action, Drama, Fantasy, and Thriller.

Ed McDonnell
President
imdb.com/name/nm0568093

MARC PLATT PRODUCTIONS

100 Universal City Plaza
North Hollywood, CA 91608
818-777-1122

imdb.com/company/co0093810

Accepts query letter from unproduced, unrepresented writers. Project types include Feature Films and TV. Preferred genres include Action, Comedy, Crime,

Drama, Family, Fantasy, Horror, Romance, and Thriller.

Adam Siegel
President
818-777-9544
imdb.com/name/nm2132113

Jared LeBoff
818-777-9961
imdb.com/name/nm1545176

Marc Platt
Producer
818-777-1122
platt@nbcuni.com
imdb.com/name/nm0686887
facebook.com/pages/Marc-E-Platt/112127405470433
Assistant: Joey Levy

MARDEORO FILMS

826 Winthrop Rd
San Marino, CA 91108
626-799-1388 (phone)
626-799-2388 (fax)

mardeoro@mardeorofilms.com
mardeorofilms.com
imdb.com/company/co0176050

Does not accept any unsolicited material. Project types include Feature Films. Preferred genres include Drama.

Oscar Luis Costo
Producer/Director/Writer
imdb.com/name/nm0182724

Vivian Wu
Producer
imdb.com/name/nm0943180

MARK VICTOR PRODUCTIONS

2932 Wilshire Blvd, Suite 201
Santa Monica, CA 90403
310-828-3339 (phone)
310-828-9588 (fax)

info@markvictorproductions.com
markvictorproductions.com
imdb.com/company/co0184007

Accepts query letter from unproduced, unrepresented writers via email. Project types include Feature Films and TV. Preferred genres include Action, Animation, Horror, Non-Fiction, Reality, and Thriller.

Sarah Johnson
Director of Development
310-828-3339
imdb.com/name/nm1154417

Mark Victor
310-828-3339
markvictorproductions@hotmail.com
imdb.com/name/nm0896131

MARK YELLEN PRODUCTION

183 S Orange Dr
Los Angeles, CA 90036
323-935-5525 (phone)
323-935-5755 (fax)

Accepts query letter from unproduced, unrepresented writers via email. Project types include Feature Films, TV, and Commercials. Preferred genres include Action and Family. Established in 2003.

Mark Yellen
Producer
323-935-5525
mark@myfilmconsult.com
imdb.com/name/nm0947390
linkedin.com/in/markyellen

MARLBORO ROAD GANG PRODUCTIONS

334 E 90th St
New York, NY 10128
212-996-7932 (phone)
310-451-4000 (fax)

imdb.com/company/co0123076

Does not accept any unsolicited material. Project types include Feature Films and TV. Preferred genres include Crime and Drama.

Aaron Lubin
Producer
imdb.com/name/nm0523892

Ed Burns
Actor/Writer/Director/Producer
imdb.com/name/nm0122654

MAROBRU PRODUCTIONS

515 W 57th St, 3rd Floor
New York, NY 10019
212-265-3600

marobru.net

Does not accept any unsolicited material. Project types
include TV. Preferred genres include Comedy.

Michele Armour
Producer
imdb.com/name/nm1723268

MARSH ENTERTAINMENT

12444 Ventura Blvd., Suite 203
Studio City, CA 91604
818-509-1135

imdb.com/company/co0005422

Does not accept any unsolicited material. Project types
include TV. Preferred genres include Drama.

Sherry Marsh
Producer/Manager
imdb.com/name/nm1639567

MARTIN CHASE PRODUCTIONS

500 S Buena Vista St
Burbank, CA 91521
818-560-3952 (phone)
818-560-5113 (fax)

imdb.com/company/co0110950
facebook.com/martinchaseproductions

Does not accept any unsolicited material. Project types
include Feature Films and TV. Preferred genres
include Family. Established in 2000.

Debra Chase
Founder
818-526-4252
imdb.com/name/nm0153744

MARTY KATZ PRODUCTIONS

22337 Pacific Coast Highway #327
Malibu, CA 90265
310-589-1560 (phone)
310-589-1565 (fax)

martykatzproductions@earthlink.net
martykatzproductions.com
imdb.com/name/nm0441794
facebook.com/martykatzproductions
twitter.com/martykatzprods
linkedin.com/company/marty-katz-productions-inc

Accepts query letter from unproduced, unrepresented
writers via email. Project types include Feature Films.
Preferred genres include Action, Comedy, Drama, and
Romance. Established in 1996.

Campbell Katz
Vice President of Production & Development
imdb.com/name/nm0441645

Marty Katz
Producer
imdb.com/name/nm0441794
linkedin.com/pub/marty-katz/8/9a2/481

MARVISTA ENTERTAINMENT

10277 W Olympic Blvd
Los Angeles, CA 90067
424-274-3000 (phone)
424-274-3050 (fax)

info@marvista.net
marvista.net
imdb.com/company/co0118519
twitter.com/MarVistaEnt
facebook.com/MarVistaEntertainment
linkedin.com/company/mar-vista-entertainment-inc.

Accepts query letter from unproduced, unrepresented
writers via email. Project types include Feature Films
and TV.

Fernando Szew
CEO
310-737-0950
fszew@marvista.net
imdb.com/name/nm2280496
linkedin.com/pub/fernando-szew/3b/511/7a8

Joseph Szew
Partner

Susan Young
CFO

Vanessa Shapiro
Executive Vice President, Distribution

Sharon Bordas
Executive Vice-President Production and
Development

Stephanie Slack
Sr. Vice-President

Peggy Lisberger
Sr. Vice-President

Robyn Snyder
Executive Vice-President Production and
Development
310-737-0950
rsnyder@marvista.net
imdb.com/name/nm2237557

MAS AND MORE ENTERTAINMENT

674 Echo Park Ave
Los Angeles, CA 90026
213-250-9162

mas@masandmore.com
masandmore.com

Does not accept any unsolicited material. Project types
include Feature Films. Preferred genres include
Drama.

Miguel Mas
CEO/Director
imdb.com/company/co0137420

Ricardo Ochoa Fernandez
VP
imdb.com/name/nm2808010

MASIMEDIA

11620 Oxnard St
North Hollywood, California 91606
818-358-4803

submissions@masimedia.net

masimedia.net
imdb.com/company/co0155931

Accepts scripts from unproduced, unrepresented
writers via email. Project types include Feature Films
and TV. Preferred genres include Documentary and
Horror. Established in 2006.

Anthony Masi
President
818-358-4803
anthony@masimedia.net
imdb.com/name/nm1502845
twitter.com/MasiMedia

MASS HYSTERIA ENTERTAINMENT

2920 W. Olive Ave. #208
Burbank, CA 91505
818-459-8200

info@masshysteriafilms.com
masshysteriafilms.com

Accepts query letter from unproduced, unrepresented
writers via email. Project types include Feature Films
and TV.

Daniel Grodnik
President
310-285-7800
grodzilla@earthlink.net
imdb.com/name/nm0342841
linkedin.com/pub/dan-grodnik/9/176/44

MASSIVE

618 Indiana Ave #1
Venice, CA 90291
310-908-9004

info@massive.la
massive.xn--la-pt3n

Does not accept any unsolicited material. Project types
include Feature Films. Preferred genres include
Drama.

Andy Kleinman
Producer
imdb.com/name/nm2035742

MATADOR PICTURES

20 Gloucester Place
London W1U 8HA
011-442-077344544 (phone)
011-442-077347794 (fax)

admin@matadorpictures.com
matadorpictures.com
imdb.com/company/co0045407
facebook.com/pages/London-United-Kingdom/
    Matador-Pictures/206766474356
twitter.com/matadorpictures

Does not accept any unsolicited material. Project types include Feature Films. Preferred genres include Action, Comedy, Drama, and Romance. Established in 1999.

Nigel Thomas
Producer
+44 (0) 20-7009-9640
imdb.com/name/nm0859302

Orlando Cubit
Development Executive
+44 (0) 20-7009-9640
imdb.com/name/nm4919747

Lucia Lopez
+44 (0) 20-7009-9640
imdb.com/name/nm2389416

MATRIARCH MULTIMEDIA GROUP

1150 S. LaBrea Ave
Los Angeles, CA 90019
323-963-8717

info@matriarchmultimedia.com
imdb.com/company/co0312785
matriarchmultimedia.com

Does not accept any unsolicited material. Project types include Feature Films and TV. Preferred genres include Comedy and Horror.

Cassandra Cooper
Founder/CEO/Producer
imdb.com/name/nm2111621

MAVEN PICTURES

148 Spring St
New York, NY 10012

info@mavenfilmsllc.com
imdb.com/company/co0337243
facebook.com/MavenPictures
mavenfilmsllc.com
twitter.com/Maven_Pictures

Does not accept any unsolicited material. Project types include Feature Films. Preferred genres include Action, Comedy, Drama, Romance, and Thriller. Established in 2011.

Celine Rattray
Producer
imdb.com/name/nm1488027

Alex Francis
Producer
imdb.com/name/nm2123360

Jenny Halper
Development Executive
imdb.com/name/nm3794516
linkedin.com/pub/jenny-halper/42/6a7/12

Nic Marshall
Director of Operations
imdb.com/name/nm2090942
linkedin.com/pub/nic-marshall/a/254/971

Trudie Styler
CEO
imdb.com/name/nm0836548
linkedin.com/pub/trudie-styler/70/653/702

Hardy Justice
Sr. Vice-President
imdb.com/name/nm1155511
linkedin.com/pub/hardy-justice/47/16a/486

MAVERICK ENTERTAINMENT GROUP

1191 E Newport Center Dr., Suite 210
Deerfield Beach, FL 33442
954-422-8811 (phone)
954-429-0565 (fax)

info@maverickentertainment.cc
maverickentertainment.cc
imdb.com/company/co0060687

Accepts scripts from unproduced, unrepresented writers via email. Project types include Feature Films. Preferred genres include Action, Comedy, and Horror.

Doug Schwab
President
imdb.com/name/nm0776979

Pam White
Vice President
imdb.com/name/nm4983373

MAXIMUM FILMS & MANAGEMENT

33 W 17th St, 11th Floor
New York, NY 10011
212-414-4801 (phone)
212-414-4803 (fax)

lauren@maximumfilmsny.com
imdb.com/company/co0223939

Does not accept any unsolicited material. Project types include Feature Films, TV, and Theater.

Marcy Drogin
212-414-4801
imdb.com/name/nm1216320

MAYA ENTERTAINMENT GROUP

1201 W 5th St, Suite T210
Los Angeles, CA 90017
213-542-4420 (phone)
213-534-3846 (fax)

info@maya-entertainment.com
mayaentertainment.com
linkedin.com/company/maya-entertainment

Accepts query letter from unproduced, unrepresented writers via email. Project types include Feature Films and TV. Preferred genres include Comedy, Drama, Non-Fiction, and Reality. Established in 2008.

Christina Hirigoyen
Development Executive
213-542-4420
imdb.com/name/nm3491113

Moctesuma Esparza
213-542-4420
imdb.com/name/nm0260800
linkedin.com/pub/moctesuma-esparza/32/938/678

MAYHEM PICTURES

725 Arizona Ave, Suite 402
Santa Monica, CA 90401
310-393-5005 (phone)
310-393-5017 (fax)

imdb.com/company/co0093869

Does not accept any unsolicited material. Project types include Feature Films and TV. Preferred genres include Comedy, Family, Non-Fiction, and Reality. Established in 2003.

Mark Ciardi
Producer
310-393-5005
mark@mayhempictures.com
imdb.com/name/nm0161891

Brad Butler
Creative Executive
310-393-5005
brad@mayhempictures.com
imdb.com/name/nm2744089
linkedin.com/pub/brad-butler/44/159/48a

MBST ENTERTAINMENT

345 N Maple Dr, Suite 200
Beverly Hills, CA 90210
310-385-1820 (phone)
310-385-1834 (fax)

imdb.com/company/co0057791

Accepts query letter from unproduced, unrepresented writers. Project types include Feature Films, TV, and Theater. Preferred genres include Action, Comedy, Drama, and Romance. Established in 2005.

Jonathan Brandstein
Partner
310-385-1820
imdb.com/name/nm0104844

Larry Brezner
Partner
310-385-1820
imdb.com/name/nm010836
linkedin.com/pub/larry-brezner/11/b49/844

MECHANIKS

905 Electric Ave
Venice , CA 90291
310-460-7280 (phone)
310-396-7566 (fax)

works@mechaniks.com
mechaniks.com
imdb.com/company/co0119989

Does not accept any unsolicited material. Project types include Feature Films. Preferred genres include Drama.

Andrea Kikot
Producer
imdb.com/name/nm1118602

MEDIA 8 ENTERTAINMENT

15260 Ventura Blvd., Suite 710
Sherman Oaks, CA 91403
818-325-8000 (phone)
818-325-8020 (fax)

info@media8ent.com
media8entertainment.com
imdb.com/company/co0051264

Does not accept any unsolicited material. Project types include Feature Films. Preferred genres include Action, Comedy, Drama, and Thriller.

Stewart Hall
President and Board Member
imdb.com/name/nm1279593

MEDIA HOUSE CAPITAL

15260 Ventura Blvd., Suite 1040
Sherman Oaks, CA 91403
310-890-4137 (phone)
818-382-7811 (fax)

5542 Short St
Burnaby, British Columbia, V5J 1L9
604-419-8178 (phone)
604-435-4384 (fax)

imdb.com/company/co0311137
mediahousecapital.com

Does not accept any unsolicited material. Project types include Feature Films. Preferred genres include Drama and Romance.

Aaron L. Gilbert
Managing Director
imdb.com/name/nm0317943

David Bodanis
COO
imdb.com/name/nm2034591

MEDIA NATION PMC

414 S Irving Blvd.
Los Angeles, CA 90020
323-931-1141

medianation.biz

Does not accept any unsolicited material. Project types include TV. Preferred genres include Drama.

Linda Berman
Executive Producer
imdb.com/name/nm0075802

David Craig
Executive Producer
imdb.com/name/nm0185829

MEDIA RIGHTS CAPITAL

9665 Wilshire Blvd
2nd Floor
Beverly Hills, CA 90212
310-786-1600 (phone)
310-786-1601 (fax)

info@mrclp.com
mrcstudios.com
imdb.com/company/co0194736

Does not accept any unsolicited material. Project types include Feature Films and TV. Preferred genres

include Animation, Comedy, Drama, Romance, and Thriller.

Alex Jackson
Creative Executive

Brye Adler

Joe Hipps

Whitney Timmons
Director of Television
linkedin.com/pub/whitney-timmons/9/707/4a2

Modi Wiczyk
imdb.com/name/nm1582943
Assistant: Maggie Settli

Asif Satchu
www.imdb.com/name/nm2640007
Assistant: Maggie Settli

Charlie Goldstein
imdb.com/name/nm0326177

MEDIA TALENT GROUP

9200 Sunset Blvd, Suite 550
West Hollywood, CA 90069
310-275-7900 (phone)
310-275-7910 (fax)

imdb.com/company/co0130439

Accepts query letter from unproduced, unrepresented writers. Project types include Feature Films and TV. Established in 2009.

Geyer Kosinski
310-275-7900
imdb.com/name/nm0467083

Chris Davey
310-275-7900
imdb.com/name/nm1312702
linkedin.com/pub/chris-davey/3/a24/641

MEDUSA FILM

Via Aurelia Antica 422/424
Rome, Lazio 00165
Italy
+39-06-663-901 (phone)
+39-06-66-39-04-50 (fax)

info.medusa@medusa.it
medusa.it
imdb.com/company/co0117688
twitter.com/medusa_film
facebook.com/medusafilm

Does not accept any unsolicited material. Project types include Feature Films. Preferred genres include Comedy, Crime, Documentary, Drama, Family, Horror, Romance, and Thriller. Established in 1916.

Faruk Alatan
imdb.com/name/nm0016092

Luciana Migliavacca
imdb.com/name/nm3096618

Pier Paolo Zerilli
imdb.com/name/nm1047259
linkedin.com/pub/pier-paolo-zerilli/7/95a/a05

MEGA FILMS

1411 Broadway
New York, NY 10018
212-819-9446 (phone)
212-819-1498 (fax)

imdb.com/company/co0089752

Does not accept any unsolicited material. Preferred genres include Drama and Thriller.

Morris S. Levy
Producer
imdb.com/name/nm1459257

MEGALOMEDIA

6207 Bee Cave Rd, Suite 125
Austin, TX 78746
512-347-9901

info@megalomedia.com
imdb.com/company/co0070416
megalomedia.com

Does not accept any unsolicited material. Project types include TV.

MELEE ENTERTAINMENT

144 S Beverly Dr, Suite 402
Beverly Hills, CA 90212
310-248-3931 (phone)
310-248-3921 (fax)

acquisitions@melee.com
melee.com
facebook.com/pages/Melee-Entertainment
twitter.com/MeleeEnt
imdb.com/company/co0109181

Does not accept any unsolicited material. Project types include Feature Films. Established in 2003.

Brittany Williams
Creative Executive
310-248-3931
imdb.com/name/nm2950356

Bryan Turner
CEO
310-248-3931
imdb.com/name/nm0877440
linkedin.com/pub/bryan-turner/1b/3a7/952

MENO FILM COMPANY

1300 NW Northrup Ave
Portland, OR 97209

122 Hudson St, 5th Floor
New York, NY 10013
646-613-1260

imdb.com/company/co0156951

Does not accept any unsolicited material. Project types include Feature Films. Preferred genres include Horror and Science Fiction.

Gus Van Sant
Director
imdb.com/name/nm0001814

MERCHANT IVORY PRODUCTIONS

250 W. 57th St.
Suite 1825
New York, NY 10019
212-582-8049 (phone)
212-706-8340 (fax)

contact@merchantivory.com
merchantivory.com
facebook.com/pages/Merchant-Ivory-Productions/
    105682432798518
imdb.com/company/co0055367

Accepts query letter from unproduced, unrepresented writers via email. Project types include Feature Films and TV. Preferred genres include Drama, Non-Fiction, and Reality. Established in 1961.

Simon Oxley
Producer
simon@merchantivory.co.uk
imdb.com/name/nm1774746
linkedin.com/pub/simon-oxley/35/b59/64b

Neil Jesuele
Director of Development
212-582-8049
njesuele@merchantivory.com
imdb.com/name/nm3134373
linkedin.com/pub/neil-jesuele/19/80b/a70

Paul Bradley
Producer
paul@merchantivory.co.uk
imdb.com/name/nm0103364

James Ivory
Principle
imdb.com/name/nm0412465

MERV GRIFFIN ENTERTAINMENT

130 S El Camino Dr
Beverly Hills, CA 90212
310-385-2700 (phone)
310-385-2728 (fax)

imdb.com/company/co0093384

Does not accept any unsolicited material. Project types include Feature Films, Short Films, and TV. Preferred genres include Action, Comedy, Crime, Documentary, Drama, Non-Fiction, Period, Reality, Romance, and Thriller. Established in 1964.

Tony Griffin
imdb.com/name/nm0341389

Mike Eyre

Ron Ward
Vice Chairman
imdb.com/name/nm2302243

Robert Pritchard
President
imdb.com/name/nm2923017
linkedin.com/pub/rob-pritchard/5/425/a26

METAMORPHIC FILMS

9107 Wilshire Blvd.
Los Angeles, CA 90210
310-461-3530

info@metamorphicfilms.com
metamorphicfilms.com
twitter.com/MetamorphicFilm

Does not accept any unsolicited material. Project types include Feature Films. Preferred genres include Horror and Science Fiction.

Teresa Zales
Producer
imdb.com/name/nm1536187

METATV PRODUCTIONS

1149 N. Gower St, #106E
Los Angeles, CA 90038
323-785-2233

metatv@metatvproductions.com
metatvproductions.com

Does not accept any unsolicited material. Project types include TV.

Jean-Michel Michenaud
Producer
imdb.com/title/tt0243345

Charles Duncombe
Producer
imdb.com/name/nm5720358

METRO-GOLDWYN MEYER (MGM)

245 N Beverly Dr
Beverly Hills, CA 90210
310-449-3000

mgm.com
twitter.com/MGM_Studios
facebook.com/mgm

Does not accept any unsolicited material. Project types include Feature Films. Preferred genres include Action, Comedy, Crime, Drama, Family, Horror, Myth, Romance, Science Fiction, and Thriller.

Dene Stratton
CFO
310-449-3000
imdb.com/name/nm4682676

Gary Barber
310-449-3000
imdb.com/name/nm0053388

Cassidy Lange
310-449-3000
imdb.com/name/nm3719738

MGA ENTERTAINMENT

16300 Roscoe Blvd., Suite 150
Van Nuys, CA 91406
818-894-2525 (phone)
800-222-4685 (fax)

mgae.com
imdb.com/company/co0124725

Does not accept any unsolicited material. Project types include Feature Films. Preferred genres include Family.

Issac Larin
Producer
imdb.com/title/tt2034403

MGMT. ENTERTAINMENT

9220 W Sunset Blvd, Suite 106
West Hollywood, CA 90069
310-558-2540

imdb.com/name/nm2889228
facebook.com/mgmtent

Does not accept any unsolicited material.

David Schiff
Partner/Producer/Manager
imdb.com/name/nm0771467

MICHAEL DE LUCA PRODUCTIONS

10202 W Washington Blvd
Astaire Building, Suite 3028
Culver City, CA 90232
310-244-4990 (phone)
310-244-0449 (fax)

imdb.com/company/co0174505

Does not accept any unsolicited material. Project types include Feature Films. Preferred genres include Action, Comedy, Drama, and Thriller.

Michael De Luca
Producer
310-244-4990
imdb.com/name/nm0006894
Assistant: Kristen Detwiler

Josh Bratman
Development Executive
310-244-4916
imdb.com/name/nm2302300
Assistant: Sandy Yep

Alissa Phillips
310-244-4918
imdb.com/name/nm1913014
Assistant: Bill Karesh

MICHAEL GRAIS PRODUCTIONS

321 S Beverly Dr, Suite M
Beverly Hills, CA 90210
323-857-4510 (phone)
323-319-4002 (fax)

michael.grais@gmail.com
imdb.com/company/co0177680
michaelgrais.com

Accepts query letter from unproduced, unrepresented writers via email. Project types include Feature Films and TV. Preferred genres include Horror and Thriller.

Michael Grais
323-857-4510
michaelgrais@yahoo.com
michaelgrais.com
imdb.com/name/nm0334457

MICHAEL MAILER FILMS

81 Worth St
New York, NY 10013
212-966-9494 (phone)
212-966-9490 (fax)

michaelmailerfilms.com
imdb.com/company/co0160601

Does not accept any unsolicited material. Project types include Feature Films. Preferred genres include Thriller.

Michael Mailer
President, Producer
imdb.com/name/nm0537550

Allison Keir
Creative Executive
imdb.com/name/nm2608240

MICHAEL MELTZER PRODUCTIONS

12207 Riverside Dr, Suite 208
Valley Village, CA 91607
818-766-8339

Does not accept any unsolicited material. Project types include Feature Films. Preferred genres include Comedy, Drama, and Horror.

Michael L. Meltzer
Owner/Producer
imdb.com/name/nm0578444

MICHAEL TAYLOR PRODUCTIONS

2370 Bowmont Dr
Beverly Hills, CA 90210
954-749-5141 (phone)
213-740-3395 (fax)

taycoprod@aol.com
mt@mtjibs.com
imdb.com/company/co0183466

Accepts query letter from unproduced, unrepresented writers via email. Project types include Feature Films and TV. Preferred genres include Non-Fiction and Reality.

Michael Taylor

Producer

213-821-3113

mtjibs.com

imdb.com/name/nm0852888

Assistant: Yolanda Rodriguez

MICHELLE KRUMM PRODUCTIONS

3826 Clayton Ave

Los Angeles, CA 90027

imdb.com/company/co0292601

Does not accept any unsolicited material. Project types include Feature Films. Preferred genres include Drama and Thriller.

Michelle Krumm

Producer

imdb.com/name/nm2325301

MIDDKID PRODUCTIONS

10202 W Washington Blvd

Fred Astaire Building, Suite 2010

Culver City, CA 90232

310-244-2688 (phone)

310-244-2603 (fax)

imdb.com/company/co0177102

Accepts query letter from unproduced, unrepresented writers. Project types include TV. Preferred genres include Crime, Detective, and Drama.

Shawn Ryan

imdb.com/name/nm0752841

Assistant: Kent Rotherham

Marney Hochman Nash

imdb.com/name/nm2701117

Assistant: Kent Rotherham

MIDNIGHT SUN PICTURES

10960 Wilshire Blvd, Suite 700

Los Angeles, CA 90024

310-902-0431 (phone)

310-450-4988 (fax)

imdb.com/company/co0071900

Accepts query letter from produced or represented writers. Project types include Feature Films and TV. Preferred genres include Comedy, Drama, Horror, and Romance.

Renny Harlin

310-902-0431

imdb.com/name/nm0001317

MIKE LOBELL PRODUCTIONS

9477 Lloydcrest Dr

Beverly Hills, CA 90210

323-822-2910 (phone)

310-205-2767 (fax)

imdb.com/company/co0007564

Accepts query letter from unproduced, unrepresented writers. Project types include Feature Films. Preferred genres include Action, Comedy, Drama, and Romance. Established in 1973.

Mike Lobell

Producer

323-822-2910

imdb.com/name/nm0516465

Assistant: JanetChiarabaglio

MIKE'S MOVIES

627 N. Las Palmas

Los Angeles , CA 90004

323-462-4690 (phone)

323-462-4699 (fax)

Does not accept any unsolicited material. Project types include Feature Films.

Michael Peyser

Producer

imdb.com/name/nm0679017

MILK & MEDIA

3450 Cahuenga Blvd., West #604

Los Angeles, CA 90068

323-851-4800 (phone)

323-851-4808 (fax)

imdb.com/company/co0268194

milkandmedia.com

Accepts query letter from unproduced, unrepresented writers via email. Project types include Feature Films and TV. Preferred genres include Drama, Horror, and Thriller.

Elton Brand
Producer
imdb.com/name/nm1580954

Harry Knapp
Producer
imdb.com/name/nm0460485

MILLAR/GOUGH INK

500 S Buena Vista St
Animation Building 1E16
Burbank, CA 91521
818-560-4260 (phone)
818-560-4216 (fax)

imdb.com/company/co0188223

Accepts query letter from unproduced, unrepresented writers. Project types include Feature Films and TV. Preferred genres include Action, Drama, Family, and Science Fiction.

Miles Millar
818-560-4260
imdb.com/name/nm0587692
Assistant: Mal Stares

Alfred Gough
818-560-4260
imdb.com/name/nm0332184
Assistant: Mal Stares

MILLENNIUM FILMS

6423 Wilshire Blvd
Los Angeles, CA 90048
310-388-6900 (phone)
310-388-6901 (fax)

info@millenniumfilms.com
millenniumfilms.com
imdb.com/company/co0002572
twitter.com/MillenniumFilms
facebook.com/OfficialMillenniumfilms

Accepts query letter from unproduced, unrepresented writers via email. Project types include Feature Films.

Preferred genres include Action, Comedy, Detective, Drama, Fantasy, Non-Fiction, Science Fiction, and Thriller. Established in 1992.

Avi Lerner
Founder
imdb.com/name/nm0503592

Trevor Short
CFO
imdb.com/name/nm0795121

Boaz Davidson
Head of Development & Creative Affairs
imdb.com/name/nm0203246

Mark Gill
President

John Fremes
President of International

John Thompson
Head of Production

Frank Demartini
Legal Counsel

Lonnie Ramati
Executive Vice President of Business & Legal Affairs

MIMRAN SCHUR PICTURES

1411 5th St
Suite 200
Santa Monica, CA 90401
310-526-5410 (phone)
310-526-5405 (fax)

info@mimranschurpictures.com
mimranschurpictures.com
imdb.com/company/co0272027
twitter.com/mimranschur
facebook.com/pages/Mimran-Schur-Pictures/
    210823324999

Accepts query letter from produced or represented writers. Project types include Feature Films. Preferred genres include Drama. Established in 2009.

Jordan Schur
310-526-5410
imdb.com/name/nm2028525
linkedin.com/pub/jordan-schur/78/747/6b1

Lauren Pettit
Creative Executive
310-526-5410
imdb.com/name/nm2335692
linkedin.com/pub/lauren-pettit/13/aa8/241
twitter.com/LaLaLaLooo

David Mimran
310-526-5410
imdb.com/name/nm3450764
linkedin.com/pub/jordan-schur/78/747/6b1
Assistant: Caroline Haubold

MIRADA

4235 Redwood Ave
Los Angeles, CA 90066
424-216-7470

mirada.com
facebook.com/MiradaStudios
twitter.com/miradastudios

Does not accept any unsolicited material. Project types include Feature Films, TV, and Theater. Preferred genres include Animation, Drama, Fantasy, and Myth. Established in 2010.

Guillermo del Toro
imdb.com/name/nm0868219

Guillermo Navarro
imdb.com/name/nm0622897

Javier Jimenez
imdb.com/name/nm3901643

MIRANDA ENTERTAINMENT

7337 Pacific View Dr
Los Angeles, CA 90068
323-874-3600 (phone)
323-851-5350 (fax)

imdb.com/company/co0067754

Does not accept any unsolicited material. Project types include Feature Films and TV. Preferred genres include Comedy, Horror, and Thriller.

Carsten Lorenz
Producer
323-874-3600
clorenz1@aol.com
imdb.com/name/nm0520696

MISHER FILMS

12233 Olympic Blvd, Suite 354
Los Angeles, CA 90064
310-405-7999 (phone)
310-405-7991 (fax)

misherfilms.com
imdb.com/company/co0085725

Does not accept any unsolicited material. Project types include Feature Films and TV. Preferred genres include Action, Crime, and Drama.

Kevin Misher
310-405-7999
kevin.misher@misherfilms.com
imdb.com/name/nm0592746
Assistant: Sarah Ezrin

MOCKINGBIRD PICTURES

Los Angeles, CA

info@mockingbirdpictures.com
mockingbirdpictures.com
twitter.com/mockingbirdpics

Accepts query letter from unproduced, unrepresented writers via email. Project types include Feature Films. Preferred genres include Drama.

Bonnie Curtis
imdb.com/name/nm0193268

Julie Lynn
imdb.com/name/nm0528724

Kelly Thomas
Executive Producer
imdb.com/name/nm1684437
twitter.com/Tom_Tom_Kel

MODERCINE

18 4th Place, Suite 2
Brooklyn, NY 11231

info@moderncine.com
moderncine.com/index.php
imdb.com/company/co0100731
facebook.com/moderncine

Does not accept any unsolicited material. Project types include Feature Films and Short Films. Preferred genres include Comedy, Crime, Horror, and Thriller.

Robert Tonino
CFO
imdb.com/name/nm1720736

Andrew van den Houten
CEO
imdb.com/name/nm0886156
linkedin.com/pub/andrew-van-den-houten/b/530/ba1
facebook.com/andrew.vanhouten

MOJO FILMS

4024 Radford Ave.
Bungalow 1
Studio City, CA 91604
818-655-6292

imdb.com/company/co0042403

Accepts query letter from unproduced, unrepresented writers. Project types include Feature Films and TV. Established in 2007.

Mary-Beth Basile
Producer
imdb.com/name/nm1039389

Gary Fleder
Director
818-655-6292
garyfleder.com
imdb.com/name/nm0001219
linkedin.com/pub/gary-fleder/a/17/35

MOMENTUM WORLDWIDE

250 Hudson St
2nd Floor
New York, NY 10013
646-638-5400

imdb.com/company/co0268253
momentumww.com
twitter.com/MomentumWW

facebook.com/MomentumWorldwide
linkedin.com/company/2593

Accepts query letter from unproduced, unrepresented writers via email. Project types include TV and Commercials. Preferred genres include Action, Animation, Comedy, Crime, Detective, Drama, Family, Fantasy, Horror, Myth, Non-Fiction, Reality, Romance, Science Fiction, Sociocultural, and Thriller.

Chris Weil
CEO

MONSTERFOOT PRODUCTIONS

3450 Cahuenga Blvd West
Loft 105
Los Angeles, CA 90068
323-850-6116 (phone)
323-378-5232 (fax)

imdb.com/company/co0275343
facebook.com/MonsterfootProductions
twitter.com/MONSTERFOOTprod
linkedin.com/company/monsterfoot-productions

Accepts query letter from unproduced, unrepresented writers. Project types include Feature Films and TV. Preferred genres include Non-Fiction and Reality. Established in 2006.

Ahmet Zappa
CEO
323-850-6116
ahmetzappa.com
imdb.com/name/nm0953257
linkedin.com/in/ahmetzappa
twitter.com/AhmetZappa

MONTAGE ENTERTAINMENT

2118 Wilshire Blvd. Suite 297
Santa Monica, CA 90403
310-966-0222

david@montageentertainment.com
imdb.com/company/co0100820
montageentertainment.com

Accepts query letter from unproduced, unrepresented writers via email. Project types include Feature Films and TV.

David Peters
Producer
310-966-0222
david@montageentertainment.com
imdb.com/name/nm0007070

Bill Ewart
Producer
310-966-0222
bill@montageentertainment.com
imdb.com/name/nm0263867

MONTECITO PICTURES

9465 Wilshire Blvd, Suite 920
Beverly Hills, CA 90212
310-247-9880 (phone)
310-247-9498 (fax)

1482 E. Valley Rd
Suite 477
Montecito, CA 93108
805-565-8590 (phone)
805-565-1893 (fax)

montecitopicturecompany.com
imdb.com/company/co0118469

Accepts query letter from unproduced, unrepresented writers. Project types include Feature Films and TV. Preferred genres include Action, Comedy, Drama, Family, Non-Fiction, Period, and Thriller. Established in 2000.

Ivan Reitman
Partner
imdb.com/name/nm0718645
Assistant: Eric Reich

Alex Plapinger
Executive Vice President of Production
310-247-9880
imdb.com/name/nm3292687
linkedin.com/pub/alex-plapinger/4/544/808

Tom Pollock
Partner
imdb.com/name/nm0689696
Assistant: Krystee Morgan

Joe Medjuck
Partner
imdb.com/name/nm0575817

MONTONE/YORN (UNNAMED YORN PRODUCTION COMPANY)

2000 Ave of the Stars
3rd Floor North Tower
Los Angeles, CA 90067

Accepts query letter from unproduced, unrepresented writers. Preferred genres include Action, Comedy, Family, and Fantasy. Established in 2008.

Rick Yorn
imdb.com/name/nm0948833

MOONSTONE ENTERTAINMENT

PO Box 7400
Studio City, CA 91614
818-985-3003 (phone)
818-985-3009 (fax)

submissions@moonstonefilms.com
moonstonefilms.com
imdb.com/company/co0023327
facebook.com/MoonstoneEntertainment

Accepts query letter from unproduced, unrepresented writers via email. Project types include Feature Films. Established in 1992.

Shahar Stroh
Director Development & Acquisitions
818-985-3003
shahar@moonstonefilms.com
imdb.com/name/nm2325576

Yael Stroh
President
yaels@moonstonefilms.com
imdb.com/name/nm0834806

MORGAN CREEK PRODUCTIONS

10351 Santa Monica Blvd
Los Angeles, CA 90025
310-432-4848 (phone)
310-432-4844 (fax)

morgancreek.com
facebook.com/morgancreekproductions
twitter.com/Morgan__Creek

Accepts query letter from unproduced, unrepresented writers. Project types include Feature Films. Established in 1988.

Andrew Moncrief
Creative Executive
linkedin.com/pub/andrew-moncrief/11/262/325

MORNINGSTAR ENTERTAINMENT

350 N Glenoaks Blvd
Suite 300
Burbank, CA 91502
818-559-7255 (phonc)
818-559-7551 (fax)

mstar@morningstarentertainment.com
morningstarentertainment.com
facebook.com/pages/Morningstar-Entertainment/
  91568286971
imdb.com/company/co0050956
linkedin.com/companies/morningstar-entertainment

Accepts query letter from unproduced, unrepresented writers via email. Project types include TV. Preferred genres include Non-Fiction and Reality. Established in 1980.

Paninee Theeranuntawat
CFO

Gary Tarpinian
President
linkedin.com/pub/gary-tarpinian/33/3a/367

MORTON JANKEL ZANDER (MJZ)

2201 S Carmelina Ave
Los Angeles, CA 90064
310-826-6200 (phone)
310-826-6219 (fax)

facebook.com/MJZ.MJZ
mjz.com
twitter.com/MJZitter
imdb.com/company/co0102914
facebook.com/MJZ.MJZ

Does not accept any unsolicited material. Project types include Short Films and Commercials. Established in 1990.

Scott Howard
Executive Producer

Kate Leahy
Executive Producer

David Zander
President
imdb.com/name/nm1536307

MOSAIC MEDIA GROUP

9200 W Sunset Blvd
10th Floor
Los Angeles, CA 90069
310-786-4900 (phone)
310-777-2185 (fax)

imdb.com/company/co0037759

Accepts query letter from unproduced, unrepresented writers. Project types include Feature Films and TV. Preferred genres include Action, Comedy, Drama, Family, and Myth.

David Householter
310-786-4900
dhouseholter@mosaicla.com
imdb.com/name/nm0396720
Assistant: Brendan Clougherty

Mike Falbo
310-786-4900
mfalbo@mosaicla.com
imdb.com/name/nm3824648
Assistant: Mark Acomb

Jimmy Miller
310-786-4900
jmiller@mosaicla.com
imdb.com/name/nm0588612
Assistant: Alyx Carr

MOSHAG PRODUCTIONS

1531 Wellesley Ave
Los Angeles, CA 90025
310-820-6760 (phone)
310-820-6960 (fax)

moshag@aol.com
imdb.com/company/co0061487

Accepts query letter from unproduced, unrepresented writers via email. Project types include Feature Films and TV.

Mark Mower
Producer
imdb.com/name/nm0610272

MOTT STREET PICTURES

801 N. Fairfax Ave, Suite 322
Los Angeles, CA 90046
310-279-9797

mottstreetpictures.com
imdb.com/company/co0321036

Does not accept any unsolicited material. Project types include Feature Films. Preferred genres include Drama and Fantasy.

Alex Sagalchik
Producer
imdb.com/name/nm4215812

MOVIE MOGUL, INC.

9100 Wilshire Blvd
Suite 520E
Beverly Hills, California
90210
424-245-4331

mogul-inc.com

Does not accept any unsolicited material. Project types include Feature Films.

Deborah Harpur
CEO
imdb.com/name/nm2970095

MOVIE PACKAGE COMPANY

287 S Robertson Blvd., Suite 101
Beverly Hills, CA 90211

Does not accept any unsolicited material. Project types include Feature Films.

Shaun Redick
Producer
imdb.com/name/nm2211720

Ray Mansfield
Producer
imdb.com/name/nm1796751

MOVING PICTURES

8447 Wilshire Blvd., Suite 212
Beverly Hills, CA 90212
310-288-5464

imdb.com/name/nm3082970

Does not accept any unsolicited material. Project types include Feature Films and TV. Preferred genres include Comedy and Romance.

Peter Jaysen
Head/Producer
imdb.com/name/nm0419779

MOXIE PICTURES

5890 W Jefferson Blvd
Los Angeles, CA 90016
310-857-1000 (phone)
310-857-1004 (fax)

18 E. 16th St.
4th Floor
New York City, NY 10003
212-807-6901 (phone)
212-807-1456 (fax)

info@moxiepictures.com
moxiepictures.com
imdb.com/company/co0119462
facebook.com/moxiepictures
twitter.com/MoxiePictures
linkedin.com/company/moxie-pictures

Does not accept any unsolicited material. Project types include Feature Films and TV. Preferred genres include Comedy, Documentary, Drama, Reality, and Romance. Established in 2005.

Robert Fernandez
CEO
fernandez@moxiepictures.com
imdb.com/name/nm0273045

Katie Connell
Head of Production
katie@moxiepictures.com

Dan Levinson
President
danny@moxiepictures.com
imdb.com/name/nm1829495
linkedin.com/pub/dan-levinson/6/91b/1a5

MOZARK PRODUCTIONS

4024 Radford Ave, Bldg. 5
Studio City, CA 91604
818-655-5779 (phone)
818-655-5129 (fax)

imdb.com/company/co0023587

Does not accept any unsolicited material. Project types
include Feature Films and TV. Preferred genres
include Comedy and Drama.

Linda Bloodworth Thomason
Writer/Producer/Director
imdb.com/name/nm0089124

MPI MEDIA GROUP

16101 S 108th Ave
Orland Park, IL 60467
800-777-2223

info@mpimedia.com
mpimedia.com
imdb.com/company/co0028092

Does not accept any unsolicited material. Project types
include TV. Preferred genres include Comedy, Drama,
and Horror.

Malik Ali
Founder
imdb.com/name/nm5307398

Greg Newman
EVP
imdb.com/name/nm0628103

MRB PRODUCTIONS

311 N. Robertson Blvd., #513
Beverly HIlls, CA 90211
323-965-8881 (phone)
323-965-8882 (fax)

mrbproductions.com

twitter.com/MRBProductions1
facebook.com/pages/MRB-Productions-Inc/
   113037758751306
imdb.com/company/co0122884
linkedin.com/company/mrb-productions

Does not accept any unsolicited material. Project types
include Feature Films and TV. Preferred genres
include Comedy, Documentary, Drama, Romance,
and Thriller. Established in 2001.

Astrid Downs
Executive Producer
astrid@mrbproductions.com

Matthew Brady
Executive Producer
matthew@mrbproductions.com
imdb.com/name/nm0103683

Brenda Bank
Producer
brenda@mrbproductions.com
imdb.com/name/nm1870773
Assistant: Erica Weiss

Luke Watson
Vice-President
luke@mrbproductions.com
imdb.com/name/nm2362830
linkedin.com/pub/luke-watson/15/60a/683

MR. MUDD

137 N Larchmont Blvd, #113
Los Angeles, CA 9004
323-932-5656 (phone)
323-932-5666 (fax)

mrmudd.com

Does not accept any unsolicited material. Project types
include Feature Films. Preferred genres include
Comedy, Drama, Family, and Romance. Established
in 1998.

Lianne Halfon
Producer
imdb.com/name/nm0355147

John Malkovich
imdb.com/name/nm0000518

Russell Smith
Producer
imdb.com/name/nm0809833
linkedin.com/pub/russell-smith/2a/687/39

MTV ANIMATION

1515 Broadway, 25th Floor
New York , NY 10128

imdb.com/company/co0054176

Does not accept any unsolicited material.

Chris Lin
SVP of Production/Series Development
imdb.com/name/nm4930153

MULTI-VALENCE PRODUCTIONS

2005 Palo Verde, Suite 200
Long Beach, CA 90815
562-208-0476

alexandergarcia06@gmail.com
imdb.com/company/co0315075

Does not accept any unsolicited material. Project types include Feature Films. Preferred genres include Drama and Fantasy.

Alexander Garcia
Producer/Writer
imdb.com/name/nm0305094

MULTIVISIONNAIRE PICTURES

3080 W Valley Blvd., Suite B
Alhambra, CA 91803
626-737-8357 (phone)
626-727-8642 (fax)

multivisionnaire.com

Does not accept any unsolicited material. Project types include Feature Films.

Erika Kao-Haley
Executive Producer
imdb.com/name/nm2537107

MUSE PRODUCTIONS

15-B Brooks Ave
Venice, CA 90291
310-306-2001 (phone)
310-574-2614 (fax)

imdb.com/company/co0019350
musefilm.com

Does not accept any unsolicited material. Project types include Feature Films. Preferred genres include Drama and Thriller.

MUTUAL FILM COMPANY

150 S. Rodeo Dr, Suite 120
Beverly Hills, CA 90212
310-855-7355 (phone)
310-855-7356 (fax)

imdb.com/company/co0007500

Does not accept any unsolicited material. Project types include Feature Films and TV.

Gary Levinshohn
Producer
imdb.com/name/nm0506013

Shelly Clippard
VP of Production & Development
imdb.com/name/nm0166953

MXN

1930 Curson Ave
Los Angeles, CA 90046
323-977-0377

imdb.com/company/co0237694

Does not accept any unsolicited material. Project types include Feature Films and TV. Preferred genres include Comedy.

Mason Novick
Producer/Manager
imdb.com/name/nm1259504

MY2CENTENCES

9229 Sunset Blvd., Suite 601
West Hollywood, CA 90069

310-777-0323 (phone)
310-777-0324 (fax)

info@my2c.com
my2centences.com
imdb.com/company/co0077666

Does not accept any unsolicited material. Project types include Feature Films. Preferred genres include Drama.

Chris Williams
Partner
imdb.com/name/nm0930282

Craig Singer
Partner
imdb.com/name/nm0801916

MYRIAD PICTURES

3015 Main St, Suite 400
Santa Monica, CA 90405
310-279-4000 (phone)
310-279-4001 (fax)

info@myriadpictures.com
imdb.com/company/co0033226
myriadpictures.com
twitter.com/MyriadPictures
facebook.com/MyriadPictures1

Does not accept any unsolicited material. Project types include Feature Films. Preferred genres include Comedy, Drama, Fantasy, Horror, Non-Fiction, and Romance. Established in 1998.

Kirk D'Amico
CEO
imdb.com/name/nm0195136
linkedin.com/pub/kirk-d-amico/10/bb2/180
twitter.com/kirkdamico

MYSTICARTS PICTURES

1918 W. Magnolia Blvd., Suite 206
Burbank, CA 91505
818-563-4121 (phone)
818-563-4318 (fax)

mysticartpictures.com
imdb.com/company/co0053465

Does not accept any unsolicited material. Project types include Feature Films and TV. Preferred genres include Drama.

Katy Wallin
CEO/President/Producer
imdb.com/name/nm0002359

MYTHIC FILMS

20501 Ventura Blvd., Ste 325
Woodland Hills, CA 91364
323-660-9441 (phone)
323-660-9450 (fax)

mythicfilms.com
imdb.com/company/co0235454

Does not accept any unsolicited material. Project types include Feature Films. Preferred genres include Drama and Non-Fiction.

Ralph Hemecker
Producer, Writer, Director
imdb.com/name/nm0375973

NABU FILMS

7125 Lennox Ave Int 156
Van Nuys, CA 91405
818-646-0354

info@nabufilms.com
imdb.com/company/co0238576
nabufilms.com

Does not accept any unsolicited material.

Jessica Villegas
Producer
imdb.com/name/nm3096521

NALA FILMS

2016 Broadway Pl.
Santa Monica, CA 90404
310-264-2555

info@nalafilms.com
nalafilms.com
twitter.com/nalafilms
facebook.com/NALAFilms

Does not accept any unsolicited material. Project types include Feature Films and TV. Preferred genres include Drama and Thriller.

Emilio Barroso
CEO
imdb.com/name/nm1950898

NAMANCO PRODUCTIONS

300 E 51st St, Apt 11A
New York, NY 10022
212-688-6310

7 Audubon Pl
New Orleans, LA 70118
504-866-2888

imdb.com/company/co0010060

Does not accept any unsolicited material. Project types include Feature Films. Preferred genres include Drama.

Jimmy Walsh
Executive Producer
imdb.com/name/nm1255801

NANCY TENENBAUM FILMS

43 Lyons Plain Rd
Weston, CT 06883
203-221-6830 (phone)
203-221-6832 (fax)

ntfilms2@aol.com
imdb.com/company/co0012648
facebook.com/pages/Nancy-Tenenbaum-Films/
   159473827409156

Accepts query letter from unproduced, unrepresented writers via email. Project types include Feature Films. Preferred genres include Comedy and Drama. Established in 1996.

Meredith Hall
Director of Development

Nancy Tenenbaum
President
imdb.com/name/nm085494
Assistant: Lyndsy Celestino

NBC PRODUCTIONS

3000 W Alameda Ave
Burbank, CA 91523-0001
USA
818-840-4444

nbcuni.com
imdb.com/company/co0065874

Docs not accept any unsolicited material. Project types include Feature Films and TV. Preferred genres include Action, Comedy, Crime, Documentary, Drama, Family, Fantasy, Horror, Non-Fiction, Romance, Science Fiction, and Thriller. Established in 1947.

NBC STUDIOS

3000 W Alameda Ave
Burbank, CA 91523-0001
USA
818-526-7000

nbcuni.com
imdb.com/company/co0022762
twitter.com/nbcstudiotour

Does not accept any unsolicited material. Project types include Feature Films and TV. Preferred genres include Action, Comedy, Crime, Detective, Documentary, Drama, Non-Fiction, and Thriller. Established in 1950.

NBC UNIVERSAL

30 Rockefeller Plaza
New York, NY 10112
212-664-4444

nbcumv.com/mediavillage

Project types include Feature Films and TV. Preferred genres include Comedy, Crime, Documentary, Drama, Period, Reality, and Thriller. Established in 2009.

Jessica Franks
Development Executive

Steve Burke
President
imdb.com/name/nm4446434

Marci Klein
Executive Producer
imdb.com/name/nm0458885

Josie Ventura

Dan Berkowitz

Jon Dakss
Vice President

Pearlena Igbokwe
imdb.com/name/nm2303684

NBC UNIVERSAL TELEVISION DISTRIBUTION

3400 W. Olive Ave.
Burbank, CA 91505
818-840-4444 (phone)
818-866-1430 (fax)

30 Rockafeller Plaza
New York City, NY 10112
212-664-4444

454 N. Columbus Dr.
5th Floor
Chicago, IL 60611
312-836-5725

3340 Peachtree Rd. NE
Suite 711
Atlanta, GA 30326
404-812-3712

nbcuni.com
imdb.com/company/co0129175

Does not accept any unsolicited material. Project types include Feature Films and TV. Preferred genres include Action, Animation, Comedy, Crime, Detective, Documentary, Drama, Family, Fantasy, Horror, Reality, Science Fiction, and Thriller. Established in 1971.

Jerry DiCanio
imdb.com/name/nm3034292

Jennifer Nicholson-Salke
President
imdb.com/name/nm2323622
linkedin.com/pub/jennifer-vessio/6/b6b/436

NECROPIA ENTERTAINMENT

9171 Wilshire Blvd, Suite 300
Beverly Hills, CA 9021
323-865-0547

imdb.com/company/co0368091

Does not accept any unsolicited material. Project types include Feature Films. Preferred genres include Action, Fantasy, Horror, Myth, and Science Fiction.

Guillermo de Toro
Director
imdb.com/name/nm0868219

NEO ART & LOGIC

5225 Wilshire Blvd Ste. 501
Los Angeles, CA 90036
323-451-2040

aaron@neoartandlogic.com
imdb.com/company/co0038165

Accepts query letter from unproduced, unrepresented writers via email. Project types include Feature Films and TV. Preferred genres include Action, Animation, Comedy, Documentary, Drama, Family, Fantasy, Horror, Science Fiction, and Thriller. Established in 2000.

Kirk Morri
Executive
imdb.com/name/nm0606294

W. K. Border
imdb.com/name/nm0096176

Joel Soisson
imdb.com/name/nm0812373

Aaron Ockman
imdb.com/name/nm1845744
linkedin.com/pub/aaron-ockman/7/530/94b

NEVER NOMINATED PRODUCTIONS

6565 Sunset Blvd.
Los Angeles, CA
323-466-9200

imdb.com/company/co0422094

Does not accept any unsolicited material. Project types include TV.

Courtland Cox
SVP of Development
imdb.com/name/nm1202338

NEW AMSTERDAM ENTERTAINMENT

142 W 44th St, PH-2
New York, NY 10036
212-922-1930 (phone)
212-997-1936 (fax)

mail@newamsterdamnyc.com
newamsterdamnyc.com
imdb.com/company/co0010962
twitter.com/wix
facebook.com/pages/New-Amsterdam-Entertainment-
    Inc

Does not accept any unsolicited material. Project types include Feature Films and TV. Preferred genres include Action, Documentary, Drama, Fantasy, Horror, Science Fiction, and Thriller. Established in 1996.

Richard Rubinstein
CEO
imdb.com/name/nm0748283

Katherine Kolbert
imdb.com/name/nm0463946

Michael Messina
imdb.com/name/nm0582175

Sara Reiner
imdb.com/name/nm2200017
linkedin.com/pub/dir/Sara/Reiner

NEW ARTISTS ALLIANCE

16633 Ventura Blvd, #1440
Encino, CA 91436
818-784-8341

info@naafilms.com
newartistsalliance.com
imdb.com/company/co0237280
facebook.com/naafilms
twitter.com/naafilms

Accepts query letter from unproduced, unrepresented writers via email. Project types include Feature Films. Preferred genres include Action, Drama, Horror, and Thriller. Established in 2003.

John Suits
john@naafilms.com
imdb.com/name/nm2986811

Gabe Cowan
gabe@naafilms.com
imdb.com/name/nm1410462
linkedin.com/pub/gabriel-cowan/79/849/863

NEW CRIME PRODUCTIONS

1041 N Formosa Ave
Formosa Building, Room 219
West Hollywood, CA 90016
323-850-2525

newcrime@aol.com
imdb.com/company/co0079035

Accepts query letter from unproduced, unrepresented writers via email. Project types include Feature Films. Preferred genres include Comedy, Drama, Romance, and Thriller.

John Cusack
Executive
imdb.com/name/nm0000131
facebook.com/pages/John-Cusack/176246839075056

NEW FILMS INTERNATIONAL

14320 Ventura Blvd. # 619
Sherman Oaks, CA 91423
818-501-2720 (phone)
818-501-2780 (fax)

info@newfilmsint.com
newfilmsint.com

Does not accept any unsolicited material. Project types include Feature Films. Preferred genres include Drama, Romance, and Thriller.

Nesim Hason
President

Serap Acuner
COO

NEW HORIZONS

11600 San Vicente Blvd.
Los Angeles, CA 9004
310-820-6733 (phone)
310-207-6819 (fax)

submissions@newhorizonspix.com
newhorizonspix.com

Does not accept any unsolicited material. Project types include Feature Films and TV. Preferred genres include Action, Horror, Science Fiction, and Thriller.

Roger Corman
President/Executive Producer

Julie Corman
Sr.Exec VP/ Executive Producer

NEW LEAF LITERARY & MEDIA

110 W 40th St, Suite 410
New York, NY 10018
646-248-7989 (phone)
646-861-4654 (fax)

assist@newleafliterary.com
newleafliterary.com
facebook.com/NewLeafLiterary
twitter.com/NewLeafLiterary

Does not accept any unsolicited material. Project types include Feature Films.

Joanna Volpe
President/Agent

Pouya Shahbazian
Head of Film & TV Division/Producer

NEW LINE CINEMA

116 N Robertson Blvd
Los Angeles, CA 90048
310-854-5811 (phone)
310-854-1824 (fax)

warnerbros.com
imdb.com/company/co0046718
facebook.com/warnerbrosent
twitter.com/Warnerbrosent
linkedin.com/company/2470

Does not accept any unsolicited material. Project types include Feature Films and TV. Preferred genres include Action, Comedy, Crime, Documentary, Drama, Family, Fantasy, Non-Fiction, Period, Romance, Science Fiction, and Thriller. Established in 1967.

Andrea Johnston
Creative Executive

Michael Disco

Toby Emmerich
President
imdb.com/name/nm0256497
Assistant: Joshua Mack

Richard Brener
imdb.com/name/nm0107196
Assistant: Kristin Schmidt

Sam Brown
imdb.com/name/nm1354041
Assistant: Celia Khong

Walter Hamada
imdb.com/name/nm1023578

NEW REDEMPTION PICTURES

3000 W. Olympic Blvd, Bldg. 3
Santa Monica, CA 90404
310-315-4820

Does not accept any unsolicited material. Project types include Feature Films and TV. Preferred genres include Comedy.

John Herzfeld
Partner/Producer

NEW REGENCY FILMS

10201 W Pico Blvd
Bldg 12
Los Angeles, CA 90035
310-369-8300 (phone)
310-969-0470 (fax)

270 Lafayette St.
Suite 1505
New York City, NY 10012

212-966-3166 (phone)
212-966-3443 (fax)

info@newregency.com
newregency.com

Project types include Feature Films. Preferred genres include Action, Comedy, Crime, Drama, Family, Romance, and Science Fiction.

Justin Lam
Creative Executive
imdb.com/name/nm3528759

Arnon Milchan
Chairman
imdb.com/name/nm0586969

Mimi Tseng
CFO
imdb.com/name/nm2303729

David Manpearl
imdb.com/name/nm1818404

NEW RENAISSANCE PICTURES

15346 Saranac Dr
Whittier, CA 90604
650-722-2082

contact@newrenaissanceonline.com
newrenaissanceonline.com

Does not accept any unsolicited material. Project types include Feature Films and TV. Preferred genres include Comedy, Horror, and Science Fiction.

NEW SCHOOL MEDIA, LLC

9229 Sunset Blvd, Suite 301
West Hollywood, CA 90069
310-858-2989 (phone)
310-858-1841 (fax)

facebook.com/pages/New-School-Media-LLC/
    115508901796269/RK=0/
    RS=iOlGZEFKcSNyOB5RdRwP6zDcS3I-

Accepts query letter from unproduced, unrepresented writers. Project types include Feature Films.

Brian Levy
imdb.com/name/nm2546392
linkedin.com/pub/brian-levy/92/3b4/816

NEW WAVE ENTERTAINMENT

2660 W Olive Ave
Burbank, CA 91505
818-295-5000 (phone)
818-295-5002 (fax)

35 W. 36th St.
10th Floor
New York, NY 10018
212-594-2414 (phone)
212-239-1034 (fax)

nwe.com
imdb.com/company/co0024003
facebook.com/NewWaveEntertainment
twitter.com/NWESocial

Does not accept any unsolicited material. Project types include Feature Films, TV, and Commercials. Preferred genres include Action, Animation, Comedy, Crime, Detective, Drama, Family, Fantasy, Horror, Myth, Non-Fiction, Reality, Romance, Science Fiction, Sociocultural, and Thriller.

Paul Apel
CEO
818-295-5000
imdb.com/name/nm1318269
linkedin.com/pub/paul-apel/4/b10/682

Gregory Woertz
EVP Chief Financial Office
818-295-5000
gwoertz@nwe.com
imdb.com/name/nm0937343

NICK WECHSLER PRODUCTIONS

Santa Monica, CA
310-309-5759 (phone)
310-309-5716 (fax)

info@nwprods.com
nwprods.com
imdb.com/company/co0156991

Does not accept any unsolicited material. Project types include Feature Films and TV. Preferred genres include Action, Animation, Comedy, Crime, Drama, Family, Fantasy, Horror, Science Fiction, and Thriller. Established in 2005.

Nick Wechsler
nick@nwprods.com
imdb.com/name/nm0917059

Elizabeth Bradford
Director of Development
lizzy@nwprods.com
imdb.com/name/nm4504768
linkedin.com/pub/elizabeth-bradford/82/857/9

Felicity Aldridge
Creative Executive
felicity@nwprods.com
imdb.com/name/nm4504820
linkedin.com/pub/felicity-aldridge/98/615/923

NIGHT AND DAY PICTURES

527 W. 7th St.
Suite 402
Los Angeles, CA 90036
323-930-2212

info@nightanddaypictures.com
imdb.com/company/co0253348
nightanddaypictures.com

Accepts query letter from unproduced, unrepresented writers via email. Project types include Feature Films.

Michael Roiff
President
michael@nightanddaypictures.com
imdb.com/name/nm1988698

Rachel Berk
Creative Executive
imdb.com/company/co0157684
linkedin.com/pub/rachel-berk/29/2a9/812

NINJAS RUNNIN' WILD PRODUCTIONS

7024 Melrose Ave, Suite 420
Los Angeles, CA 90038
323-937-6100

imdb.com/company/co0308755

Accepts scripts from produced or represented writers. Project types include Feature Films.

Jason Barrett
Producer
imdb.com/name/nm2249074

Zac Effron
imdb.com/name/nm1374980

NORTH BY NORTHWEST ENTERTAINMENT

601 W. Board St
Boise, ID 83702
208-345-7870 (phone)
208-345-7999 (fax)

100 Andover Park West
Suite 150-121
Tukwila, WA 98188
206-293-8860 (phone)
206-293-8860 (fax)

903 W Broadway
Spokane, WA 99201
509-324-2949 (phone)
509-324-2959 (fax)

moviesales@nxnw.net
contact@nxnw.net
nxnw.net

Does not accept any unsolicited material. Project types include Feature Films. Preferred genres include Thriller.

Dave Tanner
CEO/Partner
509-252-2570
dtanner@nxnw.net

NOVA PICTURES

6496 Ivarene Ave.
Los Angeles, CA 90068
323-462-5502 (phone)
323-463-8903 (fax)

pbarnett@novapictures.com
info@novapictures.com
novapictures.com

Accepts query letter from unproduced, unrepresented writers via email. Project types include Feature Films.

Peter Barnett
Executive Producer
imdb.com/name/nm0055963

NUBIA FILMWORKS LLC

1516 K St S.E, Suite #303
Washington, DC 20003
202-547-1591 (phone)
202-547-0013 (fax)

info@nubiafilmworks.com
facebook.com/NocturnalAgony
nubiafilmworks.com
twitter.com/nubiafilmllc

Accepts query letter from unproduced, unrepresented writers. Project types include Feature Films and TV. Preferred genres include Drama.

Calvin "C-Note" Jackson
Development Executive
calvinj@nubiafilmworks.com

Mary Colbert
Creative Executive
240-432-6265
maryj@nubiafilmworks.com

Tara Hayman
Creative Executive
tarah@nubiafilmworks.com

Shuaib Mitchell
President
imdb.com/name/nm2712648
linkedin.com/pub/shuaib-mitchell/7/2b6/72b
facebook.com/shuaib.mitchellnubiafilmworks

NU IMAGE FILMS

6423 Wilshire Blvd
Los Angeles, CA 90048
310-388-6900 (phone)
310-388-6901 (fax)

info@millenniumfilms.com
millenniumfilms.com
imdb.com/company/co0024720
twitter.com/MillenniumFilms

facebook.com/OfficialMillenniumfilms

Does not accept any unsolicited material. Preferred genres include Action, Comedy, Drama, and Science Fiction.

Christine Crow
Director of Development
310-388-6900
imdb.com/name/nm4579268

Mark Gill
President
310-388-6900
imdb.com/name/nm1247584

John Thompson
Head of Development
310-388-6900
imdb.com/name/nm0860315

Boaz Davidson
310-388-6900
imdb.com/name/nm0203246

NUYORICAN PRODUCTIONS

1100 Glendon Ave, Suite 920
Los Angeles, CA 90024
310-943-6600 (phone)
310-943-6609 (fax)

imdb.com/company/co0021149

Does not accept any unsolicited material. Project types include Feature Films, TV, and Commercials. Preferred genres include Action, Comedy, Drama, Non-Fiction, and Reality.

Jennifer Lopez
imdb.com/name/nm0000182

Tiana Rios
Creative Executive
imdb.com/name/nm1018804

O2 FILMES

Rua Baumann, 930
Vila Leopoldina
São Paulo, SP 05318-000
Brazil

+55 1138 39 94 00 (phone)
+55 11 38 32 48 11 (fax)

O2 FILMES / RIO DE JANEIRO
Rua Pereira da Silva, 602
Laranjeiras
22221-140 Rio De Janeiro - RJ
Brasil
+55 21 31 72 99 00

faleconosco@o2filmes.com
o2filmes.com.br
imdb.com/company/co006939
twitter.com/o2filmes
facebook.com/o2filmes

Does not accept any unsolicited material. Project types include Feature Films. Preferred genres include Documentary and Drama.

Paulo Morelli
imdb.com/name/nm0603758
linkedin.com/pub/paulo-o2-filmes/22/118/41a
twitter.com/paulomorelli

OAKDALE PICTURES

15450 Kivett Ln
Reno, NV 89521
775-225-4447 (phone)
775-852-6259 (fax)

info@oakdalepictures.us
oakdalepictures.us

Does not accept any unsolicited material. Project types include Feature Films. Preferred genres include Drama.

Dana MacDuff
Producer

Brandon MacDuff
Producer

OCCUPANT FILMS

5225 Wilshire Blvd., Suite 600
Los Angeles , CA 90036
323-934-9106 (phone)
323-937-0550 (fax)

joe@occupantfilms.com
occupantfilms.com

Does not accept any unsolicited material. Project types include Feature Films. Preferred genres include Comedy, Family, and Horror.

Felipe Marino
Partner/Producer

Joe Neurauter
Partner/Producer

Kate Sharp
Production Executive

OCEAN PICTURES

9830 Wilshire Blvd.
Beverly Hills, CA 90212

Does not accept any unsolicited material. Project types include Feature Films.

Harold Ramis
Director/Writer/Producer

Suzanne Herrington
Development

Laurel Ward
Development

OCEAN SKY ENTERTAINMENT

12021 Wilshire Blvd., Suite 117
Los Angeles, CA 90025
310-472-7096

oceanskyentertainment.com
facebook.com/pages/Ocean-Sky-Entertainment/
360929067560

Does not accept any unsolicited material. Project types include Feature Films. Preferred genres include Drama and Romance.

ODDLOT ENTERTAINMENT

9601 Jefferson Blvd, Suite A
Culver City, CA 90232
310-652-0999 (phone)
310-652-0718 (fax)

2141 N. Southport Ave.
Chicago, IL 60614

info@oddlotent.com
oddlotent.com
facebook.com/oddlotent
imdb.com/company/co0113140

Does not accept any unsolicited material. Project types include Feature Films. Preferred genres include Drama.

Gigi Pritzker
CEO
imdb.com/name/nm0698133

Stacy Keppler
Director of Development
imdb.com/name/nm4139143

ODENKIRK PROVISSIERO ENTERTAINMENT

650 N Bronson Ave. Suite B-145
Los Angeles, CA 90004
323-960-4777 (phone)
323-960-4772 (fax)

info@odenkirktalent.com
odenkirktalent.com

Does not accept any unsolicited material. Project types include TV. Preferred genres include Comedy.

Naomi Odenkirk
Partner/Producer/Manager

Marc Provissiero
Partner/Producer/Manager

ODNA ENTERTAINMENT

12233 W. Olympic Blvd. Ste. 260
Los Angeles, CA 90064
310-777-3555

Does not accept any unsolicited material. Project types include Feature Films. Preferred genres include Action, Drama, and Thriller.

Moritz Borman
Producer

O ENTERTAINMENT

31878 Camino Capistrano, Suite 101
San Juan Capistrano, CA 92675
949-443-3222 (phone)
949-443-3223 (fax)

oentertainment.com

Does not accept any unsolicited material. Project types include Feature Films and TV. Preferred genres include Comedy.

Steve Oedekerk
Director/Writer/Producer/Actor

OFFSPRING ENTERTAINMENT

8755 Colgate Ave
Los Angeles, CA 90048
310-247-0019 (phone)
310-550-6908 (fax)

imdb.com/company/co0163665
facebook.com/pages/Offspring-Entertainment

Does not accept any unsolicited material. Project types include Feature Films. Preferred genres include Comedy, Drama, and Family.

Adam Shankman
Executive
imdb.com/name/nm0788202

Jennifer Gibgot
Producer
imdb.com/name/nm0316774
linkedin.com/pub/jennifer-gibgot/73/184/435

OFRENDA

3467 N. Knoll Dr
Los Angeles, CA 90068
323-851-6145

donna@ofrenda.com
ofrenda.com

Does not accept any unsolicited material. Project types include Feature Films. Preferred genres include Drama.

Luis Aira
Founder/Director

Donna Casey
Executive Producer

OLD CHARLIE PRODUCTIONS

10100 Santa Monica Blvd. Suite 1300
Los Angeles, CA 90067

Does not accept any unsolicited material. Project types include TV. Preferred genres include Comedy.

Mike Sikowitz
President/Producer/Writer

OLD CITY ENTERTAINMENT

453 S. Spring St
Suite 439
Los Angeles, CA 90013
213-465-4822

wjsaunders@oldcityentertainment.com
williamjsaunders.com
imdb.com/company/co0271474

Does not accept any unsolicited material. Project types include Feature Films, Short Films, TV, and Commercials.

William Saunders
Director
wjsaunders@oldcityentertainment.com
linkedin.com/pub/william-saunders/50/703/a32

OLIVE BRIDGE ENTERTAINMENT

10202 W Washington Blvd
Culver City, CA 90232
310-244-1269

olivebridge.com
imdb.com/company/co0219609

Does not accept any unsolicited material. Project types include Feature Films and TV. Preferred genres include Action, Comedy, Drama, Period, and Romance. Established in 2003.

Will Gluck
imdb.com/name/nm0323239

Alicia Emmrich
imdb.com/name/nm1445355

Jodi Hildebrand
imdb.com/name/nm1637492

Richard Schwartz
imdb.com/name/nm1108160
linkedin.com/pub/dir/Richard/Schwartz

OLMOS PRODUCTIONS INC.

500 S Buena Vista St
Old Animation Building, Suite 1G
Burbank, CA 91521
818-560-8651 (phone)
818-560-8655 (fax)

olmosonline@yahoo.com
edwardjamesolmos.com/fvcs
twitter.com/edwardjolmos
facebook.com/people/Edward-James-Olmos/
    1777260806
imdb.com/company/co0000821

Does not accept any unsolicited material. Project types include Feature Films, TV, and Commercials. Preferred genres include Comedy, Drama, Family, Non-Fiction, and Reality. Established in 1980.

Edward Olmos
President
edwardjamesolmos.com
imdb.com/name/nm0001579
facebook.com/EdwardJOlmos

OLYMPUS PICTURES

12424 Whilshire Blvd.
Suite 1120
Los Angeles, CA 90025
310-452-3335 (phone)
310-452-0108 (fax)

getinfo@olympuspics.com
olympuspics.com

Does not accept any unsolicited material. Project types include Feature Films. Established in 2007.

Leslie Urdang
imdb.com/name/nm0881811

Amanda Beckner
Creative Executive
rrdecter@olympuspics.com
linkedin.com/pub/amanda-beckner/43/a2a/924

O'MALLEY PRODUCTIONS

20335 Ventura Blvd., #416
Woodland Hills, CA 91364
818-884-7012 (phone)
818-884-7031 (fax)

info@omalleyproductions.com
omalleyproductions.com
facebook.com/pages/OMalley-Productions/
    106897616017333

Does not accept any unsolicited material. Project types
include TV.

OMANTRA FILMS

9415 Culver Blvd.
Culver City, CA 90232
310-558-0606 (fax)

raj@omantrafilms.com
omantrafilms.com
facebook.com/omantraraj
twitter.com/omantrafilms

Does not accept any unsolicited material. Project types
include Feature Films. Preferred genres include
Drama, Family, and Romance.

OMBRA FILMS

12444 Ventura Blvd, Suite 103
Studio City, CA 91604
818-509-0552

info@ombrafilms.com
imdb.com/company/co002701

Accepts query letter from unproduced, unrepresented
writers via email. Project types include Feature Films
and TV. Preferred genres include Fantasy, Horror, and
Thriller. Established in 2011.

Juan Sola
Producer
imdb.com/name/nm4928159

Jaume Collet-Serra
Producer
imdb.com/name/nm1429471

Pablo Larcuen
Producer
imdb.com/name/nm3631130

O.N.C. ENTERTAINMENT INC

11150 Santa Monica Blvd, Suite 450
Los Angeles, CA 90025
310-477-0670 (phone)
310-477-7710 (fax)

imdb.com/company/co0176401

Does not accept any unsolicited material. Project types
include Feature Films. Preferred genres include Action,
Comedy, Crime, Family, Romance, and Thriller.

Michael Nathanson
President
michaelnathanson@oncentertainment.com
imdb.com/name/nm0622296
linkedin.com/pub/michael-nathanson/6/20/a15
Assistant: Robyn Altman

ONEIDA INDIAN NATION

2037 Dream Catcher Plaza
Oneida, NY 13421
315-829-8900

info@oneida-nation.org
oneidaindiannation.com

Does not accept any unsolicited material. Project types
include Feature Films. Preferred genres include
Drama.

Arthur Raymond Halbritter
CEO/Producer

ONE RACE FILMS

9100 Wilshire Blvd
East Tower, Suite 535
Beverly Hills, CA 90212
310-401-6880 (phone)
310-401-6890 (fax)

info@oneracefilms.com

imdb.com/company/co0313548
vindiesel.com
oneracefilms.com

Accepts query letter from unproduced, unrepresented writers via email. Project types include Feature Films and TV. Preferred genres include Action, Crime, Drama, Science Fiction, and Thriller. Established in 1995.

Vin Diesel
imdb.com/name/nm0004874

Samantha Vincent
samantha@oneracefilms.com
imdb.com/name/nm2176972
linkedin.com/pub/samantha-vincent/6/4b0/7b0

Thyrale Thai
thyrale@oneracefilms.com
imdb.com/name/nm1394166
linkedin.com/pub/thyrale-thai/9/1b6/3a5

ONEZERO FILMS

8285 W Sunset Blvd, #2
West Hollywood, CA 90046
323-656-5852

info@onezerofilms.com

Does not accept any unsolicited material. Project types include Feature Films. Preferred genres include Drama.

Louise Runge
Founder/Partner/Producer

Samantha Housman
Partner/Producer

OOPS DOUGHNUTS PRODUCTIONS

6030 Wilshire Blvd.
Suite 101
Los Angeles, CA 90036
323-936-9811 (phone)
818-560-6185 (fax)

imdb.com/company/co0248742
facebook.com/OopsDoughnuts

Accepts query letter from unproduced, unrepresented writers. Project types include Feature Films, TV, and Commercials.

Andy Fickman
imdb.com/name/nm0275698
Assistant: Whitney Engstrom

Betsy Sullenger
Producer
imdb.com/name/nm0998095

OPEN CITY FILMS

122 Hudson St.
5th Floor
New York, NY 10013
212-255-0500 (phone)
212-255-0455 (fax)

oc@opencityfilms.com
imdb.com/company/co0091401
twitter.com/opencityfilms

Accepts query letter from unproduced, unrepresented writers via email. Project types include Feature Films and TV. Preferred genres include Non-Fiction and Reality.

Jason Kilot
imdb.com/name/nm0459852

Joana Vicente
linkedin.com/pub/jason-kliot/49/a39/982

OPENING NIGHT PRODUCTIONS

939 8th Ave, Suite #400
New York, NY 10019
212-757-8155 (phone)
212-757-8156 (fax)

info@openingnightproductions.com
openingnightproductions.com

Does not accept any unsolicited material. Project types include Feature Films. Preferred genres include Science Fiction.

Yaron Zilberman
Writer/Director/Producer

OPEN ROAD FILMS

12301 Wilshire Blvd.
Suite 600
Los Angeles, CA 90025
310-696-7575

imdb.com/company/co0178575
openroadfilms.com
twitter.com/OpenRoadFilms
facebook.com/OpenRoadFilms

Does not accept any unsolicited material. Project types include Feature Films, Short Films, and TV. Preferred genres include Action, Crime, Documentary, and Drama. Established in 2002.

Keri Safran
VP Media
imdb.com/name/nm1518819

ORBIT FILMS

137 N Larchmont Blvd. Suite 459
Los Angeles, CA 90004
323-837-5009 (phone)
323-464-4577 (fax)

info@orbit-films.com
orbit-films.com

Does not accept any unsolicited material. Project types include Feature Films. Preferred genres include Drama and Thriller.

Dror Soref
Producer/Director

ORBIT PICTURES

11755 Wilshire Blvd. Suite 2400
Los Angeles, CA 90025
310-914-4999 (phone)
310-914-4996 (fax)

phillip@orbitpics.com
orbitpics.com

Does not accept any unsolicited material. Project types include Feature Films.

ORIGINAL FILM

5930 W Jefferson Blvd
Los Angeles, CA 90016
310-445-9000 (phone)
310-575-6990 (fax)

perry@schafferrogers.com
originalfilm.com
facebook.com/OriginalFilm
imdb.com/company/co0011134

Accepts query letter from unproduced, unrepresented writers. Project types include Feature Films. Preferred genres include Action, Comedy, and Drama.

Bruce Mellon
Executive Producer
bruce@originalfilm.com
imdb.com/name/nm0578089
linkedin.com/pub/bruce-mellon/1/3a2/730

Joe Piccirillo
Executive Producer
joe@originalfilm.com
imdb.com/name/nm6311600
linkedin.com/pub/joseph-piccirillo/6/2a2/7a5

ORIGINAL MEDIA

175 Varick St
7th Floor
New York, NY 10014
212-683-3086 (phone)
212-683-3162 (fax)

933 N. La Brea Ave.
Suite 400
Los Angeles, CA 90038
323-850-7809

originalmedia.com
facebook.com/pages/Original-Media/
    119848194726628
twitter.com/OriginalMediaTV

Accepts scripts from unproduced, unrepresented writers. Project types include Feature Films and TV. Preferred genres include Comedy, Drama, Family, Romance, and Thriller.

Chelsey Trowbridge
imdb.com/name/nm2399791

Charlie Corwin
Co Creator
imdb.com/name/nm1231965

Michael Saffran
COO
linkedin.com/pub/michael-saffran/27/242/5b9

Patrick Moses
SVP Current Series and Development
linkedin.com/pub/dir/patrick/moses

Colleen Ocean Hall
SVP Unscripted Development
imdb.com/name/nm5066841
linkedin.com/pub/dir/Colleen/Hall

Jessica Matthews
VP Scripted Development
linkedin.com/pub/jessica-matthews/7b/6b8/b24

ORION ENTERTAINMENT

10397 W. Centennial Rd
Littleton, CO 80127
720-891-4839

orionentertainment.com
facebook.com/orionmultimedia
twitter.com/orionmultimedia

Does not accept any unsolicited material. Project types include TV.

Chris Dorsey
CEO and President

Larry Sletten
VP of Videography

ORLANDO ENTERTAINMENT

307 W. 6th St., Ste. 207
Royal Oak, MI 48067
310-403-2003 (phone)
313-255-1020 (fax)

orlandoent@sbcglobal.net

Does not accept any unsolicited material. Project types include Feature Films and TV. Preferred genres include Horror.

Vince Orlando
Producer

ORPHANAGE ANIMATION STUDIOS

6725 Sunset Blvd., Suite 220
Los Angeles, CA 90028
323-469-6700

theorphanage.com

Does not accept any unsolicited material. Project types include Feature Films. Preferred genres include Animation.

OSCILLOSCOPE PICTURES

511 Canal St Suite 5E
New York City, NY 10013
212-219-4029 (phone)
212-219-9538 (fax)

info@oscilloscope.net
oscilloscope.net
twitter.com/oscopelabs
facebook.com/oscopelabs
imdb.com/company/co0230412

Does not accept any unsolicited material. Project types include Feature Films. Preferred genres include Drama and Romance.

Aaron Katz
Executive

Tom Sladek
linkedin.com/pub/tom-sladek/7/388/4a9

Dan Berger
imdb.com/name/nm3088964
linkedin.com/pub/dan-berger/8/83B/93A

David Laub
imdb.com/name/nm3000864

Amanda Lebow
imdb.com/name/nm4144904

O'TAYE PRODUCTIONS

12001 Ventura Place
Suite 340
Studio City, CA 91604

USA
818-232-8580 (phone)
818-232-8108 (fax)

imdb.com/company/co0201867

Accepts query letter from unproduced, unrepresented writers. Project types include TV.

Taye Diggs
imdb.com/name/nm0004875

Jennifer Bozell
Head of Development
linkedin.com/pub/jennifer-bozell/5/74b/876

OUTERBANK ENTERTAINMENT

4000 Warner Blvd.
Burbank, CA 91522
818-954-3281 (phone)
818-977-9990 (fax)

imdb.com/company/co0048032

Accepts query letter from unproduced, unrepresented writers via email. Project types include Feature Films and TV.

Kevin Williamson
President
310-858-8711
kevin@outerbanks-ent.com
imdb.com/name/nm0932078

OUTLAW PRODUCTIONS

11054 Cashmere St
Los Angeles, CA 90049
310-476-9891

outlawfilm.com

Does not accept any unsolicited material. Project types include TV. Preferred genres include Action, Comedy, Drama, and Horror.

Deborah Jelin Newmyer
President/Producer

Michael Glassman
VP of Developement & Production

OUT OF THE BLUE ENTERTAINMENT

c/o Sony Pictures Entertainment
10202 W Washington Blvd
Astaire Building, Suite 1200
Culver City, CA 90232-3195
310-244-7811 (phone)
310-244-1539 (fax)

info@outoftheblueent.com
outoftheblueent.com
imdb.com/company/co0052395

Accepts query letter from unproduced, unrepresented writers via email. Project types include Feature Films and TV.

Toby Conroy
Creative Executive
imdb.com/name/nm1926762

Sidney Ganis
imdb.com/name/nm0304398
linkedin.com/pub/sidney-ganis/4/143/315

OVATION STUDIOS

2850 Ocean Park Blvd
Santa Monica, CA 90405
310-430-7575

ovationtv.com

Does not accept any unsolicited material. Project types include TV.

Rob Canter
SVP, Head of Production & Media Services

OVERBROOK ENTERTAINMENT

10202 W. Washington Blvd.
Poitier Building
Culver City, CA 90232
310-432-2400 (phone)
310-432-2401 (fax)

overbrookent.com
imdb.com/company/co0072775
twitter.com/officialjaden

Accepts query letter from unproduced, unrepresented writers. Project types include Feature Films and TV. Established in 1998.

Gary Glushon
310-432-2400
imdb.com/name/nm2237223
linkedin.com/pub/gary-glushon/a/270/455

Will Smith
310-432-2400
imdb.com/name/nm0000226

OVERNIGHT PRODUCTIONS

15 Mercer St, Suite 4
New York, NY 10013
212-625-0530

overnightprod.co

Does not accept any unsolicited material. Project types include Feature Films. Established in 2008.

Rick Schwartz
212-625-0530
imdb.com/name/nm0777408
linkedin.com/in/rickschwartzproducer

OWN: OPRAH WINFREY NETWORK

5700 Wilshire Blvd
Ste 120
Los Angeles, CA 90036
323-602-5500

oprah.com/own
linkedin.com/company/oprah-winfrey-network
facebook.com/ownTV
twitter.com/OprahWinfreyNet

Does not accept any unsolicited material. Preferred genres include Animation, Documentary, Family, and Reality.

Oprah Winfrey
CEO
imdb.com/name/nm0001856
twitter.com/oPRAH

OZLA PICTURES INC.

1800 Camino Palmero St
Los Angeles, CA 90046
323-876-0180 (phone)
323-876-0189 (fax)

ozla@ozla.com
imdb.com/company/co0131306

Does not accept any unsolicited material. Project types include Feature Films and TV. Established in 1992.

Takashige Ichise
Producer
323-876-0180
imdb.com/name/nm0406772
Assistant: Chiaki Yanagimoto

PACIFICA INTERNATIONAL FILM & TV CORPORATION

PO Box 8329
Northridge, CA 91237
818-831-0360 (phone)
818-831-0352 (fax)

imdb.com/company/co018571

Does not accept any unsolicited material.

Christine Iso
Executive Producer
imdb.com/name/nm1259606

PACIFIC STANDARD

9720 Wilshire Blvd
4th Floor
Beverly Hills, CA 90212
310-777-3119 (phone)
310-777-0150 (fax)

imdb.com/company/co0373561

Does not accept any unsolicited material. Project types include Feature Films. Established in 2012.

Reese Witherspoon
imdb.com/name/nm0000702

Bruna Papandrea
imdb.com/name/nm0660295

PACK CREEK PRODUCTIONS

70 Desert Solitaire
Moab, UT 84532
435-259-0924 (phone)
435-259-3594 (fax)

info@packcreekproductions.com
packcreekproductions.com
imdb.com/company/co0433125

Accepts scripts from unproduced, unrepresented writers. Project types include Feature Films and TV. Preferred genres include Documentary. Established in 2001.

Sheila Canavan
Producer
imdb.com/name/nm2614103

Michael Chandler
Producer
imdb.com/name/nm0151434

PAGE PRODUCTIONS

12800 Industrial Park Blvd. Suite 135
Plymouth, MN 55441
763-383-9400 (phone)
763-383-9500 (fax)

info@pageprod.com
pageprod.com

Accepts query letter from unproduced, unrepresented writers via email. Project types include TV.

David Page
President/Executive Producer

Roberta Brackman
VP

PAINLESS PRODUCTIONS

1410 S Centinela Ave
Los Angeles, CA 90025
310-839-9900 (phone)
310-943-8178 (fax)

painless.tv

Does not accept any unsolicited material. Project types include TV.

Jim Casey
President

Ross Kaiman
VP of Development

PALERMO PRODUCTIONS

c/o Twentieth Century Fox
10201 W Pico Blvd
Building 52, Room 103
Los Angeles, CA 90064
310-369-1900

imdb.com/company/co031209

Accepts query letter from unproduced, unrepresented writers. Project types include Feature Films and TV.

John Palermo
Producer
310-369-1911
imdb.com/name/nm0657561
Assistant: Mike Belyea

PALMSTAR ENTERTAINMENT

14622 Ventura Blvd.
Suite 755
Sherman Oaks, CA 91403
646-277-7356 (phone)
310-469-7855 (fax)

contact@palmstar.com
facebook.com/PalmStarEntertainment
linkedin.com/company/palmstar-entertainment
twitter.com/Palmstar
imdb.com/company/co0037203

Does not accept any unsolicited material. Project types include Feature Films. Preferred genres include Action, Comedy, Drama, Family, Non-Fiction, Romance, and Thriller. Established in 2004.

Michael Bassick
Co-CEO
imdb.com/name/nm2471372

Kevin Scott Frakes
CEO
imdb.com/name/nm0289694

Stephan Paternot
Chairman
imdb.com/name/nm0665456
linkedin.com/in/stephanpaternot
facebook.com/paternot

PALOMAR PICTURES

PO Box 491986
Los Angeles, CA 90049
310-440-3494

ad@palomarpics.com
imdb.com/company/co0009947

Does not accept any unsolicited material. Project types include Feature Films and TV. Established in 1992.

Joni Sighvatsson
310-440-3494
imdb.com/name/nm0797451

Aditya Ezhuthachan
Head of Development
310-440-3494
imdb.com/name/nm2149074
linkedin.com/pub/aditya-ezhuthachan/8/769/419

PANAMAX FILMS

2000 Ponce de Leon Blvd, Suite 500
Coral Gables, FL 33134

9 DesBrosses st, 2nd flr
New York, NY 10013

info@panamaxfilms.com
panamaxfilms.com

Accepts scripts from produced or represented writers. Project types include Feature Films.

James M. McNamara
Founder and Chairman

Benjamin Odell
Head of Development & Production

PANAY FILMS

500 S Buena Vista
Old Animation Bldg, Rm 3c-6
Burbank, CA 91521
818-560-4265

imdb.com/company/co0282368

Does not accept any unsolicited material. Project types include Feature Films. Preferred genres include Action, Comedy, Drama, and Fantasy.

Andrew Panay
imdb.com/name/nm0659123
Assistant: Lukas Stuart-Fry

Adam Blum
imdb.com/name/nm3597471

PANDEMONIUM

9777 Wilshire Blvd, Suite 700
Beverly Hills, CA 90212
310-550-9900 (phone)
310-550-9910 (fax)

Accepts query letter from unproduced, unrepresented writers via email. Project types include Feature Films.

Bill Mechanic
310-550-9900
imdb.com/name/nm0575312
Assistant: David Freedman

Suzanne Warren
310-550-9900
imdb.com/name/nm0913049

PANTELION FILMS

2700 Colorado Ave.
Suite 200
Santa Monica, CA 90404
310-449-9200 (phone)
310-255-3870 (fax)

1601 Cloverfield Blvd.
Suite 200
South Tower
Santa Monica, CA 90404
310-255-3000 (phone)
310-255-3908 (fax)

2000 Avendia Vasco de Quiroga
Álvaro Obregón, Mexico 01210
011-525-552612000

info@pantelionfilms.com
pantelionfilms.com
facebook.com/PantelionFilms
imdb.com/company/co0325194

Does not accept any unsolicited material. Project types include Feature Films and TV. Preferred genres

include Action, Comedy, Drama, Family, Romance, and Science Fiction. Established in 2010.

James McNamara
Chairman
imdb.com/name/nm2241044
linkedin.com/pub/jim-mcnamara/6/316/388
facebook.com/james.mcnamara.50115

Ben Odell
Head of Production & Development
310-255-5778
imdb.com/name/nm0643967
linkedin.com/pub/benjamin-odell/6/648/784
facebook.com/ben.odell.52

Paul Presburger
CEO
imdb.com/name/nm0643967
linkedin.com/pub/paul-presburger/1/569/723

Sandra Condito
President (Acquisitions & Production)
imdb.com/name/nm1354700
linkedin.com/pub/sandra-condito/2a/bb2/3a9

PANTHERA FILM FINANCE

15675 Spaulding St
Omaha, NE 68116

pantherafilm@gmail.com
pantherafilmfinance.com

Does not accept any unsolicited material. Project types include Feature Films. Preferred genres include Comedy and Family.

Edward Jarzobski
Producer

PANTHER FILMS

1888 Century Park East
14th Floor
Los Angeles, CA 90067
424-202-6630 (phone)
310-887-1001 (fax)

imdb.com/title/tt0114084

Does not accept any unsolicited material. Project types include Feature Films.

Lindsay Culpepper
424-202-6630
imdb.com/name/nm0258431
linkedin.com/pub/lindsay-culpepper/6/580/594

Brad Epstein
Producer
424-202-6630
imdb.com/name/nm0258431
linkedin.com/pub/brad-epstein/53/a35/86a

PAPA JOE ENTERTAINMENT

14804 Greenleaf St
Sherman Oaks, CA 91403
818-788-7608 (phone)
818-788-7612 (fax)

info@papjoefilms.com

Accepts query letter from unproduced, unrepresented writers via email. Project types include Feature Films and TV.

Joe Simpson
CEO
818-788-7608
imdb.com/name/nm1471425
Assistant: Heath Pliler

Erin Alexander
818-788-7608
imdb.com/name/nm0018408
Assistant: Amelia Garrison

PAPER CRANE PRODUCTIONS

Los Angeles, CA

papercraneproductions.net
imdb.com/company/co0353174
facebook.com/papercraneproductions
twitter.com/PaperCraneLA

Does not accept any unsolicited material. Project types include Feature Films, Short Films, and TV. Preferred genres include Drama.

Angelo Salvatore Restaino
Partner
angelo-restaino.com
imdb.com/name/nm1913564
facebook.com/angelo.restaino.14
twitter.com/jellostack

Emily Moss Wilson
Partner
emosswilson@gmail.com
emosswilson.com
imdb.com/name/nm2672860
linkedin.com/pub/emily-moss-wilson/7/983/881
facebook.com/emosswilson
twitter.com/emosswilson

Hugo Perez
Producer
newzdude.tumblr.com
imdb.com/name/nm3348137
linkedin.com/in/newzdude
facebook.com/newzdude
twitter.com/newzdude

Greg Wilson
Producer
imdb.com/name/nm2745424
linkedin.com/pub/greg-wilson/4/9a4/18
facebook.com/edcotafloata

Ryan Cheevers
Producer
imdb.com/name/nm2122043
linkedin.com/pub/ryan-cheevers/b0/3b3/b12
facebook.com/ryanwilliamcheevers
twitter.com/Ryan_Cheevers

PAPER STREET FILMS

265 Canal St., Suite 212
New York, NY 10013
646-524-6954 (phone)
646-417-6460 (fax)

info@paperstreetfilms.com
paperstreetfilms.com
imdb.com/company/co0222800

Does not accept any unsolicited material. Project types include Feature Films. Preferred genres include Comedy, Drama, Horror, and Thriller. Established in 2007.

Emily Buder
Creative Executive
imdb.com/name/nm1692758

Benji Kohn
Partner
imdb.com/name/nm2803928

Bingo Gubelmann
Partner
imdb.com/name/nm1292502

Austin Stark
Partner
imdb.com/name/nm0823133

Chris Papavasiliou
Partner
imdb.com/name/nm2830113

PARADIGM STUDIO

2701 2nd Ave North
Seattle, WA 98109
206-282-2161 (phone)
206-283-6433 (fax)

info@paradigmstudio.com
paradigmstudio.com
linkedin.com/in/jcomerford

Accepts query letter from unproduced, unrepresented writers via email. Project types include Feature Films and TV.

John Comerford
President
206-282-2161
imdb.com/name/nm0173766
linkedin.com/pub/dir/John/Comerford

B Dahlia
Manager
206-282-2161
imdb.com/name/nm1148338
linkedin.com/pub/b-dahlia/40/258/970

PARADOX ENTERTAINMENT

9107 Wilshire Blvd, Suite 600
Beverly Hills, CA 90210
310-271-1355 (phone)
323-655-1720 (fax)

info@paradoxent.com
imdb.com/company/co0036328

Does not accept any unsolicited material. Project types include Feature Films. Preferred genres include Action, Comedy, Drama, Fantasy, Romance, and Science Fiction.

Janet Sheppard
CFO
imdb.com/name/nm5128822

Fredrik Malmberg
imdb.com/name/nm1573406

PARALLEL MEDIA

301 N Canon Dr,
Suite 223
Beverly Hills, CA 90210
310-858-3003 (phone)
310-858-3034 (fax)

11054 Ventura Blvd.
Suite 371
Studio City, CA 91604
323-319-3944 (phone)
323-843-9921 (fax)

info@parallelmediallc.com
parallelmediafilms.com
imdb.com/company/co0198771

Does not accept any unsolicited material. Project types include Feature Films. Established in 2006.

Armen Mahdessian
Executive
linkedin.com/pub/dir/%20/Mahdessian

PARAMEDIA INC.

2120 Colorado Ave, Suite 200
Santa Monica, CA 90404

Does not accept any unsolicited material. Project types include TV.

Jim Paratore
President/Producer

Susan Favre
VP of Development

PARAMOUNT PICTURES

5555 Melrose Ave
Los Angeles, CA 90038
323-956-5000

paramount.com
twitter.com/ParamountPics
facebook.com/Paramount

Docs not accept any unsolicited material. Project types include Feature Films.

Allison Small
Creative Executive
imdb.com/name/nm1861333

Marc Evans
imdb.com/name/nm0263010

Ashley Brucks
imdb.com/name/nm2087318

PARAMYTH FILMS

264 S. La Cienega Blvd., Suite 148
Beverly Hills, CA 90211

nika@paramythfilms.com
paramythfilms.com

Accepts scripts from produced or represented writers. Project types include Feature Films. Preferred genres include Action, Drama, and Thriller.

Nika Agiashvili
Producer/Director/Writer

David Agiashvili
Producer

PARIAH

9229 Sunset Blvd
Ste 208
West Hollywood, CA 90069
USA
310-461-3460 (phone)
310-246-9622 (fax)

Does not accept any unsolicited material. Project types include Feature Films and TV.

Gavin Polone
Owner
310-461-3460
imdb.com/name/nm0689780
Assistant: Stephen Iwanyk

PARKCHESTER PICTURES

8750 Wilshire Blvd., Suite 301
Los Angeles, CA 90211
310-289-5988

Does not accept any unsolicited material. Project types include TV. Preferred genres include Drama.

Jerry Offsay
Producer

PARKER ENTERTAINMENT GROUP

8306 Wilshire Blvd
Suite #1904
Beverly Hills, CA 90211
323-400-6622 (phone)
323-400-6655 (fax)

cparker@parkerentgroup.com
info@parkerentgroup.com
parkerentgroup.com
facebook.com/parkerentgroup
imdb.com/company/co0270280

Accepts scripts from produced or represented writers. Project types include Feature Films. Established in 2008.

Gregory Parker
CEO
323-400-6622
gparker@parkerentgroup.com
imdb.com/name/nm2027023

Christopher Parker
President
cparker@parkerentgroup.com
imdb.com/name/nm2034521
twitter.com/indianapapi

PARKER FILM COMPANY

1101 Fifth Ave Suite 300
San Rafael, CA 94901

parkerfilmcompany.com

Does not accept any unsolicited material. Project types include Feature Films. Preferred genres include Drama.

Jonathan Parker
Writer/Director

Catherine di Napoli
Writer/Producer

PARKES/MACDONALD PRODUCTIONS

1663 Euclid St
Santa Monica, CA 90404
310-581-5990 (phone)
310-581-5999 (fax)

imdb.com/company/co0112928

Accepts query letter from unproduced, unrepresented writers. Project types include Feature Films and TV. Established in 2007.

Laurie MacDonald
Producer
310-581-5990
imdb.com/name/nm0531827

Walter Parkes
Producer
310-581-5990
imdb.com/name/nm0662748
linkedin.com/pub/dir/walter/parkes

PARKWAY PRODUCTIONS

7095 Hollywood Blvd, Suite 1009
Hollywood, CA 90028
323-874-6207

parkwayprods@aol.com
imdb.com/company/co0063736

Accepts query letter from unproduced, unrepresented writers via email. Project types include Feature Films and TV.

Penny Marshall
323-874-6207
imdb.com/name/nm0001508

PARTICIPANT MEDIA

331 Foothill Rd
3rd Floor
Beverly Hills, CA 90210
310-550-5100 (phone)
310-550-5106 (fax)

info@participantproductions.com
participantmedia.com
imdb.com/company/co013277
facebook.com/ParticipantMedia
twitter.com/_Participant

Does not accept any unsolicited material. Project types include Feature Films and TV. Preferred genres include Non-Fiction and Reality. Established in 2004.

Erik Andreasen
310-550-5100
imdb.com/name/nm1849675

Jonathan King
Executive Vice President of Production
310-550-5100
imdb.com/name/nm2622896
linkedin.com/pub/jonathan-king/B/A60/1B0

PARTIZAN ENTERTAINMENT

1545 Wilcox Ave Suite 200
Hollywood, CA 90028
323-468-0123 (phone)
323-468-0129 (fax)

285 W. Broadway
Suite 330
New York, NY 10013
212-388-0123 (phone)
212-625-2040 (fax)

Feature%20Films,%20Television
partizan.com
facebook.com/partizan
twitter.com/wearepartizan

Does not accept any unsolicited material. Project types include Feature Films and TV. Preferred genres include Action, Animation, Comedy, Crime, Drama, Fantasy, Horror, Romance, Science Fiction, and Thriller. Established in 1991.

Lori Stonebraker
lstonebraker@partizan.us

Matt Tucker
matt.tucker@partizan.com

Sheila Stepanek
Executive Producer
sstepanek@partizan.us

Li-Wei Chu
Head of Production & Development
liwei.chu@partizan.us
linkedin.com/in/liweichu

PARTS AND LABOR FILMS

177 N 10th St
Brooklyn, NY 11211
718-599-5244

Does not accept any unsolicited material. Project types include Feature Films. Preferred genres include Drama and Romance.

Jay Van Hoy
Producer

Lars Knudsen
Producer

PATHE PICTURES

6 Ramillies St
4th Floor
London W1F 7TY
United Kingdom
442-073-235151 (phone)
+44207-631-3568 (fax)

reception.desk@pathe-uk.com
pathe-uk.com

Does not accept any unsolicited material. Project types include Feature Films and TV. Preferred genres include Non-Fiction and Reality.

Bradley Quirk
Creative Executive
imdb.com/name/nm1574955
facebook.com/bradley.quirk

PATRICIA K. MEYER PRODUCTIONS

511 Hill St #313
Santa Monica , CA 90405
310-392-0422

imdb.com/company/co0061979

Does not accept any unsolicited material. Project types include Feature Films and TV.

Patricia K. Meyer
Writer/Producer/Director
imdb.com/name/nm0583307

PATRIOT PICTURES

PO Box 46100
West Hollywood, CA 90046
323-874-8850 (phone)
323-874-8851 (fax)

info@patriotpictures.com
contact@patriotpictures.com
patriotpictures.com

Accepts query letter from unproduced, unrepresented writers via email. Project types include Feature Films and TV. Preferred genres include Non-Fiction and Reality.

Michael Mendelsohn
323-874-8850
imdb.com/name/nm0578861
linkedin.com/pub/michael-mendelsohn/19/5/b74

PAURA PRODUCTIONS

11150 Santa Monica Blvd, Suite 450
Los Angeles, CA 90025
310-477-7776 (phone)
310-477-7710 (fax)

info@pauraprod.com
imdb.com/company/co0134381
pauraprod.com
facebook.com/pages/Paura-Productions/
    100226523363013

Accepts query letter from unproduced, unrepresented writers via email. Project types include Feature Films. Preferred genres include Comedy, Crime, Drama, and Thriller.

Catherine Paura
Executive
imdb.com/name/nm0667474

Wayne Kline
Executive
imdb.com/name/nm0459679

Joseph Farrell
Executive

PCH FILM

3380 Motor Ave
Los Angeles, CA 90034
310-841-5817

info@pchfilm.com
pchfilms.com
imdb.com/company/co0127673

Accepts scripts from unproduced, unrepresented writers via email. Project types include Feature Films. Preferred genres include Comedy and Romance.

Kayla Thorton
310-841-5817
kayla@pchfilm.com
imdb.com/name/nm4267414
linkedin.com/pub/kayla-thornton/6/911/378

PEACE ARCH ENTERTAINMENT

4640 Admiralty Way, Suite 710
Marina del Rey, CA 90292
310-776-7200 (phone)
310-823-7147 (fax)

info@peacearch.com
imdb.com/company/co0078130

Does not accept any unsolicited material. Project types include Feature Films and TV. Established in 1986.

Sudhanshu Saria
310-776-7200
ssaria@peacearch.com
imdb.com/name/nm2738818

PEACE BY PEACE PRODUCTIONS

14757 Royal Way;
Truckee, CA 96161
530-582-8000

peacebypeace1@mac.com
peaceproductions.org

Accepts query letter from unproduced, unrepresented writers via email. Project types include Feature Films and TV.

Alyssa Milano
Producer
323-552-1097
imdb.com/name/nm0000192
Assistant: Kelly Kall

PEACEOUT PRODUCTIONS

1299 Ocean Ave, Suite 333
Santa Monica, CA 90401

Does not accept any unsolicited material. Project types include TV. Preferred genres include Crime, Drama, and Romance.

Judith Verno
President/Producer

PEARL PICTURES

10956 Weyburn Ave, Suite 200
Los Angeles, CA 90024
310-443-7773

pearlpics.com

Does not accept any unsolicited material. Project types include TV.

Gary Pearl
Producer

PEGGY RAJSKI PRODUCTIONS

2 Washington Square Village
Suite 14I
New York, NY 10012
323-634-7020 (phone)
323-634-7021 (fax)

imdb.com/company/co0011800

Does not accept any unsolicited material. Project types include Feature Films and TV. Preferred genres include Non-Fiction and Reality.

Peggy Rajski
Producer
323-634-7020
rajskip@aol.com
imdb.com/name/nm0707475

PERFECT STORM ENTERTAINMENT

1850 Industrial St, Penthouse
Los Angeles, CA 90021

info@theperfectstorment.com
perfectstorment.com

Does not accept any unsolicited material. Project types include Feature Films.

Justin Lin
Director
imdb.com/name/nm0510912

PERISCOPE ENTERTAINMENT

2340 Kenilworth Ave
Los Angeles, CA 90039
323-663-4657 (phone)
323-663-6326 (fax)

periscopeentertainment.com

Does not accept any unsolicited material. Project types include Feature Films.

David Guy Levy
Executive Producer

Ryle Eddings
SVP of Development

PERMUT PRESENTATIONS

3535 Hayden Ave
4th Floor
Culver City, CA 90232
USA
310-838-0100 (phone)
310-838-0105 (fax)

info@permutpres.com

imdb.com/company/co0011800

Accepts query letter from unproduced, unrepresented writers. Project types include Feature Films and TV.

Chris Mangano
Development Executive
310-248-2792
imdb.com/name/nm2032016

David Permut
310-248-2792
imdb.com/name/nm0674303

PERSISTENT ENTERTAINMENT

10960 Wilshire Blvd. Suite 700
Los Angeles, CA 90024
310-777-0126 (phone)
310-777-5259 (fax)

info@persistent-ent.com
persistentpictures.com

Accepts query letter from produced or represented writers. Project types include Feature Films. Preferred genres include Drama.

PETER ENGEL PRODUCTIONS

2660 W Olive Ave
Burbank, CA 91505
818-295-5000

imdb.com/company/co0033113

Does not accept any unsolicited material. Project types include TV. Preferred genres include Comedy.

Peter Engel
Principal, Producer
imdb.com/name/nm0257137

PETERS ENTERTAINMENT

21731 Ventura Blvd.
Woodland Hills, CA 91364

Does not accept any unsolicited material. Project types include Feature Films.

Jon Peters
Producer

Adele Heydenrich
VP

PFEFFER FILM

500 S. Buena Vista Blvd. Animation Bldg.
Burbank, CA 91521
818-560-3177 (phone)
818-843-7485 (fax)

Does not accept any unsolicited material. Project types include Feature Films. Preferred genres include Drama, Romance, and Thriller.

Rachel Pfeffer
Producer

PHOENIX PICTURES

10203 Santa Monica Blvd
Suite 400
Los Angeles, CA 90067
424-298-2788 (phone)
424-298-2588 (fax)

info@phoenixpictures.com
phoenixpictures.com

Accepts query letter from unproduced, unrepresented writers via email. Project types include Feature Films and TV.

Ali Toukan
Creative Executive
424-298-2788
imdb.com/name/nm4371255

Edward McGurn
424-298-2788
imdb.com/name/nm0570342

Douglas McKay
424-298-2788
imdb.com/name/nm1305822

PIC AGENCY

6161 Santa Monica Blvd Suite 300
Hollywood, CA 90038
323-461-2900 (phone)
323-461-2909 (fax)

info@picagency.com

picagency.com

Does not accept any unsolicited material. Project types include Feature Films. Preferred genres include Drama.

PICTURE ENTERTAINMENT

3400 Airport Ave
Santa Monica, CA 90405
310-397-7150

info@pictureentertainment.com
pictureentertainment.com

Does not accept any unsolicited material. Project types include Feature Films and TV. Preferred genres include Drama.

Lee Caplin
Chairman/Manager/Producer

Sonia Mintz
Development

PICTUREMAKER PRODUCTIONS

13949 Ventura Blvd. Suite 205
Sherman Oaks, CA 91423
818-783-8400 (phone)
818-783-8401 (fax)

Does not accept any unsolicited material. Project types include TV. Preferred genres include Drama.

Glenn Gordon Caron
Writer/Producer

PICTURE SHACK ENTERTAINMENT

115 W 30th St, 6th Floor
New York, NY 10001
646-674-3050

info@pictureshackentertainment.com
pictureshackentertainment.com

Does not accept any unsolicited material. Project types include TV. Preferred genres include Comedy, Horror, and Thriller.

George Plamondon
Producer

Betsy Schechter
Producer

PIERCE WILLIAMS ENTERTAINMENT

1531 14th St
Santa Monica, CA 90404
310-656-9440 (phone)
310-656-9441 (fax)

imdb.com/company/co0009226

Project types include Feature Films. Preferred genres include Drama, Horror, and Thriller.

Mark Williams
Executive Producer
imdb.com/name/nm0931251

PIERPOLINE FILMS

17 W 24th St, Suit 305
New York, NY 10010
212-255-2340

info@pierpolinefilms.com
pierpolinefilms.com

Does not accept any unsolicited material. Project types include Feature Films. Preferred genres include Drama and Thriller.

Joyce Pierpoline
Producer

PILLER/SEGAN/SHEPHERD

7025 Santa Monica Blvd
Hollywood, CA 90038
323-817-1100 (phone)
323-817-1131 (fax)

imdb.com/company/co0310765

Accepts query letter from unproduced, unrepresented writers. Project types include Feature Films and TV. Established in 2010.

Shawn Piller
323-817-1100
imdb.com/name/nm0683525

Scott Shepherd
323-817-1100
imdb.com/name/nm0791863

Lloyd Segan
323-817-1100
imdb.com/name/nm0781912
linkedin.com/pub/lloyd-segan/59/991/427

PINE STREET ENTERTAINMENT

4000 Warner Blvd. Bldg. 146 Rm. 204
Burbank, CA 91522
818-954-3279 (phone)
818-977-9713 (fax)

general.info@pinestreetent.com
pinestreetent.com

Does not accept any unsolicited material. Project types include TV.

PINK SLIP PICTURES

1314 N. Coronado St.
Los Angeles, CA 90026
USA
213-483-7100 (phone)
213-483-7200 (fax)

pinkslip@earthlink.net
imdb.com/company/co0123114

Does not accept any unsolicited material. Project types include Feature Films and TV.

Max Wong
Producer
213-483-7100
imdb.com/name/nm0939246

Karen Firestone
Producer
949-228-2354
karenfirestone@hotmail.com
imdb.com/name/nm0278652

PIONEER PICTURES

9229 W. Sunset Blvd. Suite 608
West Hollywood, CA 90069

310-273-8825 (phone)
310-273-8842 (fax)

pioneer-pictures.com

Does not accept any unsolicited material. Project types include Feature Films and TV. Preferred genres include Drama.

Robert Kravis
Producer

Karl Herrmann
Producer

PIPELINE ENTERTAINMENT INC.

330 W 42nd St
Suite 1106
New York, NY 10036
212-372-7509

pipeline-talent.com
imdb.com/company/co0215262

Accepts query letter from unproduced, unrepresented writers. Project types include Feature Films and TV. Preferred genres include Action, Comedy, Crime, Drama, and Thriller.

Dan De Fillipo
Manager
dan@pipeline-talent.com
imdb.com/name/nm2496568

Virginia Donovan
Director of Film Financing
virginia@pipeline-talent.com
imdb.com/name/nm3270342

Dave Marken
Manager
dave@pipeline-talent.com
imdb.com/name/nm2441741

PIXAR

1200 Park Ave
Emeryville, CA 94608
510-922-3000 (phone)
510-922-3151 (fax)

publicity@pixar.com
imdb.com/company/co0017902

pixar.com
facebook.com/DisneyPixar
twitter.com/disneypixar

Does not accept any unsolicited material. Project types include Feature Films. Preferred genres include Animation, Comedy, Family, and Fantasy.

Jim Morris
Producer
imdb.com/name/nm0606640

John Lasseter
imdb.com/name/nm0005124

Ed Catmull
President
imdb.com/name/nm0146216
twitter.com/edcatmull

PLAN B ENTERTAINMENT

9150 Wilshire Blvd
Beverly Hills, CA 90212
310-205-5166 (phone)
310-275-5234 (fax)

imdb.com/company/co0136967
facebook.com/pages/Plan-B-Entertainment/
    104009369636628

Does not accept any unsolicited material. Project types include Feature Films and TV. Preferred genres include Action, Animation, Drama, Fantasy, and Myth. Established in 2004.

Sarah Esberg
Producer
310-275-6135
imdb.com/name/nm1209665

Brad Pitt
Producer
310-275-6135
imdb.com/name/nm0000093

Jeremy Kleiner
Producer
imdb.com/name/nm1250070

PLATFORM ENTERTAINMENT

128 Sierra St
El Segundo, CA 90425
310-322-3737 (phone)
310-322-3729 (fax)

imdb.com/company/co0085659

Accepts query letter from unproduced, unrepresented writers. Project types include Feature Films. Established in 1998.

Daniel Levin
Producer
310-322-3737
imdb.com/name/nm0505575

Larry Gabriel
Producer
310-322-3737
imdb.com/name/nm0300181

Scott Sorrentino
Producer
310-322-3737
imdb.com/name/nm1391744

PLATINUM DUNES

631 Colorado Ave
Santa Monica, CA 90401
310-319-6565 (phone)
310-319-6570 (fax)

imdb.com/company/co0071240
twitter.com/platinumdunes
facebook.com/pages/Platinum-Dunes/
    108426449182341

Does not accept any unsolicited material. Project types include Feature Films and TV. Established in 2001.

Michael Bay
Partner
imdb.com/name/nm0000881

Bradley Fuller
Producer
imdb.com/name/nm0298181

Andrew Form
Producer
imdb.com/name/nm0286320

PLATINUM STUDIOS

2029 S Westgate Ave
Los Angeles, CA 90025
United States
310-807-8100 (phone)
310-887-3943 (fax)

info@platinumstudios.com
platinumstudios.com

Does not accept any unsolicited material. Project types include Feature Films. Preferred genres include Science Fiction.

Scott Mitchell Rosenberg
Producer

Dave Collins
Director of Film & Television

PLAYTONE PRODUCTIONS

PO Box 7340
Santa Monica, CA 90406
310-394-5700 (phone)
310-394-4466 (fax)

playtone.com
imdb.com/company/co0101441
facebook.com/TomHanks
twitter.com/tomhanks

Does not accept any unsolicited material. Project types include Feature Films and TV. Established in 1996.

Tom Hanks
Partner
310-394-5700
imdb.com/name/nm0000158

PLUM PICTURES

Plum Pictures
33 Oval Rd
London NW1 7EA
+44 (0207-184-5700

info@plumpictures.co.uk
imdb.com/company/co0284770
plumpictures.co.uk
twitter.com/plumpictures
facebook.com/plum.pictures.7

Does not accept any unsolicited material. Project types include Feature Films. Preferred genres include Comedy and Drama. Established in 2007.

Will Daws
Managing Director

Stuart Cabb
Managing Director

Rob White
Head of Development

Kari Lia
Producer

Mark Jones
Executive Producer

Victoria Moss
Head of Production

Dan Lewis
Producer

Max Andrews
Producer

Paul Cohen
Director

Andy Dugdale
Finance Director

Carly Shear
Legal & Business Affairs Manager

Kate Wilson
Director of Operations

Nicholas Berry
Editor

POILEYWOOD ENTERTAINMENT

200 Grandview Place
Longwood, FL 32712

scottpoiley@poileywood.com
poileywood.com

Does not accept any unsolicited material. Project types include Feature Films. Preferred genres include Horror and Thriller.

POINT ROAD FILMS

1041 N. Formosa Ave., Writer's Bldg., Suite 9
West Hollywood, 90046

Does not accept any unsolicited material. Project types include Feature Films. Preferred genres include Action, Drama, and Horror.

John Moore
Partner/Director/Producer

Peter Veverk
Partner/Producer

POINTS WEST PICTURES

9100 Wilshire Blvd. Suite 1000w
Beverly Hills, CA 90212

Does not accept any unsolicited material. Project types include Feature Films and TV. Preferred genres include Comedy and Drama.

Jon Hamm
Actor/Producer

Jennifer Westfeldt
President/Actor/Producer/Writer

POKER PRODUCTIONS

3395 S Jones Blvd. Ste 318
Las Vegas, NV 89146
701-221-9252

pokerprod.com

Does not accept any unsolicited material. Project types include TV.

Mori Eskandani
President

POLSKY FILMS

8938 Keith Ave
West Hollywood, CA 90069
310-278-1454

info@polskyfilms.com
imdb.com/company/co0202713
facebook.com/pages/Polsky-Films/139696959381434

Does not accept any unsolicited material. Project types include Feature Films. Preferred genres include Crime, Documentary, and Drama.

Alan Polsky
Producer
imdb.com/name/nm2611223

Gabe Polsky
Producer
imdb.com/name/nm2126907

Liam Satre-Meloy
Executive
imdb.com/name/nm3176310

POLYMORPHIC PICTURES

4000 Warner Blvd
Building 81, Suite 212
Burbank, CA 91522
818-954-3822

imdb.com/company/co0297133

Does not accept any unsolicited material. Project types include Feature Films. Established in 2010.

Polly Johnsen
Producer
imdb.com/name/nm1480881

Sarah Emerson
Creative Assistant

POPART FILM FACTORY

23679 Calabasas Rd, Suite 686
Calabasas, CA 91302

popartfilms@earthlink.net
popartfilmfactory.com

Does not accept any unsolicited material. Project types include Feature Films. Preferred genres include Action, Crime, Drama, and Science Fiction.

PORCHLIGHT ENTERTAINMENT

11050 Santa Monica Blvd., 3rd Floor
Los Angeles , CA 90025
310-477-8400 (phone)
310-477-5555 (fax)

info@porchlight.com
porchlight.com

Does not accept any unsolicited material. Project types include Feature Films and TV.

Bruce D. Johnson
CEO/President

PORCHLIGHT FILMS

94 Oxford St
Suite 31
Darlinghurst NSW 2010
Australia
61-2-9326-9916 (phone)
61-2-9357-1479 (fax)

admin@porchlightfilms.com.au
porchlightfilms.com.au
imdb.com/company/co0141203
twitter.com/porchlightfilms

Project types include Feature Films and TV. Preferred genres include Comedy, Crime, Drama, Horror, and Thriller. Established in 1996.

Vincent Sheehan
Producer
vincent@porchlightfilms.com.au
imdb.com/name/nm0790636

Anita Sheehan
Producer
imdb.com/name/nm1618460

Liz Watts
Producer
imdb.com/name/nm0915192

PORTERGELLER ENTERTAINMENT

6352 De Longpre Ave
Los Angeles, CA 90028
323-822-4400 (phone)
323-822-7270 (fax)

info@portergeller.com
imdb.com/company/co0220606

Does not accept any unsolicited material. Project types include Feature Films and TV.

Darryl Porter
Producer
imdb.com/name/nm0692080

Michael Tyree
Producer
imdb.com/name/nm2699784

POW! ENTERTAINMENT

9440 Santa Monica Blvd, Suite 620
Beverly Hills, CA 90210
310-275-9933 (phone)
310-285-9955 (fax)

info@powentertainment.com
powentertainment.com
imdb.com/company/co0109379
linkedin.com/company/stan-lee's-pow-entertainment
facebook.com/pages/POW-Entertainment/
    114580325221034

Accepts query letter from unproduced, unrepresented writers via email. Project types include Feature Films and TV. Established in 2001.

Gill Champion
CEO

Stan Lee
CCO
imdb.com/name/nm0498278
twitter.com/TheRealStanLee

POWER UP FILMS

419 N Larchmont Blvd #283
Los Angeles, CA 90004
323-463-3154

info@powerupfilms.org
powerupfilms.org
imdb.com/company/co0026662
twitter.com/thrashPOWrUPfLm
facebook.com/pages/POWER-UP-films/99261618727

Accepts query letter from unproduced, unrepresented writers via email. Project types include Feature Films and TV. Established in 2000.

Stacy Codikow
Founder
imdb.com/name/nm0168499

Lisa Thrasher
President of Film Production
imdb.com/name/nm1511212

PRACTICAL PICTURES

2211 Corinth Ave
Los Angeles, CA 90064
310-405-7777

imdb.com/company/co0172687
facebook.com/pages/Practical-Pictures/
  160830843940750

Does not accept any unsolicited material.

Jason Koffeman
Creative Executive
imdb.com/name/nm1788896

PRANA STUDIOS

1145 N McCadden Place
Los Angeles, CA 90038
323-645-6500 (phone)
323-645-6510 (fax)

info@pranastudios.com
pranastudios.com
imdb.com/company/co0206196
facebook.com/PRANASTUDIOS

Project types include Feature Films. Preferred genres include Action, Animation, Comedy, Drama, Family, and Fantasy.

Danielle Sterling
VP of Development
imdb.com/name/nm1306678

Kristin Dornig
Co-Creative Director & CEO
imdb.com/name/nm0233921

Samir Hoon
President
tescom.rs/3/samir-hoon
imdb.com/name/nm0393696
linkedin.com/pub/dir/Samir/Hoon

Arish Fyzee
Creative Director
imdb.com/name/nm0299564
linkedin.com/pub/arish-fyzee/14/38B/9A5

PREFERRED CONTENT

6363 Wilshire Blvd, Suite 350
Los Angeles, CA 90048
323-782-9193

info@preferredcontent.net
imdb.com/company/co0323647
preferredcontent.net
facebook.com/preferredcontent
linkedin.com/company/preferred-content

Does not accept any unsolicited material. Project types include Feature Films. Preferred genres include Action. Established in 2010.

Trace Sheehan
Producer
imdb.com/name/nm2618717

Ross Dinerstein
Producer
imdb.com/name/nm1895871

Kevin Iwashina
Producer
imdb.com/name/nm2250990

PREFERRED FILM & TV

6363 Wilshire Blvd
Los Angeles, CA 90048
323-782-9193

facebook.com/PreferredFilmTv

Does not accept any unsolicited material. Project types include Feature Films and TV. Preferred genres include Horror and Thriller.

Ross Dinerstein
Partner/Producer

PREGER ENTERTAINMENT

6175 NW 167th St, Suite G10
Hialeah, FL 33015
305-893-0207

info@pregerentertainment.com
pregerentertainment.com

Does not accept any unsolicited material. Project types include Feature Films. Preferred genres include Drama and Horror.

Michael Preger
Producer

David Norton
Production Executive

PRELUDE PICTURES

1711 Worthington Rd., Suite 108
West Palm Beach, FL 33409
561-683-6614 (phone)
561-683-6615 (fax)

preludepictures.com

Does not accept any unsolicited material. Project types include Feature Films. Preferred genres include Comedy and Drama.

PRETTY MATCHES PRODUCTIONS

1790 Broadway, 20th Floor
New York, New York 10019
212-512-5755

imdb.com/company/co0173730

Accepts query letter from unproduced, unrepresented writers. Project types include Feature Films and TV. Preferred genres include Comedy, Non-Fiction, Reality, and Romance. Established in 2005.

Sarah Parker
Principal
imdb.com/name/nm0000572

Alison Benson
Producer
imdb.com/name/nm3929030
linkedin.com/pub/alison-benson/45/930/826
Assistant: Matt Nathanson

PRETTY PICTURES

100 Universal City Plaza
Building 2352-A, 3rd Floor

Universal City, CA 91608
818-733-0926 (phone)
818-866-0847 (fax)

imdb.com/company/co0011868

Does not accept any unsolicited material. Project types include Feature Films and TV. Preferred genres include Comedy, Drama, Non-Fiction, Romance, and Thriller.

Gail Mutrux
Producer
imdb.com/name/nm0616153

Tore Schmidt
Producer
imdb.com/name/nm1664013

PRIMARY PRODUCTIONS

440 Lafayette St, 6th Floor
New York, NY 10003
212-674-1400

Does not accept any unsolicited material. Project types include Feature Films. Preferred genres include Comedy and Family.

Amy Kaufman
Producer

Nick Kreiss
Creative Executive

PRINCIPATO-YOUNG ENTERTAINMENT

9465 Wilshire Blvd, Suite 900
Beverly Hills, CA 90212
310-274-4474

261 Madison Ave.
9th Floor
New York, NY 10016
212-725-0010

imdb.com/company/co0049718
principatoyoung.com
linkedin.com/company/principato-young-
    entertainment
facebook.com/pages/Principato-Young-Entertainment/
    199597900062880
twitter.com/PYE_Digital

Accepts query letter from unproduced, unrepresented writers. Project types include Feature Films and TV. Preferred genres include Comedy.

Peter Principato
Partner
imdb.com/name/nm1213782
Assistant: Max Suchov

Paul Young
Partner
imdb.com/name/nm1116986

David Gardner
Partner
imdb.com/name/nm2148266

Brian Dobbins
Partner
imdb.com/name/nm1827666

Allen Fischer
Partner
imdb.com/name/nm1461672

PROCESS MEDIA

225 Broadway
New York, NY 10007
212-219-3209 (phone)
212-219-3417 (fax)

info@process-media.com
process-media.com

Does not accept any unsolicited material. Preferred genres include Comedy and Drama.

Tim Perell
Producer

PRODCO, INC.

427 S Victory Blvd
Burbank, CA 91502

Does not accept any unsolicited material. Project types include TV. Preferred genres include Comedy, Drama, and Family.

Lindsay Dwyer
Production Coordinator

PRODUCTION POINT

1223 Wilshire Blvd. Suite #947
Santa Monica, CA 90403
310-459-8989 (phone)
310-496-2780 (fax)

productionpoint.com

Does not accept any unsolicited material. Project types include Feature Films. Preferred genres include Drama.

Brandon Hooper
President

Jason McClaren
Vice President

PROFILES TELEVISION PRODUCTIONS

200 N. Continental Blvd., 3rd Floor
El Segundo, CA 90245

facebook.com/pages/Profiles-Television-Productions-LLC/130341067065498

Does not accept any unsolicited material. Project types include TV.

Bertram van Munster
Co-Founder/Executive Producer

Elise Doganieri
Co-Founder/Executive Producer

PROLIFIC ENTERTAINMENT

25 Broadway
New York, NY 10004
212-412-9188 (phone)
347-287-6702 (fax)

general@prolific-ent.com
prolific-ent.com

Does not accept any unsolicited material. Project types include Feature Films. Preferred genres include Science Fiction.

Will Rowbotham
Producer/Manager

PROMETHEUS ENTERTAINMENT

6430 Sunset Blvd., Suite 1450
Los Angeles, CA 90028
323-769-4000 (phone)
323-769-4060 (fax)

prometheusentertainment.com

Does not accept any unsolicited material. Project types include Feature Films and TV. Preferred genres include Drama and Science Fiction.

Kevin J. Burns
President

Scott Hartford
EVP of Development & Production

PROSPECTOR PRODUCTIONS

1495 Hancock St
Quincy, MA
617-328-1467

info@prospectorproductions.com
prospectorproductions.com

Does not accept any unsolicited material. Project types include TV.

PROSPECT PARK

2049 Century Park East #2550
Century City, CA 90067
310-746-4900 (phone)
310-746-4890 (fax)

imdb.com/company/co0276484

Accepts query letter from unproduced, unrepresented writers via email. Project types include Feature Films and TV. Preferred genres include Drama, Non-Fiction, and Reality.

Jeff Kwatinetz
Executive Producer
imdb.com/name/nm0477153

Paul Frank
imdb.com/name/nm1899773

PROTOZOA PICTURES

104 N 7th St
Brooklyn, NY 11211
718-388-5280 (phone)
718-388-5425 (fax)

imdb.com/company/co0062935

Does not accept any unsolicited material. Project types include Feature Films. Preferred genres include Action, Fantasy, Horror, Science Fiction, and Thriller.

Darren Aronofsky
imdb.com/name/nm0004716

PUNCHED IN THE HEAD PRODUCTIONS

540 President St, Suite #1D
Brooklyn, NY 11215
718-422-0704

punchedinthehead.com

Does not accept any unsolicited material. Project types include TV.

Craig D'Entrone
Producer/Director

Amelia D'Entrone
Producer

PUNCH PRODUCTIONS

11661 San Vincente Blvd., Suite 222
Los Angeles , CA 90049
310-442-4880 (phone)
310-442-4884 (fax)

Does not accept any unsolicited material. Preferred genres include Comedy and Drama.

Dustin Hoffman
Actor/Owner

PURE GRASS FILMS, LTD.

1st Floor, 16 Manette St
London, W1D 4AR

info@puregrassfilms.com
puregrassfilms.com

facebook.com/puregrassfilms
twitter.com/puregrassfilms

Does not accept any unsolicited material. Project types include Feature Films. Preferred genres include Action, Drama, Horror, Non-Fiction, Science Fiction, and Thriller.

Ben Grass
imdb.com/name/nm2447240

PURPLE ROSE FILMS

137 Park St
Chelsea, MI 48118
734-433-7782

purplerosefilms@aol.com

Does not accept any unsolicited material. Project types include Feature Films.

Jeff Daniels
Partner

PUSH IT PRODUCTIONS

121 W. Lexington Dr, Suite 635
Glendale, CA 91203
818-480-6519

page@pushitprods.com
pushitprods.com

Does not accept any unsolicited material. Project types include TV. Preferred genres include Comedy.

Wanda Sykes
Actor/Host/Producer

Page Hurwitz
Producer

QED INTERNATIONAL

1800 N Highland Ave, 5th Floor
Los Angeles, CA 90028
323-785-7900 (phone)
323-785-7901 (fax)

info@qedintl.com
qedintl.com
imdb.com/company/co0178111

facebook.com/pages/QED-International/
97974558257
twitter.com/QEDIntl

Accepts scripts from unproduced, unrepresented writers. Project types include Feature Films. Preferred genres include Action, Comedy, Crime, Drama, Fantasy, Horror, Myth, Romance, and Thriller. Established in 2005.

Bill Block
imdb.com/name/nm1088848

QUADRANT PICTURES

9229 Sunset Blvd, Suite 225
West Hollywood, CA 90069
424-244-1860

assistant@quadrantpictures.com
imdb.com/company/co0316578

Accepts query letter from unproduced, unrepresented writers via email. Project types include Feature Films and TV. Preferred genres include Action, Drama, Family, Horror, Science Fiction, and Thriller. Established in 2011.

John Schwartz
Producer
imdb.com/name/nm1862748

Doug Davison
imdb.com/name/nm0205713

QUATTRO MEDIA

171 Pier Ave, #328
Santa Monica, CA 90405
United States
323-828-2289

Does not accept any unsolicited material. Project types include Feature Films.

James Strader
Producer/Manager

QUINCY PICTURES

1645 Vine St
Los Angeles, CA 90028

United States
323-798-4681

quincypics.com

Does not accept any unsolicited material. Project types include Feature Films. Preferred genres include Horror.

Allene Quincy
Founder/CEO

QUORUM ENTERTAINMENT

1041 N Formosa Ave., Pickford Bldg. Room 204
West Hollywood, CA 90046
United States
310-594-5727

Does not accept any unsolicited material. Project types include Feature Films. Preferred genres include Crime, Drama, and Horror.

Brett Donowho
Founder/Producer/Director

R2 (R SQUARED)

9242 Beverly Blvd. Suite 300
Beverly Hills, CA 90210
United States
310-724-7700

relativitymedia.com

Does not accept any unsolicited material. Project types include Feature Films. Preferred genres include Drama.

Ryan Kavanaugh
CEO

Robbie Brenner
Head

RABBIT BANDINI PRODUCTIONS

3500 W Olive Ave
Ste 1470
Burbank, CA 91505
818-953-7510

imdb.com/company/co0132192
rabbitbandiniproductions.com

Does not accept any unsolicited material. Project types include Feature Films. Preferred genres include Thriller.

James Franco
imdb.com/name/nm0290556

Vince Jolivette
vince@rabbitbandini.com
imdb.com/name/nm0006683

RABBIT HOLE PICTURES

1041 N. Formosa Ave.
West Hollywood, CA 90046
United States
323-850-2727

Does not accept any unsolicited material. Project types include Feature Films. Preferred genres include Action and Science Fiction.

Louis Leterrier
Director

Nick Miller
Executive

RADAR PICTURES

10900 Wilshire Blvd, Suite 1400
Los Angeles, CA 90024
310-208-8525 (phone)
310-208-1764 (fax)

info@radarpictures.com
imdb.com/company/co0023815
radarpictures.com
facebook.com/pages/Radar-Pictures/
   156573061049054

Does not accept any unsolicited material. Project types include Feature Films. Preferred genres include Action and Drama.

Ted Field
CEO
imdb.com/name/nm0276059

RADIANT PRODUCTIONS

914 Montana Ave., 2nd Floor
Santa Monica , CA 90403

United States
310-656-1400 (phone)
310-656-1408 (fax)

Does not accept any unsolicited material. Project types include Feature Films and TV. Preferred genres include Action and Drama.

Wolfgang Peterson
Director/Producer

Kimberly Miller
President/Producer

Rachel Walens
VP

@RADICAL MEDIA

1630 12th St
Santa Monica, CA 90404
310-664-4500 (phone)
310-664-4600 (fax)

435 Hudson St, 6th Floor
New York, NY 10014
212-462-1500 (phone)
212-462-1600 (fax)

info@radicalmedia.com
ckim@radicalmedia.com
radicalmedia.com
imdb.com/company/co0029540

Accepts query letter from unproduced, unrepresented writers.

Frank Scherma
President
scherma@radicalmedia.com
imdb.com/name/nm0771075
linkedin.com/pub/frank-scherma/0/332/440
facebook.com/frank.scherma.1
twitter.com/schermarad

Jon Kamen
Chairman
carden@radicalmedia.com
imdb.com/name/nm3885651

Brent Eveleth
Creative Director (Group)
eveleth@radicalmedia.com
brenteveleth.com
linkedin.com/in/brenteveleth

Sidney Beaumont
Executive Producer
beaumont@radicalmedia.com
imdb.com/name/nm1359013
linkedin.com/pub/sidney-beaumont/29/806/221
facebook.com/sydney.beaumont.3
twitter.com/sydneybeaumont

Bob Stein
Head (Production, Media and Entertainment)
stein@radicalmedia.com
imdb.com/name/nm6539622
linkedin.com/pub/bob-stein/12/437/4AA

Justin Wilkes
President (Media and Entertainment)
310-664-4500
wilkes@radicalmedia.com
imdb.com/name/nm1461710
linkedin.com/pub/justin-wilkes/26/2/430
facebook.com/justin.wilkes.7
twitter.com/justinwilkes

Adam Neuhaus
310-664-4500
neuhaus@radicalmedia.com
imdb.com/name/nm2732887
linkedin.com/pub/adam-neuhaus/4/9a4/91b
twitter.com/AdamNeuhaus

RADIOACTIVEGIANT

3000 Olympic Blvd, Suite 2100
Los Angeles, CA 90404
United States
310-954-9353

404-890-5502

radioactivegiant.com
facebook.com/pages/RadioactiveGiant/
    130232493665021
twitter.com/RGTVnews

Does not accept any unsolicited material. Project types include Feature Films. Preferred genres include Thriller.

Albert Sandoval
CEO/Producer

Tom Somerset
CMO/Producer

Daemon Hillin
Head of Development & Production

RADIUS ENTERTAINMENT

9229 Sunset Blvd, Suite 301
Los Angeles, CA 90069
United States
310-858-2989 (phone)
310-858-1841 (fax)

asst@radius-ent.com
radius-ent.com

Does not accept any unsolicited material. Project types include TV. Preferred genres include Comedy, Drama, and Romance.

Carol Bodie
Producer

RAFFAELLA PRODUCTIONS

14320 Ventura Blvd., Suite 617
Sherman Oaks, CA 91423
United States
310-472-0466

Does not accept any unsolicited material. Project types include Feature Films. Preferred genres include Action and Science Fiction.

Raffaella Laurentiis
Producer

Hester Aupetit
EVP

Matthew Feitshans
VP of Development

RAINBOW FILM COMPANY/ RAINBOW RELEASING

1301 Montanta Ave, Suite A
Santa Monica, CA 90403
310-271-0202 (phone)
424-238-5682 (fax)

therainbowfilmco@aol.com
imdb.com/company/co0061144
rainbowreleasing.com
facebook.com/pages/Rainbow-Film-Company/
    110015385727699
imdb.com/company/co0067478
rainbowfilms.com

Accepts query letter from unproduced, unrepresented writers via email. Project types include Feature Films. Preferred genres include Comedy, Drama, Non-Fiction, and Romance.

Henry Jaglom
President
imdb.com/name/nm0415617

Sharon Lester
Distributor

RAINMAKER ENTERTAINMENT

200-2025 W Broadway
Vancouver, BC
Canada
V6J 1Z6
604-714-2600 (phone)
604-714-2641 (fax)

imdb.com/company/co0298750
rainmaker.com
facebook.com/RainmakerEnt
twitter.com/rainmakerent
linkedin.com/company/rainmaker-entertainment-inc

Does not accept any unsolicited material. Project types include Feature Films and TV. Preferred genres include Animation, Family, and Fantasy.

Craig Graham
Executive Chairman & CEO
imdb.com/name/nm0333981

Michael Hefferon
President
imdb.com/name/nm1803236
linkedin.com/in/michaelhefferon
facebook.com/hefferon

RAINMAKER FILMS INC.

4212 San Felipe St 399
Houston, TX 77027
832-287-9372

rainmaker.inc@gmail.com
imdb.com/company/co0147298

Accepts query letter from unproduced, unrepresented writers via email. Project types include Feature Films. Preferred genres include Science Fiction.

Grant Gurthie
President - Executive Producer
imdb.com/name/nm0349262
linkedin.com/pub/grant-guthrie/8/149/b90

RAIN MANAGEMENT GROUP

1631 21st St
Santa Monica, CA 90404
United States
310-954-9520 (phone)
310-496-2769 fax (fax)

rainmanagementgroup.com

Does not accept any unsolicited material. Project types include TV. Preferred genres include Drama.

Jonathan Baruch
Producer/Manager

Rob Wolken
Producer/Head of Operations/Manager

RAINSTORM ENTERTAINMENT, INC.

345 N Maple Dr, Suite 105
Beverly Hills, CA 90210
818-269-3300 (phone)
310-496-0223 (fax)

info@rainstormentertainment.com
steve@rainstormentertainment.com
rainstormentertainment.com

imdb.com/company/co0010764
linkedin.com/company/rainstorm-entertainment

Accepts query letter from unproduced, unrepresented writers via email. Project types include Feature Films and TV. Preferred genres include Non-Fiction and Reality.

Alec Rossel
Development Executive
818-269-3300
imdb.com/name/nm1952377

RAMOS AND SPARKS GROUP

122 S Calhoun St
Tallahassee, FL 32301
United States
850-412-1060

Does not accept any unsolicited material. Project types include Feature Films. Preferred genres include Drama.

Bob Sparks
Partner

Rich Ramos
Partner

RAMPAGE ENTERTAINMENT

2412 Columbia St, 2nd Floor
Vancouver, BC V5Y 3E6
Canada
604-684-8618

info@rampage-entertainment.com
rampage-entertainment.com

Does not accept any unsolicited material. Project types include Feature Films. Preferred genres include Comedy, Drama, and Horror.

Gavin Wilding
Producer/Director

Jessica Drillon
Executive

Eric Edmeades
Executive

RANDOM HOUSE STUDIO

1745 Broadway
New York, NY 10019
212-782-9000

Accepts query letter from unproduced, unrepresented writers. Project types include Feature Films. Established in 2007.

Valerie Cates
Executive Story Editor
212-782-9000
imdb.com/name/nm1161200

Brady Emerson
212-782-9000
imdb.com/name/nm3031708

RANDOM HOUSE TELEVISION

4000 W Alameda Ave, 3rd Floor
Burbank , CA 91505
United States
818-748-1100

Does not accept any unsolicited material. Project types include TV. Preferred genres include Crime, Drama, and Thriller.

Peter Gethers
President of Random House Studio

Jeffrey Levine
Head of Television

Christina Malach
Executive Story Editor

RAQUEL PRODUCTIONS

51 W. 52nd St
New York, NY 10019
United States

Does not accept any unsolicited material. Project types include TV. Preferred genres include Reality.

Bruce Taub
President

RAT ENTERTAINMENT

150 S Rodeo Dr
Beverly Hills, CA 90212
818-733-4603 (phone)
818-733-4612 (fax)

imdb.com/company/co0026594

Accepts query letter from unproduced, unrepresented writers. Project types include Feature Films and TV. Preferred genres include Non-Fiction and Reality. Established in 2002.

Brett Ratner
Producer
imdb.com/name/nm0711840
Assistant: Anita S. Chang

John Cheng
Producer
imdb.com/name/nm1766738

RATIO PICTURES

23875 Ventura Blvd., Suite 202B
Calabasas, CA 91302
United States
818-222-2403

general@ratiopictures.com
ratiopictures.com

Does not accept any unsolicited material. Project types include Feature Films. Preferred genres include Fantasy and Thriller.

Brian Metcalf
Director, Producer, Writer

Karoline Kautz
Producer

RAVEN BANNER ENTERTAINMENT

177 Drayton Ave
Toronto, ON M4C 3M1
Canada

ravenbannerentertainment.com
facebook.com/RavenBannerEntertainment
twitter.com/RavenBanner

Project types include Feature Films. Preferred genres include Horror and Thriller.

Michael Paszt
Partner/Producer

James Fler
Partner/Producer

Andrew Hunt
Partner/Producer

RCR MEDIA GROUP

421 S Beverly Dr.
Beverly Hills, CA 90212

1169 Loma Linda Dr,
Beverly Hills, CA 90210
310-273-3888 (phone)
310-273-2888 (fax)

info@rcrmg.com
rcrmediagroup.com
facebook.com/rcrmediagroup
linkedin.com/company/rcr-media-group
twitter.com/rcrmediagroup

Does not accept any unsolicited material. Project types include Feature Films. Preferred genres include Action, Comedy, Crime, Drama, Horror, Romance, Science Fiction, and Thriller.

Rui Costa Reis
Chairman
imdb.com/name/nm3926066

Eliad Josephson
CEO
imdb.com/name/nm4035615
linkedin.com/in/eliadjosephson
facebook.com/eliad.josephson

Ricardo Costa Reis
Producer/Creative Executive
imdb.com/name/nm4579160
facebook.com/notes/rcr-media-group/ricardo-costa

RCR PICTURES

8840 Wilshire Blvd
Beverly Hills, CA 90211

310-358-3234 (phone)
310-358-3109 (fax)

imdb.com/company/co0301318

Accepts query letter from unproduced, unrepresented writers. Project types include Feature Films. Preferred genres include Crime, Drama, Romance, and Science Fiction.

Robin Schorr
Producer
imdb.com/name/nm0774908

REBELLION PICTURES

12100 N.E. 16th Ave, Suite 208
North Miami, FL 33161
305-895-3737 (phone)
305-895-3701 (fax)

rp@rebellionpictures.com
rebellionpictures.com

Does not accept any unsolicited material.

Adam Hammel
Writer/Director

Lucy Hammel
Writer/Director

RECORDED PICTURE COMPANY

24 Hanway St
London W1T 1UH
United Kingdom
+44 20-7636-2251 (phone)
+44 20-7636-2261 (fax)

rpc@recordedpicture.com
recordedpicture.com
imdb.com/company/co0029168
twitter.com/recordedpicture

Accepts scripts from produced or represented writers. Project types include Feature Films.

Jeremy Thomas
+44 20 7636 2251
imdb.com/name/nm0859016
Assistant: Karin Padgham

Alainee Kent
+44 20 7636 2251
imdb.com/name/nm1599134

Peter Watson
+44 20 7636 2251
imdb.com/name/nm0914838

RED BOARD PRODUCTIONS

3000 W. Olympic Blvd., Bldg. 4 Suite 1200
Santa Monica, CA 90404
310-264-4285 (phone)
310-264-4286 (fax)

Does not accept any unsolicited material. Project types
include TV. Preferred genres include Drama.

David Milch
Producer/Writer

RED CROWN PRODUCTIONS

630 5th Ave, Suite 2505
New York, NY 10111
212-355-9200 (phone)
212-719-7029 (fax)

info@redcrownproductions.com
redcrownproductions.com
imdb.com/company/co0308277
facebook.com/redcrownproductions
twitter.com/RedCrownProd

Does not accept any unsolicited material. Project types
include Feature Films. Preferred genres include
Comedy and Drama. Established in 2010.

Riva Marker
Head of Production & Development
riva@redcrownproductions.com
imdb.com/name/nm1889450

Alish Erman
Creative Executive
alish@redcrownproductions.com
imdb.com/name/nm2289542

Daniel Crown
212-355-9200
dcrown@crownnyc.com
imdb.com/name/nm3259054

RED GIANT MEDIA

535 5th Ave, 5th Floor
New York, NY 10017
212-989-7200 (phone)
212-937-3505 (fax)

info@redgiantmedia.com
imdb.com/company/co0228962

Does not accept any unsolicited material. Project types
include Feature Films. Preferred genres include Science
Fiction. Established in 2008.

Aimee Schoof
Producer
imdb.com/name/nm0774779
facebook.com/aimee.schoof
twitter.com/linkedin.compubaimee-schoof475853a

Isen Robbins
Producer
imdb.com/name/nm0730358
twitter.com/isen1

Kevin Fox
imdb.com/name/nm0289100
linkedin.com/in/person
twitter.com/kfury

RED GRANITE PICTURES

9255 Sunset Blvd, Suite 710
Los Angeles, CA 90069
310-703-5800 (phone)
310-246-3849 (fax)

imdb.com/company/co0325207
redgranitepictures.com

Does not accept any unsolicited material. Project types
include Feature Films. Preferred genres include
Drama.

Riza Aziz
CEO
imdb.com/name/nm4265383

Joe Gatta
imdb.com/name/nm2211910

RED HEN PRODUCTIONS

3607 W Magnolia
Ste. L
Burbank, CA 91505
818-563-3600 (phone)
818-787-6637 (fax)

imdb.com/company/co0021072

Accepts query letter from unproduced, unrepresented writers. Preferred genres include Drama and Thriller.

Stuart Gordon
818-563-3600
imdb.com/name/nm0002340

RED HOUR FILMS

629 N La Brea Ave
Los Angeles, CA 90036
323-602-5000 (phone)
323-602-5001 (fax)

redhourfilms.com
imdb.com/company/co0039303
facebook.com/RedHourFilms
twitter.com/RedHourFilms

Does not accept any unsolicited material. Project types include Feature Films and TV. Preferred genres include Action, Comedy, Family, Fantasy, and Science Fiction.

Ben Stiller
imdb.com/name/nm0001774

Robin Mabrito
robin@redhourfilms.com
imdb.com/name/nm3142663

RED LINE FILMS

304 Hudson St
New York, NY 10013
212-257-6230

info@redlinefilms.net
redlinefilms.net

Does not accept any unsolicited material. Project types include TV.

Peter Franchella
Co-Founder/Producer

Al Szymanski
Co-Founder/Producer

RED OM FILMS, INC.

3000 Olympic Blvd
Building 3, Suite 2330
Santa Monica, CA 90404
310-594-3467

imdb.com/company/co0087432

Does not accept any unsolicited material. Project types include Feature Films and TV. Preferred genres include Action, Comedy, Drama, and Family.

Lisa Gillian
Producer
imdb.com/name/nm0731359

Philip Rose
Producer
imdb.com/name/nm0741615

Julia Roberts
imdb.com/name/nm0000210

RED PLANET PICTURES

2nd Floor, Axtell House, 23-24 Warwick St
London
W1B 5NQ
+44-0-20-3551-9080 (phone)
+44-0-20-3701-4780 (fax)

info@redplanetpictures.co.uk
redplanetpictures.co.uk
imdb.com/company/co0213314

Does not accept any unsolicited material. Project types include TV. Preferred genres include Crime and Drama.

Simon Winstone
Director of Development
simonwinstone@redplanetpictures.co.uk
imdb.com/name/nm0935654

RED ROVER FILMS

8265 Sunset Blvd, Suite 202
Los Angeles, CA 90046
323-461-8686

contact@redroverfilms.com
redroverfilms.com

Does not accept any unsolicited material. Project types include Feature Films. Preferred genres include Thriller.

Todd Traina
Principal, Producer

RED STROKES ENTERTAINMENT

9465 Wilshire Blvd. Suite 319
Beverly Hills, CA 90212
310-786-7887 (phone)
310-786-7827 (fax)

Does not accept any unsolicited material. Project types include Feature Films.

Garth Brooks
Partner/Producer

Lisa Sanderson
Partner/Producer

RED WAGON ENTERTAINMENT

8931 Ellis Ave.
Los Angeles, CA 90034
310-853-4600

imdb.com/company/co0093794
redwagonentertainment.com

Does not accept any unsolicited material. Project types include Feature Films and TV. Preferred genres include Animation, Drama, Fantasy, and Horror.

Douglas Wick
Producer
310-244-4466
imdb.com/name/nm0926824

Lucy Fisher
Producer
310-244-4466
imdb.com/name/nm0279651

REEL FX

2115 Colorado Ave
Santa Monica, CA 90404
310-264-6440

reelfx.com

Does not accept any unsolicited material. Project types include Feature Films. Preferred genres include Action, Drama, and Horror.

Aron Warner
President of Animation

Lisa Zambri
Development Executive

REEL ONE ENTERTAINMENT

591 N. Irving Blvd.
Los Angeles, CA 90004
323-460-4090

Does not accept any unsolicited material. Project types include Feature Films. Preferred genres include Drama.

Tom Berry
President/Producer

REFUGEE PRODUCTIONS

500 S. Buena Vista St, Old Animation Building
Burbank, CA 91521
818-560-3870 (phone)
818-560-3990 (fax)

Does not accept any unsolicited material. Project types include TV. Preferred genres include Drama.

Jessika Borsiczky
Producer

REGENCY ENTERPRISES

10201 W. Pico Blvd., Bldg. 12
Los Angeles, CA 90035
310-369-8300 (phone)
310-969-0470 (fax)

Does not accept any unsolicited material. Project types include Feature Films.

Thomas Imperato
EVP/Head of Production

Kara Francis
EVP of Production

REGENT ENTERTAINMENT

10940 Wilshire Blvd, Suite 1600
Los Angeles, CA 90024
310-806-4290 (phone)
310-443-4296 (fax)

info@regententertainment.com
regententertainment.com
imdb.com/company/co0045895

Accepts query letter from unproduced, unrepresented writers via email. Project types include Feature Films and TV. Preferred genres include Action, Drama, Horror, and Science Fiction.

David Millbern
Director of Development
310-806-4290
imdb.com/name/nm0587778

Roxana Vatan
imdb.com/name/nm2985872

REHAB ENTERTAINMENT

1416 N La Brea Ave
Hollywood, CA 90028
323-645-6444 (phone)
323-645-6445 (fax)

info@rehabent.com
rehabent.com
imdb.com/company/co0235838

Accepts query letter from unproduced, unrepresented writers via email. Project types include Feature Films.

John Hyde
President

Brett Coker
imdb.com/name/nm1832709

REHME PRODUCTIONS

10956 1/2 Weyburn Ave
Los Angeles, CA 90024
310-824-3371

Does not accept any unsolicited material. Project types include Feature Films and TV.

Robert Rehme
President

Nick Grillo
Producer

REINER/GREISMAN

9169 W. Sunset Blvd.
West Hollywood, CA 90069
310-285-2300 (phone)
310-285-2345 (fax)

imdb.com/company/co0185376

Accepts query letter from unproduced, unrepresented writers. Project types include Feature Films. Preferred genres include Comedy and Drama.

Rob Reiner
310-285-2328
imdb.com/name/nm0001661
Assistant: Pam Jones

Alan Greisman
Producer
310-205-2766
imdb.com/name/nm0340112

RELATIVITY MEDIA, LLC

9242 Beverly Blvd, Suite 300
Beverly Hills, CA 90210
310-724-7700 (phone)
310-724-7701 (fax)

imdb.com/company/co0125319
facebook.com/relativity
twitter.com/relativity

Accepts query letter from produced or represented writers. Project types include Feature Films, TV, and Commercials. Preferred genres include Non-Fiction and Reality.

Jonathan Karsh
imdb.com/name/nm1285615

Julie Link
facebook.com/julie.link5

RELEVE ENTERTAINMENT

6255 W. Sunset Blvd., Ste 923
Hollywood, CA 90028
323-468-9470

releve-ent.com

Does not accept any unsolicited material. Project types include Feature Films. Preferred genres include Drama.

Holly Davis-Carter
Producer, Manager

REMEMBER DREAMING, LLC

8252 1/2 Santa Monica Blvd, Suite B
West Hollywood, CA 90046
323-654-3333

Accepts query letter from unproduced, unrepresented writers. Project types include Feature Films and TV. Preferred genres include Non-Fiction and Reality.

Stan Spry
President
imdb.com/name/nm1413593
twitter.com/stanspry

Courtney Brin
courtney@freefall-films.com
imdb.com/name/nm2831504
linkedin.com/pub/courtney-brin/14/31a/27a

RENAISSANCE PICTURES

315 S Beverly Dr, Suite 216
Beverly Hills, CA 90210
310-785-3900 (phone)
310-785-9176 (fax)

imdb.com/company/co0047594

Accepts query letter from unproduced, unrepresented writers. Project types include Feature Films and TV.

Preferred genres include Action, Drama, Fantasy, and Horror.

Sam Raimi
imdb.com/name/nm0000600

Robert Tapert
Partner
imdb.com/name/nm0849964

RENART FILMS

135 Grand St.
3rd Floor
New York, NY 10013
212-274-8224 (phone)
212-274-8229 (fax)

info@renartfilms.com
imdb.com/company/co0199700

Accepts query letter from produced or represented writers. Project types include Feature Films. Preferred genres include Comedy, Drama, and Romance.

TJ Federico
tj@renartfilms.com
imdb.com/name/nm2077416
linkedin.com/pub/tj-federico/70/a38/64b

Dan Schechter
dan@renartfilms.com
imdb.com/name/nm1633080

Julie Christeas
julie@renartfilms.com
imdb.com/name/nm2184127

Caroline Dillon
Creative Director
caroline@renartfilms.com
imdb.com/name/nm0226974

Timothy Duff
President
tim@renartfilms.com
imdb.com/name/nm2178779
linkedin.com/pub/timothy-duff/5/7a5/5b4

RENEE MISSEL MANAGEMENT

2376 Adrian St, Suite A
Newbury Park, CA 91320

310-463-0638 (phone)
805-669-4511 (fax)

fi lmtao@aol.com
imdb.com/name/nm0592911
twitter.com/reneemissel

Accepts query letter from unproduced, unrepresented writers via email. Project types include Feature Films. Established in 1983.

Bridget Stone

Renee Missel
Producer
imdb.com/name/nm0592911
twitter.com/reneemissel

RENEE VALENTE PRODUCTIONS

9000 Sunset Blvd
Los Angeles, CA 90069
310-472-5342

valenteprod@aol.com
imdb.com/company/co0112475

Accepts query letter from unproduced, unrepresented writers via email. Project types include Feature Films and TV. Established in 1980.

Renee Valente
Executive Producer
imdb.com/name/nm0884095

RENEGADE 83

121 W Lexington Dr. Bldg. 413
Glendale, CA 91203
818-480-3112 (phone)
818-480-3192 (fax)

showinfo@renegade83.com
renegade83.com

Does not accept any unsolicited material. Project types include TV.

David Garfinkle
Partner

Todd Cohen
Development

RENEGADE ANIMATION, INC.

111 E Broadway, Suite 208
Glendale, CA 91205
818-551-2351 (phone)
818-551-2350 (fax)

contactus@renegadeanimation.com
renegadeanimation.com

Accepts query letter from unproduced, unrepresented writers via email. Project types include TV.

Darrell Van Citters
imdb.com/name/nm0885864

Ashley Postlewaite
imdb.com/name/nm1041234
linkedin.com/pub/ashley-postlewaite/0/66a/950
facebook.com/ashley.postlewaite

Alec Megibben
Storyboard Artist
linkedin.com/in/alecanimates

RENFIELD PRODUCTIONS

c/o The Lot
1041 N Formosa Ave
Writers Building, Suite 321
West Hollywood, CA 90046
323-850-3907 (fax)

development@renfieldproductions.com
renfieldproductions.com
facebook.com/RenfieldProductions
twitter.com/renfieldprods
imdb.com/company/co0034557

Accepts query letter from unproduced, unrepresented writers via email. Project types include TV. Preferred genres include Action, Animation, Comedy, Drama, Family, Horror, Non-Fiction, and Reality

Mike Finnell
Producer
imdb.com/name/nm0278228

Joe Dante
Director
imdb.com/name/nm0001102
facebook.com/directorjoedante
twitter.com/joe_dante

RENO PRODUCTIONS

311 W 43rd St, Suite 1104
New York, NY 10036

info@renoproductionsinc.com
renoproductionsinc.com

Does not accept any unsolicited material. Project types
include Feature Films. Preferred genres include Crime,
Drama, and Thriller.

Peter Askin
Partner/Director/Writer/Producer

Will Battersby
Partner/Producer

RESERVE ENTERTAINMENT GROUP

269 S Beverly Dr, Suite 1122
Beverly Hills, CA 90210
310-360-4397 (phone)
310-388-5853 (fax)

info@thereserveent.com
thereserveent.com

Accepts query letter from unproduced, unrepresented
writers via email. Project types include Feature Films.
Preferred genres include Drama.

LaMont T. Cain
CEO/Producer

Allan B. Bates
President/Executive Producer

REVEILLE, LLC/ SHINE INTERNATIONAL

1741 Ivar Ave
Los Angeles, CA 90028
323-790-8000 (phone)
323-790-8399 (fax)

Does not accept any unsolicited material. Project types
include TV. Preferred genres include Non-Fiction and
Reality.

Carolyn Bernstein
Executive Vice-President, Scripted TV
imdb.com/name/nm3009190

Rob Cohen
imdb.com/name/nm0003418

Todd Cohen
imdb.com/name/nm1537619
linkedin.com/in/trcohen

REVEK ENTERTAINMENT

12100 Wilshire Blvd, Suite 819
Los Angeles, CA 90025
310-845-6356

asst@revekentertainment.com
revekentertainment.com
twitter.com/RevekEntertain
facebook.com/pages/Revek-Entertainment/
351904838248753

Does not accept any unsolicited material. Project types
include Feature Films. Preferred genres include
Drama, Horror, and Thriller.

Gabriela Revilla
Producer/Writer

REVELATIONS ENTERTAINMENT

1221 Second St
4th Floor
Santa Monica, CA 90401
310-394-3131 (phone)
310-394-3133 (fax)

info@revelationsent.com
revelationsent.com
linkedin.com/company/revelations-entertainment
facebook.com/pages/Revelations-Entertainment/
110579179025356
imdb.com/company/co0075256

Does not accept any unsolicited material. Project types
include Feature Films and TV. Preferred genres
include Action, Detective, Drama, and Family.
Established in 1996.

Morgan Freeman
President
imdb.com/name/nm0000151

Lori McCreary
CEO
imdb.com/name/nm0566975
twitter.com/LoriMcCreary

Tracy Mercer
VP of Development
imdb.com/name/nm0580312

James Younger
EVP of Factual Productions

Leif Lillehaugen
Creative Executive

Megan Parlen
Sr. Director of Factual Productions

John Kaiser
Production Associate

Marcus Mucha
VP of Business Development

REVOLUTION FILMS

9-A Dallington St
London EC1Z 0BQ
UK
+44-20-7566-0700

email@revolution-films.com
imdb.com/company/co0103733
facebook.com/revolutionfilms

Does not accept any unsolicited material. Project types include Feature Films. Preferred genres include Action, Comedy, Drama, Non-Fiction, Period, and Thriller. Established in 1994.

Michael Winterbottom
Producer
imdb.com/name/nm0935863

Andrew Eaton
Producer
imdb.com/name/nm0247787

REVOLUTION MEDIA

8383 Wilshire Blvd., Suite 310
Beverly Hills, CA 90211
323-883-0056

Does not accept any unsolicited material. Project types include TV. Preferred genres include Comedy and Drama.

Michael Benaroya
Partner/Producer

REVOLVER PICTURE COMPANY

6338 Wilshire Blvd.
Los Angeles, CA 90048
323-782-4933

facebook.com/RevolverPictureCompany

Does not accept any unsolicited material. Project types include Feature Films. Preferred genres include Horror.

Nick Phillips
EVP/Producer

Kelly Martin Wagner
Producer

RG ENTERTAINMENT LTD.

9595 Wilshire Blvd., Ste 900
Beverly Hills, CA 90212
310-246-1442 (phone)
310-246-1474 (fax)

Does not accept any unsolicited material. Project types include Feature Films. Preferred genres include Animation and Fantasy.

Ray Griggs
President

RHINO FILMS

10501 Wilshire Blvd, Suite 814
Los Angeles, CA 90024
310-441-6557 (phone)
310-441-6584 (fax)

contact@rhinofilms.com
rhinofilms.com
imdb.com/company/co0032380
facebook.com/RhinoFilmProductions

Does not accept any unsolicited material. Project types include Feature Films.

RHOMBUS MEDIA, INC.

99 Spadina Ave. Unit#600
Toronto, Ontario
M5V 3P8
Canada
416-971-7856 (phone)
416-971-9647 (fax)

info@rhombusmedia.com
rhombusmedia.com
imdb.com/company/co0010810
linkedin.com/company/rhombus-media-inc.
facebook.com/rhombusmedia
twitter.com/rhombusmedia

Does not accept any unsolicited material. Project types include Feature Films. Preferred genres include Action, Comedy, Crime, Horror, Science Fiction, and Thriller. Established in 1979.

Larry Weistein
Producer
imdb.com/name/nm0918452

Niv Fichman
Producer
imdb.com/name/nm0275651

RHYTHM & HUES STUDIOS

2100 E Grand Ave
El Segundo, CA 90245
310-448-7500 (phone)
310-448-7600 (fax)

Prism Tower, A-Wing, 3rd Floor
Goregaon-Malad Link Rd
Goregaon (West), Mumbai 400062
India
+91 22 40388888

The V, Vega Block, 11th Floor, Left Wing, Plot No - 17
Software Units Layout, HITEC City
Madhapur, Hyderabad - 500 081
India
+91 40 40334567

401 W Georgia St, Suites No. 500 & 600
Vancouver, BC V6B 5A1, Canada
604-288-8745

info-la@rhythm.com

rhythm.com
imdb.com/company/co0075252
linkedin.com/company/rhythm-&-hues
facebook.com/RhythmAndHues
twitter.com/RhythmAndHues

Does not accept any unsolicited material. Project types include Feature Films. Preferred genres include Action, Comedy, Crime, Drama, Family, Fantasy, Romance, and Science Fiction. Established in 1987.

Heather Jennings
imdb.com/name/nm0997142

Gautham Krishnamurti
Chief Technology Officer

Gary Nolan
Visual Effects Producer

Derek Spears
Visual Effects Supervisor

Ray Chen
Visual Effects Supervisor

Pauline Ts'o
Lighting Supervisor
imdb.com/name/nm1173396

RICE & BEANS PRODUCTIONS

30 N Raymond Ave, Suite 605
Pasadena, CA 91103
626-792-9171

vin88@pacbell.net
imdb.com/company/co0094899

Accepts query letter from unproduced, unrepresented writers via email. Project types include Feature Films and TV. Preferred genres include Comedy and Drama.

Vince Cheung
Producer
imdb.com/name/nm0156588

Ben Montanio
Producer
imdb.com/name/nm0598996

RICHE PRODUCTIONS

9336 W Washington Blvd
Stage 4, Room 201
Culver City, CA 90232
310-202-4850

imdb.com/company/co0176392

Accepts query letter from unproduced, unrepresented writers. Project types include Feature Films and TV. Preferred genres include Action and Family.

Alan Riche

Partner
imdb.com/name/nm0724843
Assistant: Adrienne Novelly

Peter Riche

Partner
imdb.com/name/nm0724855
linkedin.com/pub/peter-riche/70/414/ab4

RICH HIPPIE PRODUCTIONS

Rich Hippie Productions
332 S. Beverly Dr, Suite 101
Beverly Hills, CA 90212
United States

nfo@richhippieproductions.com
richhippieproductions.com

Does not accept any unsolicited material. Preferred genres include Drama and Thriller.

Sydney Holland

Founder/CEO

Erik Fleming

Head of Development

RIDGEROCK ENTERTAINMENT GROUP

3945 Ceanothus Place
Calabasas, CA 91302
615-489-6350 (phone)
888-735-1901 (fax)

rigderockentertainment.com

Does not accept any unsolicited material. Project types include Feature Films. Preferred genres include Drama.

Brett Granstaff

Producer

RIGHT COAST PRODUCTIONS

289 Springs Fireplace Rd
East Hampton, NY 11937
631-329-1200

Does not accept any unsolicited material. Project types include Feature Films. Preferred genres include Comedy, Drama, Family, and Romance.

Barry Sonnenfeld

Director/Producer

RINGLEADER STUDIOS

8840 Wilshire Blvd., Third Floor
Beverly Hills, CA 90211

ringleaderstudios.com

Does not accept any unsolicited material. Project types include TV. Preferred genres include Horror and Science Fiction.

Steve Harris

Producer

RIP CORD PRODUCTIONS

5555 Melrose Ave., Dressing Rm 115
Hollywood, CA 90038
323-956-3800 (phone)
323-862-2294 (fax)

Project types include Feature Films and TV. Preferred genres include Comedy.

Mike White

Writer/Director/Producer

RITCHIE/WIGRAM PRODUCTIONS

4000 Warner Blvd.
Burbank, CA 91522
818-954-2412 (phone)
818-954-6538 (fax)

Does not accept any unsolicited material.

Guy Ritchie
Director

Lionel Wigram
Producer

RIVAL PICTURES

2121 Cloverfield Blvd., Suite 116
Santa Monica, CA 90404
310-664-1954 (phone)
310-388-0536 (fax)

edparks@rivalpictures.net
rivalpictures.net

Does not accept any unsolicited material. Project types include Feature Films. Preferred genres include Drama and Thriller.

Ed Parks
Founder/Producer

RIVE GAUCHE TELEVISION

15442 Ventura Blvd.
Ste. 507
Sherman Oaks, CA 91403
818-784-9912 (phone)
818-784-9916 (fax)

rgtvsales@rgitv.com
rgitv.com
imdb.com/company/co0010886
linkedin.com/company/rive-gauche-television
twitter.com/RiveGaucheTV
facebook.com/pages/Rive-Gauche-Television/
    174496655908588

Project types include Feature Films. Preferred genres include Documentary. Established in 1994.

Jonathan Kramer
CEO
818-386-1035
jon@rgitv.com
imdb.com/name/nm2883855

David Auerbach
President
818-530-7917
david@rgitv.com

Jay Behling
CFO
818-530-7908
jay@rgitv.com

Laurie Carreira
Manager, Distribution Services
818-784-9917
laurie@rgitv.com

Bryan Gabourie
Vice President, International Distribution
818-784-9912
bryan@rgitv.com

Marine Ksadzhikyan
Senior Vice President, International Distribution
818-784-2237
marine@rgitv.com

Ashley Lewelling
Director of Development
818-530-7913
ashley@rgitv.com

Antonia Lianos
Director of Contract Administration
818-784-2094
antonia@rgitv.com

Tomas Silva
Vice President, International Sales
305-803-3090
tomas@rgitv.com

Devin Sunseri
Director of Development
818-784-9912
devin@rgitv.com

Sylvia Wadzinski
Assistant, International Sales & Production
818-784-9912
sylvia@rgitv.com

RIVER ROAD ENTERTAINMENT

2000 Ave of the Stars, Suite 620-N
Los Angeles, CA 90067
213-253-4610 (phone)
310-843-9551 (fax)

imdb.com/company/co0120121

linkedin.com/company/river-road-entertainment

Does not accept any unsolicited material. Project types include Feature Films and TV. Preferred genres include Comedy, Drama, Non-Fiction, and Reality.

Tom Skapars
Creative Executive
imdb.com/name/nm2799570
linkedin.com/pub/tom-skapars/0/139/52

RKO PICTURES, INC.

2034 Broadway
Santa Monica, CA 90404
310-277-0707

info@rko.com
rko.com

Does not accept any unsolicited material. Project types include Feature Films and TV. Preferred genres include Action, Animation, Drama, and Thriller.

Ted Hartley
Chairman

Vanessa Coifman
EVP of Production

ROADSIDE ATTRACTIONS

7920 Sunset Blvd
Suite 402
Los Angeles, CA 90046
323-882-8490

info@roadsideattractions.com
roadsideattractions.com
imdb.com/company/co0017716
twitter.com/roadsidetweets
facebook.com/RoadsideAttractionsFilms
linkedin.com/company/roadside-attractions

Accepts query letter from produced or represented writers. Project types include Feature Films. Preferred genres include Comedy, Drama, Horror, and Thriller.

Howard Cohen
Founder
imdb.com/name/nm1383518

Eric d'Arbeloff
Founder
imdb.com/name/nm0195396

Gail Blumenthal
Distributor
imdb.com/name/nm0089812

ROAR

9701 Wilshire Blvd. 8th Floor
Beverly Hills , CA 90212
310-586-8222 (phone)
310-586-8147 (fax)

roar.la

Does not accept any unsolicited material. Project types include Feature Films and TV. Preferred genres include Action, Comedy, Drama, and Thriller.

Bernie Cahill
Partner/Producer

Jay Froberg
Partner

ROBERT CORT PRODUCTIONS

1041 N Formosa Ave
West Hollywood, CA 90046
323-850-2644 (phone)
323-850-2634 (fax)

imdb.com/company/co0094924

Accepts query letter from unproduced, unrepresented writers. Project types include Feature Films and TV. Preferred genres include Comedy and Drama.

Robert Cort
Producer
imdb.com/name/nm0181202
Assistant: Maritza Berta

Eric Hetzel
Producer
imdb.com/name/nm0381796

ROBERT GREENWALD PRODUCTIONS

10510 Culver Blvd
Culver City, CA 90232-3400

310-204-0404 (phone)
310-204-0174 (fax)

info@rgpinc.com
imdb.com/company/co0056700

Does not accept any unsolicited material. Project types include Feature Films and TV. Preferred genres include Comedy, Drama, and Non-Fiction.

Robert Greenwald
imdb.com/name/nm0339254

Philip Kleinbart
imdb.com/name/nm0459036

ROBERT KOSBERG PRODUCTIONS

1438 N. Gower St, Bldg. 35, Box 10
Hollywood, CA 90028
323-468-4513

bobkosberg@nashentertainment.com
bobkosberg@yahoo.com
imdb.com/company/co0094875

Accepts query letter from unproduced, unrepresented writers via email. Project types include Feature Films and TV.

Robert Kosberg
Producer
imdb.com/name/nm0466946

Jane Moore
Development
imdb.com/name/nm0601327

ROBERT LAWRENCE PRODUCTIONS

1810 14th St
Suite 102
Santa Monica, CA 90404
310-399-2762

imdb.com/company/co0021936
linkedin.com/company/robert-lawrence-productions

Accepts query letter from unproduced, unrepresented writers. Project types include Feature Films. Preferred genres include Action, Comedy, and Drama.

Robert Lawrence
President
imdb.com/name/nm0492994

ROBERTS/DAVID FILMS INC.

100 Universal City Plaza
Bldg. 1320
Universal City, CA 91608
323-574-1700 (phone)
818-733-1551 (fax)

robertsdavid.com
linkedin.com/company/roberts-david-films-inc.
imdb.com/company/co0109061

Does not accept any unsolicited material. Project types include Feature Films and TV. Preferred genres include Comedy, Non-Fiction, and Reality.

Mark Roberts
Partner
mark@robertsdavid.com

Lorena David
Partner
lorena@robertsdavid.com

ROBERT SIMONDS COMPANY

10202 Washington Blvd
Robert Young Building
Suite 3510
Culver City, CA 90232
310-244-5222 (phone)
310-244-0348 (fax)

imdb.com/company/co0033486

Does not accept any unsolicited material. Project types include Feature Films. Preferred genres include Action, Comedy, Family, and Thriller. Established in 2012.

Robert Simonds
CEO
rasst@rscfilms.com
imdb.com/name/nm0800465
Assistant: Jennifer Jiang

ROCKET SCIENCE PRODUCTIONS

11601 Wilshire Blvd., Suite 2200
Los Angeles, CA 90025

Does not accept any unsolicited material. Project types include TV. Preferred genres include Drama.

Harvey Myman
President/Producer

ROCKLIN/ FAUST

10390 Santa Monica Blvd, Suite 200
Los Angeles, CA 90025
310-800-5140 (phone)
310-789-3060 (fax)

imdb.com/company/co0299281
linkedin.com/pub/nicole-rocklin/1b/a90/462

Does not accept any unsolicited material. Project types include Feature Films and TV. Preferred genres include Animation, Comedy, Drama, Non-Fiction, and Reality.

Blye Pagon Faust
Producer
imdb.com/name/nm1421308

ROCK'N ROBIN PRODUCTIONS

555 W 57th St, Suite 1701
New York, NY 10019
212-246-4367

info@rocknrobin.tv
rocknrobin.tv
facebook.com/pages/Rockn-Robin-Productions/
    1508332256051557
twitter.com/rocknrobintv

Does not accept any unsolicited material.

Robin Roberts
Host/President/Producer

John Palacio
Creative Director

RODDENBERRY ENTERTAINMENT

4400 Coldwater Canyon Blvd, Suite #100
Studio City, CA 91604

866-979-9979 (phone)
818-487-9440 (fax)

roddenberry.com

Does not accept any unsolicited material. Project types include Feature Films and TV. Preferred genres include Drama and Science Fiction.

Rod Roddenberry
Producer

Trevor Roth
COO/Head of Development

ROGUE STATE PRODUCTIONS

2000 Ave of the Stars, 3rd Floor
Los Angeles, CA 90067

Does not accept any unsolicited material. Project types include TV.

Eli Frankel
Producer

ROLLMAN ENTERTAINMENT

6767 Forest Lawn Dr, Suite 210
Los Angeles, CA 90068
323-850-7655

eric@rollmanent.com
rollmanent.com

Does not accept any unsolicited material. Project types include Feature Films. Preferred genres include Animation and Family.

Eric Rollman
CEO

ROOM 101, INC.

9677 Charleville Blvd.
Beverly Hills 90212
310-271-1130

imdb.com/company/co0203017
linkedin.com/company/room-101-inc.

Accepts query letter from unproduced, unrepresented writers. Project types include Feature Films and TV. Preferred genres include Crime, Drama, and Horror.

Steven Schneider
Producer
imdb.com/name/nm2124081

ROOM 5 FILMS

373 Broadway, E22
New York, NY 10013
212-343-2800

contact@room5films.com
room5films.com
facebook.com/pages/Room-5-Films/
    266636396750533
imdb.com/company/co0267662

Does not accept any unsolicited material. Preferred
genres include Documentary and Drama. Established
in 2011.

Heather Smith
Producer
imdb.com/name/nm3150253

ROOM 9 ENTERTAINMENT, LLC

9229 Sunset Blvd, Suite 505
West Hollywood, CA 90069
310-651-2001 (phone)
310-651-2010 (fax)

info@room9entertainment.com
imdb.com/company/co0122495

Does not accept any unsolicited material. Project types
include Feature Films and TV. Preferred genres
include Drama and Non-Fiction.

David O. Sacks
CEO
imdb.com/name/nm1616294

Michael R. Newman
imdb.com/name/nm1616293

Daniel Brunt
imdb.com/name/nm1616292

ROOS MEDIA GROUP

1818 7th Ave. S
Fargo, ND 58103

roosmediagroup.com

Does not accept any unsolicited material. Project types
include Feature Films. Preferred genres include
Comedy.

Kirk Roos
Owner/Producer

ROSA ENTERTAINMENT

7288 Sunset Blvd, Suite 208
Los Angeles, CA 90046
310-470-3506 (phone)
310-470-3509 (fax)

info@rosaentertainment.com
rosaentertainment.com
imdb.com/company/co0182149
facebook.com/pages/Rosa-Entertainment/
    180064202005686

Does not accept any unsolicited material. Project types
include Feature Films and TV. Preferred genres
include Comedy and Drama.

Sidney Sherman
Producer
sidney@rosaentertainment.com
imdb.com/name/nm0792587

ROSEBLOOD MOVIE CO.

1875 Century Park East, Suite 2140
Los Angeles, CA 90067

info@rko.com
rko.com/roseblood.asp

Does not accept any unsolicited material. Project types
include Feature Films. Preferred genres include Crime,
Drama, Horror, and Thriller.

ROSEROCK FILMS

4000 Warner Blvd
Building 81
Suite 216
Burbank, CA 91522
818-954-7528 (phone)
818-954-6658 (fax)

imdb.com/company/co0182148

facebook.com/roserockfilms
twitter.com/roserock_films

Does not accept any unsolicited material. Project types include Feature Films.

Patricia Reed
Director of Development
818-954-7673
imdb.com/name/nm0715623

Hunt Lowry
Producer
imdb.com/name/nm0523324
linkedin.com/pub/hunt-lowry/a/841/2b8

ROTH FILMS

2900 W Olympic Blvd
Santa Monica, CA 90404
310-255-7000

imdb.com/company/co0268489

Accepts query letter from unproduced, unrepresented writers. Project types include Feature Films.

Joe Roth
Producer
imdb.com/name/nm0005387

Palak Patel
imdb.com/name/nm2026983

ROUGH DIAMOND PRODUCTIONS

1424 N. Kings Rd
Los Angeles, CA 90069
323-848-2900

julia@juliaverdin.com
juliaverdin.com

Does not accept any unsolicited material. Project types include Feature Films. Preferred genres include Drama, Horror, and Thriller.

Julia Verdin
Producer

Bill Kravitz
Producer

ROUGHHOUSE

1722 Whitley Ave
Hollywood, CA 90028
323-469-3161

Accepts scripts from produced or represented writers. Project types include Feature Films. Preferred genres include Drama and Romance.

David Green
imdb.com/name/nm0337773

ROUNDTABLE ENTERTAINMENT

5300 Melrose Ave, Suite E 331
Hollywood, CA 90038
323-769-2567

Does not accept any unsolicited material. Project types include Feature Films. Preferred genres include Comedy and Drama.

Gina Matthews
Partner, Producer

Grant Scharbo
Partner, Producer

ROUTE ONE FILMS

1041 N Formosa Ave
Santa Monica East #200
West Hollywood, CA 90046
323-850-3855 (phone)
323-850-3866 (fax)

1620 Montgomery St. #250
San Francisco, CA 94111
415-449-9122

routeonefilms.com
imdb.com/company/co0316867

Does not accept any unsolicited material. Project types include Feature Films.

Jay Stern
imdb.com/name/nm0827731

Russell Levine
imdb.com/name/nm4149902

Chip Diggins
imdb.com/name/nm0226505

ROXWELL FILMS

650 Rose Ave, Suite 2
Venice, CA 90291
310-399-7895

info@roxwell.net
roxwell.net
facebook.com/RoxwellFilms

Does not accept any unsolicited material. Project types include Feature Films. Preferred genres include Crime, Drama, and Thriller.

Kevin Shulman
Producer/Director

Jeremy Rosen
Producer

ROYAL TIES PRODUCTIONS

5700 Canoga Ave, Suite 300
Woodland Hills, CA 91367

Does not accept any unsolicited material. Project types include TV. Preferred genres include Drama.

Regina King
Actor/Producer/Director

Reina King
Producer

RUBICON ENTERTAINMENT

3406 Tareco Dr.
Los Angeles, CA 90068
323-850-9200 (phone)
323-378-5584 (fax)

submissions@rubiconentertainment.com
rubiconentertainment.com
imdb.com/company/co0476567
linkedin.com/company/rubicon-entertainment-llc

Accepts query letter from unproduced, unrepresented writers via email. Project types include Feature Films. Preferred genres include Comedy and Drama.

RUBY-SPEARS PRODUCTIONS

3500 W. Olive Ave., Suite 300
Burbank , CA 91505
818-840-1234

info@rubyspears.com
rubyspears.com

Does not accept any unsolicited material. Project types include Feature Films and TV. Preferred genres include Animation.

Joseph Ruby
President

Kenneth Spears
Vice President

RUCKUSFILM

4610 Charlotte Ave.
Nashville, TN 37209
615-298-5818 (phone)
615-292-0204 (fax)

clarke@ruckusfilm.com
ruckusfilm.com

Does not accept any unsolicited material. Project types include Feature Films and TV. Preferred genres include Comedy, Family, and Fantasy.

Clarke Gallivan
Producer

Coke Sams
Producer

RUMPUS ENTERTAINMENT

8630 Pine Tree Place
Los Angeles, CA 90069
323-774-5245

pete@rumpusla.com
rumpusla.com

Does not accept any unsolicited material. Project types include Feature Films. Preferred genres include Comedy and Romance.

Steve Carr
Partner/Director/Producer

Jason Taragon
Partner/Producer

RUNAWAY PRODUCTIONS

7336 Santa Monica Blvd.
Ste 751
West Hollywood, CA 90046
310-801-0885

lindapalmer@runawayproductions.tv
runawaylp@gmail.com
facebook.com/runawayproduct
runawayproductions.tv

Accepts query letter from unproduced, unrepresented writers via email. Project types include Feature Films and TV. Preferred genres include Comedy.

Linda Palmer
imdb.com/name/nm1881313

Todd Wade
imdb.com/name/nm0905520

RYAN MURPHY PRODUCTIONS

5555 Melrose Ave Modular Building, First Floor
Los Angeles, CA 90038
323-956-2408 (phone)
323-862-2235 (fax)

imdb.com/company/co0156994

Does not accept any unsolicited material. Project types include Feature Films and TV. Preferred genres include Comedy, Documentary, Drama, Horror, Non-Fiction, Science Fiction, and Thriller. Established in 2008.

Dante Di Loreto
President
imdb.com/name/nm0223994

Ryan Murphy
imdb.com/name/nm0614682

S3 ENTERTAINMENT GROUP

1100 Woodward Heights
Ferndale, MI 48220
248-547-7334 (phone)
248-547-8909 (fax)

info@s3eg.com
s3eg.com

Does not accept any unsolicited material. Project types include Feature Films. Preferred genres include Thriller.

Jeff Stern
Producer

Jeff Spillman
Producer

SACRED DOGS ENTERTAINMENT LLC

311 N Robertson Blvd.
Ste. 249
Beverly Hills, CA 90211
323-656-6900

victory@sacreddogs.com
studio@sacreddogs.com
sacreddogs.com
imdb.com/company/co0121976
facebook.com/Victory.Tischler.Blue
twitter.com/vtb1

Project types include Feature Films. Preferred genres include Documentary.

Arden Brotman
323-656-6900
imdb.com/name/nm2231224

Victory Tischler-Blue
Owner
323-656-6900
imdb.com/name/nm0089548

SAFADY ENTERTAINMENT

9663 Santa Monica Blvd, Suite 406
Beverly Hills, CA 90210

safadyentertainment.com

Does not accept any unsolicited material. Project types include Feature Films. Preferred genres include Action, Drama, Horror, and Thriller.

Gary Safady
President/Producer

Craig Chapman
EVP/Producer

SALTIRE ENTERTAINMENT

6352 De Longpre Ave
Los Angeles, CA 90028

imdb.com/company/co0104114

Does not accept any unsolicited material. Project types include Feature Films. Preferred genres include Drama, Myth, and Science Fiction.

Stuart Pollok
Producer
imdb.com/name/nm0689415

SALTY FEATURES

135 W 20th St. – 5th fl.
New York, NY 10011
212.604.9700
212-924-1601 (phone)
212-924-2306 (fax)

info@saltyfeatures.com
saltyfeatures.com
facebook.com/SaltyFeatures
twitter.com/saltyfeatures

Does not accept any unsolicited material. Project types include Feature Films and TV. Preferred genres include Non-Fiction and Reality.

Yael Melamede
Producer
imdb.com/name/nm0577336

Eva Kolodner
imdb.com/name/nm0464286

SALVATORE/ORNSTON PRODUCTIONS

5650 Camellia Ave
North Hollywood, CA 91601
310-466-8980 (phone)
818-752-9321 (fax)

imdb.com/company/co0223789

Accepts query letter from produced or represented writers. Project types include Feature Films. Preferred genres include Action, Animation, Comedy, Crime, Drama, Romance, and Thriller.

Richard Salvatore
Executive
imdb.com/name/nm0759363

David E. Ornston
Executive
imdb.com/name/nm0650361

SAMACO FILMS

12400 Wilshire Blvd, Suite 1300
Los Angeles, CA 90025
310-979-9971 (phone)
310-979-9973 (fax)

franco@samacoproductions.com
samacofilms.com

Does not accept any unsolicited material. Project types include Feature Films. Preferred genres include Action, Drama, and Thriller.

Franco Sama
Producer

SAMUELS MEDIA

345 N Canon Dr, Suite 202
Beverly Hills, CA 90210
310-395-1280

Does not accept any unsolicited material. Project types include Feature Films. Preferred genres include Drama and Thriller.

Steve Samuels
Producer

SAMUELSON PRODUCTIONS LIMITED

10401 Wyton Dr
Los Angeles, CA 90024-2527
310-208-1000 (phone)
323-315-5188 (fax)

info@samuelson.la
samuelson.la
imdb.com/company/co0182558

linkedin.com/company/samuelson-productions-limited

Does not accept any unsolicited material. Project types include Feature Films and TV. Preferred genres include Action, Comedy, and Drama.

Peter Samuelson
Owner
imdb.com/name/nm0006873
Assistant: Brian Casey

Marc Samuelson
imdb.com/name/nm0760555

Renato Celani
imdb.com/name/nm1954607

Josie Law
imdb.com/name/nm1656468

Saryl Hirsch
imdb.com/name/nm1950244

SANDBAR PICTURES

1145 N. McCadden Place
Hollywood, CA 90038
323-337-1183 (phone)
323-337-1434 (fax)

4111 W. Alameda Ave Ste 505
Burbank, CA 91505
415-398-0780 (phone)
415-398-1598 (fax)

info@sandbarpictures.net
sandbarpictures.net
imdb.com/company/co0171098

Does not accept any unsolicited material. Project types include Feature Films. Preferred genres include Drama, Horror, and Thriller. Established in 2005.

Greg Little
Founder
imdb.com/name/nm0514571

Elizabeth Zox Friedman
Founder
imdb.com/name/nm0295288
linkedin.com/pub/lizzie-friedman/72/7b6/536
twitter.com/Frizzie93

SANDER/MOSES PRODUCTIONS

The Lot 1041 N. Formosa Ave
Formosa Building
Suite 7
West Hollywood, CA 90046
818-560-4500 (phone)
818-860-6284 (fax)

info@sandermoses.com
sandermoses.com
imdb.com/company/co0028175
facebook.com/SanderMosesProductions

Accepts query letter from unproduced, unrepresented writers via email. Project types include Feature Films, TV, and Commercials. Preferred genres include Drama, Non-Fiction, and Reality.

Kim Moses
imdb.com/name/nm0608593

Ian Sander
imdb.com/name/nm0761401
twitter.com/IanSander

SANDERS/ARMSTRONG MANAGEMENT

2120 Colorado Ave
Santa Monica, CA
310-315-2100

Does not accept any unsolicited material. Project types include TV. Preferred genres include Drama.

Nancy Sanders
Producer/Talent Manager

Mark Armstrong
Producer/Talent Manager

SANDIA MEDIA

6100 4th St. NW, Suite A109
Los Ranchos, NM 87107
505-345-2135 (phone)
505-814-5703 (fax)

info@sandiamedia.com
sandiamedia.com

Does not accept any unsolicited material. Project types include Feature Films. Preferred genres include Comedy.

Peter Touche
Founder/CEO/Producer

SANITSKY COMPANY

9200 Sunset Blvd.
Los Angeles, CA 90069
310-274-0120 (phone)
310-274-1455 (fax)

imdb.com/company/co0059772

Does not accept any unsolicited material. Project types include TV. Preferred genres include Drama.

Larry Sanitsky
President
imdb.com/name/nm0762792

SARABANDE PRODUCTIONS

715 Broadway, Suite 210
Santa Monica, CA 90401
310-395-4842

Does not accept any unsolicited material. Project types include TV. Preferred genres include Drama.

David Manson
Writer/Producer

Arla Sorkin Manson
EVP

SARGENT HALL PRODUCTIONS

9229 Sunset Blvd. Suite 620
West Hollywood, CA 90069
310-550-9002

Does not accept any unsolicited material. Project types include Feature Films and TV. Preferred genres include Comedy and Drama.

Topher Grace
Actor/Producer

Gordon Kaywin
Producer

SATURN FILMS

9000 Sunset Blvd., #911
West Hollywood , CA 90069
310-887-0900 (phone)
310-248-2965 (fax)

saturnfilms.com

Does not accept any unsolicited material. Project types include Feature Films. Preferred genres include Action and Drama.

Nicolas Cage
Partner/Producer/Actor

Kelly Moore
Development

SAWBONE FILMS

10 Cottage Rd
South Portland, ME 04106
207-799-9500

Does not accept any unsolicited material. Project types include TV. Preferred genres include Drama.

Lisa Quijano Wolfinger
President/Founder/Producer

SBK PICTURES

c/o Simone Sheffield PO Box 256
Palm Springs, CA 92263
310-295-0796

sbk-pictures.com

Accepts query letter from unproduced, unrepresented writers via email. Project types include Feature Films and TV. Preferred genres include Drama.

Ben Kingsley
Actor/Producer

Valerie Hoffman
Producer

SCARLET FIRE ENTERTAINMENT

561 28th Ave
Venice, CA 90291

310-302-1001 (phone)
310-302-1002 (fax)

imdb.com/company/co0052256

Does not accept any unsolicited material. Project types include Feature Films and TV. Preferred genres include Comedy.

Allen Loeb
Producer
310-302-1001
imdb.com/name/nm1615610

Steven Pearl
Producer
310-302-1001
imdb.com/name/nm0669093

SCARPE DIEM PRODUCTIONS

408 Greenwich St
New York, NY 10013
212-966-3292

Does not accept any unsolicited material. Project types include Feature Films. Preferred genres include Drama.

SCARY MADISON

10202 W Washington Blvd., Judy Garland Bldg.
Culver City, CA 90232

Does not accept any unsolicited material. Project types include Feature Films. Preferred genres include Thriller.

Adam Sandler
Producer

Scott Sandler
Producer

SCIENTIFIC GAMES CORPORATION

750 Lexington Ave
New York, NY 10022
212-754-2233

scientificgames.com
twitter.com/ScientificGames

Does not accept any unsolicited material. Project types include TV.

Ronald O. Perelman
Chairman

David L. Kennedy
Exec. Vice Chairman of Scientific Games

SCOOTY WOOP ENTERTAINMENT

8228 Sunset Blvd., Suite 300
West Hollywood, CA 90046
310-654-6978

info@scootywoopentertainment.com
scootywoopentertainment.com
facebook.com/ScootyWoopEntertainment
twitter.com/ScootyWoopEnt

Mary Cybriwsky
Partner/Producer/Manager

Frankie Lindquist
Partner/Producer/Manager

SCORE PRODUCTIONS, INC.

2401 Main St.
Santa Monica, CA 90405
604-868-7377

score@scoreproductions.com
scoreproductions.com
imdb.com/company/co0128322

Accepts query letter from produced or represented writers. Project types include Feature Films and TV. Preferred genres include Detective, Drama, Fantasy, and Science Fiction.

SCOTT FREE PRODUCTIONS

614 N. La Peer Dr.
Los Angeles, CA 90069
310-360-2250 (phone)
310-360-2251 (fax)

imdb.com/company/co0074212

Does not accept any unsolicited material. Project types include Feature Films and TV. Preferred genres

include Action, Animation, Crime, Detective, Drama, Non-Fiction, Reality, and Thriller.

Ridley Scott
imdb.com/name/nm0000631
Assistant: Nancy Ryan

David Zucker
imdb.com/name/nm0001878
Assistant: Mark Pfeffer

SCOTT RUDIN PRODUCTIONS

120 W 45th St
10th Floor
New York, NY 10036
212-704-4600

imdb.com/company/co0093765
linkedin.com/company/scott-rudin-productions

Accepts query letter from unproduced, unrepresented writers. Project types include Feature Films. Established in 1993.

Scott Rudin
Producer
212-704-4600
imdb.com/name/nm0748784

Eli Bush
Executive
212-704-4600
eli@scottrudinprod.com
imdb.com/name/nm4791912

SCOTT SANDERS PRODUCTIONS

322 8th Ave, 14th Floor
New York, NY 10001
212-792-6390

scottsandersproductions.com
imdb.com/company/co0326530

Accepts query letter from unproduced, unrepresented writers. Project types include Feature Films and TV.

Scott Sanders
imdb.com/name/nm0761712
Assistant: Jaime Quiroz

Bryan Kalfus
imdb.com/name/nm0435729

SCREEN DOOR ENTERTAINMENT

15223 Burbank Blvd.
Sherman Oaks, CA 91411
818-781-5600 (phone)
818-781-5601 (fax)

info@sdetv.com
sdetv.com
imdb.com/company/co0099778

Accepts query letter from unproduced, unrepresented writers. Project types include TV. Preferred genres include Reality. Established in 2001.

Joel Rizor
President
imdb.com/name/nm1381432

M. Alessandra Ascoli
generalinfo@sdetv.com
imdb.com/name/nm0038529

Dave Shikiar
imdb.com/name/nm0793434

SCREEN GEMS

10202 W Washington Blvd
Culver City, CA 90232
310-244-4000 (phone)
310-244-2037 (fax)

imdb.com/company/co0010568

Does not accept any unsolicited material. Project types include Feature Films, Short Films, and TV. Preferred genres include Action, Comedy, Documentary, Drama, Fantasy, Horror, Reality, Romance, Science Fiction, and Thriller. Established in 1926.

Clint Culpepper
President
imdb.com/name/nm0191695

Scott Strauss
Executive Vice President of Production
imdb.com/name/nm0833873

Pamela Kunath
imdb.com/name/nm2242666

Loren Schwartz
imdb.com/name/nm2817219

James Lopez
imdb.com/name/nm5144603

Eric Paquette
imdb.com/name/nm1789841

Glenn Gainor
imdb.com/name/nm0004636

Carol Smithson
imdb.com/name/nm2972574
linkedin.com/pub/carol-smithson/10/762/7b2

SE8 GROUP

PO Box 691763
West Hollywood, CA 90069
310-285-6090 (phone)
310-285-6097 (fax)

imdb.com/company/co0103782

Accepts query letter from unproduced, unrepresented writers. Project types include Feature Films. Preferred genres include Drama and Thriller.

Douglas Urbanski
Producer
imdb.com/name/nm0881703

Gary Oldman
imdb.com/name/nm0000198

SECOND AND 10TH INC.

51 MacDougal St, Suite 383
New York, NY 10012
347-882-4493

Does not accept any unsolicited material. Project types include Feature Films. Preferred genres include Drama.

Anne Carey
Producer
imdb.com/name/nm0136904
linkedin.com/pub/anne-carey/28/237/661

SEISMIC PICTURES

Raleigh Studios
5358 Melrose Ave.
Suite 218W

Hollywood, CA 90028
323-960-3449

info@seismicpictures.com
seismicpictures.com
imdb.com/company/co0203691

Does not accept any unsolicited material. Project types include Feature Films and TV. Preferred genres include Comedy, Drama, Non-Fiction, and Reality.

Alejandro Laguette
Director of Development
imdb.com/name/nm1657781

Robert Schwartz
imdb.com/name/nm0777412

SELF-RELIANT FILM

info@selfreliantfilm.com
selfreliantfilm.com
facebook.com/selfreliantfilm
twitter.com/selfreliantfilm
imdb.com/company/co0422279

Accepts query letter from unproduced, unrepresented writers via email. Project types include Feature Films and Short Films. Preferred genres include Documentary and Drama. Established in 2010.

Paul Harrill
Founder
imdb.com/name/nm0364204

Ashley Maynor
Founder
imdb.com/name/nm3579482

SENART FILMS

555 W 25th St, 4th Floor
New York, NY 10001
212-406-9610 (phone)
212-406-9581 (fax)

info@senartfilms.com
senartfilms.com
imdb.com/company/co0081078
facebook.com/senartfilms

Does not accept any unsolicited material. Project types include Feature Films and TV. Preferred genres include Drama, Non-Fiction, and Reality.

Robert May
Producer
imdb.com/name/nm1254338

SERAPHIM FILMS

310-888-4200 or 310-246-0050

assistant@seraphimfilms.com
seraphimfilms.com
imdb.com/company/co0045933

Does not accept any unsolicited material. Project types include Feature Films. Preferred genres include Animation, Drama, Fantasy, and Horror.

Clive Barker
President
imdb.com/name/nm0000850
facebook.com/officialclivebarker

Mark Miller
Vice-President

SERENDIPITY POINT FILMS

9 Price St
Toronto, ON M4W 1Z1
Canada
416-960-0300 (phone)
416-960-8656 (fax)

serendipitypoint.com
imdb.com/company/co0016814
facebook.com/SerendipityPointFilms
twitter.com/SerendipityPnt

Does not accept any unsolicited material. Project types include Feature Films and TV. Preferred genres include Action, Comedy, Drama, and Thriller.

Robert Lantos
Producer
imdb.com/name/nm0487190
Assistant: Cherri Campbell

Wendy Saffer
imdb.com/name/nm2194201

SERENDIPITY PRODUCTIONS, INC.

15260 Ventura Blvd, Suite 1040
Sherman Oaks, CA 91403
818-789-3035 (phone)
818-235-0150 (fax)

imdb.com/company/co0119340

Does not accept any unsolicited material. Project types include Feature Films and TV. Preferred genres include Drama, Horror, and Non-Fiction.

Ketura Kestin
keturak@gmail.com
imdb.com/name/nm3109585

Daniel Heffner
danheffner@earthlink.net
imdb.com/name/nm0004527

SEVEN ARTS PICTURES

1801 Century Park East
Suite 1830
Lost Angeles, CA 90067
323-372-3080 (phone)
323-372-3088 (fax)

136-144 New Kings Rd
London, United Kingdom, SW6 4LZ
011-442-030068222 (phone)
011-442-030068220 (fax)

8721 Sunset Blvd
Suite 209
Los Angeles, CA 90069

info@7artspictures.com
7artspictures.com
imdb.com/company/co0045848

Does not accept any unsolicited material. Project types include Feature Films. Preferred genres include Comedy, Drama, Science Fiction, and Thriller.

Peter Hoffman
CEO
imdb.com/name/nm0389056

SHADOWCATCHER ENTERTAINMENT

4701 SW Admiral Way
Box 32

Seattle, WA 98116
206-328-6266 (phone)
206-447-1462 (fax)

kate@shadowcatcherent.com
facebook.com/ShadowCatcherEntertainment
shadowcatcherent.com

Does not accept any unsolicited material. Project types include Feature Films, TV, and Theater. Preferred genres include Animation, Comedy, Drama, Non-Fiction, and Reality.

David Skinner
Executive Producer
imdb.com/name/nm1623496

Norman Stephens
Producer
imdb.com/name/nm1017457

Tom Gorai
Producer
imdb.com/name/nm0329753
linkedin.com/pub/tom-gorai/9/553/b86

SHAFTESBURY FILMS

163 Queen St East Suite 100
Toronto, ON, Canada, M5A 1S1
416-363-1411 (phone)
416-363-1428 (fax)

4370 Tujunga Ave Suite 300
Studio City, CA 91604
818-505-3361 (phone)
818-505-3511 (fax)

info@shaftesbury.ca
facebook.com/ShaftesburyTV
twitter.com/shaftesburytv
shaftesbury.ca
linkedin.com/company/shaftesbury-films-inc.
imdb.com/company/co0014501

Does not accept any unsolicited material. Project types include Feature Films and TV. Preferred genres include Action, Animation, Comedy, Drama, Family, Romance, and Thriller. Established in 1987.

Adam Haight
Senior Vice President, Scripted Content
ahaight@shaftesbury.ca

Christina Jennings
Chairman & CEO
cjennings@shaftesbury.ca
imdb.com/name/nm0421126
twitter.com/CJShaftesbury

Julie Lacey
Vice President, Creative Affairs
jlacey@shaftesbury.ca
imdb.com/name/nm0479936

SHAUN CASSIDY PRODUCTIONS

Los Angeles, CA
818-733-5976

imdb.com/company/co0000380

Accepts query letter from unproduced, unrepresented writers. Project types include TV. Preferred genres include Comedy and Drama.

Shaun Cassidy
imdb.com/name/nm0001027

SHEEP NOIR FILMS

438 W 17th Ave
Vancouver, BC V5Y 2A2
604-762-8933 (fax)

info@sheepnoir.com
sheepnoir.com
imdb.com/company/co0047875

Does not accept any unsolicited material. Project types include Feature Films and TV. Preferred genres include Drama.

Wendy Hyman
Producer
imdb.com/name/nm0405207

Nathaniel Geary
imdb.com/name/nm0311303

Marc Stephenson
Producer
604-762-8933
marc@sheepnoir.com
imdb.com/name/nm0827287
facebook.com/marc.stephenson.353

SHEPHARD/ROBIN COMPANY

c/o Raleigh Studios
5300 Melrose Ave, Suite 225E
Los Angeles, CA 90038
323-871-4412 (phone)
323-871-4418 (fax)

imdb.com/company/co0035643

Does not accept any unsolicited material. Project types
include TV. Preferred genres include Drama.

Greer Shephard
Principle
imdb.com/name/nm0791709

Michael Robin
Principle
imdb.com/name/nm0732218

SHOE MONEY PRODUCTIONS

10202 W Washington Blvd
Poitier Building, Suite 3100
Culver City, CA 90232
310-244-6188

shoemoneyproductions@mac.com
imdb.com/company/co0126698
facebook.com/pages/ShoeMoney-Productions/
    6624704006

Accepts query letter from unproduced, unrepresented
writers via email. Project types include Feature Films
and TV. Preferred genres include Drama.

Thomas Schlamme
imdb.com/name/nm0772095

Julie DeJoie
Head of Production & Development
imdb.com/name/nm1264807

SHONDALAND

323-671-4650

facebook.com/ShondaLand
imdb.com/company/co0170849

Does not accept any unsolicited material. Project types
include Feature Films and TV. Preferred genres
include Comedy and Drama.

Betsy Beers
Producer
imdb.com/name/nm0066530
twitter.com/BeersBetsy

Shonda Rhimes
imdb.com/name/nm0722274
twitter.com/shondarhimes

Alison Eakle
Executive
imdb.com/name/nm2300208

SHORELINE ENTERTAINMENT

1875 Century Park East, Suite 600
Los Angeles, CA 90067
310-551-2060 (phone)
310-201-0729 (fax)

info@shorelineentertainment.com
shorelineentertainment.com
imdb.com/company/co0074988
facebook.com/ShorelineEntertainment

Does not accept any unsolicited material. Project types
include Feature Films and TV. Preferred genres
include Drama, Horror, Non-Fiction, Reality, Science
Fiction, and Thriller.

Morris Ruskin
CEO
imdb.com/name/nm0750830

Sam Eigen
imdb.com/name/nm2073662
linkedin.com/pub/sam-eigen/1/777/256

SHOWTIME NETWORKS

10880 Wilshire Blvd
Ste 1600
Los Angeles, CA 90024
310-234-5200

1633 Broadway
New York, NY 10019
212-708-1600

sho.com
linkedin.com/company/showtime-networks
facebook.com/showtime
imdb.com/company/co0075105

Does not accept any unsolicited material. Project types include Feature Films and TV. Preferred genres include Action, Animation, Comedy, Crime, Detective, Drama, Family, Fantasy, Horror, Myth, Non-Fiction, Romance, Science Fiction, and Thriller.

Tim Delaney
imdb.com/name/nm2303906

Matthew Blank
CEO
imdb.com/name/nm2303194

Joan Boorstein
imdb.com/name/nm1140886

Christina Spade
CFO
imdb.com/name/nm5268270
linkedin.com/pub/chris-spade/11/b35/a00

SIDNEY KIMMEL ENTERTAINMENT

9460 Wilshire Blvd., Suite 500
Beverly Hills, CA 90212
310-777-8818 (phone)
310-777-8892 (fax)

reception@skefilms.com
skefilms.com
imdb.com/company/co0015447
linkedin.com/company/sidney-kimmel-entertainment

Does not accept any unsolicited material. Project types include Feature Films. Preferred genres include Comedy, Crime, Drama, and Romance. Established in 2004.

Matt Berenson
President
imdb.com/name/nm0073554

Sidney Kimmel
Chairman
imdb.com/name/nm0454004

Jim Tauber
CCO
imdb.com/name/nm0851433

Mark Mikutowicz
Vice-President
imdb.com/name/nm2963870

SIERRA/ AFFINITY

9378 Wilshire Blvd.
Suite 210
Beverly Hills, CA 90212
424-253-1060 (phone)
424-653-1977 (fax)

info@sierra-affinity.com
sierra-affinity.com
imdb.com/company/co0276464
linkedin.com/company/sierra-affinity

Does not accept any unsolicited material. Project types include Feature Films. Preferred genres include Action, Comedy, Crime, Detective, Drama, Fantasy, Horror, Romance, Science Fiction, and Thriller.

Nicholas Meyer
CEO
imdb.com/name/nm0583293

Kelly McCormick
Sr. Vice-President
imdb.com/name/nm0566555

Jen Gorton
Creative Executive
imdb.com/name/nm4224815
facebook.com/jen.gorton.9

SIGNATURE PICTURES

8285 W Sunset Blvd, Suite 7
West Hollywood, CA 90046
323-848-9005 (phone)
323-848-9305 (fax)

james@signaturepictures.com
signaturepictures.com
imdb.com/company/co0119730
twitter.com/sigpix
facebook.com/SigPix
linkedin.com/company/signature-pictures

Does not accept any unsolicited material. Project types include Feature Films. Preferred genres include Action, Drama, Non-Fiction, Romance, and Thriller.

Moshe Diamant
Partner
imdb.com/name/nm0224537

Illana Diamant
Partner
imdb.com/name/nm0224532

SIKELIA PRODUCTIONS

110 W 57th St
5th Floor
New York, NY 10019
212-906-8800 (phone)
212-906-8891 (fax)

imdb.com/company/co0141038

Does not accept any unsolicited material. Project types include Feature Films. Preferred genres include Action, Crime, Drama, Romance, and Thriller.

Emma Koskoff
President
imdb.com/name/nm0863374

Martin Scorsese
Principle
imdb.com/name/nm0000217
facebook.com/scorsese

Margaret Bodde
Executive Producer
imdb.com/name/nm0090784

SILVER DREAM PRODUCTIONS

3452 E Foothill Blvd, Suite 620
Pasadena, CA 91107
626-799-3880 (phone)
626-799-5363 (fax)

luoyan@silverdreamprods.com
silverdreamprods.com
imdb.com/company/co0182728

Accepts query letter from unproduced, unrepresented writers via email. Project types include Feature Films. Preferred genres include Drama and Myth.

Luo Yan
imdb.com/name/nm0526839
Assistant: Diana Chin

SILVER/KOSTER PRODUCTIONS

353 S Reeves Dr, Penthouse
Beverly Hills, CA 90212
310-551-5245

skfilmco@aol.com
silvers-koster.com

Accepts query letter from unproduced, unrepresented writers via email. Project types include Feature Films, TV, and Commercials. Preferred genres include Non-Fiction and Reality.

Iren Koster
President
imdb.com/name/nm0467397
linkedin.com/pub/iren-koster/44/ba8/824

Karen Corcoran
Vice-President
facebook.com/karen.corcoran.505

Tracey Silvers
Chairman
imdb.com/name/nm0799016
facebook.com/tracey.silvers.3

SILVER NITRATE ENTERTAINMENT

12268 Ventura Blvd
Studio City, CA 91604
818-762-9559 (phone)
818-762-9177 (fax)

imdb.com/company/co0093834
linkedin.com/company/silver-nitrate

Does not accept any unsolicited material. Project types include Feature Films. Preferred genres include Animation, Comedy, Drama, and Science Fiction.

Ash Shah
Principle
ash@silvernitrate.net
imdb.com/name/nm0787420

SILVER PICTURES

2434 Main St.
Santa Monica, CA 90405
310-566-6100 (phone)
310-566-6188 (fax)

imdb.com/company/co0019968

Accepts query letter from unproduced, unrepresented writers. Project types include Feature Films and TV. Preferred genres include Action, Animation, Drama, Family, Non-Fiction, Reality, Science Fiction, and Thriller.

Joel Silver
Chairman
imdb.com/name/nm0005428

Alex Heineman
imdb.com/name/nm2670366

Sarah Meyer
Director of Development
imdb.com/name/nm1060895
twitter.com/sarahjeanious

SIMONSAYS ENTERTAINMENT

12 Desbrosses St
New York, NY 10013
917-797-9704

info@simonsaysentertainment.net
simonsaysentertainment.net
imdb.com/company/co0278962

Accepts scripts from unproduced, unrepresented writers. Project types include Feature Films. Preferred genres include Crime, Drama, and Romance.

Ron Simons
Principle
imdb.com/name/nm1839399

April Yvette Thompson
imdb.com/name/nm1690743
facebook.com/aprilyvettethompson

SIMON WEST PRODUCTIONS

3450 Cahuenga Blvd West
Building 510
Los Angeles, CA 90068
323-845-0821 (phone)
323-845-4582 (fax)

submissions@simonwestproductions.com
imdb.com/company/co0093861
simonwestproductions.com

Accepts query letter from unproduced, unrepresented writers. Project types include Feature Films and TV. Preferred genres include Action, Drama, and Science Fiction.

Simon West
Principle
imdb.com/name/nm0922346

Jib Polhemus
President
imdb.com/name/nm1015441
linkedin.com/pub/jib-polhemus/87/189/167

SIMSIE FILMS/ MEDIA SAVANT PICTURES

2934 1/2 Beverly Glen Circle
Suite 264
Los Angeles, CA 90077

simsiefilms@mac.com
imdb.com/company/co0182824

Accepts query letter from unproduced, unrepresented writers. Project types include Feature Films. Preferred genres include Comedy and Drama.

Gwen Field
Partner
imdb.com/name/nm0275947
linkedin.com/in/gwenfield

SINGE CELL PICTURES

PO Box 69691
West Hollywood, CA 90069
USA
310-360-7600 (phone)
310-360-7011 (fax)

imdb.com/company/co0079704

Accepts query letter from unproduced, unrepresented writers. Project types include Feature Films and TV. Preferred genres include Comedy and Drama.

Michael Stipe
Principle
imdb.com/name/nm0005468

Sandy Stern
Principle
imdb.com/name/nm0827840

SINOVOI ENTERTAINMENT

1317 N San Fernando Blvd, Suite 395
Burbank, CA 91504
818-562-6404 (phone)
818-567-0104 (fax)

maxwell@sinovoientertainment.com
imdb.com/company/co0020398

Accepts query letter from unproduced, unrepresented writers via email. Project types include Feature Films. Preferred genres include Comedy, Drama, and Horror.

Maxwell Sinovoi
Principle
imdb.com/name/nm0802511

Kimberly Estrada
imdb.com/name/nm1538997
facebook.com/KimberlyEstradaFanPage
twitter.com/kimberlyestrada

SIXTH SENSE PRODUCTIONS, INC.

269 S Beverly Dr, Suite 1297
Beverly Hills, CA 90212
310-247-2790 (phone)
310-247-2791 (fax)

info@sixthsenseproductions.com
scripts@sixthsenseproductions.com
sixthsenseproductions.com

Accepts scripts from unproduced, unrepresented writers via email. Project types include Feature Films. Preferred genres include Action, Drama, and Sociocultural.

Richard Harding
CEO
imdb.com/name/nm1502749
linkedin.com/pub/richard-harding/8/406/7B0
twitter.com/rhssp

SKETCH FILMS

B54
Ugli Campus
56 Wood Ln
London, W12 7SB
+44203-096-1225

hello@sketchfilms.co.uk
imdb.com/company/co0262357
sketchfilms.co.uk
twitter.com/sketchfilm
facebook.com/SketchLondon
linkedin.com/company/sketch-films

Does not accept any unsolicited material. Project types include Feature Films. Preferred genres include Action, Fantasy, Horror, Myth, and Science Fiction. Established in 2009.

Len Wiseman
Writer
imdb.com/name/nm0936482

Jason Brooks
Producer

Christian Jaroljmek
Digital Producer

Luke Scully
Director

Pierangelo Pirak
Producer

Jeremy Riggall
Owner
jeremy@sketchfilms.co.uk

SKYDANCE PRODUCTIONS

5555 Melrose Ave
Dean Martin Building
2nd Floor
Hollywood, CA 90038
310-314-9900

hello@skydance.com
imdb.com/company/co0152219
skydance.com
facebook.com/SkydanceProductions
twitter.com/Skydance
linkedin.com/company/skydance-productions

Accepts scripts from produced or represented writers. Project types include Feature Films and TV. Preferred genres include Action, Comedy, Drama, Family, Fantasy, Myth, Science Fiction, and Thriller.

Jesse Sisgold
COO

Marcy Ross
President

David Ellison
CEO
imdb.com/name/nm1911103
Assistant: Bill Bost

Dana Goldberg
CCO
imdb.com/name/nm1602154
Assistant: Matt Grimm

SKYLARK ENTERTAINMENT, INC.

12405 Venice Blvd, Suite 237
Los Angeles, CA 90066
310-390-2659

imdb.com/company/co0021365

Does not accept any unsolicited material. Project types include Feature Films and TV. Preferred genres include Comedy, Drama, and Non-Fiction.

SKY ONE

9220 Sunset Blvd, Suite 230
West Hollywood, CA 90069
310-860-2740 (phone)
310-860-2471 (fax)

sky.com

Accepts query letter from unproduced, unrepresented writers. Project types include TV. Preferred genres include Action and Science Fiction.

Rebecca Siegal
Sr. Vice-President

SMART ENTERTAINMENT

9595 Wilshire Blvd, Suite 900
Beverly Hills, CA 90212

310-205-6090 (phone)
310-205-6093 (fax)

assistant@smartentertainment.com
smartentertainment.com
imdb.com/company/co0158519
linkedin.com/company/smart-entertainment

Accepts query letter from unproduced, unrepresented writers via email. Project types include Feature Films and TV. Preferred genres include Comedy, Horror, Non-Fiction, Reality, and Thriller.

John Jacobs
President
john@smartentertainment.com
imdb.com/name/nm0414481

Zac Unterman
zac@smartentertainment.com
imdb.com/name/nm2303352

SMASH MEDIA FILMS

1208 Georgina Ave
Santa Monica, CA 90402
310-395-0058 (phone)
310-395-8850 (fax)

info@smashmediafilms.com
smashmediafilms.com

Accepts query letter from unproduced, unrepresented writers via email. Project types include Feature Films and TV. Preferred genres include Comedy, Drama, and Science Fiction.

Shelley Hack
Vice-President
shelley.hack@smashmediafi lms.com

Harry Winer
President
harry.winer@smashmediafi lms.com
linkedin.com/pub/harry-winer/11/3ab/900

SMOKEHOUSE PICTURES

12001 Ventura Pl., Suite 200
Studio City, CA 91604
818-432-0330 (phone)
818-432-0337 (fax)

imdb.com/company/co0184096

Does not accept any unsolicited material. Project types include Feature Films. Preferred genres include Comedy, Drama, and Thriller.

George Clooney
Partner
imdb.com/name/nm0000123

Grant Heslov
Partner
imdb.com/name/nm0381416
Assistant: Tara Oslin

Katie Murphy
Creative Executive
imdb.com/name/nm3682023
linkedin.com/pub/katie-murphy/3/a40/659

SNEAK PREVIEW ENTERTAINMENT

6705 Sunset Blvd
2nd Floor
Hollywood, CA 90028
323-962-0295 (phone)
323-962-0372 (fax)

indiefilm@sneakpreviewentertain.com
sneakpreviewentertain.com
imdb.com/company/co0061839
linkedin.com/company/sneak-preview-entertainment

Accepts query letter from unproduced, unrepresented writers via email. Project types include Feature Films. Established in 1991.

Steven Wolfe
CEO
323-962-0295
sjwolfe@sneakpreviewentertain.com
imdb.com/name/nm0938145

Chris Hazzard
Director of Development
323-962-0295
ch@sneakpe.com
imdb.com/name/nm3302502
linkedin.com/pub/chris-hazzard/5/543/6b3
twitter.com/ChrisHazzardSF

SOBE BROOKE STUDIOS

255 Alhambra Circle
Suite # 1160
Coral Gables, FL 33134
305-602-0312

10900 Wilshire Blvd.
Suite # 1400
Los Angeles, CA 90024
305-602-0312

1230 Peachtree St North East, 19th Floor Atlanta, GA 30309
305-602-0312

sobebrooke.com
twitter.com/sobebrooke
facebook.com/SobeBrookeStudios

Accepts scripts from unproduced, unrepresented writers. Project types include Feature Films. Preferred genres include Action and Drama.

Justin Shaner
CEO
imdb.com/name/nm5232783
linkedin.com/in/justinshaner
facebook.com/jshaner1

Jose Yacaman
Executive Vice President of Production
imdb.com/name/nm2499513
linkedin.com/pub/jose-yacaman/8/b1a/55a
facebook.com/jose.d.yacaman
twitter.com/JDYacaman

Carla Pimentel
imdb.com/name/nm4520475
linkedin.com/pub/carla-carolina-pimentel/35/438/4b8
facebook.com/carla.c.pimentel

Fernando Rojas
COO
linkedin.com/pub/fernando-rojas/49/873/4a8
facebook.com/frojash

SOBINI FILMS

10203 Santa Monica Blvd
Suite 300B
Los Angeles, CA 90067

310-432-6900 (phone)
310-432-6939 (fax)

sobini.com
imdb.com/company/co0086773
twitter.com/sobinifilms

Does not accept any unsolicited material. Project types include Feature Films. Preferred genres include Comedy, Drama, Family, and Thriller.

David Higgin
President
imdb.com/name/nm0383371

Cami Winikoff
COO
imdb.com/name/nm0935121

Mark Amin
CEO
imdb.com/name/nm0024909
linkedin.com/in/markaminsobini

SOCIAL CAPITAL FILMS

1010 Wilshire Blvd.
Suite 507
Los Angeles, CA 90017
866-609-7098

1001 Bridgeway PMB 170
Sausalito, CA 94965
415-332-8877 (phone)
415-332-8467 (fax)

info@socialcapitalfilms.com
imdb.com/company/co0319624

Does not accept any unsolicited material. Project types include Feature Films and TV. Preferred genres include Comedy, Drama, Family, Horror, Non-Fiction, Reality, Science Fiction, and Thriller.

Martin Shore
CEO
imdb.com/name/nm2005915

SOGNO PRODUCTIONS

PO Box 55476
Portland, OR 97238
561-676-4696

imdb.com/company/co0197581

Accepts scripts from unproduced, unrepresented writers. Project types include Feature Films. Preferred genres include Action, Comedy, Documentary, Drama, Fantasy, Romance, and Thriller.

SOLIPSIST FILMS

465 N Crescent Heights Blvd
Los Angeles, CA 90048
323-272-3122 (phone)
323-375-1649 (fax)

info@solipsistfilms.com
solipsistfilms.com
imdb.com/company/co0157838

Accepts query letter from unproduced, unrepresented writers via email. Project types include Feature Films and TV. Preferred genres include Detective, Drama, Fantasy, Non-Fiction, Reality, and Thriller.

Stephen L'Heureux
Principle
imdb.com/name/nm1655017
twitter.com/SLHeureux8

David Purcell
Creative Executive
twitter.com/davepurcell

S PICTURES, INC.

4420 Hayvenhurst Ave
Encino, CA 91436
818-995-1585 (phone)
818-995-1677 (fax)

info@spictures.tv
spictures.tv

Does not accept any unsolicited material. Project types include Feature Films and TV. Preferred genres include Comedy, Non-Fiction, Reality, and Science Fiction.

Chuck Simon
818-995-1585
chuck@spictures.tv
imdb.com/name/nm1247168
facebook.com/cksimon1

SPITFIRE PICTURES

9100 Wilshire Blvd
#401e
Beverly Hills, CA 90212
310-300-9000 (phone)
310-300-9001 (fax)

710 Tenth St NW Atlanta, GA 30318
404-872-7006

spitfirepictures.com
imdb.com/company/co0091468

Does not accept any unsolicited material. Project types
include Feature Films. Preferred genres include
Documentary, Drama, Romance, and Thriller.
Established in 2003.

Nigel Sinclair
CEO
imdb.com/name/nm0801691

Nicholas Ferrall
Director
imdb.com/name/nm5909330
linkedin.com/pub/nick-ferrall/39/58b/356

SPYGLASS ENTERTAINMENT

245 N Beverly Dr
Second Floor
Beverly Hills, CA 90024
310-443-5800 (phone)
310-443-5912 (fax)

spyglassentertainment.com
imdb.com/company/co0031181
linkedin.com/company/spyglass-entertainment

Does not accept any unsolicited material. Project types
include Feature Films. Preferred genres include Action,
Comedy, Drama, Family, Horror, Non-Fiction, and
Thriller.

Gary Barber
Chairman
imdb.com/name/nm0053388

Roger Birnbaum
Chairman
imdb.com/name/nm0083696

STAGE 6 FILMS

10202 W Washington Blvd
Culver City, CA 90232
310-244-4000 (phone)
310-244-2626 (fax)

sonypicturesworldwideacquisitions.com
imdb.com/company/co0222021

Does not accept any unsolicited material. Project types
include Feature Films. Preferred genres include Action,
Animation, Comedy, Crime, Documentary, Drama,
Family, Horror, Period, Romance, Science Fiction,
and Thriller. Established in 2007.

ST. AMOS PRODUCTIONS

3480 Barham Blvd
Los Angeles, CA 90068
323-850-9872

st.amosproductions@earthlink.net
imdb.com/company/co0009925

Accepts query letter from unproduced, unrepresented
writers via email. Project types include Feature Films
and TV. Preferred genres include Comedy, Drama,
Non-Fiction, and Reality.

John Stamos
Principle
imdb.com/name/nm0001764
facebook.com/johnstamos
twitter.com/JohnStamos

STARRY NIGHT ENTERTAINMENT

975 Park AVe.
Suite 10C
New York, NY 10028
212-717-2750 (phone)
212-794-6150 (fax)

Los Angeles, CA
818-895-4916

mailbox@starrymightent.com
info@starrynightentertainment.com
imdb.com/company/co0183209
starrynightentertainment.com
facebook.com/pages/Starry-Night-Entertainment
twitter.com/StarryNightEnt

Accepts query letter from unproduced, unrepresented writers via email. Project types include Feature Films, TV, Commercials, and Theater. Preferred genres include Comedy, Drama, Non-Fiction, and Reality.

Michael Shulman
Partner (NY)
ms@starrynightentertainment.com

Craig Saavedra
Partner (LA)
cs@starrynightentertainment.com
facebook.com/craig.saavedra
twitter.com/CraigSAAVEDRA

STARS ROAD ENTERTAINMENT

10202 W Washington Blvd
David Lean Bldg, Suite 100
Culver City, CA 90232
310-244-4646

imdb.com/company/co0242736

Does not accept any unsolicited material. Project types include Feature Films. Preferred genres include Crime, Detective, Fantasy, Horror, and Thriller.

Sam Raimi
Partner
imdb.com/name/nm0000600

Joshua Donen
Partner
imdb.com/name/nm0232433

Ryan Carroll
Executive
imdb.com/name/nm1498070

STATE STREET PICTURES

9255 W. Sunset Blvd.
Suite 528
Los Angeles, CA 90069
323-556-2240 (phone)
323-556-2242 (fax)

State St Pictures
8075 W. 3rd St.
Suite 306
Los Angeles, CA
90048

statestreetpictures.com
imdb.com/company/co0068765
facebook.com/StateStreetPictures

Does not accept any unsolicited material. Project types include Feature Films and TV. Preferred genres include Comedy and Drama.

Robert Teitel
Partner
imdb.com/name/nm0854052
facebook.com/robert.teitel

Michael Flavin
Creative Executive

George Tillman, Jr.
Partner
imdb.com/name/nm0863387
facebook.com/gtillmanjr
twitter.com/George_Tillman

STEAMROLLER PRODUCTIONS, INC.

100 Universal City Plaza #7151
Universal City, CA 91608
818-733-4622 (phone)
818-733-4608 (fax)

steamrollerprod@aol.com
imdb.com/company/co0003653

Accepts query letter from unproduced, unrepresented writers via email. Project types include Feature Films and TV. Preferred genres include Action, Crime, Detective, Non-Fiction, Reality, and Thriller.

Steven Seagal
imdb.com/name/nm0000219
facebook.com/sseagalofficial
Assistant: Tracy Irvine

Binh Dang
imdb.com/name/nm0199462

STEFANIE EPSTEIN PRODUCTIONS

427 N Canon Dr, Suite 214
Beverly Hills, CA 90210
310-385-0300 (phone)
310-385-0302 (fax)

billseprods@aol.com

imdb.com/company/co0171458
twitter.com/StefanieEpstein

Accepts query letter from unproduced, unrepresented writers via email. Project types include Feature Films and TV. Preferred genres include Comedy and Drama.

Stefanie Epstein
Producer
twitter.com/StefanieEpstein

Bill Gienapp
Creative Executive
twitter.com/Type_O_Purple

STEVEN BOCHCO PRODUCTIONS

3000 Olympic Blvd, Suite 1310
Santa Monica, CA 90404
310-566-6900

yr@bochcomedia.com
imdb.com/company/co0085628
linkedin.com/company/steven-bochco-productions

Accepts query letter from unproduced, unrepresented writers. Project types include TV. Preferred genres include Crime, Detective, and Drama.

Craig Shenkler
CFO

Steven Bochco
Chairman
imdb.com/name/nm0004766

Dayna Kalins
President
imdb.com/name/nm0435861

STOKELY CHAFFIN PRODUCTIONS

1456 Sunset Plaza Dr
Los Angeles, CA 90069
310-657-4559

linkedin.com/pub/stokely-chaffin/b/a98/634
imdb.com/name/nm0149563

Accepts query letter from unproduced, unrepresented writers via email. Project types include Feature Films and TV. Preferred genres include Action, Comedy, Horror, Non-Fiction, and Thriller.

Stokely Chaffin
Principle
imdb.com/name/nm0149563
linkedin.com/pub/stokely-chaffin/b/a98/634

STONEBROOK ENTERTAINMENT

10061 Riverside Dr, Suite 813
Toluca Lake, CA 91602
818-766-8797

imdb.com/company/co0291056
linkedin.com/company/stonebrook-entertainment

Accepts query letter from unproduced, unrepresented writers via email. Project types include Feature Films and TV.

Kris Wheeler
Producer
imdb.com/name/nm2699108
facebook.com/pages/Kris-Wheeler/203421416346308
twitter.com/Wheelerkris

STONE & COMPANY ENTERTAINMENT

c/o Hollywood Center Studios
1040 N Las Palmas Ave, Building 1
Los Angeles, CA 90038
323-960-2599 (phone)
323-960-2437 (fax)

info@stonetv.com
stonetv.com/home.html
imdb.com/company/co0173288

Accepts query letter from unproduced, unrepresented writers via email. Project types include TV. Preferred genres include Non-Fiction and Reality.

Scott Stone
Principle
imdb.com/name/nm0832164

David Weintraub
Producer
imdb.com/name/nm1479111
twitter.com/dwetalent

René Brar
Development Executive
imdb.com/name/nm0105324
twitter.com/renebrar

STONE VILLAGE PICTURES

9200 W Sunset Blvd
Suite 520
West Hollywood, CA 90069
310-402-5171 (phone)
310-402-5172 (fax)

stonevillagepictures.com
imdb.com/company/co0003987

Does not accept any unsolicited material. Project types include Feature Films. Preferred genres include Drama, Romance, and Thriller.

Dylan Russell

Partner
imdb.com/name/nm1928375

Scott Steindorff

Executive Producer
imdb.com/name/nm1127589
linkedin.com/pub/scott-steindorff/21/282/454
twitter.com/Scottsteindorff

STOREFRONT PICTURES

1112 Montana Ave
Santa Monica, CA 90403
310-459-4235

betty@storefrontpics.com
storefrontpics.com
imdb.com/company/co0096868

Does not accept any unsolicited material. Project types include Feature Films. Preferred genres include Comedy, Drama, Family, Fantasy, and Romance.

Susan Cartsonis

President
imdb.com/name/nm0142134
linkedin.com/pub/susan-cartsonis/5/8/359
facebook.com/susan.cartsonis
twitter.com/SusanCartsonis

STORY AND FILM

2934 1/2 Beverly Glen Circle,
Suite 195
Los Angeles, CA 90077
310-480-8833

imdb.com/company/co0120778

Accepts query letter from unproduced, unrepresented writers via email.

Clark Peterson

Development Executive
imdb.com/name/nm0677075
linkedin.com/pub/clark-peterson/13/971/204

STORYLINE ENTERTAINMENT

8335 Sunset Blvd, Suite 207
West Hollywood, CA 90069
323-337-9045 (phone)
323-210-7263 (fax)

info@storyline-entertainment.com
imdb.com/company/co0091980
storyline-entertainment.com
facebook.com/storylineent

Does not accept any unsolicited material. Project types include Feature Films, TV, and Theater. Preferred genres include Comedy, Drama, Non-Fiction, Reality, and Romance.

Craig Zadan

Partner
323-337-9045
craig@storyline-entertainment.com

Neil Meron

Partner
323-337-9046
neil@storyline-entertainment.com

Mark Nicholson

Vice President (Development)
323-337-9047
mark@storyline-entertainment.com

STRAIGHT UP FILMS

3215 La Cienega Ave
Los Angeles, CA 90034
424-238-8470

hello@straightupfilms.com
straightupfilms.com
twitter.com/straightupfilms
imdb.com/company/co0167695

facebook.com/pages/Straight-Up-Films/
243716051911

Does not accept any unsolicited material. Project types include Feature Films and TV. Preferred genres include Comedy, Crime, and Drama.

Marisa Polvino
Co-CEO/Producer
imdb.com/name/nm0689909
linkedin.com/pub/marisa-polvino/5/413/923

Kate Cohen
Co-CEO/Producer
imdb.com/name/nm3154628

Ilane Sharone
Partner

David Boies
Partner

Katie Canright
Production Coordinator

Casey A. Carroll
Director of Development
imdb.com/name/nm3554230
linkedin.com/pub/casey-a-carroll/45/6b0/802

STRIKE ENTERTAINMENT

3000 W Olympic Blvd
Building 5, Suite 1250
Santa Monica, CA 90404
310-315-0550 (phone)
310-315-0560 (fax)

imdb.com/company/co0086710
linkedin.com/company/strike-entertainment_2

Accepts query letter from unproduced, unrepresented writers via email. Project types include Feature Films. Preferred genres include Action, Comedy, Drama, Horror, Science Fiction, and Thriller. Established in 2002.

Marc Abraham
Producer
Assistant: Jamie Zakowski

Tom Bliss
Producer
Assistant: Mark Barclay

Eric Newman
Producer
Assistant: Jesse Rose Moore

Kristel Laiblin
Assistant: Nhu Tran

STUDIOCANAL

301 N. Canon Dr.
Suite 207
Beverly Hills, CA 90210
310-247-0994 (phone)
310-247-0995 (fax)

imdb.com/company/co0047476
facebook.com/STUDIOCANAL.UK
twitter.com/StudioCanalUK

Does not accept any unsolicited material. Project types include Feature Films and TV. Preferred genres include Comedy, Crime, Drama, Fantasy, Horror, Non-Fiction, Reality, Romance, and Thriller.

Ron Halpern
Executive Vice President of Production
facebook.com/ron.halpern1

SUBMARINE ENTERTAINMENT

525 Broadway
Ste 601
New York, NY 10012
212-625-1410 (phone)
212-625-9931 (fax)

info@submarine.com
submarine.com
imdb.com/company/co0131815

Accepts query letter from produced or represented writers. Project types include Feature Films. Preferred genres include Documentary and Drama.

Josh Braun
President
josh@submarine.com
imdb.com/name/nm2248562

David Koh
Executive

Dan Braun
President
dan@submarine.com
imdb.com/name/nm2250854

SUCH MUCH FILMS

Santa Monica, CA 90405

info@suchmuchfilms.com
suchmuchfilms.com
facebook.com/suchmuchfilms
imdb.com/company/co0112289
twitter.com/SuchMuchFilms

Accepts query letter from unproduced, unrepresented writers via email. Project types include Feature Films. Preferred genres include Documentary and Drama.

Judi Levine
Principle
imdb.com/name/nm0505861
facebook.com/judi.levine.94

Ben Lewin
Principle
imdb.com/name/nm0506802

SUMMIT ENTERTAINMENT

1630 Stewart St
Ste 120
Santa Monica, CA 90404
310-309-8400 (phone)
310-828-4132 (fax)

summit-ent.com
imdb.com/company/co0046206
twitter.com/summitent

Does not accept any unsolicited material. Project types include Feature Films. Preferred genres include Action, Comedy, Crime, Drama, Fantasy, Romance, Science Fiction, and Thriller.

Rob Friedman
CEO
310-309-8400
imdb.com/name/nm2263981

Patrick Wachsberger
President
310-309-8400
imdb.com/name/nm0905163

Gillian Bohrer
Vice-President
310-309-8400
imdb.com/name/nm2023551

Merideth Milton
Sr. Vice-President
310-309-8400
imdb.com/name/nm0590693

SUNDIAL PICTURES

511 Sixth Ave., Suite 375
New York, NY 10011

info@sundialpicturesllc.com
imdb.com/company/co0259997
sundial-pictures.com

Does not accept any unsolicited material. Project types include Feature Films. Preferred genres include Comedy, Documentary, Drama, and Thriller.

Benjamin Weber
imdb.com/name/nm3373548
linkedin.com/in/benweber1
facebook.com/benjamin.weber.3557

Joey Carey
Partner
imdb.com/name/nm2909903
linkedin.com/pub/joey-carey/64/932/685
twitter.com/JoeyCareyFilms

Stefan Norwicki
President
imdb.com/name/nm3378356
twitter.com/StefanNowicki

SUNLIGHT PRODUCTIONS

854-A Fifth St
Santa Monica, CA 90403
310-899-1522 (phone)
310-899-1262 (fax)

info@sunlightproductions.com
imdb.com/company/co0028319

filmbudget.com/sunlightproductions

Does not accept any unsolicited material. Project types include Feature Films and TV. Preferred genres include Comedy, Drama, and Non-Fiction.

Mike Binder
Executive
imdb.com/name/nm0082802

Jack Binder
Executive

SUNSWEPT ENTERTAINMENT

10201 W Pico Blvd
Building 45
Los Angeles, CA 90064
310-369-0878 (phone)
310-969-0726 (fax)

Sunswept Entertainment - TV
10201 W. Pico Blvd.
Building 3/Room 204
Los Angeles, CA 90035

imdb.com/company/co0226011

Does not accept any unsolicited material. Project types include Feature Films. Preferred genres include Animation, Comedy, Family, Fantasy, and Romance. Established in 2004.

Karen Rosenfelt
Principle
imdb.com/name/nm1651942

Caroline MacVicar
Creative Executive

SUNTAUR ENTERTAINMENT

1581 N Crescent Heights Blvd.
Los Angeles, CA 90046
323-656-3800

info@suntaurent.com
imdb.com/company/co0183461
suntaurent.com

Does not accept any unsolicited material. Project types include Feature Films and TV. Preferred genres include Comedy and Drama.

Paul Aaron
Executive
imdb.com/name/nm0007477
facebook.com/aaronpaul
twitter.com/aaronpaul_8

SUPER CRISPY ENTERTAINMENT

2812 Santa Monica Blvd
Ste 205
Santa Monica, CA 90404
310-453-4545

crispyfilms@gmail.com
imdb.com/company/co0326644

Does not accept any unsolicited material. Project types include Feature Films. Preferred genres include Comedy, Drama, and Romance.

Jonathan Schwartz
Producer
310-453-4545
imdb.com/name/nm2009933

Andrea Sperling
Producer
310-453-4545
imdb.com/name/nm0818304

SUPERFINGER ENTERTAINMENT

c/o Chris Hart/UTA
9560 Wilshire Blvd
Beverly Hills, CA 90212
310-385-6715

imdb.com/company/co0181284

Accepts query letter from unproduced, unrepresented writers via email. Project types include Feature Films and TV. Preferred genres include Animation, Comedy, Non-Fiction, and Reality.

Dane Cook
imdb.com/name/nm0176981
twitter.com/DaneCook

SUZANNE DELAURENTIIS PRODUCTIONS

5555 Melrose Ave, Drier Building #217
Hollywood, CA 90036
323-956-7899

10061 Riverside Dr, Suite 101
Toluca Lake, California, 91602

delaurentiisllc@gmail.com
suzannedelaurentiisproductions.com
imdb.com/company/co0014118

Does not accept any unsolicited material. Project types include Feature Films and TV. Preferred genres include Crime and Drama.

Suzanne DeLaurentiis
Producer
imdb.com/name/nm0216560

SWEET 180

141 W 28th St #300
NYC, NY 10001
212-541-4443 (phone)
212-563-9655 (fax)

sweet180.com
twitter.com/Sweet180grados

Does not accept any unsolicited material. Project types include Feature Films and TV. Preferred genres include Comedy, Drama, Non-Fiction, Reality, and Romance.

Lillian LaSalle
Principle
lillian@sweet180.com
facebook.com/lillian.lasalle

Catherine Clausi
Assistant: Lindsay Carlson

Nina Schreiber
Manager
nina@sweet180.com

Rachel Maran
assistant@sweet180.com

TAGGART PRODUCTIONS

9000 W Sunset Blvd
Suite 1020
West Hollywood, CA 90069
424-249-3350 (phone)
424-249-3972 (fax)

taggart-productions.com
facebook.com/taggartproductions
linkedin.com/company/taggart-productions
imdb.com/company/co0316676
twitter.com/TaggartTweet

Does not accept any unsolicited material. Project types include Feature Films. Preferred genres include Action, Comedy, Crime, Drama, and Thriller. Established in 2010.

Tim Nardelli
linkedin.com/pub/tim-nardelli/22/323/550
facebook.com/tim.nardelli

Michael Nardelli
President & CEO
imdb.com/name/nm1660148
linkedin.com/pub/dir/Mike/Nardell

TAGHIT

468 N Camden Dr, Suite 200
Beverly Hills, 90210
United States

Does not accept any unsolicited material. Project types include Feature Films. Preferred genres include Drama and Thriller.

Rachid Bouchareb
Writer

Jean Brehat
Producer

TAGLINE PICTURES

9250 Wilshire Blvd
Ground Floor
Beverly Hills, CA 90212
310-595-1515 (phone)
310-595-1505 (fax)

info@taglinela.com

taglinela.com
imdb.com/company/co0183460

Does not accept any unsolicited material. Project types include TV. Preferred genres include Comedy and Drama.

William Mercer

Chris Henze
Partner
imdb.com/name/nm1771421
linkedin.com/pub/chris-henze/70/a23/78b

J.B. Roberts
Partner
facebook.com/jb.roberts.9

Ron West

Kelly Kulchak
President
imdb.com/name/nm2103544

TAILLIGHT TV

30 Middleton St
Nashville, TN 37210
United States
615-385-1034 (phone)
615-385-1024 (fax)

taillight.tv

Does not accept any unsolicited material. Project types include TV. Preferred genres include Reality.

Tom Forest
President/Executive Producer

Thom Oliphant
VP of Development/Executive Producer

TALLGRASS PICTURES

710 13th St #300
San Diego, CA 92101
United States
916-717-4483

jennifer@tallgrasspictures.com
tallgrasspictures.com

Accepts query letter from unproduced, unrepresented writers via email. Project types include Feature Films.

Preferred genres include Action, Comedy, Crime, Drama, Fantasy, Reality, Romance, and Science Fiction.

Jennifer Atlas
Development

TAMARA ASSEYEV PRODUCTION

1187 Coast Village Rd.
Suite 134
Santa Barbara, CA 93108
323-656-4731 (phone)
323-656-2211 (fax)

tamaraprod@aol.com
imdb.com/company/co0043622

Accepts query letter from unproduced, unrepresented writers. Project types include TV. Preferred genres include Drama.

Tamara Asseyev
Producer
imdb.com/name/nm0039834
linkedin.com/pub/tamara-asseyev/66/35/9b4
Assistant: Constance Mead

TANNENBAUM COMPANY

c/o CBS Studios
4024 Radford Ave, Bungalow 16
Studio City, CA 91604
818-655-7181 (phone)
818-655-7193 (fax)

imdb.com/company/
     co0099776%20%20%20Cached%20Tannenbaum%20Company,
twitter.com/tbaumco

Does not accept any unsolicited material. Project types include Feature Films and TV. Preferred genres include Comedy, Drama, Non-Fiction, and Reality.

Kim Haswell-Tannenbaum
Producer

Jason Wang
Creative Affairs
imdb.com/name/nm4867712
linkedin.com/pub/jason-wang/4/9A5/905

Eric Tannenbaum
Partner
imdb.com/name/nm1383548

TAPESTRY FILMS, INC.

9328 Civic Center Dr, 2nd Floor
Beverly Hills, CA 90210
310-275-1191 (phone)
310-275-1266 (fax)

imdb.com/company/co0018522
linkedin.com/company/tapestry-films

Does not accept any unsolicited material. Project types include Feature Films. Preferred genres include Action, Comedy, Family, Romance, and Thriller.

Michael Schreiber
President
imdb.com/name/nm2325100

Peter Abrams
imdb.com/name/nm0009222

Robert L. Levy
imdb.com/name/nm0506597

Kat Blasband Page
imdb.com/name/nm2321097

TAR ART

304 Hudson St, 6th Floor
New York, NY 10013
United States
212-989-7900 (phone)
212-989-7911 (fax)

inquire@tar-art.com
tar-art.com

Does not accept any unsolicited material. Project types include Feature Films. Preferred genres include Drama.

Evanly Schindler
Co-Founder

Mauriziio Marchiori
Co-Founder

TASHMOO PRODUCTIONS

1075 Duval St, Suite C21 #236
Key West, FL 33040
United States
305-294-9382

1841 Broadway, Suite 711A
New York, NY 10023
212-799-7855

info@tashmoo.com
tashmoo.com

Does not accept any unsolicited material. Project types include Feature Films. Preferred genres include Comedy and Drama.

Lawrence Blume
Producer

TAURUS ENTERTAINMENT COMPANY

5555 Melrose Ave
Marx Brothers Building, Suite 103/104
Hollywood, CA 90038
818-935-5157 (phone)
323-686-5379 (fax)

taurusentco@yahoo.com
taurusec.com
imdb.com/company/co0080449
facebook.com/TaurusEntertainmentsInc

Accepts query letter from unproduced, unrepresented writers via email. Project types include Feature Films and TV. Preferred genres include Action, Animation, Drama, and Family. Established in 1991.

James Dudelson
jgdudelson@yahoo.com
imdb.com/name/nm0240054
facebook.com/james.dudelson

Robert Dudelson
rfdudelson@mac.com
imdb.com/name/nm0240055
linkedin.com/pub/robert-dudelson/5/418/a53
facebook.com/rfdudelson

TAYLOR LANE PRODUCTIONS

2446 1/2 N Gower St
Los Angeles, CA 90068
United States
310-770-2594

Does not accept any unsolicited material. Project types include Feature Films. Preferred genres include Drama.

Christian Taylor
President, Producer

T&C PICTURES

3122 Santa Monica Blvd #200
Santa Monica, CA 90404
310-828-1340 (phone)
310-828-1581 (fax)

info@tandcpictures.com
imdb.com/company/co0207457

Accepts query letter from unproduced, unrepresented writers. Project types include Feature Films and TV. Preferred genres include Action, Comedy, Drama, Family, Non-Fiction, and Thriller.

Bill Borden
Producer
christine@tandcpictures.com
imdb.com/name/nm0096115

Barry Rosenbush
Executive
imdb.com/name/nm0742492

Arata Matsushima
310-828-7801
imdb.com/name/nm2606503

T&C PICTURES

3122 Santa Monica Blvd., Suite 200
Santa Monica, CA 90404
United States
310-828-7801

Does not accept any unsolicited material. Project types include Feature Films.

Bill Borden
Producer

Barry Rosenbush
Producer

TDJ ENTERPRISES

PO Box 763518
Dallas, TX 75376
United States
888-201-2535

info@tdjakes.com
twitter.com/bishopjakes
facebook.com/TDJenterprises
tdjakes.com

Does not accept any unsolicited material. Project types include Feature Films. Preferred genres include Drama.

Bishop T.D. Jakes
CEO/Author

Curtis Wallace
COO

TEAKWOOD LANE PRODUCTIONS

1845 W Olympic Blvd., Suite 1125W
Los Angeles, CA 90064
United States

Does not accept any unsolicited material. Project types include TV. Preferred genres include Action, Drama, and Thriller.

Howard Gordon
Producer/Writer

Hugh Fitzpatrick
Head of TV

TEAM DOWNEY

1311 Abbot Kinney
Venice, CA 90291
310-450-5100

imdb.com/company/co0306946
teamdowney.com

Does not accept any unsolicited material. Project types include Feature Films. Preferred genres include Action, Comedy, and Drama. Established in 2010.

Susan Downey
Producer
imdb.com/name/nm1206265

Robert Downey
Producer
imdb.com/name/nm0000375
facebook.com/robertdowneyjr
twitter.com/RobertDowneyJr

David Gambino
President
imdb.com/name/nm1312724
linkedin.com/pub/david-gambino/9/756/879

TEAM G

1839 Blake Ave #5 Los Angeles, CA 90039
213-915-8106 (phone)
323-843-9210 (fax)

info@teamgproductions.com
teamgproductions.com

Project types include Feature Films. Preferred genres include Comedy, Drama, and Science Fiction.

Jett Steiger
Partner
imdb.com/name/nm2532520

Trey Hock
Partner
imdb.com/name/nm2465366
twitter.com/treyhock

TEAM TODD

2900 W Olympic Blvd
Santa Monica, CA 91404
310-255-7265 (phone)
310-255-7222 (fax)

imdb.com/company/co0050544
linkedin.com/company/team-todd
facebook.com/pages/Team-Todd/25240836851

Accepts scripts from produced or represented writers. Project types include Feature Films. Preferred genres include Animation, Drama, Family, Myth, and Romance.

Julianna Hays
Creative Executive
imdb.com/name/nm3057670
linkedin.com/in/juliannahays

Suzanne Todd
Principle
imdb.com/name/nm0865297
linkedin.com/in/mssuzannetodd
twitter.com/teamsuz

TELEVISA USA

1601 Cloverfield Blvd., South Tower, Suite 200
Santa Monica, CA 90404
United States

twitter.com/TelevisaDigital
facebook.com/TelevisaPublishing
televisa.com/us

Does not accept any unsolicited material. Project types include TV. Preferred genres include Drama and Romance.

Michael Garcia
CCO

TELEVISION 360

9111 Wilshire Blvd.
Beverly Hills, CA 90210
United States
310-272-7000

Does not accept any unsolicited material. Project types include TV. Preferred genres include Comedy.

Evelyn O'Neil
Producer

Marcus Blakely
Development

TEMPLE HILL ENTERTAINMENT

9255 W Sunset Blvd
West Hollywood, CA 90069
310-270-4383 (phone)
310-270-4395 (fax)

templehillent.com
imdb.com/company/co0069651

facebook.com/pages/Temple-Hill-Entertainment/
     336532409773139
twitter.com/TempleHillEnt

Does not accept any unsolicited material. Project types
include Feature Films and TV. Preferred genres
include Comedy, Drama, Family, Fantasy, and
Thriller. Established in 2006.

Marty Bowen
Partner
imdb.com/name/nm2125212
Assistant: Charlie Morrison

Wyck Godfrey
Partner
imdb.com/name/nm0324041
twitter.com/wyckgodfrey
Assistant: Jaclyn Huntling

Tracy Nyberg
Sr. Vice-President
imdb.com/name/nm2427937

Adam Londy
Creative Executive

Isaac Klausner
Creative Executive
imdb.com/name/nm2327099
linkedin.com/pub/isaac-klausner/16/25b/151
facebook.com/isaac.klausner

TENAFLY FILM COMPANY

15 Birchwood Place
Tenafly, NJ 07670
United States
201-569-2844

info@tenaflyfilmco.com
tenaflyfilmco.com

Does not accept any unsolicited material. Project types
include Feature Films and TV. Preferred genres
include Comedy and Drama.

Eric Weber
Writer/Producer/Director

Sean Devaney
Creative Executive/Producer

TEN/FOUR PICTURES

1011 N Fuller Ave, Suite C
Los Angeles, CA 90046
United States
323-851-5400 (phone)
323-851-5401 (fax)

info@tenfourpictures.com
tenfourpictures.com

Does not accept any unsolicited material. Project types
include Feature Films.

Gil Cates
Partner/Producer

Caitlin Murney
Partner/Producer

Stephanie Hall
Creative Executive/Assistant

TEN THIRTEEN PRODUCTIONS

PO Box 900
Beverly Hills , CA 90213
United States

Does not accept any unsolicited material. Project types
include Feature Films and TV. Preferred genres
include Action and Science Fiction.

Chris Carter
Writer/Producer/Director

Gabe Rotter
Director of Development

TEN THIRTY-ONE PICTURES

P.O. Box 604
Burbank, CA 91503
United States
818-570-1031

888-896-1031

tenthirtyonepictures.com

Does not accept any unsolicited material. Project types
include Feature Films. Preferred genres include
Drama, Romance, and Thriller.

Levi Obery
Principal/Producer

David Zimmerman
Principal

Jess Brown
Principal

TERNION PRODUCTIONS

2850 Ocean Park Blvd., Suite 300
Santa Monica, CA 90405
United States

Does not accept any unsolicited material. Project types include Feature Films and TV. Preferred genres include Action, Comedy, and Drama.

Mike Judge
Writer/Director

John Altschuler
Writer/Producer

Dave Krinsky
Writer/Producer

TERRA FIRMA FILMS

3601 Wilshire Blvd
Beverly Hills, CA 90210
310-480-5676 (phone)
310-862-4717 (fax)

info@terrafirmafilms.com
imdb.com/company/co0163783
terrafirmafilms.com

Accepts query letter from unproduced, unrepresented writers via email. Project types include Feature Films. Preferred genres include Action, Comedy, Drama, Family, and Romance. Established in 2003.

Adam Herz
President
imdb.com/name/nm0381221

Josh Shader
Producer
imdb.com/name/nm1003558
linkedin.com/pub/josh-shader/9/1b8/547
twitter.com/JoshShader

TERRIMEL ENTERTAINMENT

5555 Melrose Ave, Dreier Bldg. Suite 210
Los Angeles, CA 90038
United States

terrimelentertainment.com

Does not accept any unsolicited material. Project types include Feature Films. Preferred genres include Comedy and Romance.

Terri Melkonia
Producer

THE AMERICAN FILM COMPANY

c/o Business Affairs, Inc.
2415 Main St, 2nd Floor
Santa Monica, CA 90405
310-392-0777

info@americanfilmco.com
theamericanfilmcompany.com
imdb.com/company/co0176864
facebook.com/theamericanfilmcompany
twitter.com/AmericanFilmCo

Accepts query letter from unproduced, unrepresented writers via email. Project types include Feature Films. Preferred genres include Drama, Non-Fiction, Period, and Thriller. Established in 2008.

Brian Falk
President
imdb.com/name/nm1803137
twitter.com/brifalk

THE ASYLUM

72 E Palm Ave
Burbank, CA 91502
323-850-1214 (phone)
818-260-9811 (fax)

comments@theasylum.cc
theasylum.cc
imdb.com/company/co0042909
twitter.com/theasylumcc
facebook.com/AsylumFilms
linkedin.com/company/the-asylum

Does not accept any unsolicited material. Project types include Feature Films. Preferred genres include Action,

Fantasy, Horror, Science Fiction, and Thriller. Established in 1997.

Micho Rutare
Director of Development
micho@theasylum.cc
imdb.com/name/nm3026436
twitter.com/MichoRutare

David Michael Latt
Partner
imdb.com/name/nm0490375

Mark Quod
Post Production Supervisor
quod@theasylum.cc
imdb.com/name/nm0704517

Joseph Lawson
Visual Effects Supervisor
lawson@theasylum.cc
imdb.com/name/nm1037472

David Rimawi
Partner
rimawi@theasylum.cc
imdb.com/name/nm0727235

Paul Bales
Partner
bales@theasylum.cc
imdb.com/name/nm0050097

Lisa Ries
Post Production Sound Assistant
ries@theasylum.cc
imdb.com/name/nm2917991

THE AV CLUB

2629 Main St #211
Santa Monica, CA 90405
310-396-1165

avclub.com
twitter.com/theavclub
facebook.com/theavclub

Does not accept any unsolicited material. Project types include Feature Films. Preferred genres include Comedy, Drama, Non-Fiction, Romance, and Science Fiction.

Amy Robertson
Producer
imdb.com/name/nm1516144

THE BADHAM COMPANY

c/o Rain Management
1800 Stanford St
Santa Monica, CA 90404
310-481-9800

c/o Paradigm Agency
360 N Beverly Dr
Beverly Hills CA 90210
310-288-8000

ah@badhamcompany.com
imdb.com/company/co0054883
johnbadham.com

Accepts scripts from produced or represented writers. Project types include Feature Films and TV. Preferred genres include Drama, Family, and Non-Fiction.

John Badham
Producer
imdb.com/name/nm0000824

Aif Hewitt
Vice-President

THE BRAKEFIELD COMPANY

3727 W Magnolia Blvd., #718
Burbank, CA 91505

info@thebrakefieldcompany.com
thebrakefieldcompany.com
imdb.com/company/co0344861
facebook.com/TheBrakefieldCompany
twitter.com/TheBrakefieldCo

Does not accept any unsolicited material. Project types include Feature Films. Preferred genres include Drama.

Shawna Brakefield
CEO/President
imdb.com/name/nm1113538

Jennifer Grace Cook
Creative Executive
imdb.com/name/nm1614490

THE BUENA VISTA MOTION PICTURES GROUP

500 S. Buena Vista St
Burbank, CA 91521
818-560-1000

Does not accept any unsolicited material. Project types include Feature Films.

Richard Cook
Chairman

THE BUREAU

18 Phipp St
2nd Floor
London - EC2A 4NU
United-Kingdom
+44-0207-033-0555

mail@thebureau.co.uk
thebureau.co.uk

Does not accept any unsolicited material. Project types include Feature Films. Preferred genres include Comedy, Documentary, Drama, Romance, and Thriller. Established in 2000.

Valentina Brazzini
linkedin.com/pub/valentina-brazzini/3/896/926

Bertrand Faivre
Producer
imdb.com/name/nm0265724
linkedin.com/pub/bertrand-faivre/11/2a1/b03

Soledad Gatti-Pascual
imdb.com/name/nm0309806
linkedin.com/pub/soledad-gatti-pascual/15/99/400

Tristan Golighter
Producer

Matthew de Braconier

THE EDELSTEIN COMPANY

10351 Santa Monica Blvd.
Los Angeles, CA 90035
323-933-4051

imdb.com/company/co0155498

Does not accept any unsolicited material. Project types include TV.

Michael Edelstein
Producer
imdb.com/name/nm024904

THE FRED ROGERS COMPANY

4802 Fifth Ave
Pittsburgh, PA 15213
412-687-2990

info@fci.org
fci.org

Does not accept any unsolicited material. Project types include TV. Preferred genres include Animation and Family.

William H. Isler
CEO/President

Alan Friedman
Director of Development

THE GOATSINGERS

177 W. Broadway, 2nd Floor
New York, NY 10013
212-966-3045 (phone)
212-966-4362 (fax)

imdb.com/company/co0000042

Does not accept any unsolicited material. Project types include Feature Films and TV.

Harvey Keitel
President/Actor/Producer
imdb.com/name/nm0000172

THE GOLD COMPANY

499 N Canon Dr, Suite 306
Beverly Hills, CA 90210
310-270-4653

Accepts query letter from unproduced, unrepresented writers. Project types include Feature Films. Preferred genres include Comedy.

Eric L. Gold
Principle
imdb.com/name/nm0324970
linkedin.com/pub/eric-l-townley/2/a14/63

Jessica Green
Executive Vice President of Production
imdb.com/name/nm2783652

THE GOLDSTEIN COMPANY

1644 Courtney Ave
Los Angeles, CA 90046
310-659-9511

garywgoldstein.com
linkedin.com/company/the-goldstein-company
facebook.com/garywgoldstein
twitter.com/garywgoldstein

Accepts query letter from unproduced, unrepresented
writers via email. Project types include Feature Films,
TV, and Commercials. Preferred genres include
Action, Comedy, Non-Fiction, Reality, Romance, and
Thriller.

Sandra Tomita
imdb.com/name/nm0866739

Gary Goldstein
Producer
gary@garywgoldstein.com
imdb.com/name/nm0326214
linkedin.com/in/garywgoldstein
twitter.com/garywgoldstein

THE GOODMAN COMPANY

8491 Sunset Blvd, Suite 329
Los Angeles, CA 90069
323-655-0719

ilyssagoodman@sbcglobal.net

Accepts query letter from unproduced, unrepresented
writers. Project types include Feature Films and TV.
Preferred genres include Comedy, Drama, Family,
Non-Fiction, and Reality.

Ilyssa Goodman
Executive
imdb.com/name/nm1058415
linkedin.com/in/ilyssagoodman

THE GOTHAM GROUP

9255 Sunset Blvd, Suite 515
Los Angeles, CA 90069
310-285-0001 (phone)
310-285-0077 (fax)

gotham-group.com
linkedin.com/company/the-gotham-group

Does not accept any unsolicited material. Project types
include Feature Films, TV, and Commercials.
Preferred genres include Action, Animation, Comedy,
Drama, Family, Fantasy, Non-Fiction, Reality, and
Science Fiction.

Peter McHugh
peter@gotham-group.com

Julie Kane-Ritsch
jkr@gotham-group.com
imdb.com/name/nm1415970
linkedin.com/pub/julie-kane-ritsch/a/6a9/322

Ellen Goldsmith-Vein
egv@gotham-group.com
imdb.com/name/nm1650412

THE GREENBERG GROUP

2029 S Westgate Ave
Los Angeles, CA 90025

info@greenberggroup.com
greenberggroup.com
linkedin.com/company/the-greenberg-group
facebook.com/pages/The-Greenberg-Group/
    741724785853691

Accepts query letter from unproduced, unrepresented
writers via email. Project types include Feature Films,
TV, and Commercials. Preferred genres include
Action, Non-Fiction, Reality, and Thriller.

Randy Greenberg
randy@greenberggroup.com
imdb.com/name/nm2985843
twitter.com/RandyGreenberg

THE GROUP ENTERTAINMENT

115 W 29th St #1102
New York, NY 10001

212-868-5233 (phone)
212-504-3082 (fax)

The Anchor Building
2509 Portland Ave,
Louisville KY, 40212
502-561-1162

info@thegroupentertainment.com
thegroupentertainment.com

Does not accept any unsolicited material. Project types include Feature Films and TV. Preferred genres include Action, Comedy, Drama, Non-Fiction, Reality, and Romance.

Rebecca Atwood
Creative Executive
rebecca@thegroupentertainment.com

Gil Holland
Partner
imdb.com/name/nm0390693

Jill McGrath
Partner
jill@thegroupentertainment.com

Kyle Luker
Partner
kyle@thegroupentertainment.com
imdb.com/name/nm1739392

THE HALCYON COMPANY

8455 Beverly Blvd
Penthouse
Los Angeles, CA 90048
323-650-0222

info@thehalcyoncompany.com
thehalcyoncompany.com
imdb.com/company/co0175646
facebook.com/pages/The-Halcyon-Company/
    109874619030902
twitter.com/TheHalcyonCo

Does not accept any unsolicited material. Project types include Feature Films. Preferred genres include Action, Science Fiction, and Thriller. Established in 2006.

Derek Anderson
CEO
imdb.com/name/nm2203770

Joel Michaels
President of Production

James Middleton
Creative Development & Production

Victor Kubicek
CEO
imdb.com/name/nm2127497

THE HAL LIEBERMAN COMPANY

8522 National Blvd, Suite 108
Culver City, CA 90232
310-202-1929 (phone)
323-850-5132 (fax)

imdb.com/company/co0152063

Accepts query letter from unproduced, unrepresented writers via email. Project types include Feature Films. Preferred genres include Drama, Family, Fantasy, Horror, and Thriller.

Hal Lieberman
Principle
imdb.com/name/nm0509386
linkedin.com/pub/hal-lieberman/13/a7b/5b8

Dan Scheinkman
Vice-President
linkedin.com/pub/dan-scheinkman/7/49/a59

THE HATCHERY

4751 Wilshire Blvd.
Third Floor
Los Angeles, CA 90010
323-549-4360 (phone)
818-748-4615/Attn: Dan Angel (fax)

dangel@thehatcheryllc.com
thehatcheryllc.com

Does not accept any unsolicited material. Project types include Feature Films and TV. Preferred genres include Comedy, Family, Horror, and Science Fiction.

Dan Angel
Founder
dangel@thehatcheryllc.com
imdb.com/name/nm0029445
linkedin.com/pub/dan-angel/5/74a/19a

THE HECHT COMPANY

5455 8th St #34
Carpinteria, CA 93013
805-745-1007

hechtco@aol.com
imdb.com/company/co0080878

Accepts query letter from unproduced, unrepresented writers via email. Project types include Feature Films and TV. Preferred genres include Drama, Non-Fiction, Reality, and Thriller.

Duffy Hecht
Producer
imdb.com/name/nm0372953

Steve Peterson
Director of Development

THE HELPERN COMPANY

10323 Santa Monica Blvd., Suite 101
Los Angeles, CA 90025

Does not accept any unsolicited material. Project types include Feature Films.

David Helpern
Producer
imdb.com/name/nm0375809

THE JAR

4100 W Alameda Ave. 4th Floor
Burbank, CA 91505
818-955-5400

Does not accept any unsolicited material. Project types include TV. Preferred genres include Comedy and Drama.

Tom Mazza
EVP & Head of Worldwide TV
imdb.com/name/nm2301903

THE JIM HENSON COMPANY

1416 N La Brea Ave
Hollywood, CA 90028
323-802-1500 (phone)
323-802-1825 (fax)

37-18 Northern Blvd, Suite 400
Long Island City, NY 11101
212-794-2400 (phone)
212-439-7452 (fax)

info@henson.com
henson.com
linkedin.com/company/the-jim-henson-company
facebook.com/hensoncompany
imdb.com/company/co0095015

Does not accept any unsolicited material. Project types include Feature Films, TV, Commercials, and Theater. Preferred genres include Animation, Comedy, Family, Fantasy, Non-Fiction, Reality, and Science Fiction. Established in 1958.

Brian Henson
Chairman
imdb.com/name/nm0005008

Halle Stanford
Executive Vice President of Children's Entertainment
imdb.com/name/nm1277553
linkedin.com/pub/halle-stanford/1a/22a/647

THE KONIGSBERG COMPANY

7919 W Sunset Blvd., 2nd Floor
Los Angeles, CA 90046
323-845-1000

imdb.com/company/co006938

Does not accept any unsolicited material. Project types include Feature Films and TV. Preferred genres include Drama.

Frank Konigsberg
Producer
imdb.com/name/nm0465119

THE LADD COMPANY

9255 Sunset Blvd., Suite 620
West Hollywood, CA 90069
310-777-2060 (phone)
310-777-2061 (fax)

imdb.com/company/co0042559

Does not accept any unsolicited material. Project types include Feature Films.

Alan Ladd Jr.
President
imdb.com/name/nm0480440

THE LEVINSON/FONTANA COMPANY

185 Broome St
New York, NY 10002
212-206-3585

levinson.com
tomfontana.com
imdb.com/company/co0068745

Does not accept any unsolicited material. Project types
include TV.

Tom Fontana
Writer/Executive Producer
imdb.com/name/nm0284956

Barry Levinson
Director/Writer/Executive Producer
imdb.com/name/nm0001469

THE LITTLEFIELD COMPANY

500 S Buena Vista St Animation Building, Suite 3D-2
Burbank, CA 91521
818-560-2280 (phone)
818-560-3775 (fax)

imdb.com/company/co0080851

Does not accept any unsolicited material. Project types
include TV. Preferred genres include Drama.

Warren Littlefield
Principle
818-560-2280
imdb.com/name/nm0514716
Assistant: Patricia Mann

Jill Young
Development Executive

THE LITTLE FILM COMPANY

12930 Ventura Blvd, Suite #822
Studio City, CA 91604
818-762-6999

The Little Film Company UK
5 Rama Court, Harrow on the Hill
Middlesex, HA1 3NG

info@thelittlefilmcompany.com
thelittlefilmcompany.com

Does not accept any unsolicited material. Project types
include Feature Films. Preferred genres include Action,
Comedy, Documentary, Fantasy, and Romance.

Ellen Little
Co-President

Robbie Little
Co-President
imdb.com/name/nm0514655

THE MANHATTAN PROJECT LTD.

1775 Broadway, Suite 410
New York , NY 10019
212-258-2541

imdb.com/title/tt0091472

Does not accept any unsolicited material. Project types
include Feature Films and TV.

David Brown
Producer
imdb.com/name/nm0113360

Kit Golden
President
imdb.com/name/nm0325455

THE MARK GOKDON COMPANY

12235 W Olympic Blvd, Suite 230
Los Angeles, CA 93064
310-843-6301 (phone)
310-923-103 (fax)

imdb.com/company/co0085751
linkedin.com/company/the-mark-gordon-company

Does not accept any unsolicited material. Project types
include Feature Films and TV. Preferred genres
include Action and Drama.

Mark Gordon
imdb.com/name/nm0330428

THE MAZUR/KAPLAN COMPANY

3204 Pearl St
Santa Monica, CA 90405
310 450 5838

info@mazurkaplan.com
mazurkaplan.com
imdb.com/company/co0247200

Does not accept any unsolicited material. Project types include Feature Films and TV. Preferred genres include Comedy, Family, Fantasy, Non-Fiction, Reality, Romance, and Thriller. Established in 2009.

Paula Mazur
Producer
310-450-5838
imdb.com/name/nm0563394

Kimi Armstrong Stein
Vice-President
kimi@mazurkaplan.com
imdb.com/name/nm2148964

Mitchell Kaplan
Producer
imdb.com/name/nm3125086

Ally Israelson
Creative Executive

THE OCTOBER PEOPLE, LLC

Seattle, WA
619-500-2854

San Diego, CA

info@theoctoberpeople.net
facebook.com/TheOctoberPeople
twitter.com/October_People
theoctoberpeople.net
imdb.com/company/co0397558

Does not accept any unsolicited material. Project types include Feature Films and Short Films. Preferred genres include Horror and Thriller. Established in 2013.

THE ORPHANAGE

6725 Sunset Blvd., Suite 220
Los Angeles, CA 90028

323-469-6700 (phone)
415-561-2570 (fax)

39 Mesa St, Suite 201
San Francisco, CA 94129
415-561-2570

theorphanage.com

Does not accept any unsolicited material. Project types include Feature Films.

Dan Macnamara
President

Liz Roewe
Executive Producer

THE PITT GROUP

8750 Wilshire Blvd.
Suite 301
Beverly Hills, CA 90211
310-246-4800 (phone)
310-275-9258 (fax)

imdb.com/company/co0034610

Accepts query letter from unproduced, unrepresented writers. Project types include Feature Films and TV. Preferred genres include Animation, Comedy, Crime, Detective, Drama, and Romance. Established in 2000.

Jeremy Conrady
Creative Executive
jconrady@pittgroup.com
imdb.com/name/nm262042
linkedin.com/pub/jeremy-conrady/a/b29/787

Lou Pitt
Principle
lpitt@pittgroup.com
imdb.com/name/nm2229316
linkedin.com/pub/lou-pitt/6/a28/2b5

THE RADMIN COMPANY

9201 Wilshire Blvd, Suite 102
Beverly Hills, CA 90210
310-274-9515 (phone)
310-274-0739 (fax)

queries@radmincompany.com
radmincompany.com

imdb.com/company/co0040878

Accepts query letter from unproduced, unrepresented writers via email. Project types include Feature Films. Preferred genres include Comedy, Drama, and Romance. Established in 1993.

Linne Radmin
CEO
imdb.com/name/nm0705709
linkedin.com/pub/linne-radmin/15/b75/951

Brandon Klaus
Creative Executive

THE SAFRAN COMPANY

9663 Santa Monica Blvd.
Suite 840
Beverly Hills, CA 90210
310-278-1450

imdb.com/company/co0179825

Does not accept any unsolicited material. Project types include Feature Films and TV. Preferred genres include Comedy and Family. Established in 2006.

Peter Safran
imdb.com/name/nm0755911

Joan Mao
Director of Development
imdb.com/name/nm1619641

THE SEAN DANIEL COMPANY

12429 Ventura Court, 2nd Floor
Studio City, CA 91604
818-508-8165

imdb.com/name/nm0199733

Does not accept any unsolicited material. Project types include Feature Films. Preferred genres include Action, Comedy, Horror, and Thriller.

Jason Brown
Development
imdb.com/name/nm0113798

Sean Daniel
Producer
imdb.com/name/nm0199733

THE STEVE TISCH COMPANY

10202 W Washington Blvd
Culver City, CA 90232
310-841-4330

imdb.com/company/co0024369

Accepts query letter from unproduced, unrepresented writers. Project types include Feature Films. Preferred genres include Action, Comedy, Drama, and Thriller. Established in 1984.

Steve Tisch
Chairman
imdb.com/name/nm0005494

Lacy Boughn
Director of Development
imdb.com/name/nm2064419

THE SWEET SHOP

1011 N. Fuller Ave, Suite G
West Hollywood, CA 90046
424-258-1000

thesweetshop.tv
facebook.com/thesweetshopfilms
twitter.com/_thesweetshop

Does not accept any unsolicited material. Project types include Short Films, TV, and Commercials.

Dina Morales
Producer
dmorales@thesweetshop.tv

Laura Thoel
Executive Producer
laura@thesweetshop.tv

Preston Garrett
Head of Production
pgarrett@thesweetshop.tv

THE WALT DISNEY COMPANY

500 S Buena Vista St
Burbank, CA 91521
818-560-1000 (phone)
818-560-2500 (fax)

thewaltdisneycompany.com

twitter.com/DisneyPost
linkedin.com/company/the-walt-disney-compan

Does not accept any unsolicited material. Project types include TV. Preferred genres include Action, Animation, Comedy, Drama, Family, Fantasy, Myth, and Non-Fiction. Established in 1923.

Robert Iger
President
bob.iger@disney.com
imdb.com/name/nm2250609

Mary Ann Hughes
Vice-President
imdb.com/name/nm3134377

Rita Ferro
imdb.com/name/nm3474908
linkedin.com/pub/rita-ferro/8/31a/9aa
facebook.com/rita.ferro.980

THE WEINSTEIN COMPANY

375 Greenwich St, Lobby A
New York, NY 10013-2376
212-941-3800 (phone)
212-941-3949 (fax)

9100 Wilshire Blvd, Suite 700W
Beverly Hills, CA 90212
424-204-4800

Canaletto House
39 Beak St.
London, United Kingdom, W1F 9SA
011-442-074946180

99 Hudson St.
New York, NY 10013
212-845-8600

345 Hudson St, New York, NY 10014, United States
+646-862-3400

info@weinsteinco.com
weinsteinco.com
linkedin.com/company/the-weinstein-company
imdb.com/company/co0150452
facebook.com/weinsteinco
twitter.com/WeinsteinFilms

Does not accept any unsolicited material. Project types include Feature Films and TV. Preferred genres

include Action, Animation, Comedy, Drama, Family, Myth, Non-Fiction, Romance, and Thriller. Established in 2005.

Harvey Weinstein
Co-Chairman
imdb.com/name/nm0005544
linkedin.com/pub/harvey-weinstein/91/965/aa4
Assistant: Brendon Boyea

Bob Weinstein
Co-Chairman

Collin Creighton
Vice President (Production & Development)
imdb.com/name/nm3083758

Barbara Schneeweiss
Vice President (Development & Production for TV & Film)
imdb.com/name/nm0773679
linkedin.com/pub/barbara-schneeweiss/4/360/a46

THE WOLPER ORGANIZATION

4000 Warner Blvd.
Bldg. 14, Ste. 200
Burbank, CA 91504
818-123-1421 (phone)
818-123-1593 (fax)

wolperorg.com
imdb.com/company/co0089381

Does not accept any unsolicited material. Project types include Feature Films and TV. Preferred genres include Crime, Detective, and Drama. Established in 1987.

Sam Alexander
Director of Development
sam.alexander@wbtvprod.com
imdb.com/name/nm3303012
linkedin.com/pub/sam-alexander/4/904/117

Kevin Nickldus
Creative Director
imdb.com/name/nm2102454
linkedin.com/pub/kevin-nicklaus/15/668/48B

David L. Wolper
Actor
imdb.com/name/nm0938678

Mnrkf Whlperf
Executive Producer
imdb.com/name/nm0938679

THE ZANUCK COMPANY

16 Beverly Park
Beverly Hills, CA 90210
310-248-0281 (phone)
310-203-9117 (fax)

info@zanuckco.com
imdb.com/company/co0093750
zanuckco.com

Does not accept any unsolicited material. Project types include Feature Films and TV. Preferred genres include Action, Comedy, Crime, Drama, Family, Fantasy, Period, Romance, and Thriller. Established in 1988.

Richard D Zanuck
imdb.com/name/nm0005573

Dean Zanuck
Producer
310-204-3989
imdb.com/name/nm0953124

THIRTEEN/WNET

825 Eighth Ave
New York, NY 10019
United States
212-560-1313 (phone)
212-560-1314 (fax)

programming@thirteen.org
twitter.com/thirteenny
facebook.com/wnet-thirteen
thirteen.org

Does not accept any unsolicited material. Project types include TV. Preferred genres include Drama and Family.

David Horn
Producer

THIS AMERICAN LIFE

153 W 27th St, Suite 1104
New York, NY 10001
United States

web@thislife.org
thislife.org

Does not accept any unsolicited material. Project types include Feature Films.

Ira Glass
Producer

Julie Snyder
Executive Producer

Alissa Shipp
Producer

THOMAS PRODUCTIONS, ROB

1438 N Gower St, Bldg. 62
Los Angeles, CA 90028
United States
323-468-5320

robthomasproductions.com

Project types include TV. Preferred genres include Comedy and Drama.

Rob Thomas
Writer/Producer

THOUGHT MOMENT MEDIA

5419 Hollywood Blvd, Suite C-142, Los Angeles, California, 90027
323-380-8662

info@thoughtmoment.com
thoughtmoment.com
facebook.com/pages/Thought-Moment-Media/
270162619826746
imdb.com/company/co0397382
twitter.com/ThoughtMoment

Accepts scripts from produced or represented writers. Project types include Feature Films, Short Films, and TV.

Andrea James
Producer

Jamison Hebert
Producer

THOUSAND WORDS

110 S Fairfax Ave, Suite 370
Los Angeles, CA 90036
323-936-4700 (phone)
323-936-4701 (fax)

info@thousand-words.com
imdb.com/title/tt0763831
thousand-words.com

Accepts query letter from unproduced, unrepresented writers via email. Project types include Feature Films. Preferred genres include Animation, Drama, and Thriller. Established in 2000.

Michael Van Vliet
Creative Executive
323-936-4700
info@thousand-words.com
imdb.com/name/nm2702900

Jonah Smith
Chairman
323-936-4700
info@thousand-words.com
imdb.com/name/nm0808819

Palmer West
Chairman
323-936-4700
info@thousand-words.com
imdb.com/name/nm0922279

THREE STRANGE ANGELS

8750 Wilshire Blvd., Suite 300E
Beverly Hills, CA 90211
United States
310-601-2291

Does not accept any unsolicited material. Project types include Feature Films. Preferred genres include Comedy and Fantasy.

Lindsay Doran
Producer

THREE STRONGE ANGELS, INC.

9350 W Washington Blvd
Culver City, CA 90232
310-540-8213

imdb.com/company/co0183490

Does not accept any unsolicited material. Project types include Feature Films. Preferred genres include Action, Comedy, and Fantasy.

Lindsay Doran
310-240-8213
imdb.com/name/nm0233386
Assistant: Natasha Khrolenko

THRESHOLD ENTERTAINMENT

1649 11th St
Santa Monica, CA 90404
United States
310-452-8899 (phone)
310-452-0736 (fax)

thethreshold.com

Does not accept any unsolicited material. Project types include Feature Films and TV. Preferred genres include Fantasy and Science Fiction.

Larry Kasanoff
Chairman/CEO/Producer

Michael Ross
President, Threshold Animation Studios

Amy Steele
VP of Creative & Business Development

THROUGH FILMS

137 Larmont Blvd., Suite 150
Los Angeles, CA 90004
United States
310-993-2124

marcus@throughfilms.com
throughfilms.com
facebook.com/pages/Through-Films-LLC/
    158983616009

Does not accept any unsolicited material. Project types include Feature Films. Preferred genres include Drama.

Marcus Cox
Producer

Karrie Cox
Producer/Actor/Writer

THUNDERBIRD FILMS

10675 Santa Monica Blvd
Suite B
Los Angeles, California 90025

165 Ave Rd
Suite 301
Toronto, Ontario
M5R 3S4

533 Smithe St.
Suite 401
Vancouver, British Columbia
V6B 6H1
604-683-3555 (phone)
604-707-0378 (fax)

info@hunderbirdfilms.net
imdb.com/company/co0163158
thunderbird.tv
facebook.com/pages/Thunderbird-Films
twitter.com/TbirdFilms

Does not accept any unsolicited material. Project types include TV. Preferred genres include Comedy and Drama.

Timothy Gamble
CEO
imdb.com/name/nm0303817
linkedin.com/pub/tim-gamble/66/b4b/895
facebook.com/tim.gamble.33

Alex Raffe
Head of Production & Development
alex@thunderbirdfilms.com
imdb.com/name/nm0706244
linkedin.com/pub/alex-raffe/2/65b/509
twitter.com/thunderbird.tvteam

Danielle Kreinik
Head of Development
imdb.com/name/nm2315742
linkedin.com/in/daniellekreinik

THUNDER ROAD PICTURES

1411 5th St Suite 400
Santa Monica, CA 90401
310-573-8885

imdb.com/company/co0172670

Does not accept any unsolicited material. Project types include Feature Films and TV. Preferred genres include Action, Crime, Detective, Drama, Non-Fiction, and Thriller. Established in 2003.

Kent Kubena
Sr. VP, Film & TV Development & Production
imdb.com/name/nm0473423
linkedin.com/in/kentkubena
Assistant: Noah Winter

Basil Iwanyk
Owner
imdb.com/name/nm0412588

Erica Lee
Vice-President
imdb.com/name/nm3102707

Peter Lawson
President of Production
imdb.com/name/nm4498662
linkedin.com/pub/peter-j-lawson/6b/b11/282

TIG PRODUCTIONS, INC.

4450 Lakeside Dr, Suite 225
Burbank, CA 91505
United States
818-260-8707 (phone)
818-260-0440 (fax)

Project types include Feature Films. Preferred genres include Drama and Thriller.

Kevin Costner
Producer/Director/Actor

Jasa Abreo
Development

TIMBERGROVE ENTERTAINMENT

505 Avondale Ave., Suite D
Los Angeles, CA 90049
United States
310-458-8007 (phone)
310-393-9188 (fax)

Does not accept any unsolicited material. Project types
include Feature Films. Preferred genres include
Comedy.

David Koplan
Producer

TIM BURTON PRODUCTIONS

8033 Sunset Blvd, Suite 7500
West Hollywood, CA 90046
310-300-1670 (phone)
310-300-1671 (fax)

timburton.com
imdb.com/company/co0081851

Does not accept any unsolicited material. Project types
include Feature Films. Preferred genres include Action,
Family, and Fantasy. Established in 1989.

Tim Burton
Principle
310-300-1670
kory.edwrds@timburton.com
imdb.com/name/nm0000318

Derek Frey
Executive
derek@lazerfilm.com
imdb.com/name/nm0294553
linkedin.com/in/derekfreyfilms
facebook.com/DerekFreyFilms

TIME INC. STUDIOS

135 W 50th St, 10th Floor
New York, NY 10020
United States
212-522-0064

Does not accept any unsolicited material. Project types
include Feature Films and TV. Preferred genres
include Drama.

Paul Speaker
President/Producer

TITMOUSE, INC.

6616 Lexington Ave
Hollywood, CA 90038
United States
32-466-7800

sales@titmouse.net
titmouse.net

Does not accept any unsolicited material. Project types
include TV. Preferred genres include Animation and
Comedy.

TIWARY ENTERTAINMENT GROUP

1 Irving Place, Suite P8C
New York, NY 10003
United States
212-477-6698 (phone)
212-477-5259 (fax)

info@tiwaryent.com
tiwaryent.com

Does not accept any unsolicited material. Project types
include Feature Films. Preferred genres include
Drama.

Vivek Tiwary
President/CEO/Producer/Writer

TMC ENTERTAINMENT

12200 W Olympic Blvd., Suite 470
Los Angeles, CA 90064
United States
310-806-4400 (phone)
310-806-4401 (fax)

contact@tmcent.tv
tmcent.tv

Does not accept any unsolicited material. Project types
include Feature Films and TV. Preferred genres
include Comedy, Drama, and Family.

Drew S. Levin
Chairman/CEO

Tip McPartland
VP of Production & Development

TOM WELLING PRODUCTIONS

16000 Ventura Blvd
Encino, CA 91436
818-954-4012

imdb.com/company/co0314090

Does not accept any unsolicited material. Project types include TV. Preferred genres include Drama. Established in 2010.

Tom Welling
Founder
imdb.com/name/nm0919991

TONIK PRODUCTIONS

27 W 24th St. Suite 1108
New York, NY 10010
212-532-6565 (phone)
212-532-6650 (fax)

info@tonikproductions.com
tonikproductions.com/home
imdb.com/company/co0078138
twitter.com/Tonik_Films

Accepts query letter from unproduced, unrepresented writers via email. Project types include Feature Films. Preferred genres include Comedy, Drama, Family, Fantasy, and Science Fiction.

Nikki SIlver
Principle
imdb.com/name/nm1012185
linkedin.com/pub/nikki-silver/6/919/310
facebook.com/nikki.silver.75

Tonya Lewis Lee
Principle
imdb.com/name/nm1416174
linkedin.com/pub/tonya-lewis-lee/10/361/620
facebook.com/TonyaLewisLee
twitter.com/TLewisLee

TOOL OF NORTH AMERICA

2210 Broadway
Santa Monica, CA 90404
310-453-9244 (phone)
310-453-4185 (fax)

50 W 17th St, 4th Floor
New York, NY 10011
212-924-1100 (phone)
212-924-1156 (fax)

toolofna.com
facebook.com/toolofna

Accepts query letter from unproduced, unrepresented writers via email. Project types include Feature Films, TV, and Commercials. Preferred genres include Drama, Horror, Non-Fiction, Reality, and Thriller.

Dustin Callif
Executive Producer
310-453-9244
dustin@toolofna.com
imdb.com/name/nm2956668
linkedin.com/company/tool-of-north-america

Josh Gold
Executive Producer
310-453-9244
josh@toolofna.com

Oliver Fuselier
Executive Producer
310-453-9244
oliver@toolofna.com
imdb.com/name/nm0299336
linkedin.com/pub/dir/oliver/fuselier

Robert Helphand
Executive Producer
310-453-9244
robert.helphand@toolofna.com
linkedin.com/pub/robert-helphand/7/19/b76

Chris Neff
Executive Producer
310-453-9244
chris.neff@toolofna.com
linkedin.com/in/cneff08

Lori Stonebraker
Executive Producer
310-453-9244
lori.stonebraker@toolofna.com
linkedin.com/pub/lori-stonebraker/91/abb/2a8

TOWER OF BABBLE ENTERTAINMENT

854 N Spaulding Ave
Los Angeles, CA 90046
323-230-6128 (phone)
323-822-0312 (fax)

info@towerofb .com
towerofb .com
imdb.com/company/co0179064

Accepts query letter from unproduced, unrepresented writers via email. Project types include Feature Films and TV. Preferred genres include Comedy and Romance.

Jeff Wadlow
323-230-6128
info@towerofb .com
imdb.com/name/nm0905592

Beau Bauman
323-230-6128
info@towerofb .com
imdb.com/name/nm0062149

TRANCAS INTERNATIONAL FILMS, INC.

2021 Pontius Ave
2nd Floor
Los Angeles, CA 90025
310-477-6569 (phone)
310-477-7126 (fax)

info@trancasfilms.com
trancasfilms.com
imdb.com/company/co0005891
twitter.com/TrancasFilms
facebook.com/TrancasInternationalFilms

Does not accept any unsolicited material. Project types include Feature Films and TV. Preferred genres include Action, Comedy, Drama, Horror, and Thriller.

Louis Nader
imdb.com/name/nm0618868

Malek S. Akkad
President
imdb.com/name/nm0015443
linkedin.com/pub/malek-akkad/6a/a7a/376

TRANSCENDENT ENTERTAINMENT

Los Angeles, CA

transcendentent.com
imdb.com/company/co0269457

Project types include Feature Films and TV.

Danny Rodriguez
CEO
danny@transcendentent.com
linkedin.com/pub/danny-rodriguez/5/a96/817
twitter.com/officialDannyR

Wayne Little
Legal Counsel

Troy Mathis
CFO

Mickey Ha
Vice President of Transcendent Asia

TREEHOUSE FILMS

4450 Lakeside Dr
Suite 225
Burbank, CA 91505
818-260-8707 (phone)
818-260-0440 (fax)

imdb.com/company/co0077634

Does not accept any unsolicited material. Project types include Feature Films. Preferred genres include Drama and Romance.

Kevin Costner
Founder
imdb.com/name/nm0000126

Jim Wilson
Founder

TRIBECA FILMS

375 Greenwich St, 8th Floor
New York, NY 10013
212-941-2400 (phone)
212-941-3939 (fax)

345 N. Maple Dr.
Suite 202
Beverly Hills, CA 90210
310-651-8342

54 Varick St,
New York, NY 10013
212-941-2001 (phone)
212-941-3997 (fax)

info@tribecafilm.com
entries@tribecafilmfestival.org
tribecafilm.com
imdb.com
linkedin.com/company/tribeca-film-festiva

Does not accept any unsolicited material. Project types include Feature Films and TV. Preferred genres include Action, Comedy, Crime, Drama, Fantasy, Non-Fiction, Period, Romance, and Thriller. Established in 1989.

Robert De Niro

Partner
212-941-2400
imdb.com/name/nm0000134
linkedin.com/pub/robert-deniro/26/9b9/646
facebook.com/RobertDeNiroSr

Berry Welsh

Director of Development
212-941-2400
imdb.com/name/nm2654730
linkedin.com/pub/berry-welsh/4/B85/742
facebook.com/berry.welsh
twitter.com/BarryPWels

Jane Rosenthal

Partner
imdb.com/name/nm0742772
linkedin.com/pub/jane-rosenthal/15/186/3B4
facebook.com/pages/Jane-Rosenthal
twitter.com/janetribeca

TRICOAST STUDIOS

11124 Washington Blvd
Culver City, CA 90232
310-458-7707

tricoast@tricoast.com
tricoast.com
imdb.com/company/co0127287
twitter.com/TriCoastStudios
facebook.com/pages/Tricoast-Worldwide-Studios/
   140312726147049
linkedin.com/company/tricoast-studios

Does not accept any unsolicited material. Project types include Feature Films and TV. Established in 1987.

Strathford Hamilton

Founder
strath@tricoast.com
imdb.com/name/nm0358175

Marcy Hamilton

CEO
marcy@tricoast.com
imdb.com/name/nm0358036

Martin Wiley

Executive Producer
info@tricoastworldwide.com

Daisy Hamilton

Director of Business Development
daisyhamilton@tricoast.com

Andrew Williams

Sound Supervisor
andrew@tricoast.com

TRICOR ENTERTAINMENT

1613 Chelsea Rd
San Marino, CA 91108
626-356-4646 (phone)
626-356-3646 (fax)

executiveoffices@tricorentertainment.com
tricorentertainment.com
imdb.com/company/co0070488

Does not accept any unsolicited material. Project types include Feature Films. Established in 1988.

Craig Darian
CEO
323-464-0055
darian@occidentalentertainment.com
craigdarian.com
imdb.com/name/nm1545768

Howard Kazanjian
Chairman

William Wegner
Legal Counsel

Ron Mencer
Director of Development
imdb.com/name/nm1348889

TRILOGY ENTERTAINMENT GROUP

1207 4th St
Suite 400
Santa Monica, CA 90401
310-656-9733

trilogyent.com
twitter.com/PenDensham
imdb.com/company/co0078090
linkedin.com/company/trilogy-entertainment-group
facebook.com/pages/Riding-the-Alligator/
    104540316270450

Does not accept any unsolicited material. Project types include Feature Films and TV. Preferred genres include Action, Comedy, Fantasy, Romance, and Thriller.

Pen Densham
Founder
imdb.com/name/nm0219720
linkedin.com/pub/pen-densham/9/9bb/393
twitter.com/Pendensham

Nevin Densham
Producer
imdb.com/name/nm0219719

John Watson
Founder
imdb.com/name/nm2302370

TROIKA PICTURES

2019 S Westgate Ave
2nd Floor
Los Angeles, CA 90025
310-696-2859 (phone)
310-820-7310 (fax)

troikapics@gmail.com
troikapictures.com
imdb.com/company/co0246102
twitter.com/troikapictures

Does not accept any unsolicited material. Project types include Feature Films. Preferred genres include Action, Crime, Fantasy, Romance, and Thriller.

Bradley Gallo
Head of Production & Development
310-696-2859
imdb.com/name/nm0303010
linkedin.com/in/bradleygallo

Robert Stein
CEO
310-696-2859
imdb.com/name/nm3355501
linkedin.com/pub/robert-stein/41/665/405

Michael Helfant
COO
310-696-2859
imdb.com/name/nm0375033
linkedin.com/pub/michael-helfant/4/57/10a

TROMA ENTERTAINMENT

36-40 11th St
Long Island City, NY 11106
718-391-0110 (phone)
718-391-0255 (fax)

troma1@gmail.com
troma.com
imdb.com/company/co0019150
facebook.com/troma.entertainment
linkedin.com/company/troma-entertainment

Accepts scripts from unproduced, unrepresented writers. Project types include Feature Films. Preferred genres include Action, Drama, Fantasy, Horror, Science Fiction, Sociocultural, and Thriller.

Lloyd Kaufman

President
lloyd@troma.com
lloydkaufman.com
imdb.com/name/nm0442207
linkedin.com/pub/lloyd-kaufman/0/661/541
facebook.com/pages/Lloyd-Kaufman
twitter.com/witter.comlloydkaufman

Michael Herz

Vice-President
imdb.com/name/nm0381230
linkedin.com/pub/michael-herz/10/a95/a90

TURTLEBACK PRODUCTIONS, INC.

11736 Gwynne Ln
Los Angeles, CA, CA 90077
310-440-8587 (phone)
310-440-8903 (fax)

turtleback-productions-inc.hub.biz

Accepts query letter from unproduced, unrepresented writers. Project types include Feature Films and TV. Preferred genres include Crime, Drama, Fantasy, and Thriller. Established in 1988.

Howard Meltzer

President
310-440-8587
imdb.com/name/nm0578430
linkedin.com/pub/howard-meltzer/36/824/660

TV LAND

1515 Broadway 45th Floor
New York, NY 10036
212-846-3723 (phone)
201-422-6630 (fax)

info@tvland.com
tvland.com
linkedin.com/company/tv-land
facebook.com/tvland
twitter.com/tvland
imdb.com/company/co0094233

Accepts query letter from unproduced, unrepresented writers via email. Project types include TV. Preferred genres include Comedy and Drama. Established in 1996.

Larry W. Jones

President
212-846-6000
larry.jones@tvland.com
imdb.com/name/nm1511130
linkedin.com/pub/larry-jones/6/122/1a0
facebook.com/pages/Larry-W-Jones/
    579462038841440

Bradley Gardner

Producer
imdb.com/name/nm3952119

Rose Catherine Pinkney

Vice-President
imdb.com/name/nm0684384
linkedin.com/pub/rose-catherine-pinkney/38/8a2/486

Scott Gregory

Vice-President
linkedin.com/pub/scott-gregory/3/824/b94
facebook.com/scott.gregory.9619

TV ONE LLC

1010 Wayne Ave
Silver Spring, MD 20910
301-755-0400

tvoneonline.com
imdb.com/company/co0118331
facebook.com/tvonetv
twitter.com/tvonetv
linkedin.com/company/tv-one

Accepts query letter from produced or represented writers. Project types include TV. Preferred genres include Comedy and Drama. Established in 2004.

Alfred Liggins

Chairman
301-755-0400
aliggins@tv-one.tv
imdb.com/name/nm3447190

Michelle Rice

Executive Vice-President

Jubba Seyyid

Senior Director
linkedin.com/pub/jubba-seyyid/91/933/958
twitter.com/Jubbaman

Jay Schneider
Executive Vice-President

Jody Drewer
CFO

T.V. REPAIR

davidjlatt@earthlink.net
imdb.com/company/co0183810

Accepts query letter from unproduced, unrepresented writers via email. Project types include TV.

David Latt
310-459-3671
davidjlatt@earthlink.net
imdb.com/name/nm0490374

TWENTIETH CENTURY FOX FILM CORPORATION

10201 W Pico Blvd
Los Angeles, CA 90035
310-369-1000 (phone)
310-203-1558 (fax)

foxmovies@fox.com
foxstudios.com
facebook.com/20thCFoxStudios
twitter.com/foxbacklot
imdb.com/company/co0000756

Does not accept any unsolicited material. Project types include Feature Films and TV. Preferred genres include Action, Comedy, Crime, Detective, Drama, Family, Fantasy, Horror, Myth, Non-Fiction, Romance, and Thriller. Established in 1935.

Emma Watts
President

Kimberly Cooper

Ted Dodd
linkedin.com/pub/ted-dodd/5/789/801

Steve Freedman
linkedin.com/pub/steve-timinskas/3/90a/381

David A Starke
linkedin.com/company/fox-filmed-entertainment

TWENTIETH CENTURY FOX TELEVISION

10201 W Pico Blvd
Los Angeles, CA 90064
310-369-6000

info@fox.com
foxmovies.com
twitter.com/20thcenturyfox
facebook.com/foxmovies
imdb.com/company/co0056447
linkedin.com/company/fox-filmed-entertainment

Does not accept any unsolicited material. Project types include TV. Preferred genres include Comedy and Drama. Established in 1949.

Gary Newman
Chairman
gary.newman@fox.com
imdb.com/name/nm3050096
linkedin.com/pub/gary-newman/8/a67/421

Jonathan Harris
Sr. Vice President Legal Affairs
linkedin.com/pub/jonathan-harris/9/A50/2B6

Dana Walden
Executive
imdb.com/name/nm0992861

TWENTIETH TELEVISION

2121 Ave of the Stars
17th Floor
Los Angeles, CA 90067
310-369-1000 (phone)
310-369-3899 (fax)

info@fox.com
fox.com
linkedin.com/company/twentieth-television
imdb.com/company/co0161074
facebook.com/pages/20th-Television/
    112762725404025
twitter.com/FOXTV

Does not accept any unsolicited material. Project types include TV. Preferred genres include Comedy and Drama. Established in 1995.

Roger Ailes
Producer
imdb.com/name/nm0014614

TWINSTAR ENTERTAINMENT

556 S. Fair Oaks Ave, Suite 376
Pasadena, CA 91105
949-929-1200

info@twinstarentertainment.com
twinstarentertainment.com
imdb.com/company/co0144114

Accepts scripts from unproduced, unrepresented writers. Project types include TV. Preferred genres include Animation, Comedy, Drama, and Family. Established in 2003.

Russ Werdin
CEO
linkedin.com/pub/russ-werdin/18/600/5a6

Joel Valdez
Art Director

Evelyn Gabai
Writer

Chuck Powers
Director

TWISTED PICTURES

c/o Evolution Entertainment
901 N Highland Ave
Los Angeles, CA
323-850-3232

imdb.com/company/co0137447
facebook.com/pages/Twisted-Pictures/
    108186339203451

Accepts query letter from unproduced, unrepresented writers. Project types include Feature Films and TV. Preferred genres include Crime, Horror, and Thriller. Established in 2004.

Mark Burg
Founder
imdb.com/name/nm0121117

TWO TON FILMS

info@twotonfilms.com
imdb.com/company/co0188112
facebook.com/pages/Two-Ton-Films/324667725316
twotonfilms.com
twitter.com/TwoTonFilms

Accepts query letter from unproduced, unrepresented writers via email. Project types include Feature Films and TV. Preferred genres include Action, Comedy, Drama, and Family.

Justin Zackham
Partner
imdb.com/name/nm0951698

Clay Pecorin
Partner
imdb.com/name/nm2668976
linkedin.com/pub/clay-pecorin/4/98a/839

UFLAND PRODUCTIONS

963 Moraga Dr
Los Angeles, CA 90049
310-476-4520 (phone)
310-476-4891 (fax)

ufland.productions@verizon.net
imdb.com/company/co0000904

Does not accept any unsolicited material. Project types include Feature Films and TV. Preferred genres include Comedy, Drama, and Romance. Established in 1972.

Harry Ufland
Producer
imdb.com/name/nm0880036
linkedin.com/pub/harry-ufland/3b/103/843

Mary Jane Ufland
Producer
imdb.com/name/nm0880040

UNDERGROUND FILMS

447 S Highland Ave
Los Angeles, CA 90036
323-930-2588 (phone)
323-930-2334 (fax)

submissions@undergroundfilms.net
undergroundfilms.net
facebook.com/UndergroundFilmsManagement
imdb.com/company/co0118811

Accepts scripts from unproduced, unrepresented
writers via email. Project types include TV. Preferred
genres include Action, Animation, Comedy, Drama,
Family, Fantasy, Horror, Myth, Non-Fiction,
Romance, and Thriller. Established in 2003.

Trevor Engelson
Owner
trevor@undergroundfilms.net
imdb.com/name/nm0257333
linkedin.com/pub/trevor-engelson/3/a80/b75

Evan Silverberg
Producer
323-930-2588
evan@undergroundfilms.net

Austin Bedell
Development Assistant
austin@undergroundfilms.net
imdb.com/name/nm6551298
linkedin.com/in/austinchristopherbedell

Josh McGuire Turner
Producer
323-930-2435
josh@undergroundfilms.net
facebook.com/josh.t.mcguire

Chris Dennis
Manager
chris@undergroundfilms.net
imdb.com/name/nm4221802

Noah Rothman
Producer
noah@undergroundfilms.net

UNIFIED PICTURES

19773 Bahama St
Northridge, CA 91324
818-576-1006 (phone)
818-534-3347 (fax)

info@unifiedpictures.com
unifiedpictures.com
twitter.com/unifiedpictures

facebook.com/unifiedpictures

Accepts query letter from unproduced, unrepresented
writers. Project types include Feature Films. Preferred
genres include Action, Comedy, Crime, Detective,
Drama, Horror, and Thriller. Established in 2004.

Keith Kjarval
Founder/Producer
imdb.com/name/nm1761309

Paul Michael Ruffman
Senior VP Business Development
linkedin.com/pub/dir/Paul/Ruffman

Steve Goldstein
President/Business Development
imdb.com/name/nm2179640

UNION ENTERTAINMENT

9255 Sunset Blvd, Suite 528
West Hollywood, CA 90069
310-274-7040 (phone)
310-274-1065 (fax)

info@unionent.com
imdb.com/company/co0183888

Does not accept any unsolicited material. Project types
include Video Games. Preferred genres include
Animation. Established in 2006.

Richard Leibowitz
President
310-274-7040
rich@unionent.com
imdb.com/name/nm2325318
Assistant: Sarah Logie

Howard Bliss
howard@unionent.com
imdb.com/name/nm2973051
linkedin.com/pub/howard-bliss/39/b27/1b9

UNIQUE FEATURES

888 7th Ave, 16th Floor
New York, NY 10106
212-649-4980 (phone)
212-649-4999 (fax)

9200 W. Sunset Blvd.
Suite 404
West Hollywood, CA 90069
310-492-8009 (phone)
310-492-8022 (fax)

imdb.com/company/co0242085

Does not accept any unsolicited material. Project types include Feature Films and TV. Established in 2008.

Michael Lynne
Principle
310-492-8009
imdb.com/name/nm1088153

UNISON FILMS

790 Madison Ave
Suite 306
New York, NY 10065
212-226-1200 (phone)
646-349-1738 (fax)

info@unisonfilms.com
unisonfilms.com
imdb.com/company/co0143046

Project types include Feature Films. Preferred genres include Comedy, Drama, and Romance. Established in 2004.

Ryan Brooks
Executive Producer

Cliff Curtis
Producer

Cassandra Kulukundis
Producer
imdb.com/name/nm0474697

Emanuel Michael
CEO
imdb.com/name/nm1639578
linkedin.com/pub/emanuel-michael/83/863/272

UNITED ARTISTS

245 N Beverly Dr
Beverly Hills, CA 90210
310-449-3000

unitedartists.com

imdb.com/company/co0026841
facebook.com/mgm
twitter.com/MGM_Studios
linkedin.com/company/united-artists

Does not accept any unsolicited material. Project types include Feature Films and TV. Preferred genres include Action, Crime, and Drama. Established in 1919.

Gary Barber
Chairman

Jonathan Glickman
President

Roma Khanna
President

Dene Stratton
CFO

UNIVERSAL CABLE PRODUCTIONS

100 Universal City Plaza
Building 1440, 14th Floor
Universal City, CA 91608
818-840-4444

30 Rockefeller Plaza
New York, NY 10112
212-664-4444

imdb.com/company/co0242101
nbcuni.com/cable/universal-cable-productions

Accepts query letter from unproduced, unrepresented writers. Project types include TV. Preferred genres include Comedy and Drama. Established in 1997.

Alex Kerr
Development Executive
818-840-4444

UNIVERSAL STUDIOS

100 Universal City Plaza
Universal City, CA 91608
818-840-4444

universalstudios.com
imdb.com/company/co0000534

Does not accept any unsolicited material. Project types
include Feature Films and TV. Preferred genres
include Action, Animation, Comedy, Crime,
Detective, Drama, Family, Fantasy, Horror, Myth,
Non-Fiction, Romance, Science Fiction, and Thriller.
Established in 1912.

Ron Meyer
818-840-4444
imdb.com/name/nm0005228

UNIVERSAL TELEVISION

100 Universal City Plaza
Building 1360, 3rd Floor
Universal City, CA 91608
818-777-1000

universalstudios.com
imdb.com/company/co0096447

Does not accept any unsolicited material. Project types
include TV. Preferred genres include Action,
Animation, Comedy, Crime, Detective, Drama,
Family, Fantasy, Myth, Non-Fiction, Romance,
Science Fiction, and Thriller.

Stephen Burke
CEO

UNSTOPPABLE ENTERTAINMENT

c/o Independent Talent Agency
76 Oxford St
London W1D 1BS
United Kingdom

info@unstoppableentertainmentuk.com
twitter.com/UnstoppableLtd
unstoppableentertainmentuk.com
facebook.com/UnstoppableEntertainmentUK

Accepts scripts from unproduced, unrepresented
writers. Project types include Feature Films. Preferred
genres include Action, Comedy, Crime, Drama,
Romance, Science Fiction, and Thriller. Established in
2007.

Noel Clarke
Principle
noel@unstoppableentertainmentuk.com

UNTITLED ENTERTAINMENT

350 S Beverly Dr, Suite 200
Beverly Hills, CA 90212
310-601-2100

imdb.com/company/co0034249
linkedin.com/company/untitled-entertainment

Accepts query letter from unproduced, unrepresented
writers. Project types include TV. Preferred genres
include Comedy, Drama, Fantasy, Myth, Non-Fiction,
and Romance.

Jason Weinberg
Partner
linkedin.com/pub/jason-weinberg/10/643/80b

UPLOAD FILMS

9522 Brookline Ave.
Baton Rouge, LA 70809
225-610-1639

8522 National Blvd., #106
Culver City, CA 90232
310-841-5805 (phone)
310-841-5804 (fax)

uploadfilms.com/index.php
imdb.com/company/co0195173

Does not accept any unsolicited material. Project types
include Feature Films. Preferred genres include Action,
Detective, Drama, Horror, and Thriller. Established in
2006.

John Portnoy
Partner
jportnoy@uploadfilms.com
imdb.com/name/nm0692471
linkedin.com/in/johnportnoy
facebook.com/kandyd

Nick Thurlow
Producer
imdb.com/name/nm2250917
linkedin.com/pub/dir/nick/thurlow
facebook.com/nick.thurlow

Andrew Mann
Partner
7films.dendelionblu.me/andrew-mann
imdb.com/name/nm2635886
linkedin.com/in/andrewmanntci
facebook.com/andrew.mann.9

UPPITV

c/o CBS Studios
4024 Radford Ave, Bungalow 9
Studio City, CA 91604
818-655-5000

imdb.com/company/co0286875

Does not accept any unsolicited material. Project types include TV. Preferred genres include Comedy and Drama.

Samuel Jackson
818-655-5000
imdb.com/name/nm0000168
twitter.com/SamuelLJackson

Rebecca Windsor
Manager of Development
linkedin.com/pub/rebecca-windsor/11/603/998

USA NETWORK

30 Rockefeller Plaza
21st Floor
New York, NY 10112
212-664-4444 (phone)
212-703-8582 (fax)

imdb.com/company/co0014957
usanetwork.com
facebook.com/USANetwork
twitter.com/USA_Network

Does not accept any unsolicited material. Project types include TV. Preferred genres include Comedy and Drama. Established in 1971.

Sally Whitehill
212-664-4444

VALHALLA MOTION PICTURES

3201 Cahuenga Blvd W
Los Angeles, CA 90068-1301
323-850-3030 (phone)
323-850-3038 (fax)

vmp@valhallaent.com
valhallamotionpictures.com
imdb.com/company/co0092570
facebook.com/pages/Valhalla-Motion-Pictures/
    126114487446982
twitter.com/valhallapics

Does not accept any unsolicited material. Project types include Feature Films and TV. Preferred genres include Action, Drama, Fantasy, Horror, and Thriller.

Gale Hurd
CEO
323-850-3030
gah@valhallapix.com
imdb.com/name/nm0005036
twitter.com/GunnerGale

VANDERKLOOT FILM & TELEVISION

750 Ralph McGill Blvd N.E.
Atlanta, GA 30312
404-221-0236 (phone)
404-221-1057 (fax)

billvdk@gmail.com
vanderkloot.com
linkedin.com/company/vanderkloot-film-&-television-
    inc.

Does not accept any unsolicited material. Project types include Feature Films, Short Films, TV, and Commercials. Preferred genres include Action, Comedy, Drama, Family, and Non-Fiction. Established in 1976.

William VanDerKloot
404-221-0236
william@vanderkloot.com
imdb.com/name/nm0886281
linkedin.com/in/vanderkloot

Lisa Ferrell
Executive Producer
lisa@magicklantern.com

VANGUARD FILMS + ANIMATION

8703 W Olympic Blvd
Los Angeles, CA 90035
310-888-8020 (phone)
310-362-8685 (fax)

contact@vanguardanimation.com
vanguardanimation.com

Does not accept any unsolicited material. Project types include Feature Films. Preferred genres include Animation. Established in 2004.

John Williams
Chairman & CEO
310-888-8020
imdb.com/name/nm0930964

Robert Moreland
President Production & Development
310-888-8020
imdb.com/name/nm0603668
linkedin.com/pub/rob-moreland/7/903/aa0

VANGUARD PRODUCTIONS

12111 Beatrice St
Culver City, CA 90230
310-306-4910 (phone)
310-306-1978 (fax)

info@vanguardproductions.biz
vanguardproductions.biz
facebook.com/VanguardPublishing

Accepts query letter from unproduced, unrepresented writers via email. Project types include TV. Preferred genres include Action, Comedy, Drama, Family, and Non-Fiction. Established in 1986.

Terence O'Keefe
310-306-4910
terry@vanguardproductions.biz
imdb.com/name/nm0641496

VANQUISH MOTION PICTURES

10 Universal City Plaza
NBC/Universal Building, 20th Floor
Universal City, CA 91608
818-753-2319

submissions@vanquishmotionpictures.com
imdb.com/company/co0273425

Accepts query letter from unproduced, unrepresented writers via email. Project types include Feature Films and TV. Established in 2009.

Neetu Sharma
Creative Executive
818-753-2319
ns@vanquishmotionpictures.com
imdb.com/name/nm3434485

Ryan Williams
Creative Executive
818-753-2319
rs@vanquishmotionpictures.com
imdb.com/name/nm4426713

VARSITY PICTURES

11821 Mississippi Ave
Los Angeles, CA 90025
310-601-1960 (phone)
310-601-1961 (fax)

imdb.com/company/co0215791
twitter.com/varsitypictures
facebook.com/VarsityPictures

Accepts query letter from unproduced, unrepresented writers. Project types include Feature Films and TV. Established in 2007.

Carter Hansen
Creative Executive
310-601-1960
imdb.com/name/nm3255715
facebook.com/thecarterhansen
twitter.com/Carter_Hansen

Shauna Phelan
310-601-1960
imdb.com/name/nm1016912
linkedin.com/pub/shauna-phelan/5/8b5/697
facebook.com/shauna.phelan.7

VERISIMILITUDE

225 W 13th St
New York, NY 10011

212-989-1038 (phone)
212-989-1943 (fax)

info@verisimilitude.com
verisimilitude.com

Does not accept any unsolicited material. Project types
include Feature Films. Preferred genres include
Comedy, Drama, Romance, and Thriller.

Tyler Brodie
Partner
imdb.com/name/nm0110921

Hunter Gray
Partner
imdb.com/name/nm0336683

Phaedon Papadopoulos
Creative Executive
imdb.com/name/nm3011396

Alex Orlovsky
Partner
imdb.com/name/nm0650164

VÉRITÉ FILMS

15 Beaufort Rd
Toronto, ON M4E 1M6
Canada
416-693-8245

verite@veritefilms.ca
veritefilms.ca
imdb.com/company/co0121068
facebook.com/pages/V%C3%A9rit%C3%A9-Films-
    Inc/174261756027334
twitter.com/veritecanada

Accepts query letter from unproduced, unrepresented
writers. Project types include TV. Preferred genres
include Comedy, Drama, and Family. Established in
2004.

Virginia Thompson
306-585-1737
virginia@veritefilms.ca
imdb.com/name/nm1395111

VERTEBRA FILMS

250 E 33rd St.
10016
323-461-0021 (phone)
323-461-0031 (fax)

hello@vertebrafilms.com
vertebrafilms.com
imdb.com/company/co0319489
twitter.com/VertebraFilms

Does not accept any unsolicited material. Project types
include Feature Films. Preferred genres include Horror
and Thriller. Established in 2010.

Mac Cappucino
imdb.com/name/nm2225247

VERTIGO FILMS

The Big Room Studios 77 Fortess Rd
London, United Kingdom,
NW5 1AG
+44-0-20-7428-7555 (phone)
+44-0-20-7485-9713 (fax)

mail@vertigofilms.com
vertigofilms.com
imdb.com/company/co0113509
facebook.com/VertigoFilmsUK
twitter.com/vertigofilms

Does not accept any unsolicited material. Project types
include Feature Films. Preferred genres include Action,
Comedy, Crime, Drama, Fantasy, Horror, Romance,
Science Fiction, and Thriller. Established in 2002.

Allan Niblo
Producer
imdb.com/name/nm0629242

James Richardson
Producer
imdb.com/name/nm0724597

Rupert Preston
Producer
imdb.com/name/nm0696486

Jim Spencer
Producer
imdb.com/name/nm2005794

NIck Love
imdb.com/name/nm0522393

VH1

2600 Colorado Ave
Santa Monica, CA 90404
310-752-8000

info@vh1.com
vh1.com
facebook.com/VH1
twitter.com/VH1

Accepts query letter from unproduced, unrepresented writers. Project types include TV. Preferred genres include Comedy, Drama, Non-Fiction, and Romance. Established in 1986.

Van Toffler
212-846-8000
van.toffler@vh1.com
imdb.com/name/nm0865508

VIACOM INC.

1515 Broadway
New York, NY 10036
212-258-6000

viacom.com
facebook.com/viacom
twitter.com/viacom

Does not accept any unsolicited material. Project types include TV. Preferred genres include Comedy, Drama, and Non-Fiction. Established in 1971.

Philippe Dauman
212-258-6000
philippe.dauman@viacom.com
imdb.com/name/nm2449184

VILLAGE ROADSHOW PICTURES

100 N Crescent Dr, Suite 323
Beverly Hills, CA 90210
310-385-4300 (phone)
310-385-4301 (fax)

flo@gracepr.net
imdb.com/company/co0108864

vreg.com

Does not accept any unsolicited material. Project types include Feature Films. Established in 1998.

Bruce Berman
310-385-4300
imdb.com/name/nm0075732
Assistant: Suzy Figueroa

Matt Skiena
310-385-4300
mskiena@vrpe.com
imdb.com/name/nm3466832

VINCENT CIRRINCIONE ASSOCIATES

1516 N. Fairfax Ave
Los Angeles, CA 90046
323-850-8080

reception@vcassoc.com
vincentcirrincioneassociates.com
imdb.com/company/co0090082
facebook.com/vcatalent
linkedin.com/company/vincent-cirrincione-associates

Does not accept any unsolicited material. Project types include Feature Films and TV. Preferred genres include Drama and Thriller.

Vincent Cirrincione
Owner/Producer
imdb.com/name/nm0162801

VINCENT NEWMAN ENTERTAINMENT

8840 Wilshire Blvd
3rd Floor
Los Angeles, CA 90211
310-358-3050 (phone)
310-358-3289 (fax)

general@liveheart-vne.com
imdb.com/company/co0163095

Accepts query letter from unproduced, unrepresented writers via email. Project types include TV. Preferred genres include Action, Comedy, Drama, Fantasy, Myth, and Thriller. Established in 2011.

Vincent Newman
310-358-3050
vincent@liveheart-vne.com
imdb.com/name/nm0628304
Assistant: John Funk

John Funk
Director/Writer
linkedin.com/pub/john-funk/a/4a3/924

VIN DI BONA PRODUCTIONS

12233 W Olympic Blvd, Suite 170
Los Angeles, CA 90064
310-442-5600

vdbp.com
imdb.com/company/co0017060
linkedin.com/company/vin-di-bona-productions
afv.com
facebook.com/AFVOfficial

Accepts query letter from unproduced, unrepresented writers. Project types include TV. Preferred genres include Comedy. Established in 1987.

Vin DiBona
Chairman
imdb.com/name/nm0223688

Cara Di Bona
imdb.com/name/nm0223685

Joanne Moore
President
imdb.com/name/nm0601370

VINTON ENTERTAINMENT

info@vintonentertainment.com
vintonentertainment.com

Accepts scripts from unproduced, unrepresented writers. Project types include Feature Films, Short Films, TV, and Commercials. Preferred genres include Animation.

Will Vinton
CEO

John Ripper
COO

VIRGIN PRODUCED

315 S Beverly Dr, Suite 506
Beverly Hills, CA 90212
310-941-7300

903 Colorado Ave
Santa Monica CA 90401
310-941-7300

901,9th Floor, Notan Classic Bldg
F/891-B, Turner Rd, Bandra (West)
Mumbai 400 050 India

media@virginproduced.com
virginproduced.com
imdb.com/company/co0310456
twitter.com/VIRGINproduced
facebook.com/VIRGINproduced

Does not accept any unsolicited material. Project types include TV. Preferred genres include Action, Animation, Comedy, Drama, Fantasy, and Thriller. Established in 2010.

Jason Felts
CEO
310-941-7300
jfelts@virginproduced.com
imdb.com/name/nm1479777

Rebecca Farrell
imdb.com/name/nm2761874

VISION FILMS, INC.

14945 Ventura Blvd
Sherman Oaks, CA 91403
818-784-1702 (phone)
818-788-3715 (fax)

visionfilms.net
facebook.com/VisionFilmsInc
imdb.com/company/co0070863
linkedin.com/pub/vision-films/66/a61/8b1

Does not accept any unsolicited material. Project types include Feature Films, Short Films, and Commercials. Preferred genres include Documentary and Family. Established in 1997.

Lise Romanoff
CEO
lise@visionfilms.net
imdb.com/name/nm0738983

Adam Wright
Executive Vice-President
adam@visionfilms.net

Jasmine Abrams
Contract Manager
contracts@visionfilms.net

Nathan Ross
Director of Digital Operations & Servicing
nathan@visionfilms.net

Monique Green
Director of Finance
accounting@visionfilms.net

Samantha Coolbeth
Sales & Marketing Coordinator
samantha@visionfilms.net

Alex Saveliev
Director of Domestic Distribution
marketing@visionfilms.net

VOLTAGE PRODUCTIONS

116 N. Robertson Blvd., Suite 200
Los Angeles, CA 90048 USA
323-606-7630 (phone)
323-315-7115 (fax)

sales@voltagepictures.com
office@voltagepictures.com
voltagepictures.com
imdb.com/company/co0179337

Accepts scripts from produced or represented writers.
Project types include Feature Films. Preferred genres
include Action, Animation, Drama, Fantasy, Non-
Fiction, Romance, and Science Fiction. Established in
2011.

Zev Foreman
Head of Development
imdb.com/name/nm2303301

Nicolas Chartier
nicolas@voltagepictures.com
imdb.com/name/nm1291566

Craig Flores
imdb.com/name/nm1997836
Assistant: Edmond Guidry

VON ZERNECK SERTNER FILMS

c/o HCVT
11444 W Olympic Blvd
11th Floor
Los Angeles, CA 90064
310-652-3020

vzs@vzsfilms.com
imdb.com/company/co0094479
vzsfilms.com

Does not accept any unsolicited material. Preferred
genres include Crime, Detective, Drama, Non-Fiction,
and Thriller. Established in 1987.

Frank Von Zerneck
Partner
310-652-3020
vonzerneck@gmail.com
imdb.com/name/nm0903273

Robert M. Srtner
Partner
imdb.com/name/nm0785750

VOX3 FILMS

315 Bleecker St #111
New York, NY 10014
212-741-0406 (phone)
212-741-0424 (fax)

contact@vox3films.com
imdb.com/company/co0146502
vox3films.com
facebook.com/pages/Vox3-Films/110031625098

Does not accept any unsolicited material. Project types
include TV. Preferred genres include Drama,
Romance, and Thriller. Established in 2004.

Steven Shainberg
Partner
imdb.com/name/nm078760

Christina Lurie
Partner
imdb.com/name/nm1417371

Andrew Fierberg
212-741-0406
andrew.fi erberg@vox3fi lms.com
imdb.com/name/nm0276404

VULCAN PRODUCTIONS

505 Fifth Ave. S., Suite 900
Seattle WA 98104
206-342-2000

production@vulcan.com
info@vulcanproductions.com
imdb.com/company/co0042766
vulcanproductions.com
facebook.com/VulcanInc
twitter.com/VulcanInc

Does not accept any unsolicited material. Preferred
genres include Action, Non-Fiction, and Thriller.
Established in 1983.

Jody Allen
President
206-342-2277
jody@vulcan.com
imdb.com/name/nm0666580

WALDEN MEDIA

1888 Century Park East
14th Floor
Los Angeles, CA 90067
310-887-1000 (phone)
310-887-1001 (fax)

17 New England Executive Park
Suite 305
Burlington, MA 01803

info@walden.com
imdb.com/company/co0073388
walden.com
twitter.com/waldenmedia
facebook.com/waldenmedia

Accepts query letter from unproduced, unrepresented
writers via email. Project types include Feature Films.
Established in 2001.

Eric Tovell
Creative Executive
etovell@walden.com
Assistant: Carol Tang ctang@walden.com

Evan Turner
310-887-1000
imdb.com/name/nm1602263

Amanda Palmer
310-887-1000
imdb.com/name/nm2198853

WALKER/FITZGIBBON TV & FILM PRODUCTION

2399 Mt. Olympus
Los Angeles, CA 90046
323-878-0500 (phone)
305-793-3011 (fax)

mo@walkerfitzgibbon.com
imdb.com/company/co0171571
walkerfitzgibbon.com
facebook.com/WFTVF
linkedin.com/company/walker-fitzgibbon-tv-&-film
twitter.com/WalkerFitzFilm

Accepts query letter from unproduced, unrepresented
writers via email. Project types include TV. Preferred
genres include Animation, Comedy, Drama, and Non-
Fiction. Established in 1996.

Mo Fitzgibbon
323-469-6800
mo@walkerfitzgibbon.com
imdb.com/name/nm0280422

Robert W. Walker
imdb.com/name/nm0908166

WALT BECKER PRODUCTIONS

8530 Wilshire Blvd.
Suite 550
Beverly Hills, CA 90212
USA

323-871-8400 (phone)
323-871-2540 (fax)

imdb.com/company/co0236068

Does not accept any unsolicited material. Project types include TV.

Walt Becker
imdb.com/name/nm0065608

Kelly Hayes
Director of Development
imdb.com/name/nm0971886

WALT DISNEY STUDIO HOME ENTERTAINMENT

500 S. Buena Vista St.
Burbank, CA 91521-6369
USA
818-560-1000

waltdisneystudios.com
imdb.com/company/co0049546

Does not accept any unsolicited material. Project types include Feature Films, Short Films, and TV. Preferred genres include Action, Animation, Comedy, Crime, Documentary, Drama, Family, Fantasy, Horror, Non-Fiction, Romance, Science Fiction, and Thriller. Established in 1952.

WARNER BROS. TELEVISION GROUP

4000 Warner Blvd
Burbank, CA 91522-0001
818-954-6000

info@warnerbros.com
imdb.com/company/co0253255
warnerbros.com
facebook.com/warnerbrosent
twitter.com/Warnerbrosent
linkedin.com/company/2470

Does not accept any unsolicited material. Project types include TV. Preferred genres include Action, Animation, Comedy, Drama, Family, Fantasy, Myth, Non-Fiction, Romance, and Thriller. Established in 2005.

Bruce Rosenblum
President
bruce.rosenblum@warnerbros.com
imdb.com/name/nm2686463

WARNER BROTHERS ANIMATION

411 N Hollywood Way
Burbank, CA 91505
818-977-8700

info@warnerbros.com
imdb.com/company/co0072876
warnerbros.com
facebook.com/warnerbrosent
twitter.com/Warnerbrosent
linkedin.com/company/2470

Does not accept any unsolicited material. Project types include TV. Preferred genres include Animation. Established in 1930.

Sam Register
Executive Vice-President, Creative
sam.register@warnerbros.com
imdb.com/name/nm1882146

WARNER BROTHERS ENTERTAINMENT INC.

4000 Warner Blvd
Burbank, CA 91522-0001
818-954-6000

warnerbros.com
facebook.com/warnerbrosent
twitter.com/Warnerbrosent
linkedin.com/company/2470

Does not accept any unsolicited material. Project types include TV. Preferred genres include Action, Animation, Comedy, Crime, Detective, Drama, Family, Fantasy, Myth, Non-Fiction, Romance, Science Fiction, and Thriller. Established in 1923.

Barry Meyer
barry.meyer@warnerbros.com
imdb.com/name/nm0583028

WARNER BROTHERS HOME ENTERTAINMENT

4000 Warner Blvd
Burbank, CA 91522-0001
818-954-6000

info@warnerbros.com
imdb.com/company/co0200179
warnerbros.com
facebook.com/warnerbrosent
twitter.com/Warnerbrosent
linkedin.com/company/2470

Does not accept any unsolicited material. Project types include Feature Films, Short Films, and TV. Preferred genres include Action, Animation, Comedy, Crime, Drama, Family, Fantasy, Horror, Myth, Non-Fiction, Romance, Science Fiction, and Thriller. Established in 2005.

Kevin Tsujihara
President
kevin.tsujihara@warnerbros.com
imdb.com/name/nm2493597

WARNER BROTHERS PICTURES

4000 Warner Blvd
Burbank, CA 91522-0001
818-954-6000

info@warnerbros.com
imdb.com/company/co0026840
warnerbros.com
facebook.com/warnerbrosent
twitter.com/Warnerbrosent
linkedin.com/company/2470

Does not accept any unsolicited material. Project types include Feature Films. Preferred genres include Action, Animation, Comedy, Crime, Detective, Drama, Family, Fantasy, Myth, Non-Fiction, Romance, and Thriller. Established in 1923.

Jeff Robinov
President
jeff.robinov@warnerbros.com
imdb.com/name/nm0732268
Assistant: Carrie Frymer

Andrew Fischel
Assistant: Stephanie Rosenthal

Lynn Harris
Executive Vice President of Production
imdb.com/name/nm0365036
Assistant: Alexandra Amin

Racheline Benveniste
Creative Executive
imdb.com/name/nm3367909
Assistant: Matthew Crespy

Greg Silverman
imdb.com/name/nm0798909
Assistant: Cate Adams

WARNER HORIZON TELEVISION

4000 Warner Blvd
Burbank, CA 91522-0001
818-954-6000

info@warnerbros.com
imdb.com/company/co0183230
warnerbros.com
facebook.com/warnerbrosent
twitter.com/Warnerbrosent
linkedin.com/company/2470

Does not accept any unsolicited material. Project types include TV. Preferred genres include Action, Animation, Comedy, Drama, Family, Fantasy, Myth, Non-Fiction, and Romance. Established in 1999.

Peter Roth
President
818-954-6000
peter.roth@warnerbros.com
imdb.com/name/nm2325137

WARNER SISTERS PRODUCTIONS

PO Box 50104
Santa Barbara, CA 93150
818-766-6952

info@warnersisters.com
imdb.com/company/co0121034
warnersisters.com
facebook.com/cass.warner
twitter.com/cassieowarner

Does not accept any unsolicited material. Preferred genres include Documentary and Non-Fiction. Established in 2003.

Cass Warner
imdb.com/name/nm2064300

WARP FILMS

Spectrum House 32-34 Gordon House Rd
London, United Kingdom, NW5 1LP
011-442-072848350 (phone)
011-442-072848360 (fax)

info@warpfilms.co.uk
warp.net/films
imdb.com/company/co0251927

Accepts query letter from unproduced, unrepresented writers via email. Project types include Feature Films. Preferred genres include Action, Comedy, Documentary, Drama, Horror, Non-Fiction, and Romance. Established in 2004.

Mark Herbert
imdb.com/name/nm0378591

Peter Carlton
imdb.com/name/nm1275058

WARP X

Electric Works
Digital Campus
Sheffield S1 2BJ
UK
+44114-286-6280 (phone)
+44114-286-6283 (fax)

info@warpx.co.uk
warpx.co.uk
imdb.com/company/co0202028

Does not accept any unsolicited material. Project types include Feature Films. Preferred genres include Comedy, Crime, Documentary, Drama, Horror, and Thriller. Established in 2008.

Mary Burke
Producer
imdb.com/name/nm1537339

Mark Herbert
Producer
imdb.com/name/nm0378591

Robin Gutch
imdb.com/name/nm0349168

Barry Ryan
imdb.com/name/nm1419213

WARREN MILLER ENTERTAINMENT

5720 Flatiron Parkway
Boulder CO 80301
303-253-6300 (phone)
303-253-6380 (fax)

info@warrenmillertv.com
imdb.com/company/co0040142
aimstudios.tv
facebook.com/WarrenMillerEntertainment

Accepts query letter from unproduced, unrepresented writers. Project types include Feature Films and TV. Preferred genres include Action, Non-Fiction, and Reality. Established in 1952.

Jeffrey Moore
Senior Executive Producer
jmoore@aimmedia.com
imdb.com/name/nm2545455

Warren Miller

Ginger Sheehy
imdb.com/name/nm1200078
linkedin.com/pub/ginger-sheehy/3/849/5b4
twitter.com/gst916

WARRIOR POETS

407 Broome St
New York, NY 10013
212-219-7617 (phone)
212-219-2920 (fax)

em@warrior-poets.com
info@warrior-poets.com
imdb.com/company/co0169151
warrior-poets.com

Does not accept any unsolicited material. Project types include Feature Films and TV. Preferred genres include Drama and Non-Fiction. Established in 2005.

Morgan Spurlock
imdb.com/name/nm1041597
Assistant: Emmanuel Moran

Jeremy Chilnick
imdb.com/name/nm2505733
Assistant: Marjon Javadi

Ethan Goldman
imdb.com/name/nm1134121

WATER'S END PRODUCTIONS

9903 Santa Monica Blvd.
No. 822
Beverly Hills, CA 90212
424-293-0714

watersendprod.com
imdb.com/company/co0472007

Does not accept any unsolicited material. Project types include Feature Films. Preferred genres include Drama. Established in 2012.

Tom Dolby
Producer

WAYANS BROTHERS ENTERTAINMENT

8730 W Sunset Blvd, Suite 290
Los Angeles, CA 90069-2247
323-930-6720 (phone)
424-202-3520 (fax)

thawkins@wayansbros.com
imdb.com/company/co0001823

Does not accept any unsolicited material. Project types include TV. Preferred genres include Comedy, Crime, Family, and Horror. Established in 1980.

Keenan Wayans
imdb.com/name/nm0005540

Shawn Wayans
imdb.com/name/nm0915465

Rick Alvarez
imdb.com/name/nm0023315

Marlon Wayans
imdb.com/name/nm0005541
Assistant: Shane Miller

Mike Tiddes
Creative Executive
imdb.com/name/nm1639277

WAYFARE ENTERTAINMENT VENTURES LLC

435 W 19th St
4th Floor
New York, NY 10011
212-989-2200

info@wayfareentertainment.com
info@start-media.com
imdb.com/company/co0239158
wayfareentertainment.com

Does not accept any unsolicited material. Project types include Feature Films. Preferred genres include Action, Comedy, Drama, Family, Fantasy, Myth, Non-Fiction, Romance, Science Fiction, and Thriller. Established in 2008.

Ben Browning
info@wayfareentertainment.com
imdb.com/name/nm1878845

Jeremy Kipp Walker
imdb.com/name/nm0907844

Michael Maher
start-media.com/start-motion-pictures/team/michael-j-maher
imdb.com/name/nm3052130

Sarah Shepard
imdb.com/name/nm2416896
linkedin.com/pub/sarah-shepard/24/145/38b

WEED ROAD PRODUCTIONS

4000 Warner Blvd
Building 81, Suite 115
Burbank, CA 91522

818-954-3771 (phone)
818-954-3061 (fax)

imdb.com/company/co0093488

Does not accept any unsolicited material. Project types include Feature Films and TV. Preferred genres include Action, Animation, Drama, Family, Fantasy, Horror, Non-Fiction, Science Fiction, and Thriller. Established in 2004.

Akiva Goldsman
imdb.com/name/nm0326040
Assistant: Bonnie Balmos

Nicki Cortese
imdb.com/name/nm2492480
Assistant: Mike Pence

WEINSTOCK PRODUCTIONS

316 N Rossmore Ave
Los Angeles, CA 90004
323-791-1500

imdb.com/company/co0032259

Accepts query letter from unproduced, unrepresented writers. Project types include Feature Films. Preferred genres include Comedy, Crime, Drama, Family, and Thriller.

Charles Weinstock
President
imdb.com/name/nm091848
linkedin.com/pub/chuck-weinstock/19/35a/aa0

WEINTRAUB/KUHN PRODUCTIONS

1821 Wilshire Blvd, Ste 645
Santa Monica, CA 90403
310-458-3300 (phone)
310-458-3302 (fax)

imdb.com/company/co0031680

Does not accept any unsolicited material. Project types include Feature Films and TV. Preferred genres include Action, Comedy, Drama, Family, Fantasy, Myth, Non-Fiction, Romance, Science Fiction, and Thriller. Established in 1976.

Maxwell Meltzer
imdb.com/name/nm0578443

Jackie Weintraub
imdb.com/name/nm0918520

Tom Kuhn
President
imdb.com/name/nm0474166
linkedin.com/pub/tom-kuhn/18/534/292

Fred Weintraub
President
fred@fredweintraub.com
fredweintraub.com
imdb.com/name/nm0918518

WELLER/GROSSMAN PRODUCTIONS

5200 Lankershim Blvd, Fl5
North Hollywood, CA 91601
818-755-4800

contact@wellergrossman.com
imdb.com/company/co0102774

Accepts scripts from produced or represented writers. Project types include TV. Preferred genres include Animation, Comedy, Drama, and Reality. Established in 1993.

Robb Weller
contact@wellergrossman.com
imdb.com/name/nm0919888

WENDY FINERMAN PRODUCTIONS

144 S Beverly Dr, #304
Beverly Hills, CA 90212
310-694-8088 (phone)
310-694-8088 (fax)

info@wendyfinermanproductions.com
imdb.com/company/co0004317

Accepts query letter from unproduced, unrepresented writers via email. Project types include Feature Films and TV. Preferred genres include Comedy, Drama, Family, Fantasy, Period, and Romance.

Wendy Finerman
Producer
wfinerman@wendyfinermanproductions.com
imdb.com/name/nm0277704

Lisa Zupan
Vice-President
lzupan@wendyfinermanproductions.com
imdb.com/name/nm0958702

WESSLER ENTERTAINMENT

11661 San Vicente Blvd., Suite 609
Los Angeles, CA 90049

imdb.com/company/co0037906

Accepts query letter from unproduced, unrepresented writers. Project types include Feature Films. Preferred genres include Comedy and Family.

Charles B. Wessler
President
imdb.com/name/nm0921853

WE TV NETWORK

11 Penn Plaza
19th Floor
New York, NY 10001
212-324-8500 (phone)
212-324-8595 (fax)

contactwe@wetv.com
wetv.com
imdb.com/company/co0340786
facebook.com/WeTV
twitter.com/WEtv
linkedin.com/company/we-tv-network-rainbow-
    media-

Does not accept any unsolicited material. Project types include TV. Preferred genres include Comedy, Family, and Reality. Established in 1997.

Laurence Gellert
imdb.com/name/nm1557598

WHALEROCK INDUSTRIES

2900 W Olympic Blvd
3rd Floor
Sanata Monica, CA, 90404
310-255-7272 (phone)
310-255-7058 (fax)

info@bermanbraun.com

bermanbraun.com
imdb.com/company/co0199425

Does not accept any unsolicited material.

Chris Cowan
Executive, Head of Unscripted Television
imdb.com/name/nm0184544

Andrew Mittman
President
imdb.com/name/nm3879410

WHITE HORSE PICTURES

9100 Wilshire Blvd, Suite 423E, Beverly Hills, CA
90212
424-228-8000

info@whitehorsepics.com
whitehorsepics.com
facebook.com/whitehorsepics
twitter.com/whitehorsepic

Project types include Feature Films. Preferred genres include Documentary. Established in 2014.

Jeanne Elfant Festa
Producer

Nicholas Ferrall
Producer

Cassidy Hartmann
Producer

Guy East
Principal

Nigel Sinclair
Principal

WHITEWATER FILMS

11264 La Grange Ave
Los Angeles, CA 90025
310-575-5800 (phone)
310-575-5802 (fax)

info@whitewaterfilms.com
whitewaterfilms.com
imdb.com/company/co0109361
linkedin.com/company/whitewater-films
facebook.com/WhitewaterFilms

twitter.com/WhitewaterFilms

Does not accept any unsolicited material. Project types include Feature Films. Preferred genres include Comedy, Crime, Drama, Non-Fiction, Romance, and Thriller. Established in 2008.

Nick Morton
Producer
imdb.com/name/nm1134288

Bert Kern
Associate Producer
imdb.com/name/nm2817387

Trent Brion
Producer
imdb.com/name/nm116357

Rick Rosenthal
Producer
imdb.com/name/nm0742819
linkedin.com/pub/rick-rosenthal/6/491/a63

WHYADUCK PRODUCTIONS INC.

4804 Laurel Canyon Blvd
PMB 502
North Hollywood, CA 91607-3765
818-980-5355

rbw@duckprods.com
duckprods.com
imdb.com/company/co0034143

Does not accept any unsolicited material. Project types include Feature Films and TV. Preferred genres include Comedy, Drama, Non-Fiction, Romance, and Science Fiction. Established in 1981.

Robert Weide
rbw@duckprods.com
imdb.com/name/nm0004332

WIDEAWAKE, INC.

8752 Rangely Ave
Los Angeles, CA 90048
310-652-9200

imdb.com/company/co0145942

Does not accept any unsolicited material. Project types include Feature Films and TV. Preferred genres

include Action, Comedy, Family, and Romance. Established in 2004.

Luke Greenfield
imdb.com/name/nm0339004

Jake Detharidge
Creative Executive
imdb.com/name/nm4681516

WIGRAM PRODUCTIONS

4000 Warner Blvd
Building 81, Room 215
Burbank, CA 91522
818-954-2412 (phone)
818-954-6538 (fax)

imdb.com/company/co0204562

Accepts query letter from unproduced, unrepresented writers. Project types include Feature Films. Preferred genres include Action, Comedy, Crime, Fantasy, Science Fiction, and Thriller. Established in 2006.

Lionel Wigram
jeff.ludwig@wbconsultant.com
imdb.com/name/nm0927880
Assistant: Jeff Ludwig

Peter Eskelsen
Vice-President
peter.eskelsen@wbconsultant.com
imdb.com/name/nm2367411
linkedin.com/pub/peter-eskelsen/18/73a/755

WILD AT HEART FILMS

868 W Knoll Dr, Suite 9
West Hollywood, CA 90069
310-855-1538 (phone)
310-855-0177 (fax)

wildheartfilms@aol.com
info@wildatheartfilms.us
wildatheartfilms.us
imdb.com/company/co0096528
twitter.com/WildatHeartFilm

Does not accept any unsolicited material. Preferred genres include Animation, Comedy, Drama, Family, Myth, Non-Fiction, and Romance. Established in 2000.

Jewell Sparks
Head of Development
jewell@wildatheartfilms.us
imdb.com/name/nm3876152

James Egan
CEO
jamesegan@wildatheartfilms.us
imdb.com/name/nm0250680
linkedin.com/pub/james-egan/5/7a/b31

Jess Kreusler
Creative Executive
jess@wildatheartfilms.us

Tammy Hirata
Creative Executive
tammy@wildatheartfilms.us

WILDWOOD ENTERPRISES, INC.

725 Arizona Ave, Suite 306
Santa Monica, CA 90401
310-451-8050

imdb.com/company/co0034515

Does not accept any unsolicited material. Project types include Feature Films, Short Films, and TV. Preferred genres include Comedy, Crime, Drama, Fantasy, Non-Fiction, Romance, and Thriller.

Robert Redford
Owner
imdb.com/name/nm0000602

Bill Holderman
Development Executive
imdb.com/name/nm2250139

WIND DANCER FILMS

6255 W. Sunset Blvd. Suite 1100
Hollywood, CA 90028
310-601-2720 (phone)
310-601-2725 (fax)

38 Commerce St
New York, NY 10014
212-765-4772 (phone)
212-765-4785 (fax)

imdb.com/company/co0028602

winddancer.com
facebook.com/pages/Wind-Dancer-Films/
138276536219842

Does not accept any unsolicited material. Project types include Feature Films and TV. Preferred genres include Comedy, Crime, Drama, Fantasy, and Romance. Established in 1989.

Matt Williams
Principal
imdb.com/name/nm0931285
Assistant: Jake Perron

Judd Payne
Head of Production
imdb.com/name/nm1450928
linkedin.com/pub/judd-payne/5/61b/52b
twitter.com/juddpayne

Catherine Redfearn
Creative Executive
catherine_redfearn@winddancer.com
imdb.com/name/nm1976144
linkedin.com/pub/catherine-redfearn/15/19/148

David McFadzean
Principal
imdb.com/name/nm05687
Assistant: David Caruso

Dete Meserve
President
twitter.com/DeteMeserve

WINDOWSEAT, INC.

200 Pier Ave, Suite 135
Hermosa Beach, CA 90254
310-372-3650

info@windowseatpictures.com
windowseat.com/?page_id=791
linkedin.com/company/windowseatpictures
imdb.com/company/co0470347
facebook.com/windowseatpictures
twitter.com/WINDOWSEATpics

Does not accept any unsolicited material. Project types include Feature Films, TV, and Commercials. Established in 2014.

Jim Reach
Principle
310-372-3650
info@windowseat.com

Jim Ferguson

Ron Askew

W.L. Kiely

Bill Kiely
Director
imdb.com/name/nm2316469

Emiliano Haldeman
Sr. Vice-President
imdb.com/name/nm2541464
linkedin.com/pub/emiliano-haldeman/63/550/5b3

Ryan Dorff
CFO
imdb.com/name/nm6459728

Joseph McKelheer
Sr. Vice-President
joe@windowseat.com
imdb.com/name/nm1559624
linkedin.com/pub/joseph-mckelheer/6/2b1/35

WINGNUT FILMS LTD.

PO Box 15 208
Miramar
Wellington 6003
New Zealand
+64-4-388-9939 (phone)
+64-4-388-9449 (fax)

reception@wingnutfilms.co.nz
wingnutfilms.co.nz
imdb.com/company/co0046203
linkedin.com/pub/wingnut-films/6b/b04/516

Does not accept any unsolicited material. Project types include Feature Films and TV. Preferred genres include Animation, Comedy, Crime, Family, Fantasy, Horror, Non-Fiction, Romance, Science Fiction, and Thriller.

Carolynne Cunningham
Producer
imdb.com/name/nm0192254

Peter Jackson
imdb.com/name/nm0001392

WINKLER FILMS

190 N Canon Dr Suite 500 Penthouse
Beverly Hills, CA 90210
310-858-5780 (phone)
310-858-5799 (fax)

winklerfilms@sbcglobal.net
winklerfilms.com
imdb.com/company/co0049390

Accepts query letter from unproduced, unrepresented writers. Project types include Feature Films and TV. Preferred genres include Action, Crime, Drama, and Romance.

Irwin Winkler
CEO
310-858-5780
imdb.com/name/nm0005563
Assistant: Selina Gomeau

David Winkler
Producer
310-858-5780
imdb.com/name/nm0935210

Charles Winkler
310-858-5780
imdb.com/name/nm0935203
Assistant: Jose Ruisanchez

Jill Cutler
President
imdb.com/name/nm1384594

WINSOME PRODUCTIONS

PO Box 2071
Santa Monica, CA 90406
310-656-3300

info@winsomeprods.com
imdb.com/company/co0129854
winsomeprods.com
facebook.com/pages/Winsome-Productions/
    19789808323

Does not accept any unsolicited material. Project types include Feature Films and TV. Preferred genres

include Action, Comedy, Drama, and Non-Fiction. Established in 1989.

A.D. Oppenheim
info@winsomeprods.com
imdb.com/name/nm0649148

Daniel Oppenheim
imdb.com/name/nm0649151

WITT-THOMAS PRODUCTIONS

11901 Santa Monica Blvd, Suite 596
Los Angeles, CA 90025
310-472-6004 (phone)
310-476-5015 (fax)

pwittproductions@aol.com
imdb.com/company/co0083928

Does not accept any unsolicited material. Project types include Feature Films. Preferred genres include Action, Comedy, Crime, Drama, Period, and Romance. Established in 2010.

Tony Thomas
Partner
imdb.com/name/nm0859597
Assistant: Marlene Fuentes

Paul Witt
Partner
pwittproductions@aol.com
imdb.com/name/nm0432625
Assistant: Ellen Benjamin

W!LDBRAIN ENTERTAINMENT, INC.

15000 Ventura Blvd
3rd Floor
Sherman Oaks, CA 91403
818-290-7080

info@wildbrain.com
wildbrain.com
imdb.com/company/co0077172
linkedin.com/company/wild-brain

Accepts query letter from produced or represented writers. Project types include Feature Films, Short Films, and TV. Preferred genres include Animation, Comedy, Family, and Fantasy. Established in 1994.

Michael Polis
President
mpolis@wildbrain.com
imdb.com/name/nm1277040

Bob Higgins
imdb.com/name/nm0383338

Lisa Ullmann
imdb.com/name/nm0880520

WOLF FILMS, INC.

100 Universal City Plaza #2252
Universal City, CA 91608-1085
818-777-6969 (phone)
818-866-1446 (fax)

imdb.com/company/co0019598

Does not accept any unsolicited material. Project types include Feature Films, Short Films, and TV. Preferred genres include Drama and Non-Fiction.

Dick Wolf
CEO
imdb.com/name/nm0937725

Danielle Gelber
Executive Producer
imdb.com/name/nm1891764

Tony Ganz
imdb.com/name/nm0304673

WOLFMILL ENTERTAINMENT

9027 Larke Ellen Circle
Los Angeles, CA 90035
310-559-1622 (phone)
310-559-1623 (fax)

info@wolfmill.com
imdb.com/company/co0184078
wolfmill.com

Accepts query letter from unproduced, unrepresented writers via email. Project types include Feature Films and TV. Preferred genres include Animation. Established in 1997.

Marv Wolfman
Partner
marv@wolfmill.com
imdb.com/name/nm0938379

Craig Miller
Partner
craig@wolfmill.com
imdb.com/name/nm0003653

WONDERLAND SOUND AND VISION

8739 Sunset Blvd
West Hollywood, CA 90069
310-659-4451 (phone)
310-659-4451 (fax)

hello@wonderlandsoundandvision.com
wonderlandsoundandvision.com
imdb.com/company/co0080859
facebook.com/wonderlandsav
twitter.com/mcgswonderland

Does not accept any unsolicited material. Project types include Feature Films and TV. Preferred genres include Action, Comedy, Crime, Drama, Horror, Non-Fiction, Romance, and Science Fiction. Established in 2000.

Steven Bello
Creative Executive
imdb.com/name/nm2086605

Mary Viola
imdb.com/name/nm0899193

WONDERPHIL PRODUCTIONS, LLC

1032 Irving St., #130
San Francisco, CA. 94122
310-482-1324

phil@wonderphil.biz
wonderphil.biz
imdb.com/company/co0115133

Accepts scripts from unproduced, unrepresented writers. Project types include Feature Films. Preferred genres include Action, Drama, Fantasy, Horror, Science Fiction, and Thriller.

Phil Gorn
CEO
phil@wonderphil.biz
imdb.com/name/nm1486721

Sanders Robinson
President
925-525-7583
sandman@wonderphil.biz
facebook.com/sanders.robinson.50

WORKING TITLE FILMS

9720 Wilshire Blvd
4th Floor
Beverly Hills, CA 90212
310-777-3100 (phone)
310-777-5243 (fax)

imdb.com/company/co0057311
workingtitlefilms.com
twitter.com/Working_Title
facebook.com/WorkingTitleFilms

Does not accept any unsolicited material. Project types include Feature Films, Short Films, and TV. Preferred genres include Action, Comedy, Crime, Drama, Family, Fantasy, Non-Fiction, Romance, Science Fiction, and Thriller. Established in 1983.

Amelia Granger
+44 20 7307 3000
imdb.com/name/nm0335028

Liza Chasin
liza.chasin@workingtitlefilms.com
imdb.com/name/nm0153877
Assistant: Johanna Byer

Michelle Wright
imdb.com/name/nm0942657

Tim Bevan
Co-Chairman
imdb.com/name/nm0079677

Eric Fellner
Co-Chairman
imdb.com/name/nm0271479

WORLD FILM SERVICES, INC.

150 E 58th St
29th Floor
New York, NY 10155
212-632-3456 (phone)
212-632-3457 (fax)

imdb.com/company/co0184077

Accepts query letter from unproduced, unrepresented writers. Project types include Feature Films and TV. Preferred genres include Action, Comedy, Crime, Drama, Family, Fantasy, Horror, Non-Fiction, Romance, Science Fiction, and Thriller.

John Heyman
CEO
imdb.com/name/nm0382274

Dahlia Heyman
Creative Executive
imdb.com/name/nm3101094

Pamela Osowski
Creative Executive
imdb.com/name/nm1948494

WORLD OF WONDER PRODUCTIONS

6650 Hollywood Blvd, Suite 400
Hollywood, CA 90028
323-603-6300 (phone)
323-603-6301 (fax)

support@worldofwonder.net
worldofwonder.net
imdb.com/company/co0093416
facebook.com/pages/World-of-Wonder-Productions/
    187007651324618
twitter.com/worldofwonder

Does not accept any unsolicited material. Project types include Feature Films and TV. Preferred genres include Action, Comedy, Crime, Drama, Family, Non-Fiction, Period, and Reality. Established in 1990.

Fenton Bailey
imdb.com/name/nm0047259

Tom Campbell
imdb.com/name/nm1737859

Chris Skura
imdb.com/name/nm1048940

WORLDVIEW ENTERTAINMENT, INC.

1384 Broadway
25th Floor
New York, NY 10018
212-431-3090 (phone)
212-431-0390 (fax)

info@worldviewent.com
worldviewent.com
imdb.com/company/co0001099
twitter.com/worldviewent
facebook.com/worldviewent

Does not accept any unsolicited material. Project types include Feature Films. Preferred genres include Action, Comedy, Documentary, Drama, and Romance. Established in 2007.

Sarah Johnson Redlich
Partner
imdb.com/name/nm3164071

Christopher Woodrow
imdb.com/name/nm2002108

Amanda Bowers
imdb.com/name/nm4112873

Maria Cestone
imdb.com/name/nm2906036

WORLDWIDE BIGGIES

545 W 45th St
5th Floor
New York, NY 10036
646-442-1700 (phone)
646-557-0019 (fax)

info@wwbiggies.com
kari@wwbiggies.com
wwbiggies.com
imdb.com/company/co0173152

Does not accept any unsolicited material. Project types include Feature Films and TV. Preferred genres include Action, Animation, Comedy, Drama, Family, Fantasy, Non-Fiction, and Reality. Established in 2007.

Albie Hecht
CEO
imdb.com/name/nm0372935

Scott Webb
imdb.com/name/nm1274591

Kari Kim
kari@wwbiggies.com
imdb.com/name/nm2004613

WORLDWIDE PANTS INC.

1697 Broadway
New York, NY 10019
212-975-5300 (phone)
212-975-4780 (fax)

imdb.com/company/co0066959

Does not accept any unsolicited material. Project types
include Feature Films and TV. Preferred genres
include Action, Animation, Comedy, Drama, Non-
Fiction, and Romance.

Rob Burnett
imdb.com/name/nm0122427

Tom Keaney
Executive
imdb.com/name/nm3174758

David Letterman
imdb.com/name/nm0001468

WWE STUDIOS

12424 Wilshire Blvd, Suite 1400
Los Angeles, CA 90025
310-481-9370 (phone)
310-481-9369 (fax)

WWE Corporate Headquarters
Attention: (please include Department)
1241 E Main St
Stamford, CT 06902

talent.marketing@wwe.com
wwe.com
imdb.com/company/co0242604
twitter.com/WWEStudios

Does not accept any unsolicited material. Project types
include Feature Films and TV. Preferred genres

include Action, Comedy, Crime, Detective, Drama,
Family, Horror, Non-Fiction, Science Fiction, and
Thriller. Established in 2002.

Michael Luisi
President
imdb.com/name/nm0525405

Richard Lowell
imdb.com/name/nm1144067
Assistant: Cherie Harris Cherie.harris@wwecorp.com

X FILME CREATIVE POOL

Kurfuerstenstrasse 57
10785 Berlin
Germany
49-30-230-833-11 (phone)
49-30-230-833-22 (fax)

Niederlassung München
Tölzer Straße 5
82031 Grünwald
Deutschland
49-89-6494-6324 (phone)
49-89-6494-5820 (fax)

x-filme@x-filme.de
x-filme.de
imdb.com/company/co0055954

Does not accept any unsolicited material. Preferred
genres include Action, Comedy, Drama, Family, and
Romance. Established in 1994.

Stefan Arndt
stefan.arndt@x-filme.de
imdb.com/name/nm0036155

Wolfgang Becker
imdb.com/name/nm0065615

Dani Levy
imdb.com/name/nm0506374

XINGU FILMS LTD.

12 Cleveland Row
St. James
London SW1A 1DH
United Kingdom
44-20-7451-0600 (phone)
44-20-7451-0601 (fax)

mail@xingufilms.com
xingufilms.com
imdb.com/company/co0068740

Does not accept any unsolicited material. Project types include TV. Preferred genres include Action, Animation, Comedy, Crime, Detective, Drama, Family, Fantasy, Horror, Myth, Non-Fiction, Romance, Science Fiction, and Thriller. Established in 1993.

Trudie Styler
trudie@xingufilms.com
imdb.com/name/nm0836548

Alex Francis
Producer
imdb.com/name/nm2123360

Kate Henderson

Anita Sumner
imdb.com/name/nm0838856

XIX ENTERTAINMENT

9000 W Sunset Blvd, Penthouse
West Hollywood, CA 90069
310-746-1919 (phone)
310-746-1920 (fax)

33 Ransomes Dock
35-37 Parkgate Rd
London SW11 4NP
44-20-7801-1919 (phone)
44-20-7801-1920 (fax)

info@xixentertainment.com
xixentertainment.com

Does not accept any unsolicited material. Project types include Feature Films and TV. Preferred genres include Drama, Non-Fiction, Period, Reality, Romance, and Thriller. Established in 2010.

Robert Dodds
CEO
robert.dodds@xixentertainment.com
imdb.com/name/nm2142323

XYZ FILMS

4223 Glencoe Ave, Suite B119
Marina del Rey, CA 90292
310-956-1550 (phone)
310-827-7690 (fax)

team@xyzfilms.com
xyzfilms.com
imdb.com/company/co0244345
facebook.com/xyzfilms
twitter.com/xyzfilms

Does not accept any unsolicited material. Project types include Feature Films. Preferred genres include Action, Comedy, Crime, Drama, Horror, Non-Fiction, Science Fiction, and Thriller.

Nate Bolotin
Partner
nate@xyzfilms.com
imdb.com/name/nm1924867

Todd Brown
Partner
info@xyzfilms.com
imdb.com/name/nm1458075

Kyle Franke
Head of Development
310-359-9099
kyle@xyzfilms.com
imdb.com/name/nm3733941

YAHOO!

2400 Broadway
1st Floor
Santa Monica, CA 90404
310-907-2700 (phone)
310-907-2701 (fax)

yahoo.com
imdb.com/company/co0054481

Accepts query letter from unproduced, unrepresented writers. Project types include Short Films, TV, and Commercials. Preferred genres include Comedy, Family, Non-Fiction, and Reality. Established in 1995.

David Filo
Founder

Ryan Clifford

Jacqueline Reses

YARI FILM GROUP

10850 Wilshire Blvd
6th Floor
Los Angeles, CA 90024
310-689-1450 (phone)
310-234-8975 (fax)

info@yarifilmgroup.com
reception@yarifilmgroup.com
imdb.com/company/co0136740
yarifilmgroup.com

Does not accept any unsolicited material. Project types include Feature Films and TV. Preferred genres include Action, Animation, Comedy, Crime, Drama, Family, Romance, and Thriller.

Bob Yari
byari@yarifilmgroup.com
imdb.com/name/nm0946441
Assistant: Julie Milstead

Ethen Adams
imdb.com/name/nm2319337

David Clark
imdb.com/name/nm1354046

YORK SQUARE PRODUCTIONS

17328 Ventura Blvd, Suite 370
Encino, CA 91316
818-789-7372

assistant@yorksquareproductions.com
yorksquareproductions.com
imdb.com/company/co0378544

Accepts query letter from unproduced, unrepresented writers via email. Project types include Feature Films, TV, and Commercials. Preferred genres include Comedy and Drama.

Jonathan Mostow
Executive
imdb.com/name/nm0609236
Assistant: Emily Somers

YORKTOWN PRODUCTIONS

18 Gloucester Ln
4th Floor
Toronto ON M4Y 1L5
Canada
416-923-2787 (phone)
416-923-8580 (fax)

imdb.com/company/co0184088

Does not accept any unsolicited material. Project types include Feature Films, Short Films, and TV. Preferred genres include Action, Comedy, Drama, Family, Fantasy, Romance, and Science Fiction. Established in 1986.

Norman Jewison
Founder
416-923-2787
imdb.com/name/nm0422484

Michael Jewison
Producer
imdb.com/name/nm0422483

YOURFACE GOES HERE ENTERTAINMENT

1041 N Formosa Ave
Santa Monica Bldg W, #7
West Hollywood, CA 90046
323-850-2433

imdb.com/company/co0247237

Does not accept any unsolicited material. Project types include TV. Preferred genres include Drama, Fantasy, Horror, Romance, Science Fiction, and Thriller.

Alan Ball
323-850-2433
imdb.com/name/nm0050332

ZACHARY FEUER FILMS

9348 Civic Center Dr, 3rd Floor
Beverly Hills, CA 90210
310-729-2110 (phone)
310-820-7535 (fax)

Accepts query letter from unproduced, unrepresented writers. Project types include TV. Preferred genres include Action, Comedy, Drama, and Thriller.

Zachary Feuer
Producer
imdb.com/name/nm0275400

ZAK PENN'S COMPANY

6240 W. Third St., Ste. 421
Los Angeles, CA 90036
323-939-1700

imdb.com/company/co0185423
linkedin.com/company/zak-penn's-company

Does not accept any unsolicited material. Project types include Feature Films and TV. Preferred genres include Comedy, Family, Fantasy, Non-Fiction, Science Fiction, and Thriller.

Zak Penn
Producer
zak.penn@fox.com
zakpenn.blogspot.com
imdb.com/name/nm0672015
twitter.com/zakpenn
Assistant: Hannah Rosner

ZANUCK INDEPENDENT

1951 N Beverly Dr
Beverly Hills, CA 90210
310-274-5735 (phone)
310-273-9217 (fax)

imdb.com/company/co0279611

Accepts query letter from unproduced, unrepresented writers. Project types include Feature Films. Preferred genres include Action, Comedy, Drama, and Thriller.

Dean Zanuck
Founder
imdb.com/name/nm0953124

ZEMECKIS/NEMEROFF FILMS

264 S La Cienega Blvd, Suite 238
Beverly Hills, CA 90211
310-736-6586

imdb.com/company/co0141237

Does not accept any unsolicited material. Project types include Feature Films. Preferred genres include Comedy and Drama.

Leslie Zemeckis
Producer
imdb.com/name/nm0366667

Terry Nemeroff
Producer
imdb.com/name/nm0625892

ZENTROPA ENTERTAINMENT

Filmbyen 22
2650 Hvidovre
Denmark
+45-36-86-87-88

receptionen@filmbyen.dk
zentropa.dk
linkedin.com/company/zentropa
imdb.com/company/co0136662
facebook.com/Zentropaproductions
twitter.com/ZentropaNews

Accepts scripts from unproduced, unrepresented writers. Project types include Feature Films. Preferred genres include Action, Comedy, Crime, Drama, Family, Fantasy, Horror, Non-Fiction, Romance, Science Fiction, and Thriller. Established in 1992.

Peter Aalbaek Jensen
CEO
peter.aalbaek.jensen@filmbyen.dk
imdb.com/name/nm0421639

Frederik Nemeth
CFO
frederik.nemeth@filmbyen.dk

ZEPHYR FILMS

48a Goodge St
London
W1T 4LX
UK
+440207-794-0011

info@zephyrfilms.co.uk
zephyrfilms.co.uk

Does not accept any unsolicited material. Project types include Feature Films and TV. Preferred genres include Action, Animation, Comedy, Crime, Drama, Family, Fantasy, Horror, Romance, and Thriller.

Phil Robertson
Producer
imdb.com/name/nm0731990

Chris Curling
Producer
imdb.com/name/nm0192770
linkedin.com/pub/chris-curling/15/53/BB7

ZETA ENTERTAINMENT

3422 Rowena Ave
Los Angeles, CA 90027
310-595-0494

imdb.com/company/co0037026

Does not accept any unsolicited material. Project types include Feature Films and TV. Preferred genres include Action, Comedy, Crime, Drama, Family, Fantasy, Horror, and Thriller.

Zane Levitt
President
zanewlevitt@gmail.com
imdb.com/name/nm0506254
linkedin.com/pub/zane-levitt/30/3b1/552

ZIEGER PRODUCTIONS

310-476-1679 (phone)
310-476-7928 (fax)

imdb.com/company/co0114742
zieglerfilms.com/zieglerproductions.html

Accepts query letter from unproduced, unrepresented writers.

Michele Colucci-Zieger
Producer
imdb.com/name/nm1024135

ZING PRODUCTIONS, INC.

220 S Van Ness Ave
Hollywood, CA 90004
323-466-9464

Bauman Management
947 S Windsor Blvd.
Los Angeles, CA 90019
310-210-4728

jbauman@baumanmgt.com
zinghollywood.com

Does not accept any unsolicited material. Project types include Feature Films, Short Films, and TV. Preferred genres include Animation, Comedy, Drama, Family, Fantasy, Reality, and Romance.

Rob Loos
President
rob@zinghollywood.com
imdb.com/name/nm0519763
linkedin.com/pub/rob-loos/5/426

ZODIAK USA

520 Broadway Suite 500
Santa Monica, CA 90401
310-460-4490 (phone)
310-460-4494 (fax)

contact@zodiakusa.com
zodiakusa.com
imdb.com/company/co0314564
linkedin.com/company/zodiak-usa

Accepts query letter from unproduced, unrepresented writers via email. Project types include TV. Preferred genres include Animation, Comedy, Non-Fiction, Reality, and Romance.

Natalka Znak
CEO
imdb.com/name/nm1273500

Timothy Sullivan
212-488-1699
imdb.com/name/nm2432438

ZUCKER PRODUCTIONS

Los Angeles, CA
310-656-9202 (phone)
310-656-9220 (fax)

imdb.com/company/co0110404
facebook.com/pages/Zucker-Productions/
    253063648039987

Accepts query letter from unproduced, unrepresented writers. Project types include TV. Preferred genres include Comedy, Drama, Fantasy, Romance, and Thriller. Established in 1972.

Farrell Ingle
Creative Executive
imdb.com/name/nm3377346
linkedin.com/pub/farrell-ingle/12/3a0/2b9

Jerry Zucker
Partner
imdb.com/name/nm0958387

Janet Zucker
Partner
imdb.com/name/nm0958384

Index by Company Name

Find software, books, courses and more on WritersStore.com

Find software, books, courses and more on WritersStore.com

Find software, books, courses and more on WritersStore.com

Find software, books, courses and more on WritersStore.com

Index by Contact Name

Find software, books, courses and more on WritersStore.com

Find software, books, courses and more on WritersStore.com

Find software, books, courses and more on WritersStore.com

Herzfeld, John, 310
Heslov, Grant, 382
Heston, Fraser, 71
Hetzel, Eric, 361
Hevert, Jeff, 188
Hewitt, Aif, 398
Heydenrich, Adele, 332
Heyman, David, 233
Heyman, John, 439
Heyman, Dahlia, 439
Heyward, Andy, 94
Heyward, Amy Moynihan, 94
Hicks, Kevin, 80
Higgin, David, 383
Higgins, Bob, 437
Higgins, David, 267
Higgins, Angelique, 267
High, Joel C., 153
Hikaka, Kimberly, 136
Hildebrand, Jodi, 316
Hill, Norm, 65
Hill, John, 109
Hillary, David, 167
Hillin, Daemon, 346
Hinojosa, David, 258
Hipps, Joe, 293
Hirata, Tammy, 435
Hirigoyen, Christina, 291
Hirsch, Saryl, 369
Hirschorn, Michael, 249
Ho, Jennifer, 215
Hobbs, Rebecca, 198
Hoberman, David, 285
Hochman Nash, Marney, 297
Hock, Trey, 395
Hoerr, Mark, 230
Hoffman, Peter, 374
Hoffman, Dustin, 342
Hoffman, Gary, 211
Hoffman, Todd, 131
Hoffman, Valerie, 370
Hoffman, Phillip, 151
Hogan, Justin, 269
Hogan, Justin, 258
Holbrook, Boyd, 280

Holderman, Bill, 435
Holland, Todd, 161
Holland, Gil, 401
Holland, Sydney, 359
Holleran, Leslie, 264
Homan, Eric, 206
Honovic, Matthew, 223
Hoon, Samir, 339
Hooper, Brandon, 341
Hopwood, David, 96
Hori, Takeo, 86
Horn, David, 407
Horowitz, Jordan, 215
Horowitz, Mark, 110
Horwitz, Andy, 95
Householter, David, 302
Housman, Samantha, 318
Howard, Ron, 240
Howard, Max, 194
Howard, Scott, 302
Howell, Lynette, 182
Howsam, Erik, 167
Huang, Joan, 141
Hudson, Brett, 118
Hughes, Mary Ann, 406
Hughes, Patrick, 236
Hume, John, 260
Hunt, David, 204
Hunt, Andrew, 349
Hunter, Alan, 237
Hunter, Hugh, 237
Hunter, Dave, 226
Hurd, Gale, 421
Hurvitz, Rick, 128
Hurwitz, Peter, 56
Hurwitz, David, 116
Hurwitz, Page, 343
Husney, Evan, 73
Huston, Anjelica, 222
Hyde, John, 353
Hyman, Kevin, 97
Hyman, Wendy, 375
I., T., 221
Ianno, Dominic, 243
Ichise, Takashige, 322

Igbokwe, Pearlena, 308
Iger, Robert, 406
Imani Cameron, Kisha, 149
Imbert, Frederic, 173
Imperato, Thomas, 353
Infantolino, Joseph, 109
Ingle, Farrell, 445
Inglott, Joanne, 118
Ingold, Jeff, 172
Irwin, John, 248
Irwin, Molly, 87
Isaacs, Stanley, 55
Isler, William H., 399
Iso, Christine, 322
Israel, Jesse, 243
Israelson, Ally, 404
Istock, Steven, 134
Ivory, James, 294
Iwanter, Sidney, 95
Iwanyk, Basil, 409
Iwashina, Kevin, 339
Iwerks, Leslie, 270
Izaac, Raymond, 219
Jablin, Burton, 233
Jackman, Michael A., 83
Jacks, James, 207
Jackson, Randy, 174
Jackson, Peter, 436
Jackson, Rick, 196
Jackson, Samuel, 421
Jackson, Alex, 293
Jackson, Calvin "C-Note", 313
Jackson, Aaron, 164
Jackson, Ian, 197
Jacobs, Andrew, 95
Jacobs, Katie, 231
Jacobs, John, 381
Jacobs Miller, Nancy, 199
Jacobson, David, 267
Jacobson, Ross, 58
Jacobson, Danny, 245
Jacobson, Nina, 148
Jaffe, Michael, 249
Jaglom, Henry, 346

Find software, books, courses and more on WritersStore.com

Find software, books, courses and more on WritersStore.com

Liman, Doug, 237
Lin, Chris, 305
Lin, Dan, 272
Lin, Justin, 331
Linde, David, 268
Lindenberg, Ryan, 113
Lindquist, Frankie, 371
Lingg, Kathy, 100
Link, Julie, 354
Linnen, Nik, 127
Lisberger, Peggy, 289
Little, Robbie, 403
Little, Ellen, 403
Little, Wayne, 412
Little, Greg, 369
Littlefield, Warren, 403
Litto, George, 212
Litto, Andria, 212
Livadory, Matt, 87
Lizette, Melina, 245
Lloyd, Lauren, 275
Lobell, Mike, 297
Lockridge, Tom, 278
Loeb, Allen, 371
Lomuscio, Alyssa, 155
Londy, Adam, 396
Loos, Rob, 444
Lopez, Lucia, 290
Lopez, James, 373
Lopez, Jennifer, 313
Lorenz, Robert, 283
Lorenz, Carsten, 299
Lorre, Chuck, 143
Louzil, Eric, 178
Love, Sandi, 184
Love, NIck, 424
Lowe, Andrew, 183
Lowell, Richard, 440
Lowry, Hunt, 365
Luber, Matt, 263
Lubetkin, Dan, 98
Lubin, Aaron, 287
Lucas, George, 277
Ludlow, Graham, 148
Lui, Cybill, 85

Lui, Cybill, 85
Luisi, Michael, 440
Luker, Kyle, 401
Lundberg, Robert, 265
Luong, David, 63
Lupovitz, Dan, 159
Lurie, Christina, 427
Lurie, Rod, 105
Lynch, David, 65
Lynn, Julie, 299
Lynne, Michael, 419
Lyons, Charlie, 235
Mabrito, Robin, 351
Macari, Mike, 279
Macauley, Scott, 202
Macdonald, Andrew, 171
MacDonald, Laurie, 328
MacDuff, Dana, 314
MacDuff, Brandon, 314
Mace, Dave, 275
MacFarlane, Seth, 210
Maciejewicz, Berenika, 282
Mackay, David, 104
Macletchie, Donna, 250
Macnamara, Dan, 404
MacVicar, Caroline, 390
Macy, Trevor, 246
Maddox, Anthony, 99
Maggini, Tia, 254
Magiday, Lee, 183
Magielnicki, Matt, 158
Mahdessian, Armen, 327
Maher, Michael, 431
Mailer, Michael, 296
Maisel, Ileen, 79
Malach, Christina, 348
Malatesta, Catherine, 268
Malkovich, John, 304
Malloy, Royal, 79
Malmberg, Fredrik, 327
Malone, Patrick, 218
Mancini, Val, 216
Mancuso, Frank, 125
Mandabach, Caryn, 137
Mangano, Chris, 332

Maniscalco, Mia, 175
Mankoff, Douglas, 179
Mann, Michael, 204
Mann, Thea, 151
Mann, Andrew, 421
Manpearl, David, 311
Mansfield, Ray, 303
Manson, David, 370
Manson, Arla Sorkin, 370
Mao, Joan, 405
Maran, Rachel, 391
Marashlian, Paul, 91
March, Daniel, 177
Marchand, Xavier, 76
Marchiori, Mauriziio, 393
Marciano, Nathalie, 57
Marcus, Jay, 195
Marcus, Deborah, 64
Marcus, Michael, 152
Margolies, Rob, 167
Marguilies, Alan, 81
Marin, Mindy, 122
Marino, Felipe, 314
Mark, Laurence, 267
Markel, Heidi Jo, 179
Marken, Dave, 334
Marker, Riva, 350
Markus, David, 82
Marmor, Jennifer, 154
Marsh, Sherry, 288
Marshall, Amanda, 79
Marshall, Edwin, 228
Marshall, Garry, 232
Marshall, Frank, 257
Marshall, Nic, 290
Marshall, Penny, 328
Marshall-Green, Logan, 95
Martin, James, 234
Martin, Nichola, 106
Martin, Franklin, 177
Martin, David, 98
Martinez, John Torres, 286
Martinez, Philippe, 105
Martinez, Philippe, 277
Marx, Hilary, 253

Find software, books, courses and more on WritersStore.com

Find software, books, courses and more on WritersStore.com

Find software, books, courses and more on WritersStore.com

Find software, books, courses and more on WritersStore.com

Find software, books, courses and more on WritersStore.com

Index by Submission Policy

Accepts query letter from produced or represented writers

Accepts query letter from unproduced, unrepresented writers

Accepts query letter from unproduced, unrepresented writers via email

Accepts scripts from produced or represented writers

Accepts scripts from unproduced, unrepresented writers

Accepts scripts from unproduced, unrepresented writers via email

Does not accept any unsolicited material

Find software, books, courses and more on WritersStore.com

Find software, books, courses and more on WritersStore.com

Find software, books, courses and more on WritersStore.com

Find software, books, courses and more on WritersStore.com